THE UNIVERSITY OF CHIC/

ORIENTAL INSTITUTE NUBIAN E

VOLUME IX

EXCAVATIONS BETWEEN
AND THE SUDAN FF

NOUBADIAN X-GROUP REMAINS FF

CEMETERIES Q AND 219 AND FF

Q, R, V, W, B, J, AND M AT

Thomas

with the assist

CAMPAGNE INTERNATIONALE POUR LA SAUVEGARDE
DES MONUMENTS DE LA NUBIE

THE UNIVERSITY OF CHICAGO
ORIENTAL INSTITUTE NUBIAN EXPEDITION
VOLUME IX

EXCAVATIONS BETWEEN ABU SIMBEL AND THE SUDAN FRONTIER

KEITH C. SEELE, *DIRECTOR*

PART 9:

NOUBADIAN X-GROUP REMAINS FROM ROYAL COMPLEXES IN
CEMETERIES Q AND 219 AND FROM PRIVATE CEMETERIES
Q, R, V, W, B, J, AND M AT QUSTUL AND BALLANA

by

BRUCE BEYER WILLIAMS

THE ORIENTAL INSTITUTE OF THE UNIVERSITY OF CHICAGO
CHICAGO • ILLINOIS

Library of Congress Catalog Card Number 91–61754

ISBN: 0–918986–74–5

The Oriental Institute

Published 1991. Printed in the United States of America.

TABLE OF CONTENTS

LIST OF FIGURES

LIST OF TABLES

LIST OF PLATES

LIST OF TEXT AND REGISTER ABBREVIATIONS

Ag.	silver or silvered		lt.	light
alt.	alternated, alternating, alternate		max.	maximum
am.	amethyst		med.	medium
approx.	approximate, approximately		Mer.	Meroitic
bk.	black		min.	miniature
bl.	blue		N	north, northward, northern, northernmost
bn.	brown			
ca.	circa		N/A	not available for study
car.	carnelian		NID	not identified
CAT	catalog entry, Mayer-Thurman and Williams 1979		no.	number
			op.	opaque
cb.	crude brick, mudbrick		ord.	ordinary
cem.	cemetery		os. egg.	ostrich eggshell
dec.	decorated, decoration		pk.	pink
diam.	diameter		pl.	plate
dim.	dimensions		pt.	paint, painted
disc.	discarded		qz.	quartz
dist.	disturbed		R	right
dk.	dark		rect.	rectangular
E	east, eastward, eastern, easternmost		S	south, southward, southern, southernmost
Eg.	Egyptian			
ext.	extended		samp.	sample
fa.	faience		std.	standard decoration
fig.	figure		S. J. E.	Scandinavian Joint Expedition
gl.	glass		tr.	translucent
gn.	green		unc.	uncertain
gt.	gilt (gilded glass)		undec.	undecorated
hor.	horizontal		vert.	vertical, vertically
inc.	incised		W	west, westward, western, westernmost
irreg.	irregular, irregularly		wh.	white
Ku. wm.	Kushite Wheelmade		X-Gr.	X-Group
L	left		ye.	yellow

BIBLIOGRAPHY

Abd el-Moneim Abu Bakr

    1967   "Rapport préliminaire sur les résultats des fouilles entreprises par la mission archéologique de l'Université du Caire dans la région d'Aniba en Nubie saison 1961–1962," *Fouilles en Nubie 1961–1963*. Cairo: Organisme général des imprimeries gouvernmentales, pp. 1–26.

Acland, P. E. B.

    1932   "Notes on the Camel in the Eastern Sudan," *Sudan Notes and Records* 15: 119–49.

Adams, William Y.

    1961   "The Christian Potteries at Faras," *Kush* 9: 30–43.

    1962   "Pottery Kiln Excavations," *Kush* 10: 62–75.

    1964   "Post–Pharaonic Nubia in the Light of Archaeology I," *JEA* 50: 102–20.

    1977   *Nubia, Corridor to Africa.* Princeton: Princeton University Press.

    1986   *The Ceramic Industries of Medieval Nubia.* Lexington: The University of Kentucky.

Addison, Frank

    1949   *Jebel Moya,* The Wellcome Excavations in the Sudan. London: Oxford University Press.

    1956   "Second Thoughts on Gebel Moya," *Kush* 4: 4–18.

Almagro, Martín

    1965   *La necrópolis meroítica de Nag Gamus (Masmás, Nubia Egipcia),* Memorias de la Misión Arqueológica, vol. 8, Madrid: Ministerio de Asuntos Exteriores and Ministerio de Educación Nacional.

Anonymous, ed.

    1979   *Africa in Antiquity; the Arts of Ancient Nubia and the Sudan,* vols. I (The Essays) and II (The Catalogue, by Steffen Wenig), Brooklyn: The Brooklyn Museum.

Arkell, Anthony J.

    1949   *Early Khartoum: An Account of the Excavation of an Early Occupation Site Carried out by the Sudan Government Antiquities Service in 1944–5.* London: Oxford University Press.

    1953   *Shaheinab: An Account of the Excavation of a Neolithic Occupation Site Carried out for the Sudan Antiquities Service in 1949–50.* London: Oxford University Press.

Bates, Oric and Dunham, Dows
    1927   *Excavations at Gamai.* in *Varia Africana, Vol. 4*, edited by E. A. Hooton and
            Natica I. Bates. Harvard African Studies, vol. 8. Cambridge, MA: Harvard University
            Press, pp. 1–122.

Bietak, Manfred
    1968   *Studien zur Chronologie der Nubischen C-Gruppe: Ein Beitrag zur Frühgeschichte
            Unternubiens zwischen 2200 und 1550 vor Chr.* Berichte des Österreichischen
            Nationalkomitees der UNESCO-Aktion für die Rettung der Nubischen Altertümer, vol. 5.
            Österreichische Akademie der Wissenschaften, Phil.-hist. Klasse, Denkschriften, vol. 97.
            Vienna: Hermann Böhlaus Nachf.

Bonnet, Charles
    1978   "Fouilles archéologiques à Kerma (Soudan). Rapport préliminaire de la campagne 1977–
            1978." *Genava* n.s. 26: 107–34.

    1980   "Les fouilles archéologiques de Kerma (Soudan). Rapport préliminaire des campagnes de
            1978–1979 et de 1979–1980," *Genava* n.s. 28: 31–62.

    1982   "Les fouilles archéologiques de Kerma (Soudan). Rapport préliminaire des campagnes de
            1980–1981 et de 1981–1982." *Genava* n.s. 30: 29–53.

    1986   "Les fouilles archéologiques de Kerma (Soudan). Rapport préliminaire sur les campagnes
            de 1984–1985 et 1985–1986," *Genava* n.s. 34: 5–20.

Breasted, James Henry
    1906–7 *Ancient Records of Egypt*, 5 vols. Chicago: The University of Chicago Press.

Burckhardt, Johannes
    1822   *Travels in Nubia*, 2d ed. London: John Murray.

Carter, William H. (Col.)
    1902   *Horses Saddles and Bridles.* Baltimore: The Lord Baltimore Press.

Chappel, T. G. H.
    1977   *Decorated gourds in north-eastern Nigeria.* Lagos: The Nigerian Museum.

Chittick, H. N.
    1982   "Ethiopia and the Nile Valley," *Meroitica* 6: 50–54.

Crawford, O. G. S. and Addison, Frank
    1951   *Abu Geili and Saqadi & Dar el Mek*, The Wellcome Excavations in the Sudan, vol. 3.
            London: Oxford University Press.

Davies, Nina de Garis
    1926   *The Tomb of Huy; Viceroy of Nubia in the Reign of Tutankhamun.* London: EES.

Dinkler, Erich

1977   "König Ezqana von Aksum und das Christentum," in *Ägypten und Kusch; Festschrift Fritz Hintze*, edited by E. Endesfelder, K-H Priese, F. Reinecke, and S. Wenig. Schriften zur Geschichte und Kultur des alten Orients, vol. 13. Berlin: Akademie-Verlag: 121–132.

Du Bois-Aymé, M.

1822   "Memoire sur la ville de Qoceir et ses environs et sur les peuples nomades," *Descrption de l'Égypte*, vol. 11. *État moderne*. Paris: C. L. F. Panckoucke, pp. 383–400.

Dunham, Dows

1950   *El Kurru*. The Royal Cemeteries of Kush, vol. I. Cambridge, MA: Harvard University Press.

1957   *Royal Tombs of Meroe and Barkal*. Royal Cemeteries of Kush, vol. IV. Boston: The Museum of Fine Arts.

1963   *The West and South Cemeteries at Meroe*. The Royal Cemeteries of Kush, vol. V. Boston: The Museum of Fine Arts.

1982   *Excavations at Kerma. Part VI*. Boston: The Museum of Fine Arts.

Dziobek, Eberhard

n.d.   "Eine Grabpyramide des frühen NR in Theben."

Edwards, Amelia

1899   *A Thousand Miles up the Nile*. London: George Routledge and Sons.

Egloff, Michel

1977   *Kellia; La Poterie Copte*. Recherches suisses d'archéologie copte, vol. 3. Geneva: Georg.

Emery, Walter B.

1954   *Great Tombs of the First Dynasty II*. EES memoir 46. London: Oxford University Press.

Emery, W. B. and Kirwan, L. P

1935   *The Excavations and Survey between Wadi es-Sebua and Adindan 1929–1931*. Service des antiquités de l'Égypte, Mission archéologique de Nubie, 1929–1934. Cairo: Government Press, Bulaq.

1938   *The Royal Tombs of Ballana and Qustul*. Cairo: Government Press.

Fathi Afifi Bedawi

1976   *Die Römische Gräberfelder fon Sayala-Nubien*. Österreichischen Akademie der Wissenschaften, Phil-hist. Klasse, Denkschriften, vol. 126. Vienna: Österreichischen Akademie der Wissenschaften.

Fattovich, Rodolfo

1989   "The Stelae of Kassala: A New Type of funerary Monuments in the Eastern Sudan," *Archéologie du Nil Moyen* 3: 55–70.

Firth, C. M.

1912   *The Archaeological Survey of Nubia, Report for 1908–1909.* Cairo: Government Press.

1915   *The Archaeological Survey of Nubia, Report for 1909–1910.* Cairo: Government Press.

1927   *The Archaeological Survey of Nubia, Report for 1910–1911.* Cairo: Government Press.

Frend, W. H. C.

1978   "The Christian Period in Mediterranean Africa, ca. A.D. 200 to 800," in *The Cambridge History of Africa*, vol. 2, edited by J. D. Fage. Cambridge: Cambridge University Press, pp. 410–78.

Garstang, John; Sayce, A. H.; and Griffith, F. Ll.

1911   *Meroe: The City of the Ethiopians.* Oxford: The Clarendon Press.

Godlewski, W.

1986   "Remarks on the Art of Nobadia (V–VIII Century)," in *Nubische Studien: Tagungsakten der 5. internationalen Konferenz der International Society for Nubian Studies, Heidelberg, 22.–25. September 1982*, edited by Martin Krause. Mainz am Rhein: Philipp von Zabern, pp. 269–80.

Griffith, F. Ll.

1911   *Karanog: The Meroitic Inscriptions of Shablul and Karanog.* The University of Pennsylvania Egyptian Department of the University Museum. Eckley B. Coxe, Junior Expedition to Nubia, vol. VI. Philadelphia: The University Museum.

1926   "Oxford Excavations in Nubia. XL; Meroitic Antiquities at Faras and other Sites," *LAAA* 13: 17–35

Hintze, Fritz

1962   "Preliminary Report on the Excavations at Musawwarat es Sufra, 1960–61," *Kush* 10: 170–202.

1967   "Meroe und die Noba," *ZÄS* 94: 79–86.

1971   *Musawwarat es Sufra.* Vol. I, 2. *Der Löwentempel, Tafelband.* With contributions by Ursula Hintze, Karl-Heinz Priese, and Kurt Stark. Berlin: Akademie-Verlag.

Hoffman, M. A.; Lupton, C.; and Adams, B.

1982   *The Predynastic of Hierakonpolis—an Interim Report.* Egyptian Studies Association, Publication No. 1. Cairo: Cairo University Herbarium.

Hofmann, Inge

1967   *Die Kulturen des Niltals von Aswan bis Sennar vom Mesolithikum bis zum Ende der Christlichen Epoche.* Monographien zur Völkerkunde, vol. 4. Hamburg: Kommissionverlag Cram de Gruyter and Co.

1982   "Bemerkungen zum Ende des meroitischen Reiches," *Meroitica* 6: 232–34.

Hofmann, Inge; Tomandl, Herbert; and Zach, Michael

1989 "Beitrag zur Geschichte der Nubier," *Meroitica* 10: 269–98.

Hofmann, Inge and Vorbichler, A.

1979 *Der Äthiopenlogos bei Herodot.* Beiträge zur Afrikanistik, vol. 3. Vienna: Institute für Afrikanistik und Ägyptologie der Universität Wien.

Hölscher, Uvo

1954 *The Excavation of Medinet Habu V: Post-Ramessid Remains.* OIP 66. Chicago: The University of Chicago Press.

Hughes, George R.

1963 "Serra East: The University of Chicago Excavations, 1961–62; A Preliminary Report on the First Season's Work," *Kush* 11: 121–30.

Johnson, Barbara

1981 *Pottery from Karanis Excavations of the University of Michigan.* Ann Arbor: The University of Michigan.

Kaiser, Werner

1969 "Zu den königlichen Talbezirken der I. und II. Dynastie in Abydos und zur Baugeschichte des Djoser-Grabmals," *MDAIK* 25: 1–21.

Kaiser, Werner and Dreyer, Günter

1982 "Nachuntersuchungen im frühzeitlichen Königsfriedhof. 2. Vorbericht," *MDAIK* 38: 211–69.

Kelley, Alan

1976 *The Pottery of Ancient Egypt Dynasty I to Roman Times.* Toronto: Royal Ontario Museum.

Kemp, Barry J.

1966 "Abydos and the Royal Tombs of the First Dynasty," *JEA* 52: 13–22.

Kirwan, Sir Laurence P.

1939 *The Oxford University Excavations at Firka.* London: Oxford University Press.

1982 "The X-Group Problem," *Meroitica* 6: 191–204.

Kromer, Karl

1967 *Römische Weinstuben in Sayala (Nubien),* Österreichischen Akademie der Wissenschaften, Phil.-hist. Klasse, Denkschriften, vol. 95. Vienna: Hemann Böhlaus Nachf.

Lenoble, Patrice

1989 "'A New type of Mound-Grave' (continued) le tumulus à enciente d'Umm Makharoqa, pres d'el Hobagi (A.M.S. NE-36-0/7-0-3)," *Archéologie du Nil Moyen* 3: 93–120.

Macleod, W.

1970   *Composite Bows from the Tomb of Tutankhamun.* Tutankhamun's Tomb Series, vol. 3, Oxford: Griffith Institute.

Macramallah, Rizkallah

1940   *Un cimetière archaïque de la classe moyenne du peuple à Saqqarah.* Cairo: Imprimerie Nationale, Boulaq.

Marshall, K. and Abd el Rahman Adam

1953   "Excavation of a Mound Grave Near Ushara," *Kush* 1: 40–46.

Mayer-Thurman, Christa and Williams, Bruce

1979   *Ancient Textiles from Nubia.* Chicago: The Art Institute of Chicago and The Oriental Institute of The University of Chicago.

Michalowski, Kazimierz

1970   "Open Problems of Nubian Art and Culture in the Light of the Discoveries at Faras," in *Kunst und Geschichte Nubiens in Christlicher Zeit*, edited by E. Dinkler. Recklinghausen: Aurel Bongers, pp. 111–28.

Millet, Nicholas B.

1963   "Gebel Adda: Preliminary Report for 1963," *JARCE* 2: 147–65.

1967   "Gebel Adda: Preliminary Report, 1965–1966," *JARCE* 6: 53–63.

1968   "Meroitic Nubia," Ph.D. dissertation, Yale University.

1984   "Meroitic Religion," *Meroitica* 7: 111–21.

Mills, A. J.

1982   *The Cemeteries of Qasr Ibrim; a Report of the Excavations conducted by W. B. Emery in 1961.* EES memoir 51. London: EES.

Mond, Sir Robert and Myers, Oliver H.

1934   *The Bucheum.* EES memoir 41 (3 vols.) London: EES.

Nordström, Hans-Åke

1972   *Neolithic and A-Group Sites.* The Scandinavian Joint Expedition to Sudanese Nubia, vol. 3. Copenhagen, Oslo, and Stockholm: Scandinavian University Books.

O'Connor, David

1989   "New Funerary Enclosures (*Talbezirke*) of the Early Dynastic Period at Abydos," *JARCE* 26: 51–86.

Osing, Jürgen

1976   "Ächtungstexte aus dem Alten Reich (II)," *MDAIK* 32: 133–185.

Paul, Andrew

1954   *A History of the Beja Tribes of the Sudan.* Cambridge: Cambridge University Press. (reprinted 1971).

Pellicer, Manuel; Llongueras, Miguel; Zozaya, Juan; and Vasquez de Acuña, I.

    1965   *Las necrópolis meroíticas del Grupo "X," y cristianas de Nag el Arab (Argín, Sudán),*
            Memorias de las Misión Arqueológica, vol. 5. Madrid: Ministerio de Asuntos Exteriores.

Plumley, J. Martin

    1982   "Preliminary Remarks on four 5th Century Mss. from Qasr Ibrim," *Meroitica* 6: 218–21.

Potratz, Johannes A. H.

    1966   *Die Pferdetrensen des alten Orient.* Analecta Orientalia, vol. 41. Rome: Pontificum
            Institutum Biblicum.

Presedo Velo, Francisco J.; Blanco y Caro, R.; and Pellicer Catalán, Manuel

    1970   *La necrópolis de Mirmad (Argín Sur-Nubia sudanesa).* Memorias de las Misión
            Arqueológica, vol. 11. Madrid: Ministerio de Asuntos Exteriores.

Randall-MacIver, D., and Woolley, C. Leonard

    1911   *Buhen.* The University of Pennsylvania Egyptian Department of the University
            Museum. Eckley B. Coxe, Junior Expedition to Nubia, vols. 7–8 Philadelphia: The
            University Museum.

Reisner, G. A.

    1910   *The Archaeological Survey of Nubia, Report for 1907–1908.* Vol. I *Archaeological
            Report.* Cairo: National Printing Department.

    1923   *Excavations at Kerma, Parts I–V.* Harvard African Studies, vols. 5–6. Cambridge, MA:
            Peabody Museum of Harvard University.

Ricke, Herbert

    1967   *Ausgrabungen von Khor-Dehmit bis Bet el Wali.* Oriental Institute Nubian Expedition,
            vol. 2. Chicago: The University of Chicago Press.

Säve-Söderbergh, Torgny

    1963   "The tomb of the Prince of Teh-Khet Amenemhat," *Kush* 11: 159–74.

Säve-Söderbergh, Torgny; Englund, Gertie; and Nordström, Hans-Åke, eds.

    1982   *Late Nubian Cemeteries.* Scandinavian Joint Expedition to Sudanese Nubia, vol. 6.
            Copenhagen, Oslo, and Stockholm: Scandinavian University Books.

Schäfer, Heinrich

    1905   *Urkunden der Älteren Äthiopenkönige I.* Urkunden des ägyptischen Altertums, vol. 3,
            part 1. Leipzig: J. C. Hinric'sche Buchhandlung.

Schiff Giorgini, Michela

    1971   *Soleb II. Les Nécropoles.* Florence: Sansoni.

Schweinfurth, Georg

    1899   "Bega-Gräber," *Zeitschrift für Ethnologie* 31: 538–54.

    1922   *Auf unbetretenen Wegen in Aegypten.* Hamburg and Berlin: Hoffmann und Campe
            Verlag.

Seele, Keith C.

1974   "University of Chicago Oriental Institute Nubian Expedition: Excavations between Abu Simbel and the Sudan Border, Preliminary Report," *JNES* 33: 1–43.

Seligman, C. G.

1916   "A Prehistoric Site in Northern Kordofan," *LAAA* 7: 107–14.

Shafiq Farid

1963a   *Excavations at Ballana 1958–1959.* Cairo: General Organisation for Government Printing Offices.

1963b   "Excavations of the Antiquities Department at Ballana," in *Fouilles en Nubie 1959–1961.* Cairo: Organisme général des imprimeries gouvernmentales, pp. 89–94.

1973   "Excavations of the Antiquities Department at Qustul, Preliminary Report," *ASAE* 61: 30–35.

Shinnie, Peter

1954   "Excavations at Tanqasi, 1953," *Kush* 2: 66–85.

1978a   "The Nilotic Sudan and Ethiopia, c. 660 B.C. to A.D. 600," in *The Cambridge History of Africa*, vol. 2, edited by J. D. Fage Cambridge: Cambridge University Press, pp. 210–71.

1978b   "Christian Nubia," in *The Cambridge History of Africa*, vol. 2, edited by J. D. Fage Cambridge: Cambridge University Press, pp. 556–88.

Skeat, T. C.

1977   "A Letter from the King of the Blemmyes to the King of the Noubades," *JEA* 63: 159–70.

Smith, H. S.

1962   *Preliminary Report of the Egypt Exploration Society's Nubian Survey.* Cairo: General Organization for Government Printing Offices.

1976   *The Fortress of Buhen: the Inscriptions.* EES, vol. 48. London: EES.

Smither, Paul C.

1945   "The Semnah Dispatches," *JEA* 31: 3–10.

Snowden, Frank M.

1970   *Blacks in Antiquity; Ethiopians in the Greco-Roman Experience.* Cambridge, MA: Belknap Press of Harvard University.

Steffen, Randy

1973   *United States Military Saddles 1812–1843.* Norman, OK: University of Oklahoma Press.

Steindorff, Georg

1935   *Aniba, erster Band.* Glückstadt and Hamburg: J. J. Augustin.

Streck, Bernhard

1982   *Sudan: Steinernde Gräber und lebendige Kulturen am Nil.* Cologne: Dumont
Buchverlag.

Strouhal, Eugen

1984   *Wadi Kitna and Kalabsha South.* Vol. 1. *Archaeology.* Prague: Charles University.

Török, László

1979   "The Art of the Ballana Culture and its Relation to Late Antique Art,"
Meroitica 5: 85–100.

1988   *Late Antique Nubia: History and archaeology of the southern neighbor of Egypt in the
4th–6th c. A.D.* Antaeus; Communicationes ex Instituto Archaeologico Academiae
Scientarum Hungaricae 16. Budapest: Archaeological Institute of the Hungarian
Academy of Sciences.

Tomandl, Herbert

1987   "Tradierung und Bedeutung eines religiosen Motiv von der meroitischen bis zur
christlichen Periode." *Beiträge zur Sudanforschung* 2: 107–26.

Trigger, Bruce G.

1965   *History and Settlement in Nubia.* Yale University Publications in Anthropology, no. 69.
New Haven: Department of Anthropology, Yale University.

1967   *The Late Nubian Settlement at Arminna West.* Publications of the Pennsylvania-Yale
Expedition to Egypt, no. 2. New Haven and Philadelphia: The Peabody Museum of
Natural History of Yale University and the University Museum of the University of
Pennsylvania.

1969   "The Royal Tombs at Qustul and Ballana and their Meroitic Antecedents,"
JEA 55: 117–28.

1984   "History and Settlement in Lower Nubia in the Perspective of Fifteen Years,"
Meroitica 7: 367–80.

Updegraff, Robert Timothy

1978   "A Study of the Blemmyes," Ph.D. Dissertation, Brandeis University.

Verwers, Jan

1962   "The Survey from Fasras to Gezira Dabarosa." in "The Archaeological Survey on the
West Bank of the Nile." *Kush* 10: 19–33.

Vila, Andre

1975   *PASCAD,* Fascicule 2: *les districts de Dal (rive gauche) et de Sarkamatto (rive droite).*
Paris: Centre nationale de la recherche scientifique.

1976   *PASCAD,* Fascicule 4: *district de Mograkka (Est et Ouest), District de Kosha (Est et
Ouest).* Paris: Centre nationale de la recherche scientifique.

1977   *PASCAD*, Fascicule 8: *le district d'Amara Est*. Paris: Centre nationale de la recherche scientifique.

1978a   *PASCAD*, Fascicule 9: *l'ile d'Arnyatta; le district d'Abri (Est et Ouest); le district de Tabaj (est et Ouest)*. Paris: Centre nationale de la recherche scientifique.

1978b   *PASCAD*, Fascicule 10: *le district de Koyekka (rive droite); les districts de Morka et de Hamid (rive gauche); l'ile de Nilwatti*. Paris: Centre nationale de la recherche scientifique.

1980   *PASCAD*, Fascicule 12: *la nécropole de Missiminia I, les sépultures napatéennes*. Paris: Centre nationale de la recherche scientifique.

1982   *PASCAD*, Fascicule 13: *la nécropole de Missiminia II, les sépultures méroïtique*. Paris: Centre nationale de la recherche scientifique.

1984   *PASCAD*, Fascicule 14: *la nécropole de Missiminia. III. Les sépultures ballanéennes. IV. Les sépultures chrêtiennes*. Paris: Centre nationale de la recherche scientifique.

Whitcomb, Donald S. and Johnson, Janet H.
1979   *Quseir el Qadim 1978: Preliminary Report*. American Research Center in Egypt Reports, vol. 1. Cairo: ARCE.

1982   *Quseir el Qadim 1980: Preliminary Report*. American Research Center in Egypt Reports, vol. 7. Malibu: Undena.

Williams, Bruce
1985   "A Chronology of Meroitic Occupation below the Fourth Cataract," *JARCE* 22: 149–95.

n.d.   "The Late Nubian Pottery: a Review of *The Ceramic Industries of Medieval Nubia* by W. Y. Adams."

Woolley, C. Leonard and Randall-MacIver, D.
1910   *Karanog: The Romano-Nubian Cemetery*. The University of Pennsylvania Egyptian Department of the University Museum. Eckley B. Coxe, Junior Expedition to Nubia, vols. 3–4. Philadelphia: The University Museum.

LIST OF BIBLIOGRAPHICAL ABBREVIATIONS

ARCE   American Research Center in Egypt.

EES   Egypt Exploration Society.

JARCE   *Journal of the American Research Center in Egypt*, New York.

JEA   *Journal of Egyptian Archaeology*, London.

JNES   *Journal of Near Eastern Studies*, Chicago.

LAAA   *University of Liverpool Annals of Archaeology and Anthropology*, Liverpool .

Meroitica 2   W. Y. Adams et al., *Meroitic North and South. A Study in Cultural Contrasts. Meroitica. Schriften zur altsudanesischen Geschichte und Archäologie*. Vol. 2. Berlin: Akademie-Verlag, 1976.

Meroitica 5   *Africa in Antiquity; the Arts of Ancient Nubia and the Sudan. Proceedings of the Symposium Held in Conjunction with the Exhibition, Brooklyn, September 29– October 1, 1978*, edited by Fritz Hintze. Meroitica. Schriften zur altsudanesischen Geschichte und Archäologie. Vol. 5. Berlin: Akademie-Verlag, 1979

Meroitica 6   *Meroitic Studies: Proceedings of the Third International Meroitic Conference, Toronto 1977*, edited by N. B. Millet and A. L. Kelley. Meroitica. Schriften zur altsudanesischen Geschichte und Archäologie. Vol. 6. Berlin: Akademie-Verlag, 1982.

Meroitica 7   *Meroitistische Forschungen 1980; Akten der 4. Internationalen Tagung für Meroitistische Forschungen vom 24. bis 29. November 1980 in Berlin*, edited by Fritz Hintze. Meroitica. Schriften zur altsudanesischen Geschichte und Archäologie. Berlin: Akademie-Verlag, 1984.

Meroitica 10   *Studia Meroitica 1984: Proceedings of the Fifth International Conference of Meroitic Studies. Rome 1984*, edited by Sergio Donadoni and Steffen Wenig. Meroitica. Schriften zur altsudanesischen Geschichte und Archäologie. Vol. 10. Berlin: Akademie-Verlag 1989.

MDAIK   *Mitteilungen des Deutschen Archäologischen Instituts Abteilung Kairo*, Mainz am Rhein.

OINE III   Bruce Beyer Williams, *Excavations Between Abu Simbel and the Sudan Frontier,*
                  Keith C. Seele, Director. Part 1: The A-Group Royal Cemetery at Qustul: Cemetery
                  L. The Oriental Institute Nubian Expedition, vol. III. Chicago: The Oriental Institute,
                  1986.

OINE IV   Bruce Beyer Williams, *Excavations Between Abu Simbel and the Sudan Frontier,*
                  Keith C. Seele, Director. Parts 2, 3, and 4: Neolithic, A-Group, and Post-A-Group
                  Remains from Cemeteries W, V, S, Q, T, and a Cave East of Cemetery K. The
                  Oriental Institute Nubian Expedition, vol. IV. Chicago: The Oriental Institute, 1989.

OINE V   Bruce Williams, *Excavations Between Abu Simbel and the Sudan Frontier, Keith C.*
                  Seele, Director. Part 5: C-Group, Pan Grave, and Kerma Remains at Adindan
                  Cemeteries T, K, U, and J. The Oriental Institute Nubian Expedition, vol. V. Chicago:
                  The Oriental Institute, 1983.

OINE VII   Bruce Beyer Williams, *Excavations Between Abu Simbel and the Sudan Frontier,*
                  Keith C. Seele, Director. Part 7: Twenty-fifth Dynasty and Napatan Remains at
                  Qustul: Cemeteries W and V. The Oriental Institute Nubian Expedition, vol. VII.
                  Chicago: The Oriental Institute, 1990.

OINE VIII   Bruce Beyer Williams, *Excavations Between Abu Simbel and the Sudan Frontier,*
                  Keith C. Seele, Director. Part 8: Meroitic Remains from Cemetery Q at Qustul and
                  Cemetery B and a Settlement at Ballana. The Oriental Institute Nubian Expedition,
                  vol. VIII. Chicago: The Oriental Institute, 1991.

PASCAD   *La prospection archéologique de la valée du Nil au sud de la cataracte de Dal (Nubie*
                  soudanaise).

ZÄS   *Zeitschrift für Ägyptische Sprache und Altertumskunde.* Leipzig, Berlin.

ACKNOWLEDGMENTS

The excavations of the Oriental Institute Nubian Expedition were made possible by a grant from the United States Department of State and support from Mr. William Boyd. Research for the present volume was supported by a grant from the National Endowment for the Humanities. Publications were assisted by a gift from Mr. and Mrs. John Leslie. Without the help of these people and institutions, the project could not have been carried forward, and their help is gratefully acknowledged.

Many have aided this publication by contributing time and effort. Their number is too large for me to record here, and I can mention only those who played a role in forwarding this book. Artists were Lisa Heidorn, who also undertook most of the production, and Carol Abraczinskas; Peter Zale prepared the concession map. Photographers were Jean Grant, Jennifer Christiano, and Ursula Schneider. Major assistance in preparing and checking the manuscript was done by Leanne Galvin. Special care shown by Lynn Michaels of Color Concept Company made possible the halftone reproduction of painted pottery drawings. Pottery was mended by Mrs. Elizabeth Tieken and Mrs. Corsin Ellis. Objects were conserved, cleaned, and sometimes reassembled by Donald Hansen, Barbara Hall, Laura D'Alessandro, and Mrs. Carolyn Livingood. Text editing was done by Mrs. Sally Zimmerman, Mrs. Beverly Wilson, and the staff of the Publications Office. Valuable volunteer assistance was rendered by John Robb, Deborah Schwartz, and Patrick Zak. The staff of the Oriental Institute Museum has been a constant source of help, notably Raymond Tindel, John Larson, Honorio Torres, and the curator, Karen Wilson. The registry volunteers deserve special thanks for their continuous care and patience, as does Karen Bradley, who placed the objects in storage with care and precision. Very special thanks must be given to Mrs. Camilla Fano whose devotion and care in checking and registering objects have contributed greatly to the series, and to John Ellsworth for his great care and skill in pasting up the figures and plates for this volume. The directors and faculty of the Oriental Institute are owed deep gratitude for making the present series possible.

PREFACE

This volume completes a cycle of reports presenting the pre-Christian remains excavated by the Oriental Institute Nubian Expedition between Abu Simbel and the Sudan frontier. A number of Christian contexts were excavated also, but they were quite fragmentary and may be incorporated into future works.

The present volume contains two major groups of materials: remains of complexes that were associated with the royal tombs of Qustul and Ballana and private tombs. The former are of special interest because they show that the tumuli were the centers of continuing cults, and because they are related to earlier developments in Nubian funerary complexes, a topic which is reviewed briefly in *Chapter 1*. The second body of materials, from private burials, supports and augments the remains already published from the royal cemeteries, and the reader is referred to those works as often as comparisons permit.

CHAPTER 1

X-GROUP REMAINS AT QUSTUL AND BALLANA: CHRONOLOGY AND BURIAL CUSTOMS

One of the largest and most important bodies of material excavated by the Oriental Institute Nubian Expedition is assigned to the time between the Meroitic and Christian periods in Lower Nubia. Materials of this period were originally designated X-Group, as one of a series of letters used to indicate Nubian cultures that could not be given definite names.[1] Although letters assigned to earlier cultures, A-Group and C-Group, remain in current use, objections to the title X-Group have led to a number of alternative proposals, including Ballana Culture, Post-Meroitic, and Post-Pyramidal.[2] However, the term "group" has been revived as an archaeological designation for a body of materials that could be distinguished from others, even in cases where a direct succession of cultures may be assumed.[3] The alternative designations have the disadvantage of imputing local or cultural characteristics, a problem which the term "X-Group" does not have. The present work will therefore use X-Group as the term to refer to the major archaeological cultures in Nubia and Sudan in the fourth–sixth centuries A.D.[4]

A. THE EXPLORATION OF X-GROUP REMAINS AT QUSTUL AND BALLANA

Of all the major hidden remains of ancient civilization on the Nile, the latest great creations of pharaonic culture, the X-Group royal tumuli of Ballana and Qustul, were among the earliest detected. Burckhardt noted the Qustul tumuli and speculated on their contents with prescient accuracy;[5] Vyse observed the tumuli and attempted to excavate one;[6] Amelia Edwards observed both the Qustul and Ballana tumuli, scouted the Qustul cemetery and tried to excavate one of the smaller tumuli.[7] Subsequent travellers and researchers made no attempt to excavate the tumuli until Emery and Kirwan in 1931 began the first of four seasons on behalf of the Antiquities Service.[8] After their publication, no further work was attempted until three decades later, when Shafiq Farid excavated other large tumuli at Qustul and Ballana, again for the Antiquities Organization. So far, his work at Ballana has been published.[9] Although the area had been intensively explored, the possibility that the tumuli were the core elements of larger complexes was not considered.

1. See Reisner 1910, p. 345 for the genesis of the term X-Group.

2. Török 1988, p. 19 (Post-Meroitic); Trigger 1965, p. 132 (Ballana Culture, Tanqasi Culture); Adams 1977, p. 392 (X-Horizon, but also Post-Meroitic); see now Lenoble 1989, pp. 106–07 (Nubo-Meroitic for the culture or Post-pyramidal Meroitic).

3. See Fattovich 1989, pp. 55–56 for the use of Gash Group and Jebel Mokram Group.

4. See pp. 3–4 below for the problem of continuity.

5. Burckhardt 1822, pp. 36–37.

6. Edwards 1899, p. 322.

7. Ibid., pp. 314 and 322.

8. Emery and Kirwan 1938, pp. 1–4.

9. Shafiq Farid 1963a, 1963b, and 1973.

When the Oriental Institute Nubian Expedition began work in the Qustul Cemetery, the intention was to seek out burials of courtiers, officials, and other non-royal contemporaries of the owners of the great tumuli.[10] However, the opening of wide areas in the cemetery had unexpected results for part of the area had been previously used for caches and burials, and later for Christian burials. Most interesting, however, was the discovery that the great tumuli were parts of large complexes.[11] The earliest installations consisted of several groups of cache pits found just north of a shallow *khor* that divided the later X-Group cemetery. They dated to A-Group, and, as in the case with such pits elsewhere, they were used primarily for the storage of pottery and household objects.[12] No activity was in evidence after the A-Group until the early Meroitic Period, when the area near the already ancient cache pits began to be used for burials. These rapidly accumulated, and a large cemetery spread far to the west by late Meroitic times, although it ceased to be important well before the end of Meroitic Lower Nubia.[13]

At this point, a discrepancy should be noted between the locations of Cemeteries Q (220) at Qustul and 219 at Ballana as given by the original excavators and as determined by the Oriental Institute Nubian Expedition. The necessary revision for Cemetery Q was made based on large scale maps made by the Documentation Center and on aerial photographs as well as the expedition survey. However, the position of 219 was also displaced. Since The Oriental Institute did not excavate extensively in 219, the outline cannot be adjusted precisely. A revised location may be keyed approximately by identifying the row of four tumuli near the southeast edge of 219 on plate 1 as Ba. 3, 6, 9, and 37, respectively. Immediately to the west are Ba. 4, 10, and 47, with 2 and 1 in the more confused area just to the south. The isolated tumulus to the north is Ba. 80. None of the large tombs near the northern end of the cemetery is clearly identifiable in the photographs. The circular structure BA was thus probably associated with Ba. 80.

It was only in the earlier part of the X-Group period that the Qustul cemetery was used.[14] The first X-Group royal tumuli were erected in the southern part of the cemetery (Qu. 3, 14, 2, and 17);[15] at least some of them and some private tumuli had been built as complexes. There were sufficient changes in the burials between these southern tumuli, and those found in the northern sector, to suggest a different period for their placement. At the same time, the clearly successive erection of the northern complexes (Qu. 31, 48, and 36) would indicate that the Qustul Cemetery expanded from south to north. Approximately seven royal tombs were found altogether as well as numerous smaller tumuli. Changes in substructures and objects indicate a similar development in the Ballana necropolis,[16] but The Oriental Institute was unable to excavate in that cemetery (except for a single enigmatic structure) and this could not be verified from the development of complexes. Later, several small plots of Christian tombs were placed in Cemetery Q, but no evidence of transition between the two phases was recovered.

As the operations of the expedition expanded to other sites in the concession, X-Group tumuli and other graves were found in several places, most notably Cemeteries W, V, and R. Some remains in these cemeteries were later than those in the royal cemeteries. The area of Cemetery Q was excavated extensively in the 1962–1963 season, yielding several different kinds of loci. Their presentation requires a more complex series of prefix abbreviations than those used in previous volumes and are explained in the following table 1.

---

10. Seele 1974, pp. 2–3

11. See pp. 5–10 below.

12. OINE IV, pp. 105–12.

13. The remains are discussed in detail in OINE VIII; see also Williams 1985, pp. 149–70 for the chronology of Meroitic remains.

14. See pp. 12–15 below. The latest tombs in the concession, in Cemeteries R and V still did not contain the latest materials that can be dated to X-Group at Firka and Ibrim.

15. Tombs and loci were numbered consecutively Q 1–684. Surface installations were distinguished by upper case letters, A–H and numbers. The following are dealt with in this volume: Area B consists of chapels for Qu. 35; Area C consists of chapels assigned to Qu. 48; Area E is a single chapel assigned to Qu. 56. Area F is a series of chapels assigned to Qu. 36 (see tab. 1).

16. See pp. 4–5, 26–27 below.

Table 1. Tombs and Loci in Cemetery Q (220).

Seele Locus	Prefix Here	Number	Identification
—	Qu.	1–	Tumuli as numbered by Emery and Kirwan or Shafiq Farid
Q	Q	1–684	Tombs and other deposit loci excavated by the OINE
A	A	—	Building west of Q, not in this volume
B	QB	1–54	Row of chapels associated with Qu. 31
C	QC	1–57	Row of chapels associated with Qu. 48
D	QD	1–18	Superstructures of Meroitic tombs near Qu. 48; not considered in this volume
E	QE	1	Chapel/pit associated with Qu. 56
F	QF	1–14	Chapels associated with Qu. 36
G	G		Building, not in this volume
H	H		Area excavated, not in this volume

Note that the Qustul cemetery areas excavated were presented on field sheets designated A–F by Seele and Knudstad. They do not correspond to the locus designations given in this table. Private tombs on these field sheets are presented together under the headings Area Q*A* through Area Q*F*.

B. PROBLEMS IN X-GROUP ARCHAEOLOGY

CONTINUITY AND CHRONOLOGY

X-Group materials[17] found in the earliest season of excavation in Nubia differed considerably from those of contemporary Egypt, and also those of the Ptolemaic-Roman and Christian Periods in Nubia.[18] X-Group remains also differ from those of Meroitic Nubia south of the Dodekaschoinos, a contrast emphasized by the burials Emery and Kirwan found in the great tumuli of Qustul and Ballana. Not belonging to any traditional continuum in the area, X-Group left researchers with the problem of identifying the culture with one or more of the various groups known to have occupied the region in late Roman and Byzantine times.[19] Despite the resolution of the ensuing controversy in favor of identifying the royalty buried at Qustul and Ballana as Noubadian, a discrepancy remained between the testimony of ancient writers that two peoples occupied Lower Nubia and the appearance of only one archaeological culture in the region.[20] In addition, many X-Group cemeteries were located near or at Meroitic burial grounds and some settlements seemed to continue without interruption.[21] A number of common X-Group objects and practices also had antecedents in the earlier period. Because of the apparent unity of culture in the region and the continuity between periods, Lower Nubia between A.D. 100 and 570 was often viewed as a continuous series of developments.[22] However, some problems undermined this assumption that a homogeneous Nubian culture gradually evolved during X-Group. While it is true that numerous sites were used in both Meroitic and X-Group times, this could be due to the fact that the region offered such restricted opportunities for settlement and burial that many areas would inevitably be reused. Even so, many sites were begun or abandoned between Meroitic and

17. See note 1 above.

18. Reisner 1910, pp. 313–47.

19. Emery and Kirwan 1938, pp. 5–24, especially 18–24; Kirwan 1982.

20. Adams 1977, p. 420.

21. Török 1988, pp. 176–78, 199–207; Adams 1977, pp. 393–95.

22. Török 1988, pp. 211–19 summarizes a major discussion of the evidence. See also Adams 1977, pp. 393–95.

X-Group periods.[23] One other major argument for a direct transition between the two cultures must be rejected because it was based on sherds from occupation debris that actually contained material of several phases.[24] Inasmuch as a detailed examination of chronology had never been presented, chronological details of Meroitic and X-Group materials were not sufficiently well known to determine which were actually chronologically juxtaposed.

EVIDENCE FOR CULTURAL DIVERSITY

Although unacknowledged for some time, this question became more crucial in the 1960s when a major culture was clearly identified by Prof. Ricke in the Dodekaschoinos.[25] This culture, dated by associated coins and objects to the middle of the fourth century A.D., could be attributed to the Blemmyes. Although it contained imports that corresponded generally to those found in X-Group remains from the south, they did not correspond precisely enough to be considered contemporary, either with the X-Group of Qustul type, or with Meroitic materials.

C. ROYAL TOMBS AND THE CHRONOLOGY OF X-GROUP

Until recently, the chronology of X-Group in published discussions has not been closely reasoned or carefully documented. When first discovered, there was little with which to compare the X-Group. Early and late limits were set by the "donation of Diocletian" and the establishment of Christianity, while a positive historical correlation with the era of greatest Blemmye and Noubadian activity in Egypt, seemed convincing. The coin of Valens in Qu. 14 provided more positive corroboration. Although it sufficed to give a general date to X-Group, this chronology was not detailed enough to deal with the question of continuity.[26]

Sherds from stratified debris were used to construct chronology during the 1960s rescue, based on the implied belief that controlled excavation would produce controlled groups of more or less contemporary material. However, these expectations did not materialize. The strata were not carefully followed, while some collections of material as were presented as chronological groups that were, in their own time, either surface materials or the products of uncontrolled digging, i.e. fill. Thus broad transitional phases presented in the archaeological literature include pottery that varies in date from the middle of the Meroitic period to the middle of the X-Group period.[27] It was thus clear that neither Nubian comparisons alone, nor Nubian stratified sites, could produce a reliable and detailed chronology for either the Meroitic or X-Group periods.[28]

QUSTUL, BALLANA, AND THE CHRONOLOGY OF X-GROUP

Realizing the weakness of the various attempts to date Noubadian X-Group remains, Török undertook a major critical re-examination of the chronology of the Qustul and Ballana tumuli which have been at the center of chronological debate. Based largely on the development of the tombs, changes in the most elaborate deposits, and evidence furnished by northern imports, he established seven major phases, with eleven generations of rulers. Since this should produce periods of twenty years or less in length, such a

---

23. Adams 1977, pp. 393–95; for sites published after Adams' discussion, see table 9 below.

24. Trigger 1967, pp. 65–67; see OINE VIII, *Chapter 1* for a discussion of the chronological evaluation of occupation debris in this period.

25. Ricke 1967, pp. 37–42.

26. See Trigger 1969, pp. 121–22, 124–25; Török 1979, pp. 85–100 and 1988, pp. 75–207 for a detailed examination of the problems of chronology.

27. See note 26. In one proposed chronology of Meroitic pottery, phenomena associated with a middle phase was dated after the late phase. Since this late phase, at Karanog and elsewhere, can be correlated to later third century A.D. documents, this later phase was dated later, in the fourth century. Since it contained many northern imports that were antecedent to certain imported X-Group vessels, the chronological placement of this phase seemed to corroborate the belief in direct continuity between Meroitic and X-Group materials. See OINE VIII, *Appendix A*, p. 181.

28. OINE VIII, *Chapter 1*, pp. 4–6, Williams 1985, pp. 150–51.

detailed chronology was not necessary for the present report. Moreover, it was not applied directly to details of pottery types, nor was the important evidence yielded by complexes at Qustul available to him. Török's chronology could therefore not be accepted, without a procedure that would at once check the general order of his phases, and develop a chronology with broader chronological bands more useful in archaeological correlation. In the present case, simpler criteria, the substructures of the great tombs, changes in pottery, and the development of the Qustul cemetery were used to establish a chronology. Although this process was applied before the publication of Török's chronology, comparisons between the results produced by both inquiries were only differences in detail; they agree in all major respects. Only the status of Qu. 31 and Qu. 48, which are considered royal here, and the date of Ba. 80, which is considered late here, are at issue, but neither change overturns Török's outline of X-Group tomb typology or chronology. Other differences of detail that might be construed are herein held insignificant.

THE ORDER OF THE QUSTUL AND BALLANA CEMETERIES

The most important evidence discovered by The Oriental Institute for judging the chronology of the Qustul cemetery was the sequential development of complexes that accompanied several major tumuli, notably cult installations located north, and sometimes northeast of the tumuli. These became progressively more complex, beginning with a deposit of simple stone and crude mud cups near Qu. 14, and continuing with simple chapels (more than 50) in a row north of Qu. 31, to more elaborate ones north of Qu. 48, and still more complex chapels (14) north of Qu. 36. (pls. 2, 7–9). The progressive changes indicated that Qu. 14, Qu. 31, Qu. 48, and Qu. 36 were comparable royal tombs made in order. Although no attempt was made to distinguish royal, from other tombs presented in previous publications, it should be clear that Qu. 31 and Qu. 48 must be admitted to royal rank because of their important chapel rows. The lack of wealth in Qu. 31 may be attributed to plundering and the lack of size, wealth, and elaboration in the substructure of Qu. 48 may have been due both to hasty construction and plundering.

SUBSTRUCTURES

The complexes established the general chronological direction at Qustul, which could be extended to Ballana by tracing other developments in substructures, objects, pottery and aspects of the burials. Török traced the development of six types of major tomb substructure (A–F with numerous subdivisions and another type for smaller tombs (Z). These could be correlated with major tomb classes and one subdivision, which were plotted on maps of the cemetery in the present work (see tab. 2). Despite the complexity of development in the substructures of Qustul and Ballana, the types used by Török and types used here corresponded very closely, as did the chronology. The differences proposed here are not significant enough to propose a new series of royal generations, and the chronological correspondence between Török's eleven royal generations in fifteen phases (I–VII with subdivisions) and the major divisions developed for plotting is, except for Ba. 80, exact.[29]

29. Only Qu. 48, which is considered a hastily finished substructure in this work, was assigned to the great tomb series with Török's C–C/3. His late classes C/4–5 were grouped with F. The Qustul C–C/3 tombs all had long corridor dromos approaches from the east which were recurved to connect additional chambers on the north (right) side of the axis. The Ballana C/4–5 tombs all had a direct axis from the south leading to an outer (burial) chamber and an inner room. Chambers on the east (right) side of the axis were connected directly to the outer chamber. The plan of Qu. 2 (Török 1988, pl. 6), with its corridor leading from the burial chamber to a third (north) room is derived from Qu. 17 (ibid., pl. 5) and belongs to the Qustul C class, while that of Ba. 80 (ibid., pl. 6) has three additional chambers, two linked to the main chamber, following the plan of the Ballana C class (ibid., pl. 10). This arrangement appears to modify the axial plans of group F (ibid., pl. 9) which normally (except Ba. 73) have the third (transverse) chamber connected to the inner room by making them parallel and connecting them with the burial chamber. As a group, the amount of space devoted to these side chambers in the Ballana C group is much greater than that at Qustul, and the placement of the corridors differs.

Figure 1. The Occurrence of Royal Substructure Types in Cemetery Q (220).

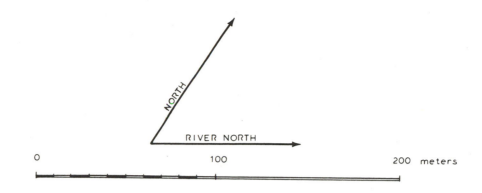

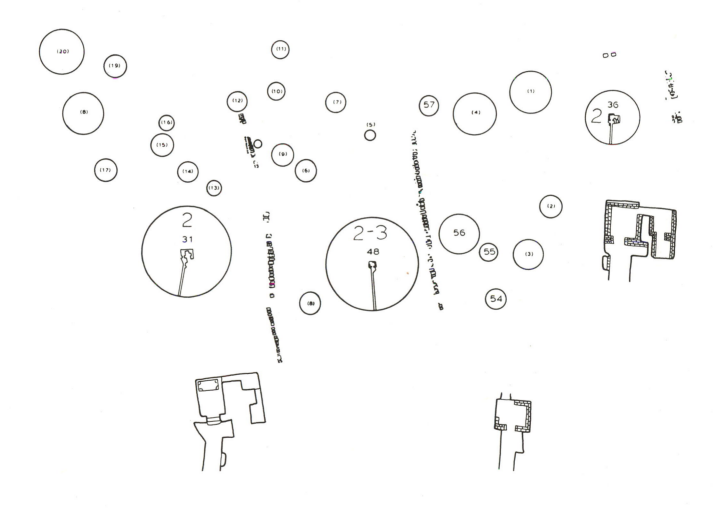

KEY

Tomb Number	Qu. 3	Qu. 14	Qu. 31	Qu. 36	Qu. 48
Török Group	B	A	C	C	Z/1
OINE Group	IA2	IA1	IB3	IB3	IB4
MAP INDEX	1	1	2	2	2

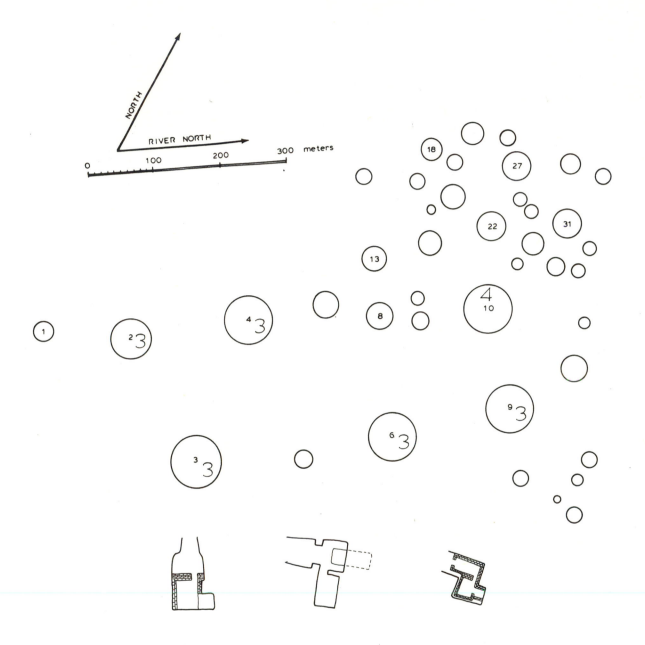

Figure 2. The Occurrence of Royal Substructure Types in Cemetery 219.

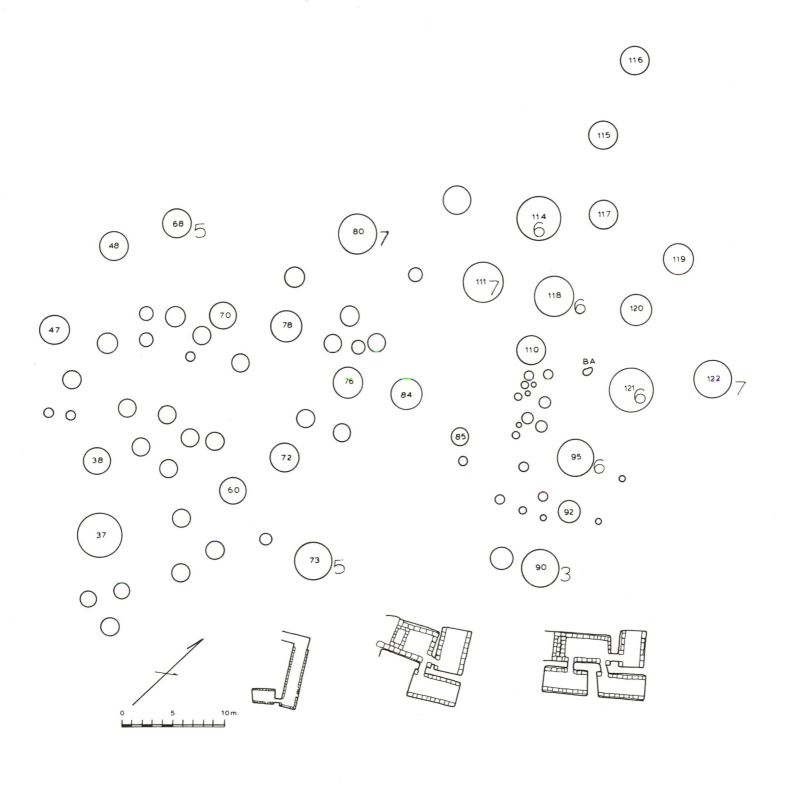

KEY

Tomb Number	Ba. 2	Ba. 6	Ba. 37	Ba. 3	Ba. 118	Ba. 80
Török Group	D	D	E	F	C	C
OINE Group	IIA	IIA	IIB	IIIA	IIIB1	IIIB2
MAP INDEX	3	3	4	5	6	7

Several kinds of substructure, indicated on table 2, could be plotted on the plans of the royal cemeteries to verify chronological development (figs. 1–2).[30] In both cemeteries, incremental changes in the substructures were arranged roughly in directions, first from south to north, then from east to west. These may be summarized as early experiments (1), tombs with the axis recurved to the north (2), a second series of experiments (3), the development of an axial approach to the burial (4), a straight axis with a single transverse side room (5), and a straight axis with a parallel side room or rooms (6).

The sequence of distribution agreed with the sequence of complexes, and the earliest stage also had a substructure (Qu. 3) most closely related to Meroitic mudbrick substructures.

Table 2. Substructures of X-Group Royal Tombs at Ballana and Qustul.

Key No.	Török Type	Török Plate	Outline			Remarks and Tombs
			I			Qustul stages (Török phases Ia–IIIa)
1				A		Shaft entered from the east with a large transverse rectangular pit
	A	4			1	Structure only a wall (Qu. 14)
	B	4			2	Construction within pit with two small subsidiary chambers (Qu. 3); see Karanog for Meroitic precedent[a]
2				B		Shaft entered from the east with longitudinal pit, axis recurved to the north; two well-defined chambers to the north, cb. lined
	C/3	6			1	Separate corridor to northeast chamber (Qu. 2)
	C[b]	5			2	North chamber linked to bent axis (Qu. 17)
	C	5			3	Same as 2, with a bed pit (Qu. 31, Qu. 36)
	Z/1	6			4	Unfinished (Qu. 48)
			II			
3	D/1–4	7		A		Axial approach to chamber, indirect to subsidiary chambers, burial pit virtually a chamber; partition still partly cut (Ba. 2 [indirect axis], Ba. 4, Ba. 9 [indirect axis], Ba. 6, Ba. 90)
4	E[c]	8		B		Indirect axis, partitions built (Ba. 47, Ba. 10, Ba. 37 [transitional to III A])
			III			Corridor bent or straight, but burial and second chamber axial (Phases VI–VII)
5	F	9		A		Storage jar chamber transverse to left beyond burial at slight angle (Ba. 3, Ba. 48, Ba. 68, Ba. 73)
				B		
6	C/5	10			1	Outer burial chamber, inner transverse chamber, longitudinal side chamber parallel (Ba. 95, Ba. 114, Ba. 118, Ba. 121)
7	C/4–5	6, 10			2	Side chamber(s) long, one double (Ba. 80, Ba. 111, Ba. 122)

a. Woolley and Randall-MacIver 1910, figs. A–B, tomb G 64.
b. C/1, C.
c. E, D/F, D/3.

Note that this table is drawn from Emery and Kirwan 1938, pp. 27–160. The numbers in the left column indicate tombs with the designated substructure in figures 1 and 2 in the present volume. For the second and third columns, see Török 1988, pp. 72–92, table 1, p. 154, and plates 4–10.

30. Emery and Kirwan 1938, pp. 27–160, plans. In addition, tumuli are added from Shafiq Farid's excavations.

OBJECTS

The Török chronology was verified using the distribution of substructure types, but its original construction was based as much on the occurrence and development of objects as on architecture.[31] However, the most important of these objects were imported, or made for special purposes, or even based on Meroitic prototypes. They were very important for developing a chronology of the royal cemeteries, where they occurred in large numbers and where they can serve as a check on the chronological vagueness of luxury goods in Nubia. Elsewhere, they were much less common, and difficult to use in extending the phasing from royal to private cemeteries, since objects of this kind tended to be used for longer periods than simple domestic pieces, or to be plundered and reused. Moreover, imports and elaborately made pieces tended to be much less common in private, than in royal tombs. The purpose of presenting the Oriental Institute's excavations required common objects that changed fairly rapidly and were not frequently reused.

POTTERY

The most reliable links between the royal and private tombs were found among common pottery vessels. These were especially useful because the tombs themselves were not often reused in X-Group, thus providing numerous unmixed collections of vessels. Among the various shapes, two major groups changed often enough, and occurred frequently enough, to provide reliable correlations between tombs and sites.[32]

NARROW-NECKED BOTTLE-JARS

Ovoid bottle-jars with tall, narrow necks and flaring rims were among the most common typical vessels of X-Group (fig. 14). Corresponding vessels in Meroitic times were very different; the profiles were globular and baggy, and the necks short and straight. Jars with this general gourd-like profile occur as early as A-Group.[33]

Although gourd-like vessels were made by most of the ancient cultures of Nubia, bottle-jars of almost every culture were given distinctive features of shape and decoration. In this case, the X-Group bottle-jar has distinctive features of shape that can be traced to an origin in the Tanqasi culture.[34] However, the simplest bottle-jar from the royal tombs has a neck of medium width that flares slightly at the rim. Decoration consists of a single row of blob-beads on a single string.[35] Despite changes in the neck, the vessel is clearly derived in shape and decoration from the latest Meroitic jars of fine/ordinary pottery.[36] Here it occurs in tombs of type I. The narrow-necked bottle-jars derived from Tanqasi prototypes at Ushara and Meroe appear in one tomb of type IB (Qu. 36). This vessel was common throughout the Ballana cemetery.[37]

GOBLETS

The second group of pottery vessels that were important chronologically were goblets. As the second element in the jar/cup combination that occurs in almost every period in Nubia, goblets are common in Lower Nubian X-Group. Two major forms of goblet were used in X-Group. Like bottle-jars, goblets were not derived from local antecedents but from Late Roman/Byzantine period Egyptian tradition. The process of

---

31. Török 1988, pp. 93–154. For his review of earlier opinion, see pp. 75–81. Both Millet (1968, p. 193) and Török (1979) had previously noted important differences between the types of objects found at Qustul and Ballana.

32. See Emery and Kirwan 1938, pp. 386–99; Török 1988, table 6; and Adams 1986, pp. 469–70 (mostly R1). See *Chapter 2*, pp. 39–42 below.

33. OINE IV, pp. 136–37 for pottery in A-Group and Neolithic times. Several vessels itemized on table 26 were also based on gourds or parts of gourds. See also figs. 6g–j and 30j, for example.

34. For the date of the Tanqasi Culture (X-Group of Noba tradition) and its jars, see Török 1988, pp. 195–99. See also *Chapter 2*, p. 40, n. 23 below.

35. Emery and Kirwan 1938, pl. 112:22.

36. OINE VIII, fig. 6j.

37. Emery and Kirwan 1938, pl. 112:28–38. For the occurrences, see pp. 27–74 (Qustul) and 75–160, tombs cited here in table 2. The incised grooves often made at the base of the neck may be simplified Upper Nubian decoration; See *Chapter 2*, p. 40.

adoption may have been rather complex, for goblets occur in metal, as do bottle-jars.[38] The finest, a straight-rimmed goblet, first appeared almost as broad as a bowl, with a ring base, a somewhat ribbed lower side, and a short, smooth, slightly inverted, almost vertical rim (fig. 7e). The first of these to appear at Qustul were equally tall and wide, while those found in the Ballana cemetery were taller, and narrower, with a smooth lower side and wider lip. The earlier type continued to occur in type IIA groups (Török's phase IIIb and later) Even taller goblets occurred in private tombs in Cemetery Q, Cemetery R, and other sites. Some of these have narrow, inverted rims.[39] The second type of goblet, a constricted vessel, has a tapered lower side, bulged shoulder, and a short vertical rim with a diameter smaller than the shoulder (fig. 7o–x). It, too, became taller and more slender in later groups, although the difference in the royal cemeteries was not so pronounced as elsewhere.[40]

POTTERY SUMMARY

The pottery from the royal tombs at Qustul and Ballana, as illustrated by the private tombs presented in this volume, thus revealed two phases in the development of bottle-jars and goblets, one corresponding roughly to the late fourth century A.D., the other to the fifth century A.D.[41] In addition, an earlier phase, with very broad, open goblets, corresponding to the middle of the fourth century A.D., could be distinguished in the Dodekaschoinos.[42] Also, a later phase, with very tall goblets, some with sharply inverted rims, and bottle-jars with elaborate rims, could be distinguished at Firka[43] and Ibrim.[44] This latter phase is probably dated to the late fifth and sixth centuries A.D. The four phases—Kalabsha (main period ca. A.D. 330/340–370/380), Qustul (ca. A.D. 370/380–410), Ballana (ca. A.D. 410–490), and Firka/Ibrim (ca. A.D. 490–570) describe the general chronology of X-Group in northern Nubia as used in this volume. However, the scheme has only a limited value for dating materials in southern Nubia and the Butana.[45]

E. THE DATE OF PRIVATE TOMBS AND CEMETERIES AT QUSTUL AND BALLANA

The large concentrations of tombs that characterized the Meroitic period in this region were essentially replaced by scattered burial plots or clusters. A few X-Group burials were found at Ballana, dispersed to the south of the Meroitic cemetery, and even at the Meroitic cemetery of Qustul, X-Group tombs were not placed in groups that continued the Meroitic cemetery. The various scattered tombs, plots, and clusters are identified within the larger cemetery areas here by a second letter, which is italicized for Cemetery Q (V*A*–V*H* and Q*A*–Q*E*). Stages in the development of each cluster or plot indicated by the distribution of tomb types, are distinguished by number and given an approximate range of dates by the contents of the best preserved tombs. These indicate that most of the clusters can be dated with some confidence within the X-Group phases of the royal cemeteries (table 3). The largest clusters are as follows: (Q*A* stage 1, sixteen early [?] tombs; Q*B*–Q*C* stage 1, twenty-one early to middle X-Group tombs; Q*E* stage 4, fourteen early tombs; Q*E* stage 5, fifteen early tombs; R stage 1, eighteen early to middle X-Group tombs, R stage 3, forty-seven middle to late X-Group tombs, W2 west stage, sixteen middle X-Group tombs, and B stages 2–3, scattered X-Group tombs.

These dated tombs offer some evidence for the chronology of tomb types in the area. In early Noubadian X-Group (second of the four phases), shafts were almost exclusively oriented north-south with a chamber on

---

38. For various metal prototypes of pottery vessels, see Emery and Kirwan 1938, pls. 64, 66, and 71.

39. Ibid., pl. 114:80–86; the two poles of the progression in the royal tombs are 83 and 80d.

40. Ibid., pl. 114:87.

41. See Török 1988, p. 154, table 1 for a summary of evidence developed in pp. 78–153.

42. Ricke 1967, fig. 72 above. Compare these with fig. 7a and e. Evidence for the date is summarized by Török 1988, pp. 178–81. Well-dated positive evidence consisting of coins, glass, and amphorae, was confined to the mid-late fourth century. Török also redates the Sayala cist tumuli, pp. 181–82. See Fathi Afifi Badawi 1976.

43. Kirwan 1939, pl. XXV:21, 14e–f, and 15. See Török 1988, pp. 189–93.

44. Mills 1982, pl. XIII:11.9, 11.11, and 12.2, for example. See Török 1988, pp. 182–84. The cemeteries began slightly earlier than Firka B, but the latest goblets are comparable.

45. Török 1988, pp. 195–98. Dates between A.D. 300 and 500 fit with the limited number of imports.

the west side. This type predominated into the middle phase (see Cemetery W2; this is the third phase). One or two early tombs may have been oriented east-west, but these may also have been reused Meroitic tombs (Q*E* stage 3). In Middle X-Group, the east-west direction came to predominate, and by the end (R stage 3), almost all tombs were so oriented. Few of the vaulted tombs found here could be dated, but these were middle and late X-Group.

Burials on hides occur early, and were replaced by bed burials in the middle and late phases, sometimes indicated only by trenches cut to allow the legs to pass into the chamber.

Table 3. The Three Major Substructure Types in the Cemetery Areas at Qustul.

| | *Location* | | | | | | |
	QA	QB	QC	QD	QE	R	W
North-South Shaft							
Late 4th Century	1,2[a]	1,2	1	1	3, 4[b] 5, (6)	1	—
Early 5th Century	3	1,3	1	1,2	—	3	2
Late 5th– 6th Century	—	—	—	—	—	—	—
East-West Shaft							
Late 4th Century	—	—	—	—	3[c]	—	—
Early 5th Century	3	1/1	2	—	4?	1,3	2
Late 5th– 6th Century	—	—	—	—	—	3[d]	—
Vault							
Late 4th Century	—	—	—	—	—	—	—
Early 5th Century	[4][e]	—	—	3	—	3	—
Late 5th– 6th Century	—	—	—	—	—	2, 3	—

a. Note that numbers indicate stages in Cemeteries Q and R.
b. Two undated east-west tombs; (6) is probably with 5.
c. One tomb.
d. Only important late occurrence.
e. Uncertain date.

CEMETERY Q

QA

Apart from the complexes, X-Group tombs occurred in four groups in Q*A*. To the east was a group of early medium- to small-sized tombs, all north-south shafts with chambers on the west side. Immediately to the west was a small group of five larger early tombs, also all with north-south shafts. Stage 3 consisted of seven middle X-Group tombs, mostly oriented east-west, just to the west of stage 2. Three shafts (north-south) with ledges and vaults to the northwest probably date to X-Group (stage 4). For the assignment of specific tombs, see table 30.

Table 4. Dated Private Tombs in the Stage-Clusters of Cemetery Q.

	QA 1 (16)	2 (5)	3 (6)	4 (4)	QB 1 (8)	2 (4)	3 (1)
Late 4th Century	12, 33	6, 8, 9			-- 70	62, 74	
Early 5th Century			1, 2, 3, 18	?	70 --		78
Late 5th– 6th Century							

	QC 1 (13)	2 (8)	QD 1 (4)	2 (3)	3 (2)		
Late 4th Century	------ 66, 67	--?-- -----	-----			51–53,	82
Early 5th Century	58, 227 ------	502 -----	-----	117 -----	143 -----		
Late 5th– 6th Century							

	QE 1 (4)	2 (4)	3 (18)	4 (14)	5 (15)	6 (3)
Late 4th Century	-----		----- 434	344, 388 192	161, 196 316, 338	134
Early 5th Century	-----	147, 148	-----			?
Late 5th– 6th Century						

Note that the number in parentheses in the heading gives the approximate number of tombs in the cluster. Numbers opposite time-phases are dated tombs. Dashed lines give the chronological boundaries for clusters not confined to a single time phase.

QB

Located east of QA, QB contained animal pits associated with three early tumuli and three groups or stages of private tombs. The largest was a group that extended along the eastern edge of the cemetery in QB and the area immediately to the north, QC, which dated to both early and middle X-Group. The second was a group of north-south shafts that extended in a line between Qu. 54/60 and Qu. 4. The third was an isolated middle X-Group tomb, Q 78. For tombs in the various stages, see table 32.

QC

The group of tombs in QB stage 1 continued to the north, where more tombs were dated. In addition, there was a group of tumuli west of Qu. 19 of which only two were dated. For dated tombs, see table 34.

Q*D*

The area near Qu. 31 contained a number of X-Group tombs, but none of the clusters were very large. One group consisted of isolated north-south shafts west of Qu. 31, which apparently once had small tumuli. Three small north-south tombs were found southwest of Qu. 48, and there were two isolated tumulus tombs west of Qu. 33 of middle X-Group date, with ledges, vaults, and end-niches. For dated tombs, see table 36.

Q*E*

More X-Group tombs were found near Qu. 48 than any of the other great tumuli. These can be considered in six groups whose location, date, and major tombs are summarized in tables 37 and 38. Most of the tombs were early, and located north and west of Qu. 48, in the area bounded by that tumulus and Qu. 54, Qu. 51, Qu. 50, Qu. 35, and Qu. 49 (stages 2, 3, and 4).

Table 5. Stages and Tomb Types in Cemetery R.

	R 1 (18)	R 2 (5)	R 3 (47)	
Late 4th Century	----- 111, 118	-----		
				110
Early 5th Century	-----		60, 66, 49, 24 22, 23, 62, 65	
				11
Late 5th– 6th Century		-----	2, 8, 15, 51, 64, 89, 95	

	Shaft types				
	1:N-S	*1:E-W*	*3:N-S*	*3:E-W*	*Vault/Niche*
Late Meroitic					
Early 4th Century					
Mid 4th Century					
Late 4th Century	x				
Early 5th Century		x	x	xx	
Late 5th– 6th Century				xx	xx

CEMETERY R

Cemetery R includes a number of groups that were not originally related, notably a group of early to middle X-Group tombs to the north, scattered early and middle (and one late) tombs to the west, and a large group of middle and late tombs to the east. This last group extended across a New Kingdom cemetery located toward the south and east of the area, and a few Christian burials were located there also. For dated stages and tomb types, see tables 5 and 41.

CEMETERY V

VA–VI

The plain north of R was sparsely dotted with burials of A-Group, New Kingdom, and X-Group date (tables 6, and 43–49). There was one cluster of Christian tombs, and circular pits were also found. Most of the earlier tombs and X-Group burials were found in small clusters. The only remarkable feature in X-Group was a stepped pit in VB, lined with stones on three sides.

Table 6. Types and Tombs in Cemetery V.

	VA (4)	VB (1)	VC (2)	VF (1)	VG (3)	VH (4)	VI (3)
Late 4th Century	----- 14				36 (E-W)		
Early 5th Century	-----		41 probably 42	68?			
Late 5th– 6th Century	X?ᵃ 95, 96	X?ᵇ	N-S		89 (N-S)	N-S shaftᶜ	3 E-W not located

a. 9, N-S with wide trench, 13, N-S.
b. Stepped pit, uncertain date.
c. 122–124, 127; others Christian?

CEMETERY W2

W2 consisted of two clusters of tombs (table 50), the westernmost of which was substantially X-Group in date. All but four of the X-Group tombs were oriented north-south.

CEMETERY J

Only three X-Group tombs were located in Cemetery J, which was a small area with tombs of the C-Group, X-Group, and Christian periods (tables 7 and 51).

Table 7. Cemeteries W2 and J.

	W2 (16)	J (3)
Late 4th Century	?	
Early 5th Century	74, 57?, 58?	3?
Late 5th– 6th Century		3, 7, 8

F. THE QUSTUL-BALLANA SEQUENCE AND OTHER SITES

The chronological progression of the royal cemeteries was originally indicated by changes in the substructures, the development of complexes, and the distribution of elaborate imported objects. The sequence was extended, using these features, and validated by plotting only tombs that appeared to be royal. However, only pottery occurred elsewhere, with enough frequency to make it useful as a standard to establish the dates of other sites, although Török used elaborate, but less common objects.[46]

As discussed above, two major phases of X-Group pottery can be detected in material found elsewhere, which are not represented in the royal tumuli (table 8). First, the broadest goblets with very narrow rims were found in the Dodekaschoinos, in Blemmye remains near Bab Kalabsha, and in the "taverns" and graves at Sayala.[47] A stage later than the royal cemeteries is represented by the tall goblets with concave lower sides, narrow profiles, and rather sharply in-turned rims. This stage, also characterized by bottle-jars with complex rim profiles and sometimes elaborately painted decoration, is most prominently documented at Abri, Firka, and the cemeteries at Ibrim.[48]

G. THE HISTORICAL CHRONOLOGY OF X-GROUP

Inasmuch as each of the major phases can be identified quite rapidly in well-controlled groups that include pottery, they are easily correlated with major X-Group sites. However, because Nubia made so little use of coinage, correlations with the Mediterranean world have been more problematical until recently.[49] Very early materials from the Kalabsha area were associated with coins of Constantius II, and Constantinopolis coins were also present, indicating a date in the second third of the fourth century A.D.[50] A coin of Valens in the mound of tumulus Qu. 14 indicates a date in the last quarter of the century for that early X-Group tomb.[51] This rather meager evidence was supplemented by large amounts of elaborate imported goods, but the discussion of these objects has sometimes been contradictory, and the results of important studies and comparisons have been widely ignored.[52] Török's wide-ranging, and elaborate discussion of the available parallels has established patterns of evidence to date the four phases recognized in this work.[53] His results agree with dates that can be derived directly from the coins; they agree generally with the historical situation, as reconstructed in his work, but also as construed by others.[54] Because there is no space here to examine the details of Török's comparisons and because this writer believes that his dates are unlikely to be

46. 1988, pp. 176–207.

47. See note 43 above. Ricke 1967, fig. 72:B8/2, 3, 4; B6/1; Török 1988, p. 179; see p. 157 below.

48. See notes 44 and 45 above for Firka and Ibrim. For Abri-Missiminia, see Vila 1984 and Török 1988, p. 188 and especially pls. 159–60.

49. Trigger 1969, p. 125. He recognized the chronological position of the royal cemeteries but could not distinguish a progression in the material.

50. Ricke 1967, p. 39; Strouhal 1984, p. 230; Török 1988, p. 179.

51. Emery and Kirwan 1938, p. 398; Török 1988, p. 94.

52. Török 1988, pp. 75–78.

53. For the earliest phase in the Kalabsha area (and Sayala), see Török 1988, pp. 178–82, the most important evidence being discussed on p. 179. For the "taverns," which probably served for some kind of funerary meal, at the cemeteries, see Kromer 1967, pp. 77–102, also Fathi Afifi Badawi 1976. At least some of the "taverns" and tumuli appear to begin earlier than A.D. 330, although the pottery differs from Meroitic remains just to the south (see OINE VIII, *Chapter 2*). Although not all of the tombs and contexts date to the period ca. A.D. 330–380, this culture is certainly displaced by the Noubadian X-Group of the Triakontaschoinos by ca. A.D. 420 (middle X-Group).

  For the second and third phases, the early (ca. A.D. 370–410) and middle (ca. A.D. 410–490) X-Group (Noubadian), see Török 1988 (superseding 1979), pp. 75–109 (Qustul) and pp. 109–54 (Ballana), summarized in table 1, p. 154. Note that the first decade or so of the fifth century would probably form a transitional period in archaeological groups, especially pottery.

  For the fourth phase, the late X-Group (Noubadian), see Török 1988, p. 193 (Firka Cemetery B), 182–84 (Ibrim; much material is middle X-Group), and 188 (Abri-Missiminia).

54. Török 1988, pp. 219–34. For a review of sources and opinions, see pp. 22–73.

substantially changed, the chronology advanced in *Late Antique Nubia* has been adopted. Of the four phases, the first three are linked with historical evidence from the Mediterranean, but the last, the Firka/Ibrim phase, has not been precisely correlated. Its beginning is established by the end of the Ballana cemetery, but the archaeological transition to the Christian Period cannot be dated.

Table 8. The Chronology of X-Group in Lower Nubia.

Location	Triakontaschoinos	Dodekaschoinos	Date
Late Meroitic	Karanog, Ibrim, Ballana		
			ca. A.D. 300
Early 4th Century		Sayala tumuli, "taverns"	
			ca. A.D. 300
Mid 4th Century		Bab Kalabsha, Wadi Kitna	
			ca. A.D. 370
Late 4th Century	Qustul (220), Gamai	possibly same, continued	
			ca. A.D. 410
Early 5th Century	Ballana (219)	112, 122, 34	
			ca. A.D. 490
Late 5th– 6th Century	Ibrim, Firka, late groups to S	same continued	

H. CHRONOLOGY AND THE OCCUPATION OF X-GROUP NUBIA

As accepted in this work and indicted in table 9, X-Group Nubia has five phases. The first two occurred in the Dodekaschoinos, in the taverns and cell-tumuli of Sayala,[55] and the cemeteries near Kalabsha (Kalabsha and Wadi Kitna).[56] These sites were not matched chronologically in the Triakontaschoinos, where no cemeteries yielded remains that could be dated between about A.D. 300 and 370. Since none of the settlement sites were excavated by methods that would distinguish deposits of different eras,[57] and since debris in Nubia tends to contain material of different ages,[58] the various transitions between the Meroitic and X-Group of Lower Nubia derived from these occupation sites should be rejected.[59] There is a gap in the known archaeology of the valley south of Sayala during the first three quarters of the fourth century A.D. The Qustul cemetery began in the late fourth century, followed by the Ballana cemetery in the fifth. Both of these phases are strongly represented in the Triakontaschoinos, but only the second appears in the Dodekaschoinos. This suggests that there may have been a hiatus of uncertain duration and significance in its occupation. However, the table includes a number of undated sites that could have emanated from this period.

During the main period of the Ballana royal cemetery (middle X-Group), the large cemeteries at Ibrim were begun, and sites in the Dodekaschoinos can be assigned to the same culture. The great mounds at Gamai ceased to be made and some probably had been used for new burials. However, great mounds were

55. Kromer 1967, pp. 77–102; Fathi Afifi Badawi 1978, pp. 1–35, pls. 28–29; see also Török 1988, pp. 181–82. For the shapes of the burials, see figs. 3–4. Rubble tumuli are still used by the Bedja (Schweinfurth 1899, pp. 538–54; 1920, pp. 270–80; Updegraff 1979, pp. 200–01).

56. Ricke 1967, pp. 37–70; Strouhal 1984; Török 1988, pp. 178–81. The executioners' trenches at Shellal very probably date to this period or slightly later, based on the fact that Shellal was the frontier only after the beginning of the fourth century, and also from a coin found in one of the trenches. (Reisner 1910, pp. 72–73).

57. See table 9 above, Arminna settlement, for example.

58. See pp. 3–4 above and Williams 1985, p. 150.

59. Following Török 1988, pp. 201–07, 211, citing the major sites and sources.

now erected at Kosha East and at Firka, indicating the rise of a center there, possibly a continuation of the series at Gamai.

By late X-Group, the royal cemetery at Ballana ceased to be used, even though, based on published evidence, this was the great age of the Gebel Ada X-Group cemeteries. Most of the X-Group remains at Ibrim date to this period, and new, large cemeteries appear at the Wadi Allaqi. The end of the Ballana royal cemetery was not an isolated event, for the great tombs at Firka, Kosha, and Gamai were replaced by considerable, but less imposing tumuli in several places, especially Wadi Allaqi, Ibrim, and Gebel Ada.

Although archaeological evidence seems to indicate that Lower Nubia was densely occupied between A.D. 350 and 370, it is probably based on too few and too elaborate tombs to adequately represent the general population.[60] Even the evidence from fragmentary settlements that suggests a smaller and poorer population than existed in late Meroitic times indicates a larger number of inhabitants than the tumuli. Three regional cultures can now be identified in this period, (1) the culture of the fourth century Dodekaschoinos, (2) the "Noubadian X-Group" proper of the fourth to the sixth centuries, extending to the south of Abri, and (3) an uncertain number of cultures in Sudan which have been grouped under the Tanqasi label.[61] Although the identification of these three cultures has been disputed, their separate archaeological identity is clear. Generally Noba (Nubian) traditions seem to have been responsible for the Sudanese sites, whether or not they overlapped with the Meroitic period.[62] The larger of the two Lower Nubian cultures certainly produced the material culture of the Noubadians, as they identified themselves.[63] Although it has been compared to Meroitic culture and to Noba remains in Sudan, the culture of the Dodekaschoinos differs appreciably in burial types[64] and pottery[65] from both Meroitic and Noba traditions. Rather, the tumuli belong to the tradition of the Eastern Desert or Atbai. In this work, the three traditions are known as X-Group of Blemmye,[66] Noubadian, and Noba tradition, respectively.

60. Török 1988, pp. 212–13. On pp. 186–88, he compares the findings of the Franco-Sudanese Survey with Trigger's estimates for population in the same region, with considerable divergence.

61. Ibid., p. 219.

62. Ibid., pp. 195–99.

63. The definite nature of the boundary between Lower Nubia and the south was pointed out by Török (ibid., pp. 219–20) rather diffidently, despite the close relationship. The term Noubades was repeatedly used for the Lower Nubian kingdom, even by its own rulers, such as Silko and Abourni. See ibid., pp. 51–59.

64. See ibid., pp. 178–81. Compare Ricke 1967, figs. 59–63 and Strouhal 1984, pp. 21–81; see also Updegraff 1978, pp. 200–04 and Schweinfurth 1899, pp. 538–54. The type of tomb superstructure was characteristic in the Eastern Desert and along the desert edges in Upper Egypt, territory associated with the Blemmyes, but never the Noubades.

65. Compare Ricke 1967, figs. 73–76, pls. 24–28 (various) with Garstang, Sayce, and Griffith 1911, pls. XLI–XLII (various). The pottery differs considerably from Adams' H11.

66. Török (1988, pp. 31–51) believed that the Kalabsha groups belonged to the Meroites rather than the Blemmyes because the Meroitic kingdom existed well into the later fourth century (p. 37, see also p. 45). Note, however, that the Meroites and Blemmyes were associated in the embassy of A.D. 336 (pp. 31–32 but the "Meroites" are actually called Ethiopians). The Kasu and Bedja were claimed together as subjects by Ezana of Aksum (p. 33) who made a practice of confirming subject local rulers in Arabia (p. 44, quoting Burstein). If Kharamdeye's name associates him with the Blemmyes named in Gebelein Document 6. SB III 6257 (p. 66; for a discussion, see Millet 1968, pp. 272–304), one more item connects the Blemmyes and Meroites. This connection, under Axumite suzerainty, could account for all of the events Török cites without the existence of an organized Meroitic province of Lower Nubia in the fourth century. In sharp contrast to the third century, there are no datable Meroitic records or archaeological contexts from the Triakontaschoinos in the first seventy years of the fourth century (OINE VIII, *Chapter 1* and Williams 1985, pp. 191–95). That province had probably ceased to exist and had become a "no-man's land." Review of other events should stress that the base of Blemmye (Bedja) power was, and is, in the vast expanse of the Atbai (Paul 1954, Updegraff 1979, pp. 10–13), and occupation of the Valley was probably incidental; even the location of their cemeteries reflects this circumstance. The Noubadian kingdom and its successors were centered on the valley.

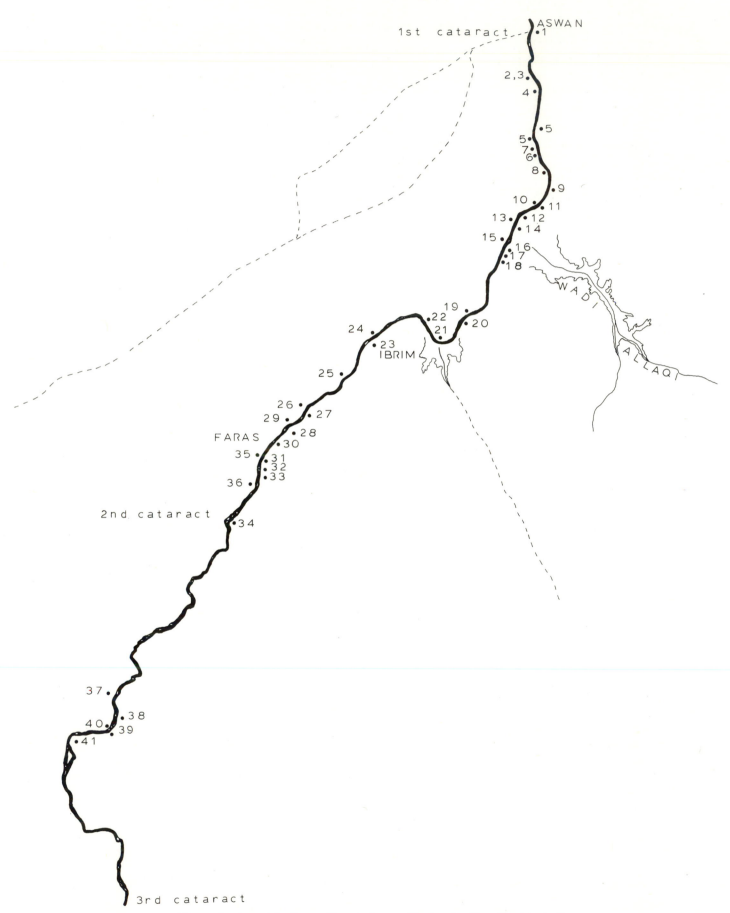

Figure 3. Map of X-Group Sites in Lower Nubia. For Key See Table 9.

Table 9. The Relative Chronology of X-Group Sites.

Map Key	Location	Size/ Type	Late Meroitic	Early 4th Century	Mid 4th Century	Late 4th Century	Early 5th Century	Late 5th– 6th Century
1	15[a]	40–50					x	x
2	34[b]	40–50					x	x
3	35[c]	Few, ?					?	
4	41:1[d]	ca. 40+					x	x
5	B[e]	Rulers			x			
5	C Taphis[f]	1 ruler			x			
5	A–E[g]	500			x			
6	W. Kitna[h]	Very large		x				
7	59[i] Kalabsha	2						
8	63[j] Dendur	Traces						
9	68[k] Moalla	1						
10	72[l] Gerf Hussein	180+					x[m]	x[n]
10	74[o] Gerf Hussein	Few						
11	75[p] Gerf Hussein	Cemetery						
12	92[q] Aman Daud	—					x	?

a. Reisner 1910, pp. 149–55.

b. Ibid., pp. 199–203.

c. Ibid.

d. Ibid., pp. 207–08.

e. Ricke 1967, pp. 37–45, 55–63. Török 1988, pp. 178–81.

f. Ricke 1967, pp. 42, 65–68, and Török 1988, pp. 178–81.

g. Ricke 1967, p. 37 and Török 1988, pp. 178–81.

h. Strouhal 1984, and Török 1988, pp. 178–81.

i. Firth 1912, p. 36.

j. Ibid., p. 37.

k. Ibid., p. 66.

l. Ibid., pp. 88–98.

m. Ibid., tombs 93 and 166 for example.

n. Ibid., tombs 60, 64, and 162.

o. Ibid., pp. 108–09.

p. Ibid., p. 110.

q. Ibid., pp. 201–03.

Table 9. The Relative Chronology of X-Group Sites (*cont.*).

Map Key	Location	Size/Type	Late Meroitic	Early 4th Century	Mid 4th Century	Late 4th Century	Early 5th Century	Late 5th–6th Century
13	100 Pselchis[r]	—	x	x				
14	112–113[s] W. Allaqi	120						x
15	122[t]	140					x?	x
16	132[u]	34–35					x?	x
17	137[v] Sayala N.	Few						
—	143/147[w]	?[x]						
18	Sayala Taverns[y]	—		x				
18	Tumuli[z]	Cemetery		x				
19	Wadi el Arab[aa]	Settlement		House 1, room 1			House 22	
19	154[bb]	40						
20	156[cc]	?						
21	163[dd]					64		
22	169[ee]					Pit		
23	192 Ibrim[ff]	200					Many	Very many
23	193[gg]	165					x	Very many

r. Firth 1915, pp. 25–29. This belongs to the Dodekaschoinos tradition if Roman; note the early *qadus*.

s. Firth 1927, pp. 112–24, see pp. 112–17, tombs 10, 43, 47, and 84.

t. Ibid., pp. 156–65.

u. Ibid., pp. 188–90.

v. Ibid., p. 212.

w. Ibid., p. 45.

x. Uncertain occurrence, taken from the survey, not the grave register.

y. Kromer 1967, from the Dodekaschoinos tradition.

z. Fathi Afifi Badawi 1976; Török 1988, pp. 181–82.

aa. Emery and Kirwan 1935, pp. 108–22. For the Dodekaschoinos tradition, see figs. 94:1, 99:5, and fig. 103:13. For early Noubadian X-Group, see fig. 107, for example.

bb. Ibid., p. 124, fig. 3; p. 136, fig. 122; pp. 138–48, various.

cc. Ibid., p. 148.

dd. Ibid., p. 159, mixed with Meroitic phase III material.

ee. Ibid., pp. 199–200. The pit was reused.

ff. Mills 1982, pp. 9–35. See Török 1988, pp. 182–84 for the Ibrim cemeteries.

gg. Mills 1982, pp. 47–67.

Table 9. The Relative Chronology of X-Group Sites (*cont.*).

Map Key	Location	Size/ Type	Late Meroitic	Early 4th Century	Mid 4th Century	Late 4th Century	Early 5th Century	Late 5th– 6th Century
24	200[hh]	12?				93, 96	89	
23	192c[ii]	5	x					
26	214[jj]	Few				6?, 157		
24	Masmas[kk]	1				46		
25	Arminna[ll]	Settlement	Mixed			Mixed	Mixed	
24	Aniba[mm]					x		x
27	Ada[nn] Cemetery					x		x
27	Ada[oo] Fortress		x			?		
28	Q, R, W Qustul					x	x	?
29	219 Ballana					x		
30	195[pp] Faras	—						18
30	Site 19[qq]	—					x	
31	25[rr] Serra	—				25, 117, 143		7, 27, 127
32	350[ss]	—				VIII		
33	63[tt]	—					1A?	1
34	163[uu]	—				2		

hh. Emery and Kirwan 1935, pp. 294–311.

ii. Mills 1982, pp. 44–45.

jj. Emery and Kirwan 1935, pp. 417–50. The cemetery is largely Meroitic.

kk. Almagro 1965, p. 113. This is a Meroitic Cemetery of some 150 tombs.

ll. Trigger 1967. For late X-Group, see fig. 20:5 and 6 (House X); see also the stratigraphic summary, pp. 58–70. Fine Meroitic cups (Trigger's 1A) occur in levels II and III with Middle (2A) and Late (2B) X-Group goblets. See also Török 1988, pp. 203–04.

mm. See Abd el–Moneim Abu Bakr 1967, pl. XXXIV above center; for late material, see pl. XXXIII above center.

nn. For early tombs, see Millet 1963, pp. 154–64 (Cemetery 3); for later materials, see ibid., fig. 4 (Cemetery 1) and Mostapha el-Amir 1963, pls. IX above, X below, and XI.

oo. The X-Group installations in the fortress have not been dated within the period. See Millet 1968, pp. 193–94 and Török 1988, p. 205.

pp. Säve-Söderbergh, Englund, and Nordström, eds. 1981, pp. 65–67, pl. 20.

qq. Ibid., p. 68, pl. 21.

rr. Ibid., pp. 70–127, pls. 33–38. Note that groups are not complete.

ss. Ibid., pp. 130–32, pl. 42.

tt. Ibid., pp. 139–42, pl. 49.

uu. Ibid., pp. 178–79, pl. 68.

Table 9. The Relative Chronology of X-Group Sites (*cont.*).

Map Key	Location	Size/Type	Late Meroitic	Early 4th Century	Mid 4th Century	Late 4th Century	Early 5th Century	Late 5th–6th Century
34	Gamai[vv]	—				x		
35	Serra West[ww]	—					x	x
36	Argin Mirmad[xx]	Cemetery				1, 8, 9	23	24, 27
36	Nag el Arab[yy]	Cemetery				x	x	x
38	Firka[zz]	Cemetery					A	B
37	Dal[aaa]	Cemetery						x
37	Mog-rakka[bbb]	Cemetery						x
39	Kosha East[ccc]	Cemetery					x	
40	Kosha West[ddd]	Cemetery					2	
41[eee]	Amara Dambo	40						x
2-R-48[fff]	Shaboon	50						x
2-S-11[ggg]	Olleg	15					x unc.	
2-S-23[hhh]	Yaren	2–3					x unc.	
2-S-24[iii]	Saadee	Few?					x unc.	

vv. Bates and Dunham 1927, Mounds B, C, E, A, U, and Y. Mound J has two horse burials in a pit to the west, note also animals in the shaft of Y1, p. 89.

ww. Verwers 1962, pl. V.

xx. Presedo Velo, Blanco y Caro, and Pellicer Catalán 1970; note the tombs below by number.

yy. Pellicer and Llongueras 1965, for the late fourth century, see fig. 18:1, for the early-mid fifth century, see fig. 18:4, 11, 13, and 14; for the late fifth-sixth century, see figs. 18:3, 5, 8, 9, and 10.

zz. Kirwan 1939, for earlier large tombs in Cemetery A, see pp. 1–12; for later tombs in Cemetery B, see pp. 12–18. See Török 1988, pp. 189–93 for a discussion.

aaa. See Vila 1975, pp. 40–42 (3-B-10), 92–93 (3-B-38), and 73–75 (3-B-26). For a discussion of the entire region between Dal and Abri, see Török 1988, pp. 186–88.

bbb. Vila 1976, pp. 48–50 (3-L-16).

ccc. Kirwan 1937, pp. 24–27. K 1 and 2 were very large; Vila 1976, pp. 74–78. See Török 1988, pp. 193–94.

ddd. Vila 1976, pp. 104–05.

eee. Vila 1977, pp. 74–75. From this point forward, sites are not placed on the map individually. The map key refers to the location as recorded by the Franco-Sudanese survey.

fff. Ibid., pp. 89–91.

ggg. Ibid., pp. 104–05.

hhh. Ibid., pp. 114–15.

iii. Ibid., pp. 116–17.

Table 9. The Relative Chronology of X-Group Sites (*cont.*).

Map Key	Location	Size/ Type	Late Meroitic	Early 4th Century	Mid 4th Century	Late 4th Century	Early 5th Century	Late 5th– 6th Century
2-S-25[iii]	Kada	7					x unc.	.
2-S-26[kkk]		20					x unc.	
2-S-30[lll]	Adjej	20 + Ch.					x unc.	
2-V-6 (40)[mmm]	Abri Miss-iminia	260					x unc.	x imp.
2-V-13[nnn]	S. el Abd	Small						
2-V-21[ooo]	Tabaj Serrana	200				x		x
8-B-22[ppp]	Damnei	40				x		
8-B-34[qqq]	el Beleh	75					x unc.	
8-G-14[rrr]	Koyyekka Meter	10+					x unc.	
8-L-4[sss]	Kodiya	150						x?
8-B-27[ttt]	Morka Irki Saab	30				x		
8-G-33[uuu]	Hamid Abjaber	?					x unc.	
8-L-3[vvv]	Nilwatti Nobrayin/ Kudee-Kullu	30 + Ch.						x imp.

Note that sites·are number-keyed to numbers given in the first column in table 9. Some sites were clustered too closely to be given individual numbers, as at Ibrim, Qustul, and in the area between Dal and the south end of Sai Island (see note eee). The sites are only those included in the present scheme of chronology. Thus the region between Gamai and Dal, from which little evidence has been identified, contains no sites.

jjj. Vila 1977, p. 118.

kkk. Ibid., p. 119.

lll. Ibid., pp. 124–25.

mmm. Vila 1984, pp. 6–177; see Török 1988, pp. 188–93.

nnn. Vila 1978a, pp. 46–48.

ooo. Ibid., pp. 95–97.

ppp. Ibid., pp. 112–13.

qqq. Ibid., pp. 115–16.

rrr. Vila 1978b, pp. 34–35.

sss. Ibid., pp. 43–44.

ttt. Ibid., pp. 62–63.

uuu. Ibid., p. 95.

vvv. Ibid., pp. 108–09.

I. THE ROYAL COMPLEXES OF QUSTUL

The most important discovery of the Oriental Institute Nubian Expedition in Noubadian X-Group was the discovery that the great royal tumuli, and at least some of the smaller tombs of the Noubades, were parts of complexes. Although three expeditions have explored the royal cemeteries of Qustul and Ballana, the first two treated the tumuli essentially as isolated barrows. It was not until Seele undertook to discover remains associated with the royal tumuli, that his broad surface clearance yielded subsidiary pits, chapels, and other evidence for the development of complexes, both royal and non-royal. The complete royal complex was found by The Oriental Institute to have three permanent parts: the tumulus (the one indispensable feature, and the focus of the complex), animal burial pits, and the chapels.

Chapels were placed to the north of the tumulus, with the door facing southward. These chapels were arranged in a row, the longest having fifty-seven chapels that extended for one hundred meters.

ANIMAL PITS

Between one and three pits were placed to the west for the burial of horses, donkeys, and camels. Pits that contained the intact, decapitated, dismembered, or partly burned remains of riding or baggage animals were found directly west of the main tumuli at distances that varied from 20 to 45 meters. At Qu. 3 and Qu. 10, they were oriented east-west; at Qu. 36, they were oriented north-south. The remains contained in the pits differed considerably from the substructure sacrifices in the tumuli.

Three pits, Q 5, Q 20, and Q 26, were associated with Qu. 3. The southern two each contained two layers of animal bones on a layer of clean sand, separated by a second layer of sand. Above the upper layer in the southern pit was a third layer of sand. The middle pit contained a jumbled mass of brick and stone that may have belonged to a structure that was demolished at the time of the final burial. The pits contained the remains of many horses, a few donkeys, and several camels. The bodies were dismembered and jumbled, and the number of hooves was insufficient to account for the total number of individual animals present. The eight to ten horses in each pit had been decapitated and the heads were missing. Remains of trappings were present, but damaged. Wooden parts of the saddle trees were charred, but remains of textiles and rope survived, as well as some incidental objects such as metal cups. The northern pit was actually a pair of pits. The western pit was empty, but the eastern pit contained four horses that had been killed and dumped directly into the eastern side of the pit from the northeast. The only objects found were pieces of rope bridles. The two animal pits of complex Qu. 36 contained five camels and five horses each, with remains of a camel saddle and trappings. Q 39, associated with Qu. 10, contained remains of at least one horse, a donkey, and two camels, as well as parts of saddles and associated textiles.

CHAPELS

The cult element of the complex was a series of chapels placed in an east-west row facing southward, and passing north of the tumulus. Fifty-one chapels were found at Qu. 31, and fifty-four were found north of Qu. 48; Qu. 36 had remains of fourteen chapels. The chapels were denuded almost to ground level and many plans were fragmentary, but many were complete. The rows may originally have had a few more chapels than were preserved, but the symmetrical layout of the rows north of the mid-points of the tumuli indicate that they were substantially complete. The rows were not uniformly straight, and most chapels had slight individual variations; some had been rebuilt. The row at Qu. 31 was laid out in three shorter segments, each on a slightly different axis. One other feature indicates that some special grouping occurred—small pedestals for libation tables were constructed in front of chapels near the western end of the row, but not in the other segments. The chapel row of Qu. 48 was more fragmentary, but most identifiable altars were near the western end. At Qu. 36, the pedestals were long brick benches, which were near the western end of the row.

The chapels themselves were rectangular mudbrick structures about two by three meters wide. They were constructed of a single thickness of brick stretchers, and occasionally they had a single short buttress stub in the middle of each side wall. The doors were in the south end, as revealed by the remains of wooden thresholds and stone door sockets, as well as doors lying where they had fallen. In addition, there were remains of stone jambs and lintels, part of a small sandstone sphinx, and an obelisk about one meter in height. Two sandstone plaques with painted decoration were found, and there may have been other decorations, inasmuch as (or since) some bowls containing the residue of green and white pigments were also recovered. In no case was a remnant of a fallen roof preserved, nor was there any trace of a fallen or ruined wall, which may be explained by a heap of bricks in chapel row Qu. 48, suggesting that building materials were removed for use elsewhere. It is possible, of course, that the chapels were open courts, or, if there were roofs, that they may have been only light screens of matting on poles, since a single thickness of brick wall would not have supported a vault.

At Qu. 31, the side walls of some chapels projected south of the doorways, creating either shallow porches or antae; some of these, in Qu. 48 and the chapel row of Qu. 36, were longer and thicker than the wall itself. Sometimes the area in front of the chapels was paved with mud; one pavement extended across the frontage of several chapels in the Qu. 31 row.

As pointed out above, certain chapels had libation tables placed on small brick podia in front of the door. At Qu. 36, the podia were enlarged and made into benches that extended almost the width of the chapel itself. In at least two cases, libation tables were found on the podia. In other cases, they were on the ground at the center of the back wall of the chapel where they may have been placed for safekeeping. Pottery associated with the chapels was contemporary with the royal tombs, and it included remains of goblets and bottle-jars as well as bowls, cooking pots, and amphorae.

Except for the three rows of chapels, no other evidence of permanent ceremonial installations was discovered at the royal tombs. There was, however, some evidence that these chapel rows were permanent facilities built to accommodate ceremonies that had existed without special structures. Two small deposits of votive and ordinary pottery, one of them placed on a stone, were found northeast of tumulus Qu. 14, at what was approximately (equivalent to) the east end of a chapel row. The most coherent deposit (Q 51) consisted of a jar with twenty-five small, handmade clay cups. In addition, in one private tomb (Q 227) there was a deposit of vessels at the northeast side of the tumulus.

A number of explanations could be advanced for the chapels, but most leave some features unexplained. They may have been built at one time by the king as cult places for his court or for assembled gods, but the chapels would probably be structurally uniform. Were the chapels built by the king for the court, we would expect to find a similar regularity and some special chapel for the king. If the chapels had been built for the king in sequence by successors for periodic ceremonies, they would not necessarily be uniform, but some chapels were rebuilt, indicating they were used for some time. Moreover, the libation tables are made in imitation of Meroitic private libation tables. Most probably, the chapels were built by permission of a king to worship the deceased king on behalf of members of the court. This would account for all of the conditions stated, and it would allow for some chapels to serve as cult places for sacrificed persons in the tumulus. Since the king would be the central focus of each cult, no special offering place would be required at the tumulus.

BALLANA CEMETERY 219: ENCLOSURE BA

The chapel rows of Qustul clearly show that a regular cult was carried out at the great tumuli in which libations and food offerings were made. In such circumstances, it would be difficult to believe that no central cult existed for the main tumulus. The one area excavated at Ballana in Cemetery 219 uncovered a large circular structure some 90 m east of a tumulus in the northern part of the cemetery, probably Ba. 80 (the location is marked on plate 1 according to a plan of Cemetery 219 prepared by Shafiq Farid).[67] The location alone would indicate some ritual purpose for the structure, a use also indicated by a libation table, amphorae, and a tubular stand or pipe found there.

The main part of the building was a roughly kidney-shaped enclosure of mud brick or puddled mud. The northern part of the structure was lined with two lower walls that formed smaller arcs with it. A spur wall led southward from an opening, and, to the northwest, facing the tumulus, the structure had some involved reconstruction or repair and buttress walls, as found in the chapels.

---

67. The tumulus was recorded as 114, but the location and dimensions of the enclosure would then conflict with 118. Because Cemetery 219 was displaced by earlier excavators, the tumulus is probably to be identified as Ba. 80.

THE CULTURAL SETTING OF THE COMPLEXES

Although hardly unambiguous, the chapels do offer major new information about the Noubadian Kingdom. For example, the number of chapels in each row should or could reflect in some way the size of the court, while the consistent size and placement of the chapels tells much about its relation to the king. However, some thematic links may be found in earlier complexes, although they are separated from Qustul by many centuries. At Kerma,[68] for example, complexes include the main ring tumulus with a long east-west corridor, external sacrifices, and royal chapels, placed to the north of a direct approach from the river facing south (fig. 4). Smaller chapels accompanied one of the great royal chapels, arranged approximately as were the rows at Qustul.[69] The low ring tumulus[70] contained a long corridor which leads to side chambers[71] containing the burial of the ruler on a bed.[72] Both humans[73] and animals accompanied the deceased; those buried inside were intact, while those outside were decapitated or dismembered.[74]

68. Reisner 1923 I–III, pp. 61–98.

69. The great funerary chapels of Kerma are closely related in outer plan to the city temple of Lower Deffufa, which also originally had an apse (Bonnet 1978, pp. 113–16; 1980, pp. 43–50). Placed north of an east-west approach from the river, their doors opened southward to face the route to the tomb they served. In addition to these main chapels, subsidiary chapels were constructed north of the tumulus of KX. These were assigned by the excavator to the tumuli immediately north, but their logical association would follow that of the large structures and they should therefore be assigned to the time of KX.

Table 10. Tumuli and Chapels at Kerma.

Tumulus	Main Chapel	Subsidiary Chapel
KIII	II	—
KIV	—[a]	—
KX	XI	XIV A–B[b]
	XV A–D	
	XVI A–B	
XVI	XXXIIIA[c]	
—[d]	X core	—
XXXVII 3706[e]—		

a. For an example of one ruler appropriating part of another's complex, see Abusir.
b. Reisner 1923 I–III, pp. 477–81. Considerable amounts of material were deposited in and around these chapels. Chapel XV D had traces of three columns in a north-south row in the center (pp. 482–84).
c. The great deposit of pottery and objects was directly to the south (pp. 470–76, 498).
d. No tumulus was ever built; possibly a short-lived ruler?
e. This chapel is axial; contents were not described here, or in Dunham 1982. See Reisner 1923 I–III, plans III, IV, VI, and tumuli cited.

70. As in private X-Group tumuli. Rings around tumuli occur in Sudan, at Tanqasi and Hobaji.

71. Reisner 1923 I–III, plan III. This produced a circulation approach which was important in earlier X-Group burials in Sudan and at Qustul, even if the burial was on the south rather than the north side of the corridor.

72. Ibid., p. 79. The bed burial was also preceded by burials on hides, or even between hides, at Kerma. The bed burial was also found in C-Group (Bietak 1968, IIb/3), presumably as an imitation of Kerma practice, but the hide burial had been known in C-Group before, and large hides have been found in C-Group burials (OINE V, table 27, pp. 66–67).

73. Reisner 1923 I–III, pp. 65–79. Emery and Kirwan 1938, p. 26. They were not previously dispatched as at Qustul.

74. Reisner 1923 I–III, p. 78; pp. 272–315, various. Deposits of bovine heads were sometimes made south of C-Group tumuli at Serra East (Hughes 1963, p. 122). At Serra, these dated to IB. Note the chariot pulled by oxen in the tomb of Huy (Davies 1926, pl. XXVIII). Were these to be sacrificed?

Figure 4. The Complexes at Kerma.

The elaborate complexes of Kerma had antecedents both in the Kerma Culture itself, and in the C-Group of lower Nubia. Pottery was deposited at the northeast (or east) side of the tumulus.[75] Paddle-shaped stelae were used in both cultures to mark the cult direction; the one place where this was preserved, Aniba, had them placed just north of an axis leading from an early tomb to the river, facing south (fig. 5). Later, chapels were erected to accommodate the cult, making a sequence with the pottery deposit and stelae[76] that parallels the increasing permanence of the cult noted at Kerma and at X-Group Qustul.

Although the comparisons cannot be extended to every detail, it should be noted that the related complexes of customs linked in a traditional series in Nubia interacted closely with Egyptian funerary customs.[77] For example, early Napatan ring tumuli at el Kurru covered trenches with side chambers that

75. OINE V, p. 23; Bonnet 1982, fig. 11.

76. Steindorff 1935, Blatt 5; Bietak 1968, p. 94, 1a/4 and similar.

77. This relationship may extend to the A-Group period and before, with some features that re-emerged in the complexes discussed immediately above and below. The features shared with Egypt were generally altered almost beyond recognition, but some aspects played an enduring role in Egypt's funerary traditions.

contained bed burials.[78] Downstream of the main axis was a cemetery for horses. The animals were buried with some jewelry and objects, and they were apparently decapitated.[79] Later, the tumulus with its curved enclosure was replaced by a pyramid, and the substructures made axial, with a long stepped trench leading to the burial chambers from the direction of the river. The transition was actually marked by structures that combined the square and circular elements, reinforcing an identification of pyramid and tumulus in Nubia.[80] Later in the transition, bed burials were replaced by more strictly Egyptianized coffin burials.

The transition between tumulus and pyramid had been made once before, when local rulers under Egyptian control, adopted the structure as a central element in their burial complexes, replacing late C-Group or Kerma tumuli with chapels.[81] At Serra East, a local ruler in the early New Kingdom had a paved ring tumulus erected over an Egyptian style shaft and chamber complex with a brick chapel. In subsequent complexes, the tumulus was replaced by a pyramid,[82] possibly the first erected away from the capital,[83] but the chapels remained separate from the pyramid.[84] Had the pyramid replaced the tumulus only once, the relationship between the two structures could be dismissed as incidental borrowing. However, the use of the pyramid in the New Kingdom cemeteries may well have been the first, away from the royal cemeteries of Egypt, and the second use of pyramids occurred when they were no longer used for royal burials in Egypt. A typological, if not chronological, sequence appears in Nubia, from ring tumulus to conical tumulus,[85] to stepped tumulus,[86] to stepped pyramid,[87] to pyramid.

Certain royal tombs that preceded the series at Abydos were identical in Egypt and Nubia. The royal burial at Qustul in late A-Group (OINE III, *Chapter 1*) and at Hierakonpolis (Hoffman 1982, pp. 48–50) in Upper Egypt was made in a long trench with a chamber cut from one side. Although experiments were made with paired chambers and groups of shafts, by the First Dynasty, the typical substructure was fundamentally a long trench with a burial in the center, sometimes in a deeper pit (Kaiser and Dreyer 1982, fig. 13). Beds were deposited in both countries (OINE III, *Chapter 1*). Although the royal burial was now nested in the trench, as in the tomb of Khasekhemwy (Kaiser and Dreyer 1982, fig. 13), the north-south axis of the trench was retained.

Ring tumuli existed in both Egypt and A-Group Nubia, but they could not have covered the entire tomb at Qustul (Smith 1962, pp. 64–69, Rizkallah Macramallah 1940, p. 8, Type I; tomb 223). In the First Dynasty, the process of developing the pyramid was well under way in Egypt, within the rectangular paneled enclosures (Kaiser 1969, gives a discussion of the complex's development).

The sacrifices of archaic Egypt are well known (Kemp 1966, and works cited) and one of the features most often cited as a link with customs practiced in more recent Africa. Those preserved were placed around, rather than in, the tomb, but evidence from the substructures is incomplete.

Tombs at Qustul were earlier, and the sacrifices preserved were cattle, decapitated and buried outside the shaft in the direction of the river (OINE III, *Chapter 1*). The use of severed heads is illustrated by the rows of bulls' heads modeled on the bench of a First Dynasty tomb at Saqqara, and paralleled by the boucrania deposited at C-Group and Kerma tumuli (Bonnet 1982, fig. 22; Emery 1954, plates VI, VII, and I).

At Abydos, royal cult places were surrounded by rectangular paneled enclosures and sacrifice burials. These paneled enclosures were separated from the burial place, located to the north of an axis leading to the royal cemetery from the river—an axis verified by the orientation of the tombs and the enclosures (Kemp 1966; O'Connor 1989, figs. 1 and 2; the enclosures were placed just north of a direct axis to the royal cemetery and they were entered at the south end). Entered near the south end of the east wall, the plan parallels the paneled mastabas elsewhere.

78. Dunham 1950, Ku. 3, 4, and 10, for example; see also Chart II.

79. Ibid., pp. 110–17.

80. Ibid., Ku. 14; see also Chart I.

81. Bietak 1968, pl. 9–10, IIB/4.

82. Hughes 1963, pl. XXVIb. These may be the earliest private pyramids erected away from the capital.

83. Dziobek n.d.

84. Säve-Söderbergh 1963, figs. 1–2.

85. Williams 1984, register; Steindorff 1935, N916, 561, 344.

86. Bonnet 1982, pp. 40–43.

87. Schiff Giorgini 1971, fig. 322.

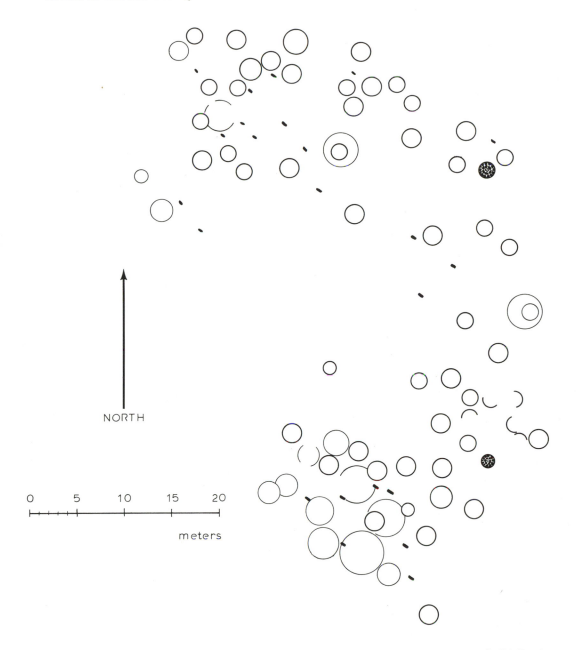

Figure 5. Stelae and Tumuli in the C-Group Cemetery. Stelae are Indicated by Solid Ovals.

J. NOBA TRADITIONS AND THE DEVELOPMENT OF THE NOUBADIAN X-GROUP BURIAL COMPLEX

Immediate antecedents of the Noubadian X-Group burial can be sought in the simpler burials of the Tanqasi culture. Although some features of the burial resemble those found in Meroitic Lower Nubia, and some objects are Meroitic, these burials differ from Meroitic tombs in design and most contents (fig. 6).

USHARA

The simplest burial that can be related to the Noubadian X-Group tomb was the mound grave at Ushara, just south of Khartoum, and west of the White Nile.[88] The objects found in this tumulus seem to be Meroitic,

---

88. Marshall and Abd el Rahman Adam 1953; Addison 1949, pl. XCII, R.2, R.3; pl. XCIII, T10; See Garstang, Sayce, and Griffith 1911, plates XXXVIII–XLV for tombs and pottery.

but the pottery appears to be intermediate in type between that of Gebel Moya and the Post-Meroitic Aloa Pottery.

A low mound covered a beehive-shaped chamber which was approached by a long, rectangular trench. The burial was placed against the south side, body contracted on the right side, with the hands before the face. Although the head was east, the local river direction could indicate a southeastern or southern direction for the actual intended orientation. Three large pots were placed in a group near the feet, four small vessels near the north side opposite the face, and two near the head. Small objects were placed near the hands and in front of the knees. This simple chamber arrangement, roughly like that used in early Kerma, was expanded in later burials at Tanqasi, Meroe, and Hobaji.

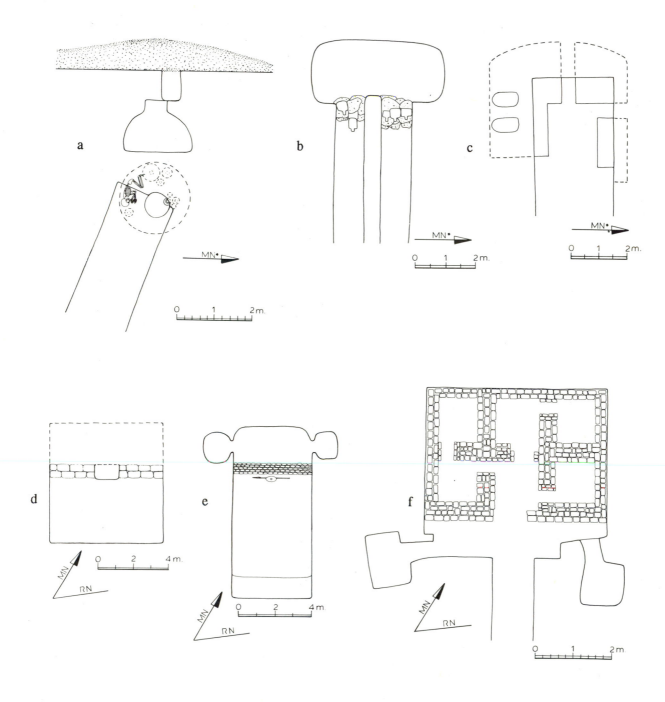

Figure 6. Burials in Sudan and X-Group Substructures: (a) Ushara,
(b) Meroe, (c) Tanqasi, (d–f) Qustul. Scales Indicated.

TANQASI

Two different tomb designs were found at Tanqasi, both of which contributed to the development of the Noubadian X-Group substructure.[89] The simpler burial was a shaft with a chamber excavated from the south side. The shaft was relatively regular and the chamber oval. The body probably had been contracted in the center of the chamber, with pottery placed at either end. The shape of this tomb is almost intermediate between the beehive and the shaft with side chamber, typical of Noubadian X-Group.

The substructure of the largest tomb, Mound I, had three chambers in a radial arrangement that could be considered an intermediate development between the beehive tomb and the tomb with recurved axis. The mound itself had a stone ring around the base and covered a long trench. Toward the west, the trench had three chambers arranged around the end, cut into its bottom and sides, and apparently blocked with mudbrick. There were two rectangular chambers, one on a side, and one at the end of the trench. The third, an L-shaped chamber, was also cut into the end on the opposite side; inside it were two hide-shaped pits for burials.

MEROE

Two different precedents for the royal burials at Qustul can be seen at Meroe. In the first, a normal late Meroitic structure (W 122, a rubble pyramid) was adapted to an entirely different kind of burial.[90] It covered a ramp that led to chambers arranged in a straight axis, and contained the burials of two oxen and a calf. Six contracted burials, with the bones somewhat confused, were deposited on the north side of the outer chamber. More bones, completely confused, were found against the south wall (a radial arrangement?). Pottery was placed in front of each group of bodies, against the west wall, and in the rear chamber. The main burial was extended in the center of the outer chamber, with one companion. Whether actually slain to accompany the main burial or not, the bodies against the wall were arranged as sacrifices. Such a practice was entirely uncharacteristic at Meroe in this period, but it closely resembles the Noubadian X-Group burials at Qustul and Ballana.

The post-Meroitic cemeteries actually contained a modification of the elaborate Tanqasi substructure.[91] Two ramps were dug, side-by-side, leaving a partition between them. The chamber, containing a north-south bed burial, was as wide as both ramps and the residual partition.

HOBAJI

A tumulus recently excavated near Khartoum belongs to the complex Sudanese traditions. Surrounded by an enclosure wall, the oval burial chamber was reached by a vertical cylindrical shaft. Made on a bed, the burial was accompanied by a large amount of grave goods, particularly weapons and covered with a (cow?) hide. The tomb is still not completely explored.[92]

SUDANESE TRADITIONS AND QUSTUL

Early substructures at Qustul are logical developments of this sequence, as they are also north-south chambers approached from the east by a broad trench or ramp (Qu. 14, also Qu. 6, Qu. 9, Qu. 10, Qu. 11, Qu. 12, and Qu. 15). At the bottom, the space in front of the main chamber served also as a transverse antechamber.[93] In some of the earliest private tombs, access to the chamber was divided by a residual or brick pillar in the center of the opening, apparently a development of the partition at Meroe.[94] In other tombs, the entry had no dividing pillar, but two small chambers on either side of the main axis preserved the radial

---

89. Shinnie 1954, figs. 3, 6; compare Emery and Kirwan 1938, fig. 26.

90. Dunham 1963, pp. 203–06 (W 122).

91. Garstang, Sayce, and Griffith 1911, pp. 29–47.

92. Lenoble 1989, pp. 93–120.

93. Emery and Kirwan 1938, Qu. 3, Qu. 14, and Qu. 25.

94. Ibid., Qu. 22 and Qu. 25, for example.

arrangement of Tanqasi tumulus I (Qu. 14). This arrangement was carried a step further in Qu. 3, which contained an entire brick structure instead of the main room, though the small chambers were retained. This brick structure was derived from a similar construction in the latest Meroitic tombs,[95] though its burial here simply replaces a major chamber of the radial group with a complex. In subsequent royal tombs, the arrangement of chambers and construction followed a recurved axis (Qu. 31, Qu. 36, Qu. 17, and Qu. 2, for example). Nevertheless, if the original radial arrangement derived from the beehive is often difficult to recognize, still all of the large tombs maintained the tradition of the radial or recurved axis to the end of the Ballana cemetery.[96]

K. NOUBADIAN X-GROUP PRIVATE BURIALS

THE DEVELOPMENT OF PRIVATE BURIALS

Noubadian X-Group burials underwent major changes during the two centuries after the establishment of the kingdom. The earliest X-Group burials at Qustul were a few rather hasty interments in the reused shafts of Meroitic tombs, or in shallow, irregular graves.[97] Thereafter, until the end of X-Group, single burials were the rule, and new tombs were almost always made. Most burials were placed on the side, thighs either straight or slightly bent, legs bent almost to a right angle, and hands before the upper body or face.[98] Early burials were placed on hides, while later ones were often placed on beds.[99] Deposits included personal jewelry, clothing, other textiles, and weapons. Tools also appear occasionally.

CEMETERIES AND STRUCTURES

The royal cemetery of Qustul was actually established to the south of the Meroitic cemetery where these early burials were made; it was the tumuli of later rulers that spread the cemetery to the north.[100] Although the establishment of cult installations and other pits near the tombs indicates that the area near each royal tomb was not intended to be used for private burials, private tumuli were soon erected there in areas of the Qustul cemetery not in current use.[101] These continued the X-Group cemetery after the transfer of the main royal necropolis to Ballana.

The most impressive of these tumuli covered stepped shafts with chambers excavated from the western side.[102] The steps are large enough to extend the top of the shaft far to the east; the simple outline appears to

---

95. Woolley and Randall-MacIver 1910, fig. A (Karanog G 64).

96. See, for example, Török 1988, pls. 4–10.

97. See tomb Q 152.

98. Extended burials appear quite early in sacrifice burials (Qu. 3; Emery and Kirwan 1938, fig. 8), but contracted burials also continued for some time (Qu. 36; ibid., fig. 28: body K; see also Ba. 9, fig. 42, main burial). Postures are mixed for sacrifice burials in Ba. 10, where the main burial is on the side (ibid., fig. 44) and Ba. 47, where the main burial is on the back (ibid., fig. 52). This situation continues through Ba. 80 (ibid., fig. 64), 95 (no main burial, ibid., fig. 68), 114 (main burial disturbed, ibid., fig. 72), and 118 (same, ibid., fig. 74); in Ba. 121, the main burial is still semi-contracted (ibid., fig. 76).

99. For one earlier example of this development, see Bonnet 1982, figs. 17–19. A number of Meroitic bed burials were cited by Török (1988, p. 214), many are not actually Meroitic in date or culture. For example, the series cited by Hofmann (1967, p. 379). The Gamai tomb is probably X-Group (Bates and Dunham 1927, E 53), as is that from Gebel Adda (Millet 1963, p. 163); northern examples include Ptolemaic or Roman (Firth 1912, p. 34; 1915, p. 161, probably connected to biers shown on Ptolemaic monuments) and Napatan (Firth 1927, p. 155; OINE VII, *Chapter 4*) burials. The large number of Meroitic graves from Ballana and Qustul contained no real beds (OINE VIII, *Chapter 2*), while they are not mentioned from Karanog (Woolley and Randall-MacIver 1910). The bed burial is not a Meroitic custom.

100. See pp. 5–10 above.

101. See pp. 12–15 above.

102. See tomb Q 133, for example.

show it as an east-west shaft. This is, however, an approach, and the shaft proper is oriented north-south. The shafts were very deep, and the chambers were blocked with mudbrick, which often filled much of the shaft.

Many tumuli, especially later ones, were quite difficult to recognize, and there was some doubt as to whether they were really tumuli or just low heaps of earth thrown up from the shaft. However, the tombs in Cemetery Q continued to be spaced fairly far apart, indicating that they were intended to be recognizable tumuli. Many tombs were not recorded with tumuli and a tumulus has had to be reconstructed based on photographs.

In addition to the early east-west dromos with broad chambers, some longitudinal tombs were also made, often with bed burials. In most cases, these were shafts with vaults set into the side, and niches cut into the end. In addition, deep shafts with side chambers, some also with vaults, were made.

BURIAL EQUIPMENT

In the early tombs, very few burials were made on beds, although the body was sometimes placed on a large hide. Most often, however, it was wrapped in a textile mantle or sheet, whose material, texture, and colors indicate that it was made locally.[103] Pottery, if present, usually included at least a bottle-jar and a goblet, although many large groups of vessels were deposited.[104] Jewelry consisted mostly of strings of beads, much cruder than Meroitic ones, when they were not actually reused Meroitic beads. Earrings of early Byzantine type were also present, and some rings were found. Amulets were reused and rare. Jewelry objects were definitely less varied and numerous than they had been in Meroitic times. Cosmetic objects followed much the same trend as the jewelry. The most common objects were household implements for minor surgery and depilation, the chatelaine or "thorn set." Kohl sticks and tubes of distinctive design also occur, but not as frequently as in Meroitic times.

A major new group of objects to appear was tools made of iron. Most often, these were saws or short, toothed sickles, adzes, hammers, and axes. These were not heavy duty implements, but rather light ones sized almost to be a kit for easy transportation. These tools were not models, however, but well-used ones—saw teeth were often worn, and the hammers were splayed from frequent and heavy use. Weapons also appeared in many tombs, often derived from Meroitic period forms. They were mostly equipment for archery, such as quivers, arrows, looses, and occasionally a brace. Although an early tomb contained a self bow, a new type of bow which appeared, made of leather and horn on a fibrous core, was one of the most important and interesting technological discoveries of the project. In addition, javelin heads, remains of sheaths for the short sword and sections of a large blade were also found in this material, as well as some leather pieces which may have been parts of armor.

Apart from the wrappings, which were often items of clothing, apparel consisted of sandals. This exhausts the equipment of the average X-Group burial at Qustul. More elaborate objects, such as boxes and vessels of bronze and stone did occur, but they were unusual and probably unusual in the original burials as well. We cannot reliably date the first appearance of the bed in private burials at Qustul, but it had certainly appeared in royal burials by the time of Qu. 31 in the early phase, and it was possibly preceded in private burials by the hide. Later, the bed became more common in private tombs, along with the royal burial posture: on the back, extended. The change from the contracted to the extended burial may not have been fully completed in X-Group; late tombs still contained burials on the side. An east-west orientation also began to replace the north-south direction of the shaft. This, too, was not completed until the latest X-Group, for late north-south shafts were made at Ibrim.

During middle and late X-Group, the normal substructure changed as well as the direction. To the shaft with a side chamber was added a shaft with a vault built on walls, or ledges cut in the sides. In some cases the end of the shaft was also undercut, making a combined vault and end-niche tomb. In one variation, a shaft was deepened in the middle; the residual ledges were used to support either a vault or a covering of stone slabs. The side chamber tomb which continued to be used; was now, however, often blocked with stone slabs.

---

103. Mayer-Thurman and Williams 1979, pp. 36–40.

104. See tombs Q 1 and R 4A of middle X-Group, for example.

CHAPTER 2

POTTERY

The simple pottery found in most tombs at the end of the Meroitic period offers a limited precedent for the pottery of X-Group, whether found in the Dodekaschoinos or the area to the south. Technologically, it contrasts even more with the pottery from Upper Nubia and Sudan assigned to the so-called Tanqasi culture.[1] Some groups of vessels important in Meroitic times had disappeared from the repertoire and others were combined into new groups,[2] while others, once quite diversified, now contained fewer shapes.[3] Once elaborate painted decoration was drastically simplified.[4] A bold, rather crude decoration in red and white occurs on some Egyptian imported pottery, and some of its elements, such as arches and swags, may have influenced X-Group decoration.[5]

Local handmade pottery continued to be produced, the jars probably derived from Sudan.[6] However, one of the most interesting groups of pottery in Meroitic times, the dark-faced incised-impressed pottery, disappeared without being replaced.[7]

Manufacturing techniques used in Meroitic times were also used in X-Group, but they may have been reintroduced from Upper Egypt[8] along with such shapes as the goblet.[9] The major groups of vessels include an X-Group fine pottery, which continued to be made of gray white clay (from the Nubian Sandstone?), X-Group ordinary pottery, which included most of the vessels deposited in tombs, and storage jars.

Three patterns of manufacture can be distinguished as traditions: the groups of vessels from Coptic period Egypt, Noubadian X-Group wheelmade, and Noubadian X-Group handmade. Coptic period Egyptian

1. Cultural relations are a different matter; see p. 49 below.

2. Kushite wheelmade and black incised vessels ceased to be made; see OINE VIII, *Chapter 1*, p. 8 and *Chapter 2*, pp. 32–34, 72–73..

3. Fine pottery was reduced in importance; see p. 43 below.

4. A new style partly derived from Meroitic decoration was introduced later in X-Group. It is actually related to several kinds of decoration: Coptic painting (even possibly wall painting); X-Group decorated objects; and earlier incised-impressed decoration on pottery (Mills 1982, pls. LXVII–LXXX). For the chronology, see Török 1988, pp. 182–84.

5. Emery and Kirwan 1938, pl. 113:44–48 for example. See Egloff 1977, pls. 1–3, 23, and various pieces on pls. 62–73, for example. Arches and swags are normally more regular in X-Group painted pottery, however, and are accompanied by vertical lines. This combination may be derived from earlier pottery decoration in Sudan (Arkell 1953, pl. 43:9; 1949, pl. 108:4) where such combinations are common.

6. See p. 63, n. 133 below.

7. The handmade pottery of the Kalabsha sites, with its red and grey surfaces and grey fabric as well as its new repertoire of shapes must be distinguished from the fine handmade pottery of Meroitic Nubia and Sudan, following Török (1988, pp. 179–80). Compare Strouhal 1984, pp. 157–77 and Ricke 1967, pls. 25–28 with Randall-MacIver and Woolley 1911, pl. 69. The survival of a few Meroitic motifs is slight compared to the abandonment of the repertoire of pharaonic decoration that dominated Meroitic painted pottery. The situation can be explained by the lack of exclusive cultural boundaries in Nubia.

8. See Adams 1986, p. 58 for a discussion of the occurrence of R 25 (a fine Egyptian/Nubian pottery made of alluvial clay), for example.

9. See Hölscher 1954, pl. 48:Q′6 and Q′9.

vessels had their own connections that need not be followed here, but the relationships of Noubadian X-Group pottery that are explored briefly in the remarks on pottery corpora.

Previous volumes in this series cite reasons why classifications now in use for the pottery do not elucidate but rather obscure the intentions that actually produced objects.[10] Although the classification proposed for late pottery makes use of definite choices in materials, processes, forms, and decoration, the organization of these choices into classes often created groups that either combined objects that were intended to be distinguished or separated pieces that were intended to belong together.[11] The classification used in the present volume therefore follows previous reports of this series and attempts to distinguish intentional groups in three levels—traditions, groups of instrumental categories (form groups or wares), and instrumental categories (forms). Despite the difference of approach, most vessels classified according to the OINE categories can be assigned to groups in Adams's classification and will be noted where appropriate.[12]

10. OINE V, pp. 25–28; OINE III, pp. 191–95.

11. See Williams n.d. for a discussion of the classification proposed in Adams 1986.

12. The following table correlates pottery form groups from the Meroitic period with X-Group form groups.

Table 11. Meroitic and X-Group Pottery Groups.

Meroitic Period (OINE VIII)	*X-Group Period Counterpart (OINE IX)*
MEROITIC POTTERY	X-GROUP POTTERY
I. Meroitic Fine/Ord.	I. X-Group Ord.
	II. X-Group Fine
II. Kushite Wheelmade	—
III. Storage Jar	III. Storage Jar
IV. Kushite Wheelmade Utility	—
V. Handmade	—
SUDANESE-SAHARAN POTTERY	—
EGYPTIAN POTTERY	COPTIC PERIOD EGYPTIAN POTTERY
I. Egyptian Fine/Ord.	I. Coptic Period Egyptian Fine/Ord.
II–III. Egyptian Utility	II–III. Coptic Period Egyptian Utility
OTHER GROUPS	— (FINE/ORDINARY II JUGLET?)

The following table correlates OINE categories with the taxothetic-taxonomic classification of Adams (1986; see also 1964 and 1973; for specific vessels, see Säve-Söderbergh, Englund, and Nordström eds. 1982).

Table 12. Adams' Wares and OINE Groups.

Adams		OINE	*Vessels and Remarks*
R 1	I.	X-Group Ord.	Goblets, cups, some bowls, bottle-jars, spouted jars (pp. 469–70)
	I.	Coptic Period Egyptian Fine/Ord.	Handled jugs, juglets, wide bowls
R 25	I.	X-Group Ord.	Goblets, some cups, bowls (pp. 468–69)
	I.	Coptic Period Egyptian Fine/Ord.	Handled jugs, juglets, cooking pots, wide bowls, pilgrim bottles
	III.	X-Group storage Jars	Storage jars
R 30	I.	Coptic Period Egyptian Fine/Ord.	Almost entire group, continues from Meroitic period (pp. 534–36)
	II–III.	Coptic Period Egyptian Utility	Cooking pots and *amphoriskoi*
U 1		Uncertain, *Qawadus*	Only possibly I X-Gr. ord. (pp. 515–16)
U 4		Amphorae only	(pp. 567–68)
U 16		Amphorae only	(pp. 575–76)
U 3		Amphora	(p. 580)
U 18		Amphora and Monophora	(pp. 581–82)
W 11	II–III.	Coptic Period Egyptian Utility	Painted, both examples (pp. 470–72)
W 28	III.	X-Group Storage Jars	Storage jars, white coated (pp. 566–67)
	II–III.	Coptic Period Egyptian Utility	*Amphoriskoi*, coated, in S. J. E., all chaffy (III)
W 29	I.	X-Group Ord.	Entire group (pp. 472–73)
W 30	II.	X-Group Fine	Cups only (p. 440)
D.II		Handmade	H 2 (uncoated), H 2 (red-topped), H 3 (red coat), H 13 (white paint on red) (pp. 421–25)

Note that assignments in parentheses are hypothetical. R 1, "Classic X-Group Red Ware"; R 2, "Transitional Red Ware"; R 25, "Middle Egyptian Fine Brown Ware"; R 30, "Aswan Graeco-Roman Red Ware"; U 1, "Meroitic and

Although the vessels of X-Group differ from those of Meroitic times, most of the choices of materials and techniques remained similar. These fundamental choices are outlined in the previous volume and will not be repeated here.[13] Despite a general continuity of materials and techniques, the shapes and decoration are so different that a new outline of the shapes is required to distinguish meaningful categories. This has resulted in an entirely different set of divisions, even for pottery imported from Egypt. For example, open X-Group ordinary vessels include goblets, cups, and bowls, while those of Meroitic times are grouped under a single category that includes both bowls and cups. The divisions are configured in this way because the goblets were derived from Egyptian vessels, while the cups appear to have had a Meroitic background. Table 13 is a presentation of the OINE material in an orderly manner and not a systematic analysis of X-Group pottery.

A. WHEELMADE POTTERY OF NOUBADIAN X-GROUP TRADITION

Only three groups remained in the locally manufactured wheelmade vessels of Nubia. The most important was the ordinary pottery, made with much the same materials and techniques as the latest Meroitic ordinary pottery.[14] The second group consisted only of cups, while the third included storage jars derived from late Meroitic counterparts.

FORM GROUP I: NOUBADIAN X-GROUP ORDINARY POTTERY

One of the changes from Meroitic to X-Group pottery was the elimination of the imperceptible gradation between Meroitic fine and ordinary pottery that included vessels of both kinds in a single group (pls. 41; 42a, e-h; 43, and 44). The red ordinary pottery increased greatly in relative numbers and was used for most of the purposes previously served by Meroitic and Roman period Egyptian cups and jars. Adams expressed some uncertainty about assigning some of the vessels a Nubian or Egyptian origin,[15] but after the earliest phase the goblets differ from contemporary Egyptian vessels, while the cups and bottle-jars have a definitely Nubian origin. Therefore only the early goblets, some miniature bottles, and some bowls may be either of Nubian or Egyptian origin.[16]

X-Group Brown Utility Ware"; U 4, "Middle Egyptian Brown Utility Ware"; W 11, "X-Group White Ware"; W 28, "Middle Egyptian Plain White Ware"; W 29, "X-Group White Ware"; W 26, "Meroitic Fine White Ware"; W 27, "Meroitic Pale Pink Ware."

Not in present collection: (R 2, I. X-Group Ord., p. 470)

Note that the table is based on the present classification and the assignments of specific vessels to classes in Säve-Söderbergh, Englund, and Nordström eds. 1982.

13. OINE VIII, *Chapter 2.* Throughout this work, as in the previous volume, choices of materials and techniques are discussed only to permit reference to the detailed descriptions found in Adams 1986 (pp. 405–583) or to point out differences between observations made in Adams's work and those made in the course of preparing the OINE volumes.

14. Adams (1986, pp. 468–70), parts of Wares R 25, R 1, and R 2, also part of Ware W 29 (pp. 472–73).

15. Adams 1986, pp. 468–69, 562; see also note 12.

16. See p. 53, n. 84 below and Mond and Myers 1934, pl. CXXXVII:45E, F, and L for examples. The vessels correspond to the very earliest and simplest found in X-Group.

The present group includes most of Adams's [1986] Ware R 1 (Classic X-Group Red Ware, pp. 469–70), much of his R 25 (early X-Group Brown Ware, pp. 468–69), and part of R 2 (Transitional Red Ware, p. 470), in addition to a number of white coated vessels. There is often no real difference in the fabric of vessels assigned to R 25 and R 1. For example, rib-rimmed goblets (B) were assigned to Adams R 25, "Middle Egyptian Fine Brown Ware" (25/46:3) because the base was cut with a string. Since this is simply an unfinished base, the feature should have no effect on the "ware" classification and R 1 is, in fact, given as an alternative class. In any case, this writer could detect no difference in the fabric or details of shaping, coating, and firing. As indicated by the classification of numerous vessels in Säve-Söderbergh, Englund, and Nordström eds. 1982, white coated vessels (Adams 1986, pp. 472–73, Ware W 29, X-Group Ordinary White Ware) includes imitations of X-Group fine (II; Säve-Söderbergh, Englund, and Nordström eds. 1982, see pls. 73–4:25/4/10 and 25/208:4) and white coated bottles (none illustrated, see Adams 1986, fig. 271:38). In the present classification of X-Group pottery, the white coat is treated as a decoration. Vessels with white coats are not generally separated from similar vessels with other coats or no coatings since their shape and decoration indicate that they were intended to be grouped together.

CLAY

As with Meroitic and Roman period Egyptian fine/ordinary pottery, the clay may have been a mixture of alluvium and clay from deposits in the Nubian Sandstone. Generally it appears fine and well sorted, indicating that the clay was carefully cleaned and levigated. The appearance is dominated by alluvium; flecks of mica are prominent and the vessels are generally fired to a dark red in the breaks.[17]

TEMPER

Smaller vessels were given a fine mineral temper much like that of ordinary pottery in Meroitic times; ground sherds, or grog temper, may also have been used. Larger vessels contained some chaff, probably dung and some sandy material. The particles in larger vessels were perhaps somewhat larger than before. The surfaces of many vessels have a glossy polished appearance.

SHAPING

Vessels were thrown on the fast wheel. Their shapes had three major origins that were modified into shapes characteristic of X-Group. For example, the goblets originated in Upper Egypt[18] while most of the cups have shapes that occur in Meroitic contexts or the Kalabsha groups.[19] Most bottle-jars, on the other hand, were derived from Sudanese prototypes.[20]

SURFACE TREATMENT

Most of the vessels were coated red; some later vessels were coated white. The red coats often have an even, glossy surface which was produced by polishing with a soft material.[21] However, some unfired pieces are also glossy (pl. 48). This gloss must have been produced by the clay and temper, perhaps by using ash as a flux which would peptize the clay.

DECORATION

Horizontal grooves and painting were both used to decorate vessels. In addition the rims of jars were modeled, sometimes given projecting ribs and even complex shapes. The shallow ribs or grooves found on the lower sides of some bottle-jars and goblets are not decoration however, but a surface treatment which was probably intended to ensure a better grip on the vessel. Decorative incised grooves occur singly on cups and in groups on the bodies of jars, especially at the base of the neck and at the shoulder. Together with the modeled rim, these grooves seem to be a simplified form of the decoration used by potters in Sudan. Here it may appear as an imitation of a metal prototype[22] that was an adaptation of a handmade pottery vessel used as a substitute for a leather bottle or gourd.[23] The painted decoration is considered below.

17. The clay is considered alluvial by Adams (1986, pp. 467–68), and the dark red or brown appearance of the fired pottery indicates that alluvium was at least predominant. For remarks on mixtures, see OINE VIII, *Chapter 2*, pp. 28–29.

18. See Hölscher 1954, pl. 48:Q'6 and Q'9 and Mond and Myers 1934, pls. CXXXVI:41J, L; CXXXVII:45L, Q and 48G, H, for example.

19. See OINE VIII, *Chapter 2*, pp. 32–34; Ricke 1967, figs. 73–74.

20. See pp. 72–73 below.

21. For a discussion of polishing, see Adams 1986, p. 85; Firth 1912, p. 52, refers to polish as a close burnish.

22. Emery and Kirwan 1938, pl. 66:E–F.

23. Garstang, Sayce, and Griffith 1911, pl. XLI:1–5. For gourds, including some with the shape of the bottle with bulged rim, see Chappel 1977, especially fig. 82. For scoops of types with ancient connections in the Nile Valley, see figs. 23–31. For colors, red, tan, brown, black, and occasional white fill, see the color plates.

FIRING

The color and physical properties of the pottery are essentially the same as similarly treated Meroitic and Egyptian vessels. Thus firing would have been much the same, in closed kilns of the type found at Faras,[24] with a neutral or oxidizing atmosphere. A few fire blooms on the sides of the vessels indicate that some irregularities existed in the atmosphere, but the dark red color is generally uniform through the break.

PAINTED DESIGNS

Early Noubadian X-Group painted decoration included simplified late Meroitic designs, designs from Egypt, and possibly new designs from Sudan. Black and white were painted on the red ground, a common combination in late Meroitic painting. The designs were not just simplified versions of earlier decoration, for common motifs such as arches and swags may have been derived from Coptic period Egypt, and used as a substitute for motifs with a similar configuration from Upper Nubia.[25]

The decoration of bottle-jars was generally put on the shoulder or upper body of the vessel and sometimes at the base of the neck. In a few cases, the neck itself was painted. The decoration of goblets is almost always above the carination. The catalogue of basic motifs in the present collection is not extensive.

BANDS

Bands and lines occur alone and in combination. On bottle-jars they occur on the body alone, in double groups of two or three, or in single groups of three or more. Horizontal bands and lines do not generally occur on cups of this group except on white coated imitations of fine pottery (fig. 9i–k).

BURST VINE

The previous volume traced a series of changes in vine decoration on pottery from Roman period Egypt that included the elimination of the vine and the reduction of the leaves to teardrop-shaped spots.[26] In X-Group, groups of horizontal teardrop-shaped blobs were arranged in more or less vertical rows of two, three, or even more spots on both local and Coptic period Egyptian wheelmade pottery. The paint is white, or black, or alternating columns of white and black spots. The vine leaf spots were painted on the shoulders or upper bodies of jars, sometimes with horizontal lines; they were also painted on goblets.[27]

BLOB-BEAD

Some bottle-jars have black or alternating black and white spots at the base of the neck or on the shoulder. Sometimes these are arranged in a line or framed band. The origin of the motif in common Meroitic decoration is quite clear.[28]

VERTICAL LINE-GROUPS

In X-Group, vertical lines occur in groups on the upper bodies of goblets and are sometimes used to frame swags. Generally there are three lines—black, white, or alternating black and white in each group. In a few cases, lines were extended onto the bases of cups. The painted pottery of contemporary Egypt is sometimes decorated with vertical lines, but the device may have been used in Nubia because it resembles a device combining vertical framing with the tassels used to decorate incised pottery in Sudan.[29]

---

24. Griffith 1926, pp. 63–65 and plates XLI–XLV. Adams, 1961, pp. 30–43; 1962, pp. 66–70; and 1986, pp. 13–25, 31–33.

25. See note 5 above.

26. For the development of the vine in Meroitic Lower Nubia, see OINE VIII, *Chapter 2*, pp. 65–67; for its significance, see Millet 1984, pp. 114–15.

27. The complete vine was revived in the elaborate style of late X-Group; see Mills 1982, pl. LXXVII:192.14.3, 193.156.1 and 193.122.8. The vines and their leaves are dissimilar.

28. OINE VIII, *Chapter 2*, p. 48.

29. Addison 1949, pl. CI, for example. See Mond and Myers 1934, pl. CXXXVII:45E1.

ZIGZAGS IN GROUPS

Groups of parallel zigzags were common in Meroitic incised pottery, but they also occurred in painted pottery.[30]

ZIGZAGS WITH BALLS AT THE INTERSECTIONS

Meroitic painted pottery and Blemmye incised pottery both were decorated with zigzags that have balls at the intersections, either alone, or, more often, crossed to make a series of St. Andrew's crosses.[31]

"TREES"

This simple motif occurred on pottery in Late Meroitic times in one color or with alternating black and white diagonal lines.[32]

CROSSHATCHED TRIANGLES

Used to fill vertical fields that hang from bands at the base of the neck, crosshatched triangles appear in the same position as used in Sudan.[33]

SWAGS AND ARCHES

Swags and arches were frequently painted in black and white on the upper zones of cups and were frequently bounded by vertical lines. Less frequently, they are found inside the rims of open bowls. Swags and arches appear frequently in the painted decoration of Coptic period Egypt, but their use here is in a rather confined space. In combination with the vertical lines they resemble the more disciplined decoration of eyes and tassels that occurs in the pottery decoration of Upper Nubia.[34]

SPECIAL GROUPS

The decoration of early and middle X-Group pottery was augmented in late X-Group times by a much more elaborate decoration found especially at Qasr Ibrim.[35] At the same time, many more of the jars were given a white or cream slip suitable as a background. Vessels with this decoration were not common in the present material and were not especially elaborate. Tomb Q 3 contained three globular bottle-jars that might be considered transitional to this style. One (Q 3—6) has black and white rosettes below white beads on the shoulder with alternating columns of black and white drop-shaped leaves on the body. The second (Q 3—2) has a black and white zigzag in a framed band on the shoulder below black and white beads on the neck; the third (Q 3—5) has a confused vine or zigzag with dots on the shoulder below white beads with alternating columns of black and white drop beads on the body. A fine cup (Q 3—A) has horizontal trefoil flowers.

For the colors of this group see QB 52–53—A (with paint), Chapel E1 Surface—1 (with paint), —5, Surface SW of Q 422—1, Q 1—14 (with paint), —15, —16 (with paint), —17, —20 (white coat, red rim), —21 (white coat, red rim), —22 (white coat, red rim); Q 2—5, —8 (with paint), Q 6—3 (with paint), Q 9—1, —3 (with paint), —7 (with paint), Q 12—2; Q 18—5, —7; Q 19—3 (with paint), Q 61—8 (with paint), —10; Q 62—12 (with paint), —16, —19; Q 70—1, —4; Q 74—10; Q 78—1 (with paint), —2, —4; Q 66—1; Q 67—10; Q 503—1, —4; Q 504—1 (with paint), —4; Q 82—3; Q 107—1; Q 134—7, —8; Q 147—1; Q 148—7 (white coat); Q 161—3, —4; Q 164—4; Q 320—2; and Q 361—2.

---

30. OINE VIII, *Chapter 2*, p. 49; Adams 1986, fig. 146:5-1.

31. Ricke 1967, fig. 75:B2/1i; see Adams 1986, fig. 146:22-1, -2, for example.

32. OINE VIII, *Chapter 2*, p. 47; not in Adams 1986, Styles N.II.

33. Garstang, Sayce, and Griffith 1911, pls. XLI:2, XLIII:7–8. Not in Adams 1986, N.II; see horizontal band of crosshatched triangles (pendant), fig. 146:5-2.

34. Arkell 1953, pls. 43–9; 1949, pls. 107:8; 108; Crawford and Addison 1951, pl. XXII:B6; Garstang, Sayce, and Griffith 1911, pl. XLII:2. For broad arches, see Egloff 1977, pls. 62–64, various. For small swags however, see, Hölscher 1954, pl. 48:Q'9.

35. Mills 1982, pls. LXXVII–LXXX.

FORM GROUP II: NOUBADIAN X-GROUP FINE POTTERY

Gray-white pottery was used only for certain cups and related goblets. Relatively little of this pottery is known from early or middle X-Group, but later in the phase an important series of fine cups was made in this form group (pl. 42e–f).[36]

CLAY

The basic raw material for these cups was the gray-white clay from the Nubian Sandstone; a complete unfired vessel and fragments of another (pl. 48) were found in Cemetery R. The clay was thoroughly cleaned and the fabric of the vessels is essentially the same as the equivalent Meroitic pottery.[37]

TEMPER

A few very small voids can be seen in the breaks and these sometimes have a spongy appearance, indicating, perhaps, that some ash was used in the clay. Otherwise, no intentional inclusions could be identified.

SHAPING

The pottery was shaped on the fast wheel. Most vessels are convex, V-shaped, sinuous, or sinuous-carinated cups with ring bases. A few have everted rims, and a few have round bases. Several cups had shapes common in the fourth century Dodekaschoinos groups, the most interesting is a concave-sided cup with convex base.[38]

SURFACE

Most of the vessels have smoothed matte surfaces.

DECORATION

Red and black paint was applied in narrow bands of hatching, crosshatching, bead motifs, and rim-ticking. This narrow band style differs considerably from the broad bands and large motifs found on the red pottery. Neither Meroitic nor X-Group nor Byzantine period Egyptian pottery was decorated in this way, but some of the cups from the Dodekaschoinos had the decoration similarly concentrated at the rim.[39] Late in the period, goblets in this fabric or in a white coated imitation made of ordinary pottery were given decoration in large motifs similar to the bottle-jars of Ibrim.[40] One cup from Tomb Q 3 was painted with red horizontal trefoil flowers, as discussed in the preceding section.

FIRING

Firing was essentially the same as for the red pottery; it may have had a slightly higher temperature but was not sufficiently oxidizing to damage the paint.

For the colors of X-Group fine pottery, see Q 3—3 (with paint), Q 8—1, Q 144—3, Q 148—3, —4 (with paint), —5, and —6 (with paint).

---

36. These are well represented at Ibrim, Mills 1982, pl. XXIV:25.3–5, 26.1. Pottery of this group was not common in the S. J. E. materials and there was a certain confusion in its classification. In one later X-Group context, it was taken for an early X-Group Meroitic survival and assigned to two groups: W 26 ("Meroitic Fine White Ware," pl. 4:A16, with a variant of the eye and tassel design) and W 27 ("Meroitic Pale Pink Ware," a cylindrical cup, pl. 5:B25). In another context, a convex cup of our C1–3 shape was not given a designation (pl. 4:B1, 25/177:4; "most nearly resembles Lower Egyptian Family LS"). All of these appear to be assignable to the X-Group fine category; variations in color can be attributed to minor variations in firing or the composition of the clay deposit. Adams (1986, pp. 435–40) points out that his W 27 may not have a separate existence. Except for the discrepancies in vessels actually assigned by Adams to various groups in Säve-Söderbergh, Englund, and Nordström eds. 1982, the description of W 30 would be appropriate for all of the fine white vessels from X-Group.

37. See OINE VIII, *Chapter 2*, p. 29.

38. Ricke 1967, figs. 73–76.

39. Ricke 1967, fig. 74:B11/3, B7/3h, B7/3b.

40. Mills 1982, pls. XXXVII:192.126.2; LXVII:192.138.2, 192.138.a, 192.138.b, 192.138.1, for example.

FORM GROUP III: STORAGE JARS

The large and complex group of Meroitic vessels called Kushite Wheelmade in OINE VIII disappeared by X-Group. Storage jars, however, continued to be made in the same tradition, (pl. 47a).[41] Their manufacture differed in no major way from the smaller wheelmade vessels except for their size and thickness. The surfaces were smoothed, and they were decorated only with bands of grooves.

For the colors of storage jars, see Q 33—3.

B. HANDMADE POTTERY

Handmade vessels, bowls and jars, form a fairly large category among the vessels made in X-Group (pl. 45).[42] Some of the jars (pl. 45d) seem to be related to jars found in Sudan.

CLAY

The raw material was the alluvial clay common in the valley that was normally used for handmade pottery, though some gray-white clay may have been added.

TEMPER

Sand and chaff or dung temper were used in the clay as in earlier groups of coarse handmade pottery.

SHAPING

X-Group handmade vessels appear to have been shaped in the same way as most earlier handmade vessels in Nubia.[43] Common shapes include deep bowls or cups, medium-sized globular, baggy, or biconical jars, and large ovoid jars with almost cylindrical necks. The sides of some jars were brought to a low neck that resembles those of Sudanese-Saharan jars from the later Meroitic period [44] Other jars in this group have taller, narrow necks, sometimes with dotted impressed zigzags around the base. Large jars appear to have been made in sections, the neck and rim added to the shoulder. Sometimes a jar has a roll of clay at the base of the neck marked by finger impressions, probably related to the collar necks that occur on jars in Sudan.

SURFACES

In most cases, the surfaces were simply smoothed, but some vessels were given a lightly burnished brown slip. Other vessels have mat-impressed bodies and a lightly polished red coat on the rim and neck.[45]

DECORATION

Some of the jars in the group were decorated with impressions in vertical trees, fronds, or zigzags on the shoulder or at the neck (fig. 141c). In addition to the impressed collar-row mentioned above, some vessels

---

41. OINE VIII, *Chapter 2*, pp. 59–60. Storage jars did not occur frequently enough in the S. J. E. materials to be identified separately. Uncoated examples were assigned to W 25 ("Middle Egyptian Fine Brown Ware"; pl. 83–2:25/264:2; with four handles at the neck), while white coated jars were assigned to W 28 ("Middle Egyptian Plain White Ware", pl. 83:1 W 14, 401/4:3; pl. 83:3 W 15, 401/11:1; see also the drawing on pl. 11). This group of vessels continued from Meroitic antecedents and has no comparable forms in the major collections of Egyptian pottery. See Kelley 1976, and Egloff 1977. Despite their ascription to an Egyptian origin, they were probably local. Adams (1986, fig. 78) places shape W 14 in U 4 (Middle Egyptian Brown Utility Ware), but the profile is difficult to compare with the S. J. E. photograph or the drawing. Shape W 13, however, which also resembles the S. J. E. vessels, is assigned partly to R 32 ordinary Meroitic pottery.

42. Emery and Kirwan 1938, pls. 111–14:15a, b, 23–27, 76a–b. Handmade vessels of these types do not occur in the Ibrim cemeteries except in 192.45, and the jar cited there is also different. This and two other tombs nearby are unusual and apparently date to the Twenty-fifth Dynasty/Napatan period (Mills 1982, p. 24; in addition, 192.41.3 could be A-Group reused. See pl. XXVIII and Vila, 1982, fig. 64 for a very late reuse of a Naqada period vessel). The handmade pottery in this collection includes the groups assigned in S. J. E. materials to Nubian handmade in X-Group. For other descriptive details, see Adams 1986, pp. 420–22, wares H 1 and H 18 with some vessels of H 2, primarily from Serra East.

43. OINE V, pp. 29–36.

44. OINE VIII, *Chapter 2*, p. 87.

45. See OINE X, forthcoming. See Adams 1986, pp. 423–24.

have small lugs. Two jars were coated red and painted in white, the decoration consisting of vertical panels of dots framed with dot chains alternating with panels framed and divided by white lines.[46]

FIRING

Handmade vessels in the present collection appear to have been evenly fired at the rather low temperature characteristic of pit firing.[47] The brown vessels seem not to have the fire blooms so often found on pit-fired vessels.

POST FIRING TREATMENT

Some vessels have a thick incrustation on the bottom apparently made by plastering the vessel with mud before using it as a cooking pot. Both the shape and the incrustation resemble much earlier vessels from Kerma.[48]

For the colors of handmade pottery, see Q 345—6 (miniature lamp), Q 356—4 (red coated jar with white paint); other vessels in the group were discolored by fire, and the miniatures were made of unfired dark grey clay.

C. POTTERY OF COPTIC PERIOD EGYPTIAN TRADITION

The major groups of pottery exported from Egypt to Nubia in the Meroitic period—fine/ordinary, simple utility, chaffy utility, and various amphorae—appear also in X-Group. The relative importance of various groups changed (pls. 46, 47c) and some new treatments and types of vessels appeared.

FORM GROUP I: FINE/ORDINARY POTTERY

Fine/ordinary pottery from Egypt almost disappeared in X-Group. Only two of the most common shapes continued to occur in X-Group times: the juglet and the single-handled wine jar with a stump base. The royal tombs contained a wider variety of vessels including handleless jars, *amphoriskoi*, tall convex jars, and pilgrim bottles or *zemzemiyya*. Otherwise, the large group of klepsydrai, cups, jugs, jars, and even larger juglets disappeared.[49]

Although other elements of manufacturing resembled those of Meroitic times, decoration changed. In the earliest stages, painted decoration appears, most often consisting of groups of black horizontal lines (fig. 187a), arches, spots (fig. 157c), or spirals (figs. 117a, 188b). A few very elaborately painted vessels also

46. Decoration of handmade pots, incised and painted.

47. Nordström 1972, pp. 52–53, fabrics IIC and IIE, at ca. 650°–700° Celsius, for example; Adams 1986, p. 32, estimates ca. 850° Celsius for kiln firing.

48. Reisner 1923, IV–V, fig. 324; note also mat impressions.

49. Emery and Kirwan 1938, pl. 113:43–48, 55, 56a. Coptic period Egyptian fine/ordinary pottery makes up a part of Adams R 30 (1986, pp. 534–36, "Aswan Graeco-Roman Red Ware" which continues from Meroitic times as the major pottery made from gray-white clay). In this period, the two groups in the different classifications correspond closely. In addition, however, some simple utility pottery was assigned to this R 30 group, and a Meroitic cooking pot is included in it (Säve-Söderbergh, Englund, and Nordström 1982; see 280/241:1, pl. 81:3). Two one-handled jugs assigned to R 25 (Middle Egyptian Fine Brown Ware, Ibid., pl. 8:3, 25/304:1, pl. 77:4, 25/65:1) should probably be assigned to Form group I. The creation of the dark brown color in the firing process is dealt with in OINE VIII *Chapter 2*, pp. 63–64.

   In the OINE classifications only "table pottery" is assigned to the fine/ordinary groups; cooking vessels were all placed in utility categories. However, Adams put some Egyptian cooking pots in R 30 (1986, fig. 300:U.11), which here is divided between Egyptian form groups I (fine/ordinary) and II (non-chaffy utility). A number of painted vessels assigned by Adams to W 11, "X-Group White Ware" would be assigned to II or III (Coptic period Egyptian utility and utility chaffy; Adams 1986, pp. 470–72, 562, where he suggests it was an import; see Säve-Söderbergh, Englund, and Nordström eds. 1982, pl. 86:3 X14, 178/24:3; pl. 86:3, probably III, pl. 78:4, J4, 25/159:4; the type occurs at Armant (Kelley 1976, 98.18).

   Many *amphoriskoi* in this pottery were white coated; these were assigned to W 28 (Adams 1986, pp. 566–67), "Middle Egyptian Plain White Ware" (Säve-Söderbergh, Englund, and Nordström eds. 1982, pl. 78:2, J4, 25/41:1; pl. 80:1, J14, 25/245:3, with spout). These would also be assigned to Coptic period Egyptian utility group, probably III, chaffy utility.

appear.[50] In addition, some juglets have branches painted with relatively fine lines on the body and shoulder (figs. 104b, 119c).[51]

In addition to painting, incised decoration appears on the shoulders of some juglets that parallels the development of arches in painted decoration. It is sometimes simple curved and straight lines but often it consists of branches (figs. 103c [with impressed circles; the handle has a pair of "tails"] and 131f) and of vines enclosed in panels framed by bands of impressed circles and slashes (fig. 116a).[52]

For the colors of Coptic fine/ordinary pottery, see Q 1—24, Q 18—4, Q 32—1 (white coat), Q 61—11, Q 70—3, Q 82—1, 2; Q 134—11 (red coat), Q 146—1, Q 161—5 (red coat), and Q 164—3.

FORM GROUPS II AND III: SIMPLE AND CHAFFY UTILITY POTTERY

The two most common kinds of utility pottery in Meroitic times continued to occur in X-Group—the simple utility or unsmoothed ordinary and chaffy.[53] As given in the previous volume, both kinds of pottery are discussed together here because some vessels, especially *amphoriskoi*, occur in both fabric types. At this time, vessels in these groups were almost always given light slips and were often decorated; the shapes are sometimes more elaborate than those of their counterparts from Meroitic times.

SHAPING

Vessels from the Qustul groups include ovoid or pyriform *amphoriskoi*, jugs, and *lekythoi*. The wide variety of open jars and cooking pots that dominated the material in earlier times was not present; vessels of these groups imported to Nubia were less diverse. One major new form, the *qadus*, appears, either in these utility form groups, or as a Nubian adoption. Although it has been found in occupation debris attributed to the Meroitic Period, the *qadus* has not been found in undisturbed tomb groups before X-Group.

DECORATION

The most remarkable change in these ceramics was the introduction of painted decoration. Often complex and atectonic, elements of style and motifs appear to anticipate some developments in local painted decoration. However, even the pottery from the royal tombs contained only a selection of the variety of vessels available in Egypt[54] and no classification of this decoration would be appropriate here. One *amphoriskos* (pl. 46f) has bold, short overlapping vine leaves around the body in red. Another *amphoriskos* is decorated with splashes or blobs of paint (fig. 193a).

For the colors of utility pottery, see Q 134—6 (white coat), Q 37—2 (with white coat and paint), Q 62—5 (with white coat and paint).

---

50. Not in the present material; see Emery and Kirwan 1938, pl. 113:43–46, 48, and 56 (some are utility vessels). For other red and black decorated vessels on a white ground, see Egloff 1977, pls. 1, 3, 23–27, 32, 62–70, of varying dates, some in utility pottery.

51. Emery and Kirwan 1938, pl. 113: 57a–b; Hölscher 1954, pl. 48:Y'9, Y'10 (cup stands); Reisner 1910, fig. 330:16–17.

52. Johnson 1981, cats. 11, 12; note the elaborate plastic decoration of pl. 21 right. See also the elaborate incised and plastic decoration of the lamp in Shafiq Farid 1963, fig. 67B.

53. OINE VIII, *Chapter 2*, pp. 67–69. The vessels are assigned by Adams (1986, figs. 266 and 299; see J 12 and J 8) to R 1 and R 30, the most common Nubian X-Group pottery and the early "Aswan" fabric (pp. 468–69 and 534–36, respectively). The variance between a Nile clay based pottery and one derived from the Nubian sandstone is probably due to a varying clay mixture. The lighter clay tends to predominate in most vessels in The Oriental Institute Museum collection.

54. For an approximation of the range of types available in Egypt, see Mond and Myers 1934, pls. CXXXIV–CLIV and Egloff 1977, Tableau 7.

FORM GROUP IV: FINE POTTERY

Only one small vessel of fine white fabric, a small two-handled juglet, was found in the present collection. It was decorated on the shoulder with a red band framed by black lines (Q 33—1, colors noted).[55]

AMPHORAE

Amphorae for storing and shipping wine were a major part of the deposits in the Noubadian X-Group royal tombs.[56] They occurred less frequently in private burials. Despite the large number of vessels from the region, the variety is only a small selection of the number of shapes and fabrics produced in Egypt and no new classification will be attempted.[57] Some amphorae were also decorated, with simple bands (fig. 24d), spot leaves, and a geometric emblem or standard (fig. 130e) in black. Decoration in white and black also occurred, consisting of crosshatching or zigzags, sometimes with dots at the intersections and vertical or diagonal lines. The design appears to depict an altar (figs. 117b and 135c).[58]

For colors of amphorae and related vessels, see Q 134—2 and Q 385—1.

D. POTTERY CORPORA

The X-Group pottery of Qustul and Adindan is presented here in four corpus sections, for X-Group wheelmade, handmade, handmade votive, and Coptic period Egyptian pottery respectively. Of these sections, only the X-Group wheelmade and handmade could be considered diverse enough to be a corpus. Only a few different shapes of votive cup were found and they generally belong to the handmade group, although the shapes are not miniaturizations of handmade pottery. Amphorae and high quality imports would be presented separately in their own corpus sections, but the latter did not occur at all in the present material and the former were not varied enough to establish classes.

As mentioned above, pottery in each of these corpora had antecedents in Meroitic times. The X-Group wheelmade pottery included three form groups—ordinary, fine, and storage jars within a single tradition of pottery making. Two of these groups were treated separately in the Meroitic corpora, as they represent significantly different developments in a much more complex ceramic tradition.

Since no single site from Egypt or Nubia has yielded a comprehensive body of material, the corpora are not complete. Because the material is limited, the classification of X-Group pottery at Qustul has been established to take into account the incompleteness of the local record. Within the larger traditional groups, pottery is assigned to major forms, each designated by a name. The major forms are subdivided by outline. The subdivisions have been made to take into account the occurrence of variants in other locations as much as possible. Some uncommon vessels might be given additional subdivision elsewhere.

55. For the pottery, see OINE VIII *Chapter 2*, p. 71 (Fine/Ordinary IIA). See Adams 1986, fig. 254:G16, p. 438. Vessels of the equivalent Meroitic group were included in the Nubian fine category (W 26), which they closely resemble in appearance.

56. Emery and Kirwan 1938, various and pl. 111. Amphorae in the present collection correspond to U 4 ("Middle Egyptian Brown Utility Ware," Adams 1986, pp. 567–68; Säve-Söderbergh, Englund, and Nordström eds. 1982, pl. 86:4, 25/43:1), sherds of which are especially common at Roman period sites in Egypt (see Adams 1986, pp. 567–68). In most cases, this appears to be a smother kiln variant of utility pottery. Adams (R 30, 1986, fig. 300:Z5 and Z7, pp. 534–36) assigned some of the amphorae to his Aswan pottery, here Coptic period Egyptian Form group II. For amphorae not in the present collection, see U 16 (Adams 1986, pp. 575–76), U 3 (p. 580), and U 18 (pp. 581–82).

57. See Adams 1986, pp. 525–83 generally.

58. For a large example, see Shafiq Farid 1963, fig. 73 and Firth 1927, p. 158, cem. 122:16.3. Sherds from an amphora found in the shafts of tombs Q 36 and 37 had part of an altar of this type (fig. 117b).

NOUBADIAN X-GROUP WHEELMADE POTTERY

GOBLETS

Most of the goblets were red coated as were almost all of the earlier bottle-necked jars with which they occur. Each of these groups has counterparts in the metal vessels of the royal tombs. Both of the goblet types were derived from Egyptian imports, but have shapes and decorations not found in Egypt.

GOBLET A: THE STRAIGHT-RIMMED GOBLET (fig. 7)

With its companions, the rib-rimmed goblet and the bottle-jar, the straight-rimmed goblet is the most characteristic pottery vessel of X-Group Nubia. Its appearance is as readily recognizable as a Kerma Beaker, and it probably had much the same significance. It did not, however, derive directly from Nubian antecedents, but from Egyptian imports in the fourth-century Dodekaschoinos. The earliest goblets of this kind were simple cups, with tapered, usually ribbed, lower sides, ring bases, and slightly inverted upper sides or rims which were smoothed to accommodate the user's lip.[59] Over time, the rim tended to become progressively broader, the body relatively narrower and deeper, and the bend at the waist more pronounced. The lower and upper sides were smoothed, the only remaining vestige of wheel marks being one or two incised grooves at the waist. Later, the lower side was made narrower and slightly recurved. In the late stages of X-Group, the curved or tapered lower side was emphasized; the bend became much sharper, and the rim narrower until the proportions were exaggerated.

After the earliest examples in the Dodekaschoinos, goblets were red coated. Painted decoration was simple, most frequently a design based on the burst vine consisting of columns of horizontal white and black drop-shapes which often alternated. White or white and black swags follow the rim. These also sometimes have vertical or splayed pendent lines where the swags joined the rim. Later the swags were abbreviated and the number of drops in the drop-row or burst vine was increased to four or five while the size of the motifs was reduced, giving them relatively more space.

GOBLET B: THE RIB-RIMMED GOBLET (fig. 8)

The career of the second goblet closely paralleled the development of the straight-rimmed goblet. The rib-rimmed goblet first appears in groups from the fourth century Dodekaschoinos. There the vessel had a tapered convex lower side and a low upturned rim.[60] Like the straight-rimmed goblet, the rim was smoothed while the lower body was sharply wheel-marked or ribbed. The base was always a stump. Over time, the vessel became taller and narrower and the portion of the shoulder that was smoothed increased; sometimes the tip of the rim was beveled. Subsequently the entire vessel was smoothed and some of the latest examples were given ring bases.[61] The vessels were red coated from the first but were almost never painted.

CUPS (fig. 9)

The development of various cups was complex. A few of them seem to have originated in the ring-based, straight-sided cups of the Meroitic period. Some cups possibly originated in the wide-bottomed, round-based vessels common in handmade pottery. Most, however, seem to have originated in the concave and straight-sided cups of the Dodekaschoinos.[62] Most originally were convex or flat-based, but a few, especially E (see tab. 13), were given disc, ring, or even pedestal bases. Unlike the chalices, most cups were white, either made of the fine white clay from the Nubian Sandstone or of alluvial clay with a white coat. A few were red coated. Apart from grooves below the rim and at the waist, decoration was painted in red or black, mostly in narrow bands framed with single, double, or sometimes triple lines. Located at the rim and sometimes on the lower body, these bands mostly contain hatching and crosshatching. Often, narrow or framing bands occur alone. In a few cases, broad red bands were painted at the rim and at a rib on the side. Red and black are combined, but rarely. The more elaborate painted style of late X-Group on bottle-necked jars was also put on cylindrical cups (fig. 105d–f).

59. See Ricke 1967, pl. 29.

60. Ricke 1967, pl. 23.

61. Mills 1982, pl. XXV:192.28.2, .3, .5, .6, and .4, for example.

62. See Ricke 1967, figs. 73–74, for example.

BOWLS (fig. 10)

Bowls were not common in X-Group and tend to have shapes like handmade bowls. Most are deep and convex, with slightly flattened bases or with the widest point near the bottom (*bombenformige*). Some have conical sides and some are convex with everted rims and disc bases. These shapes are probably of Egyptian origin.[63] Most bowls were red coated. Some were painted with typical X-Group designs vertical lines that sometimes alternated black and white, rim bands or swags painted in pairs inside the rim.

SPOUTED JARS (fig. 11)

A globular or ovoid spouted jar with a wide, straight neck and a short spout on the shoulder has a counterpart in metal, and parallels in the handmade pottery of Sudan.[64] A band of white spots may imitate the plastic decoration of a Sudanese jar.

WIDEMOUTHED JARS (fig. 12)

Jars with wide mouths are not common in X-Group materials; they seem to have varied origins, both in Nubia and in Egypt.

BOTTLE-NECKED JARS (figs. 13–15)

By far the most important group of jars was intended only to contain liquids and to dispense them by pouring. Four major categories could be distinguished from two cultural traditions.

BOTTLE-JARS OF MEROITIC BACKGROUND (figs. 13, 14e)

One of the major categories consists of broad ovoid, globular, or even somewhat baggy jars with moderately sized openings and cylindrical or slightly everted necks. These were brought up more or less abruptly from the shoulder. The rims are either straight, grooved, or simply slightly thickened. Occasionally, there is a rib at the base of the neck or on the shoulder—a rib that was once a prominent feature of Kushite wheelmade pottery in Meroitic times.

Almost all of the vessels had been smoothed and given a red coat. Decoration was painted in white and/or black. This decoration was quite simple and sometimes consisted only of pairs of bands on the body or a band at the rim. Most often, however, the decoration consists of alternating white and black ovals or blobs at the base of the neck, a simplification of the Meroitic bead motif. Although this motif does occur on the other group of bottle-jars, it is not common on them. Together with the shape, this motif helps to indicate that the present group was derived from Meroitic jars.

BOTTLE-JARS OF NOBA BACKGROUND (fig. 14a–d, f–n)

The most characteristic container used in X-Group times is a globular or ovoid vessel with a tall, constricted neck and an everted or modeled rim. Simple rims are unusual; most were candlestick rims, or some modification of the type, with one or more projecting ribs below. Later, some rims were modeled into impressive cuplike shapes. In addition to the rim, plastic decoration was also common, most frequently occurring as a rib at the base of the neck and a band of horizontal grooves on the shoulder. Although the basic shape is characteristic of Nubia, the tall bottle-neck, modeled rim, and incised bands do not occur in Meroitic pottery. Each of these features is characteristic of the tradition of Upper Nubia which we attribute to the Noba, i.e. the Tanqasi Culture. The same features are also found on the metal versions of the same vessels.

The early vessels were given red coats with white coats becoming popular later. Bottle-neck jars were frequently decorated with horizontal black bands or vertical groups of drop shapes of the same kind that occur on the goblets. Sometimes, painted decoration included bands of crosshatching, hatching, crosshatched triangles, or circles, on the shoulder. Swags, arches, and trees or branches occur less frequently. Rarely a band of black and white beads was painted around the neck. Late in the period, a new elaborate style appeared painted in black or black and red on a white background. This style, also found in bands on cups, is common at Ibrim, but rare in the present material. Designs are a combination of older Kushite decoration, Roman period Egyptian motifs, Coptic designs, and Sudanese-Saharan designs. The style does not occur fully developed in the present material.

63. See Hölscher 1954, pl. 48, shape R, and Mond and Myers 1934, pl. CXXXV:26, for example.

64. Emery and Kirwan 1938, pl. 66G; Garstang, Sayce, and Griffith 1911, pl. XLII:5 (right) and 7 (left).

STORAGE JARS (fig. 16)

The storage jars were derived from counterparts in Meroitic times. The most typical storage jar at this time was the large, almost tubular vessel with short, sloping neck and everted or angled rim.

MINIATURE VESSELS (fig. 17)

As discussed in the first chapter, unbaked miniature cups were found in surface deposits. The cups were V-shaped or convex, sometimes with a short pedestal. A shallow dish and small jar were also found. In addition to votive vessels, crude shallow lamps were handmade and lightly fired.

HANDMADE VESSELS (figs. 19–20)

Although simple coarse handmade bowls and jars continued to be made, the well-made burnished black incised pottery of Meroitic times was no longer made in X-Group. The jars seem to have included a number of vessels that represent a transition between the vessels of Sudan and the mass-produced wheelmade bottle-jars of Lower Nubia.

COPTIC PERIOD EGYPTIAN POTTERY (figs. 21–25)

Egyptian pottery found in X-Group contexts is partly comparable with important collections from Egypt, notably from Karanis,[65] Armant,[66] Medinet Habu,[67] Quseir,[68] and Kellia.[69] The Egyptian pottery appears to have developed from one period to the next without a major break. However, a new painted decoration appeared that makes X-Group imports distinct from those of earlier periods.[70] Boldly painted monochrome designs, in purple or black on a white ground found on utility pottery are especially important (fig. 122a), and now there are painted (fig. 186b) and incised juglets (fig. 116a).

As pointed out in the previous volume, the variety of Egyptian pottery in late antique Nubia is sharply limited. Only a few types from the wide variety of vessels were ever exported and the period of export need not have corresponded to the period of manufacture. Thus changes between the Roman period Egyptian and the Coptic or Byzantine period Egyptian groups in Nubia are more abrupt than they were in Egypt, an abruptness emphasized by the chronological gap between the two periods.

E. POTTERY AND THE ECONOMIC LIFE OF LATE NUBIA

The pottery of X-Group differs substantially from that of Meroitic times in all major sites and areas of the Triakontaschoinos. The abruptness of the changes south of the anti-Diocletianic border is paralleled by more abrupt changes in the ceramics of the Dodekaschoinos itself. In both regions, most important changes are in shapes and decoration, aesthetic qualities most likely to reflect some major change in the culture of the population. In the earliest groups from the Dodekaschoinos, this change is accompanied by changes in the technique of manufacturing and decorating pottery that clearly reflect a major new influence, which has been identified as Blemmyan. Changes in the Noubadian-dominated Triakontaschoinos were just as far-reaching, but the widespread preference for certain general kinds of vessel among the peoples of Nubia, and the manufacture of vessels of different cultural backgrounds in a single form group, have tended to mask the significance of the changes. However the changes were abrupt; the latest groups of the Meroitic period contained typical vessels[71] that could not be mistaken for any common early X-Group despite the red coat they have in common. The earliest X-Group burials at Qustul contained no pottery vessels, and it is possible

65. Johnson 1981.
66. Mond and Myers 1934, pls. CXVIII–CLIV.
67. Hölscher 1954, pl. 48.
68. Whitcomb and Johnson 1979, pp. 67–103; 1982, pp. 51–115.
69. Egloff 1977.
70. Emery and Kirwan 1938, pls. 113:42a, 43, 45, 46, 48, 55, and 56.
71. For example, Mills 1982, pl. XLIX; the cups have angled sides.

that, such pottery as was made and used in the Triakontaschoinos at this time was not sufficiently distinctive for archaeologists to detect it in the mixed material of occupation debris.

Table 13. Pottery of X-Group Nubia.

NOUBADIAN X-GROUP WHEELMADE POTTERY

GOBLETS

A. Approximately biconical; ring base, smoothed upper side, smoothed or slightly ribbed lower side. Often painted (fig. 7).
    1. Low to medium height, straight lower side[72]
        a. low
            i. open, narrow rim (lower body unfinished, ridged; 84c)
            ii. rim slightly inverted and narrow to moderate
                alpha. curved (85d)
                  beta. carinated (83, 86a) or almost, more inverted
            iii. bend at midpoint or below (85a–i)[73]
        b. low-moderate with side angled at or near midpoint
            i. low, angle at or above midpoint
                alpha. angle slight[74]
                  beta. angle sharper, at midpoint (84)[75]
            ii. moderate, angle below waist (82a–c)[76]
        c. medium to tall, all sharply angled
            i. angle above midpoint[77]
            ii. angle at midpoint (80 a–d)[78]
            iii. bulged waist? (81)[79]
    2. Lower side profile slightly curved; calyciform
        a. low, wide, inverted at upper third (86b?)
        b. tall, angle just above midpoint[80]
        c. tall, angle or grooves at midpoint, incurved lower side distinct[81]
            i. moderately incurved
            ii. strongly incurved

---

72. Säve-Söderbergh, Englund, and Nordström 1982, corpus, pls. 4–5:B14, B15, B17; "Classic X-Group Red Ware R 1," photographs, pls. 72:3, 4; 73:1.

73. Kirwan 1939, corpus, pls. 22–26:20a–b (hereafter cited only by number); Shafiq Farid 1963, corpus, figs. 70–72: ca. 43–44 (hereafter cited only by number).

74. Kirwan 1939, corpus 20c.

75. Kirwan 1939, corpus 20d, Shafiq Farid 1963, corpus ca. 45.

76. Kirwan 1939, corpus, no equivalent; Shafiq Farid 1963, corpus ca. 38.

77. Kirwan 1939, corpus 20e.

78. Kirwan 1939, corpus 20d(?), Shafiq Farid 1963, corpus ca. 41, 45, and 46.

79. Kirwan 1939, corpus 20f; Shafiq Farid 1963, corpus ca. 47; Mills 1982, tomb 192.2.18, .60, .61.

80. Kirwan 1939, corpus, between 20e and 21, more like 20e; Shafiq Farid 1963, corpus ca. 38b.

81. Kirwan 1939, corpus, between 20f and 21a.

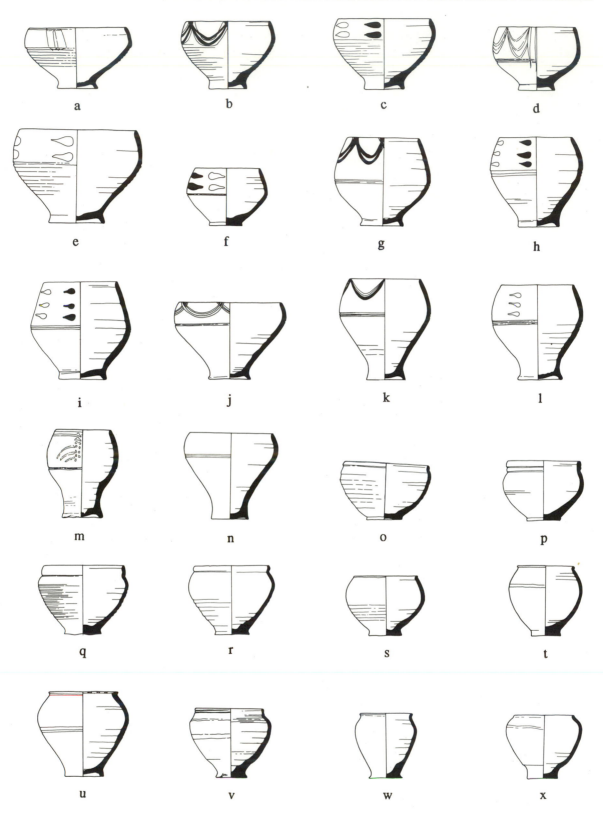

Figure 7. X-Group Goblets: (*a*) A1ai, R 111—2; (*b*) A1aii *alpha*, Q 9—3; (*c*) A1aii *beta*, Q 9—7; (*d*) A1aiii, Q 62—9; (*e*) A1bi *alpha*, Q 338 S—1; (*f*) A1bi *beta*, Q 62—18; (*g*) A1bii, Q 52—9; (*h*) A1ci, Q 1—16; (*i*) A1cii, Q 2—4; (*j*) A2a, R 4A—18; (*k*) A2b, R 2—3; (*l*) A2ci, R 2—4; (*m*) A2cii, R 11—4; (*n*) A2di, R 11—3; (*o*) B1ai?, Q 164—G; (*p*) B1a(i), Q 7—4; (*q*) B1b, Q 67—10; (*r*) B1c, Q 9—2; (*s*) B2ai, Q 52—11; (*t*) B2aii, Q 19—5; (*u*) B2aiii, Q 1—15; (*v*) B2bi, Q 390—4; (*w*) B2bii, Q 58—1; (*x*) B2biv, R 36—4. Scale 1:5.

Table 13. Pottery of X-Group Nubia (*cont.*).

GOBLETS (*cont.*)

d. tall, lower side strongly but evenly curved angle of rim, sharp, at upper third or quarter of height
    i. open[82]
    ii. narrow, thin-walled (none present)[83]

B. Tapered convex side, disc base, vertical or rib rim. Normally unpainted[84] (fig. 8)
  1. Low, rim relatively prominent, side often ridged
    a. rim almost at maximum diameter, side convex (87d[?]–e)
    b. rim more prominent, side more tapered (87c)
    c. side tapered from very distinct shoulder, shorter rim (87a)
  2. Moderate-tall, rim very low, surface finished
    a. convex-biconical, bend at or just above midpoint (87b)
      i.
      ii.
      iii.
      iv.[85]

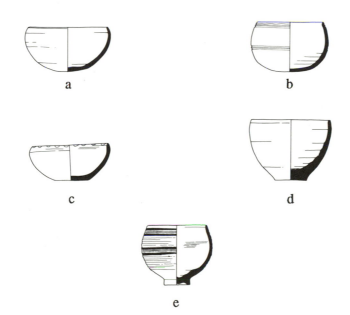

Figure 8. X-Group Cups: (*a*) A1a, Q 148—3; (*b*) A1b, R 24—4; (*c*) A2a, Q 19—3; (*d*) B1, Q 326—1; (*e*) C2, Q 54—6. Scale 1:5.

82. Kirwan 1939, corpus, between 21a and b.

83. Kirwan 1939, corpus 21c–e; Mills 1982, tomb 192.12.1, .3; 192.11.7, .9; 192.18.3; and 192.28.7.

84. Säve-Söderbergh, Englund, and Nordström 1982, corpus B9, pl. 4; pl. 72:2, B7; in the text of the entries, these are assigned both to "ware R 1" and to "Coptic Middle Egyptian Fine Brown Ware, alternatively R 1." The alluvial clay with red coat is the same as that used for A and other ordinary vessels. Both major goblet types were derived from Egypt but soon diverged from their prototypes. See Hölscher 1954, pl. 48:V′1 and Q′6; for parallel cup shapes, see S 2–5.

85. Mills 1982, tomb 192.17.3; 192.23.27.

Table 13. Pottery of X-Group Nubia (*cont.*).

GOBLETS (*cont.*)

    b. bend well above midpoint

        i. slightly concave shoulder, convex lower side (63)

        ii. biconical or slightly convex above and below bend

        iii. incurved lower side[86]

        iv. convex above and below bend sharp incurve just above base

   3. Evenly curved convex side (none present)[87]

   4. Elaborate tall variant with broad groove at midpoint, biconical (Ibrim only) (none present)[88]

CUPS[89] (fig. 9)

  A. Convex cups, rim slightly incurved

    1. Round base

      a. high waist

      b. low waist[90]

    2. Flat base, low

  B. Convex cup, rim at or about the same size as maximum diameter[91]

    1. Taper to base (59a?)

    2. Disc base (59c) (none present)

    3. Pedestal? (59b) (none present)

  C. Convex cups, diameter at rim less than waist (with base)[92]

    1. High waist (66b) (none present)

    2. Waist at midpoint (66a)

    3. Low waist (none present)

  D. Tapered cylindrical cups

    1. Flattened base

      a. low

      b. moderate

    2. Slightly convex base

      a. narrow base

      b. wide base

    3. Convex base, curve to side[93]

      a. tapered

      b. almost vertical side

---

86. Mills 1982, tomb 192.13.4.

87. Mills 1982, tomb 192.51.4.

88. Mills 1982, tomb 192.2.1.

89. Cups occur in X-Group ordinary (Adams 1986, pp. 468–69, R 1/R 25) and the bluish to white X-Group fine (essentially Adams 1986, pp. 439–40, Ware W 30, possibly some W 27; a few vessels were made in W 29 [pp. 472–73], an ordinary pottery with a white coat) pottery. Several shapes, especially concave-sided cups, have prototypes in the Blemmye materials of the Dodekaschoinos; see Ricke 1967, fig. 73. The vessels are sometimes painted, with either X-Group simple patterns, linear decoration (on white cups), and later, the elaborate decoration found at Ibrim. See Säve-Söderbergh, Englund, and Nordström 1982, corpus B–D, pls. 4–6.

90. Säve-Söderbergh, Englund, and Nordström 1982, corpus C5.

91. Säve-Söderbergh, Englund, and Nordström 1982, corpus ca. B22A.

92. Säve-Söderbergh, Englund, and Nordström 1982, corpus, approximately B1 "most nearly resembles lower Egyptian family LS." Actually the white clay from the Nubian Sandstone was used.

93. Säve-Söderbergh, Englund, and Nordström 1982, corpus A16, pl. 4. Called ware W 26, Meroitic Fine White Ware and assigned to Meroitic style; see, however, Mills 1982, tomb 193.38.a.

Table 13. Pottery of X-Group Nubia (*cont.*).

CUPS (*cont.*)

    4. Disc base

        a. tapered

        b. side nearly vertical

    5. Tall disc or pedestal base (60b?)

        a. moderate (60a)[94]

        b. tall

           i.

           ii. with a rib

E. Concave-sided cups

    1. Low

        a. convex base (65b)

        b. disc base (61c) (none present)[95]

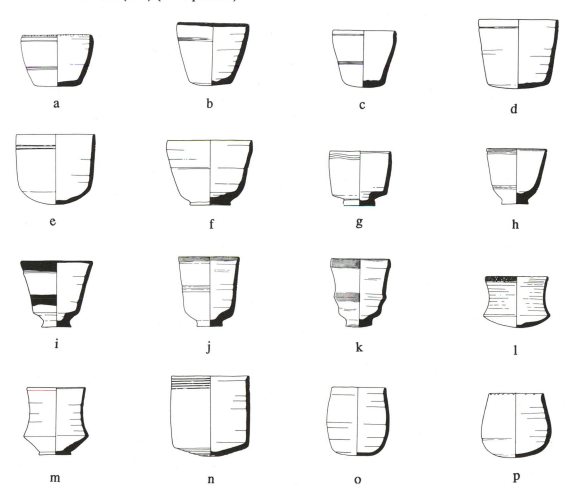

Figure 9. X-Group Cups (*cont.*): (*a*) D1a, Q 148—6; (*b*) D1b, Q 144—3; (*c*) D2a, VG 97—1; (*d*) D2b, R 4A—4; (*e*) D3b, R 4A—7; (*f*) D4a, Q 361—2; (*g*) D4b, Q 148—7; (*h*) D5a, Q 1—23; (*i*) D5a, Q 148—4; (*j*) D5bi, Q 1—19; (*k*) D5bii, Q 1—21; (*l*) E1a, Q 3—3; (*m*) E2a, Q 8—1; (*n*) F1a, Q 134—7; (*o*) G1b, Q 1—17; (*p*) G1a, Q 18—6. Scale 1:5.

94. Säve-Söderbergh, Englund, and Nordström 1982, corpus approximately B22, from 25/219:1 (called W27, Meroitic Pale Pink Ware which is the same as X-Group fine; the tomb is actually X-Group).

95. Shafiq Farid 1963, corpus 55.

Table 13. Pottery of X-Group Nubia (*cont.*).

CUPS (*cont.*)

    2. Moderate height, disc base

        a. simple (61b)[96]

        b. ridge below rim (62) (none present)[97]

        c. incurved at rim (61c) (none present)[98]

        d. no carination (61a) (none present)

    3. Zigzag profile (none present)[99]

  F. Straight-sided or inward-tapered cups

    1. Vertical side with convex or ribbed convex base or disc

        a. convex or ribbed convex base (72c)[100]

        b. disc base (65a) (none present)[101]

    2. Slight inward taper, carination at convex base (72a–b) (none present)

    3. Slightly tapered or vertical side, ring-pedestal base (none present)[102]

  G. Broad bottom, low waist

    1.[103]

        a. wide

        b. narrow

    2. Broad (73 a, d) (none present)

    3. Sharply incurved side (73h) (none present)

BOWLS (fig. 10)

  A. Convex, deep

    1. Simple convex (none present)

    2. End between bottom and side[104]

  B. Angled side

    1. Deep, broad bottom, nearly conical (75a)[105]

    2. Conical, narrow bottom[106]

        a. flat base (71a) (none present)

        b. ring base (71b) (none present)

  C. Broad-bottomed (*bombenformige*)

    1. Curved (73a, rib rim 73c)

    2. Bend between bottom and side

96. Shafiq Farid 1963, corpus 57.

97. Säve-Söderbergh, Englund, and Nordström 1982, corpus B26, 2 examples, W 29, X-Group Ordinary White Ware and W 27, Meroitic Pale Pink Ware; OINE examples are all X-Group fine. Shafiq Farid 1963, corpus 58a. Pamela Rose, personal communication and Adams 1986, pp. 472–73 and 440. W 29 is Nile silt with white slip; the fine ware equivalent is W 30.

98. Mills 1982, tomb 192.94.3; Shafiq Farid 1963, corpus approximately 57b.

99. Mills 1982, tomb 192.15.4.

100. Shafiq Farid 1963, corpus 52.

101. Säve-Söderbergh, Englund, and Nordström 1982, corpus B25, pl. 5, probably Meroitic.

102. Mills 1982, tomb 192.21.10; 192.23.3, .7, .10, .15.

103. Säve-Söderbergh, Englund, and Nordström 1982, corpus A1 or A8, pl. 4. Shafiq Farid 1963, corpus 58 Bowls.

104. Säve-Söderbergh, Englund, and Nordström 1982, corpus C11 or C12, pl. 5.

105. Säve-Söderbergh, Englund, and Nordström 1982, corpus approximately C46, pl. 6.

106. Kirwan 1939, corpus 26b.

Table 13. Pottery of X-Group Nubia (*cont.*).

BOWLS (*cont.*)

   D. Bowls with flared rims

       1. Medium height, incurved to base

           a. rim carinated outward (67) (none present)

           b. smooth profile (68) (none present)

       2. Wide bowl, slightly angled rim (70) (none present)

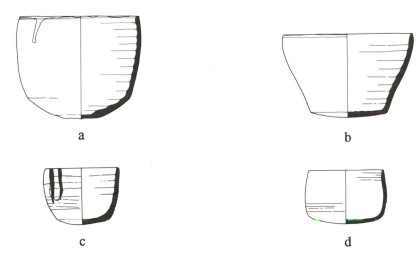

Figure 10. X-Group Bowls: (*a*) A2, Q 140—1; (*b*) B1, Q 14—3; (*c*) C1, VG 95—1; (*d*) C2, Q 12—2. Scale 1:5.

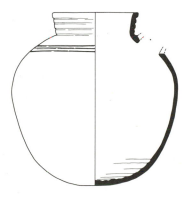

Figure 11. X-Group Ordinary Spouted Jar I—A (Q 6—4). Scale 1:5.

Figure 12. X-Group Ordinary Convex Jar I—C with Short Neck and Modeled Rim (Q 328—3). Scale 1:5.

JARS[107]

   Spouted Jars (fig. 11)

      A. Low, globular to barrel shaped, round base, short spout and vert. rim (79)[108]

      B. Tall, ring-based[109]

   Convex-broad-bottomed jar (fig. 12)

      A. As described above (74)

107. Few jars with wide rims occur in X-Group. The two major types presented here are not really a group, but represent two different major forms.

108. Low, globular to barrel-shaped: Ricke 1967, fig. 76:B8/6; Shafiq Farid 1963, corpus 49; handmade versions occur in the Tanqasi culture and the ultimate antecedent is probably the Kerma spouted jar; Reisner 1923, IV–V, figs. 283–85.

109. Firth 1927, p. 125, fig. 5:39–42.

Table 13. Pottery of X-Group Nubia (*cont.*).

JARS (*cont.*)

Tall, convex jar, tapered to base (51a–b) (none present)

Medium-necked bottle-jar (Decoration in this group consists of spot or blob-bead decoration at the base of the neck; figs. 13, 14e)

    A. Globular-baggy with relatively wide necks

        1. Low straight neck

            a. simple rim[110]

            b. bow or bulged neck

            c. roll rim[111]

        2. Flared rim (18; only bulged neck type present)

    B. Globular-baggy with necks of medium width

        1. Straight neck (mostly with groove outside rim)

        2. Conical neck (22c)[112]

        3. Flared neck

            a. neck conical (22b)

            b. neck has concave or nearly cylindrical profile (2nd)[113]

    C. Taller, narrower neck, flared

        1. Smooth profile[114]

        2. Carination at neck

            a. simple rim (35a) (none present)

            b. grooved rim (22a) (none present)

    D. Barrel shaped, carinated near base or flat-bottomed, more angular profile (none in present material)[115]

Bottle-necked jars of Noba background (fig. 14a–d, f–n)[116]

    A. Curved profile, globular, ovoid or baggy, narrow short-medium neck[117]

        1. Globular

        2. Barrel-shaped

        3. Baggy

    B. Barrel-shaped, tall, concave neck, sometimes with special articulation, rim broadly splayed, or complex[118]

        1. Smooth profile, "candlestick rim"

            a. rim bulged (28a).

            b. rim kinked (28b, 28c) (none present)

        2. Angular rim (none present)

        3. Pyriform, with cupped, complex or very broad rim (one flat-based; not in present material)[119]

110. Säve-Söderbergh, Englund, and Nordström 1982, corpus W, nearest W34, pl. 13.

111. Säve-Söderbergh, Englund, and Nordström 1982, corpus W33, pl. 13.

112. Firth 1927, fig. 5:22–23, very approximate parallels.

113. Säve-Söderbergh, Englund, and Nordström 1982, corpus W24 (?), pl. 12, Note that the jar resembles utility jar III—A (fig. 16a, c), except that the latter are smaller, and tend to have shorter necks and flatter bases.

114. Säve-Söderbergh, Englund, and Nordström 1982, corpus W33, pl. 13; Firth 1927 fig. 5:20.

115. Mills 1982, tomb 192.20.1; 192.21.7.

116. Shafiq Farid 1963, corpus 13–24.

117. Säve-Söderbergh, Englund, and Nordström 1982, corpus W38, pl. 13.

118. Kirwan 1939, corpus jars 14 and 15 here, mostly in B2.

119. Mills 1982, tomb 192.12.2; 192.23.2 (flat base); 192.52.2; 192.57.1; 192.59.1; 192.67.3; 192.80.1.

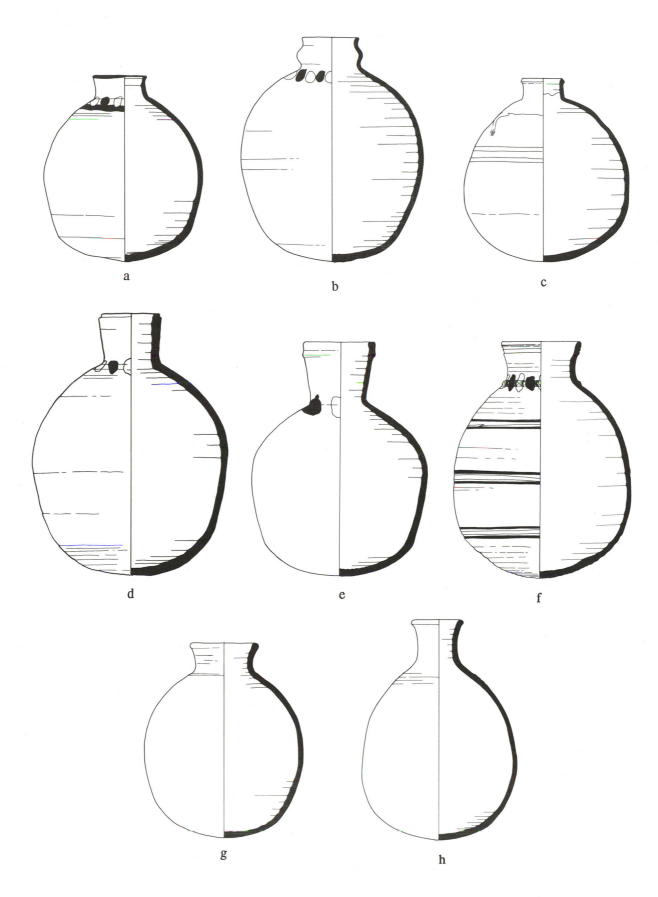

Figure 13. X-Group Medium-Necked Bottle-Jars: (*a*) A1a, Q 6—2; (*b*) A1b, W 74—3; (*c*) A1c, Q 67—7; (*d*) B1, Q 316—1; (*e*) B2, Q 37—1; (*f*) B3a, Q 164—5; (*g*) B3b, Q 44—3; (*h*) C1, Q 38—3. Scale 1:5.

Figure 14. X-Group Narrow-Necked Bottle-Jars: (*a*) A1, Q 3—2; (*b*) A2, Q 1—10; (*c*) A3, Q 148—1; (*d*) B1a, R 50—6; (*e*) C1, Q 54—1; (*f*) C2, R 4A—17; (*g*) C3, R 82—1; (*h*) C4, R 66—1; (*i*) D1, Q 2—1; (*j*) D2, Q 227—4; (*k*) C3, Q 18—3; (*l*) E1a, Q 78—3; (*m*) E1b, Q 53—2; (*n*) E3, Q 1—8. Scale 1:5.

Table 13. Pottery of X-Group Nubia (*cont.*).

JARS (*cont.*)

    C. Barrel-shaped, tall cylindrical neck, relatively narrow[120]
        1. Straight cylinder (31a)
        2. Everted rim (31b)
        3. Candlestick or ribbed rim (32, 33a, 33b, 38c)
        4. With added handle
    D. Barrel-shaped, low to medium but narrow neck
        1. Everted or rib-rimmed (29)
        2. Ridged or collar-neck
        3. Ridged or modeled rim (30a, b, 37b)
    E. Small, globular-barrel-shaped, medium length straight or concave neck with everted, rib, rectangular, or ridged rim
        1. Everted rim
           a. simple rim(34b)
           b. rib or flattened rim
        2. Vertical "rectangle" rim
        3. Ridged rim
    F. Broad-based (not in present material)[121]
    G. Very elongated ovoid or barrel-shaped (not in present material)[122]

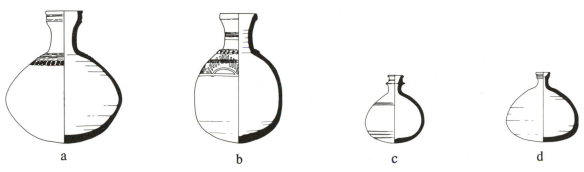

          a   b   c   d

Figure 15. X-Group Half-Size and Miniature Bottle-Jars: (*a*) A1, R 106—1; (*b*) A2, R 53—1; (*c*) B1, Q 143—7; (*d*) B2a, Q 78—4. Scale 1:5.

Half-size and Miniature Bottle-jars (fig. 15)[123]

    A. Half-size jars[124]
        1. Biconical
        2. Ovoid-tubular
    B. Miniature (juglet size)[125]
        1. Globular (57b)
        2. Broad-bottomed
           a. baggy (57d–f)[126]
           b. flat-based (58) (none present)
           c. shouldered (57a, c) (none present)[127]

120. Firth 1927, fig. 5: cem. 122:13–14; fig. 4: cem. 112:14–19, 21.

121. Mills 1982, tomb 192.23.4.

122. Mills 1982, tomb 192.34.1–3; 192.14.11; 192.15.3.

123. All belong to Säve-Söderbergh, Englund, and Nordström 1982, corpus mostly G10, G31, pl. 7.

124. Mills 1982, tomb 192.78.1; 192.85.1; 192.94.1.

125. Hölscher 1954, pl. 48:X′3–4. See also Coptic period Egyptian miniatures.

126. Shafiq Farid 1963, corpus 32–33.

127. Shafiq Farid 1963, corpus 34a.

Table 13. Pottery of X-Group Nubia (*cont.*).

JARS (*cont.*)

Utility Storage Jars of Kushite-Meroitic Background (fig. 16)

Barrel-shaped jars with medium-wide necks of short or moderate length, concave or flared, with everted or roll-rims[128]

    A. Small[129]

    B. Medium-large (20a–b)[130]

    C. Large (16a–b)[131]

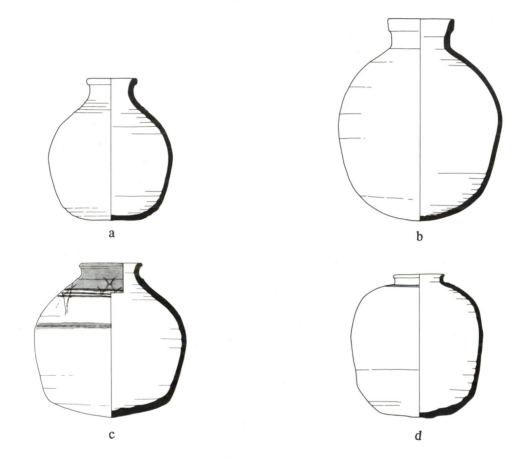

Figure 16. Utility Storage Jars of Meroitic Background: (*a*) A, Q 34—1; (*b*) B, Q 196—5;
(*c*) A, Q 149—4; (*d*) C, Q 54—14. Scale 1:5.

128. Insufficient numbers of these vessels were found to subdivide the categories.

129. Firth 1927, fig. 5: cem. 122, 2, 4; Säve-Söderbergh, Englund, and Nordström 1982, corpus W4, pl. 11, not precise. See medium-neck bottle-jars I—B3b.

130. Kirwan 1939, corpus 12b–c, but no precise parallels; Firth 1927, fig. 4:22; fig. 5:9, 12, also fig. on p. 159:2; Shafiq Farid 1963, corpus 10, approximately; Säve-Söderbergh, Englund, and Nordström 1982, corpus approximately W24, pl. 12.

131. Firth 1927, fig. 5: cem. 122:9; Säve-Söderbergh, Englund, and Nordström 1982, corpus W2, W13 (in Meroitic tomb), and W14, pls. 10, 11. In the entry for 25/264:2, the pottery is assigned to R25 "Middle Egyptian Fine Brown Ware," which was also used to designate some of the goblets (B). Since this is actually simply alluvial clay, the regional assignment cannot be made on the basis of material. It is the same as X-Group ordinary pottery. (Pamela Rose, personal communication, but separated on the basis of mica content, which appears to be higher in Egyptian pots. See Adams 1986, pp. 468, 562; he remarks that none of the criteria are absolutely diagnostic. For example, mica appears in Nubia quite often, see Nordström 1972, pp. 48–53).

Table 13. Pottery of X-Group Nubia (*cont.*).

MINIATURES — VOTIVE (fig. 17)[132]

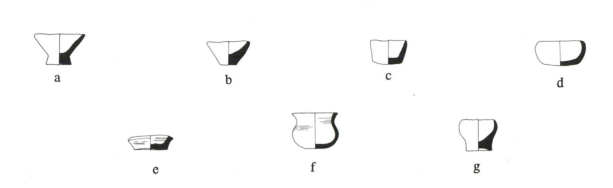

Figure 17. X-Group Votive Miniatures from Tombs Q 51 and VA 14: (*a*) Q 51—5; (*b*) Q 51—16; (*c*) Q 51—14; (*d*) Q 51—22; (*e*) Q 52—12; (*f*) VA 14—7; (*g*) Q 51—4. Scale 1:5.

Figure 18. Lamp, Q 345—6. Scale 1:5.

HANDMADE POTTERY

I. HANDMADE DOMESTIC UTILITY (both rough and burnished, rarely coated)

II. COOKING POTS (both rough and burnished, rarely coated, sometimes plastered with mud; they include the shapes of bowls B and jars A1 and C)

BOWLS (fig. 19)

    A. V-shaped (uncertain in present material)

    B. Over-hemispherical

         1. Small (cup)

         2. Large (76a)[133]

Figure 19. Handmade Bowls: (*a*) B1, Q 360 S—2; (*b*) B2, Q 62—13. Scale 1:5.

132. Säve-Söderbergh, Englund, and Nordström 1982, corpus C57, C77, pl. 6; Mills 1982, tomb 192.31.1; 192.36.1 (the interior profiles are probably not precisely drawn). These occurred in only two deposits at Qustul, and the varied group is not subdivided.

133. Kirwan 1939, corpus 27; Shafiq Farid 1963, corpus 35; in Tanqasi groups at Meroe (Garstang, Sayce, and Griffith 1911, pl. XLII:9/48).

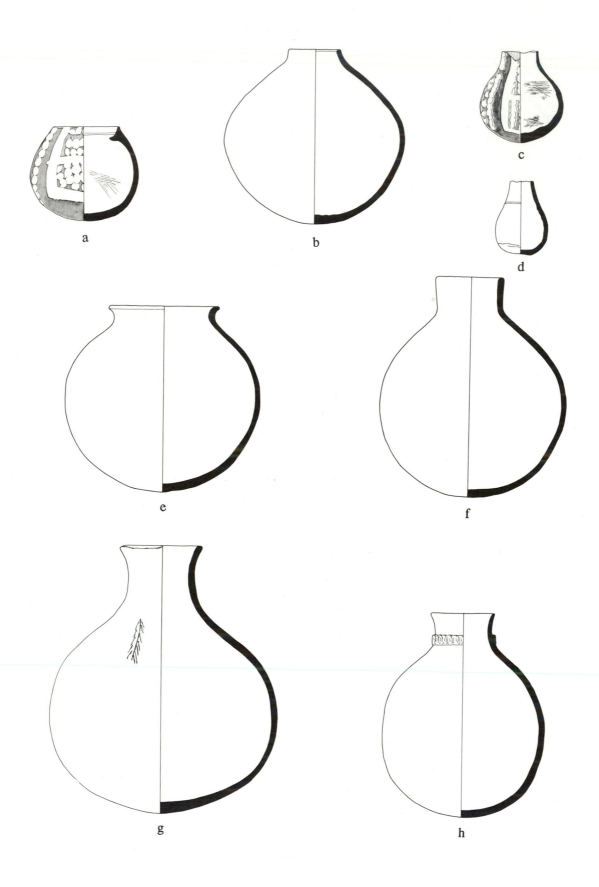

Figure 20. Handmade Jars: (*a*) A1, Q 504—2; (*b*) A2, Q 19—6; (*c*) B1, Q 356—4; (*d*) B2, Q 20—8; (*e*) C, Q 20—A; (*f*) D1a, Q 49—1; (*g*) D2, Q 186—2; (*h*) D3, Q 68—2. Scale 1:5.

Table 13. Pottery of X-Group Nubia (*cont.*).

JARS (fig. 20)

    A. Globular-almost biconical, low, almost straight neck-rim

        1. Squat (76b)[134]

        2. Medium height (26a–b)[135]

    B. Small, smooth profile to short, straight neck; globular-baggy[136]

    C. Globular, wide, everted neck

    D. Large globular jar with medium-tall neck

        1. Cylindrical neck

            a. simple[137]

            b. roll-rim (27) (none present)

        2. Smooth profile, concave neck, minor variants a–c (25, 15b, 24)[138]

        3. Rib or collar at base of neck, splayed neck,[139] variants a–c (17a–b)[140]

BINS

POTTERY OF COPTIC EGYPT

BOWLS

    A. Convex base, V-shaped side, ledge rim (78) (none present)[141]

    B. Broad bottom, convex, everted rim (77) (none present)

    C. Carinated (69) (none present)

LIDS[142]

JARS

    A. Globular-convex (none present)

    B. Tall, convex, two handles, ring base (53) (none present)

    C. Medium convex-tapered, with everted rim and ring or disc base, resembles goblet B (52) (none present)[143]

    D. Tall, tapered-convex to disc base, vertical rim; possibly N. K. reused (none present)[144]

134. Mills 1982, tomb 192.23.50.

135. Säve-Söderbergh, Englund, and Nordström 1982, corpus W17 "Early Domestic Plain Utility Ware H 1"; Shafiq Farid 1963, corpus 12; see also Säve-Söderbergh, Englund, and Nordström 1982, corpus W16.

136. Säve-Söderbergh, Englund, and Nordström 1982, corpus W16, pl. 12 (much larger), here with a red coat and white paint.

137. Kirwan 1939, corpus 11c; Firth 1927, fig. 4:11.

138. Säve-Söderbergh, Englund, and Nordström 1982, corpus W18, pl. 12.

139. Firth 1927, fig. 5: cem. 122:4.

140. Firth 1927, fig. 4:3, 5, 1.

141. Hölscher 1954, pl. 48:R'9 (rim not truly ledge).

142. See Egloff 1977, pl. 55; Johnson 1981, cat. 613, and other lids, pl. 75.

143. Kirwan 1939, corpus 18b.

144. Egloff 1977, pl. 74:2.

Table 13. Pottery of X-Group Nubia (*cont.*).

JARS (*cont.*)

Pitcher jugs and *amphoriskos* pitcher-jugs

    A. One-handled pitcher jugs (48)[145]

    B. Cylindrical bodies

        1. One handle (49) (none present)[146]

        2. Two handles (45, 55) (none present)[147]

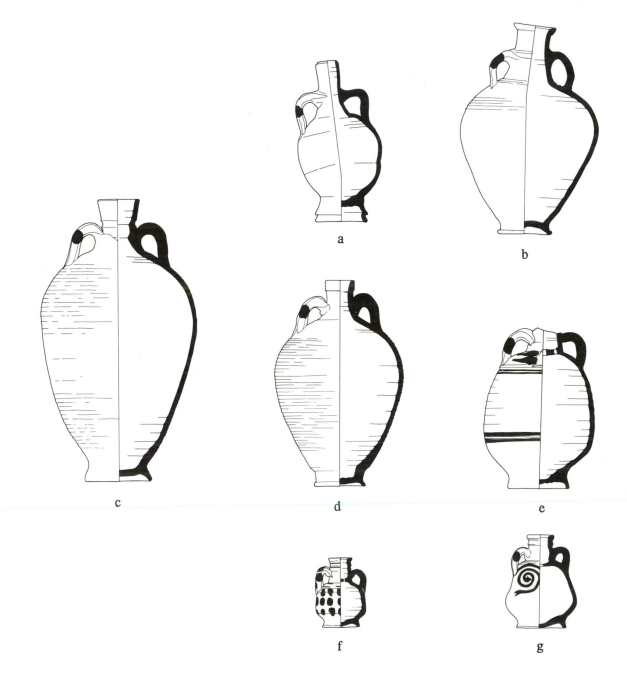

Figure 21. Coptic Period Egyptian *Amphoriskos*-Jugs and Flasks: (*a*) A, R 103—1; (*b*) B, Q 356—3; (*c*) C, Q 62—6; (*d*) C, Q 32—1; (*e*) D1a, R 1—1; (*f*) D2a, Q 196—6; (*g*) D2b, VA 14—6. Scale 1:5.

145. Säve-Söderbergh, Englund, and Nordström 1982, corpus I14, I12., pl. 7

146. Firth 1927, fig. 5: cem. 122:24.

147. Säve-Söderbergh, Englund, and Nordström 1982, corpus J, pl. 8.

Table 13. Pottery of X-Group Nubia (*cont.*).

JARS (*cont.*)

Amphoriskos-jugs or bottles and flasks (fig. 21)[148]

    A. Globular or convex body (43a–b)

    B. Pyriform body, broad candlestick rim (46, 47a)[149]

    C. Pyriform body, simple, V-shaped everted, or rectangular rim (40–42)[150]

    D. Barrel shaped with broad ring base (sometimes with filter neck)

        1. Normal size[151]

            a. carinated profile, or slightly tapered

            b. sharply tapered wide at lower bend (39)

        2. Small (half size or smaller)

            a. carinated or almost cylindrical[152]

            b. wide at lower bend

    E. Baggy, spouted (none present)[153]

    F. *Zemzemiyya* flask (none present)

        1. Handle attached to neck and shoulder (56a)

        2. Handle attached at the base of the neck and the shoulder (56b)[154]

JUGLETS (fig. 22)[155]

    A. Broad, ring-based, pyriform (50a)[156]

        1. Straight neck, simple base

            a. straight rim

            b. thickened for beak

            c. rib below rim[157]

        2. Constriction above base

            a. straight rim[158]

            b. thickened rim[159]

            c. beak

        3. Angular profile

            a. straight rim

            b. thickened rim

         4. Tall

    B. Flat base

148. See Firth 1927, fig. 4, 26; fig. 5: cem. 122:20–21; Säve-Söderbergh, Englund, and Nordström 1982, corpus J4, J13, and J14, pl. 8, X-Group Red Ware, X-Group White Ware, Middle Egyptian Plain White Ware, and Aswan Graeco-Roman Red Ware. Here, they are Coptic period Egyptian Ordinary with red or white coat.

149. Shafiq Farid 1963, corpus 30 (nearest type); Kirwan 1939, corpus 6, but tapered neck.

150. Hölscher 1954, pl. 48:L´7; Kirwan 1939, corpus 8d, C3; Shafiq Farid 1963, corpus 27–29; Kirwan 1939, corpus 9.

151. Mills 1982, tombs 192A.4.5 and 192A.17.2; Hölscher 1954, pl. 48:L´6.

152. Mills 1982, tomb 192.74.2; Kirwan 1939, corpus 8b–c.

153. Mills 1982, tomb 192.113.1.

154. Firth 1927, fig. 4:30, fig. 5: cem. 122:23; the rims differ on both.

155. Generally, Firth 1927, fig. 4:35–37, fig. 5: cem. 122:25; at Karanis, all comparable examples are Johnson 1981, cats. 4–12, Egyptian red slip A. Here, they are all uncoated fine/ord.

156. Kirwan 1939, corpus 10; Shafiq Farid 1963, corpus 31a.

157. See Johnson 1981, cat. 9.

158. For simplified forms of the decoration, see Johnson 1981, cats. 11–12 and Egloff 1977, pl. 73:10.

159. See Johnson 1981, cat. 12, approximate.

Table 13. Pottery of X-Group Nubia (*cont.*).

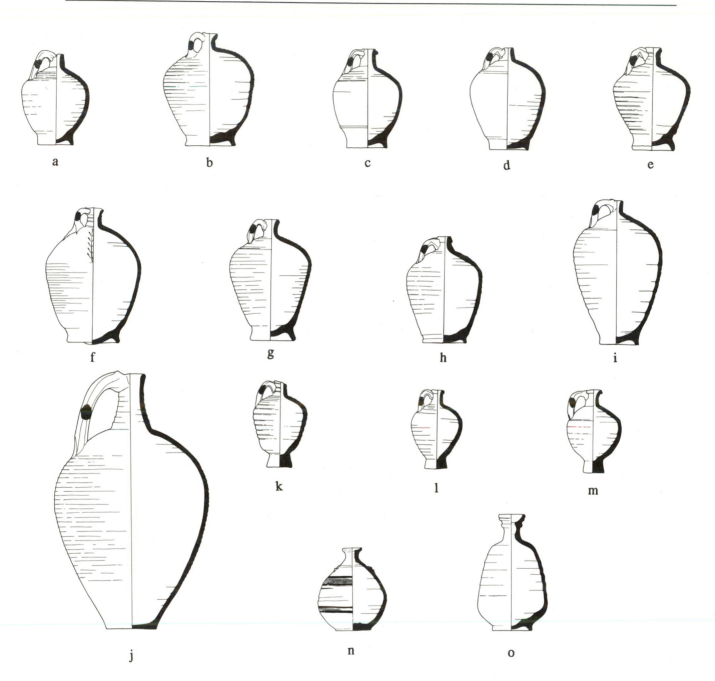

Figure 22. Coptic Period Egyptian Juglets: (*a*) A1a, Q 161—5; (*b*) A1b, Q 54—7; (*c*) A1c, Q 67—9; (*d*) A2ai, Q 3—1; (*e*) A2b, Q 82—2; (*f*) A2c, Q 52—8; (*g*) A3a, Q 62—14; (*h*) A3b, W 74—5; (*i*) A4, Q 40—1; (*j*) B, Q 136—4; (*k*) C1, Q 143—5; (*l*) C2, Q 1—25; (*m*) C3, Q 164—6; (*n*) D, Q 33—1; (*o*) E1, Q 82—1. Scale 1:5.

JUGLETS (*cont.*)

    C. Stump base (50b–c)

        1. Straight rim[160]

        2. Thickened rim[161]

        3. Beak[162]

160. See Johnson 1981, cats. 10 and 7.

161. See Johnson 1981, cat. 6.

162. See Johnson 1981, cat. 8.

Table 13. Pottery of X-Group Nubia (*cont.*).

JUGLETS (*cont.*)

   D. Two-handled juglets[163]

   E. Tapered cylindrical, handleless

      1. (44a)[164]

      2. Broad at lower bend (44b) (not present)

      3. Narrow, cupped rim (not present)[165]

MINIATURE JUGLETS (fig. 23)[166]

a   b

Figure 23. Coptic Period Egyptian Miniature Juglets from Tombs Q 143 and Q 146:
(*a*) Q 146—1; (*b*) Q 143—6. Scale 1:2.

AMPHORAE (Actually shipping and storage vessels of various fabrics; so few occurred in the present material, no independent classification is attempted; fig. 24)

   A. Two-handled storage jars of normal size (numerical breakdown according to Emery and Kirwan)[167]

      4. (b) Broad, tapers out to bend, lower side sharply incurved to short stump base, neck-shoulder handles

163. Mills 1982, tomb 192.36.2; 192.6.2; 192A.4.4.

164. See Johnson 1981, cat. 13, decoration, 114–115 (on larger vessels); Mills 1982, tomb 192.111.1.

165. Mills 1982, tomb 192.23.51.

166. Säve-Söderbergh, Englund, and Nordström 1982, corpus 25/47:2, R 31, Aswan Flaky Pink Ware; 25/19:2a, Aswan Flaky Pink Ware; 25/7:6, W 26, Meroitic Fine White Ware; here Coptic period Egyptian Fine, which can fire pink to grayish cream. See Johnson 1981, cats. (A) 1–3, (B) 34–36; Hölscher 1954, pl. 48:X′3–4; Shafiq Farid 1963, corpus 34b; Firth 1927, fig. 4, no subscript, tomb 112.78, fig. 5: cem. 122:26.

167. The Emery-Kirwan corpus corresponds to occurrences in Kirwan 1939, corpus and in Shafiq Farid's corpus as follows (other occurrences are also indicated):

Type 1: Kirwan 1939, corpus 1, Shafiq Farid 1963, corpus 2;

Type 2. Kirwan 1939, corpus 1b (no ring on base);

Type 3: Kirwan 1939, corpus 1b (different rim);

Type 4a: Kirwan 1939, corpus 1, but not precise; Shafiq Farid 1963, corpus 1, 2 (approximate); Mills 1982, tomb 192.2.59;

Type 4b: Firth 1927, fig. 5: cem. 122:19; Mills 1982, tomb 192A.24.1 (Adams R 1);

Type 6: Kirwan 1939, corpus 4; Shafiq Farid 1963, corpus 6; Mills 1982, tomb 192.13.7, variant with curved handles, tapered lower side and indented stump base;

Type 7a: Kirwan 1939, corpus 3;

Type 7b: Kirwan 1939, corpus 3; Shafiq Farid 1963, corpus 7a–b; 7b handles are extended farther;

Type 7c: Shafiq Farid 1963, corpus 7d approximately; Mills 1982, tomb 192.23 18;

Type 10: Shafiq Farid 1963, corpus 8;

Type 13a: Kirwan 1939, corpus 5; Shafiq Farid 1963, corpus 9a–c var.; Mills 1982, tomb 193.162.11. In addition, at Ibrim, there was an amphora with a simple triangular profile and small handles that were attached at the neck and the shoulder, 192.14.1.

Table 13. Pottery of X-Group Nubia (*cont.*).

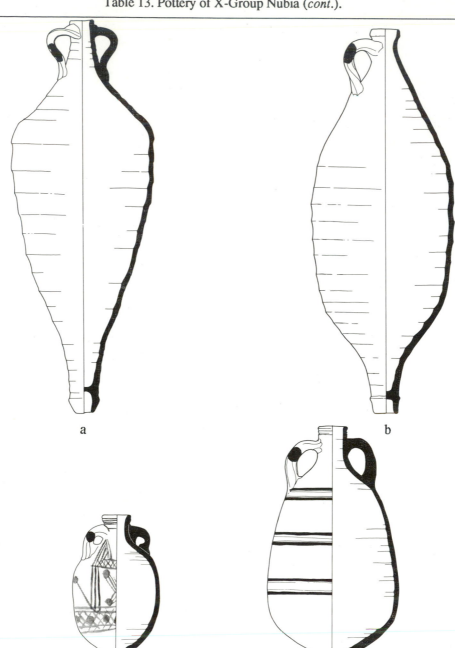

a

b

c

d

Figure 24. Imported Amphorae from Tombs Q 54, Q 56, Q 134, and Q 388: (*a*) A [13a], Q 54—8; (*b*) C, Q 134—2; (*c*) B1, Q 56—1; (*d*) A [4b], Q 388—5. Scale 1:5.

AMPHORAE (*cont.*)

   7. Medium width, tapered barrel-shaped body to short button base, neck-shoulder handle (a–c variants) (Q 51a–1)
   13. Narrow neck, handles on neck, long, concave lower side tapered to stump base, ribbed
       a. widest at shoulder, taper to base (here, hollow foot)
   B. Miniatures (classed as A)
       1. Barrel-shaped body, short stump base, neck-shoulder handle
   C. One-handled storage jars of normal size; one type here, narrow barrel-shaped body with long tapered shoulder and lower side, hollowed stump base (exterior indentation also), neck-shoulder handle (Equivalent of A13)

Table 13. Pottery of X-Group Nubia (*cont.*).

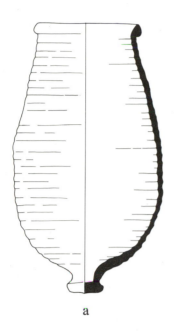

a   b

Figure 25. *Qawadus* from Tombs Q 14 and Q 381: (*a*) A, Q 14—2; (*b*) B, Q 381—2. Scale 1:5.

QAWADUS (fig. 25)

  A. Tall, sinuous side, knob-base hollowed inside, rim ribbed or grooved[168]

  B. Small, no knob, probably not intended for use on *saqia*[169]

LAMPS (treated as clay objects; see fig. 18)[170]

SPECIAL IMPORTS (NONE IN PRESENT MATERIAL)

Vessel types that correspond to those from the royal tombs are indicated by the appropriate Arabic numeral in parentheses (See Emery and Kirwan, 1938, pls. 111–114).

Note that X-Group Fine pottery is confined to cups. Handmade pottery includes handmade domestic utility and cooking pots.

Note that reference to Adams's shape corpus (1986, figs. 18–94) is made through the corpus presented in Säve-Söderbergh, Englund, and Nordström 1982, pls. 4–14 because the shapes are more precisely depicted.

168. Säve-Söderbergh, Englund, and Nordström 1982, corpus, pl. 10, V here all U1 "Meroitic and X-Group Brown Utility Ware," i.e. ordinary (Adams 1986, pp. 515–16, "Pre-Christian Brown Utility Ware"); Kirwan 1939, corpus 17; Firth 1927, fig. 4:43; fig. 5: cem. 122:6; Johnson 1981, cat. 580. Early Qawadus at Karanis have distinctive profiles much different from Nubian examples which seem to be later.

169. Firth 1927, fig. 4:29 (?), fig. 5: cem. 122:7.

170. See Q 8—7, Q 35—2, Q 72—6, Q 345—6, and Q 501A.

CHAPTER 3

OBJECTS

Although many objects in Noubadian X-Group were derived from Meroitic objects,[1] major changes took place both in the objects and in the way they were deposited. Some changes resulted from changes in technology and trade, but many differences were due to a major change in the meaning of the burial. Simplified stone offering tables alone remained of the Meroitic cult furniture. The panoply of Meroitic amuletic devices also played a sharply reduced role.[2] Jewelry occurred less frequently and was much cruder, although exceptions occurred. Cosmetic equipment was relatively rare and simple, while weapons became much more common and elaborate. Furniture (primarily beds) appeared, as did iron tools.[3]

The following discussions and tables deal with the most important objects, but they do not comprise a comprehensive and detailed discussion of every small object or fragment found in the X-Group tombs.

A. STONE FUNERARY OBJECTS AND FITTINGS

The chapel rows of Cemetery Q were equipped with a number of stone objects and fittings that were of special religious significance.

OFFERING TABLES

In the Qustul cemetery, stone offering tables[4] were found on small brick podia or altars erected in front of the chapels, placed with the spout facing the door (pl. 15a). Some offering tables (pl. 15b–c) were found placed against the back wall of the chapel, where they may have been deposited for safekeeping. Stone offering tables were known also in Sudan, for they were reused to block tombs,[5] but it is not certain that they were ever deposited as offering tables. Offering tables were used, sometimes in rows, in the fourth century shrines of the Dodekaschoinos.[6]

One of the offering tables was oval (fig. 72d) but most were rectangular (figs. 72a–c, 74, 85a), almost square, and smaller than Meroitic offering tables, but sometimes with the same thickness.[7] The tables were often outlined with a pair of framing lines (fig. 73b–d). Some were decorated with diagonal lines either in the framing band or on either side of it. These probably indicate a palm frond (fig. 72a–c); one had an oval basin. The oval table (fig. 72d) has two Isis-garlands on either side of the reservoir with a third inside it at the spout. One rectangular table has framing grooves and angled lines in red paint (fig. 73a from Chapel QB 4).

---

1. See p. 76 below.

2. Except for a few objects that may have been reused from pillaged Meroitic tombs.

3. See also OINE VIII, *Chapter 3.*

4. OINE VIII, *Chapter 3*, pp. 93–95.

5. Garstang, Sayce, and Griffith 1911, pl. XL.

6. Ricke 1967, Abb. 26; Griffith 1911, pl. 8, Kar. 39; pair only.

7. The size is paralleled by one small offering table from Cemetery B, and the tables made in series at the shrines of Bab Kalabsha.

Several of the offering tables were undecorated (figs. 73b–d, 74c–e). X-Group offering tables were found in the following locations: in Chapels QB 4, QB 5, QB 41, QB 42, and QB 52; north of tumulus Qu. 31 (OIM 20193); in the Christian cemetery west of tumulus Qu. 31 (OIM 20164, 20206, 20280, 20273, and 20261); and in chapel row QC at chapel QC 11 (QC 44—1).

OBELISK

Although tapered stone "obelisks" and garland-pillars occur in Meroitic funerary contexts,[8] regular stone obelisks do not. One example (QC 17—2) was found broken into two pieces at the top of a Meroitic shaft immediately in front of a chapel. It was clearly part of that chapel complex and possibly one of a pair.

SPHINX

A fragment making up somewhat less than half of the head and neck of a small seated sphinx was found lying just in front of chapel QC 22 (4) along with a lintel (1), doorjambs (2–3), and tumbled brick. It was probably one of a pair.[9]

JAMBS AND LINTELS

Although they belong more strictly to the class of architecture, jambs, and lintels were special fittings and their occurrence should be noted here. In the QB chapel row, some buildings were equipped with wooden doorjambs (Chapels QB 50–51, 52–53) in addition to wooden thresholds (Chapels QB 14, 16, 55) and stone sockets. A fragment of one stone jamb decorated with the Isis garland in raised relief (Chapels row QB —2) was found in a Christian superstructure nearby. In the QC chapel row, there were several complete and partial sets of jambs and lintels (Chapels QC 1–3—Uncertain, Chapel QC 20—1–2, Chapel QC 22—1–3), one with the Isis-garland (QC 17—1).[10]

PLAQUES

Remains of stone plaques or corner insets were found in the QF chapel row. A corner inset was incised with the profile of a warrior wearing a topknot and carrying a bow (QF 11—1, fig. 84b). A second plaque was painted with an *ankh* or *sa* flanked by *was*-scepters, all on a *neb*-sign (fig. 84c). The signs were painted in red and the *neb*, and possibly the *sa*, were filled in green on a white ground.[11]

SUMMARY REMARKS

The stone objects and fittings reveal a continuing commitment to the pharaonic impulse and a consistent selection of motifs. A special relation with the Isis cult is indicated in the use of the notched frond.

B. FURNITURE

The royal tombs contained a large and varied collection of furniture, but the private tombs seem only to have had beds, large chests, caskets, and lamps.

---

8. Vila 1982, fig. 38.

9. Emery and Kirwan 1938, pl. 86:B–C.

10. Emery and Kirwan 1938, pl. 27D; the "lintel" was actually a jamb turned on its side. It probably belonged to an earlier X-Group chapel, for no Meroitic chapels were equipped with such jambs. A similar jamb was found reused at Arminna West (Trigger 1967, pp. 77–78) and should be assigned a similar date despite the nearby Meroitic cemetery.

11. Anonymous Editor. 1979, p. 178; wall plaques occur at Meroe in the "Nymphaeum," and even earlier at Kerma. See also Hintze 1962, pl. LXIIIa for a plaque with an *ankh* painted on it.

Table 14. Register of Beds.

Tomb and Number	Object	Illustration
Q 1—1	Leg and fragments	
Q 4—2	Wood remains	
Q 40—6	Matting, wooden frame	pl. 49
Q 41—7	Remains	
Q 59—1	Matting	pl. 50a
Q 68—8	Matting	pl. 50b
Q 134—19	Fragments	
Q 144—1	Fragments	
Q 148—8	Fragments	
Q 316—6	Fragments	
Q 343—1	Matting	pl. 50c
Q 349—2?	Wood remains	
Q 454—1	Leg	
Q 463—1	Decayed wood	
R 2—10	Wood remains	
R 7—2	Wood remains	

BEDS AND HIDES

Beds were an important recurring feature in burials in Nubia beginning in A-Group[12] and including Kerma,[13] the Twenty-Fifth Dynasty,[14] the Noba tombs of Meroe, and Noubadian X-Group Qustul (tab. 20).[15]

Some burials at Qustul were made on hides, probably of cattle, a type of burial that preceded the bed burial elsewhere in Nubia.[16] These are unhaired rawhides; perforations for carrying or suspension were made at the corners and along the sides. The example best preserved was stretched to the shape of the body and the edges were pulled at the perforations. Some edges had been rolled to strengthen them, and a rawhide thong was passed through one of the perforations (See Qu. 7—1, Q 55—1, Q 184—1, and Q 343—2).

The X-Group bed was a simple low *angareb* with turned wooden legs, crudely finished rails, and a webbing of matting or twine apparently woven directly on the rails. Some beds and fragments were preserved well enough for some details to be studied. On one bed with twine webbing, the warp was looped over the ends; the woof strings were looped around the side rails and interlaced with the warp in a chevron twill. The middle part of the webbing had no woof for about 25 cm. In this example, the legs and their joints were not preserved.

BOXES

Caskets and boxes for storing small objects of value are characteristic but not common objects in X-Group. Some of these were inlaid with ivory panels and figures. The motifs are both Meroitic and

12. OINE III, pp. 14, 128; OINE IV, p. 14; and Nordström 1972, pl. 67.

13. Reisner 1923 IV–V, pp. 208–27 for beds and their occurrence, Dunham 1982, figs. 5, 6; Bonnet 1986, fig. 17; and Bietak 1968, pp. 123–27, for Kerma practices generally.

14. Dunham 1950, pp. 27, 30; Vila 1980, p. 33, 2-V-6/3; p. 62, 2-V-6/186; and OINE VII, p. 1, for example.

15. Garstang, Sayce, and Griffith 1911, pl. XXXVIII; Emery and Kirwan 1938, various.

16. The burial on a hide preceded bed burials in the Kerma culture, and there were hide-shaped burial pits at Tanqasi. See Bonnet 1982, fig. 11; fig. 16, transitional hide-bed burial(?); figs. 17–19 (fig. 18, with pillow and feather fan); Shinnie 1954, tomb 1.

Hellenistic, mostly combined in ways familiar from the previous period.[17] Hellenistic motifs such as the vine, long a part of Meroitic decoration continued, but the newly Hellenized art of Coptic period Egypt occurs alone, indicating, perhaps, that such pieces were imported.[18] Boxes with inlays, kohl tubes, and a few other objects such as a faience vessel from Ibrim,[19] are the only objects in ordinary tombs that have remnants of Meroitic pharaonic decoration; it is possible that these objects were plundered and reused.

Termites were active in the area and many wooden objects were consumed so thoroughly that the remains were irregular spongy masses. Many objects were probably not identified in the detritus of the tombs.

BOX WITH IVORY INLAYS: Q 67—5

One box had been inlaid in ivory so that remains were easily recognizable. Unfortunately, neither the structure of the box nor the design could be recovered (pls. 51–53). Strings of beads among the fragments show that it contained jewelry. Inlay fragments included lozenges, triangles, rosette-petals, columns, cavetto cornices, *neb* signs, *wedjat* eyes, *hemhem* crowns, a bird, and a bunch of grapes. A few pieces were still set in the wood; the edge of a panel was marked by two lines of lozenges. One row was made up of reversed light and dark triangles. Another fragment has a petal and two curved rows of lozenges with a *wedjat* eye; beyond the eye was an undecorated area. Still another fragment with rows of lozenges was also marked with grooves; above is a large undecorated area, possibly in another wood. Two cornices were still imbedded in wood; one has a lozenge directly above it. The fragments resemble architectural inlays on the great chest from tumulus Qu. 14, as does the bunch of grapes, although there were no large plaques. Another inlaid chest was found at Ibrim, with columns and lozenges.[20] A second wooden container, Q 350—2, was too badly damaged for the shape to be determined.

CIRCULAR BOX; W 74—6 (discarded)

Remains of this box were not recoverable. It was about 35 cm in diameter by 16 cm high and 3–5 cm thick. In addition to the box, a fragmentary circular ivory pyxis was found in tomb Q 37 (3).

C. MILITARY EQUIPMENT

The amount and variety of weapons and other actual or potential military equipment that occurs in X-Group tombs is greater than any other phase in Lower Nubia. Hand weapons, pole arms, and archery equipment appear regularly in wealthy burials, and bows and arrows appear in humbler tombs. In addition, items of kit, especially iron tools, occur regularly. Saddlery occurs with the horse burials. The complexity of the weapons implies a corresponding social elaboration, for several different crafts involving many skills must have been necessary. Actual crafts probably included bow-makers, sword smiths, ordinary smiths, saddlers, leather workers, and the various occupations that produced stocks of raw material to make the actual objects.

Many of the weapons had antecedents in the Meroitic period, and either the crafts continued or they were shared between the Meroites and their neighbors.[21] Some weapons such as the composite bow were innovations. In general, weapons occur much more frequently and with much greater variety in X-Group, perhaps reflecting a difference in the type of afterlife expected in the Meroitic and X-Group periods.

17. Remains of boxes of this kind were found at Ibrim (Mills 1982, pl. VII:2.22; XXI:23.47). Panels from boxes were found by Emery and Kirwan (1938, pp. 282, 383–84).

18. Emery and Kirwan 1938, pl. 109.

19. Mills 1982, pl. VI:192.2.11, 2.12.

20. Emery and Kirwan 1938, pl. 109; Mills 1982, pl. VII, 192.2.22.

21. OINE VIII, pp. 104–07, arrows; pp. 104–05, quivers; p. 106, loose. The quiver is probably the type carried by Apedemak on the ring bezel (pl. 75). Arrows held in a pelt with the tail hanging from the front are shown grasped by Apedemak at Musawwarat es Sufra (Hintze 1971, pls. 17, 25, 51–3, 53, 67, 71, 89 [center right]). Elements preserved in Meroitic period Noba-type burials include arrowheads and looses (Marshall and Abd el Rahman 1953). The continuing special significance of the bow is made clear by the incised stone from Q*F* and by its use as an attribute of the god in the glyptic from Gamai (Bates and Dunham 1927, pl. XXXIII:B, D).

Table 15. Crafts and Military Equipment.

Object	*Craft*	*Remarks*
Archery:		
Bow	Bow-maker	Several materials
Arrow	Sword smith Fletcher	Two major processes
Loose	See remarks	Lathe-turned wood, stone, or bone
Quiver	Leather worker	Tanned leather
Guard	Leather worker	Rawhide
Hand weapons:		
Short sword	Sword smith	Blade and handle
Sheath	Leather worker Silversmith	Inner wrap Outer metal
Spear-sword	Sword smith	
Javelin	Sword smith	
Armor:		
Cuirass	Leather worker	Rosettes used for studs
Shield	Leather worker	
Kit:		
Water bag	Leather worker	
Kit bag	Leather worker	
Tools	Smith	Simple iron tools different from blades
Saddlery:		
Bridle	Saddler	Major work also by Silversmith and/or smith for rings and fittings
Saddle	Saddler	Same as for bridle

ARCHERY

Although other arms occur, only archer's equipment is common in tombs of Noubadian X-Group. The Meroitic and X-Group archer loosed short arrows (ca. 50 cm) with small, very sharp points, generally with barbs. The thumb ring indicates that the so-called Mongolian draw to the chest was used, for the arrows were far too short for a draw to the angle of the jaw to be practicable. At first, a wooden self bow (Q 152—5, Q 378—8) was used, but early in X-Group, a remarkable composite bow was introduced that may have been known more widely.[22] Even so, the operating range must have been quite short, and the archer had to rely on his mobility as well as the reach of his weapon for security. In addition, poison may have been used.[23] The archer was not furtive, however, for the complete equipment, bow, arrow, quiver, thumb loose, and brace, is complex, elaborate, and sometimes of quite striking appearance.

QUIVERS

The most easily recognized military equipment commonly found in the tombs was the quiver. Like the ordinary Meroitic quivers, these were made entirely of leather.[24] The quivers had a complex structure that

22. Snowden 1970, fig 18. Herodotus (VII, 69) refers to Ethiopians using bows of palm. See Hofmann and Vorbichler 1979, p. 153. The frond can be quite tough and elastic, but it becomes quite brittle.

23. Dunham 1963, p. 205, fig. 148:b–c (W 122).

24. See OINE VIII, *Chapter 3*, pp. 104–05. Quivers have been found with some frequency, but not often completely published (Pellicer et al. 1965, fig. 34:4; Millet 1967, fig. 7; Säve-Söderbergh, Englund, and Nordström 1982, pl. 17; Mills 1982, pl. LX:107.3).

has yet to be explained in publications. This was enhanced by decorative flaps and straps and elaborate decoration. In addition, various thongs for suspension and strips for reinforcement indicate that the quiver was an object of high value. Appliqués put on an upper flap may have been symbolic.

MATERIAL

Meroitic quivers in the present collection were made of rawhide, with the grain side inward, but in X-Group times, the quiver was made of tanned leather.

BASIC STRUCTURE

By following edges and folds, it was possible to derive the shape of the original piece of leather from which the quiver was made. As the quivers were compared with each other, it was found that this basic shape was the same in all cases, that of a hide from a long-necked animal such as a goat or a gazelle (fig. 26a), or a piece of leather cut to the shape of a smaller hide.

First, the neck was folded downward onto the spine area, grain side out. In X-Group quivers, a tuck was made at the fold to make a rib; this would help the quiver keep its shape. Next, the hide was bent so that the leg, chest, and thigh areas matched, grain side inward (fig. 26b). The hide was then sewn (and glued?) along a straight line so that a receptacle was made along the spine area. In Meroitic times, this receptacle was allowed to keep its natural teardrop shape (fig. 27), but in X-Group, the upper part was made into a cylinder, using a rib at the rim to hold the shape. The lower part of the quiver was held to an oval shape by a patch of leather several layers thick sewn to the bottom (fig. 28). The tail was left dangling from the lower end. Two broad lobes or flaps were created by joining the opposite chest and flank areas, while the legs were used to hold thongs for carrying.

Figure 26 shows how the shape of the Meroitic and X-Group quiver resulted from its construction from a single hide-shaped piece of leather. Note that the shape is inferred from the quiver and is not accurate. The neck was folded down and the hide bent to form an oval (later round) receptacle by joining the two pairs of leg areas, grain side inward.

Figure 27 shows how the quiver was completed by adding an oval patch to the bottom of the receptacle and twisted thongs, one to connect the lower and upper leg areas, and a pair twisted together attached between the ends of the legs, to carry the quiver. The tail was left on the hide, and sometimes an additional tail was put on with the patch

SUSPENSION

In Meroitic times, a pair of twisted thongs was placed with an end between each pair of legs, which were then stitched together to make a loop for carrying over the shoulder.

Figure 28 shows how the thongs of the X-Group quiver were usually made double for carrying more securely. Each leg of the hide was formed into a tube into which an end of the twisted skein was inserted; both tubes were then sewn together and reinforced with short strips.

In addition, the upper and lower flaps might be joined by a twisted thong, or a loop might be inserted into the upper flap for suspension.

ACCESSORIES

A number of useful additions were sometimes made to the basic structure of the quiver, which increased reinforcement or offered protection.

Most commonly, a rectangular piece corresponding to the upper neck-cylinder was added around the base area to protect the shafts and heads of the arrows (fig. 28, right). Often, the edges of this cylinder and the upper cylinder were held in place by narrow strips stitched to the quiver at the belly edge, for no stitching penetrated the cylinder itself.

Sometimes, an oblong piece of leather was attached to the base of the quiver by thongs, strips cut from the sides, or even by stitching part of one edge with the base-cap (figs. 46–47; see also fig. 43 for a simpler version). This flap could be folded up over the quiver to protect it when not in use.

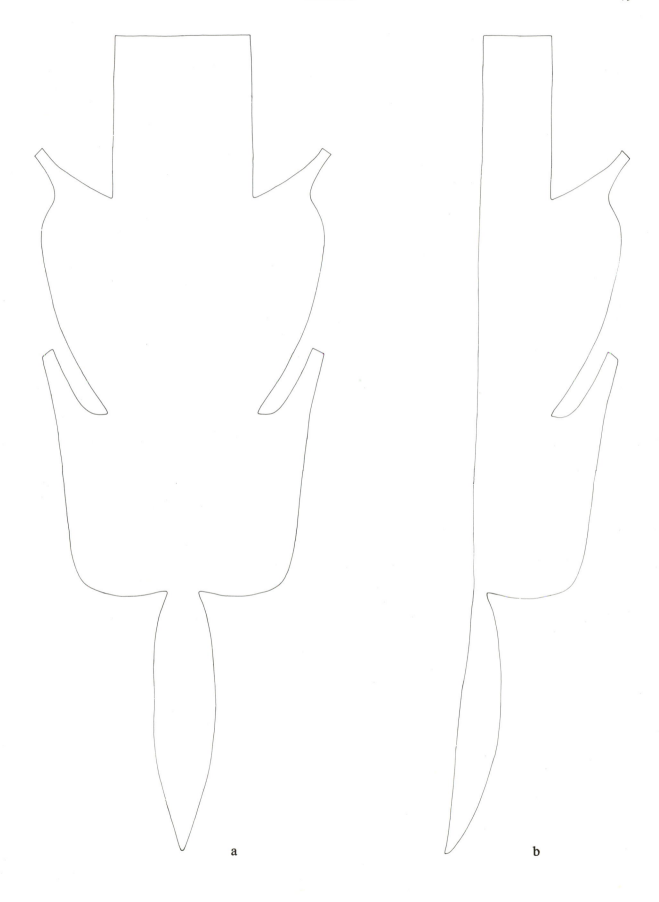

Figure 26. The Construction of an X-Group Quiver: (*a*) The Hide; (*b*) Folded. Scale 1:5.

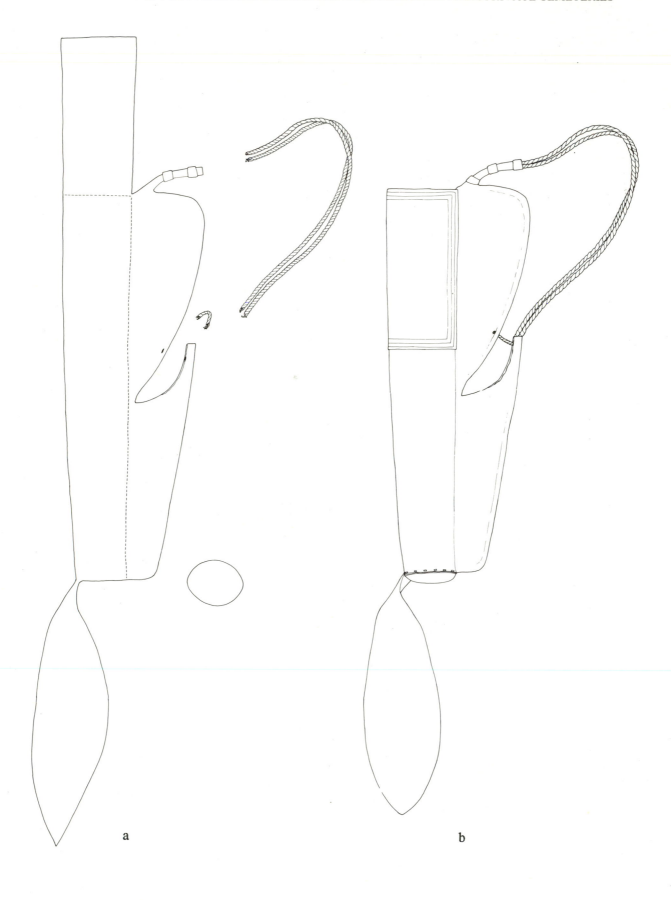

a   b

Figure 27. The Construction of a Meroitic Quiver: (a) Folding and Attachments;
(b) Completed. Scale 1:5.

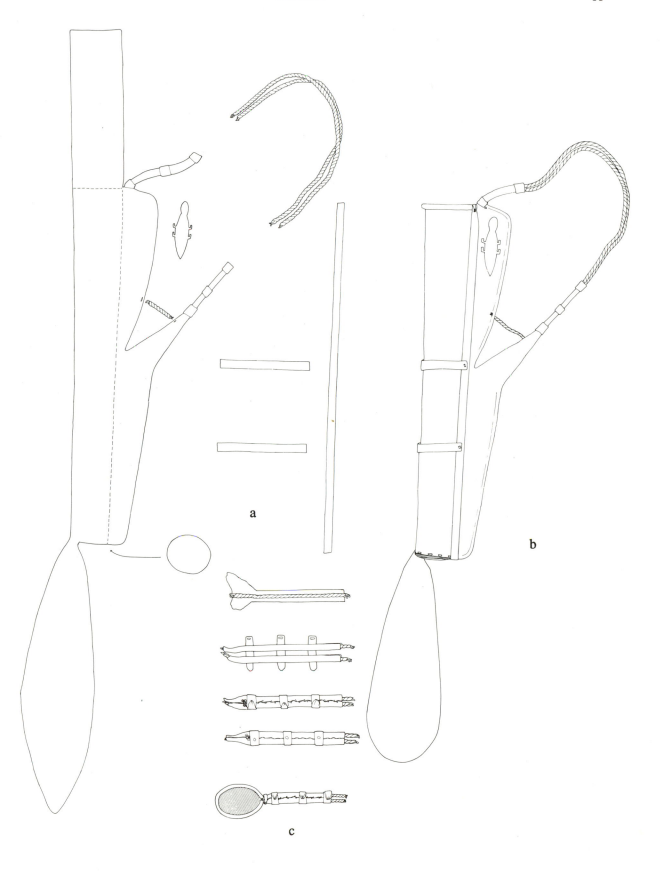

Figure 28. The Construction of an X-Group Quiver (*cont.*): (*a*) Folding and Attachments; (*b*) Completed; (*c*) The Attachment of Carrying Thongs. Scale 1:5.

Figure 29. Shapes of Decorative Flaps for X-Group Quivers. Scale 1:5.

STRUCTURAL DECORATION

A number of items were added to the quiver simply to alter its appearance. Although they may have offered a confusing silhouette of the wearer to an opponent, they were usually carefully decorated, indicating that they were primarily decorative. The added items were tail-shaped flaps, strips, and thongs (fig. 29; see also fig. 46).

The flaps and strips were most often attached to places where stitching was already present; they were often inserted into the ends or binding strips of the leg tubes. In each case, the narrow end, often cut to the width of a thong, was secured, and the broad end allowed to hang free. In some cases, the flap was cut with a tail-shape in the center and two strips on the sides, or into three strips. The ends of the strips were cut to resemble the base of a *sa* amulet. A few broad strips were found, and in some cases a thong, with an additional thong threaded through near the end, was inserted in the lower leg-flap (fig. 40).

TECHNIQUES OF DECORATION

The bodies of the quivers and various attachments were normally decorated. Most often, more than one technique of decoration was used on a quiver, but certain techniques tended to be used regularly for decorating special parts of the object.

Embossing. Stamping was used to decorate leather objects in Meroitic times, although it was not common in the decoration of X-Group leather. The upper and lower cylinders were decorated with a pointed tool which made impressions rather than incisions. These consisted of horizontal lines, herringbones, and a simple chain or guilloche, with vertical bands of similar motifs at the back (see fig. 40, for example).

Incision. In a few cases designs were actually cut into the surface of the leather. This was not the same as the impressed/embossed technique, nor did it involve the actual removal of material.

Excision. In one of the most characteristic techniques of decoration used for this material, a design was cut into the surface and the shiny grain side removed to make the actual design. This technique was used to make designs on flaps, strips, and appliqués, sometimes with incisions (figs. 40, 41).

Cut-out. Material was actually removed from some of the non-structural pieces to make serrated edges and patterns of small triangles or lozenges (figs. 47–49). The triangles or lozenges were usually arranged in lozenges or bands.

Appliqué. Small cut-out patches of leather were added to the upper flaps of some quivers on the left or outer side. These were in turn decorated with excised patterns and incision to emphasize details or even add shapes (fig. 40). In one case, the appliqué had two layers (fig. 41).

The appliqués may have had some emblematic significance. The crocodile or gecko on figure 40 has no clear meaning, but the bucranium above the lotus on figure 41 is consistent with other adaptations of pharaonic symbolism in this culture. Two discoid emblems (figs. 50–51) were removed. The use of such decoration is hardly restricted to Nubia, but the important role played by appliqué decoration in the art of Kerma should be noted.[25]

TYPES OF DECORATION

The decorative motifs used on quivers were as complex as the techniques and they were consistent with the decoration of other objects. The major elements are considered briefly below.

Filled Zones. Horizontal lines and herringbones were used to fill the upper cylinder.

Guilloche. The chain or guilloche was used most often to fill narrow framing bands or strips (fig. 44). It may be related to a single chain.

Eye or Eye and Double Tassel. The chained eye or eye and double tassel was also used to fill narrow frames or strips (figs. 40, 45a).

---

25. See Reisner 1923, pp. 172–80 for mica cut-outs applied inside pieces of leather with windows and p. 211.

Kushite-Pharaonic Motifs. In addition to the bucranium appliqué, pharaonic motifs included excised *ankhs* in bands or panels (fig. 40), the offering table of Isis (fig. 40),[26] the trefoil flower, the rosette (fig. 44) and *sa* amulet silhouettes (fig. 40).

Vine. Excised vines were used as the central motif in long strips or flaps (fig. 40, 44).

Other. Tails and flaps, as well as borders, were sometimes decorated with wavy lines or bands with wavy edges, or St. Andrew's crosses (fig. 45). These parallel the scalloped edges of many flaps (figs. 46–49). Cut-out decoration consisted mostly of rows of triangles, or lozenges, arranged diagonally in bands, or in lozenge-shaped groups (figs. 48–49).

CONDITION

Because of the plundering, most of the quivers were found in extremely fragmentary condition. After burial, they became quite brittle and, when the tombs were rifled, the lower ends were often twisted off to remove the arrowheads. From the few intact examples found at Qustul and Gebel Ada, however, it was possible to restore typical quivers which served as models to restore others (figs. 39, 46).

BOWS

Wooden self-bows have long been known from many contexts in Nubia, beginning with representations in A-Group.[27] Except for the archaic bow, these form the simple arc most commonly associated with bows made of wood. The bows from Meroitic Nubia belong to this category, and the representations of bows held by the gods also show simple arc bows. One wooden self-bow was found next to an early X-Group burial made among the Meroitic tombs of Qustul (pl. 37b). Otherwise bows have been extremely rare in X-Group materials, a surprising circumstance, considering the number of quivers, looses, and arrowheads that have been found.

Perhaps the reason bows have been so rarely reported in publications of material from this period is the fact that the typical bow was made of materials not usually well-preserved and easily mistaken for parts of quivers and other objects (figs. 30–31). Bows were not recognized in the present material until several large pieces from tomb Q 345 (7) were fitted together, leading to the identification of several fragments from other tombs. Compound bows had been known in Egypt for at least two millennia, but the examples previously reported have been shaped very much like the self bows of the same period, as single arcs.[28] The bows in the present collection were reflex bows that curved belly-out when unstrung. Since the strip of horn that provided much of the power was placed near the handle on the back of the bow, when strung, the weapon had the double-S curve conventionally associated with the well-known compound bows of Asia.

The bows in the present group were small; the one well enough preserved to obtain some indication of its original length (Q 345—7) was about a meter long. Its thickness near the center, without the strip, was about a centimeter. The bow was constructed in two halves, lashed and bound together at the center. Each of the halves was built on a fibrous vegetable core, possibly from a palm frond, a material reportedly used by ancient Ethiopian bowmen.[29] Little can be said of this core except that it was almost always completely destroyed. Only one bow actually preserved part of its core; it was round in section, although this may not have been the natural shape (fig. 30, section). The core was generally covered with a coarse textile and both were wrapped tightly in a strip of leather wound in a spiral which was presumably attached with some adhesive. A narrow strip of horn(?) about 20 to 25 cm in length was tightly bound against the belly of the bow with a narrow leather strip or thong. The two halves were strapped together without a special grip. The whole shape of the weapon was narrow and whiplike, and when unstrung, the reflex was so radical that the two tips extended well past one another.

---

26. For a discussion of this motif, see Tomandl 1987.

27. OINE III, fig. 58; Bonnet 1982, fig. 16; Smith 1976, pls. LVIII, LI:691, 732; Bates and Dunham 1927, pl. XXXIII:B, D.

28. MacLeod 1970.

29. Herodotus (VII, 69) noted Ethiopian bowmen with palm wood bows and short stone-tipped arrows. Hofmann and Vorbichler (1979, p. 173) also discuss the bows. In the same chapter they remark on the symbolism of the Ethiopians and their armament.

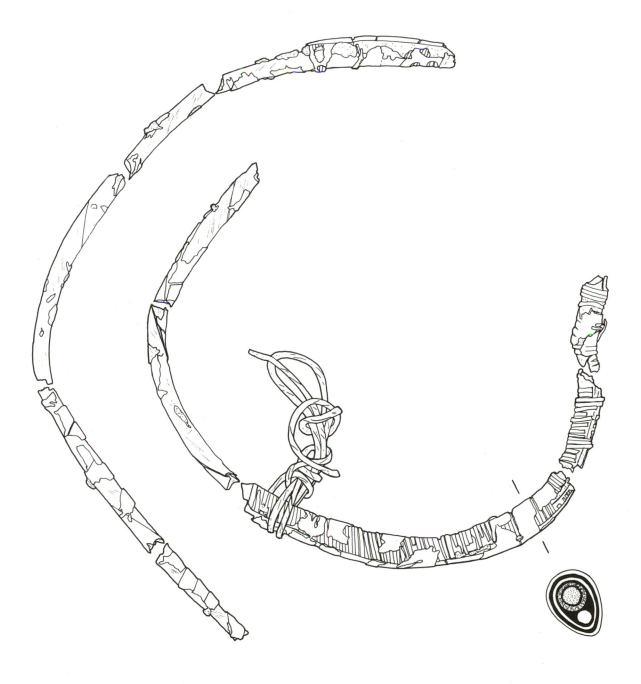

Figure 30. The Compound Bow from Tomb Q 345 (No. 7, Reconstructed Section of a Bow). Scale 1:2.

Figure 31. The Compound Bow from Tomb R 49 (No. 5c). Scale 1:2.

The size and shape of the bows in the present collection do not suggest great power, and the length of the arrows further suggests that a chest draw was used that could hardly have driven them with much force. However, the long, flexible arm of the bow also suggests that a whipping action occurred as the arrow was loosed that could give some additional propulsion to the short arrow. In any case, the small bow and short draw would be well suited to a mounted archer.

ARROWS

The quivers of Meroitic and X-Group Nubia were about 50 cm long, and feathers found inside one of the X-Group quivers indicates that was the length of the arrows (pl. 65). The arrowheads are very sharp and light with narrow protruding barbs.[30] Since the bow was light and the arrow was short, much of the effectiveness of the archer depended on the sharp edge and vicious barb of the arrowhead (pls. 64–65).

LOOSE

The archer's loose was based on the same shape as the Meroitic loose.[31] In X-Group times, however, the length increased and the side was made concave (pl. 57c–d), though a number of Meroitic looses may have been removed from tombs and reused. In this period, many looses were made of diorite (pl. 57c). Although

30. OINE VIII, p. 106; X-Group quivers are about the same length, ca. 50 cm. For arrowheads of this design in actual use in modern Sudan, see Streck 1982, pl. 32.

31. OINE VIII, p. 106.

the association of the loose with archery in Sudan has been subject to some discussion, it should be clear from the occurrence of these objects at Qustul with other elements of the archery complex that it was indeed used with the bow (Q 1—5, with bow; Q 149—3, found on a quiver; Q 196—3, with bow and quiver; Q 345—13, with bow and arrowheads; R 119—1, with arrowheads). The use of such a loose implies that the so-called Mongolian draw was employed, in which the thumb took the major stress of the draw. In this technique, arrows are released from the inside of the bow. In addition to the examples noted above, looses were found in Q 147—3 and R 65—3.

GUARD

Pieces of rawhide were cut to fit over the thumb, the back of the hand, and the upper wrist (Q 2—13, Q 61—5a, R 4A—23, R 67—2). Most guards were pierced with elaborate patterns of triangles or lozenges. Although decorative, this piercing was probably intended to allow ventilation.[32]

ARCHERY: SUMMARY REMARKS

Except for the compound bow, all of the archer's equipment had direct antecedents in Meroitic times. However, the quiver was much more elaborate and the consistency of the elaborations with the structure suggests that the archer's equipment found in Meroitic Lower Nubia and depicted on reliefs in Sudan was of Noba-Noubadian origin and adopted in Meroe.

OTHER WEAPONS

POLE ARMS

The most impressive X-Group weapons were spears and spear-swords, found in the large royal burials of Qustul and Ballana and the great tombs at Firka.[33]

SPEARHEAD

A large rectangular fragment of iron appears to extend almost from one edge to the center of the blade, where it is almost a centimeter thick (Q 62—21). The rusted remains have a fibrous texture that runs lengthwise. In addition to the large spearhead, a small spear or javelin head was found in tomb Q 378 (11).

FRAGMENTS OF A SPEAR: Q 19—8

The point and eight centimeters of a typical spear butt remain, with six small fragments of the blade.

LIGHT WEAPONS

Unlike the large blades, a characteristic Noubadian X-Group short sword was often deposited in non-royal tombs.[34] In the present material, it is represented only by remains of the scabbard (pl. 66a–b), which now consist mostly of the spirally wound rawhide lining. Part of one decorated silver cover was preserved (pl. 66b).

BODY ARMOR?

Noubadian X-Group soldiers and their leadership used shields and some body armor (pl. 66c). Although rare, shields have been found with spears.[35] In the present material, a fragment of what was probably body armor was studded with small rosettes, probably of lead (R 49—5e). The backing was made of several layers of tanned leather. Although the small fragments were not certainly identified as leather, shields were made of the material, and it would be an effective defense against the small, barbed arrows.[36] The fragment from tomb R 49 was embossed with short zigzags on one edge. Other fragments included Q 62—2, Q 74—7c, R 2—6?, R 22—5(?).

---

32. Emery and Kirwan 1938, pp. 232–33.

33. Emery and Kirwan 1938, pp. 221–32; Kirwan 1939, pl. XI-5; Mills 1982, pl. XL:7.1. For comparable, but lighter weapons in modern Sudan, see Streck 1982, pl. 38.

34. Emery and Kirwan 1938, pp. 219–21; Mills 1982, pl. VIII:2.25, for example.

35. Emery and Kirwan 1938, fig. 16.

36. Emery and Kirwan 1938, pp. 249–50.

Single weapons: Q 265—3 (arrowhead), M 1—4 (arrowhead), Q 9—8 (arrowhead), R 65—3 (loose), Q 5—7 (blade or bar[?]), 20 (iron knife blade), Q 33—5 (iron blade[?]), R 64—7 (uncertain iron object),Q 19—8 (iron spear butt with blade fragments).

Table 16. Concordance of Archery Equipment and Related Weapons.

Tomb	Quiver	Arrowhead [a]	Bow	Bowstring	Guard	Loose	Armor	Sheath	Iron
Q 1	2a		2b			5			
Q 2					13				
Q 6	8								
Q 10	1	4							
Q 11	1								
Q 14	1a		1b						
Q 32								3	
Q 38		2b							2a
Q 40	2a		2b					2c	
Q 51A	2a, c		2b, d						
Q 61		6	5b		5a				
Q 62	1a		1c				2		21
Q 64		3							
Q 66	2								
Q 68		4							
Q 74	2a, 6	3, 8	4c, 7b				7c[b]	2b	
Q 75	3	7	2b					2a	
Q 76	1	4	2						
Q 84	5	2							
Q 107	1								
Q 119	5								
Q 133		4							
Q 134	22a, b	3							5
Q 135		6							

a. All weapon points are included in this column.

b. Note also the equipment belt 4b.

Table 16. Concordance of Archery Equipment and Related Weapons (*cont.*).

Tomb	Quiver	Arrowhead	Bow	Bowstring	Guard	Loose	Armor	Sheath	Iron
Q 137		6							
Q 145		2							
Q 147						3			
Q 149	1, 2			8		3			
Q 152		6	5						
Q 196	1a	8	1b	2		3			
Q 279	1	2		1b					
Q 345		14	7	5, 7, 10					
Q 349								5	
Q 378		11, 12	8	8					
Q 381		5	7?	6					
Q 505	4a			4b[c]					
Q 594	9	12, 13, 14		10					
R 1		6?							
R 2	7			11			6?		
R 4A	24				23				
R 22	6a						5		
R 49	5a, b		5c, d				5e		
R 67				3	2				
R 119		6				1			
VA 9	3								
VH 122	4								
W 80		3b, c							

c. Other leather remains.

Table 17. Register of Leather Arms and Military Equipment (pls. 54–63).

Bow Q 1—2b (not illustrated)
    Preservation: fragments
    Core: —
    Inner Wrap: —
    Outer Wrap: single piece
    Strip: —
        Binding: —
    Bowstring: fragment

Quiver Q 1—2a (fig. 32, pl. 59a)
    Structure: not preserved
    Preservation: fragments of thongs, flaps and streamers
        Upper Cylinder: —
        Lower Cylinder: —
        Thongs: plaited
        Edging Strips: —
        Emblem Appliqué: —
        Flaps and Attachments: —
            Base-tail Flap: —
            Cover Flap: —
            Tail Flaps and Streamers:
                Tail-flap with excised square with impaled sides in double-frame square
                Streamer with two rows of excised triangles, several fragments, excised
                Streamer with single-frame rosettes, excised
    Remarks: —

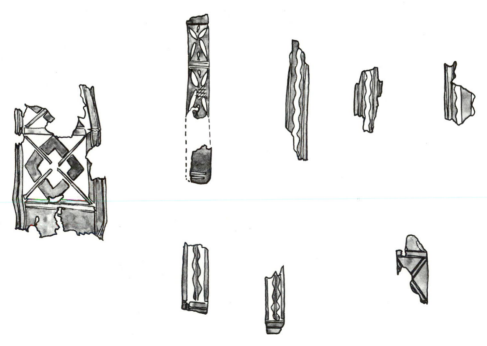

Figure 32. Quiver Fragments, Q 1—2a. Scale 1:2.

Quiver Q 6—8: (fig. 33, pl. 60a–d)
    Structure: fragments of upper cylinder, chest and flank
    Preservation: fragments with flaps and streamers
        Upper Cylinder: embossed horizontal lines, vertical lines, chain
        Lower Cylinder: —

Table 17. Register of Leather Arms and Military Equipment (*cont.*).

Quiver Q 6—8: (fig. 33, pl. 60a–d) (*cont.*)
    Thongs: twisted?
    Edging Strips: —
    Emblem Appliqué: present, uncertain shape
    Flaps and Attachments:
        Base-tail Flap: possibly fragment with vine in trapezoidal panel, incised-excised
        Cover Flap: possibly fragments with dark painted rosette, or possibly another tail-flap
        Tail Flaps and Streamers: tail flap with excised rosette in circle streamer with excised wavy
            band in single frame
    Remarks: —

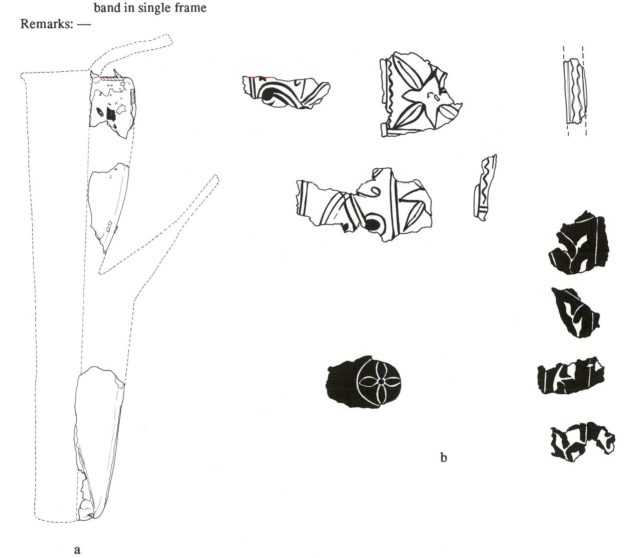

a   b

Figure 33. Quiver Fragments, Q 6—8: (*a*) Remains of quiver;
(*b*) Fragments of decorative flaps. Scales: (*a*) 1:3, (*b*) 1:2.

Quiver Q 10—1 (not illustrated)
    Structure: two cylinders, base flaps
    Preservation: fragments
        Upper Cylinder: embossed horizontal lines, medium-small herringbone with double horizontal center
            line; empty vertical band
        Lower Cylinder: plain
        Thongs: attachments only
        Edging Strips: —

Table 17. Register of Leather Arms and Military Equipment (*cont.*).

Quiver Q 10—1 (not illustrated) (*cont.*)
        Emblem Appliqué: —
        Flaps and Attachments:
            Base-tail Flap: —
            Cover Flap: perpendicular, hanging forward
            Tail Flaps and Streamers:
      Remarks: —

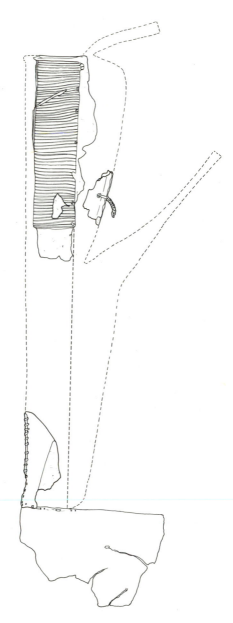

Figure 34. Quiver Fragments, Q 11—1. Scale 1:4.

Quiver Q 11—1 (fig. 34)
    Structure: two cylinders
    Preservation: fragments
        Upper Cylinder: embossed horizontal and vertical lines
        Lower Cylinder: undecorated
        Thongs: twisted
        Edging Strips: —

Table 17. Register of Leather Arms and Military Equipment (*cont.*).

Quiver Q 11—1 (fig. 34) (*cont.*)
        Emblem Appliqué: —
        Flaps and Attachments: remains of undecorated flaps
            Base-tail Flap: —
            Cover Flap: narrow, extends forward from base
            Tail Flaps and Streamers
      Remarks: —

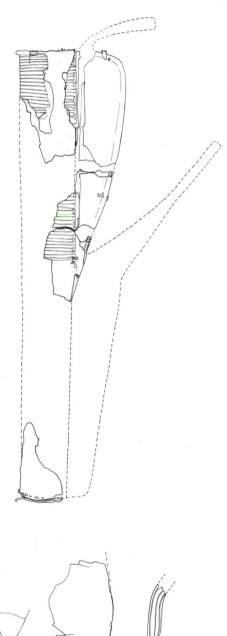

Figure 35. Quiver Fragments, Q 14—1a. Scale 1:4.

Quiver Q 14—1a (fig. 35)
     Structure: one cylinder
     Preservation: fragments

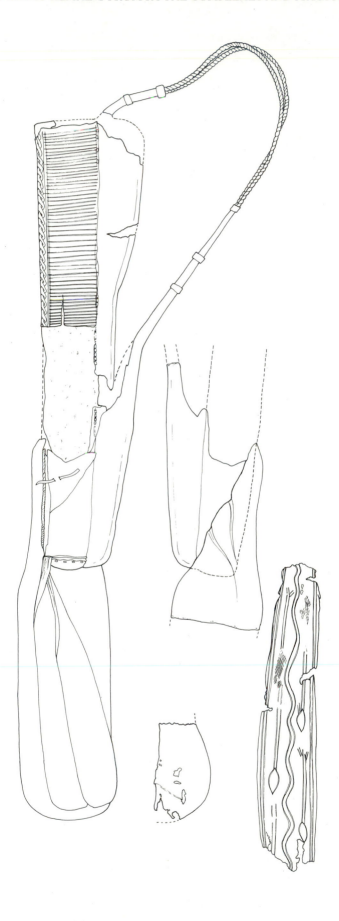

Figure 36. Quiver, Q 40—2a. Scale 1:4.

Table 17. Register of Leather Arms and Military Equipment (*cont.*).

Quiver Q 14—1a (fig. 35) (*cont.*)
      Upper Cylinder: incised horizontal lines, embossed vertical chain
      Lower Cylinder: —
      Thongs: twisted
      Edging Strips: —
      Emblem Appliqué: none
      Flaps and Attachments:
           Base-tail Flap: see tail flaps
           Cover Flap: fragments, undecorated
           Tail Flaps and Streamers: two undecorated flaps, one streamer, incised lines
    Remarks: upper cylinder contained remains of arrow shafts and fletching

Bow Q 14—1b (not illustrated)
    Preservation: fragments
    Core: —
    Inner Wrap: remains of coarse plain weave fabric present but not in leather wrapping
    Outer Wrap: fragment in poor condition
    Strip: —
      Binding: —
    Bowstring: twisted gut or rawhide, ca. 0.60 m, looped and tied at one end, broken at the other

Quiver Q 40—2a (fig. 36; pls. 58, 59b)
    Structure: double cylinder
    Preservation: broken, body substantially remaining
      Upper Cylinder: embossed horizontal lines, vertical chain on black background
      Lower Cylinder: undecorated
      Thongs: twisted
      Edging Strips: —
      Emblem Appliqué: —
      Flaps and Attachments:
           Base-tail Flap: unc., possibly reattached to lower
           Cover Flap: cylinder
           Tail Flaps and Streamers: two undecorated flaps at base, one fragment with embossed vine
    Remarks: —

Bow Q 40—2b (not illustrated)
    Preservation: fragments
    Core: —
    Inner Wrap: —
    Outer Wrap: leather fragments
    Strip: —
      Binding: —
    Bowstring: fragments
          Also tanned leather wrapping for scabbard, tied strip ca. 2–3 cm wide,
              and narrow strips ca. 0.75 cm.

Quiver Q 51A—2a (fig. 37a)
    Structure: one cylinder
    Preservation: cylinder remains and fragments
      Upper Cylinder: horizontal embossed lines, band of parallel zigzags, vertical empty band,
          triple frame
      Lower Cylinder: —
      Thongs: braided hanging loop
      Edging Strips: —
      Emblem Appliqué: —
      Flaps and Attachments:

Table 17. Register of Leather Arms and Military Equipment (*cont.*).

Quiver Q 51A—2a (fig. 37a) (*cont.*)
        Base-tail Flap: —
        Cover Flap: —
        Tail Flaps and Streamers: tail-flap with excised vine(?) another with excised
                alternating triangles
        Remarks: —

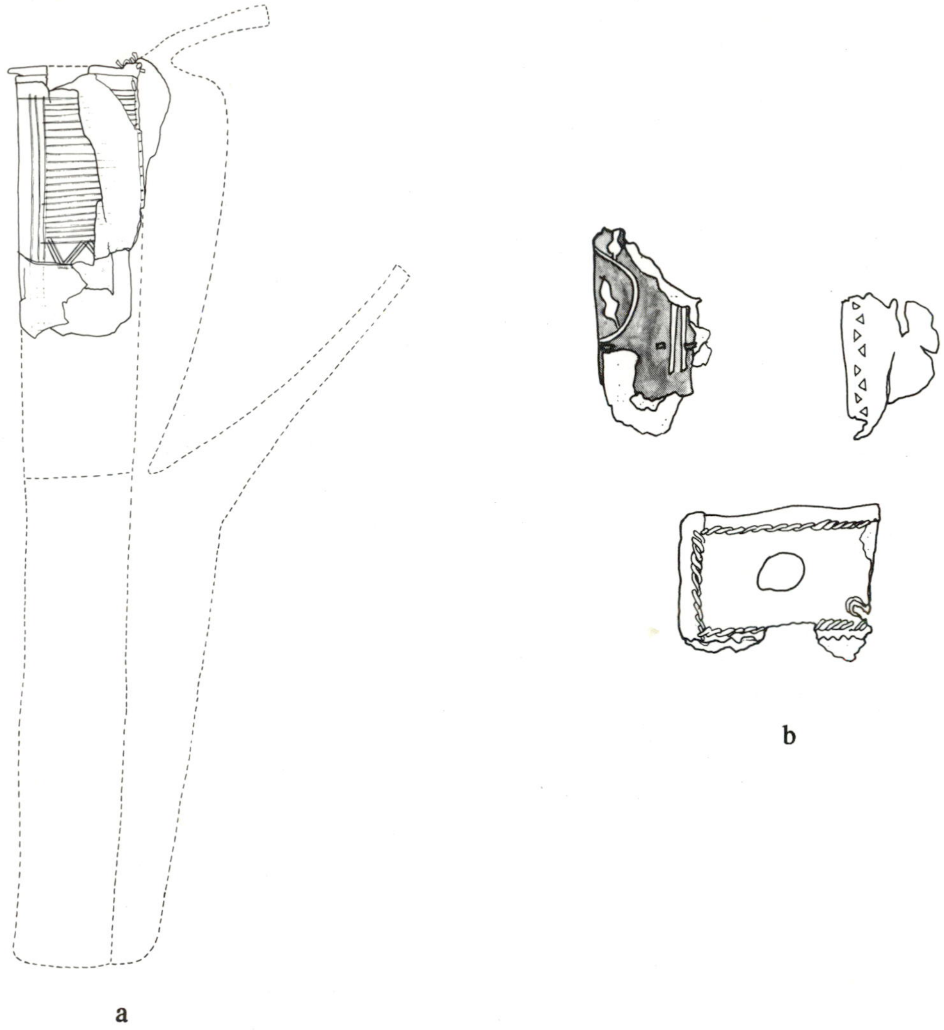

a

b

Figure 37. Quiver Fragments from Tomb Q 51A: (*a*) Quiver Fragment, No. 2a;
(*b*) Fragments of Flaps and Edge of Bag, No. 2c. Scales: (*a*) 1:4, (*b*) 1:2.

Bow Q 51A—2b (not illustrated)
   Preservation: five small fragments
   Core: —
   Inner Wrap: fabric
   Outer Wrap: present
   Strip: present
      Binding: present
   Bowstring: —
  Ca. 1.0 cm core diam. at grip; edge of bag with tie hole; rect. reinforcement lined with stitching Q 51A—2e

Quiver Q 51A—2c (fig. 37b)
   Structure: one cylinder
   Preservation: fragments
      Upper Cylinder: embossed horizontal lines

Table 17. Register of Leather Arms and Military Equipment (*cont.*).

Quiver Q 51A—2c (fig. 37b) (*cont.*)
        Lower Cylinder: —
        Thongs: —
        Edging Strips: —
        Emblem Appliqué: —
        Flaps and Attachments:
            Base-tail Flap: —
            Cover Flap: —
            Tail Flaps and Streamers: fragments, undecorated flaps, streamers
      Remarks: —

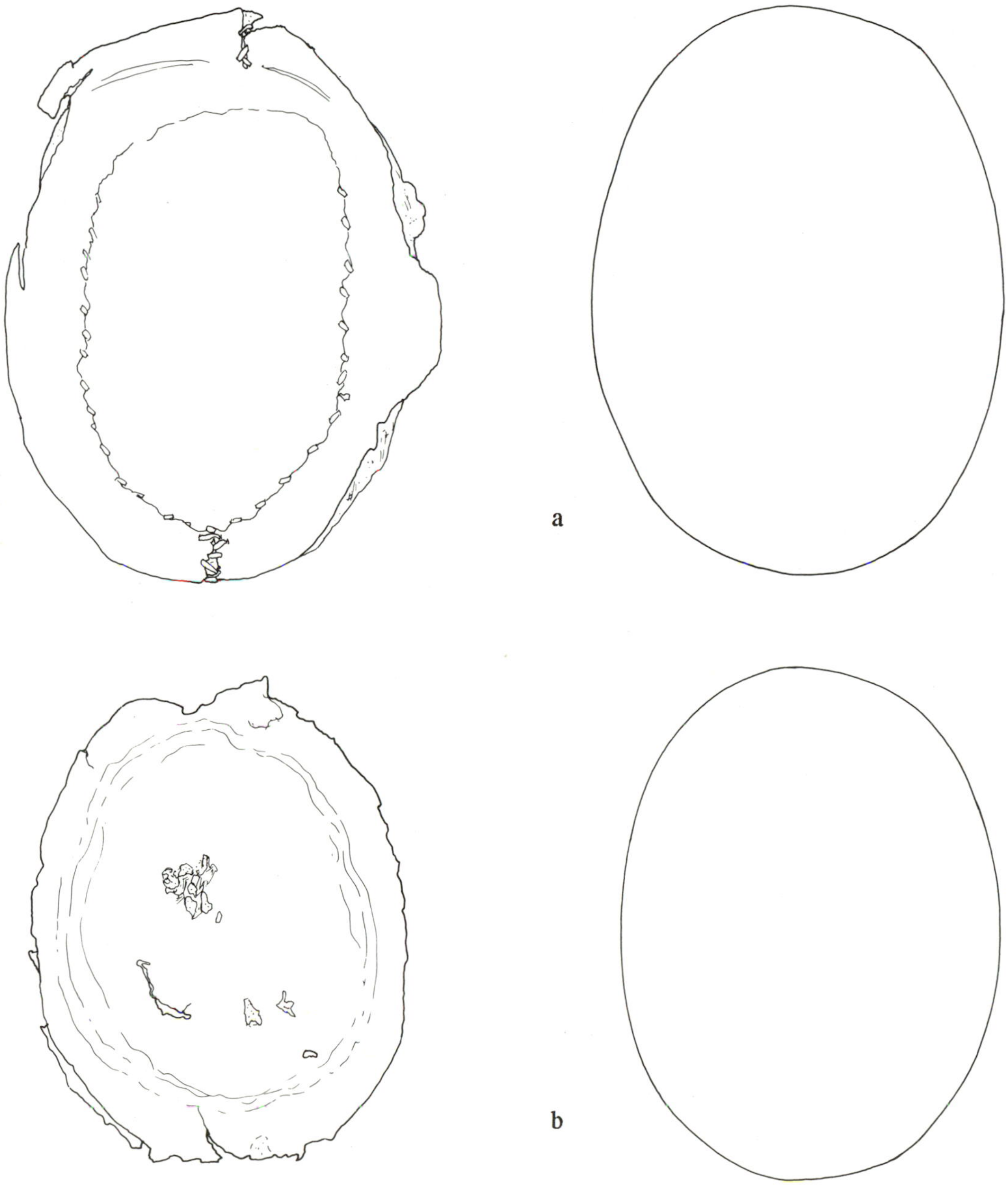

Figure 38. Leather Containers (Base Profiles) from Tombs Q 60 and Q 82:
(*a*) Q 60—4; (*b*) Q 82—7. Scale 2:5.

Table 17. Register of Leather Arms and Military Equipment (*cont.*).

Bow Q 51A—2d (not illustrated)
    Preservation: small fragments of two bows
    Core: —
    Inner Wrap: —
    Outer Wrap: small fragments
    Strip: —
        Binding: —
    Bowstring: —
    Also edge of bag with tie holes

Q 60—4 (fig. 38a)
    Leather bottle, some remains of side and oval bottom with residue

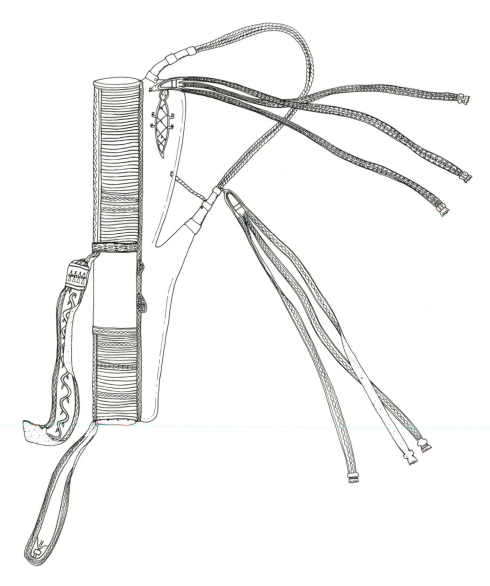

Figure 39. Quiver, Q 62—1a (reconstruction). Scale 1:5.

Quiver Q 62—1a (figs. 39–40)
    Structure: two cylinders
    Preservation: virtually complete
        Upper Cylinder: embossed horizontal lines, two bands with chains, two vertical with chains

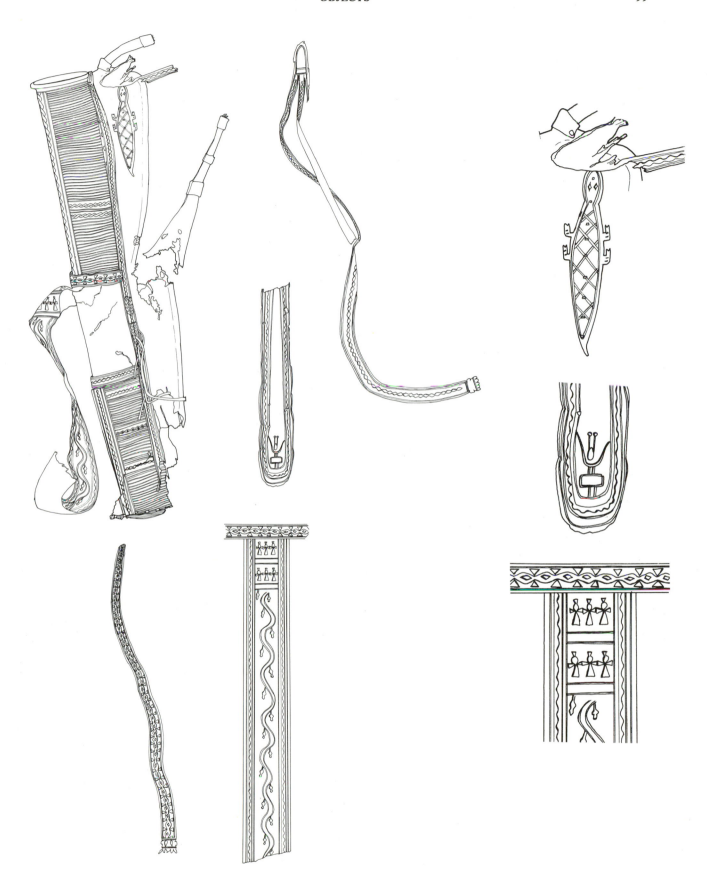

Figure 40. Quiver, Q 62—1a (as found). Scale 1:4.

Table 17. Register of Leather Arms and Military Equipment (*cont.*).

Quiver Q 62—1a (figs. 39–40) (*cont.*)
    Lower Cylinder: embossed horizontal lines, bands above, middle and below with reserve excised
        eye-chain, double frame vertical band with excised eye-chain
    Thongs: twisted
    Edging Strips: vertical, with excised eye-chain, lower edge of upper cylinder with same
    Emblem Appliqué: gecko with excised crosshatching
    Flaps and Attachments: Tail flap, front flap, streamers
        Base-tail Flap: four framing bands, Meroitic symbol with horns and sun disc '
        Cover Flap: —
        Tail Flaps and Streamers: front flap attached to upper cylinder (excised wavy vine framed by
            excised scallops; above, horizontal band of four "Nubian *ankhs*" with inverted triangles);
            three triple streamers (excised chains, ending in cut floral edges);
            single streamer (excised reserve chain with opposed triangles, floral end)
    Remarks: Q 62—1b, leather fragment, green with white stitching, may be part of an emblem (fig. 121b)

Bow Q 62—1c (pl. 62b)
    Preservation: Arm near tip and near grip, fragments
    Core: —
    Inner Wrap: —
    Outer Wrap: Wide piece of spiralling leather strap
    Strip: Impression on wrap and thong binding remains
        Binding: —
    Bowstring: None, but thong bindings near tip possibly acted as nock

Quiver Q 66—2 (not illustrated)
    Structure: uncertain
    Preservation: small fragments
    Upper Cylinder: horizontal embossed lines, vertical guilloche
    Lower Cylinder: —
    Thongs: —
    Edging Strips: —
    Emblem Appliqué: —
    Flaps and Attachments: undecorated flap
        Base-tail Flap: —
        Cover Flap: —
        Tail Flaps and Streamers: —
    Remarks: —

Quiver Q 74—2a (fig. 41; pls. 57b, 59c)
    Structure: one cylinder
    Preservation: fragmentary
    Upper Cylinder: embossed horizontal lines, vertical band with variant chain pattern
    Lower Cylinder: —
    Thongs: twisted
    Edging Strips: unc.
    Emblem Appliqué: bucranium with lotus, cut out and excised detail
    Flaps and Attachments:
        Base-tail Flap: with cut-out triangles (or possible below)
        Cover Flap: curved edges, groups of four lozenges cut-out around edge
        Tail Flaps and Streamers: tail-flaps (cut-out triangles); double-streamers (end in floral
            decoration, uncertain number of excised vines on either side of median with
            excised running lozenges)
    Remarks: This was probably originally the finest quiver in the collection; note also the sheath liner
        Q 74—2b (fig. 124d) and the leather insect Q 74—7d (fig. 55)

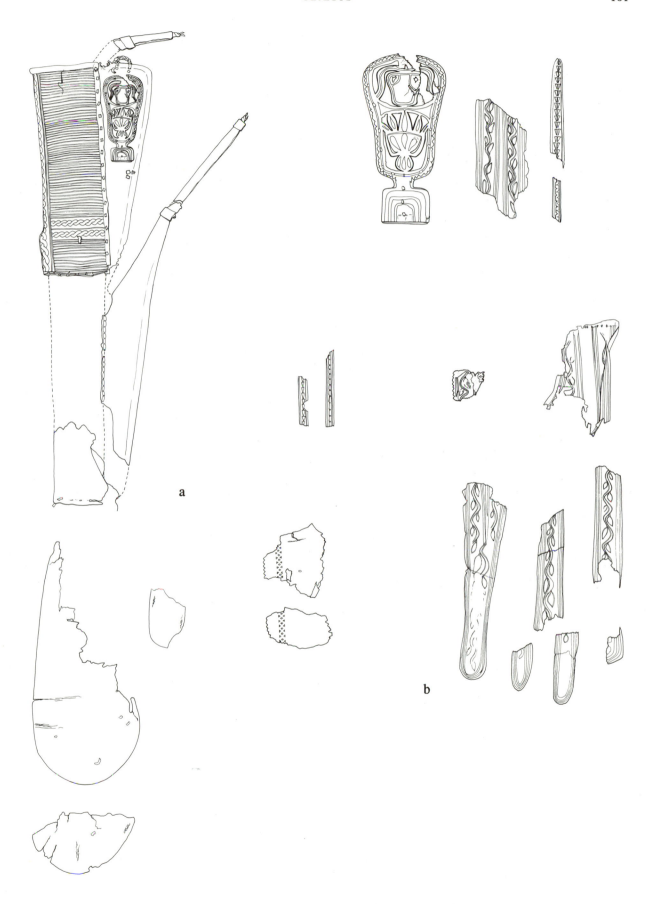

Figure 41. Quiver, Q 74—2a: (*a*) Quiver and Flaps; (*b*) Details, Emblem, and Flap. Scale 1:4.

Table 17. Register of Leather Arms and Military Equipment (*cont.*).

Bow Q 74—4c, 7b (fig. 42a)
    Preservation: only one fragment remaining
    Core: fiber
    Inner Wrap: present
    Outer Wrap: present
    Strip: —
        Binding: —
    Bowstring: two strand, fiber

Q 74—7c. Armor: Angularly-cut leather with metal (lead?) studs (not illustrated)

Q 74—4a, 7a. Bag: reinforced leather rim with holes, edges stitched; tab with hole, (fig. 42b)

Q 74—4b. Equipment strap or belt: assembled from several pieces, thongs, and strips, (fig. 42c, pl. 67b)

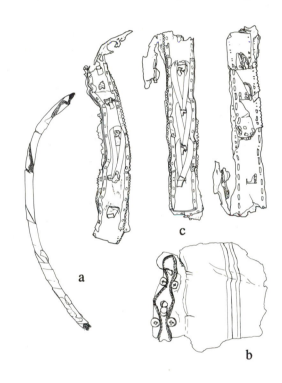

Figure 42. Leather from Tomb Q 74: (*a*) Bow, No. 4c; (*b*) Bag, No. 4a;
(*c*) Equipment Strap or Belt (Bag Edge?), No. 4b. Scale 1:4.

Quiver Q 75—3 (fig. 43)
    Structure: two cylinders
    Preservation: broken, much of body preserved
        Upper Cylinder: horizontal lines, bands of herringbone; vertical bands with chain, embossed
        Lower Cylinder: undecorated
        Thongs: twisted; hanging loop on top of chest flap
        Edging Strips: none
        Emblem Appliqué: none
        Flaps and Attachments:
            Base-tail Flap: not present
            Cover Flap: long, relatively narrow, held in place around lower cylinder rather than pendant; undecorated
            Tail Flaps and Streamers: triple streamers and tail flaps; attachments on lower part of thigh flap
    Remarks: note bag remains Q 75—4

Table 17. Register of Leather Arms and Military Equipment (*cont.*).

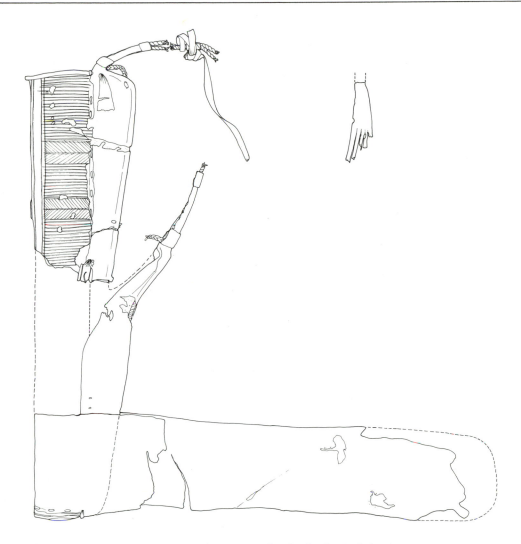

Figure 43. Quiver Remains, Q 75—3. Scale 1:4.

Bow Q 75—2b (not illustrated)
Preservation: fragments, outer arm
Core: ?
Inner Wrap: —
Outer Wrap: leather present, extra rawhide outer wrap
Strip: —
Binding: —
Bowstring: —

Short-sword sheath Q 75—2a. (fig. 125a, pl. 66a):
Inner lining, longitudinal strips of leather
Inner wrap, spirally wound rawhide strip, ca. 2 cm
Outer wrap, curved tip with broken end of wrap above

Quiver Q 76—1 (not illustrated)
Structure: uncertain
Preservation: base and cover flap only
Upper Cylinder: —
Lower Cylinder: —
Thongs: —

Table 17. Register of Leather Arms and Military Equipment (*cont.*).

Quiver Q76—1 (not illustrated) (*cont.*)
     Edging Strips: —
     Emblem Appliqué: —
     Flaps and Attachments:
         Base-tail Flap: —
         Cover Flap: fragment
         Tail Flaps and Streamers: —
   Remarks: bottom oval only

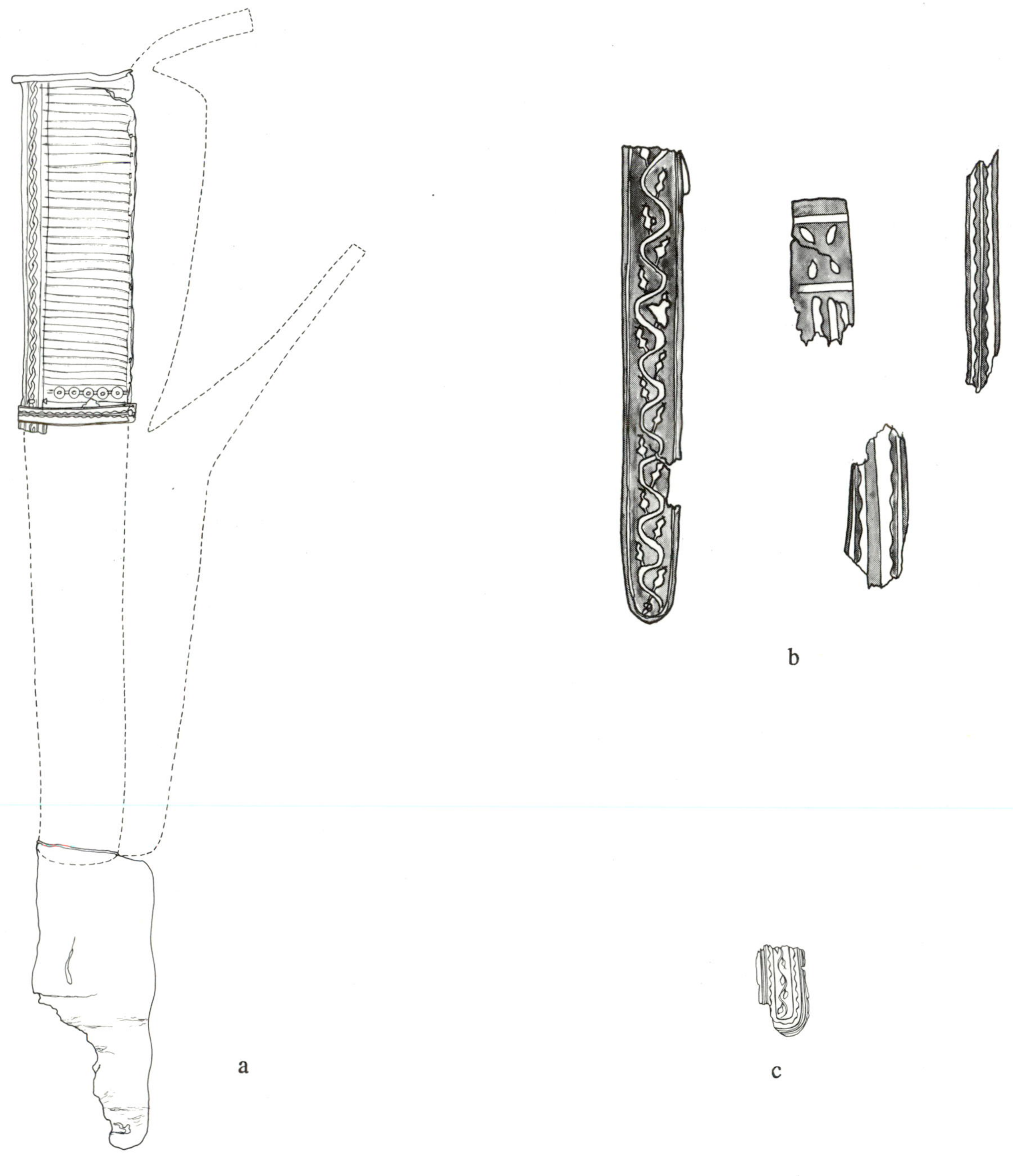

Figure 44. Quiver Remains from Tombs Q 107 and Q 119: (*a*) Quiver, Q 107—1; (*b*) Flaps, Q 107—1;
(*c*) Quiver fragment, flap, Q 119—5. Scales: (*a, c*) 1:4, (*b*) 1:2.

Table 17. Register of Leather Arms and Military Equipment (*cont.*).

Bow Q 76—2 (not illustrated)
    Preservation: fragment
    Core: —
    Inner Wrap: —
    Outer Wrap: twisted leather from near tip only
    Strip: —
        Binding: —
    Bowstring: —
    Bag: possible fragments
    Sandal: possibly tab with tied leather strap, broken

Bag Q 82—7 (fig. 38b)
    Base of oval leather container with thick residue ca. 1 cm

Quiver Q 107—1 (fig. 44a–b)
    Structure: one cylinder
    Preservation: cylinder, base, fragments
        Upper Cylinder: embossed horizontal lines, two vertical chains
        Lower Cylinder: —
        Thongs: —
        Edging Strips: at bottom of cylinder, with excised strip and two rows triangles facing inward
        Emblem Appliqué: —
        Flaps and Attachments:
            Base-tail Flap: —
            Cover Flap: attached to base, remains
            Tail Flaps and Streamers: tail-flap (very sinuous excised vine and lobed leaves); broad, medium, and narrow streamers (excised median, two rows triangles facing inward); end panel (two lozenges, framed)
    Remarks: —

Quiver Q 119—5 (fig. 44c)
    Structure: one cylinder?
    Preservation: fragments
        Upper Cylinder: embossed horizontal lines and vertical chain
        Lower Cylinder: —
        Thongs: —
        Edging Strips: —
        Emblem Appliqué: —
        Flaps and Attachments:
            Base-tail Flap: narrow, excised vine with simple leaves in triple concentric framing, curved
            Cover Flap: —
            Tail Flaps and Streamers: few fragments of various sizes
    Remarks: —

Quiver Q 134—22a (fig. 45a)
    Structure: one cylinder
    Preservation: cylinder, body broken, streamers and thongs torn away
        Upper Cylinder: embossed horizontal lines, three vertical panels, framed
        Lower Cylinder: —
        Thongs: twisted, chest and thigh areas linked
        Edging Strips: below cylinder, with excised eyes and tassels
        Emblem Appliqué: —
        Flaps and Attachments:
            Base-tail Flap: none
            Cover Flap: "leather bag or garment with pierced design and serrated edges."

Table 17. Register of Leather Arms and Military Equipment (*cont.*).

Quiver Q 134—22a (fig. 45a) (*cont.*)
>   Tail Flaps and Streamers: attachments for two; see also flap with side streamers (lotus above, flap with incised St. Andrew's crosses in frame);
>   double streamer (end plain, each with two excised rows of "triangles" facing inward);
>   end-tab (two to three incised lines around, excised band with scalloped edge for inner frame, strap, horizontal excised floral motifs);
>   end-tab (lines, lining, horizontal and angled)

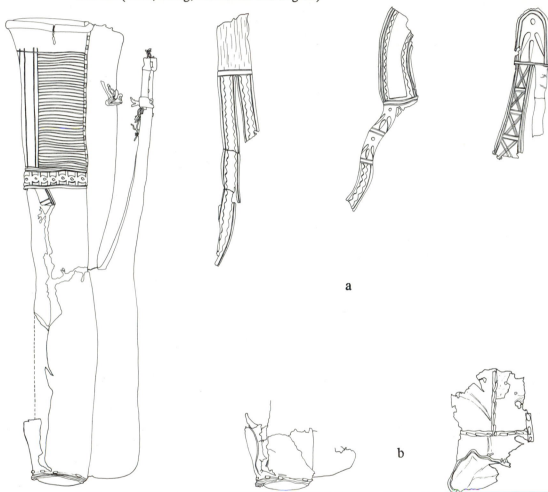

Figure 45. Quiver from Tomb Q 134: (*a*) With Streamers, No. 22a; (*b*) Base, No. 22b. Scale 1:4.

Quiver Q 134—22b (fig. 45b)
>   Structure: uncertain
>   Preservation: base only, possibly cylinder with stitched serrated edge and protective strip
>   Upper Cylinder: —
>   Lower Cylinder: —
>   Thongs: —
>   Edging Strips: —
>   Emblem Appliqué: —
>   Flaps and Attachments:
>   Base-tail Flap: —
>   Cover Flap: —
>   Tail Flaps and Streamers: —
>   Remarks: —

Table 17. Register of Leather Arms and Military Equipment (*cont.*).

Quiver Q 136—2 (not illustrated)
    Structure: one cylinder
    Preservation: fragments of cylinder, body, flaps, streamers
        Upper Cylinder: fragments
        Lower Cylinder: —
        Thongs: attachments
        Edging Strips: —
        Emblem Appliqué: —
        Flaps and Attachments:
            Base-tail Flap: —
            Cover Flap: —
            Tail Flaps and Streamers: remains of undecorated tail flaps (attachments) and streamers
    Remarks: —

Quiver Q 149—1-2 (figs. 46–49; pls. 54–55)
    Structure: one cylinder
    Preservation: complete
        Upper Cylinder: pentagonal, sewn; sides at flaps, horizontal embossed lines sides, nested rectangles
            flush at bottom end, vertical zigzag, triple framed, two panels of horizontal lines, triple framed;
            upper rib flattened
        Lower Cylinder: —
        Thongs: twisted, hanging between chest and flank areas
        Edging Strips: cut with opposed chevrons, strips with both vertical and horizontal cover stitching
        Emblem Appliqué: none
        Flaps and Attachments: very complex
            Base-tail Flap: (2) folded, decoration below
            Cover Flap: (1) broad oblong, attached to base, edges scalloped, two tie strips cut from side end
                in "Nubian *ankh*" tabs: cut-out lozenges in lozenge pattern ca. 10 cm apart
            Tail Flaps and Streamers:
                (3) twin tail flaps attached to upper thong tubes
                (4) twin tail flaps attached to lower thong tubes
                (5) twin small tail flaps attached to lower thong tubes
                (6) triple tassel on thong attached to reverse of lower chest flap
                (7) triple tassel on thong attached to reverse through vertical edging strip
                (8) triple streamer with floral-terminals, attached to lower thong tubes
                (9) triple tassel on twisted thong on upper thong tubes
    Decoration of flaps:
        1. Two parallel bands of alternating lozenges down center in angled groups of four, band of floating
            lozenges in groups of four; band of alternating lozenges, in angled rows of three alternating
            triangles and scalloped edge
        2, 3. Band of rows of triangles (six) in center, two bands of lozenge patterns on either side, scalloped
            edges
        4. Band of rows of triangles down center (four), scalloped edge
        5. Row of alternating lozenges
    Remarks: —
        The base-tail flap and tassels remained attached. The positions of the decorative streamers and tail
            flaps are indicated by broken attachments still in place, but the assignment of each group of
            streamers and flaps to any location is conjectural. One of the narrow flaps had a very long
            attachment.
        The central band of the front cylinder panel was pigmented.
        A spare bowstring is coiled about the middle.
        Note the loose Q 149—3.

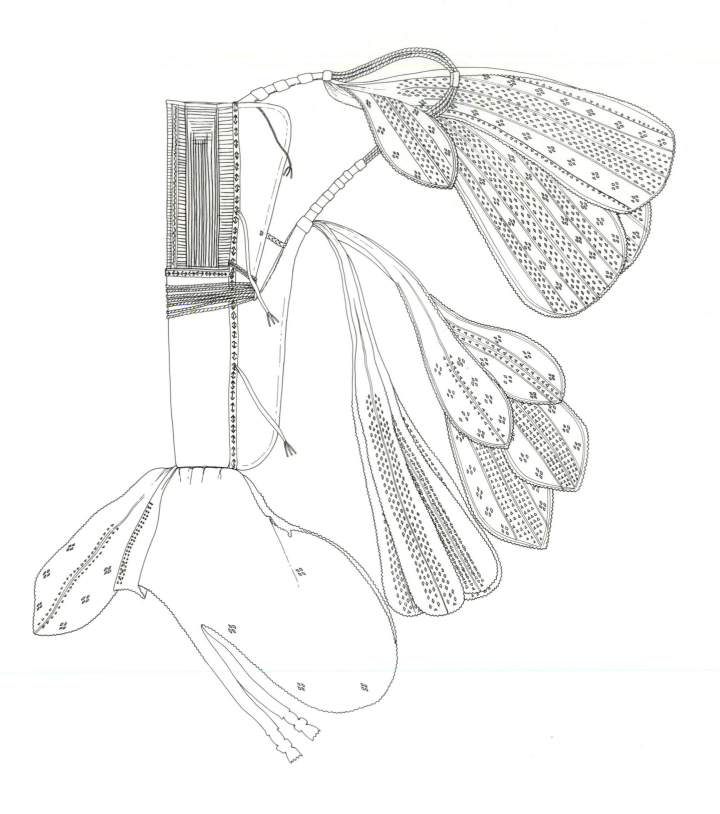

Figure 46. Quiver, Q 149—1, 2. Scale 1:5.

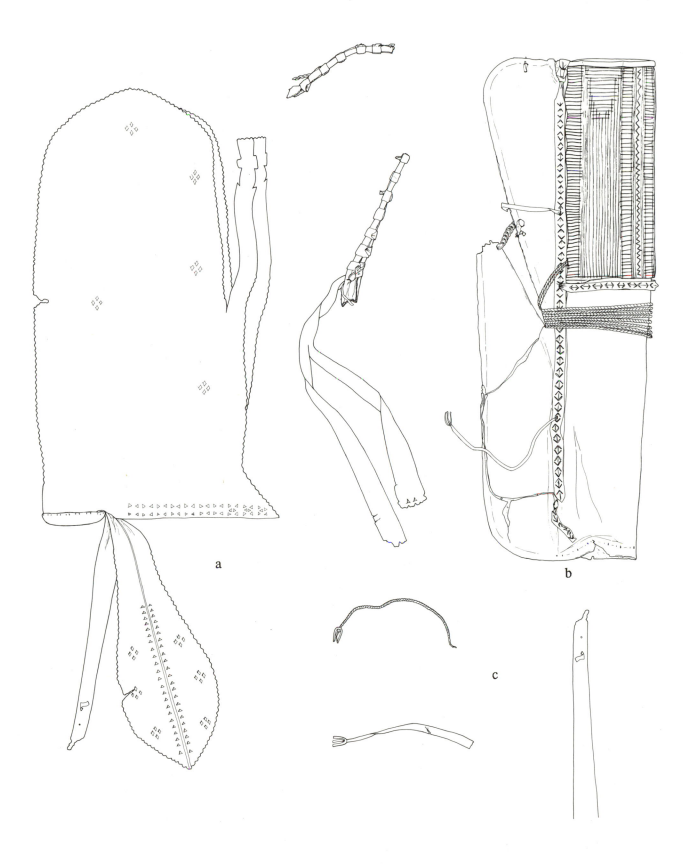

a

b

c

Figure 47. Quiver, Q 149—1, 2 (*cont.*): (*a*) Cover Flap; (*b*) Body; (*c*) Attachments. Scale 1:4.

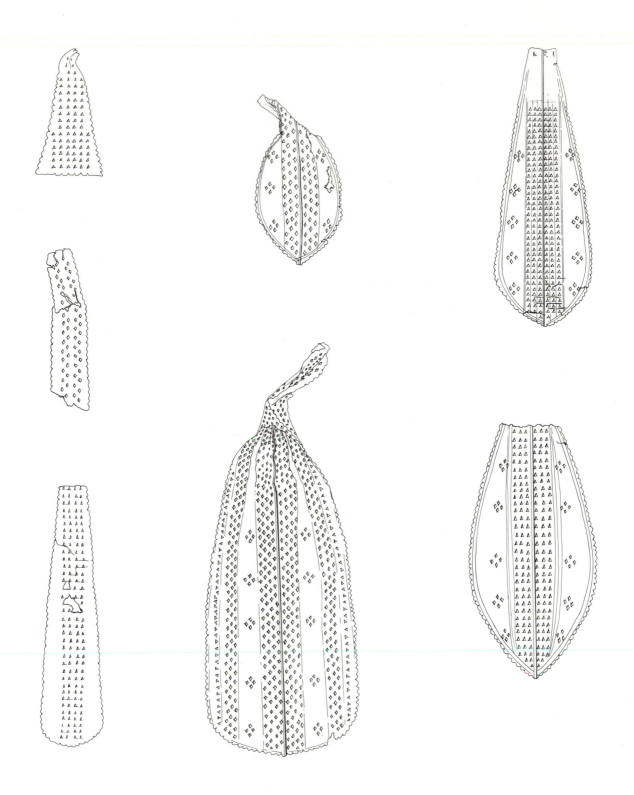

Figure 48. Quiver Flaps, Q 149—1, 2. Scale 1:4.

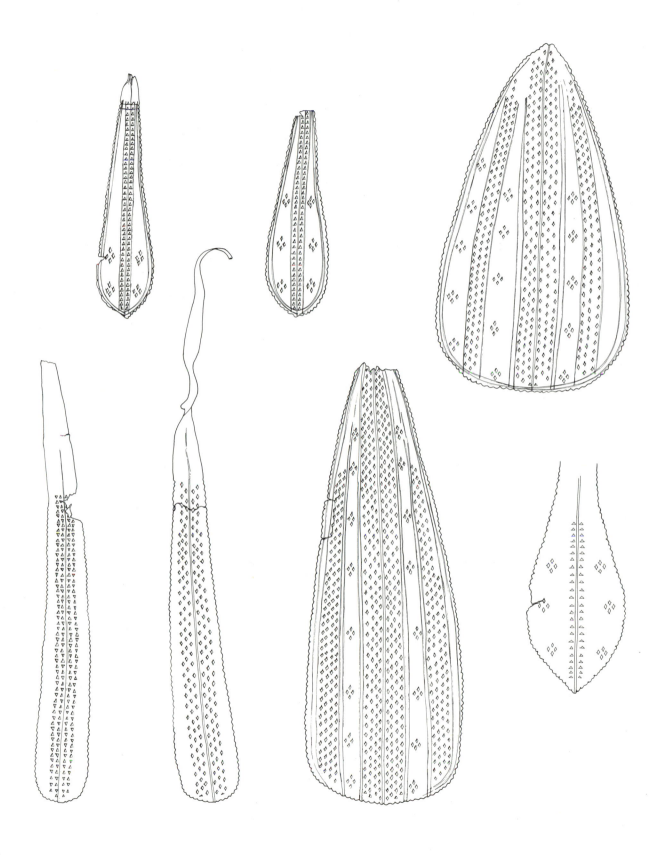

Figure 49. Quiver Flaps, Q 149—1, 2 (*cont.*). Scale 1:4.

Table 17. Register of Leather Arms and Military Equipment (*cont.*).

Quiver Q 196—1a (fig. 50; pl. 56b–c)
    Structure: two cylinders, lower secondary?
    Preservation: fragments, some large
        Upper Cylinder: embossed horizontal lines, herringbone, vertical chain
        Lower Cylinder: undecorated, probably secondary; roll stitch on the front; narrow thong passed
            through side at an angle toward lower rear (this probably held a cover flap in place)
        Thongs: twisted; thong for suspension on top of chest-flap, under tubes
        Edging Strips: horizontal at bottom of cylinder with incised chain
        Emblem Appliqué: removed; stitch-holes and residue indicate complex shape, with upper circle, two
            bulges and two pairs of holes on either side of a long tail or stalk
        Flaps and Attachments:
            Base-tail Flap: originally present but broken away
            Cover Flap: possibly attached by thong to lower cylinder
            Tail Flaps and Streamers: remains of three tail flaps and two streamers, undecorated
    Remarks: the edge of the chest-flap appears to have been stitched, in groups of three; there was no trace
        of glue

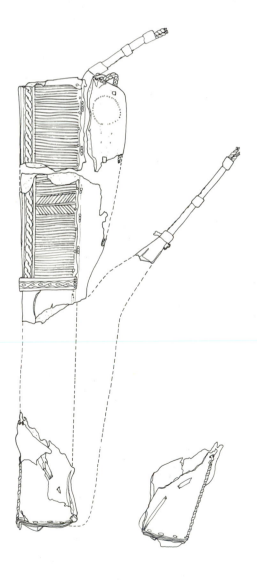

Figure 50. Quiver, Q 196—1a. Scale 1:4.

Table 17. Register of Leather Arms and Military Equipment (*cont.*).

Bow Q 196—1b (pl. 62d)
 Preservation: three fragments, at grip and arms; diameter ca. 1.0 cm at grip
 Core: fiber
 Inner Wrap: present
 Outer Wrap: present
 Strip: present
  Binding: present
 Bowstring: fragment, Q 196—2 (not illustrated)
 Loose: Q 196—3 (fig. 157b)

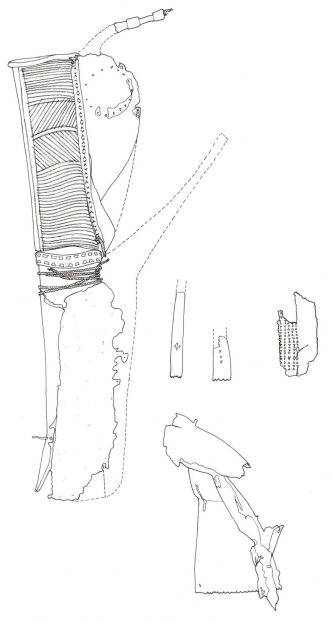

Figure 51. Quiver, Q 505—4a. Scale 1:4.

Quiver Q 505—4a (fig. 51; pl. 57a)
 Structure: one cylinder
 Preservation: body structure reconstructible, attachments removed and nearly destroyed
  Upper Cylinder: horizontal lines, herringbone, vertical lines frame empty band at front

Table 17. Register of Leather Arms and Military Equipment (*cont.*).

Quiver Q 505—4a (fig. 51; pl. 57a) (*cont.*)
        Lower Cylinder: —
        Thongs: twisted
        Edging Strips: horizontal and vertical, with angled cuts
        Emblem Appliqué: circular medallion
        Flaps and Attachments:
            Base-tail Flap: —
            Cover Flap: corner with hole, one serrated edge, other edge straight, curved fragment with row
                of lozenges
            Tail Flaps and Streamers: tail-flap with two bands of rows of three pairs of opposed triangles;
                tapered streamer with serrated end and single band of opposed triangles
      Remarks: undecorated tapered strip(s); bowstring coiled about middle of body; see also Q 505—4b

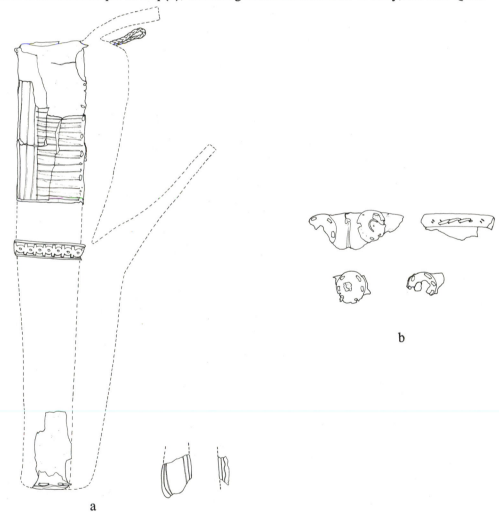

Figure 52. Leather Fragments from Tomb R 22: (*a*) Quiver, No. 6a;
(*b*) Bag Edge with Grommets, No. 6b. Scales: (*a*) 1:4, (*b*) 1:2.

Quiver R 2—7 (not illustrated)
    Structure: uncertain
    Preservation: small mixed fragments only, possibly other objects also included
        Upper Cylinder: —
        Lower Cylinder: —
        Thongs: —
        Edging Strips: —

Table 17. Register of Leather Arms and Military Equipment (*cont.*).

Quiver R 2—7 (not illustrated) (*cont.*)
    Emblem Appliqué: —
    Flaps and Attachments:
        Base-tail Flap: —
        Cover Flap: —
        Tail Flaps and Streamers: —
  Remarks: See also R 2—6, fragments of armor?

Quiver R 22—6a (fig. 52a)
  Structure: One cylinder?
  Preservation: fragmentary,
    Upper Cylinder: horizontal embossed lines, vertical band
    Lower Cylinder: —
    Thongs: braided, suspension thong
    Edging Strips: vertical, with leaning V-shaped cuts second strip with opposed pairs of sewing cuts
    Emblem Appliqué: —
    Flaps and Attachments:
        Base-tail Flap: —
        Cover Flap: —
        Tail Flaps and Streamers: tail flap with incised lines lining, double tail-streamer with excised-reserved wavy band in rectangular frame
  Remarks: also grommet from bag, round hole, pairs of stitching holes around circumference (fig. 52b)

Quivers R 49—5a, b (fig. 53a, b; pl. 60e)
  Structure: Remains of two quivers, not separable
  Preservation: fragments, mostly of attachments; register says nearly complete
    Upper Cylinder: fragments with horizontal embossed lines
    Lower Cylinder: —
    Thongs: braided
    Edging Strips: —
    Emblem Appliqué: —
    Flaps and Attachments:
        Base-tail Flap: —
        Cover Flap: fragment (serrated edge, widely-spaced lozenge-groups of cut-out lozenges; fragment (serrated edge, cut-out lozenges?)
        Tail Flaps and Streamers:
            Fragment (narrow flap with border of incised wavy line framed by two excised bands)
            Fragment (three rows cut-out triangles in bands framed by cut-out lines; flap)
            Double streamer (fine excised vine in single frame)
            Double streamer (fine excised vine in single frame)
            Two streamer fragments (excised eye and tassel in single frame, floral terminal)
            Streamer fragments (five terminals, excised running lozenges [?] in single frame, floral terminals)
            Fragment (narrow flap, running lozenges [?] in double excised border)
  Remarks: excised frame; floral terminals. The two different kinds of decoration may indicate the presence of two quivers, though this is not necessarily true

Bow R 49—5c (fig. 31; pl. 62a)
  Preservation: six fragments, including join
  Core: —
  Inner Wrap: textile present
  Outer Wrap: present
  Strip: —
    Binding: —
  Bowstring: —
  Remarks: diameter ca. 1 cm at join, normal bow size

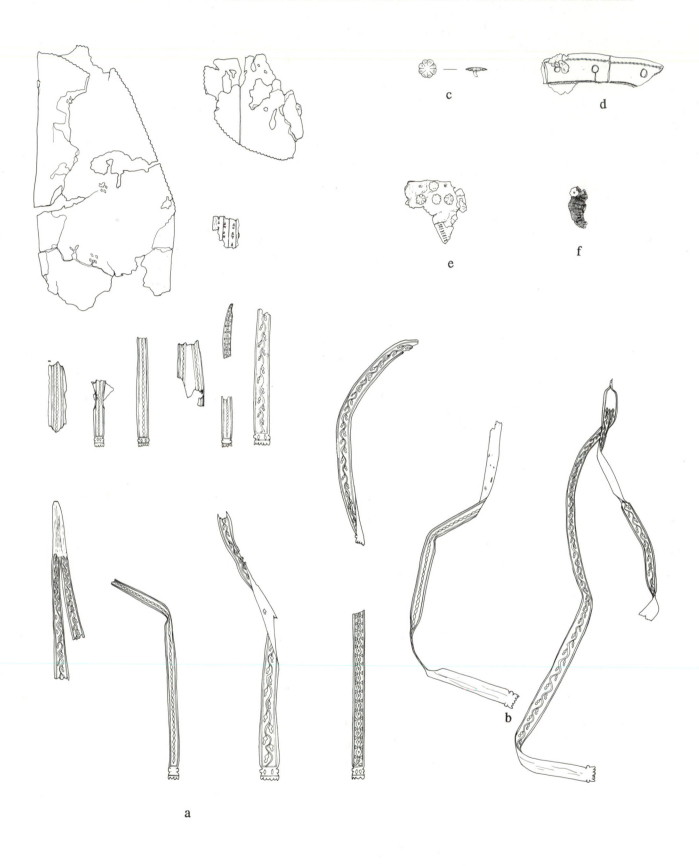

Figure 53. Leather Fragments from Tomb R 49: (*a*) Quiver Fragments, No. 5a, b; (*b*) Quiver Flaps,
No. 5a, b; (*c*) Armor Stud, No. 5e; (*d*) Bag Edge with Grommet-holes, No. 6; (*e*) Armor with
Studs, No. 5e; (*f*) Textile with Stud, nos. 5e, 7. Scales: (*a, b, d–f*)1:4, (c) 1:2.

Table 17. Register of Leather Arms and Military Equipment (*cont.*).

Bow R 49—5d (not illustrated)
 Preservation: fragments, some near grip
 Core: present
 Inner Wrap: no evidence of fabric
 Outer Wrap: very thin, leather, ca 0.5 diameter
 Strip: ca. 0.12 m on either side of join
  Binding: present
 Bowstring: —
 Remarks: Bow probably less than 0.70 m long, virtually miniature

Armor fragment R 49—5e (fig. 53c, e, f)
 Irregularly shaped dark leather with a row of zigzag punches and two rows of lead rosettes with circles
  on the petals

Bag fragment R 49—6 (fig. 53d; pl. 67c)
 Reinforced edge of bag with angled stitching and circular holes for tie

Quiver VA 9—3 (fig. 54)
 Structure: uncertain
 Preservation: remains of flaps and streamers only
  Upper Cylinder: —
  Lower Cylinder: —
  Thongs: —
  Edging Strips: —
  Emblem Appliqué: —
  Flaps and Attachments:
   Base-tail Flap: —
   Cover Flap: —
   Folded, serrated edge; remains near point, crescentic bands of triangles offset and opposed;
    band of opposed triangles on each side of fold
   Tail Flaps and Streamers: flap (broad, triangles in rows and one pattern of four in lozenge
    curved, serrated edge); medium flap (two bands of rows of three lozenges)
 Remarks: strap, rows of lozenges near edge, band of lozenges in rows of three at angle, broken at fold in
  center
 Also: sandal heel with added patch VA 9—4

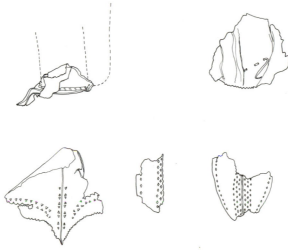

Figure 54. Quiver Fragments, VA 9—3. Scale 1:4.

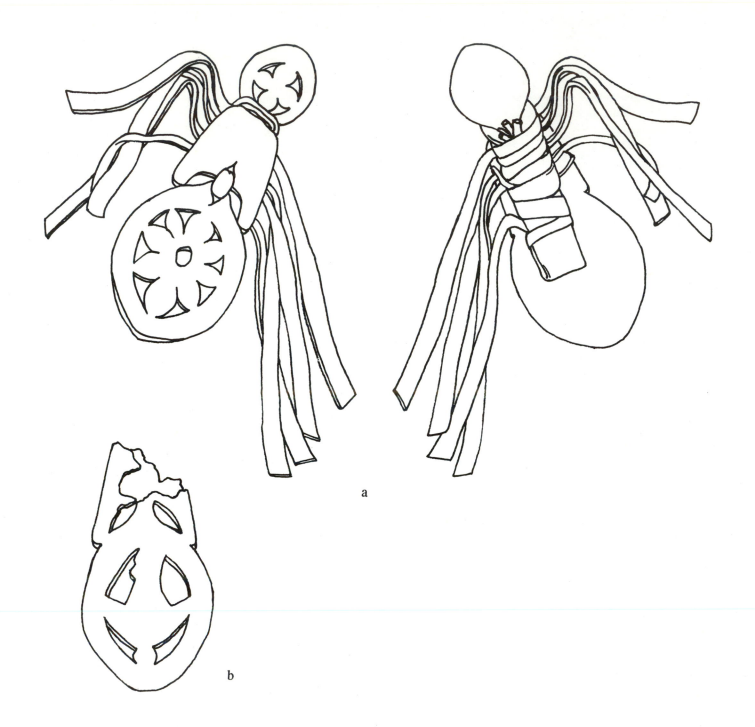

a

b

Figure 55. Leather "Bee" or "Fly," Q 74—7d. Scale 1:1.

Table 18. Register of Bags.

Tomb and Number	Descriptive Remarks
Q 1—2c	Bag with grommets, crudely sewn
Q 7—7	Upper edge of bag with drawstring
Q 39—7	Bag and other fragments
Q 51A—2e	Bag edge with tie hole
Q 60—4	Bottle or bag, some remains of side and bottom with residue
Q 74—4a	Bag with undulating strip and circles[a]
Q 74—4b	Bag edge or equipment belt
Q 74—7a	Parts of bag
Q 75—2	Bag fragments
Q 75—4	Bag remains
Q 76	Possible fragments of bag with Q 76—1
Q 79—1	Water bag(?) remains
Q 136—3	Bag fragments
Q 164—8	Bag with locking lid, two hinge straps, handle on front of lid, key lock with two slots and staples[b]
R 22—6b	Bag edge with grommets
R 49—6	Bag with folded-over edge and circular holes with tie tabs (?), water skin

a. Emery and Kirwan 1938, pl. 103-C.
b. Emery and Kirwan 1938, figs. 96, 98, 99, 116; Shafiq Farid 1963, pl. XL–XLI; for lock and straps, Kirwan 1939, pl. X-7; more elaborate, Emery and Kirwan 1938, pl. 69:A–C; also box lock, Bates and Dunham 1927, pl. XXXIII:A.

EQUIPMENT

LEATHER BAGS

The operational equipment included leather bags (pls. 67b–69), probably used to hold the iron tools common in this period. Most bags are of very dark tanned leather. Like the quivers, whose bases were often torn off to remove the arrowheads, the bodies of the bags were generally fragmentary. The bases, made of two layers, have an oval shape and the upper edges were reinforced and pierced with round holes for a drawstring. Often, these holes were protected by circular grommets. In one case, the edges of the strip undulate,[37] and small circular patches were sewn within the undulation and on the strip as a variation of the vine decoration.

One bag, with a curiously-shaped, almost gabled lid, was equipped with a lock (pl. 67a).[38]

WATER SKIN

Remains of a very large leather bag have a very smoothly bulged shape as though filled with water when deposited (pl. 69). The complete object was not preserved.[39]

SADDLES

The wooden parts of X-Group saddles as well as their remarkable decoration have been known since Emery and Kirwan excavated the royal tombs.[40] However, they were reconstructed as camel saddles which

37. Emery and Kirwan 1938, pl. 103-C.

38. For somewhat similar strap-locking devices, see Bates and Dunham 1927, pl. LXVI, fig. 17. See also Emery and Kirwan 1938, figs. 96, 98, 99, 116; Shafiq Farid 1963, pls. XL–XLI.

39. For the shape of grain and water bags as used in Sudan, see Acland 1932, pl. XXIII.

40. Emery and Kirwan 1938, pp. 259–61; for a later model, in clay, see Trigger 1967, pl. 20.

would be unsuitable for use on a horse. A saddle with its leather parts well preserved was found in animal pit Q 39 (no. 5, fig. 56) and with remains of pommels, cantles, and attachments for cinches (pls. 70, 72), it permitted a prototype horse saddle to be reconstructed. Various pads and cloths found or reconstructed by the earlier excavators were not preserved well enough to reconstruct (see pl. 29, however).

In opposition to the rigid wooden frame previously reconstructed, the version presented here is a complex and flexible military instrument. It was a successful prototype for military saddles in the Middle Ages,[41] and the major structural features were still recognizable in the latest United States cavalry saddles.[42]

The workmanship differs considerably from that of the quivers or guards; thongs are wider, holes more widely spaced and cutting much more irregular. The saddle was covered during use with pads and skins, with only the pommel and cantle projecting upward. These and a quarter strap bar were sometimes decorated with simple incised patterns. The coarser construction and simple decoration indicate that the saddles were made by different craftsmen than those who made quivers and armor.

STRUCTURE

The frame or tree of the X-Group saddle was constructed much like a skeleton, with hard parts of wood giving strength and rigidity in an otherwise flexible structure of leather.

Pommel and Cantle. As noted by Emery and Kirwan, the pommel was a symmetrically v-shaped piece of wood with a high paddle-shaped grip (fig. 57a–b). In the royal tombs this grip was sometimes decorated with elaborate silver plates. Some of the pommel-grips from the royal tombs were deeply grooved down the center. In the present material, the grip has a lower projection in front with a groove between it and the grip that apparently held the quarter strap.

Like the pommel, the cantle was a symmetrical inverted V of wood. However, instead of the paddle-shaped grip, a large ring made separately rose from the prongs.[43] The remaining fragments preserve no means of attachment; it may have been secured by the rear quarter strap.

Sidebars. Two wooden rods placed side by side and wrapped in a rectangular piece of leather with four roughly triangular skirts formed each sidebar (fig. 58). One had been repaired with a piece of rawhide.

Skirts. The triangular projections at the ends of the sidebars were sewn together with additional layers to make a boot or pocket open at the top. A prong of the pommel or cantle fit into each boot (fig. 59).

Seat. The seat of the saddle was a transverse hammock. This consisted of two rods with knobs at each end which supported a wide rectangular piece of leather wrapped and sewn around each rod. The seat rods rested on the prongs of the pommel and cantle (fig. 60).

Assembly. When removed from the horse, the seat was attached to the sidebars by partly braided thongs passed over the rods and inside the skirts (figs. 59 [left], 60). Knobs on the ends of the rods secured the thongs and kept the seat from sliding excessively.

Straps and Mounting. The X-Group saddle was held onto the back of the mount by quarter straps (braided thongs?) passed through the pommel slit and over the cantle. These quarter straps were attached to the cinch by a wooden bar with holes at each end for the quarter straps and one or two holes in the center to accept a thong or strap that held a cinch ring below. Although possibly made of multiple braided thongs or a linen strap (pl. 71, below, left), the material used for the cinch remains uncertain.

The curious wooden bar which acted as a combined quarter strap ring and safe possibly served another purpose as well (pl. 72; figs. 57, 60). To mount, the pommel and cantle ring could be grasped and the foot placed on the quarter strap bar. The bar could also make a convenient foot rest when riding at a jog-trot or using the bow.

41. See, for example Potratz 1966, fig. 35 and pp. 53–67 for the problem of riding.

42. For Bedja saddles with this general construction, with a transverse hammock seat, see du Bois-Aymé 1822, p. 390 and further notes by Acland (1932). The McClellan saddle adopted by the United States cavalry and used into World War II was adapted from the hussar saddle used in Central Europe. See Steffen 1973, especially pp. 63–73 and fig. 29; fig. 65 shows its latest use in service.

43. Emery and Kirwan 1938, p. 259 and pl. 63:A–C; remains of cantle rings found by The Oriental Institute were not preserved well enough to be restored.

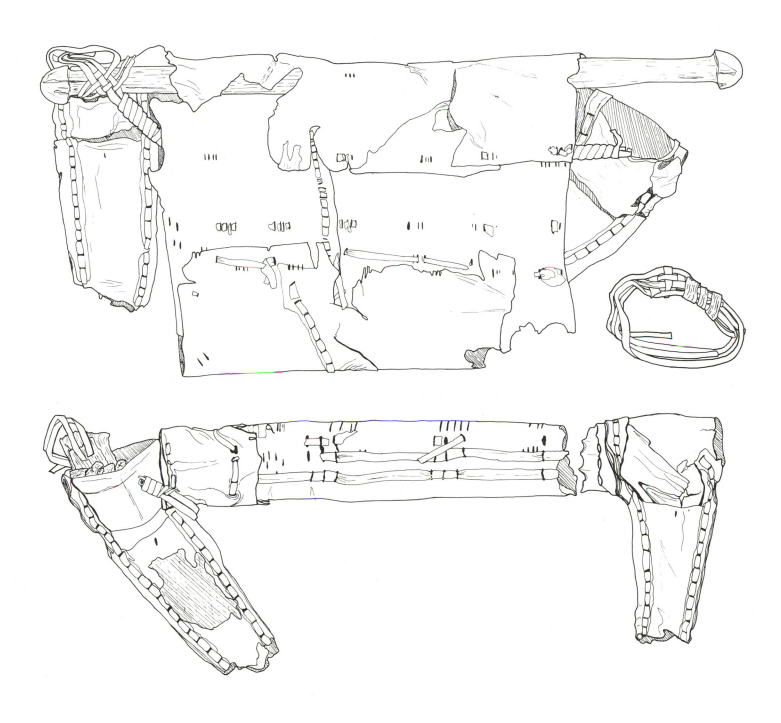

Figure 56. Saddle, Q 39—5. Scale 2:5.

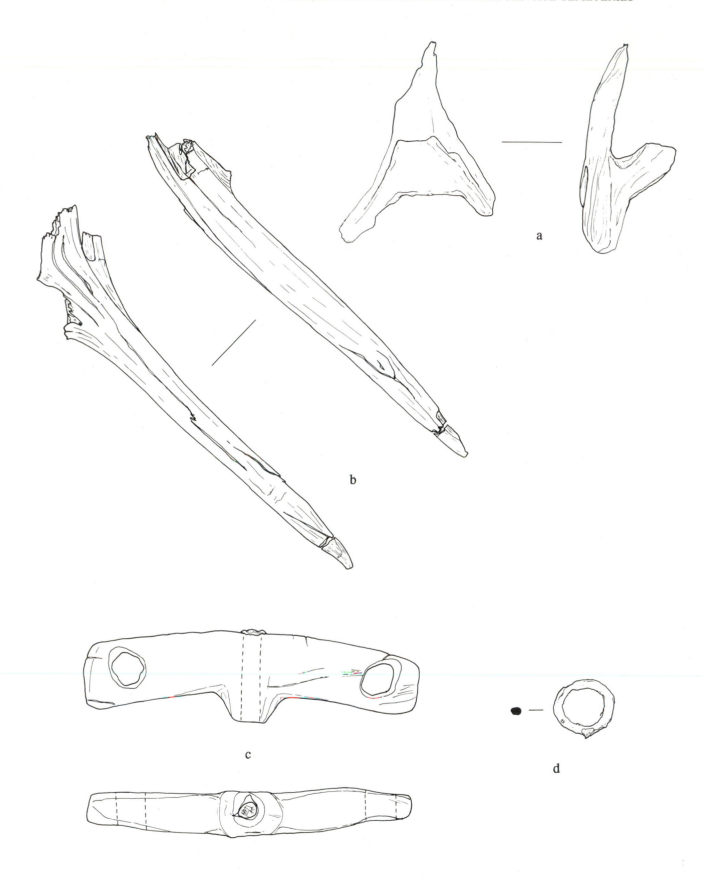

Figure 57. Fragments of Wooden Saddle Parts from Tombs Q 5, Q 39, and Q 265: (*a*) Pommel, Q 39—3d;
(*b*) Pommel, Q 5—12h; (*c*) Cinch Bar, Q 265—1; (*d*) Ring, Q 265—2a. Scale 2:5.

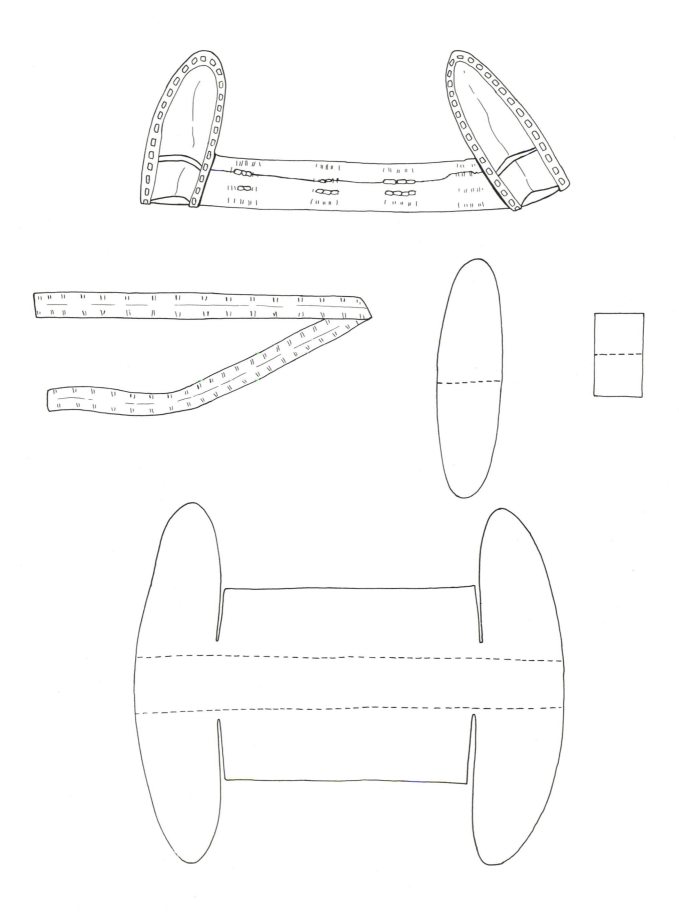

Figure 58. Construction and Assembly of a Sidebar. Scale 1:4.

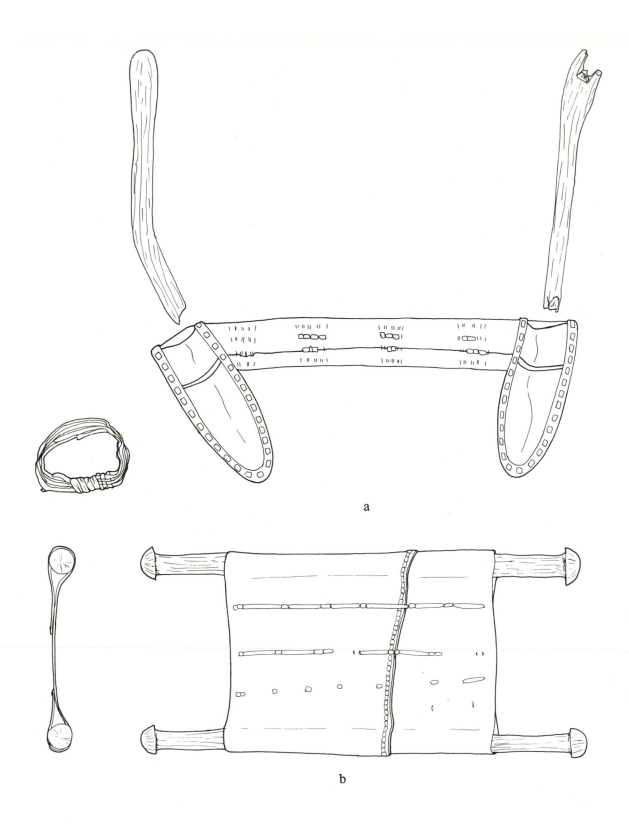

a

b

Figure 59. Assembly of a Saddle: (*a*) Addition of the Pommel and Cantle to the Saddle;
(*b*) The Hammock Seat. Scale 1:4.

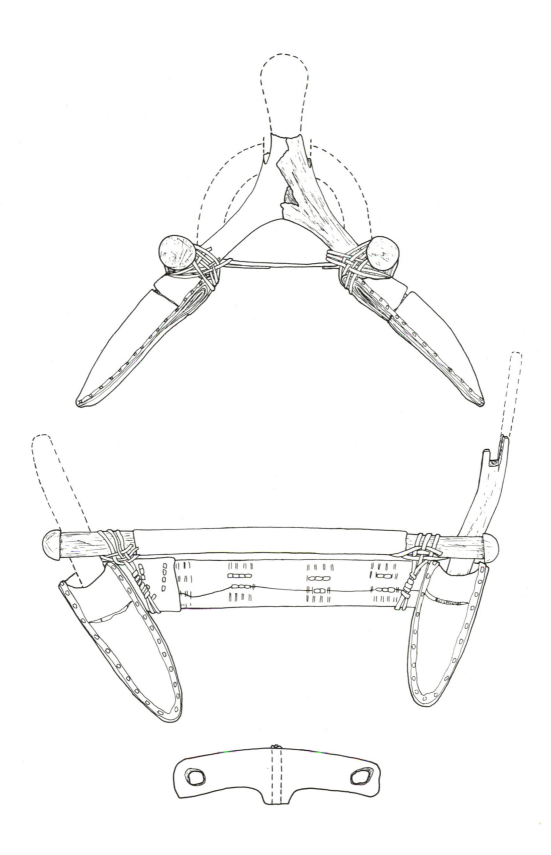

Figure 60. A Reconstruction of an X-Group Saddle (the Cinch Bar is from Tomb Q 265—1). Scale 1:4.

Table 19. Remains of Saddles.

Tomb and Object Number	Remarks
Q 5—12	
Q 5—14	
Q 5—18	
Q 20—3	
Q 20—4	
Q 39—5	Saddle with textile cover (? 2)
Q 264—1	Blanket or shabrack on A
Q 265—1	Cinch attachment

SADDLES: SUMMARY REMARKS

The X-Group saddle was closely related to the development of Eurasian saddles generally. Most of its parts were so precisely comparable to the parts of Medieval and modern (United States) cavalry saddles that saddlery terms could be applied without confusion.

HARNESS

Fragmentary remains of harness were found with the animal burials (pls. 73–75), but none were preserved well enough to indicate the structure of the bridle or the attachments of the saddle.[44] Parts of bits could be identified only by their resemblance to previously published examples.

Bits. Several fragments of Emery and Kirwan's type 3 bit, the hinged ring bit, were found in different sizes (pls. 74b, d[?], 75a–g). Corrosion prevented reliable measurement, even of the remaining fragments.

Rings. Rings were the main form of attachment in X-Group harness, and many were found in the animal burials, again of several sizes, but all large enough to receive fairly wide leather straps. In a few cases, these were locked together or still attached to loops in larger objects (pls. 73f, 74c, 75k).

Spikes. In addition to private tombs, spikes occur with the animal burials (pl. 73b–c). Here, they probably were attached to the harness in some way. It is difficult to determine how they were used.

Straps. Remains of metal straps could not be interpreted with confidence. One piece, with broadened flanges at the end, was smoothly curved (Q 5—9j). Remains of two others were straight and they narrowed toward the end where one was bent to secure a ring (Q 5—9l). Objects of this type were not published by Emery and Kirwan.

Plate(?) Remains of this object were so corroded that it could not be interpreted or restored. The remaining portion is a sickle-shaped plate, but a break at the blunt end indicates that the piece was much larger (Q 5—9i). A second curved piece may also have been attached. A ring was attached near the broken end, perhaps to a loop on one face. This object does not resemble any piece of harness previously published, but the corrosion has been so severe that it would be difficult to restore, even with comparisons.

Bells. Frequently found attached to harness, bells were also found at Meroe and Barkal. Although common in the royal tombs, only one large, bronze bell was found in this material (pl. 83g), with two small (1 × 2 cm) bronze(?) bells (pl. 83a, f), of a type also found at Firka.[45]

---

44. Emery and Kirwan 1938, pp. 251–59; Kirwan 1939, pl. XV; harness was also present at Gamai, but not preserved well enough to be reconstructed (Bates and Dunham 1927, pl. XXXVI:I).

45. Emery and Kirwan 1938, pp. 262–71; Kirwan 1939, pl. XVI; bells are well known in Kush (Dunham 1957, figs. 50, 73).

Table 20. Register of Harness Equipment.

Q 5—7	Iron bar or blade
Q 5—8	a. Fragments of bits. Four pieces.
	b. Fragments of rings. Four pieces.
	c. Fragments of block-like tool or rectangular harness-tube. Four pieces.
Q 5—9	a. Bit fragments (two)
	b. Bit fragment
	c. Double ring?
	d. Rod-end of cinch ring(?)
	e–h. Rings
	i. Uncertain flat curved piece
	j. Uncertain metal strap
	k. Bit fragment?
	l. As J(?), with two rings attached to one end
	(and various unidentified fragments)
Q 5—17	Two rings and fragments
Q 5—19	Rope remains
Q 12—3	Remains of cord (rope)
Q 12—4	Bronze ring
Q 20—2	Remains of iron rod
Q 20—5	a. Fragment of bit, L-shaped around cheek. With six fragments
	b. Fragment of bit(?). With a curve, three pieces, one with loop at end
	c. Strap or band, three pieces, one narrowed at end and bent up to secure ring
	d. Rings attached to loops. Four pieces
	e. Rings. Six complete or large fragments, nine small fragments
	f. Uncertain fragments, three pieces
	(found with and below second bone layer)
Q 26—1	Remains of rope
Q 38—2	Iron fragments
Q 39—3	a. Metal rings
	b. Leather straps
	c. Iron ring
	d. Wooden fragment
Q 39—4	Animal horns, possibly from bit (three)
Q 73—1	Rope remains
Q 73—3	Straps, bronze buckle, and iron rods
Q 148—11	Straps and bar
Q 264—2	Bronze bell of Emery-Kirwan type 12. Sound-cup with bead flange ring cast and hammered and welded to cup. The clapper is iron bar with a ring in the top hanging from a ring attached through a hole in the bell.
Q 264—3	Bridle ("of black or brown cloth with dark red 'bosses' still on skull; traces of brown cloth adhering to forehead")
Q 264—4	Ropes
Q 265—2	a. Iron ring
	b. Matting
	c. Ropes
	d. Beads
	e. Leather
Q 279—3	Small bronze hemisphere with a loop through the top, ca. 1 × 2 cm
R 4A—26	Small bronze (?) bell, as Q 279—3
Miscellaneous:	
Q 385—5a	Iron spike

D. JEWELRY

Like the cosmetic implements, jewelry in private tombs is much reduced in quantity and variety in X-Group. Moreover, the shapes were very different.

EARRINGS

The basic shape of the X-Group earring is a simple bar pointed at either end. A pendant, often welded to the bar, tapers from it to a ball terminal (fig. 61b–e, pl. 76e–g). In some cases, the ball-terminal is a bead. This earring type was derived from the Mediterranean (fig. 61a, f–h).[46]

Table 21. Register of Jewelry Objects.

Scarabs
Chapel QB 41
Q 1—6
R 67—1

Earrings
Q 38—6 (1)
Q 41—4 (1)
Q 68—6 (2)
Q 74—13 (1)
Q 75—5 (1)
Q 107—5b (1)
Q 164—15 (1)
Q 344—4 (1)
R 74—2 (1)
V 9—5 (2, iron)
V 202—2 (1, iron[?])

Bracelets and anklets
Q 41—3 (5)
Q 134—10 (1, ivory)
Q 143—2 (1, iron)
Q 143—12 (1, ivory fragment)
Q 152—3 (anklet, silver)
Q 164—10 (1, iron)
Q 378—14 (1)
Q 378—16 (1, anklet, string and feathers)

Other objects
Q 5—5 (silver stud)
Q 62—3 (silver stud or tack)
Q 137—1 (ivory lion head)
Q 137—5 (stud)
Q 164—20 (bronze fragment)
Q 320—5 (copper double coil)
Q 434—6 (damaged wedjat eye amulet)

Pendants
Q 5—6 (copper, on ring)
Q 5—16 (silver)
Q 10—5 (carnelian)
Q 27—1 (bone)
Q 107—5a (3, bone)
Q 134—18
Q 143—13 (copper *ankh*)
Q 164—11 (faience ram's head with sun disc, fragment)
Q 174—3b
Q 338—8
Q 345—16

Rings
Q 64—1
Q 84—1
Q 134—4 (5, copper)
Q 134—13 (copper wire)
Q 141—6 (2)
Q 149—6 (2)
Q 332—6 (2)
Q 349—4 (with key)
Q 350—10 (2)
Q 387—4 (iron)
Q 501—5 (silver)
R 16—1 (iron)
R 16—2 (2, iron)
R 69—2 (5)
V 12—2a (silver[?])
V 14—10
V 68—1 (3)
W 74—7

Ring-pendants
Q 344—5
Q 350—7
Q 463—2

46. Emery and Kirwan 1938, pp. 193–196, also pl. 41.

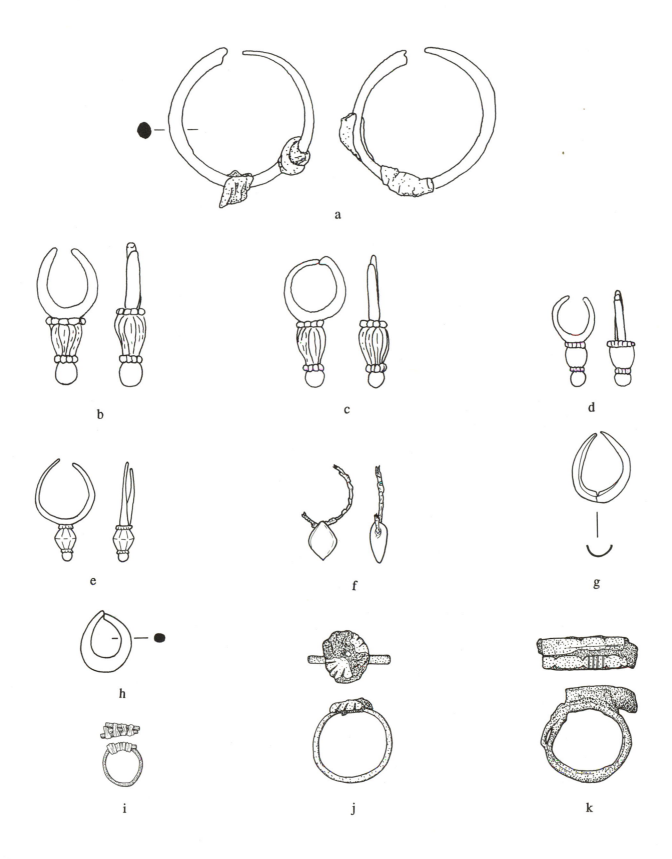

Figure 61. Jewelry: (*a*) VA 9—5; (*b*) Q 38—6; (*c*) Q 74—13; (*d*) Q 344—4; (*e*) Q 75—5; (*f*) Q 68—6; (*g*) Q 501—5; (*h*) VA 12—2a; (*i*) R 74—2; (*j*) R 16—1; (*k*) R 16—2. Scale 1:1.

RING-PENDANTS

Convex stone or glass discs with holes in the centers and slots to the edges also have pierced lugs at the top for stringing. Examples from the Ballana cemetery were parts of necklaces.[47]

OTHER PENDANTS

A variety of pendants were reused in X-Group times. This collection included a faience ram's head with a sun disc and uraei (fig. 65e) and the upper part of a deep blue Osiris (fig. 65g).

RINGS, BRACELETS, AND ANKLETS

The most common jewelry objects were simple wire-spiral rings and twisted metal rods, often with loops at the ends, used for bracelets and anklets. Most objects were iron or copper, although an anklet and some rings were silver (fig. 61i–k, pl. 77). The one unusual ring was a band with a key soldered to it (Q 349—4).

OTHER OBJECTS

Scarabs were reused and not typical of the age. One fine ivory lion's head was clearly applied to some object, but its use was not obvious (Q 137—1, fig. 149c). Although the head resembles lions on Byzantine period incense burners,[48] no parallels are obvious.

BEADS

Beads did not occur as frequently in X-Group as in Meroitic times and they tended to be larger and cruder (figs. 62–64). Ostrich eggshell beads, which were rare in Meroitic Lower Nubia, became common again, and are more numerous in this material than other kinds. The difference between Meroitic and X-Group beads therefore represents a substantial change. The types of beads closely parallel those found in the royal tombs. Table 22 assigns the beads (see the *Bead Type* number) to Emery and Kirwan's type series, indicated by simple Arabic numbers. Reused Meroitic beads are assigned to categories from Dunham's corpus, indicated by Roman numerals.[49]

Table 22. Register of Beads.

Tomb/Object Number and Bead Type	Material	Dimensions in mm	Count	Remarks
Qu. 7—3				fig. 63t
QC 4—2				
4	Orange glass	6.2 × 7.2	2	fig. 62h
37	Blue faience	6.8 × 4.9	1	
73	Blue faience	1.1 × 4.4	2	
73	Blue faience	1.8 × 2.9	3	
73	Green glass, double	4.1 × 3.0	1	
QC 9—1				Meroitic or even New Kingdom
Is	Blue and white glass, blobs	6.5 × 7.5	1	All Meroitic types
VIs	Yellow glass, double	3.3 × 2.5	3	
VIs	Red glass, quadruple	4.8 × 2.4	1	

47. Emery and Kirwan 1938, pl. 46, Ba. 47–57.

48. Emery and Kirwan 1938, pp. 362–63, pl. 96.

49. For types, see Emery and Kirwan 1938, pls. 43–44. See also OINE VIII, *Chapter 3*, pp. 111–14 for remarks on beads.

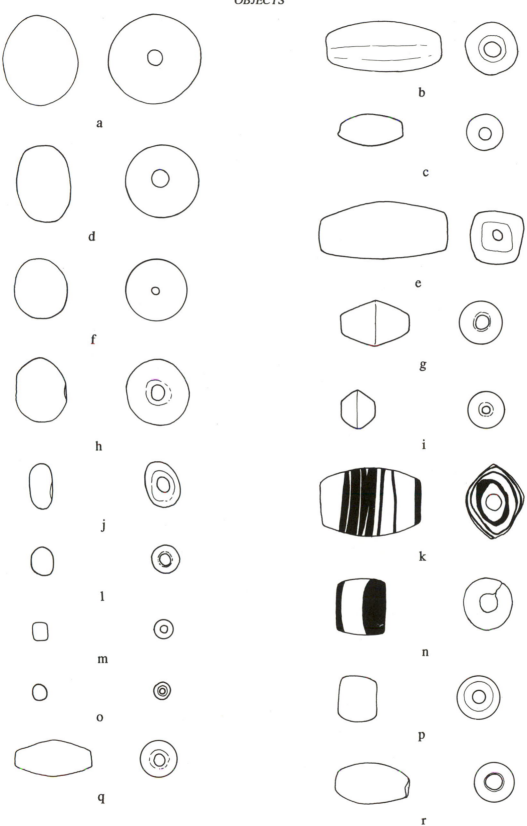

Figure 62. Beads: (*a*) 1 [Carnelian], Q 434—6; (*b*) 21 [Blue Glass], Q 64—2; (*c*) 22 [Blue Glass], Q 4—1; (*d*) 1 [Translucent Glass], Q 33—6; (*e*) 23 [White Glass], Q 434—6; (*f*) 3 [Red Glass], W 84—1; (*g*) 24 [Blue Glass], Q 434—6; (*h*) 4 [Orange Glass], QC 4—2; (*i*) 26 [Blue Faience], Q 27—1; (*j*) 11 [Red-orange Faience], Q 32—2; (*k*) 27 [Striped White Glass], Q 434—6; (*l*) 11–12 [Light Blue Faience], Q 27—1; (*m*) 14, W 74—2; (*n*) 28 [Black Glass with White Stripe], R 74—1; (*o*) 17 [Green Faience], Q 41—1; (*p*) 28 [Blue Glass], R 74—1; (*q*) 24 [Dark Blue Glass], Q 134—12; (*r*) 29 [Blue Glass], V 41—4. Scale 2:1.

Table 22. Register of Beads (*cont.*).

Tomb/Object Number and Bead Type	Material	Dimensions in mm	Count	Remarks
QC 9—1 (*cont.*)				
Va	Red glass	5.6 × 2 5	1	
VIf–i	Blue glass	1.3 × 4.5	2	
VIe–i	Blue faience	1.5 × 3.0	2	
VIe–i	Blue faience	1.5 × 2.2	4	
Ih	Gilded glass	4.6 × 6.0	1	
Q 1—3				
14	Carnelian	4.0 × 4.5	1	
14	Carnelian	3.0 × 3.7	2	
14	Blue faience	2.7 × 4.0	13	
73	Ostrich eggshell	1.6 × 3.6	4	
Q 2—10				
14	Blue faience	2.4 × 3.7	28	
73	Ostrich eggshell	1.5 × 2.4	1	
3	Black and yellow glass with white stripe	7.0 × 7.8	2	
14	Red glass	2.9 × 4.0	1	
14	White glass	3.3 × 3.9	1	
37	Quartz	6.2 × 7.3	1	
Pendant	Blue faience	3.0 × 5.3 × 4.4	1	
Q 3—7				fig. 64j
73	Ostrich eggshell	1.5 × 3.6	398	
78	Green glass	2.6 × 8.8	12	
14	Blue faience	2.8 × 3.2	1	
14	Blue glass	2.0 × 3.0	2	
14	Orange glass	2.2 × 3.0	4	
28	Red glass	3.7 × 4.0	1	
Q 4—1				
22	Blue glass	7.5 × 4.1	1	fig. 62c
Q 8—10				
80	White glass	6.0 × 9.2	1	
14	Blue faience	3.0 × 4.0	9	
73	Ostrich eggshell	1.8 × 3.4	6	
73	Ostrich eggshell	1.5 × 6.5	1	
14	Blue faience	3.4 × 4.1	5	
14	Blue faience	3.4 × 4.8	1	
11	Dark blue glass	3.9 × 6.4	1	
Q 8B—1				
3	Blue glass	7.8 × 8.2	2	
3	Green glass	7.8 × 8.2	1	
4	Glue glass	4.5 × 7.0	1	
Q 9—10				pl. 76d
52	Silver or pewter, slightly flattened, line ca. 1.0 mm	1.07 × 6.2–6.7	2	(from each end); fig. 63p
52	Agate, same as above	1.36 × 6 7	1	fig. 63r
Ir–s	Black and white striped red glass	0.94 × 1.03	1	Meroitic

Figure 63. Beads (*cont.*): (*a*) 32 [Black and White Glass], Q 30—2; (*b*) 46 [Blue Glass], W 80—4; (*c*) 30 [Brown-purple Glass], Q 33—6; (*d*) 47 [Translucent Red Glass], Q 143—1; (*e*) Pendant Bead, Q 174—3a; (*f*) 48 [Carnelian], Q 434—6; (*g*) 50 [White Glass], Q 227—6; (*h*) 36 [Blue Faience], Q 164—18; (*i*) 50 [Green Glass, Q 434—6; (*j*) Vb [Bone], Q 136—5; (*k*) 51 [Translucent Glass], Q 164—18; (*l*) 38/39 [Green Glass], Q 134—12; (*m*) 45/46 [Dark Blue Glass], Q 134—12; (*n*) 38/39 [Green Glass], Q 134—12; (*o*) 44 [Dark Blue Glass], Q 164—18; (*p*) 52 [Silver or Pewter], Q 9—10; (*q*) 44 [Opaque Red Glass], R 1—3; (*r*) 52 [Agate], Q 9—10; (*s*) 45 [Blue Glass], W 80—4; (*t*) 53, Qu. 7—3. Scale 2:1.

Table 22. Register of Beads (*cont.*).

Tomb/Object Number and Bead Type	Material	Dimensions in mm	Count	Remarks
Q 11—3				
27/37	Blue faience	6.8 × 4.8	1	
Ik	Blue faience	7.1 × 7.9	1	Meroitic
Q 13—1				
11	Blue glass	2.8 × 3.8	1	
45	Dark blue glass	3.9 × 4.4	1	
Q 14—4	Loose beads			
Q 15—1				
VIs	Gilded glass, triple	12.0 × 4.6	5	Meroitic
Q 18—12				
14	Blue glass	1.4 × 2.4	10	
14	Yellow-brown glass	2.0 × 4 0	57	
14	Yellow-brown glass, double	3.5 × 5 8	12	
14	Yellow-brown glass, triple	3.4 × 8.7	1	
14	Blue-green faience	1.8 × 3 7	26	
14	Green glass	2.2 × 3.7	4	
14	Blue glass, double	3.7 × 5.0	9	
14	Blue glass, triple	3.5 × 8.3	3	
14	Blue glass, quadruple	3.3 × 10.3	1	
14	Red glass	2.1 × 3.1	6	
14	Red glass, double	3 3 × 5.7	1	
14	Red glass, triple	4.2 × 8.8	1	
53	White glass	5.7 × 6.9		
53	Carnelian(?)	6.0 × 7.1	1	
Q 27—1				
26	Blue faience	3.8 × 4.5	2	fig. 62i
11–12	Light blue faience	3.0–3.8 × 3.2–3.9	30	fig. 62l
No type	Bone			fig. 65a, c
Q 30—2				
45	Dark blue glass	6.6 × 5.5	1	
45	Dark blue glass, red and white eyes	5.2 × 5.2	1	
32	Dark blue glass with blue and white eyes	5.0 × 5.0	1	
32	Black and white mottled glass	7.2 × 7.5	1	fig. 63a
45	Dark blue-black glass	8.0 × 8.5	1	
Q 31—1				
73	Ostrich eggshell	1.6 × 3.5	8	
Q 32—2				
28	Blue faience	3.2 × 3.5	11	
28	Green glass	3.2 × 3.5	1	
11	Red-orange faience	2.6 × 4.9	1	fig. 62j
Q 33—6				
14	Blue faience	2.5 × 4.0	255	
1	Translucent glass	7.0 × 9.0	1	fig. 62d
14	Green glass	2.3 × 3.2	1	

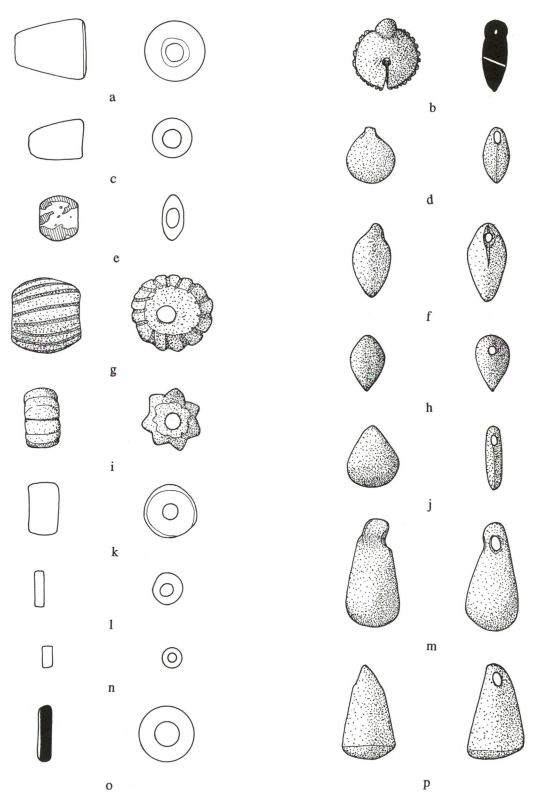

Figure 64. Beads (*cont.*) and Pendants: (*a*) 53 [Quartz], Q 68—5; (*b*) 74 [Yellow Glass Pendant], Q 344—3; (*c*) IV?, R 15—6; (*d*) 78 [White Glass], W 80—4; (*e*) 61 [Diorite], Q 143—1; (*f*) 78 [Carnelian Pendant], Q 320—5; (*g*) 68 [Dark Blue Glass], Q 136—5; (*h*) 80 [White Glass], Q 82—5; (*i*) 68 [Gilded Glass or Clear Stone], Q 136—5; (*j*) 84, Q 3—7; (*k*) 73 [Ostrich Eggshell], R 1—3; (*l*) 73 [Ostrich Eggshell], R 74—1; (*m*) 85, Q 184—2; (*n*) 14/73 [Carnelian], Q 134—12; (*o*) VI? [Black and White Stone], Q 67—13; (*p*) 85, Q 164—18. Scale 2:1.

Table 22. Register of Beads (*cont.*).

Tomb/Object Number and Bead Type	Material	Dimensions in mm	Count	Remarks
Q 33—6 (*cont.*)				
47	Orange glass	4.4 × 5.1	1	
28	Orange glass	3.4 × 4.8	1	
30	Brown-purple glass	3.4 × 3.7	1	fig. 63c
IIh	Blue glass	4.3 × 4.7	1	Meroitic
IIn	Blue glass	4.3 × 4.5	1	
Q 34—2				
28	Blue glass	8.0 × 8.7	1	
45	Bark blue glass	4.0 × 4.0	1	
Q 36—2				
14	Blue faience	2.5 × 4.0	64	
14	Green faience with two red stripes	2.5 × 4.0	1	
73	Ostrich eggshell	2.0 × 3.8	17	
Q 37—4				
28	Red faience	6.2 × 6.6	2	
Q 38—5				
28/73	Blue glass	2.6 × 3.6	6	
IVb	White glass	9.4 × 7.8	1	Meroitic
73	Ostrich eggshell	1.9 × 3.2	1,300	Approximate, still strung
Q 41—1				
73	Ostrich eggshell	ca. 1.6 × 3.6	1,500	Strung alone, many strings
17	Green faience, glass-like	0.6–1.0 × 1.5	3–500	fig. 62o
14	Green glass, translucent-opaque	2.0 × 4.0	68	Variable size, strung alone
14	Blue-green glass	1.8 × 3.3	4	
45	Dark blue glass (four facets)	2.4 × 2.6	11	
39	Orange-pink glass	3.3 × 2.3	19	Poor
No type	Rectangular bars, silver(?)	1.5 × 10.0 × 2.4	23	Three holes in each flat side for stringing; fig. 65i
Q 41—1				
73	Ostrich eggshell	1.9 × 3.0	71	Strung object, bracelet or anklet(?)
Q 41—5				
37	Carnelian(?)	5.5 × 11.8	5	
Q 42—7				
14	Blue faience	3.0 × 3.7	2	
14	Blue faience	3.1 × 4.4	1	
11	Yellow faience	2.7 × 3.5	1	
Q 42—8				
11	Light blue faience	2.8 × 4.2	1	
Q 44—2				pl. 76c
73	Ostrich eggshell	1.5 × 3.0	12	
78	Carnelian	4.5 × 8.3	5	
14	Green glass	1.4 × 1 9	1	

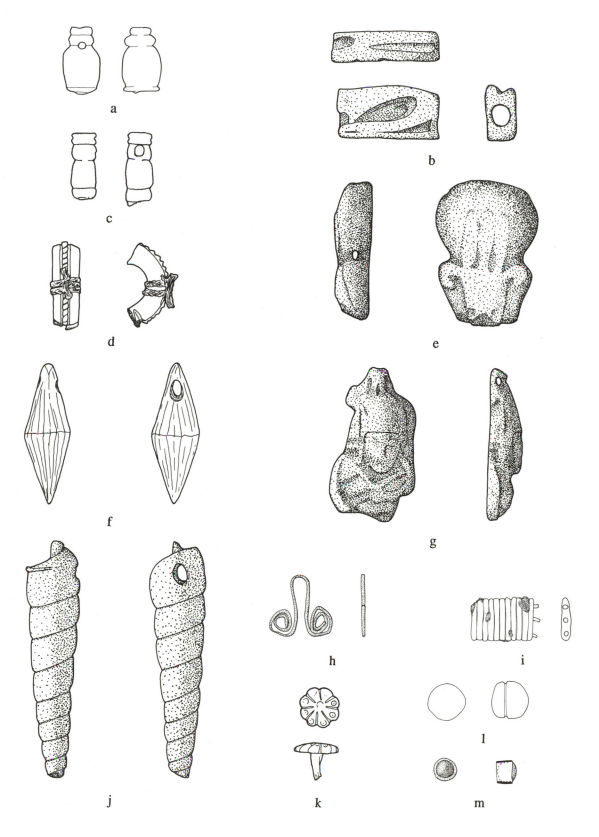

Figure 65. Various Pendants, Amulets, Hair-Ring, and Shell Jewelry Items: (*a*) Bone Pendant Q, 27—1; (*b*) Damaged *Wedjat* Eye, Q 434—6; (*c*) Bone Pendant, Q 27—1; (*d*) Faience Hair-Ring, Q 463—2; (*e*) Faience Pendant, Ram's Head with Sun Disc, Q 164—11; (*f*) Wooden Pendant, Q 345—16; (*g*) Blue Faience Pendant, Q 134—18; (*h*) Copper Double Coil, Q 320—5; (*i*) Lead(?) Spacer, Q 41—1; (*j*) Spiral Shell Pendant, Q 174—3b; (*k*) Silver Stud or "Tack," Q 62—3; (*l*) Carnelian Red Stud or Earring(?), Q 75—6; (*m*) Dark Blue Stone Set in Metal Band, Q 143—1. Scales: (*a, c, d, h–m*) 1:1, (*b, e–g*) 2:1.

Table 22. Register of Beads (*cont.*).

Tomb/Object Number and Bead Type	Material	Dimensions in mm	Count	Remarks
Q 44—2 (*cont.*)				
14	Orange-red glass	2.8 × 4.5	1	
28	Blue-black glass	5.5 × 5.6	1	
14	Blue faience	2.3 × 2.8	39	
14	Blue glass	2.5 × 3.0	11	
Pendant	Blue faience	4.5 × 13.5	1	Amun-ram with disc
Pendant	Blue faience	2.8 × 9.5	1	Rosette
39	Orange glass	3.2 × 4.0	6	
Q 49—4	Bead			
Q 51A—5				
14	Blue faience	2.9 × 3.9	12	
73	Ostrich eggshell	1.6 × 3.3	11	
73	Ostrich eggshell	1.6 × 7.0	1	

Stringing partly preserved; alternating faience, ostrich eggshell.

Tomb/Object Number and Bead Type	Material	Dimensions in mm	Count	Remarks
Q 52—4				
14	Green faience	2.7 × 3.7	47	
37	Green faience	3.6 × 4.3	11	
14	Green glass	2.6 × 4 2	1	
14	Orange glass	3.5 × 4.5	2	
14	Blue glass	3.0 × 4.0	3	
14	Blue faience	2.5 × 3.7	6	
Q 54—12	Beads (Cairo)			
Q 56—3	Bead (inside Q 56—1)			
Q 58—6				
3	Carnelian	5.5 × 6.1	1	
14	Blue faience	2.6 × 4.0	1	
14	Blue faience	2.1 × 2.4	1	
73	Ostrich eggshell	2.3 × 4.5	5	Thick
Q 58—6				
3	Carnelian	3.6 × 4.7	1	
14/17	Blue faience	2.2 × 3.0	1	
73	Ostrich eggshell	1.7 × 4.9	3	
Q 59—4				
Q 61—1, 2				Carnelian beads are possibly Q 61—2
73	Ostrich eggshell	1.5 × 3.5	92	
14	Blue faience	2.9 × 3.6	110	
14	Blue glass	2.2 × 3.5		
30	White glass	4.5 × 5 3	3	
3	White glass	4.3 × 4 7	10	
30	Gilded glass	4.0 × 4 6	5	
30	Silver glass	4.2 × 4.9	6	
3	Same	4.9 × 5.6	3	
3	Carnelian	4.6 × 5.0	18	
29	Carnelian	5.2 × 6.1	1	
80	Carnelian	5.9 × 9.6	1	
28	Quartz	4.9 × 5.0	2	

Table 22. Register of Beads (*cont.*).

Tomb/Object Number and Bead Type	Material	Dimensions in mm	Count	Remarks
Q 62—22				
1	Red glass, eye, blue, black, white, black	6.1 × 8.5	1	
27	Blue faience	5.6 × 4.1	1	
15	Blue faience	3.0 × 3.7	7	15 and 73 alternate on
73	Ostrich eggshell	1.6 × 3.4	7	twisted double strand also, silver rosette, from leather(?)
3	Carnelian	4.7 × 4.9	1	
Q 64—2				pl. 76h
14	Green faience	3.0 × 3.5	180	
21	Blue glass	7.0 × 14.0	2	fig. 62b
46	Carnelian	7.7 × 14.5	6	
47	Carnelian	3.8 × 4.6	1	
26	Carnelian	6.1 × 8.4	1	
20?	Quartz	6.1 × 10.2	1	
Q 67—5b	Strings of ostrich eggshell beads			
Q 67—13				
	Ring bead, black and white, stone(?) or glass	1.5 × 6.0 × 1.3	1	fig. 64o
Q 67—14				
Q 68—5				
53(?)	Quartz	9.6 × 8.0	7	or Meroitic IVf; fig. 64a
	Dark blue glass	9.6 × 8.0	1	
	Carnelian	9.6 × 8.0	1	
30	Red faience	5.7 × 5.6	1	
14	Blue faience	3.2 × 3.6	1	
30	Gilded glass (decomposed)	9.1 × 4.4	1	
Q 68—6				
26	Earring	7.8 × 10.3	1	Carnelian pendant added
Q 69—2				
14	Red-orange glass	2.5 × 4.0	8	
14	Blue glass	2.4 × 3.3	6	
14	Blue glass	2.4 × 3.3	3	
73	Ostrich eggshell	1.6 × 2.3	1	
Q 74—12				
27/37	Blue glass	5.4 × 4.8	1	
Q 75—6				
37	Blue glass	5.2 × 4.9	1	
11	Yellow and blue glass		1	Horizontal stripes
11	Yellow and blue glass		1	Vertical stripes
26	Earring with carnelian bead domical mottled red stud			(Q 75—5); fig. 65l
Q 76—3				
37	Blue faience	4.9 × 5.0	1	
26	Amethyst	3.9 × 4.6	1	

Table 22. Register of Beads (*cont.*).

Tomb/Object Number and Bead Type	Material	Dimensions in mm	Count	Remarks
Q 82—5				
73	Ostrich eggshell	1.9 × 3.7	93	
14	Blue faience	3.2 × 3.9	1	
80	White glass	4.9 × 7.2	1	fig. 64h
Q 82—6				Necklace, still strung
73	Ostrich eggshell	1.6 × 3.7	1000	Approximate
Q 84—4	Beads			
Q 107—5				(Q 415, Cairo 89903)
a.	Blue faience			
Q 133—1				
36	Green faience	2.8 × 1.1	2	
28	Blue glass	3.5 × 3.8	3	
27	Red glass	6.2 × 6.8	2	
14	Red glass	2.7 × 3.2	9	
4	Red glass	6.4 × 8.3	1	
3	Red glass	6.4 × 6.9	2	
Q 134—12				
51	Blue faience, short	10.5 × 15.4 × 4.7–7.1	42	Size approximate
11	Translucent glass	2.5 × 5.2	2	
45/46	Dark blue glass	5.3 × 4.0	18	fig. 63m
11	Dark blue glass	3.1 × 5.7	2	
28	Dark blue glass	4.3 × 4.7	17	
20	Dark blue glass	11.0 × 5.5	6	fig. 62q
20	Light blue glass	11.0 × 5.5	1	
14	Red glass, opaque	3.6 × 3.4	75	Crude
14	Double	3.6 × 3.4	5	
14	Dark blue glass	3.6 × 3.4	15	
14	Translucent blue and green	3.6 × 3.4	57	
38/39	Green glass	2.6 × 2.2	13	fig. 63l, n
38/39	Double	2.6 × 2.2	1	
14/73	Carnelian	6.0 × 2.1	27	New Kingdom; fig. 64n
14	Diorite	6.0 × 2.1	4	New Kingdom
14	Green glass faience, opaque	0.9 × 2.1	7	
38	Bone	4.9 × 4.5 × 1.2	9	
1/28	Green glass, opaque.	4.9 × 5.1	1	
73	Ostrich eggshell	1.9 × 4.0	17	
Q 134—18				
IIIj–k	Dark blue glass; head and torso	0.9 × 1.9 × 4.8	1	Meroitic; fig. 65g
Q 135—5				
73	Ostrich eggshell	1.5 × 3.5	113	
39	Black glass	2.2 × 2.8	5	
14	Green glass	2.0 × 3.4	59	
14	Blue faience	1.8 × 3.0	2	
14	Red glass	2.2 × 3.2	24	
14	Gilded glass	1.6 × 2.7	1	
20	Red glass	4.2 × 11 7	1	
37	Blue faience	5.4 × 9.8	15	
28	Green glass	6.6 × 7.2	1	
78	Quartz	8.3 × 10.5 × 14.6	1	

Table 22. Register of Beads (*cont.*).

Tomb/Object Number and Bead Type	Material	Dimensions in mm	Count	Remarks
Q 136—5				fig. 64g, i
Vb	Bone			fig. 63j
Q 137—4				
a.				
14	Blue faience	3.5 × 4.5	181	
80	Red glass	6.3 × 10.5	2	
80	White glass	6.7 × 10.7	2	
28	Red glass	4.3 × 4.9	1	
b.				
14	Blue faience	3.5 × 4.4	16	
78?	Blue faience	6.5 × 11.4	1	
73	Ostrich eggshell	1.5 × 3.0	2	
28	Green faience	7.7 × 9.1	1	
	Black glossy seed	3.5 × 4.2	5	
Q 141—2	Apparently the same as Q 141—5.			
Q 141—5				
14	Yellow glass	2.8 × 3.5	1	
73	Ostrich eggshell	1.5 × 3.0	92	
14	Red glass	2.2 × 2.9	88	
14	Double	2.7 × 5.7	2	
14	Blue glass	2.3 × 3.0	163	
14	Double	3.0 × 5.8	6	
14	Triple	3.5 × 5.7	1	
Q 143—1				fig. 65m
14/73	Blue-green faience	2.2 × 4.2	8–9	
	Blue faience	3.0 × 3.6	1	
28	Green glass	3.5 × 3.8	1	
28	Blue glass	3.6 × 4.1	1	Crude
VIs	Gilded glass, double	3.5 × 2.5	2	Meroitic
IVb–c	Silvered glass	6.4 × 4.6	1	Meroitic
14	Orange glass	2.5 × 4.1	1	
61	Diorite	4.7 × 5.2 × 2.2	2	fig. 64e
47	Red glass, translucent	4.0 × 5.2	1	fig. 63d
11	Red glass, opaque	3.2 × 4.1	1	
53	Red glass, opaque, elongated	8.0 × 4.9	1	
73	Ostrich eggshell	1.9 × 3.2	400	Approximate
Q 145—1	Beads			
Q 148—10				
48	Carnelian	14.9 × 7.2	1	
Xf	Gilded glass	3.4 × 2.4–4.2	1	Meroitic
Q 149—7				
73	Ostrich eggshell	1.8 × 4.1	570	Approximate
14	Blue glass	3.0 × 4.0	2	
39	Green faience	3.6 × 5.3	1	

Table 22. Register of Beads (*cont*.).

Tomb/Object Number and Bead Type	Material	Dimensions in mm	Count	Remarks
Q 152—7				Note that the beads were originally strung on a cord with a knot, but are now completely encrusted.
19/26	Wood?	7.9–12.5 × 7.4	34	Many strung
73	Ostrich eggshell	1.6 × 4.1		
14	Black glass	2.7 × 4.7	1	
37	Blue faience	9.3 × 5.8	1	
Q 161—7				
73	Ostrich eggshell	1.5 × 3.5	1,500	Approximate
Q 164—16				
14	Blue glass	2.8 × 3.4	49	
14	Red glass	3.0 × 3.5	5	
Q 164—18				
89	Blue glass, carinated below	7.5–10.5 × 10.2	Uncertain	Pendant; fig. 64p
22	Quartz	8.7 × 7.5	Uncertain	Crude
22	Tooth	5.5 × 4.8	Uncertain	Crude
84	Quartz(?)	7.8 × 9.3	Uncertain	Pendant
84	Quartz(?)	× 5.5	Uncertain	Pendant
61	Gilded glass	—	Uncertain	
14	Red glass, opaque	2.5 × 3.5	Uncertain	
14	Green glass	1.5 × 2.2–3.0	Uncertain	
73	Ostrich eggshell	1.6 × 3.4	Uncertain	
51	Translucent glass	10.0 × 2.8	Uncertain	fig. 63k
36	Blue faience	15.4 × 5.5	Uncertain	Poor; fig. 63h
37	Blue faience	6.0 × 4.0	Uncertain	
44	Dark blue glass	1.0 × 5.8	1	fig. 63o

Stringing:

Red glass beads (Type #14) alone
Green glass beads (Type #14) alone
Ostrich eggshell beads (Type #73) alone (three strands together)
Blue glass beads (Type #89) with red glass beads (Type #14) on either side
Quartz beads (Type #84) with gilded glass beads (Type #61)

Tomb/Object Number and Bead Type	Material	Dimensions in mm	Count	Remarks
Q 174—3a	Pendant bead			fig. 63e
Q 184—2, 6				fig. 64m
73	Ostrich eggshell	1.5 × 3.5	712	
37	Blue faience	5.2 × 7.3	39	
78	Blue glass	6.3 × 14.8	1	
3	Blue glass with white stripe	6.9 × 8.4	1	
14	Blue faience	3.9 × 6.6	Uncertain	
Q 186—1	Beads			
Q 192—5				
14	Gilded glass, double	2.0 × 3.3	1	
73	Ostrich eggshell	1.3 × 3.0	24	
14	Red glass	2.3 × 3.4	2	
28	Red glass	4.4 × 5.0	2	
14	Blue glass	2.5 × 3.5	52	

Table 22. Register of Beads (*cont.*).

Tomb/Object Number and Bead Type	Material	Dimensions in mm	Count	Remarks
Q 192—5 (*cont.*)				
14	Red glass, double	3.2 × 6.1	4	
14	Blue glass, double	3.0 × 6.0	3	
14	Blue glass, triple	3.0 × 8.0	1	
78	Red glass	9.3 × 14.2	1	
22	Brown seed	4.6 × 7.6	1	
47	Green glass	5.8 × 5.9	2	
28	Red, yellow, green glass	6.4 × 6.6	4	
28	Blue glass	4.7 × 6.8	7	
37	Blue faience	5.5 × 7.8	23	
39	Blue faience	4.1 × 7.7	7	
Pendant	Red glass, broken	4.6 × 7.6	1	
Q 196—7	Beads			
Q 227—1	Bead bracelet			
Q 227—6				
a.				
73	Ostrich eggshell	1.4 × 2.5	222	
3	White glass	3.5 × 3.8	2	
3	Red glass	3.5 × 3.8	1	
50	White glass	4.9 × 22.8	1	fig. 63g
50	Red glass	4.5 × 23.7	1	
b.				
50	Red glass	4.6 × 2.49	1	
50	Blue glass	5.0 × 2.3	1	
3	Quartz	3.5 × 4.0	6	
3	Carnelian	3.5 × 4.0	2	
61	Blue glass	3.4 × 5.6	2	
61	Carnelian	3.4 × 5.6	1	
61	Quartz	3.4 × 5.6	3	
VIq	Uncertain	2.8 × 5.0	1	Meroitic
Q 309—2				
73	Ostrich eggshell	1.6 × 3.5	800	Approximate; still strung
Q 316—4				
73	Ostrich eggshell	1.8 × 3.2	24	Approximate
14	Blue faience	3.5 × 3.7	35	
14	Yellow glass	3.0 × 3.4	20	
14	Yellow glass, double	2.8 × 5.6	7	
14	Yellow glass, triple	2.9 × 9.0	1	
14	Green glass	3.0 × 4.5	2	
14	Orange glass	2.9 × 3.7	1	
14	Blue glass, double	2.9 × 5.5	1	
30	Yellow glass	5.2 × 5.5	1	
Q 320—5				
73	Ostrich eggshell	1.6 × 3.3	50	Approximate; strung alone, all were encrusted.
14	Blue glass	3.0 × 4.2	5–6	
Pendant	Carnelian	4.6 × 8.2	1	Meroitic; fig. 64f
Also: copper double coil				fig. 65h

Table 22. Register of Beads (*cont.*).

Tomb/Object Number and Bead Type	Material	Dimensions in mm	Count	Remarks
Q 332—2, 4				
a.	Carnelian, hexagonal barrel			
b.	Beads			
Q 338—5				
73	Ostrich eggshell	1.8 × 3.3	90	
14	Green glass	1.2 × 2.5	46	
14	Orange glass	1.5 × 3.0	45	
78	Carnelian	9.0 × 10.4	10	
Xe(?)	Carnelian	5.8 × 12.5	1	Meroitic
78	Black glass	9.2 × 11.0	7	
78	White glass	9.2 × 10.8	18	
Q 338—6				
73	Ostrich eggshell	1.7 × 3.0	44	
14	Blue glass	2.0 × 3.2	74	
39	Blue glass	2.5 × 5.0	3	
1	Silvered glass	3.3 × 5.4	1	
1	Blue glass	3.7 × 4.8	1	
14	Green glass	2.9 × 4.0	15	
14	Orange glass	2.5 × 3.5	2	
Q 338—7				
28	Blue faience	4.3 × 4.3	49	
Q 344—3				
73	Blue glass	2.4 × 33	2	
73	Orange glass	2.7 × 3.2	3	
1	Blue faience	4.6 × 7.0	1	
37	Green faience	8.3 × 4.2	1	
74	Yellow glass pendant	5.8 × 7.6 × 6.3	1	fig. 64b
Q 345—4				
73	Ostrich eggshell	2.2 × 3.2	25	
Q 345—16				
37	Blue faience	7.3 × 3.7	1	
Pendant	Wood, biconical	0.55 × 1.57	2	fig. 65f
Q 350—3a	Beads			
Q 350—5				
73	Ostrich eggshell	1.6 × 4.7	5–10,000	Strung alone, boxful, 10.0 × 6.5 × 9.0 cm
Q 350—8				
Q 350—11				
Q 350—13				
73	Ostrich eggshell	1.5 × 3.0	382	
Q 356—1				
1	Blue faience	4.2 × 7.7	4	
Q 360—2				
14	Silvered glass	4.0 × 5.0	1	

Table 22. Register of Beads (*cont*.).

Tomb/Object Number and Bead Type	Material	Dimensions in mm	Count	Remarks
Q 361—4				
14	Red glass	2.8 × 4.1	339	
14	Dark blue glass	2.2 × 3.6	334	
14	Light blue glass	2.2 × 3.6	11	
14	Green glass	2.2 × 3.6	5	
14	Yellow glass	2.2 × 3.6	4	
73	Ostrich eggshell	1.8 × 3.7	109	
Q 377—2	Beads from burial chamber (no record)			
Q 378—15	Necklace			
Q 379—2				
VId	Dark blue glass	2.7 × 3.2	1	Meroitic
VId	Green glass	1.6 × 3.2	2	
Ii	Gilded glass	5.2 × 4.6	1	
Pendant				Meroitic
Ih	Carnelian	4.7 × 9.2	1	Strung with Ii
Ia	Blue glass	5.2 × 7.4 × 11.5	12	The count is the total for the shape: one was strung with VId
	Dark blue glass	5.2 × 7.4 × 11.5		
Q 381—3, 4				
73	Ostrich eggshell	1.5 × 3.0	126	
39	Black glass	2.0 × 2.6	2	
14	Green glass	2.4 × 4.0	15	
28	Blue faience	5.0 × 5.6	14	
37	Blue faience	6.1 × 10.2	2	
14	Red glass	2.4 × 3.6	7	
78	Black glass	6.2 × 10.4	1	
Q 385—3				
73	Ostrich eggshell	2.0 × 3.6	265	
36	Blue faience	7.5 × 15.5	2	
14	Green glass	2.3 × 3.2	3	
37	Blue faience	4.5 × 6.8	12	
Q 387—5				
28	Black glass	10.2 × 13.0	1	
Q 388—3				
14	Black glass	3.4 × 3.7	1	
73	Ostrich eggshell	1.5 × 3.0	91	
14	Blue faience	2.5 × 3.7	4	
14	Blue glass	3.0 × 4.0	3	
51	Blue glass	3.5 × 9.0	3	
26?	Blue glass	3.2 × 4.3	1(?)	
Q 434—6				fig. 65b
51	Green glass/faience	4.7 × 7.7 × 13.2	1	
27/28	Quartz	7.0 × 7.8	4	
27	Blue glass	6.5 × 9.3	1	
24	Blue glass	6.0 × 9.0	2	fig. 62g
23	White glass	8.0 × 16.6	1	fig. 62e

Table 22. Register of Beads (*cont.*).

Tomb/Object Number and Bead Type	Material	Dimensions in mm	Count	Remarks
Q 434—6 (*cont.*)				
27	White glass striped	7.6 × 9 × 12.5	4	fig. 62k
48	Carnelian	7.8 × 13.8	2	fig. 63f
27	Amethyst(?), glass	7.4 × 8.8 × 14.7	1	
21	Clear glass	8 × 10.1 × 18.2	1	
1	Red glass striped	10.2 × 12.2	1	
78(?)	Green glass	Broken	1	
Xf	Quartz	8.1 × 13.1 × 13.5	1	Meroitic
21	Carnelian	8.6 × 21.4	1	fig. 62a
IVb	Green glass	7.6 × 10.9	1	Meroitic
50	Green glass	4.9 × 10.2	1	fig. 63i
26	Blue glass	Broken	1	
Q 446—3				
14	Blue faience	4.4 × 6.0	23	
26	Green glass	6.0 × 6.5	62	
36	Blue faience	7.0 × 13.0	3	
Q 463—2	Beads			fig. 65d
Q 501—4				
73	Ostrich eggshell	1.5 × 3.0	196	
14	Blue faience	2.8 × 3.8	36	
14	Red glass	2.2 × 3.2	35	
14	Blue glass	2.0 × 3.0	6	
22	Blue glass	5.4 × 7.0	2	
47	Carnelian(?)	4.7 × 5.3	3	
	Black seed		1	
Q 503—5				
73	Ostrich eggshell	1.5 × 3.0	593	
Q 504—3				
14	Blue faience	3.7 × 4.0	4	
84/85	Red glass	4.9 × 13.3	1	
26	Blue glass	5.0 × 5.5	4	
14	Green glass	4.0 × 4.7	4	
R 1—3				
14	Red glass, opaque	2.6 × 3.2	Uncertain	
14	Dark blue glass	3.5 × 3.4	Uncertain	
37	Black glass	3.8 × 2.8	29	
37	Blue-green faience	3.8 × 2.8	21	
37	Blue faience	10.5 × 5.0	40	Approximate
37	Blue faience	5.8 × 4.6	65	Approximate
44	Quartz	11.2 × 9.8	11	
28	Quartz	9.3 × 8.9	24	
44	Green-black stone	9.5 × 8.2	8	Crude
44	Red glass, opaque	6.5 × 6.6	2	fig. 63q
48	Carnelian	1.5 × 5.7	1	
73	Ostrich eggshell	1.6 × 3.5	6	fig. 64k
85	Light blue glass	8.9 × 13.2	38	Crude
85	Dark blue glass	5.2 × 11.0	10	
14	Green glass	3.5 × 3.4	3	

Table 22. Register of Beads (*cont.*).

Tomb/Object Number and Bead Type	Material	Dimensions in mm	Count	Remarks
R 1—3 (*cont.*)				
73	Ostrich eggshell	1.6 × 3.5	3–400(?)	
14	Blue glass	2.7 × 3.2	2	
Stringing:				

Light blue glass beads (Type #85) with red beads (Type #14) and green beads (Type #14)
Blue faience beads (Type #37) with ostrich eggshell beads (Type #73), alternating
Opaque red glass beads (Type #14) alone
Light blue glass beads (Type #85) strung with dark blue glass beads (Type #14)

R 2—9	Beads and pendant			
R 6—1	Textile remains bound around waist with 4–5 beads			
R 8—3				
73	Ostrich eggshell	1.5 × 3.0	74	
R 15—6				fig. 64c
55	Green faience	6.9 × 4.4	1	
55	Blue glass	7.1 × 4.1	1	
11	Blue glass	3.7 × 4.7	2	
11	Yellow glass	3.1 × 4.4	2	
11	Blue, white, and red striped	4.6 × 5.9	1	
5/6	Green glass	5.0 × 5.6	1	
R 16—3				
73	Ostrich eggshell	1.9 × 5.0	27	
R 21—1				
73	Ostrich eggshell	1.5 × 3.0	26	
14	Red glass	2.8 × 3.5	23	
14	Blue faience	2.1 × 3.7	1	
39	Blue glass	3.4 × 5.0		
14	Blue faience	1.3 × 2.0	4	
61?	Orange glass	2.8 × 8.4	1	
61?	Green glass	3.5 × 6.6	1	
R 22—8				Strung alternating; possibly several hundred of each kind; all were encrusted with a porous material and embedded in it.
14	Blue faience(?)	2.8 × 3.6	Uncertain	
73	Ostrich eggshell	1.6 × 3.5	Uncertain	
R 27—2				
73	Ostrich eggshell	1.3 × 2.7	90	
R 36—5				
14	Blue faience	3.1 × 4.0	413	
73	Ostrich eggshell	1.6 × 2.8	30	
14	Orange glass	1.9 × 3.3	16	
14	Red glass	2.4 × 3.1	12	
14	Red glass, double	3.2 × 5.9	2	
14	Silvered glass	3.6 × 4.6	1	
R 36—6				
14	Blue faience	2.8 × 3.6	1	
73	Ostrich eggshell	1.5 × 3.0	275	

Table 22. Register of Beads (*cont.*).

Tomb/Object Number and Bead Type	Material	Dimensions in mm	Count	Remarks
R 49—3	Beads			
R 50—1a				
73	Ostrich eggshell	1.5 × 3.0	325	
14	Orange-red glass	1.3 × 2.3	2	
14	White glass	2.9 × 3.7	94	
R 50—1b				
14	Orange glass	1.7 × 2.2	510	
39	Orange glass	2.9 × 4.2	1	
14	Carnelian	2.8 × 3.6	13	
R 60—3				
73	Ostrich eggshell	1.5 × 3.0	74	
14	Red glass	2.8 × 3.5	6	
28	Green glass	4.1 × 5.2	1	
R 64—9				
73	Ostrich eggshell	1.3 × 3.2	3	
14	Blue faience	2.7 × 3.4	3	
R 65—5				
36	Dark blue glass	10.1 × 4.5	2	Very rough
IIb	Silvered glass, triple	12.2 × 3.7	1	Meroitic
28(?)	Blue faience, deformed	—	4	Decomposed
Is/t or IIq	Yellow and black glass, spiral	7.2 × 7.7	1	Meroitic
R 69—1				
36	Blue-green faience	10.7 × 7.8	20	Crude, variable size
73	Blue-green faience, double	6.2 × 8.1	1	
3–4	Yellow glass	5.0 × 6.7	1	
3–4	Blue glass	5.5 × 7.0	1	
3–4	Red glass, opaque	6.0 × 6.3	1	
Ib–i	Gilded glass	6.2 × 7.2	1	Meroitic
73	Green glass	2.4 × 3.9	17	
73	Red glass, opaque	3.1 × 3.4	23	
73	Ostrich eggshell	1.6 × 4.1	212	
R 74—1				A ring is included in this number
73	Ostrich eggshell	1.1 × 3.5	11	fig. 64l
28	Blue-green faience	3.5 × 3.5	11	
28	Black glass with white stripe	6.3 × 7.5	1	fig. 62n
28	Blue glass	5.5 × 7.3	1	fig. 62p
R 102—1	Beads			
R 103—2				
36	Brown glass	3.5–4.4 × 7.4–5.3	5	
73	Ostrich eggshell	1.6 × 2.8	3	
14	Green-blue faience	2.7 × 3.9	1	
R 106—2	Beads			
R 117—1	Beads			

Table 22. Register of Beads (*cont.*).

Tomb/Object Number and Bead Type	Material	Dimensions in mm	Count	Remarks
R 119—5				
Ie	Blue faience	1.13 × 1.42	1	Meroitic
2–3	Quartz	6.6 × 6.5		
Pendant	Dark blue glass white stripe below	4.5 × 5.9	1	Meroitic, II(?)
VA 9—6				
37	Blue faience	4.3–6.5 × 5.2–5.7	29	
28	Blue faience	7.2 × 7.9	1	
28	Green faience	8.4 × 8.8	1	
73	Ostrich eggshell	1.6 × 5.2	3	
14	Blue glass	2.4 × 3.4	?	
VA 12—2b				
14	Blue faience, rectangular	1.5–4.0 × 3.5	24	
14	Blue glass	2.1 × 4.1	1	
73	Ostrich eggshell, square	1.6 × 3.4	17	
29	Carnelian	4.8 × 3.4	1	
Note also a silver crescentic earring, and a shell token of A-Group type 3.5 × 5.2				
VA 13—3				
23	Ostrich eggshell	1.8 × 2.5	95	
VA 14—8				
73	Ostrich eggshell	1.5 × 3.5	201	
VA 14—9				
73	Ostrich eggshell	2.1 × 3.8	37	Thick!; these were found on a cord.
VB 70—1	Beads			
VC 41—4				
29	Blue glass	5.0 × 9.3	1	fig. 62r
VF 68—2	Beads			
V 202—1	(Discarded)			
a.	Blue tubes			
b.	White disc (alternating)			
c.	Blue-green drop-shaped pendant			Not in string
W 54—1				
73	Ostrich eggshell		Uncertain	
W 59—1	Beads			
W 61—1	Beads			
W 74—1				
73	Ostrich eggshell	1.5 × 3.0	694	Approximate
14	Blue glass	3.1 × 3.6	43	
14	Blue glass, double	3.4 × 7.6	1	
73	Orange glass	0.8 × 2.2	23	
14	Orange glass	2.9 × 5.0	1	
14	Blue faience	2.2 × 3.5	56	
28	Blue faience	3.8 × 4.3	20	
14	Green glass	3.3 × 5.2	1	

Table 22. Register of Beads (*cont.*).

Tomb/Object Number and Bead Type	Material	Dimensions in mm	Count	Remarks
W 74—2				fig. 62m
73	Ostrich eggshell	1.5. × 2.9	235	
W 76—3	Beads			Sample
W 80—4				
44	Blue glass	7.8 × 12.4	1	
14	Green glass	2.5 × 4.2	4	
14	Blue-green faience	2.8 × 5.1	4	
14	Blue glass	2.7 × 3.1	7	
14	Blue glass, double	2.8 × 4.9	1	
45	Blue glass	3.6 × 3.6	3	fig. 63s
78	White glass	3.9 × 6.7	1	fig. 64d
14	Red glass	2.8 × 3.3	1	
46	Blue glass	8.8 × 13	1	fig. 63b
W 84—1				
3	Red glass	6.5 × 7.5	1	fig. 64f
73	Ostrich eggshell	1.6 × 3.4	3	
14	Gilded glass, double	4.0 × 5.6	1	
14	Blue-green faience	2.6 × 3.3	11	
14	Blue faience	2.0 × 3.8	5	
30	Blue faience	4.0 × 5.4	1	
14	Red glass	2.5 × 3.0	1	
M 1—1, 3				
73	Ostrich eggshell	1.5 × 3.5	371	
14	Red glass	2.9 × 3.4	158	
14	Double	3.0 × 5.8	6	
14	Triple	3.2 × 9.0	1	
39	Black glass	2.4 × 3.0	90	
39	Double	2.4 × 6.7	8	
47	Green glass	8.1 × 8.3	12	
37	Blue faience	6.4 × 9.1	1	
14	Blue faience	1.5 × 2.5	1	
B 176A—2, 3	Beads			
B 176B—4	Bead bracelet			

E. TEXTILES

In Meroitic times, the textiles had mostly been made of linen or cotton. They were normally undyed. Some animal fiber or woollen fabrics were made, but animal fiber was mostly used for decoration. In the late Meroitic cemetery of Ballana, cotton fabrics mostly replaced linen.

By the time of the royal tumuli, animal fiber, mostly woolens, replaced linen and cotton almost completely,[50] and the fabrics were mostly dyed. Some specialty fabrics of linen were imported.

In the register of finds, textiles published in the catalogue are cited by catalogue number.[51] However, since the textile catalogue was written, the dates assigned to some tombs have been changed. For example,

50. Mayer-Thurman and Williams 1979, pp. 36–37.

51. Mayer-Thurman and Williams 1979.

tombs Q 191 and Q 301, dated to X-Group are Christian or probably Christian; tomb Q 230, dated to X-Group was probably Meroitic; tombs Q 231 and Q 332 were Meroitic tombs with X-Group burials; tomb Q 334, dated to X-Group, was a reused Meroitic tomb.[52]

F. BASKETS

Baskets were found in tombs Q 387 (2) and Q 505 (2).

G. COSMETIC IMPLEMENTS

Cosmetic implements were less common in X-Group than Meroitic contexts, although some of the finest objects were of a quality comparable to their Meroitic antecedents (pls. 80–81, 83i). They included a kohl tube, kohl sticks, wooden vessel, sets of implements on rings ("chatelaine"), tweezers, and a finely made bronze spoon (tab. 23).

KOHL TUBE

Meroitic kohl or cosmetic tubes were almost always of wood. The one tube in the collection from X-Group is ivory (Q 164—13, fig. 154b; pl. 83i). The body is conical, with a short, splayed pedestal foot; the lid was not preserved. The object was decorated with incised bands and crosshatched triangles. The shape is approximately the same as one from the royal tombs.[53] The iron kohl stick (Q 164—12), now in Cairo, was exceptionally long, some 29 cm.

---

52. The following tombs with textiles assigned to X-Group in the textile catalogue were reassigned to other periods: Q 132, with CAT 80–81 and Q 191, CAT 103 were redated to the Christian period. Q 230, CAT 106, Q 325, CAT 114, Q 334, CAT 119, and Q 600, CAT 146 were redated to the Meroitic period.

Following is a list of tombs assigned to X-Group that contained textiles. Only tombs with substantial remains were listed in the textile catalogue. The more complete list that follows contains references to the catalogue proper and to the lists of discarded textiles at the end (Mayer-Thurman and Williams 1979, p. 148).

Q 2—9 CAT 35, 15; Q 5—1 CAT 36?, 3 CAT 36, 10 CAT 37; Q 6—6 CAT 38; Q 7—1 CAT 39 (1a and b), 6; Q 9—13 CAT 40; Q 10—2 CAT 41–43, 3 CAT 44–45; Q 11—2 CAT 46, 4 CAT 47, 5 CAT 48; Q 13—3 CAT 49; Q 15—2 CAT 50; Q 16—3 CAT X-Gr.; Q 17—1 CAT 51; Q 18—8, 10 CAT 52; Q 19—9 CAT 53; Q 20—6 CAT X-Gr; Q 22—1 CAT 54, 55; Q 27—2 CAT 56–57; Q 29—1 CAT X-Gr.; Q 30—3 CAT 58, 5 CAT 59; Q 31—2 CAT X-Gr.; Q 35—3 CAT 176; Q 39—1 CAT 61, 2; Q 40—4 CAT 162; Q 41—6 CAT X-Gr.; Q 44—1 CAT 62; Q 44—5 CAT 63; Q 55—2; Q 58—4 CAT X-Gr.; Q 60—1 CAT X-Gr.; Q 62—4 CAT 64–67, 23 CAT 68; Q 65—1; Q 66—3 CAT X-Gr.; Q 68—3 CAT 69–71; Q 69—1 CAT X-Gr.; Q 71—1 CAT X-Gr.; Q 72—1 CAT X-Gr.; Q 73—2 CAT X-Gr.; Q 74—1 CAT 72, 9 CAT 73–74; Q 75—8 CAT X-Gr.; Q 78—8 CAT 75; Q 82—9 CAT 76; Q 84—3; Q 119—3 CAT 77–79; Q 133—3 CAT X-Gr.; Q 134—15 CAT 82–84; Q 135—4 CAT X-Gr.; Q 136—1 CAT 85–89; Q 137—2 CAT 90; Q 140—5 CAT unknown; Q 141—3 CAT 91–93; Q 149—9 CAT 94–98; Q 152—1 CAT 99; Q 164—19 CAT 100–102; Q 174—4 CAT 163; Q 184—3; Q 186—3 CAT 164; Q 192—4 CAT 104–105; Q 231—1 CAT 107–108; Q 279—6 CAT X-Gr.; Q 309—3 CAT X-Gr.; Q 316—5 CAT X-Gr.; Q 320—4 CAT X-Gr.; Q 321—3 CAT 111–113; Q 328—1 CAT Mer.; Q 332—5 CAT 115–118; Q 338—4 CAT 120–121; Q 344—2; Q 345—8, 12 CAT 122, 15 CAT 123; Q 348—2 CAT 167–168; Q 349—3; Q 350—6 CAT 124–127, 12; Q 356—6 CAT 128–130; Q 357—4; Q 360—1; Q 361—5; Q 378—6 CAT 131, 7 CAT 132; Q 385—4 CAT X-Gr.; Q 387—3 CAT 133–134; Q 388—2 CAT 135; Q 390—2 CAT 136; Q 391—1 CAT X-Gr.; Q 393—2 CAT 137; Q 394—2, 6 CAT 138; Q 400—2; Q 410—1 CAT X-Gr., 2; Q 422—1 CAT 139–140; Q 425—5 CAT 170–173; Q 425—6; Q 434—4 CAT X-Gr.; Q 446—2; Q 454—2 CAT X-Gr.; Q 468—1; Q 479—2 CAT 141; Q 501—7 CAT 142; Q 503—3 CAT 143; Q 580—2; Q 582—3a, 3b, 3c CAT 144; Q 594—8.

R 6—1 CAT 147; R 7—1 CAT X-Gr.; R 8—4; R 14—1 CAT X-Gr.; R 15—7 CAT 148 (number changed from 1); R 16—4 CAT 149; R 22—11 CAT 150; R 23—2 CAT X-Gr.; R 26—1 CAT X-Gr.; R 36—7 CAT X-Gr.; R 37—1; R 49—7 CAT X-Gr.; R 60—4a CAT 151, 4b CAT 152; R 62—3 CAT X-Gr.; R 82—3 CAT X-Gr.; R 111—3 CAT 153; R 113—1 CAT 154–155; R 118—3 CAT 156–157.

VA 14—12 CAT X-Gr.; VC 41—3 CAT X-Gr.; VC 42—4 CAT X-Gr.; VH 122—1 CAT 158; W 60—2 CAT X-Gr.; W 71—1; W 71—2 CAT 161; W 83—2 CAT X-Gr.; W 88—4 CAT X-Gr.

53. Royal tombs, kohl tube.

Table 23. Register of Cosmetic Implements.

Tomb and Object Number	Object
Q 2—14	Ring with tweezers and probe
Q 16—2	Tweezers
Q 61—3	Tweezers
Q 134—14	Copper spoon
Q 164—12	Kohl stick
Q 164—13	Kohl tube
Q 164—14	Bag with galena
Q 361—3	Small wooden bowl
R 2—8a	Tweezers with broad blade
R 2—8b	Ring with tweezers and two probes
R 2—8c	Two needles or probes
R 4A—25	Broad-blade tweezers with gilt glass locking band
R 6—4	Ring with tweezers, two probes and knife, braided thong
R 50—4	Iron kohl stick or probe with square section
R 51—3	Bronze tweezers and two probes on gold ring
R 64—8	Ring with tweezers and probe
V 14—11	Kohl stick or probe

RING SETS, CHATELAINES, OR THORN SETS

Although ring sets with knives continued to be used in X-Group, the three sets here included only simple narrow tweezers and iron probes. Probes also occurred alone.

TWEEZERS

In addition to the rings, simple tweezers occurred alone. Most interesting, however, was the development of a tweezers with a very broad, shovel-like blade with a locking ring to make the object usable as a clamp. One ring was made of gold.

Table 24. Register of Meroitic and X-Group Sandals.

Sandal Type, Tomb, and Number	Remarks
Group 1	Double sole, stitched around edges and down center
Q 192—2	Stitched around edge, rows down sole
Q 306—2	Edge and center reinforcement; OINE VIII
Q 574—2	Marked by lines only in center; OINE VIII
Q 670—17	Fragmentary, reinforcement at edge and short strip in center, slit to make lozenge shapes around edge; OINE VIII
Group 2 (A)	Single sole, holes for toe strap in line, two straps left on each side of ankle
B 279—5	Uncertain decoration at toes; bands of herringbone flank lozenge or lattice, broad strip with convex scallops; OINE VIII
Q 518—1	Simple, incised, with narrow bands of slashes in herringbone; OINE VIII
Group 2 (B)	Same as above, single hole for toe strap
Q 478—2	Medium painted outer band, single line incised, sole patched with three tanned pieces; OINE VIII
B 26—3	Double frame around edge with rectangular stamped *ankh*s; lattice-rhomb pattern in center with double zigzags at join (as ties[?]) and *ankh*s in spaces; zigzag at heel; OINE VIII; Appliqué: green with cutaway crescent (rhomb reserved) on red background, stitched with pinked border; two square appliqués, striding animals with white-stitched outline

Table 24. Register of Meroitic and X-Group Sandals (*cont.*).

Sandal Type, Tomb, and Number	Remarks
B 233—1	Broad, painted outer band, four lines incised inside, no center decoration(?), very broad toe strap; OINE VIII
B 297—3b	Sole almost destroyed; 2 straps attached at end; lotus appliqué, OINE VIII
Group 3	X-Group simple sandals, single thickness or patched, one or two toe strap holes, generally transverse, broad triangular flaps at ankle for straps, mostly rawhide with leather straps
Q 1—7	Simple with row of zigzag lines impressed around perimeter
Q 2—12	
Q 67—12	
Q 68—7	With tanned straps
W 88—3	Ties preserved
Q 135—7	
B 169—1	Christian; OINE VIII
Q 119—4	
Q 152—2	Simple, with rawhide straps, not unhaired
Q 149—5	
Q 345—11	Heel patched crudely
Qu. 7—2	
Q 74—5	Some parts of tie preserved
Q 49—2	
Q 350—14	
Q 378—17	Toe and heel patched crudely second sandal has a crude double sole
Q 501—3	Rawhide(?); dark surface
Qu. 7—4	Rawhide
R 22—10	Rawhide
R 49—4	Child's
R 64—5	Tanned
R 65—4	Tanned(?); simple(?)
R 66—2	Single-sole(?); tanned(?)
Other	
Q 474—4	Shoe; OINE VIII
Q 578—2	Child's sandal, small ca. 11 cm, double hole; OINE VIII
Q 164—17	Three layers, wingtip shape, single toe strap, ankle strap passed through slits in top layer
Q 501—6	Pair of shoes, small pointed, approximately wingtip; stitched at heel; remains of thongs

Sandals not examined:
Q 30—1, Q 33—4 (discarded), Q 38—7 ("leather fragments [sandals(?)]"; discarded), Q 51A—4 (N/A),
Q 55—3 (simple[?], rawhide, with tanned straps), Q 76—1 ("Note also possible fragments of bag and sandal
with 1." probably simple single-sole type), Q 184—4 (uncertain, hair present, wrapped ties), Q 394—7
(discarded), R 109—4 (sample), VA 9—4 (N/A)

H. X-GROUP SANDALS

Sandals remaining from Noubadian X-Group burials differ considerably from the Meroitic footwear.[54]
Almost all were made with a single layer, and they were not decorated. At the heel was a broad, almost
triangular area that was bent upward along each side of the ankle to attach the straps. These were secured

54. See OINE V, *Chapter 3*, pp. 71–75 for a corpus of sandals.

through two holes between (different) toes. The straps were looped or tied through holes at the ankles, and they extended around the heel. Two straps from the toe-holes met them over the instep where they were tied. In the one case where the tie was preserved, it was quite hasty, in contrast to the careful and regular leather work.

Table 25. Summary List of Tools and Vessels of Metal and Glass.

Tomb and Object Number	Remarks	Tomb and Object Number	Remarks
Tools		*Horn, etc.*	
Q 5—7	Knife blade	Q 13—2	Sheep horn
Q 5—20	Knife blade	Q 39—4	Animal horn (bit[?])
Q 6—5	Hammer (7, shaft[?])	Q 134—17	Animal horn
Q 16—1	Sickle-saw	Q 136—6	Worked horn (two)
Q 25—1	"Tool"	R 1—5	Two bone fragments
Q 33—5	Blade(?)		
Q 38—2a	Blade, 2.5 × 4.0 cm	*Pestles*	
	uncertain tool	Q 52—2	
	split rod with	R 4A—29	
	remains of blade(?)		
	three fasteners	*Whorls*	
R 4A—21	Axe[a]	QC 4—1	Pottery disc
R 4A—19	Adze[b]	Q 164—2	Two wooden
R 4A—20	Adze[c]	R 11—7	Steatite(?) with incised circles[g]
R 4A—22	Sickle-saw[d]		
R 22—7	Adze	*Metal and Glass Vessels*	
R 22—9	Sickle-saw	Q 5—2	Bronze cup fragments
R 49—2a	Sickle-saw[e]	Q 5—13	Copper/bronze bowl fragments
R 49—2b	Adze[f]	Q 5—15	Copper/bronze bowl fragments
W 80—3a	Sickle-saw	Q 20—1	Copper/bronze cup fragments
W 88—2	Sickle-saw	Q 59—2	Glass bottle shards
		Q 164—9	Bronze bowl
Fragments		Q 385—5b	Bronze bowl rim
Q 19—8	Fragment	R 64—6	Glass cup fragments
Q 20—2	Iron rod		
Q 52—3	Iron rod or probe		
R 64—7	Iron object		

a. Emery type 3, 10.5 × 6.3; back repeatedly used as a hammer, much splayed.
b. With splayed ring attachment (Emery and Kirwan, 1938, pp. 334, 704); blade decorated near top with engraved design, 13.5 × 4.6; socket, 9.5 × 3.1.
c. Called a hoe, very curved edge with ring-socket (Emery and Kirwan, p. 328, fig. 102-1); 15.0 × 5.3.
d. A curved saw with staple through hole, bent over, and wedge used to tighten ring; 17.5 × 2.5.
e. A curved saw with socket and staple; 18.4 × 2.8.
f. With an edge convex, socket forged to blade in two parts, outer folded over inner, for adjustment; 13.2 × 4.8.
g. See Garstang, Sayce, and Griffith 1911, p. 47, and Crawford and Addison 1951, pl. LVI for decorated clay whorls. They are somewhat thicker.

I. TOOLS

The addition of tools to the burial was an important change between the Meroitic period and Noubadian X-Group (pls. 82, 83b–c).[55] Most were small and light, entirely unsuited to the regular production of even modest-sized objects or use in heavy work. The most likely use, for light repairs and temporary construction

55. Emery and Kirwan 1938, pp. 327–38.

or forage, would be consistent with the emphasis on military equipment in these graves. The collection includes small sickles or saws, axes, adzes, and hammers. A set of tools found in R 4A could be considered a kit.

J. LAMPS

Lamps occurred in some of the X-Group tombs, although they were not common. In addition, some other vessels, such as miniatures, were reused as lamps. Lamps included the following: Q 8—7 (frog), Q 52—6, Q 54—2 (Christian reuse), Q 62—17, Q 135—2, Q 338—1, Q 345—6 (miniature cup used for lamp[?]; see fig. 18), Q 501—A, Q 502—3.

K. CONCLUSION: OBJECTS

As pointed out in the introductory remarks, the objects in Noubadian X-Group burials confirm the conclusion that significant cultural changes took place between Meroitic and X-Group times. The religious meaning and cultural orientation of the burial turned away from the Meroitic Osirian-mummiform and toward the ancient sleeplike burial that had persisted on the fringes of Meroitic culture. Since the equipment required for the two different kinds of burial differed sharply, the normal changes to be expected over time in burials were emphasized by qualitative changes in the equipment deposited, such as tools. Continuity was not totally lacking, especially in weapons, but the features that continued could have been derived from Sudan. However, many changes, even in such modest objects as beads, were rather abrupt.

CHAPTER 4

CONCLUSION

The most important chronological conclusion of the Oriental Institute Nubian Expedition's work in X-Group was the verification of a chronological outline for Noubadian X-Group. This consisted of an early phase and a middle phase found in the royal cemeteries and a late phase that occurs in Cemetery R and at other sites. In addition, no direct transition could be documented between the Meroitic and X-Group periods. Thus the period between A.D. 300 and about A.D. 550 can be divided into four distinct phases.[1]

A. THE MID FOURTH CENTURY A.D.

Materials datable to this phase were found in the Dodekaschoinos and the area immediately to the south. The earliest were the so-called taverns and cell-tumuli of Sayala. The large cemeteries excavated by the Oriental Institute Nubian Expedition at Bab Kalabsha and the Czechoslovakian expedition at Wadi Kitna[2] began about the same time and continued somewhat later.[3] These were accompanied by semi-permanent settlements Ricke called refuges from Nile-based banditry[4] and some religious buildings. A number of coins found in the cemeteries date to the middle years of the fourth century A.D.[5]

As pointed out in *Chapter 1*, the character of the village refuges,[6] the pottery, objects, and tumuli belong to a pagan culture so different from others in the area that it must be considered a major new archaeological group.[7] This archaeological group appeared at a time so close to major phases of Blemmye activity documented in Roman-Byzantine sources, that an identification of this culture as Blemmyan is all but assured.[8]

B. THE LATE FOURTH CENTURY A.D.

The major archaeological event of the late fourth century A.D. was the establishment of the X-Group as in the royal cemetery at Qustul. This event may have been preceded by a few simple private burials that contained no pottery, but the earliest royal tombs contained the distinctive pottery and objects of the new age.

1. See, *Chapter 1*, pp. 18–25 above.

2. See, *Chapter 1*, table 9, pp. 21–25 above.

3. See *Chapter 1*, pp. 3–5 and Török 1988, pp. 178–81.

4. Ricke 1967, pp. 33–36.

5. Ricke 1967, p. 39.

6. Ricke 1967, pp. 36–37. Blemmye raiding would occur from the desert and refuges would be built on islands as in the Christian fort on Darmus. Roman-Byzantine reprisals would generally follow the river and allow an alert to give people some chance of escape if their dwellings were not too near the river. The earnestness of these reprisals is vividly illustrated by the executioner's trenches at Shellal (Reisner 1910, p. 73). Since banditry was hardly river-borne at this period, we should probably turn from the interpretation of Ricke to that of Monneret de Villard that the villages were those of desert people; if refuges, they were from reprisals.

7. For a discussion with different conclusions see Török 1988, pp. 178–81.

8. Paully-Wissowa, "Blemyes," summarizes Greek and Latin historical and geographical writings.

X-GROUP CULTURE

In structure and contents, the tumulus complexes are not transitional, either from the local Meroitic culture of the same area or from the Blemmye culture of the Dodekaschoinos. Instead, structures and burial practices are derived primarily from post-Meroitic Sudanese tombs that were elaborations of still earlier burials which existed on the fringes of Meroitic civilization. Occasionally, features of these burials even appeared in cemeteries at the capital.[9] By close correspondence to Roman-Byzantine and Axumite sources, this Sudanese culture must be termed Noba.[10]

Although the Qustul tumuli were not transitional, the contents and the buildings of the complexes did continue pharaonic culture. For example, royal jewelry can be characterized as pharaonic and Meroitic in iconography, with Byzantine decorative elements, such as jewels,[11] and a few enigmatic elements, such as the lion bracelets.[12] At the same time, important elements of Meroitic official culture, e.g. writing, rapidly disappeared. The complex panoply of gods was reduced to a few images which were often shown in an open, spare style.[13] On one of the Gamai rings an enthroned god holds the bow, and is labeled with a rebus, a falcon on a serpent.[14] These images were also applied in new situations, such as saddle pommels.

Of all the objects found in private tombs, weapons were closest to Meroitic antecedents; arrows, quivers, and archer's braces appeared earlier, in Meroitic and in peripheral Meroitic/Noba contexts. The remarkable composite bow was previously unknown.[15]

Except for the handmade vessels, pottery is a unified industrial product. Some vessels, notably goblets, were of northern origin and a few forms were Meroitic. However, the most distinctive product, the bottle-jar, was derived from post-Meroitic Sudan, possibly ultimately from a leather or gourd original.[16] Metal vessels appear to have been derived from the same source.

Since the most important Meroitic elements in X-Group culture occur in Sudan and the burial customs and structures are Sudanese, the formative stages of this new civilization must be sought in the more transitional, tentative, and fragmented cultures of post-Meroitic Sudan. Northern elements are essentially industrial, and integrated into a mature culture at the beginning. The identification of the X-Group of the Qustul and Ballana cemeteries as Noubadian seems inescapable and a close archaeological relationship with Noba culture is affirmed.[17] In this early phase, a uniform Noubadian culture spread from south of the second Cataract to the regions north of Ibrim, in contrast to the fragmented Sudanese cultures.

C. THE EARLY FIFTH CENTURY A.D.

The second phase of Noubadian X-Group was largely contemporary with the Ballana Royal Necropolis. The tumuli were more numerous, larger and richer than those of Qustul, perhaps indicating a greater centralization of wealth and power near the capital, which was probably at Faras.[18]

---

9. Paully-Wissowa, "Noubai." Classical authors locate this people less precisely than the Blemmyes, but the general thrust was to locate them to the south and west. See also Hofmann 1982 and Hintze 1967.

10. For a discussion, see Török 1988, pp. 196–98; for a different point of view, see Lenoble 1989, especially pp. 106–07. Different cultures had coexisted for some time; see Hofmann, Tomandl, and Zach 1989, for example.

11. Emery and Kirwan 1938, pls. 32–35, 40.

12. Emery and Kirwan 1938, pl. 39.

13. Emery and Kirwan 1938, pp. 63, 133.

14. The typical Noubadian ring has a very high convex bezel (Emery and Kirwan 1938, pl. 42, B 47—2, B 42—25, Q 14—48–49). Other rings with wide cut-stone bezels may be Blemmye work (B 47—17, B 2—16; one has an altar, the other, curls and birds; see Ricke 1967, fig. 73 various, for birds and curls incised on pottery).

15. See p. 15 above.

16. See p. 40 and note 23 above.

17. Kirwan 1982.

18. Michalowski 1970, p. 12; for structural remains, see Godlewski 1986.

Apart from the removal of the royal cemetery to Ballana, Middle Noubadian X-Group did not represent a major change in the material culture. Objects produced locally were mostly modifications of early X-Group counterparts. This period, roughly the fifth century A.D., was the high point of Noubadian X-Group.

The changes that distinguish the period include both objects and the distribution of the culture. For example, a few cups made of clay from the Nubian sandstone appear to be wheelmade versions of earlier Blemmye cups from the Dodekaschoinos and these reflect the most important archaeological change of the period, the expansion of the Noubadian X-Group into the Dodekaschoinos.[19] The date of this expansion is supported by the fact that imports from the "Blemmye" sites near Kalabsha do not date late in the fifth century A.D.; it appears the X-Group culture of the Triakontaschoinos absorbed the northern region, even producing some very large tumuli near the Wadi Allaqi.[20]

Important historical events coincided with these changes. These included Noubadian-supported Blemmye intervention in Egypt after the edict of Theodosius threw that country into a religious uproar. About A.D. 410, Olympiodorus reported the Dodekaschoinos and adjacent regions of the east bank in the hands of the Blemmyes.[21] It was not, in fact until well after the fall of Africa to the Vandals that major military and financial undertakings brought about an agreement between the Noubadians and the Imperial government.[22]

The imported objects in Middle Noubadian X-Group from the Ballana Cemetery datable to the first half of the fifth century A.D. include some that may have originally belonged to churches. This and the aggressive paganism of the finds in these wealthy tumuli mirror this disturbed age as closely as history and archaeology could be expected to agree.[23]

D. THE LATE FIFTH AND SIXTH CENTURIES A.D.

The end of the royal cemetery at Ballana marks a major turning point in the archaeology of Noubadian X-Group, for the great mounds ceased to be made in Lower Nubia. Burials, such as found at Firka and Ibrim,[24] were sometimes quite wealthy, but they were no longer great monuments. The capital was apparently moved from Faras to Ibrim.[25] The changes in the cemeteries may reflect the political changes, reduction of conflict with the Empire, the growing rivalry between the Blemmye and Noubadian kingdoms and the new prominence of Ibrim.

Changes in small objects were limited, but pottery developed some exaggerated shapes. A new style of painting that combined stylistic elements from several sources also occurred.[26]

The changes between Meroitic and X-Group in Nubia and Sudan noted in this volume, OINE VIII, and other works, represent shifts in the distribution of long-existing cultural groups and religious polarities as well

---

19. See table 9, pp. 21–25 above for the chronology. The Noubadian-type material culture is in apparent contrast with the historical records, which indicate that the Blemmyes continued to control the Dodekaschoinos. However, the cups may indicate that some mutual assimilation occurred, paralleled by the adoption of Greek by both Noubadians and Blemmyes for correspondence. See Török 1988, pp. 49–51 (Olympiodorus, also pp. 46–49) and pp. 56–59 (use of Greek).

20. See *Chapter 1*, table 9, p. 22, cemeteries 112–113 (Wadi Allaqi) and 122.

21. Paully-Wissowa, "Blemyes." See also *Chapter 1*, p. 19, n. 67.

22. By about A.D. 420, the province of Africa was a major support of the Empire in religion as well as economy (Frend 1978, pp. 464, 473–78), though pagan hill tribes were a constant threat, paralleling the situation in Egypt (Frend 1978, pp. 478–79). The Vandals entered between A.D. 429–432 and finally took Carthage in A.D. 439, extending their control to Tripolitania (Frend 1978, p 480). Major Roman efforts to stabilize the Egyptian frontier began shortly thereafter, by A.D. 442.

23. Török 1979, 1988.

24. See table 9, p. 22, cemeteries 192 (Ibrim), 193 (Ibrim), and Firka.

25. Skeat 1977, pp. 159–70. In the same cache was a letter to a phylarch of the Nouba or Anouba which indicates that Ibrim was in their hands by the time of the documents. It also clearly indicates the relationship between Nouba and Noubades (Plumley 1982; see p. 219).

26. Mills 1982, pls. LXXVII–LXXVIII. See *Chapter 2*, p. 42 above.

as political conflicts. These resulted in archaeological gaps and rapid changes in cultural geography during the fourth century A.D., and economic changes reflected in the royal cemeteries.[27]

E. THE CULTURAL GEOGRAPHY OF X-GROUP NUBIA

The substantial shifts in cultural geography did not necessarily result from the introduction of new actors into the regions of Nubia and Sudan, but they were nevertheless significant because they they were part of the dissolution of antiquity.[28]

In this and previous volumes, four major cultural orientations have been noted among the archaeological remains of Nubia and Sudan. Quite remarkably, they remained recognizable despite major changes from contacts outside the region, mutual contacts within the region, and internal transformation.[29] Some, such as the Bedja (Blemmyes) and the Nuba, were peoples who remain recognizable to the present day through the transformations of Christianity and Islam. Two, Egypt and Kush, were pharaonic cultures whose continuation depended on the continuation of belief. The one has survived marginally in Coptic, but the other has not persisted. Down to the fourth century A.D., Kushite culture was supreme in and near the Nile at least as far south as Khartoum. The Napatan-Meroitic form of the culture had emerged from the formative age of Dynasty XXV and continued through a series of limited modifications as a continuation of southern pharaonic monumental civilization. The empire comprised three regions, centered on Napata, Meroe, and Lower Nubia (related in some way to the terms Akin, Aqnat, and Iken[?]). All three regions were occupied in Dynasty XXV, with a vast expansion near Meroe and a lesser one into Lower Nubia after A.D. 100. Despite changes in intensity and boundaries, the three major fields of activity endured from beginning to end.[30]

In the second century A.D., the area most intensively occupied in Kushite Lower Nubia shifted from the cataract region to the area adjacent to the Roman Frontier. Kushite occupation disappeared from Lower Nubia at or shortly after A.D. 300,[31] and its demise in the Butana dates to the later fourth century A.D.

BLEMMYES

The peoples of the Eastern Desert, Medjay (Pan-Grave), Meded, Bedja (Aksumite and Arabic) were called Blemmyes in Greek.[32] If the Kushite tradition was essentially Nilotic, even when spread into the Butana, the Bedja were consistently associated with the Eastern Desert where they were well known to Aksum and the Arabs[33] as well as the Greeks and Egyptians. Before the discovery of the Kalabsha sites, the people was really only known archaeologically from the Pan Graves, but the fourth century A.D. sites now present a vivid and coherent picture of a culture distinct from Meroe, Egypt, or the Nubians. Although devoted to the worship of Isis and associated Egyptian gods, their remains, apart from the temples themselves do not contain detailed pharaonic symbolism. The altar group of Egyptian pottery from Meroitic times and rock drawn altars of northern Lower Nubia and the Eastern Desert indicate a different approach to religious culture; in political institutions, they later imitated the Eastern Empire.

---

27. Trigger 1984, especially pp. 368–70 disparages the significance of these distributional changes, but they were of great consequence.

28. Following Trigger 1984.

29. OINE III, pp. 21–22; OINE V, pp. 118–20; OINE VII, pp. 43–44.

30. See OINE VIII, *Chapter 5*, pp. 171–73 and *Appendix A*, pp. 175–89 for the chronology of Meroitic settlement in Lower Nubia.

31. OINE VIII, *Chapter 1*, pp. 18–19.

32. Medjay are mentioned in numerous sources; for indication of location and activities, see Smither 1945. Meded is used to designate a country in the inscription of Harsiotef (Schäfer 1905, III, pp. 126–28). For Blemmyes, see Paully-Wissowa, "Blemyes," Kirwan 1982, pp. 197–98, and Skeat 1977. For Bega at Aksum, see Shinnie 1978a, pp. 260, 268; 1978b, p. 558 (Arabic).

33. Shinnie 1978a, p. 260, 1978b, p. 558.

NOBA AND NOUBADES

Even in the late Meroitic period, both the typical "pyramidal" Meroitic and "tumulus" type of burial were found in the vicinity of Meroe.[34] The most distinctive of the tumulus type burials were located generally south and west of the major centers as at Hobaji, and west of the Nile. The structure and arrangement of these tombs led directly to the tombs of Tanqasi and post-Meroitic Meroe. A form of the culture appeared subsequently at Qustul. Thus, both the original location of this cultural orientation or polarity and the expansion into Lower Nubia coincide generally although not precisely with the original location and subsequent expansion of the Noba that can be derived from historical sources.[35] Noubadian X-Group in Lower Nubia derived from the Noba of post-Meroitic Tanqasi and the Butana, and ultimately from the southern and western perimeter of the Meroitic empire.

F. GEOPOLITICS

Although several times a home of substantial states, Nubia only briefly was a power with ambitions and interests as large as the greatest states of the day. Nubia's importance depended on trade and relation to the security of Egypt.

TRADE

Pharaonic Egypt required the products of the desert, especially gold, and of the south, especially incense. Without these material supports, the authenticity of Egypt's cults was shaken[36] and the propriety of its government's claim to legitimacy was thrown into doubt. A persistent demand for certain southern products based on pharaonic culture gave Nubia a prominent positive role in Egypt's external relations. The products were derived from mines in the Atbai or by transfer along its routes; or by route in the Eastern Desert or along the river. The alternative Red Sea route hardly existed independently of the overland routes, for both passed through the desert.[37] This specialized trade was an enduring interest of Egypt and the peoples through or near whose territories it passed. With the decay and final dissolution of the pharaonic cults, however, incense and gold were less vital and the role of southern trade must have altered.

SECURITY

The reduced need for southern products meant that the policy of Egypt's rulers became primarily concerned with Nubia's potential threats to order in Egypt. Although soldiers and rulers had come from the south in many periods of disruption in Egypt, the Blemmyes became a particularly dangerous element in the third and fourth centuries A.D.[38]

Although the Kushites were sometimes provocative and required some action to keep them at a distance, their possession of the Valley checked the power of the Eastern Desert peoples well enough for trade and mining to flourish. The erosion of Meroitic power, however, and Roman internal strife offered new

34. See above, p. 33, notably the Hobaji tumulus. In addition to the material near the Butana, there are other sites at some distance. The full impact of southern and western relations cannot be explored here for lack of pertinent information in the west. (see, however, Seligman, 1916, pp. 107, 114, pls. XV–XX and Addison 1949, pl. XXX:2264, XXXIV:2193, 2000). The dates of both Faragab and Jebel Moya include many doubtful aspects (Addison 1956), but the absence of metal and parallels with sites closer to Meroe suggest dates sometime within the age of her empire are likely for much of the material.

35. Paully-Wissowa, "Noubai." The locations were indicated by Strabo (XVII, 819), Pliny (for Eratosthenes and Bion of Solai [VI-35]) and Ptolemy. Significantly, Ptolemy is the last to mention them until the time of Diocletian. The present Nuba homelands west of the Nile are well known.

36. If this seems to be a small cause, one can recall that the vast Portuguese empire was founded essentially on pepper.

37. Whitcomb and Johnson 1979, pp. 297–324. Pottery from sites surveyed in addition to that from Quseir itself has a rather narrow chronological range. It does not correspond to the Coptic period Egyptian pottery exported to X-Group Nubia. Olympiodorus reported that the emerald mines were in the hands of the Blemmyes.

38. Rise of the Blemmyes, see Török 1988, pp. 28–53; Paully-Wissowa, "Blemyes."

opportunities for peoples on the periphery. In Egypt, the Blemmyes now controlled the desert and spilled into the Nile valley, even settling there. In the end, raids and incursions went farther afield, to the Kharga oasis, and the Nile delta.[39]

The Roman response was to invite an active people to distract the invaders.[40] Although they did not appear near the frontier immediately, they entered the old Meroitic heartland, and in considerable force.[41] The new power of Aksum which apparently dominated the Blemmyes, and, perhaps, Meroe[42] acted forcefully, and it was shortly thereafter that the Noubades appear with a fully developed set of traditions in Lower Nubia.[43] The result was a dangerous combination with the Blemmyes. Egypt could have slipped from Rome's grasp like Africa had not subsidies and campaigns been applied to the problem. Thereafter, conflict between the Blemmyes and Noubades came to the fore, probably with Byzantine encouragement, which ended in a victory for the latter.[44] With the Blemmyes confined to the desert, the Nubian Valley was once again at least culturally united. It could not have been long afterward that Narses closed Philae and conversion proceeded in Nubia, with the Reconquista at least in planning stages. Justinian secured his southern flank with a series of diplomatic and religious efforts perhaps designed in part to divert the empire's southern neighbors with some of the struggles that had been so disastrous to imperial unity. In any case, the elaborate charade of competing missions of conversion took place against the backdrop of recruiting in the Nile delta for the African campaign.

The rulers of the northern Nile valley required a division of power in the south, a balance maintained by a power in the valley strong enough to keep peoples in either desert from using it as a base of activity against the north but not strong enough to dominate either one. This may explain why many important overland campaigns that resulted from considerable provocation had only punitive results.[45] The rulers of the north could not easily dispense with the warder in the south.

39. Paully-Wissowa, "Blemyes."

40. Shinnie 1978a, pp. 260–61. In addition to the cemeteries of Meroe and Tanqasi, numerous mound cemeteries remain unexplored in Sudan. See also Dinkler 1977 and Hofmann 1967, pp. 455–522, especially pp. 519–22.

41. Aksumite trade with the Nile is dealt with by Chittick (1982).

42. See Török 1988, pp. 41–44.

43. Skeat 1977. For a discussion of other documents and their relation to Noubades and Nouba or Anouba, see Plumley 1982.

44. See Török 1988, pp. 54–63 for a discussion of the conflicts.

45. This pattern would include the campaign of Psammettichus, and actions attributed to Cambyses and Petronius.

APPENDIX A

LIST OF TOMBS IN CEMETERIES Q, V, AND W BY LOCATION IN THE OINE PUBLICATION SERIES

Although the cemeteries generally contained remains from more than one period, some were unusually complex, and their remains are presented in several different volumes of the OINE series. A listing of the occurrences of tombs in the three most important cemeteries presented in this volume Q, V, and W is given below. This gives the location prefix by area and the volume which presents the tomb, if it is pre-X-Group. X-Group tombs are indicated by their cemetery area or type (animal pit), which locates their discussion here, or by "Christian" or "Uncertain," which indicates tombs not discussed in the present work.

The most difficult cemetery to index was Q. Cemetery Q was very large and complex, and many areas were excavated simultaneously resulting in widely scattered numbers. Since the Meroitic tombs essentially belonged to a single compact cemetery in Area Q*E*, sequential presentation was possible in OINE VIII. In order to present the X-Group materials in a logical order, however, Cemetery Q was broken down by areas, the tombs being presented in order within each area. The chapels and related material are presented before the X-Group private tombs. Note that surface structures were indicated by the expedition with the prefixes QA, QB, etc. A similar series of prefixes was used for cemetery areas; to distinguish the areas from the structures in the present work, the second letter of the cemetery area prefix is italicized, Q*A*, Q*B*, etc.

Table 26. List of Tomb Publications for Cemeteries Q, V, and W.

Tomb	Location/Publication	Tomb	Location/Publication
Qu. 7	Area Q*B*	Q 19	Area Q*A*
Q 1	Area Q*A*	Q 20	Animal pit, Qu. 3
Q 2	Area Q*A*	Q 21	Christian
Q 3	Area Q*A*	Q 22	Area Q*A*
Q 4	Area Q*A*	Q 23	Christian
Q 5	Animal pit, Qu. 3	Q 24	Christian
Q 6	Area Q*A*	Q 25	Area Q*A*
Q 7	Area Q*A*	Q 26	Animal pit, Qu. 3
Q 8	Area Q*A*	Q 27	Area Q*A*
Q 9	Area Q*A*	Q 28	Area Q*A*
Q 10	Area Q*A*	Q 29	Area Q*A*
Q 11	Area Q*A*	Q 30	Area Q*A*
Q 12	Area Q*A*	Q 31	Area Q*A*
Q 13	Area Q*A*	Q 32	Area Q*A*
Q 14	Area Q*A*	Q 33	Area Q*A*
Q 15	Area Q*A*	Q 34	Area Q*A*
Q 16	Area Q*A*	Q 35	Area Q*A*
Q 17	Area Q*A*	Q 36	Area Q*A*
Q 18	Area Q*A*	Q 37	Area Q*A*

Tomb	Location/Publication	Tomb	Location/Publication
Q 38	Area Q*A*	Q 85B	Christian
Q 39	Animal pit, Qu. 10	Q 86(A–C)	Christian
Q 40	Area Q*C*	Q 86A	Christian for reused object, see OINE VIII
Q 41	Area Q*C*		
Q 42	Area Q*C*	Q 87	Christian
Q 43	Area Q*C*	Q 88	Christian
Q 44	Area Q*C*	Q 89	Christian
Q 45	Christian	Q 90	Christian
Q 46	Christian	Q 91	Christian
Q 47	Christian	Q 92	Christian
Q 48	Christian	Q 93	Christian, no grave record
Q 49	Area Q*C*		
Q 50	Christian	Q 94	Christian, no grave record
Q 51	Area Q*C*		
Q 51A	Area Q*C*	Q 95	Christian, no grave record
Q 52	Area Q*C*		
Q 53	Area Q*C*	Q 96	Christian, no grave record
Q 54	Area Q*C*		
Q 55	Area Q*C*	Q 97	Christian
Q 56	Christian	Q 98	Christian
Q 57	Area Q*C*	Q 99	Christian
Q 58	Area Q*C*	Q 100	Christian
Q 59	Area Q*B*	Q 101A	Christian
Q 60	Area Q*B*	Q 101B	Christian
Q 61	Area Q*B*	Q 102	Christian
Q 62	Area Q*B*	Q 103	Christian
Q 63	Area Q*C*	Q 104	Christian
Q 64	Area Q*C*	Q 105	Christian
Q 65	Area Q*C*	Q 106	Christian, no grave record
Q 66	Area Q*C*		
Q 67	Area Q*C*	Q 107	Area Q*D*
Q 68	Area Q*B*	Q 108	Christian
Q 69	Area Q*B*	Q 109	Christian
Q 70	Area Q*B*	Q 110	Christian
Q 71	Area Q*B*	Q 111	Christian, no grave record
Q 72	Area Q*B*		
Q 73	Animal pit, Qu. 54	Q 112	Christian, no grave record
Q 74	Area Q*B*		
Q 75	Area Q*B*	Q 113	Christian, no grave record
Q 76	Area Q*B*		
Q 77	Animal pit, Qu. 60	Q 114	Christian, no grave record
Q 78	Area Q*B*		
Q 79	Animal pit, Qu. 4	Q 115	Christian, no grave record
Q 80	OINE IV		
Q 81	OINE VIII, Christian tomb	Q 116	Christian, no grave record
Q 82	Area Q*D*	Q 117	Area Q*D*
Q 83	Area Q*D*	Q 118	Christian?
Q 84	Area Q*D*	Q 119	Area Q*D*
Q 85A	Christian	Q 120	Christian
		Q 121	Christian

Tomb	Location/Publication	Tomb	Location/Publication
Q 122	Christian	Q 164	OINE VIII Area Q*E*, reused
Q 123	Christian, no grave record	Q 165	OINE VIII
Q 124	Christian	Q 166	OINE VIII
Q 125	Christian	Q 167	OINE VIII
Q 126	Christian	Q 168	OINE VIII
Q 127A	Christian	Q 169	OINE VIII
Q 127B	Christian	Q 170	OINE VIII
Q 128	Christian, no grave record	Q 171	OINE VIII
		Q 172	OINE VIII
Q 129	Christian, no grave record	Q 173	OINE VIII, OINE IX, sherds only
Q 130	Christian	Q 174	OINE VIII, Area Q*D*
Q 131	Christian	Q 175	OINE VIII
Q 132	Christian	Q 176	OINE VIII, OINE IX, sherds only
Q 133	Area Q*E*		
Q 134	Area Q*E*	Q 177	OINE VIII
Q 135	Area Q*E*	Q 178	OINE VIII
Q 136	Area Q*E*	Q 179	OINE VIII
Q 137	Area Q*E*	Q 180	OINE VIII
Q 138	OINE VIII	Q 181	OINE VIII
Q 139	OINE VIII	Q 182	OINE VIII
Q 140	Pit, chapel row QC	Q 183	OINE VIII
Q 141	Area Q*E*	Q 184	OINE VIII, Area Q*E*, reused
Q 142	Christian?		
Q 143	Area Q*D*	Q 185	OINE VIII
Q 144	Area Q*D*	Q 186	OINE VIII, Area Q*E*, reused
Q 145	Area Q*E*		
Q 146	Area Q*E*	Q 187	OINE VIII
Q 147	Area Q*E*	Q 188	OINE VIII
Q 148	Area Q*E*	Q 189	OINE VIII
Q 149	OINE VIII, Area Q*E*, reused	Q 190	OINE VIII
		Q 191	OINE VIII
Q 150	OINE VIII	Q 192	Area Q*E*
Q 151	OINE VIII	Q 193	OINE VIII, Christian?
Q 152	Area Q*E*	Q 194	OINE VIII
Q 153	OINE VIII	Q 195	Christian?
Q 154	OINE VIII	Q 196	Area Q*E*
Q 155	OINE VIII	Q 197	OINE VIII
Q 156	OINE VIII	Q 198	OINE VIII
Q 157	OINE VIII	Q 199	OINE VIII
Q 158	OINE VIII	Q 200	Christian
Q 159	OINE VIII	Q 200A	Christian
Q 160	Christian or post-Christian	Q 201	Christian
		Q 202	Christian, no grave record
Q 161	OINE VIII, Area Q*E* with Meroitic object		
		Q 203A	Christian
Q 162	OINE VIII	Q 203B	Christian
Q 163	OINE VIII	Q 204	Christian

Tomb	Location/Publication	Tomb	Location/Publication
Q 205	Christian, no grave record	Q 240	OINE VIII, OINE IX, sherds only
Q 206	Christian	Q 241	Pit, chapel row QC
Q 207	Christian	Q 242	OINE VIII
Q 208	Christian	Q 243	OINE VIII, Meroitic
Q 209	Christian, no grave record	Q 244	OINE VIII
		Q 245	OINE VIII
Q 210	Christian	Q 246	OINE VIII
Q 210A	Christian	Q 247	OINE VIII
Q 211	Christian, no grave record	Q 248	OINE VIII
		Q 249	OINE VIII
Q 212	Christian	Q 250	OINE VIII
Q 213	Christian, no grave record	Q 251	OINE VIII
		Q 252	OINE VIII
Q 214	Christian	Q 253	OINE VIII
Q 215	Christian, no grave record	Q 254	OINE VIII
		Q 255	OINE VIII
Q 216	Christian, no grave record	Q 256	OINE VIII
		Q 257	OINE VIII
Q 217	Christian, no grave record	Q 258	OINE VIII
		Q 259	OINE VIII
Q 218	Christian	Q 260	OINE VIII
Q 219	Christian, no grave record	Q 261	OINE VIII
		Q 262	OINE VIII
Q 220	Christian, no grave record	Q 263	OINE VIII
Q 221	Christian	Q 264	Animal pit, Qu. 36
Q 222	Christian, no grave record	Q 265	Animal pit, Qu. 36
		Q 266	OINE VIII
Q 223	Christian, no grave record	Q 266A	OINE VIII
		Q 267	OINE VIII
Q 224	Christian, no grave record	Q 268	OINE VIII
		Q 269	OINE VIII
Q 225	Christian, no grave record	Q 270	OINE VIII
		Q 271	OINE VIII
Q 226	Christian, no grave record	Q 272	OINE VIII
		Q 273	Christian, see OINE VIII, Q 169
Q 227	Area QC		
Q 228	OINE VIII	Q 274	OINE VIII
Q 229	OINE VIII	Q 275	OINE VIII
Q 230	OINE VIII	Q 276	OINE VIII
Q 231	Area QE	Q 277	OINE VIII
Q 232	OINE VIII	Q 278	OINE VIII
Q 233	OINE VIII	Q 279	OINE VIII, X-Group tomb QE, reused
Q 234	OINE VIII		
Q 235	OINE VIII	Q 280	OINE VIII
Q 236	OINE VIII	Q 281	OINE VIII
Q 237	OINE VIII	Q 282	Area QD
Q 238	OINE VIII, Christian tomb	Q 283	OINE VIII
		Q 284	OINE VIII
Q 239	OINE VIII	Q 285	Christian

Tomb	Location/Publication	Tomb	Location/Publication
Q 286	Christian	Q 328	OINE VIII pit, chapel row Q*C*
Q 287	OINE VIII, Christian		
Q 288	Uncertain contracted burial	Q 329	OINE VIII
		Q 330	OINE VIII
Q 289	Uncertain irregular burial	Q 331	OINE VIII
		Q 332	Area Q*E*
Q 290	OINE VIII	Q 333	OINE VIII pit, chapel row Q*C*
Q 291	OINE VIII		
Q 292	OINE VIII	Q 334	OINE VIII
Q 293	OINE VIII	Q 335	OINE VIII
Q 294	OINE VIII	Q 336	OINE VIII
Q 295	OINE VIII	Q 337	OINE VIII
Q 296	OINE VIII	Q 338	Area Q*E*
Q 297	OINE VIII	Q 339	OINE VIII, OINE IX, sherds only
Q 298	OINE VIII		
Q 299	OINE VIII	Q 340	OINE VIII
Q 300	OINE VIII	Q 341	OINE VIII
Q 301	OINE VIII	Q 342	OINE VIII
Q 302A	OINE VIII	Q 343	Area Q*E*
Q 302B	OINE VIII	Q 344	Area Q*E*
Q 303	OINE VIII, OINE IX, sherds only	Q 345	Area Q*E*
		Q 346	OINE VIII
Q 304	OINE VIII pit, chapel row Q*C*	Q 347	OINE VIII
		Q 348	Area Q*E*
Q 305	OINE VIII	Q 349	Area Q*E*
Q 306	OINE VIII	Q 350	Area Q*E*
Q 307	OINE VIII	Q 351	OINE VIII
Q 308	OINE VIII	Q 352	OINE VIII
Q 309	Area Q*E*	Q 353	OINE VIII
Q 310	OINE VIII	Q 354	OINE VIII
Q 311	OINE VIII	Q 355	OINE VIII
Q 312	OINE VIII	Q 356	Area Q*E*
Q 313	OINE VIII	Q 357	OINE VIII, Area Q*E*, reused
Q 314	OINE VIII		
Q 315	OINE VIII	Q 358	OINE VIII
Q 316	Area Q*E*	Q 359	OINE VIII
Q 317	OINE VIII pit, chapel row Q*C*	Q 360	Area Q*E*
		Q 361	Area Q*E*
Q 318	OINE VIII	Q 362	OINE VIII
Q 319	OINE VIII	Q 363	OINE VIII
Q 320	Area Q*E*	Q 363A	Post-Christian
Q 321	Area Q*E*	Q 364	OINE VIII
Q 322	OINE VIII	Q 365	OINE VIII
Q 323	OINE VIII	Q 366	OINE VIII
Q 324	OINE VIII	Q 367	OINE VIII
Q 325	OINE VIII	Q 368	OINE VIII
Q 326	Area Q*E*	Q 369	OINE VIII
Q 327	no record, burial Christian?	Q 370	OINE VIII
		Q 371	OINE VIII
		Q 372	OINE VIII

Tomb	Location/Publication	Tomb	Location/Publication
Q 373	OINE VIII	Q 421	Christian
Q 374	OINE VIII	Q 422	Area Q*E*
Q 375	OINE VIII	Q 423	OINE VIII
Q 376	Christian	Q 424	OINE VIII
Q 377	Christian	Q 425	Area Q*E*
Q 378	OINE VIII, Area Q*E*, reused	Q 426	OINE VIII
		Q 427	OINE VIII
Q 379	Area Q*E*	Q 428	OINE VIII
Q 380	Christian	Q 429	OINE VIII
Q 381	Area Q*E*	Q 430	OINE VIII
Q 382	OINE VIII	Q 431	Christian
Q 383	OINE VIII	Q 432	OINE VIII
Q 384	OINE VIII	Q 433	OINE VIII
Q 385	Area Q*E*	Q 434	OINE VIII, Area Q*E*, reused
Q 386	Christian		
Q 387	Area Q*E*	Q 435	Christian
Q 388	Area Q*E*	Q 436	Christian
Q 389	Area Q*E*	Q 437	OINE VIII
Q 390	Area Q*E*	Q 438	Christian
Q 391	Area Q*E*	Q 439	OINE VIII
Q 392	OINE VIII	Q 440	OINE VIII
Q 393	Area Q*E*	Q 441	OINE VIII
Q 394	Area Q*E*	Q 442	OINE VIII
Q 395	Christian?	Q 443	OINE VIII
Q 396	Christian	Q 444	OINE VIII
Q 397	Christian	Q 445	Christian
Q 398	Christian	Q 446	Area Q*E*
Q 399	Christian	Q 447	OINE VIII
Q 400	Area Q*E*	Q 448	OINE VIII
Q 401	Christian tomb, sherds only, Q*C* chapel row	Q 449	OINE VIII
		Q 450	OINE VIII
Q 402	OINE VIII	Q 451	Christian
Q 403	Christian	Q 452	Christian? Infant
Q 404	Christian	Q 453	Christian
Q 405	Area Q*E*	Q 454	Area Q*E* reused Christian
Q 406	OINE VIII		
Q 407	OINE VIII	Q 455	Christian
Q 408	OINE VIII	Q 456	Christian
Q 409	Christian	Q 457	A-Group cache pit, see OINE IV
Q 410	Area Q*E*		
Q 411	Christian	Q 458	OINE VIII
Q 412	Christian	Q 459	OINE VIII
Q 413	OINE VIII	Q 460	OINE VIII
Q 414	OINE VIII	Q 461	OINE VIII
Q 415	OINE VIII	Q 462	OINE VIII
Q 416	OINE VIII	Q 463	OINE VIII, Area Q*E*, reused
Q 417	OINE VIII		
Q 418	Christian	Q 464	OINE VIII
Q 419	Christian	Q 465	OINE VIII
Q 420	Christian	Q 466	OINE VIII

Tomb	Location/Publication	Tomb	Location/Publication
Q 467	OINE VIII	Q 514	OINE VIII
Q 468	Area Q*E*	Q 515	OINE VIII
Q 469	OINE VIII	Q 516	OINE VIII
Q 470	OINE VIII	Q 517	OINE VIII
Q 471	post-Christian	Q 518	OINE VIII
Q 472	OINE VIII	Q 519	OINE VIII
Q 473	Area Q*E*	Q 520	OINE VIII
Q 474	OINE VIII	Q 521	OINE VIII
Q 475	OINE VIII	Q 522	OINE VIII
Q 476	Christian	Q 523	OINE VIII
Q 477	OINE VIII	Q 524	OINE VIII
Q 478	OINE VIII	Q 525	OINE VIII
Q 479	Area Q*E*	Q 526	OINE VIII
Q 480	OINE VIII	Q 527	OINE VIII
Q 481	OINE VIII	Q 528	OINE VIII
Q 482	OINE VIII	Q 529	OINE VIII
Q 483	OINE VIII	Q 530	OINE VIII
Q 484	OINE VIII	Q 531	OINE VIII
Q 485	OINE VIII	Q 532	OINE VIII
Q 486	OINE VIII	Q 533	OINE VIII
Q 487	OINE VIII	Q 534	OINE VIII
Q 488	OINE VIII	Q 535	OINE VIII
Q 489	OINE VIII	Q 536	OINE VIII
Q 490	OINE VIII	Q 537	OINE VIII
Q 491	OINE VIII	Q 538	OINE VIII
Q 492	OINE VIII pit, chapel row Q*C*	Q 539	OINE VIII
		Q 540	OINE VIII
Q 493	OINE VIII	Q 541	OINE VIII
Q 494	OINE VIII	Q 542	OINE VIII
Q 495	OINE VIII	Q 543	OINE VIII
Q 496	OINE VIII	Q 544	OINE VIII
Q 497	OINE VIII	Q 545	Area Q*E* reused Christian
Q 498	OINE VIII		
Q 499	OINE VIII	Q 546	OINE VIII
Q 500	OINE VIII	Q 547	OINE VIII
Q 501	Area Q*C*	Q 548	OINE VIII
Q 502	Area Q*C*	Q 549	OINE VIII
Q 503	Area Q*C*	Q 550	OINE VIII
Q 504	Area Q*C*	Q 551	OINE VIII (C)
Q 505	Area Q*C*	Q 552	OINE VIII
Q 506	OINE VIII	Q 553	OINE VIII
Q 507	OINE VIII	Q 554	OINE VIII
Q 508	OINE VIII	Q 555	OINE VIII
Q 509	OINE VIII	Q 556	OINE VIII
Q 510	OINE VIII	Q 557	OINE VIII
Q 511	OINE VIII	Q 558	OINE VIII
Q 512	OINE VIII, OINE IX, sherds only	Q 559	OINE VIII
		Q 560	OINE VIII
Q 513	OINE VIII, OINE IX, sherds only	Q 561	OINE VIII
		Q 562	OINE VIII

Tomb	Location/Publication	Tomb	Location/Publication
Q 563	OINE VIII	Q 611	A-Group cache pit, see OINE IV
Q 564	OINE VIII		
Q 565	OINE VIII	Q 612	OINE VIII
Q 566	OINE VIII	Q 613	OINE VIII
Q 567	OINE VIII	Q 614	OINE VIII
Q 568	OINE VIII	Q 615	A-Group cache pit, see OINE IV
Q 569	OINE VIII		
Q 570	OINE VIII	Q 616	A-Group cache pit, see OINE IV
Q 571	OINE VIII, OINE IX, sherds only		
		Q 617	OINE VIII
Q 572	OINE VIII	Q 618	OINE VIII
Q 573	OINE VIII	Q 619	OINE VIII
Q 574	OINE VIII	Q 620	OINE VIII
Q 575	OINE VIII	Q 621	OINE VIII
Q 576	OINE VIII	Q 622	OINE VIII
Q 577	OINE VIII	Q 623	OINE VIII
Q 578	OINE VIII	Q 624	OINE VIII
Q 579	OINE VIII	Q 625	OINE VIII
Q 580	Area QE	Q 626	OINE VIII
Q 581	OINE VIII	Q 627	OINE VIII
Q 582	Area QE	Q 628	OINE VIII
Q 583	Area QE	Q 629	OINE VIII
Q 584	OINE VIII	Q 630	OINE VIII
Q 585	OINE VIII	Q 631	A-Group cache pit, see OINE IV
Q 586	OINE VIII		
Q 587	OINE VIII	Q 632	OINE VIII
Q 588	OINE VIII	Q 633	OINE VIII
Q 589	Area QE	Q 634	OINE VIII
Q 590	OINE VIII	Q 635	Christian
Q 591	OINE VIII	Q 636	OINE VIII
Q 592	OINE VIII	Q 637	OINE VIII
Q 593	OINE VIII	Q 638	OINE VIII
Q 594	OINE VIII, Area QE, reused	Q 639	OINE VIII
		Q 640	OINE VIII
Q 595	OINE VIII	Q 641	OINE VIII
Q 596	OINE VIII	Q 642	OINE VIII
Q 597	OINE VIII	Q 643	OINE VIII
Q 598	OINE VIII	Q 644	OINE VIII
Q 599	OINE VIII	Q 645	OINE VIII
Q 600	OINE VIII	Q 646	OINE VIII
Q 601	OINE VIII	Q 647	OINE VIII
Q 602	OINE VIII	Q 648	OINE VIII
Q 603	OINE VIII	Q 649	OINE VIII, OINE IX, sherds only
Q 604	OINE VIII		
Q 605	OINE VIII	Q 650	OINE VIII
Q 606	OINE VIII	Q 651	OINE VIII
Q 607	OINE VIII	Q 652	OINE VIII
Q 608	OINE VIII	Q 653	OINE VIII
Q 609	OINE VIII	Q 654	OINE VIII
Q 610	OINE VIII	Q 655	OINE VIII

Tomb	Location/Publication	Tomb	Location/Publication
Q 656	A-Group cache pit, see OINE IV	VB 25	OINE VII, OINE VI
Q 657	A-Group cache pit, see OINE IV	V 26–40	Numbers not used
		VC 41	Area VC
Q 658	OINE VIII	VC 42	Area VC
Q 659	OINE VIII	VC 43	Christian?, not on plan, rectangular grave
Q 660	OINE VIII		
Q 661	OINE VIII	VC 44	Not on plan
Q 662	A-Group cache pit, see OINE IV	VC 45	OINE VI
		VC 46	OINE VII, OINE VI
Q 663	OINE VIII	VC 47	OINE VI
Q 664	OINE VIII	VC 48	OINE VI
Q 665	OINE VIII	VC 49	OINE VI
Q 666	OINE VIII	VC 50	OINE VI
Q 667	OINE VIII	VD 51	OINE IV
Q 668	OINE VIII	VD 52	OINE IV
Q 669	OINE VIII	VD 53	OINE VI
Q 670	OINE VIII	VD 54	OINE VI
Q 671	A-Group cache pit, see OINE IV	VD 55	OINE VI
		VD 56	OINE VI
Q 672	A-Group cache pit, see OINE IV	VD 57	OINE IV
		VD 58	OINE IV
Q 673	A-Group cache pit, see OINE IV	VF 59	OINE IV
		VF 60	OINE VI
Q 674	OINE VIII	VF 61	OINE IV
Q 675	OINE VIII	VF 62	OINE VI
Q 676	OINE VIII	VF 63	OINE VI
Q 677	OINE VIII	VF 64	OINE VI
Q 678	no record	VF 65	OINE IV
Q 679	OINE VIII	VF 66	OINE VI
Q 680	OINE VIII	VF 67	OINE IV
Q 681	OINE VIII	VF 68	Area VF
Q 682	OINE VIII	VF 69	Area VF
Q 683	OINE VIII	VB 70	Area VB
Q 684	OINE VIII	VB 71	OINE VI
VA 1	Christian	VF 72	OINE VI
VA 2	OINE VII	VF 72A	OINE VII
VA 3	Christian	VF 73	OINE VI
VA 4	Christian	VF 74	OINE VI
VA 5	Christian, unexcavated	VF 75	OINE VI
VA 6	Christian, unexcavated	VF 76	OINE VI
VA 7	OINE VII	VF 77	OINE VI
VA 8	Christian	VF 78	OINE IV
VA 9	Area VA	VF 79	OINE VI
VA 10	Christian	VF 80	Two pits, A-Group?, not described
VA 11	Christian		
VA 12	Area VA	VF 81	OINE VI
VA 13	Area VA	VF 82	OINE VI
VA 14	Area VA	VF 83	OINE VI
V 15–24	Numbers not used	VG 84	OINE IV, recut Christian?

Tomb	Location/Publication
VG 85	OINE IV, recut Christian?
VG 86	Area VG
VG 87	Early pit, recut Christian?
VG 88	Christian
VG 89	Area VG, reused Christian
VG 90	Christian
VG 91	OINE VII
VG 92	OINE VI
VG 93	OINE VI
VG 94	OINE VI
VG 95	Area VG
VG 96	Area VG
VG 97	OINE VI, X-Group cup
V 98	No record, number not used?
V 99	No record, number not used?
V 100	No record, number not used?
VE 101	Christian
VE 102	Christian
VE 103	Christian
VE 104	Christian
VE 105	Christian
VE 106	Christian
VE 107	Christian
VE 108	Christian
VE 109	Christian
V 110	No record, number not used?
VH 111	OINE VII
VH 112	OINE VI, reused X-Group?, not located
VH 113	OINE VI
VH 114	OINE VII
VH 115	Area VH
VH 116	OINE VII
VH 117	Christian, cut pit
VH 118	OINE VII
VH 119	OINE VII
VH 120	OINE VI
VH 121	Christian
VH 122	Area VH
VH 123	Uncertain
VH 124	Uncertain
VH 125	OINE VII
VH 126	Christian
VH 127	Uncertain

Tomb	Location/Publication
VH 128	Christian
VH 129	Christian
VH 130	Christian
V 131–200	Numbers not used
VI 201	Area VI
VI 202	Area VI
VI 203	Area VI
W1 1	OINE VII
W1 2	OINE IV
W1 3	Pit with *qadus*, uncertain
W1 4	No record, A-Group?
W1 5	OINE IV
W1 6	OINE IV
W1 7	OINE IV
W1 8	OINE IV
W1 9	OINE IV
W1 10	OINE IV
W1 11	OINE IV
W1 12	OINE IV
W1 13	Christian
W1 14	OINE IV
W1 15	OINE IV
W1 16	OINE IV
W1 17	OINE IV
W1 18	No record, A-Group?
W1 19	OINE IV
W1 20	OINE IV
W1 21	OINE IV
W1 22	OINE IV
W1 23	OINE IV
W1 24	OINE VII
W1 25	OINE IV
W1 26	OINE IV
W1 27	OINE IV
W1 28	OINE IV
W1 28A	OINE VII
W1 29	OINE IV
W1 30	OINE IV
W1 31	OINE IV
W1 32	OINE IV
W1 33	OINE IV
W1 34	OINE VII
W1 35	OINE IV
W1 36	Christian
W1 37	Christian
W1 38	OINE IV
W1 39	OINE VII
W1 40	OINE VII
W1 41	OINE VII

Tomb	Location/Publication	Tomb	Location/Publication
W1 42	OINE VII	W2 66	Cemetery W2
W1 43	OINE VII	W2 67	Cemetery W2
W1 44	Uncertain infant burial	W2 68	OINE VI
W1 45	OINE VII	W2 69	Cemetery W2
W1 46	OINE VII	W2 70	OINE VII
W1 47	OINE VII	W2 71	Cemetery W2
W1 48	OINE VII	W2 72	OINE IV
W1 49	OINE VII	W2 73	Cemetery W2
W1 50	OINE VII	W2 74	Cemetery W2
W1 51	Uncertain late burial	W2 75	OINE VII
W2 52	OINE VI	W2 76	Cemetery W2
W2 53	Uncertain	W2 77	OINE VI
W2 54	Cemetery W2	W2 78	OINE VI
W2 55	OINE VI	W2 79	Christian
W2 56	OINE VI	W2 80	Cemetery W2
W2 57	Cemetery W2	W2 81	OINE VI
W2 58	Cemetery W2	W2 82	Uncertain
W2 59	Cemetery W2	W2 83	Cemetery W2
W2 60	Cemetery W2, reused Christian	W2 84	Cemetery W2
		W2 85	OINE VII
W2 61	Cemetery W2	W2 86	OINE VII, OINE IV (redated)
W2 62	Cemetery W2		
W2 63	Cemetery W2	W2 87	Christian
W2 64	Uncertain	W2 88	Cemetery W2
W2 65	Cemetery W2		

APPENDIX B

REGISTER OF FINDS

The X-Group materials came from a number of different types of loci. However, the register is an extension of the recording on the Oriental Institute Nubian Expedition burial sheets which describe burials and pits. Surface installations such as chapels were described only by area and often not given individual descriptive records. For the present work, descriptive entries have been assembled from notes by James Knudstad, from the detailed architectural sketches, and from the notations for sherds and registered objects and have been made to parallel the burial sheets. Apart from essential facts of burial and shape of the tomb (with a simple sketch), the burial sheets list objects found in the tombs, generally in order of their discovery. The burial sheets list complete objects, and a small label identified each object with a number (for example Q 1—1), and information on the findspot within the tomb which was later used as the basis for describing the provenience in the field register. Proveniences given to individual objects identify the tomb quite clearly, but the original location of scattered fragments within the tomb was often not indicated precisely. The register in 1962–1963 identified objects and samples. Sherds were identified only by tomb number and not registered separately. Some complete vessels were not registered. In 1963–1964, only objects were registered. Material samples and sherds were identified only as coming from a certain locus. In some cases, relatively undistinguished small objects were considered samples. Both types of recording were encountered. Although the individual objects, sherds, and samples were clearly noted by location, entries on some burial sheets, such as "sherd sample taken," indicate that the recovery of sherds was not complete and was probably haphazard. A number of items were discarded at the end of the season or were left in the tombs. A vehicle accident in 1964 resulted in the mixing of some of the sherds from Cemetery L which also mixed up sherds from the Ballana settlement with some sherds from Qasr el Wizz. Not all of the sherds from these two sites were affected.

Note that surface structures were indicated by the expedition with the prefixes QA, QB, etc. A similar series of prefixes was used for cemetery areas. To distinguish the cemetery areas from structures in the present work, the second letter of the cemetery area prefix is italicized, Q*A*, Q*B*, etc.

Tomb description: The entry gives the type of deposit, a simplified description, and dimensions as recorded in meters. Illustrations are cited in the right margin. Most of the tombs had chambers or niches (loculi) which were blocked off from the shaft. Many also had tumuli. However, these were not presented by measurement or drawing on the burial sheets. Wherever possible, tumuli have been reconstructed from photographs (pls. 33–35). These reconstructed tumuli are presented as stippled mounds on the respective cemetery plans. The plans also show tumuli in Cemeteries Q and R which were restored on the basis of tumuli preserved over nearby comparable tombs. They are indicated by dashed lines (see pls. 4–10).

Burial: The position of the body is given by four entries separated by a '/' that give the (river) direction of the head (toward the N, S, E, W, etc.), the basic position (B for back; S, R, or L for side), the position of the legs, and the position of the hands.

Body: The age and sex of the body are given as they were recorded by members of the expedition. In 1963–1964, the anthropologist was Duane Burnor (Cemeteries VH, W2, and B). The categories used were Infant I and II, Juvenile, Adult, Mature, and Senile. In doubtful cases, the categories are hyphenated. Sometimes, an estimate in years or months was indicated.

Objects: Apart from the burial and sherds, the contents of the tomb are listed under the heading "Objects." In cases where the structure of the tomb was complex or the objects were arranged in some special way, there is a subheading that indicates the location of various objects within the tomb. Important individual objects are listed, generally in the numerical order established in the field. A few objects were added to this list in Chicago, and the numbers were sometimes changed for publication (the key number for any object is the OIM number [Oriental Institute Museum, Chicago] or the field number in cases where the object was assigned to the Cairo Museum). Each object has a brief verbal descriptive designation, followed by the descriptive codes which are necessary to locate it in the appropriate discussion or table in the text; where the table is brief, codes are not indicated in the tomb register. Brief descriptive information on decorated pottery is included in the present register with Munsell color readings for selected pieces. Measurements are given for many objects that are not illustrated. Beads are indicated only by tomb and OIM number, having a separate tabular presentation in *Chapter 3* (tab. 24).

Table 27. List of Complexes.

Complexes with Chapels	
Qu. 31 Complex	pl. 7
Chapels QB 1–58	
List of stone objects and fittings	
Qu. 48 Complex	pl. 8
Chapels QC 1–54	
Pits with chapels (in order of chapel location)	
Meroitic tombs with X-Group material attributed to cult activity (in order of chapel location)	
Meroitic tombs with X-Group material and no clear relation to cult (in order of tomb number)	
Qu. 56 Complex	pl. 8
Chapel QE 1	
Deposit QE 2	
Qu. 36 Complex	pl. 9
Chapels QF 1–14	
Q 264, Animal Pit	
Q 265, Animal Pit	
Complexes without Chapels	
Qu. 3 Complex	pl. 4
Q 5, Animal Pit	
Q 20, Animal Pit	
Q 26, Animal Pit	
Qu. 54 Complex	pl. 5
Q 73, Animal Pit	
Qu. 60 Complex	pl. 5
Q 77, Animal Pit	
Qu. 4 Complex	pl. 5
Q 79, Animal Pit	
Qu. 10 Complex	
Q 39, Animal Pit	pl. 4
Cemetery 219	pl. 3
BA structure	

Textiles are discussed in Mayer-Thurman and Williams 1979. However, a number of tombs have been redated since that time. Each of the textile entries is indicated by its number (CAT 15) in the textile volume or by CAT Mer., indicating a discarded textile dated to the Meroitic period (Mayer-Thurman and Williams 1979, p. 148), CAT X-Gr., indicating one dated to the X-Group there, and CAT unc., indicating an uncertain date. A number of textiles that existed only in traces or impressions, not listed in the catalogue, are listed in this register without any CAT indication.

Pottery: Where separate lists of sherds are appended to the tomb entry, they are divided according to major cultural group and individual vessels are indicated by a Roman letter, followed by the code that refers to the text. These entries also include remarks on decoration and Munsell color readings.

Complexes: Cemetery 220 or Cemetery Q, as it was known to the Oriental Institute Nubian Expedition, was the most complex site explored. The X-Group remains alone included royal tombs and complexes with offering places, chapels, sacrifice pits, cooking pits, and private tombs, which were also sometimes complexes. The complexes and tombs were scattered unevenly across the cemetery in a number of areas. These could be broken down into phases or stages. However, the location of private tombs in the cemetery was governed by the location of complexes (table 27; note that BA is also included).

A. CEMETERY AREAS

Private burials were found in separate areas and scattered among earlier tombs at Qustul and in Cemetery B at Ballana. Since they were often clustered in areas smaller than the larger cemetery designation, they are considered in lettered areas as given in table 28 below.

Table 28. List of Cemetery Areas with Private Tombs.

Qustul South:		
Area Q*A*	(includes complexes Qu. 3 and Qu. 10)	pl. 4
Area Q*B*	(includes complexes Qu. 4, Qu. 54, and Qu. 60)	pl. 5
Area Q*C*	(includes complexes Q 51 and Q 227, Qu. 14?)	pl. 6
Qustul North:		
Area Q*D*	(includes complex Qu. 31)	pl. 7
Area Q*E*	(includes complex Qu. 48)	pl. 8
Area Q*F*	(includes complex Qu. 36)	pl. 9
Cemetery R		pl. 10
Cemetery V:		
Area VA		pl. 11a
Area VB		pl. 11b
Area VC		pl. 11c
Area VF		pl. 12a
Area VG		pl. 12b
Area VH		pl. 12c
Cemetery W2		pl. 13a
Cemetery J		pl. 13b
Tomb M 1	Not illustrated in this volume	
Cemetery B	Not illustrated in this volume	

B. CEMETERY Q (220)

As indicated above, the areas of Cemetery Q all contain more than one kind of locus, and often these included materials of different date and type within X-Group as well as earlier and later periods. The following summaries, given in tables 29–39, indicate the various categories within the areas.

SOUTH REGION, AREA Q*A* (pl. 4)

Table 29. List of Contexts in Cemetery Area Q*A*.

X-Gr. tombs:

Q 1–4, 6–19, 22
25, 27–38

Complexes:

Qu. 3:

Q 5, Animal pit
Q 20, Animal pit
Q 26, Animal pit

Qu. 10:

Q 39, Animal pit

Post-X-Gr. tombs:

Q 21
Q 23
Q 24

Table 30. Stages in Cemetery Area Q*A*.

1. Dated tombs (early): 12, 33; Other tombs: 10, 11, 13, 14, 22, 27, 29–32, 34–38, 33, 34, 32, 37; all tombs are N-S
2. Early X-Gr. tombs, dated: 6, 8, 9; other tombs: 4, 7; all are N-S
3. Middle X-Gr. tombs, dated: 1, 2, 3, 18; other tombs: 15, 16, 17; tombs 3 and 18 are N-S
4. Tombs of uncertain early or middle date with N-S shafts, ledges and vaults: 19, 25, 28

SOUTH REGION, AREA Q*B* (pl. 5)

Table 31. List of Contexts in Cemetery Area Q*B*.

X-Gr. tombs:

Qu. 7, Q 59–61, 62, 68–72, 74–76, 78

Complexes:

Qu. 60:

Q 77, Animal pit

Qu. 4:

Q 79, Animal pit

Qu. 54:

Q 73, Animal pit

Post-X-Gr. tombs:

Q 200–Q 226, small cemetery in NE part of area

Table 32. Stages in Cemetery Area Q*B*.

Subordinate tumulus to royal cemetery, larger than tumuli in private areas: Qu. 7

1. N-S tombs, dated by three tombs in continuation of area in Q*C*: 59, 60, 61B, 68, 69, 71

    E-W tombs, dated by one tomb here and six tombs in the continuation of the area; dated tomb, middle X-Gr.: 70; other tombs: 61, 72
2. N-S tombs, dated early: 62, 74; other tombs: 75, 76
3. Isolated middle X-Gr. tomb: Q 78

Animal pits:

Q 73, Q 77, and Q 79

SOUTH REGION, AREA Q*C* (pl. 6)

Table 33. List of Contexts in Cemetery Area Q*C*.

X-Gr. tombs:

Q 40–44, 49, 51, 51A–55, 57, 58, 63–67, 227, 501–505

Surface installations:

pottery deposits at tombs Q 51 and Q 227; belong either to these tombs or tumulus Qu. 14

Post-X-Gr.:

Q 46–48, 50, 56, 63 (burial)

Table 34. Stages in Cemetery Area Q*C*.

1. N-S tombs, dated early: 54, 66, 67; other tombs: 43, 57, 65

    E-W tombs, dated to middle X-Gr.: 42 (with ledges and vault), 51A, 52, 53, 58, 227; other tombs: 64
2. N-S tombs, none dated: 40, 41, 44, 55 (with ledges and vault), 505

    E-W tombs, dated to middle X-Gr.: 502, 503(?); other tombs: 501, 504

NORTH REGION, AREA Q*D* (pl. 7)

Table 35. List of Contexts in Cemetery Area Q*D*.

Pre-X-Gr.:
    Q 80 (A-Group cache pit)
X-Gr. tombs:
    Q 82-84, 107, 117, 119, 143, 144, 282
Complexes:
    Qu. 31, chapel row QB
Post-X-Gr. tombs:
    Q 85, 86-105, 108-116, 118: small cemetery
       to the W
    Q 120–131, 132: small cemetery to the E
       (not on plan)
    Q 81, 142: other tombs
Unknown:
    Q 106

Table 36. Stages in Cemetery Area Q*D*.

1. N-S shafts, dated early-middle X-Gr.: Q 82; other tombs: 83, 282
2. N-S tomb, dated early-middle X-Gr.: Q 107; dated middle X-Gr.: 117; other tomb: 119
3. Ledges, vault and niche, dated to middle X-Gr.: Q 143; other tomb: Q 144

NORTH REGION, AREA Q*E* (pl. 8)

Table 37. List of Contexts in Cemetery Area Q*E*.

Pre-X-Gr.:
    A-Group: Q 611, 615, 616, 656, 657, 662, 671–673, pit 571, pit 681
    Meroitic Cemetery (see OINE VIII)
X-Gr. tombs:
    Q 133–137, 141, 145–149, 152, 161, 164, 184, 186, 192, 196, 231, 279, 309, 316, 320, 321, 326,
    332, 338, 343–345, 348–350, 356, 357, 360, 361, 377–379, 381, 385, 387–391, 393, 394, 400,
    405, 410, 422, 425, 434, 446, 463 (Burial B), 468, 473, 479, 545, 580, 582, 583, 589,
    594 (intrusive)
X-Gr. complexes:
    Qu. 48
    Chapel row QC
    Pits, either numbered or identified by adjacent tomb: Q 140, 241, 304, 317, 324, 328, 333, 368,
      480, 492
    Qu. 56
    Chapel pit E1
Post-X-Gr. tombs: (not a list, indication of special cemetery)
    Small cemetery NW of Meroitic cemetery: Q 376, 386, 395–399, 401, 403, 404, 409, 411, 412,
      418–421, 431
Tombs that belong in sequence, found in other locations:
    Q 143–144 (Area Q*D*)
    Q 227 (Area Q*B*)
    Q 264–265 (Area Q*F*)
    Q 282 (Area Q*D*)

Table 38. Stages in Cemetery Area Q*E.*

---

1. Widely spaced tombs with long E approach to N-S chambers, directly W of Qu. 48, dated to early-middle X-Gr.: Q 134; other tombs: Q 133, 135, 136

2. Four tombs located W of Qu. 57/49, of both orientations:

   a. Long E approach with N-S chamber, dated to middle X-Gr.: Q 148

   b. N-S shafts with chambers on the W side: Q 145, 146

   c. E-W shaft with chamber on the N side, dated to middle X-Gr.: Q 147

3. Tombs scattered to the N and S of the chapel row:

   a. N-S shafts with chambers on the W side: Q 361, 137, 141, 350, 379, 479

   b. E-W shafts with chambers on the N side, dated to early X-Gr.: Q 434; other tomb: Q 345

4. A cluster of closely spaced tombs located E of Qu. 49:

   a. N-S shafts with chambers on the W side, dated to early X-Gr.: Q 192, 344, 388; other tombs: Q 356, 381, 385, 387, 390, 394, 410

   b. E-W shafts with chambers on the N side: Q 349, 389

5. A cluster of tombs with N-S shafts and chambers on the W side located between Qu. 56, 55, and 50, dated to early X-Gr.: Q 161, 196, 279 (possibly), 309 (possibly), 316, 321 (possibly), 338; other tombs: Q 326, 343, 348, 393, 422, 425, 468

6. Three tombs located E of Qu. 51, N-S shafts with chambers on the W side: Q 580, 583, 589

Note that Stage 6 is probably to be included with Stage 5. Stages 3–5 date to early X-Group. Stages 1 and 2 seem to date to middle X-Group, though the date of Stage 1 is problematical.

NORTH REGION, AREA Q*F* (pl. 9)

Table 39. List of Contexts in Cemetery Area Q*F.*

Pre-X-Gr.:

   Q 288, 289, 457

X-Gr. private tombs:

   Q 454 (X-Gr. reused by Christian)

X-Gr. complexes:

   Qu. 36

   Chapel row QF

   Animal pits: Q 264, 265

Post-X-Gr. tombs:

   Q 285, 286, 287, 435, 438, 445 (note: 435, 438, 445 in "a small plot to the S-E")

   Q 451–456 (to NE)

C. REGISTER OF FINDS

OUTLINE OF REGISTERS

X-Group remains at Qustul and Ballana are considered in the following order:

The X-Group Royal Cemetery at Qustul, Cemetery Q or 220 (table 40):

Complexes with cult structures:

Qu. 31: Chapels, pit

Qu. 48: Chapels, pits

Qu. 56: Chapel pit

Qu. 36: Chapels, Animal sacrifice burials

Complexes without cult structures:

Qu. 3

Qu. 54

Qu. 10

Private tombs

Area Q*A*

Area Q*B*

Area Q*C*

Area Q*D*

Area Q*E*

Area Q*F*

Other cemeteries:

R (table 42)

Area VA (table 43)

Area VB (table 44)

Area VC (table 45)

Area VD (No remains)

Area VE (No remains)

Area VF (table 46)

Area VG (table 47)

Area VH (table 48)

Area VI (table 49)

W2 (table 50)

J (table 51)

Tomb M 1 (table 52)

B (table 53)

The X-Group Royal Cemetery at Ballana, Cemetery 219 (table 54):

The circular structure at Ballana 4/118

CEMETERY Q (220) (pl. 14)

Table 40. Register of X-Group Finds in Cemetery Q.

Chapel	Description and Contents	Cairo	OIM	Figure/Plate
	QU. 31 COMPLEX			
I. CHAPELS Q*B*				
II. STONE OBJECTS AND FITTINGS				
I. QU. 31 COMPLEX: CHAPELS Q*B*				pl. 5
QB 1	Rectangular chapel with recessed doorway; long axis E-W; E wall thickened toward the N The chapel is much larger than others in the row.			fig. 66

Table 40. Register of X-Group Finds in Cemetery Q (*cont.*).

Chapel	Description and Contents	Cairo	OIM	Figure/Plate
QB 1 (*cont.*)				
Sherds:			33114	
	A. X-Gr. ord. body sherd			
	B. Unc. ribbed amphora body sherd			
	C. Post-X-Gr. uncoated bowl, ord.			
	D. Post-X-Gr. orange V-shaped bowl			
QB 2	Rectangular chapel with irreg. angles			fig. 66
Object:				
	Jamb with raised relief of "Isis garland"		20460	fig. 74a
Sherds:			33115	
	A. X-Gr. ord. bowl			
	B. X-Gr. ord. goblet base I—A, had been used as cooking pot			
	C. Coptic period Eg. utility *amphoriskos* II—			
Chapels 1 and 2 are separated from the main groups of the row, near the front of the tumulus. Their axis differs slightly from groups to the E and to the W.				
QB 3	Rectangular chapel with buttresses on the E, W, and N walls. The axis is the same as chapels 1 and 2, but it is separated from them.			fig. 66
Sherds:			33116	
	A. X-Gr. ord. jar			
	B. Unc. ribbed, gray amphora?			
	C. Post-X-Gr., pk. with voids and sand, body			
	D. Post-X-Gr., gray			
	E. Post-X-Gr., pk.-wh. (as C)			
	NID five sherds			

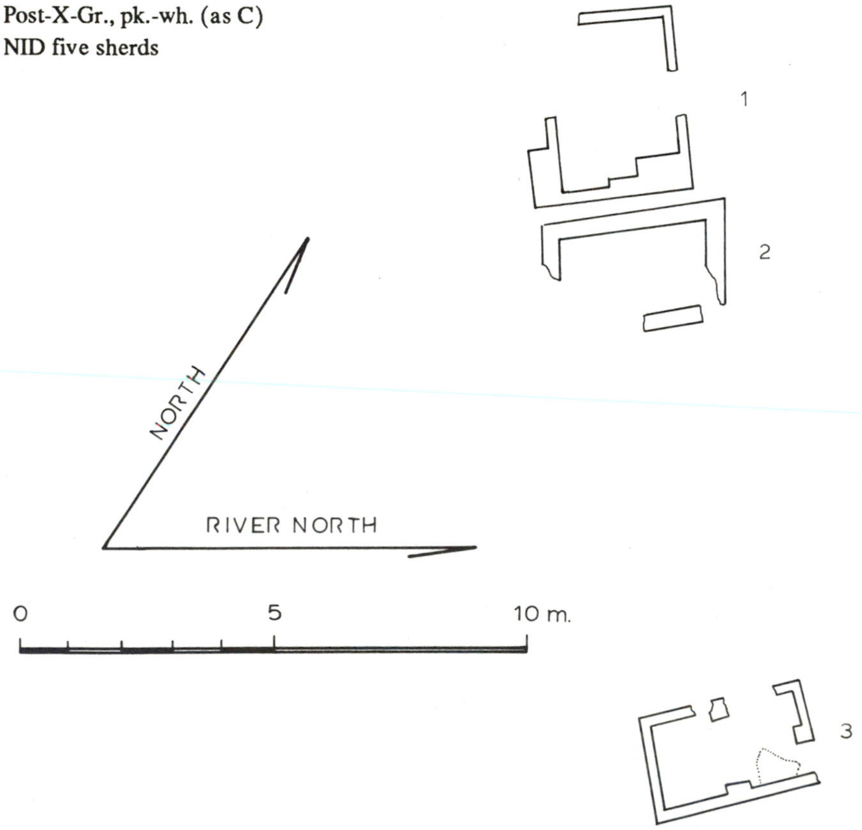

Figure 66. Plans of Chapels QB 1–3.

Table 40. Register of X-Group Finds in Cemetery Q (*cont.*).

Chapel	*Description and Contents*	*Cairo*	*OIM*	*Figure/Plate*

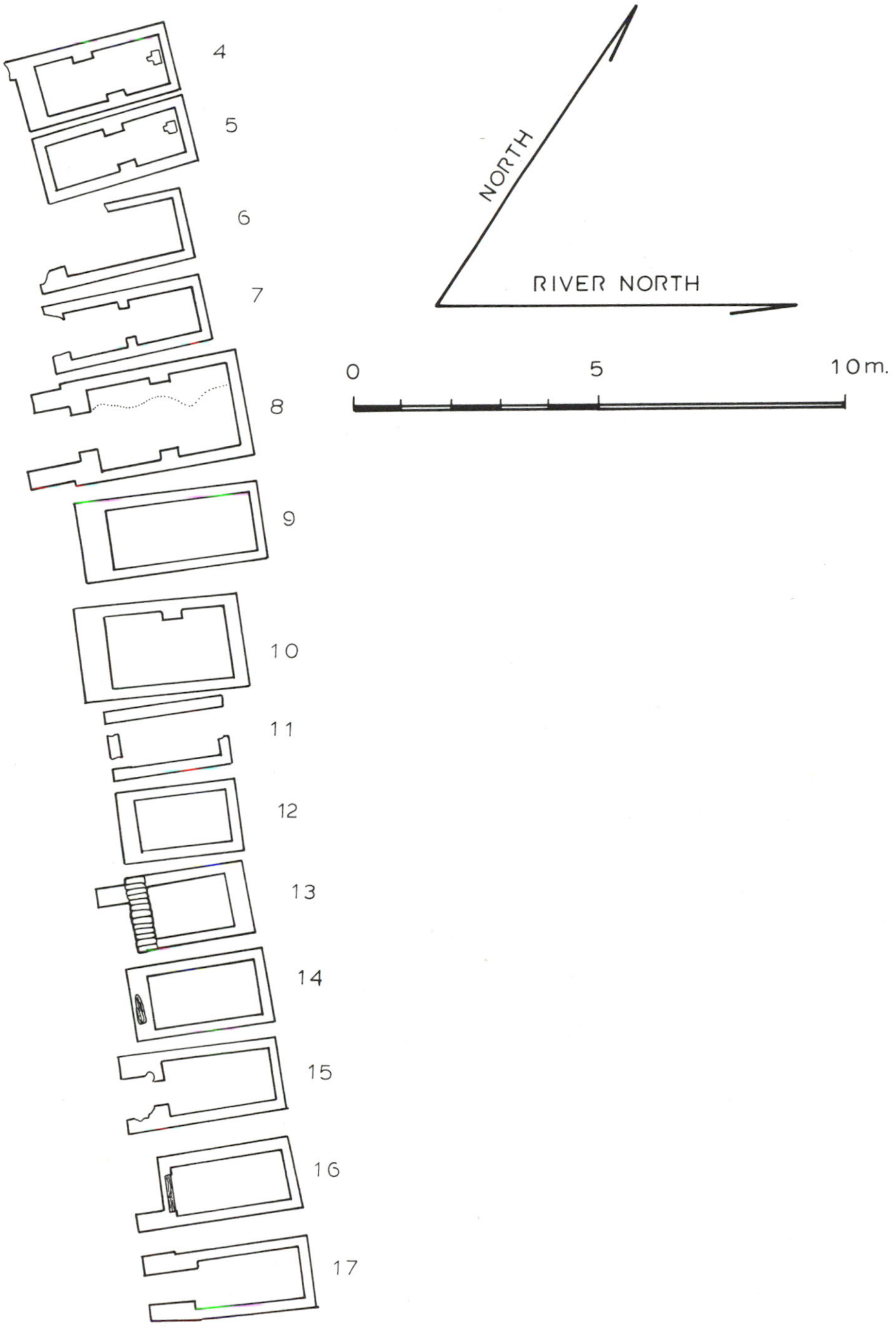

Figure 67. Plans of Chapels QB 4–17.

QB 4	Rectangular chapel with buttresses on the E and W walls, not opposed, and one anta on the W, very short. Against the rear wall was an offering table.			fig. 67
Object:				
	Offering table		20475	fig. 73a, pl. 15b

Table 40. Register of X-Group Finds in Cemetery Q (*cont.*).

Chapel	Description and Contents	Cairo	OIM	Figure/Plate
QB 4 (*cont.*)				
	Sherds:		33117	
	A. X-Gr. ord. goblet I—A			
	B. A-Gr. Eg., hard pk. bowl			
	C. Post-X-Gr. bowl with red coat, lt. rim			
QB 5	Rectangular chapel with buttresses on the E and W walls, opposed. Against the N wall was an offering table.			fig. 67
	Object:			
	Offering table		20395	fig. 73d, pl. 15b
	Chapels 4 and 5 were similar in size and axis, and both had the offering table at the N wall. They were probably a pair.			
QB 6	Rectangular chapel with thickened S wall			fig. 67
	Sherds:		33118	
	A. X-Gr. ord. goblet I—B			
	B. Mer. Ku. wm. bowl with bk. pt. bands			
QB 7	Rectangular chapel with buttresses on the E and W walls			fig. 67
	Sherds:		33119	
	A. Coptic period Eg. utility chaffy jar III—, wh. coat			
	B. Post-X-Gr. open storage vessel, abraded			
	NID one sherd			
	Chapels 6 and 7 may be a pair.			
QB 8	Rectangular chapel with buttresses, remains of paving, and a doorway in the S wall. Two long antae project from either side of the doorway.			fig. 67
	Sherds:		33120	
	A. Coptic period Eg. amphora jar, red coat			
	B. X-Gr. ord. goblet I—A1b, bk. and wh. pt. swags and tassels			
	C. X-Gr. ord. cup or bowl			
	D. X-Gr. ord. jar, wh. pt.			
QB 9	Rectangular chapel			fig. 67
	Sherds:		33121	
	A. X-Gr. ord. jar			
	B. X-Gr. ord. goblet, abraded base			
QB 10	Rectangular chapel with buttress on the N wall			fig. 67
QB 11	Rectangular chapel, plan incomplete			fig. 67
	Sherds:		33122	
	A. Post-X-Gr., pk.			
	B. Post-X-Gr. bn., sharp ridges			
	NID two sherds			
QB 12	Rectangular chapel			fig. 67
QB 13	Rectangular chapel with anta to W of S wall			fig. 67
	Sherds:		33123	
	A. X-Gr. ord. goblet I—B			
	B. Coptic period Eg. utility *amphoriskos* II—			
	C. Unc. amphora			
QB 14	Rectangular chapel with wooden threshold embedded in remains of S wall			fig. 67
QB 15	Rectangular chapel with short antae projecting from the S wall flanking a doorway. Outside the W jamb is a niche for a door-post.			fig. 67

Table 40. Register of X-Group Finds in Cemetery Q (*cont.*).

Chapel	Description and Contents	Cairo	OIM	Figure/Plate
QB 16	Rectangular chapel with wooden threshold embedded in remains of the S wall, at the inside. A long anta projects from the E end of the wall.			fig. 67
QB 17	Rectangular chapel with antae projecting from the S wall (long), flanking a doorway.			fig. 67
Sherds:			33124	
	A. X-Gr. ord. goblet I—B			
	B. Post-X-Gr., abraded			

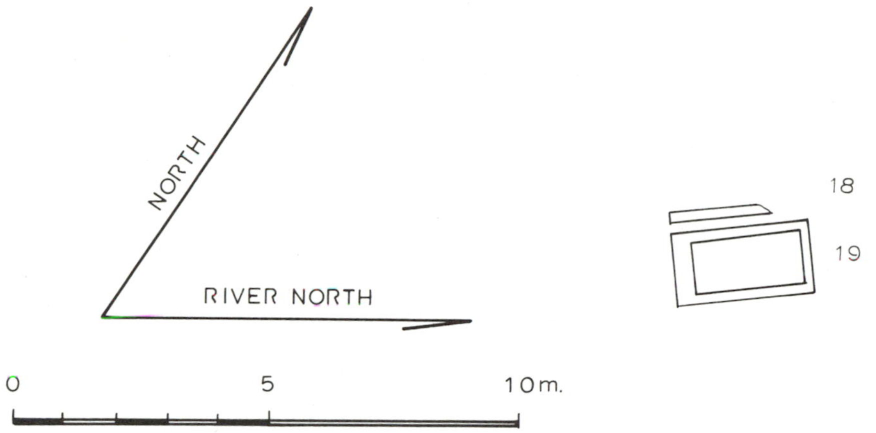

Figure 68. Plans of Chapels QB 18–19.

Chapel	Description and Contents	Cairo	OIM	Figure/Plate
QB 18	E wall of rectangular chapel			fig. 68
Sherds:			33125	
	A. Post-X-Gr. white, ribbed			
	B. Post-X-Gr. pk.			
	C. Coptic period Eg. utility *amphoriskos*, wide rim, post-X-Gr.			
	D. Handle attachment, post-X-Gr., abraded			
QB 19	Rectangular chapel			fig. 68
	Chapels 3–19 belong to a large group in the row, identified by their common axis and despite distance between 18–19 and the rest. Definite pairs are 4–5 and 18–19, but 6–7, 8–9, 14–15, and 16–17 are also probably pairs. Chapels 11–13 seem to be a subgroup of three.			
QB 20	Rectangular chapel with SW corner thickened, for door-post(?)			fig. 69
QB 21	Rectangular chapel			fig. 69
QB 22	Rectangular chapel			fig. 69
QB 23	Rectangular chapel; the E and N walls are slightly irregular			fig. 69
QB 24	Double rectangular chapel; single construction with partition wall			fig. 69
QB 25	Rectangular chapel with SE corner thickened			fig. 69
QB 26	Broad chapel, almost square; this was probably double, without partition			fig. 69
QB 27	Rectangular chapel with thickened S wall			fig. 69
QB 28	Rectangular chapel with S corners thickened			fig. 69
QB 29	Rectangular chapel			fig. 69
QB 30	Rectangular chapel			fig. 69
QB 31	Rectangular chapel with S corners thickened			fig. 69

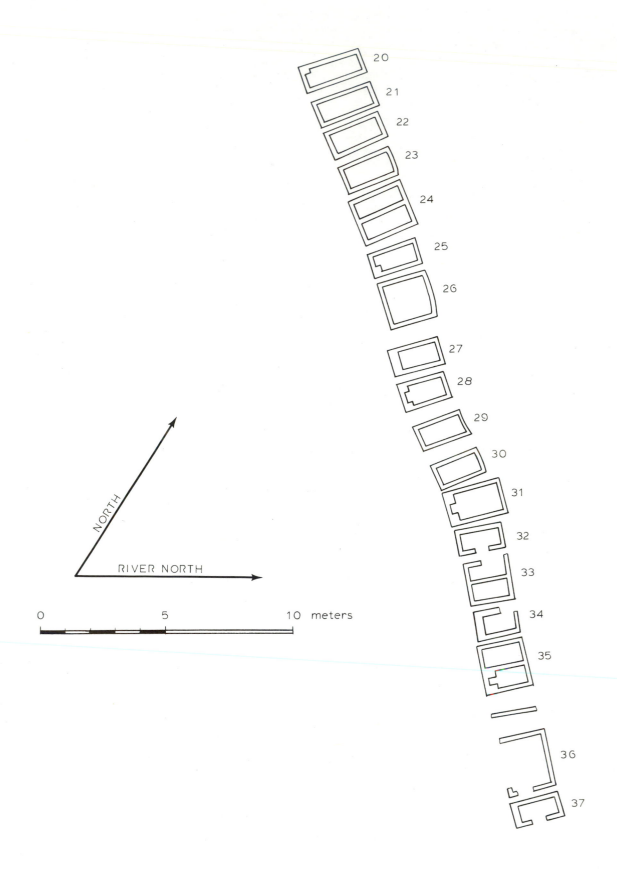

Figure 69. Plans of Chapels QB 20–37.

Table 40. Register of X-Group Finds in Cemetery Q (*cont.*).

Chapel	Description and Contents	Cairo	OIM	Figure/Plate
QB 32	Rectangular chapel with break in the E wall			fig. 69
QB 33	Double rectangular chapel; single construction with a partition wall; there is a break in the W wall			fig. 69
QB 34	Rectangular chapel; the W wall is doubled and the S wall thickened (headers)			fig. 69
QB 35	Triple rectangular chapel with end walls diverging from W to E. The center chapel's S corners are doubled and the N and S walls of the E chapel have disappeared.			fig. 69
QB 36	Broad chapel, double or triple, without partitions; the S and part of the E wall are destroyed			fig. 69
QB 37	Rectangular chapel with thickened S wall (headers); part of the E wall is destroyed			fig. 69
Sherds (Chapels 20–37):			33126	
	A. X-Gr. ord. goblet I—B			
	B. X-Gr. ord. jar			
	C. X-Gr. ord. goblet I—B?, base			
	D. X-Gr. ord. jar			
	E. Unc. ribbed, sandy, gray, one sherd			
	F. Post-X-Gr., pk., two sherds			
	G. Unc., pk.-gray, one sherd			
	Chapels 24, 26, 33, 35, and 36 are multiple or double; pairs in this group probably include 20–21, 22–23, 27–28, and 29–30. Chapels 20–37 are the E group in the row.			
QB 40–41	Double rectangular chapel, 41 the larger of the two; the N-S walls were extended 1½ bricks to make antae which were plastered with mud and whitewashed. Door sills were preserved and that of 41 was plastered. In front of the doors were low cb. podia, 35 × 38 × 20 and 40 × 37 × 20 cm high. On these podia were sandstone offering tables with the spouts directed toward the chapel.			figs. 70, 76; pl. 15a
Objects:				
QB 41	Offering table		20699	fig.73c
	Offering table		20797	fig.74e
	Scarab, 1.3 × 1.0 × 0.7		20798	
QB 42	Rectangular chapel with doorway in the S wall; the SE corner was thickened and a stone door socket was found beside the jamb. Antae were constructed on either side of the doorway, a single brick in dim. Opposite the doorway was a small podium, 38 × 38 × 15 cm, with an offering table on it, spout directed toward the chapel.			figs. 70, 76; pl. 15a
Object:				
	Offering table, carved with "Isis garland"		20787	fig. 72d
Sherd:				
	A. X-Gr. ord. goblet I—B1b, height 8.1		20780	
QB 43	Rectangular chapel with doorway in thickened S wall and reinforced S corners. A door socket was placed inside the W jamb. Antae: two cb. thick project from the S wall on either side of the doorway. In front of the doorway was a small podium, 40 × 37 × 20 cm; the podium and the antae were plastered.			fig. 70, pl. 15a
QB 44	Rectangular chapel with reinforced SE corner			fig. 70
QB 44–45	Short E-W fragment of wall just S of E-W axis of podia, opposite area without chapels.			fig. 70, pl. 16a

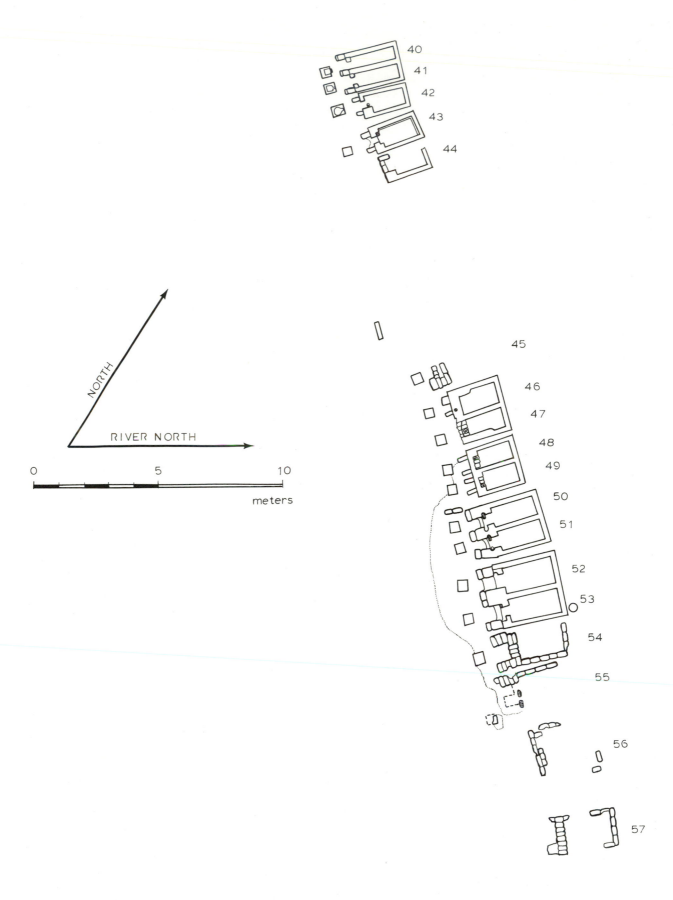

Figure 70. Plans of Chapels QB 40–57.

Table 40. Register of X-Group Finds in Cemetery Q (*cont.*).

Chapel	Description and Contents	Cairo	OIM	Figure/Plate
QB 45	Fragment of chapel; remains of reinforced SE corner and anta. Remains of podium, 43 × 43 ×? cm			fig. 70, pl. 16a
QB 46–47	Double rectangular chapel with thickened S wall and doorways. The E and W walls of the duplex were also thickened for part of their length. Door sockets were placed toward the E. The W chapel had antae on either side of the doorway, one cb. long, the W anta two cb. wide. In front of the doorways were podia, 37 × 37 cm and 34 × 36 cm			fig. 70, pl. 16a
QB 48–49	Double rectangular chapel with doorways in the S wall; the outer corners of both chapels and the inner of the E chapel were reinforced. Door sockets were placed inside the E and W jambs. Antae, a single cb. in dim., flanked the doorways; podia, 38 × 38 cm and 38 × 35 cm, are just opposite.			fig. 70, pl. 16a, b
	Object, from Chapel 48:			
	A. X-Gr. ord. goblet I—B1c, height 8.4		20736	
QB 50–51	Double rectangular chapel with doors in the S wall; reinforcement and antae made together. Antae extended at lower level by thickness of one cb. Thresholds ca. 17–20 cm wide, wooden door jamb set into W walls, niche cut in E jamb-wall for door post. Opposite doorways are podia, 40 × 40 and 40 × 43 × 18 high. Two cb. from an enclosure bound the W side.			fig. 70, pl. 16b
	Objects:			
	a. From Chapels 49–50:			
	A. X-Gr. ord. bowl I—A2, no coat, surface worn		33128	
	b. From Chapel 51:			
	A. X-Gr. ord. bowl I—A2, wh. pt. rim band and vine, in groups of three, fire discolored		33129	
	B. X-Gr. ord. goblet I—B2ai, fire discolored, height 7.4		20702	fig. 75a
	C. X-Gr. ord. goblet I—B1b, fire discolored, height 8.8		20740	
QB 52–53	Double rectangular chapel with doors in the S wall; walls reinforced at corners and antae extend S, set in slightly from the E and W walls. The antae are extended by the width of a cb. at the bottom. The doorways have niches for wooden jambs on the W side, the E anta wall is niched for a door post. Just outside 53 to the N is a small pit, 30 cm in dia., that contained a pottery vessel. Podia, 40 × 40 × 23 cm, were placed just opposite the doors. S of podium 53 were ashes and burned twigs. Inside 52 to the N was an offering table, spout outward			fig. 70, pl. 16b
	Objects:			
	a. From 52:			
	Offering table, 22 × 15.5 × 7.5		20768	
	b. From pit at 53:			
	A. X-Gr. ord. bowl I—A2, bk. and wh. pt. vine, in groups of three (2.5YR 5/6, 2.5YR 4/6, 2.5YR 3/2, 5YR 8/2), height 13.4		20735	fig. 75b
	c. From 53:			
	B. X-Gr. ord. goblet I—A1aii *beta*, bk. and wh. pt. swags		33130	

Table 40. Register of X-Group Finds in Cemetery Q (*cont.*).

Chapel	Description and Contents	Cairo	OIM	Figure/Plate
QB 54	Rectangular chapel with thickened S wall; antae flank a presumed doorway, double thickness, at the E and W walls. Opposite the doorway was a stone podium 42 × 48 cm, approx. square, with plaster			fig. 70
	Sherds:			
	A. X-Gr. ord. goblet I—B; fire discolored			
	B. X-Gr. ord. goblet I—A1bi *alpha*, wh. and bk. pt., vert. lines (wh. zone, bk. lines); fire discolored.		20751	
QB 55	Probably double rectangular chapel with doors in the S wall and antae that extended the E-W walls and thickened them at the S end. Remains of two wooden thresholds. In front of E door was a brick podium.			fig. 70
	Pavement 49–55: Much of the area immediately in front of these chapels was paved with plaster			
QB 56	Remains of probably double rectangular chapel with walls reinforced near S ends			fig. 70
QB 57	Rectangular chapel with thickened S wall; antae extended the E and W walls to the S, double thickness. The E and W walls were largely removed.			fig. 70
QB 58	NE corner of rectangular chapel			fig. 71

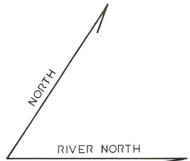

Figure 71. Plan of Chapel QB 58.

II. Qu. 31 Complex: Stone Objects and Fittings

QB 2	Jamb with raised relief of "Isis garland"		20460	fig. 74a
QB 4	Offering table		20475	fig. 73a
QB 5	Offering table		20395	fig. 73d
QB 41	Offering table		20699	fig. 73c
QB 41	Offering table		20797	fig. 74e
QB 41	Scarab, 1.3 × 1.0 × 0.7		20798	
QB 42	Offering table, carved with "Isis garland"		20787	fig. 72d
QB 52	Offering table		20768	fig. 72a, pl. 15c
Unspecified, N of Qu. 31:				
	Offering table		20193	fig. 74c
Unspecified, from Christian cemetery W of Qu. 31:				
	Offering table (Q 86–87)		20164	fig. 73b
	Offering table (Q 86), 29 × 21		20206	
	Spout from well-made and large offering table (Q 101A)		20280	fig. 72b
	Fragment of jamb with raised relief of "Isis garland"		20279	fig. 74b
	Offering table (Q 86A)		20273	fig. 72c
	Offering table (Q 110)		20261	fig. 74d

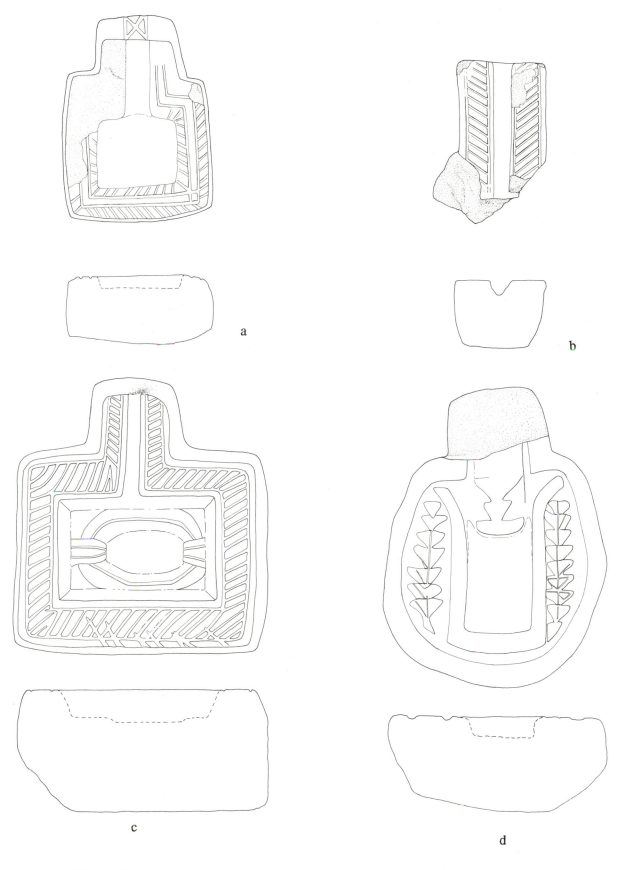

Figure 72. Offering Tables from Chapel Row Q*B*: (a) Chapel QB 52 (OIM 20768),
(*b*) Unspecified Location (OIM 20280), (*c*) Unspecified Location (OIM 20273),
(*d*) Chapel QB 42 (OIM 20787). Scale 1:4.

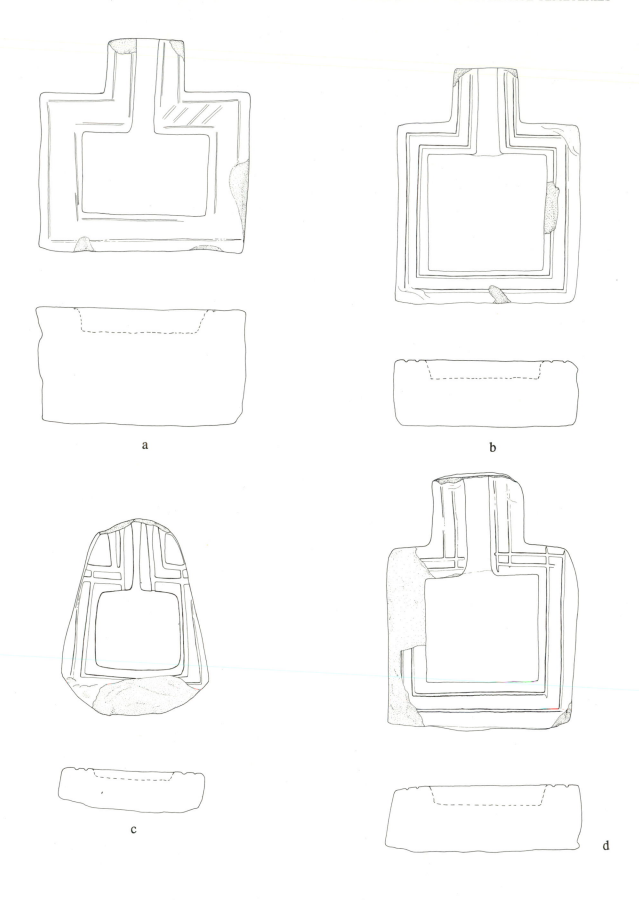

a

b

c

d

Figure 73. Offering Tables from Chapel Row Q*B* (*cont.*): (*a*) QB 4 (OIM 20475), (*b*) Q 86–87
(OIM 20164), (*c*) QB 41 (OIM 20699), (*d*) QB 5 (OIM 20395). Scale 1:4.

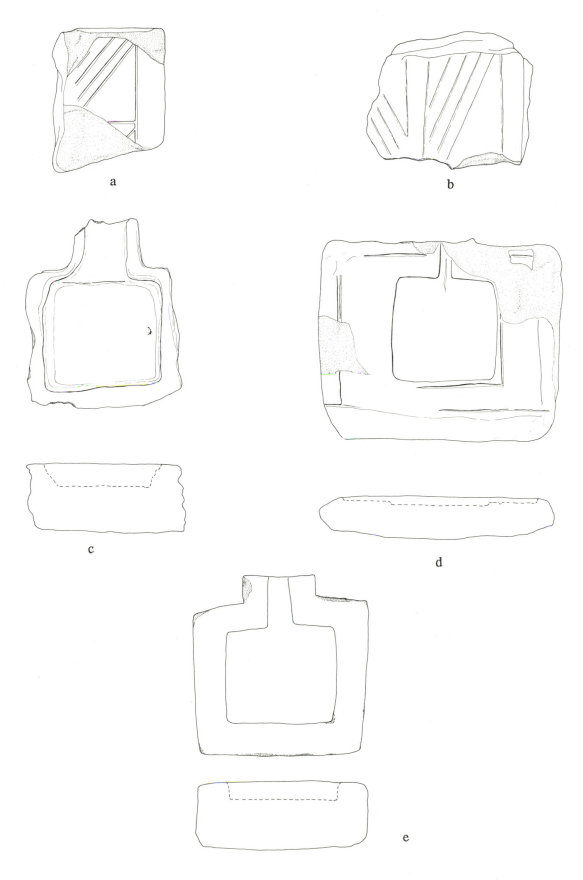

Figure 74. Incised Jambs and Offering Tables from Chapel Row Q*B*: (*a*) QB 2 (OIM 20460), (*b*) Unspecified Location (OIM 20279), (*c*) Unspecified Location (OIM 20193), (*d*) Unspecified Location (OIM 20261), (*e*) QB 41 (OIM 20797). Scale 1:4.

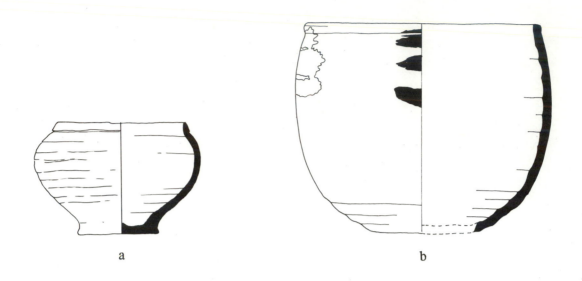

Figure 75. Pottery from Chapel Row Q*B*: (*a*) X-Gr. Ord. Goblet I—B2ai, QB 51—B;
(*b*) X-Gr. Ord. Bowl I—A2, QB 53—A. Scale 2:5.

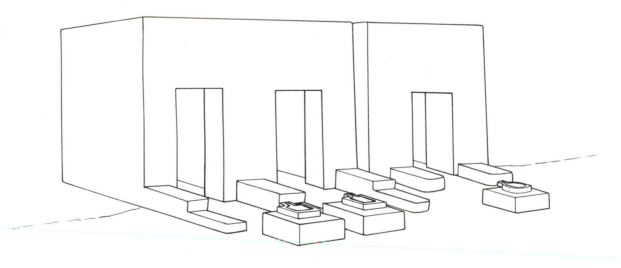

Figure 76. Conjectural Reconstructions of Chapels QB 40–42.

Table 40. Register of X-Group Finds in Cemetery Q (*cont.*).

Chapel	Description and Contents	Cairo	OIM	Figure/Plate

QU. 48 COMPLEX

I. Chapels Q*C*
II. Stone Objects and Fittings
III. Circular Pits associated with Cult
IV. Meroitic Tombs and Associated Surface Loci with X-Gr. Materials Attributed to Cult Activity
V. Meroitic Tombs and Associated Surface Loci with X-Gr. Materials with no clear Attribution to Cult Activity

I. Qu. 48 Complex: Chapels Q*C*				fig. 82, pl. 6
QC 1	Rectangular chapel, two cb. thick, foundation and one course; SW corner; a single long anta extends the E wall S			fig. 77
	Sherds:		33131	
	A. X-Gr. ord. goblet I—B			
	B. X-Gr. ord. goblet I—B1b, ribbed			
	C. X-Gr. ord. goblet I—B, base			
	D. X-Gr. fine cup V—, flattened base			
	E. X-Gr. ord. goblet I—A, wh. pt. vine, large, blackened			
	F. X-Gr. ord. bowl I—A2, wh. pt. rim band, blackened			
	G. X-Gr. ord. bowl I—A2, wh. pt. rim band, blackened			
	H. X-Gr. ord. bowl I—A2, wh. pt. rim band, blackened			
	I. X-Gr. ord. bowl I—A2, wh. pt. rim band, blackened			
	J. X-Gr. ord. bowl I—A2, wh. pt. rim band, blackened, (rim groove not present)			
	K. X-Gr. utility storage jar III—C, blackened			
	K. Unc. pk. amphora handle, spalling			
	L. Mer. Ku. wm. bowl, bk. pt. bands			
	M. Post-X-Gr. pk., knob base			
	N. Post-X-Gr. gray, base			
	O–P. Uncertain sherds			
QC 2	Rectangular chapel with thickened S wall and buttresses on the E and W walls; a foundation course for the N wall was laid rowlock. Long antae project from the S wall, set in slightly at the corners. Immediately opposite the doorway was a podium two cb. lengths wide and six cb. lengths long (at one cb. ca. 34–35 × 17–18 × 8–9 cm)			fig. 77
	Objects:			
	1. Fragment of ostrich egg		20330	
	Sherds:		33132	
	A. X-Gr. ord. goblet I—A, (large, base)			
	B. X-Gr. ord. goblet I—B, base			
	C. X-Gr. ord. bottle-jar, body sherd			
	D. X-Gr. ord. bottle-jar, body sherd			
	E. X-Gr. ord. goblet I—A, body sherd			
	F. X-Gr. ord. bowl I—A2, rim, surface damaged			
	G. X-Gr. ord. bowl I—B1(b) (lower than drawing), discolored			
	H. X-Gr. ord. bowl, body sherd, discolored			

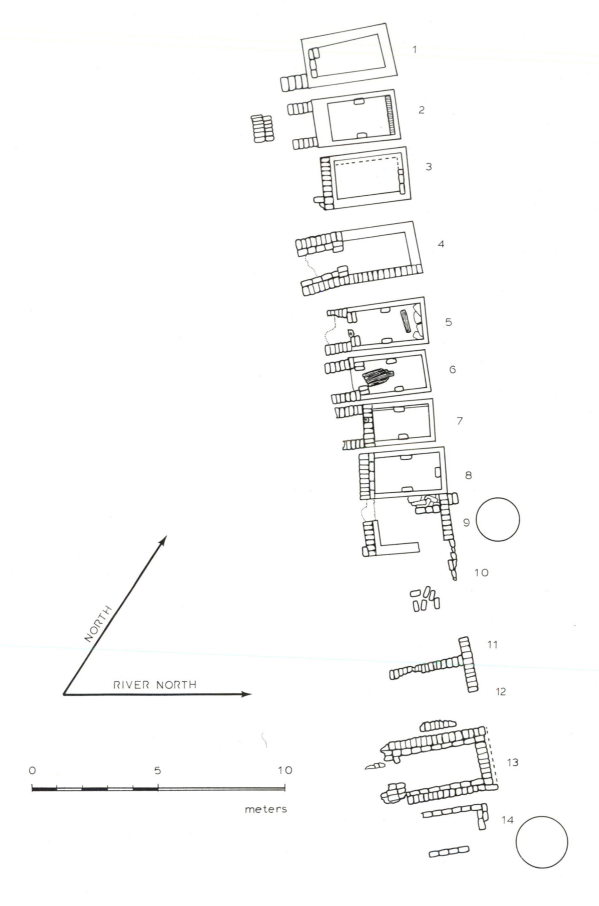

Figure 77. Plans of Chapels QC 1–14 and Associated Pits.

Table 40. Register of X-Group Finds in Cemetery Q (*cont.*).

Chapel	Description and Contents	Cairo	OIM	Figure/Plate
QC 3	Rectangular chapel, two cb. thick, with thickened S wall; part of anta projects from SE corner			fig. 77
	Sherds:		33133	
	A. X-Gr. ord. goblet I—B, base			
	B. X-Gr. ord. goblet I—A, carination and groove			
	C. X-Gr. ord. goblet I—A, carination			
	D. X-Gr. ord. goblet I—A, rim, damaged surface			
	E. X-Gr. ord. bowl I—A2, wh. pt. rim band			
	F. X-Gr. ord. bowl I—A2, wh. pt. rim band, discolored, dk.			
	G. Coptic period Eg. utility jug, ca. II—D, ring base, wh. coat			
	H. Unc. gray, many organic and mineral inclusions, red and wh. coat			
	I. X-Gr. handmade jar, parallel pairs of drop-shaped impressions			
	J. Mer. ring base, red coat			
	K. Mer. fine/ord. jar, red coat, bk. band			
QC 1–3				
	Object:			
	Fragment of door jamb with line in raised relief, probably the lower end of an "Isis garland," from top of shaft Q 267		20600	fig. 83
QC 4	Rectangular chapel, two cb. thick, with doorway in the S wall; antae project at a slight angle, extending the E and W wall lines, the longest preserved antae in the row. A mud floor extends outside.			fig. 77, pl. 17a
	Objects:			
	1. Pottery disc or spindle whorl, ground to shape, dia. 4.3		20331	
	2. Beads		21436	fig. 62h
	Sherds:		33134	
	A. X-Gr. ord. goblet I—A, bk. and wh. double swags			
	B. X-Gr. ord. goblet I—A, darkened rim			
	C. X-Gr. ord. goblet I—B, base			
	D. X-Gr. ord. goblet I—B			
	E. X-Gr. ord. goblet I—B			
	F. X-Gr. ord. goblet I—A, ring base			
	G. X-Gr. ord. goblet I—B, rib rim			
	H. X-Gr. ord. cup I—G, short, blackened			
	I. X-Gr. ord. cup I—G, short, slight discoloration			
	J. X-Gr. ord. cup I—G			
	K. X-Gr. ord. cup I—G			
	L. X-Gr. ord. cup I—G			
	M. X-Gr. ord. bottle-jar, bk. and wh. bands			
	N. Mer. fine cup, red coat			
	O. Post-X-Gr. jar or jug			
	P. Post-X-Gr. uncoated gray *qadus*			
	Q. Post-X-Gr. gray ribbed			
	R. Post-X-Gr. ord. jar rim			
	S. Post-X-Gr. pk., open burnish, shallow bowl			
QC 5	Rectangular chapel with buttresses on the E and W walls, thickened S wall with a doorway in the middle and antae that extend the side walls S. A door socket was placed at the outside edge of the E jamb. The floor was mud, extended outside. A plank, found near the rear of the chapel, may have been a lintel.			fig. 77, pl. 17a

Table 40. Register of X-Group Finds in Cemetery Q (*cont.*).

Chapel	Description and Contents	Cairo	OIM	Figure/Plate
QC 5 (*cont.*)				
	Sherds:		33135	
	A. X-Gr. ord. goblet I—A1a, bk. and wh. pt. swags			
	B. X-Gr. ord. goblet I—B, base			
	C. X-Gr. ord. goblet I—B, rim low			
	D. X-Gr. ord. cup I—G?, base			
	E. X-Gr. ord. cup I—G, rim, surface damaged			
	F. X-Gr. utility storage jar III—C, small			
	G. Uncertain handmade			
	H. Post-X-Gr. gray *qadus*			
	I. Mer. fine/ord. cup, bk. and red vine			
	J. Mer. fine/ord. cup, wh. coat			
	K. Mer. ord. jar, bk. bands			
	L. Mer. ord. jar			
	M–O. Post-X-Gr. pk.-wh.			
	P. Post-X-Gr. gray with wh. core, dk. surface, cylindrical cup			
	Q–R. Post-X-Gr. lt. coarse			
	S–T. Unc. gray-pk. ribbed			
QC 6	Rectangular chapel with buttresses on the E and W walls, thickened S wall with a door opening, and antae that extend the side walls S at a slight angle. The floor was mud, and four joined planks of a door were found just inside.			fig. 77, pls. 17a, 19a, b
	Sherds:		33136	
	A. X-Gr. ord. goblet I—B, base			
	B. X-Gr. ord. goblet I—B			
	C. Unc. handmade			
	D. Mer. fine/ord. jar, red coat, bk. bands			
	E. Mer. ord. jar			
	F. Post-X-Gr. jug handle			
	G. Unc. utility storage jar			
	H. NID rim			
QC 7	Rectangular chapel with buttresses on the E and W walls, thickened S wall with doorway, and antae that extend the side walls S. A stone door socket was placed at the S-side edge of the W jamb.			fig. 77, pl. 17a, b
	Sherds:		33137	
	A. X-Gr. ord. goblet I—A, broad, open, encrusted remains of green pigment inside (see stone from F-row)			
	B. X-Gr. ord. goblet I—A, rim			
	C. X-Gr. ord. goblet I—B, base			
	D. X-Gr. ord. goblet I—B			
	E. X-Gr. ord. goblet I—B			
	F. X-Gr. ord. bowl, discolored			
	G. X-Gr. handmade jar neck			
	H. Unc. pk. ribbed amphora			
	I. Unc. ribbed utility			
	J. Mer. ord. jar red coat, bk. bands			
	K. Mer. fine cup, red and bk. pt., part of Bes-face?			
	L. Mer. fine cup, bk. pt., moustache coil?			

Table 40. Register of X-Group Finds in Cemetery Q (*cont.*).

Chapel	Description and Contents	Cairo	OIM	Figure/Plate
QC 8	Rectangular chapel with buttresses on the side and N walls, thickened S wall.			fig. 77, pls. 17b, 18a
	Sherds:		33138	
	A. X-Gr. ord. cup I—A1a, wh. coat, red-dk. rim band			
	B. X-Gr. ord. goblet I—B, rim			
	C. X-Gr. ord. goblet I—A, worn rim			

	D. Mer. fine jar I— , red and bk. pt.,
	        Academic-Std., ankhs in petals above
	        zone with pomegranates on branches			

	E. Mer. fine cup, red and bk. pt. *sa*			
	F. Mer. fine cup, double frame and red rim band			
	G. Mer. fine cup, bk. pt., two zones			
	H. Meroitic period Sud.-Sah. bk. inc.			
	I–J. Mer. ord. jar, blob-bead pt.			
	L. Post-X-Gr. handle, worn			
	M. Post-X-Gr., red with gray surface, bowl			
	N. Post-X-Gr. wh. jar rim			
QC 9	Rectangular chapel with fragmentary plan and uncertain details. Probably built against chapel 8, W wall on foundation three cb. wide, thickened S wall. The doorway may have been offset to the W, possibly with mud paving, but worn mortar would have a similar appearance. Remains of an anta extend the E wall, and two bricks were laid against the N wall at the W end.			fig. 77 pls. 17b, 18a
	Objects:			
	1. Beads (earlier)		21438	
	Sherds:		33139	
	A. X-Gr. ord. goblet I—A			
	B. X-Gr. ord. goblet I—B, rim			
	C. X-Gr. ord. goblet I—B, rim			
	D. Mer. Eg. fine ord. cup, bk. vine dec.			
	E. Mer. Eg. fine/ord. jar, bk. bands			
	F. Mer. fine cup, bk. pt.			
	G. Post-X-Gr. gray-wh., red coat, jar base			
	H. Post-X-Gr. bn. jug, band handle			
QC 10	Remains of N wall of rectangular chapel; abuts on chapel QC 9 or was built with it as a double chapel. Loose bricks toward E from dismantling the structure			fig. 77
QC 11–12	Fragmentary pair of rectangular chapels; remains of N, E, and center walls only, headers			
QC 11				fig. 77
	Object:			
	Offering table		20444	fig. 85a
	Sherds:		33140	
	A. X-Gr. ord. bowl; rim, blackened			
	B. Mer. fine cup I—G1, red pt. rim band			
	C. Mer. fine cup, base			
	D. Mer. fine jar; fragments of QC 8—D			
	E. Mer. fine/ord. jar, red coat, three bk. lines			
	F. Mer. ord. feeding cup			
	G. Mer. Eg. fine/ord. cup, bk. pt. vine			
	H–J. Mer. Eg. fine/ord. amphora-jar, carination at waist			
	K. Mer. Eg. utility cook-pot II—			

Table 40. Register of X-Group Finds in Cemetery Q (*cont.*).

Chapel	Description and Contents	Cairo	OIM	Figure/Plate
QC 11	(*cont.*)			
	Sherds (*cont.*):			
	L. Post-X-Gr. pk. with wh. surface, beveled jar rim and handle attachment			
	M. Post-X-Gr. pk., small rim with spout			
	N. Post-X-Gr. pk., jar rim, folded, no neck			
QC 12				fig. 77
	Sherds:		33141	
	A. Mer. fine cup, red and bk. pt., stylized trefoil flower, hor.			
	B. Mer. fine cup, red coat			
	C. Mer.-X-Gr. fine feeding cup, height 5.7		21461	
	D. Post-X-Gr. gray bowl, bl. and bk. pt., wavy lines in zone			
	E. Post-X-Gr. coarse jar with everted rim, short spout, red coat			
	F. Post-X-Gr. pk.- ye., bowl with offset rib rim			
	G. Post-X-Gr. pk. jar (QC 11—N)			
	H. Mer., early, Ku. wh., wh. coat, red and bk. crosshatched zone			
QC 13	Rectangular chapel, side walls double, N wall headers and S wall formed by the ends of large antae that extend to the S.			fig. 77
QC 14	Rectangular chapel, N wall double.			fig. 77

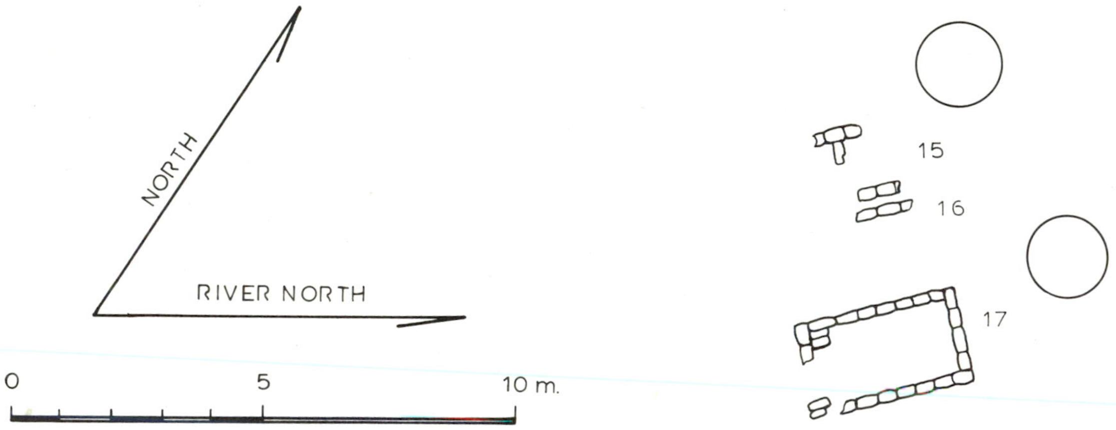

Figure 78. Plans of Chapels QC 15–17 and Associated Pits.

QC 15	Rectangular chapel with anta extending W wall to the S, fragment.			fig. 78
QC 16	Three cb. of W wall only			fig. 78
QC 17	Rectangular chapel with thickened S wall (three cb.) The structure was apparently equipped with a door jamb dec. in relief and an obelisk(s).			figs. 78, 88
	Objects:			
	1. Fragment of stone jamb with "Isis garland" in raised relief, 62 × 12.8 × 8.5 (see OINE VIII, Tomb Q 383)		21305	
	2. Sandstone obelisk from R(?) side of axis (see OINE VIII, Tomb Q 384)		21303	fig. 85b

Table 40. Register of X-Group Finds in Cemetery Q (*cont.*).

Chapel	Description and Contents	Cairo	OIM	Figure/Plate
	The following objects were found at the tops of shafts Q 383 and Q 384.			
	Sherds:		33144	
	A. A-Group or neolithic sherd with fire blooms			
	B. Meroitic period Sud.-Sah. bk. inc. jar rim			
	C. Mer. fine/ord. jar, bk. and wh. bands, discolored			
	D. Unc. handmade coarse spout			
	E. Unc. ord. bowl with groove below rim, red coat			
	F. Unc. rim			
	G. X-Gr. ord. goblet I—B3, uncoated (whole vessel)		20577	fig. 87a
QC 18	NE corner of rectangular chapel			fig. 79
QC 19	Three cb. of W wall of rectangular chapel			fig. 79, pl. 18b
QC 20	Rectangular chapel with thickened S wall			fig. 79, pl. 18b
	Objects:			
	1–2. Tapered stone jambs or broken obelisks, two sides finished, plastered and whitewashed; painted, found with bricks 9–10 × 16–17 × 35–36 with *tibn.* 14–16 × 12 × 70, 15 × 12 × 71 cm, from top of shaft Q 355		Disc.	
QC 21	Rectangular chapel with thickened S wall			fig. 79
QC 20–21				
	Sherds:		33145	
	A. Mer. Sud.-Sah. bk. inc. jar			
	B. Mer. Eg. jug or large juglet with grooved band handle and candlestick rim			
	C. X-Gr. handmade spout			
	D. Post-X-Gr. gray-wh. cup, dk. side			
	E. Unc. ord. jar neck and shoulder			
QC 22	Rectangular chapel with thickened S wall with doorway. Floor was paved with mud.			figs. 79, 89
	Objects:			
	1. Stone lintel with wh. pt. and possibly plaster			pl. 20b–c
	2–3. Stone jambs with soil rings near lower ends, finished wh. pt. and plastered on two sides		Disc.	pl. 20b–c
	4. Head of stone sphinx, R side		20811	fig. 84a, pl. 20b–c
	Sherds:		33146	
	A. Mer. Sud.-Sah. red inc. jar; rim, neck, and shoulder			
	B. Mer. fine cup with three bk. lines			
	C. Mer. Eg. cup, deep, shadow of vine dec.?			
	D. Unc. gray with lt. core, irreg. blob of purple pt.			
QC 23	Rectangular chapel with thickened S wall; fragmentary side and S walls only.			fig. 79
QC 24	Rectangular chapel with thickened S wall and short anta extending the W wall to the S. Remains of side and S walls only.			fig. 79
QC 25	Rectangular chapel; N and side walls only partially preserved			fig. 79
	Sherds:		33147	
	A. X-Gr. ord. goblet I—B, base			
	B. Mer. fine jar, bk. and red pt. zone of honeycomb with *ankhs*			
	C. Mer. Roman period Egyptian jar or jug, ring base			
	D. Unc. pk. fine			

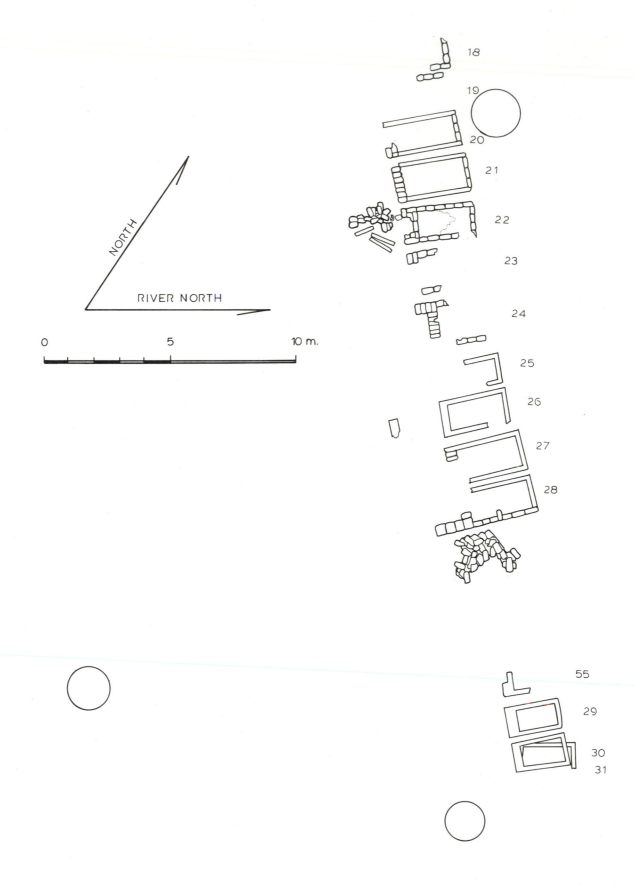

Figure 79. Plans of Chapels QC 18–31, Chapel QC 55, and Associated Pits.

Table 40. Register of X-Group Finds in Cemetery Q (*cont.*).

Chapel	Description and Contents	Cairo	OIM	Figure/Plate
QC 26	Rectangular chapel with thickened S wall, E wall broken; remains of podium S of chapel			fig. 79
QC 27	Rectangular chapel with thickened S wall, SE corner dismantled, with SW corner of chapel 28.			fig. 79
Sherds:			33148	
	A. X-Gr. ord. jar, grooved at rim, bk. and wh. spot beads			
	B. X-Gr. ord. goblet I—A with in-turned rim, bk. and wh. pt. swags			
	C. Mer. Eg. ord. jar, bk. pt. bands			
	D. Mer. Eg. ord. jar			
	E. Mer. K wh. bowl, buff surface with bk. pt. lines			
	F. Mer. Eg. utility *amphoriskos*-jug, rim-neck			
	G. Post-X-Gr.? coarse pk. jar, no neck, everted rim			
	H. Post-X-Gr. fine pk., cylindrical neck with slightly bulged rim			
	I. Unc. pk.			
QC 28	Rectangular chapel with buttress on the E wall, thickened S wall with doorway. A long anta extends the E wall S. The SW corner was dismantled, with the SE corner of chapel 27			fig. 79
QC 29	Rectangular chapel with thickened S wall			fig. 79
QC 30	Rectangular chapel with thickened S wall			fig. 79
QC 31	Rectangular chapel; preceded chapel QC 30 at axis slightly to the NE			fig. 79
QC 29–31, to S				
Object:				
	1. X-Gr. ord. goblet I—B2bi, fire blackened, height 8.6		20777	
QC 28–55	Pile of bricks with stone ring set into it. This pile was probably made of bricks from chapels in process of demolition (see 10). Note that Chapels 32–54 proceed E to W in order.			
QC 32	Two cb. from N wall of chapel only remains. To S, thickened S walls of two structures on axis to NE of row (see chapels 31, 54).			fig. 80
QC 33	Rectangular chapel with thickened S wall, N end destroyed			fig. 80
QC 34	NE corner of rectangular chapel			fig. 80
QC 35	Rectangular chapel with thickened foundation on the W side; a door socket was placed in the S wall toward the E, outside the probable doorway			fig. 80
QC 36	Rectangular chapel			fig. 80, pl. 20a
QC 37	Rectangular chapel with thickened S wall, remains of elongated podium S of chapel			fig. 80
QC 38	Rectangular chapel with originally short antae extending the side walls to the S; headers were added to enlarge these. Opposite the probable doorway was a small square podium.			fig. 80
QC 39	Rectangular chapel with thickened S wall and buttresses on the side walls. The W side of the S wall is angled N.			fig. 80

Table 40. Register of X-Group Finds in Cemetery Q (*cont.*).

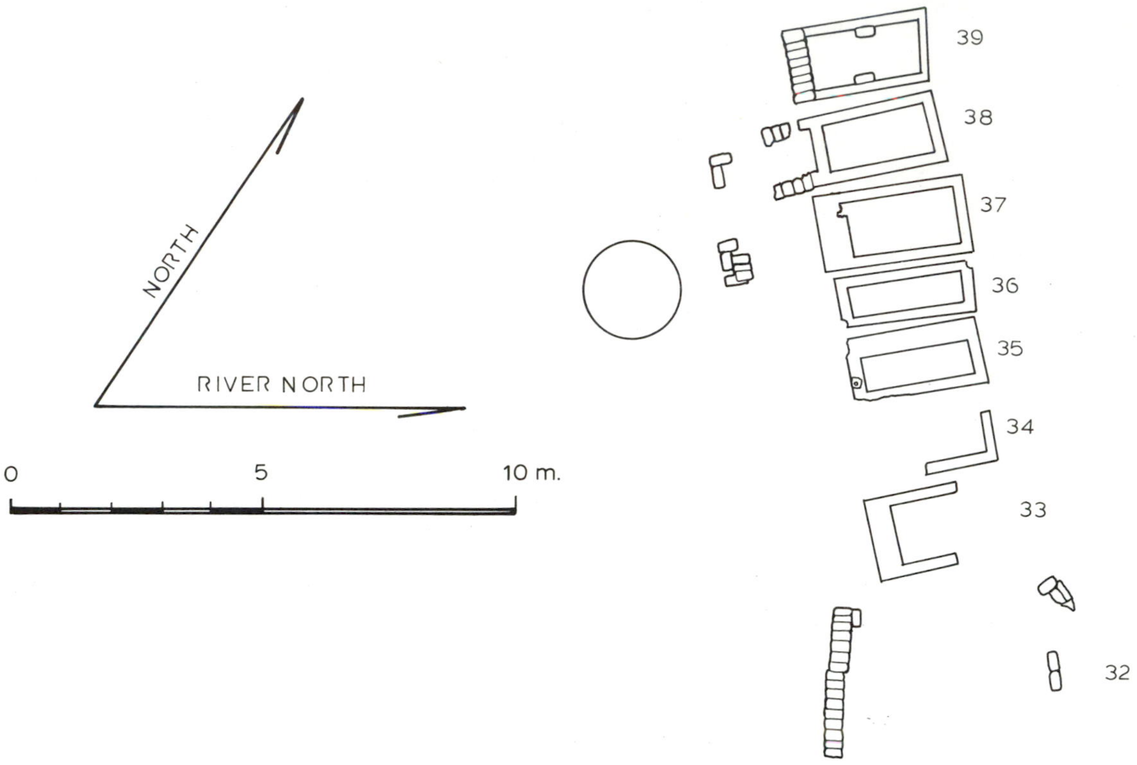

Chapel	Description and Contents	Cairo	OIM	Figure/Plate

Figure 80. Plans of Chapels QC 32–39 and Associated Pit.

Chapel	Description and Contents	Cairo	OIM	Figure/Plate
QC 40	Rectangular chapel, remains of side walls			fig. 81
QC 41	Rectangular chapel, side walls and N end only			fig. 81
QC 42	Rectangular chapel			fig. 81
QC 43	Rectangular chapel with thickened S wall (headers) and buttress on the W wall. Antae (headers) extended the side walls S.			fig. 81
QC 44	Rectangular chapel with thickened S wall (headers) and a door socket toward the W in the middle of the wall			fig. 81
	Object:			
	1. Offering table (from shaft Q 345), 15 × 22	20843		
QC 45	Rectangular chapel with thickened S wall (headers) and anta extending W wall to the S; most of W, all of N, and part of E wall destroyed			fig. 81
QC 46	Rectangular chapel with thickened S wall (headers) and anta that extends the W wall to the S; the N and part of the side walls destroyed			fig. 81
QC 47	Rectangular chapel with thickened S wall			fig. 81
QC 48	NW corner and part of N wall of rectangular chapel			fig. 81
QC 49	Anta (headers) from E wall of chapel			fig. 81
QC 50	NW corner and part of W wall of rectangular chapel			fig. 81
QC 51	N and side walls of rectangular chapel; most of W wall destroyed			fig. 81
QC 52	N and side walls of rectangular chapel; most of W wall destroyed			fig. 81
QC 53	N and N parts of side walls of rectangular chapel			fig. 81

Table 40. Register of X-Group Finds in Cemetery Q (*cont.*).

Chapel	Description and Contents	Cairo	OIM	Figure/Plate
QC 54	NE corner of rectangular chapel; axis to NE of remains of chapel row (see also chapels 31 and 32)			fig. 81

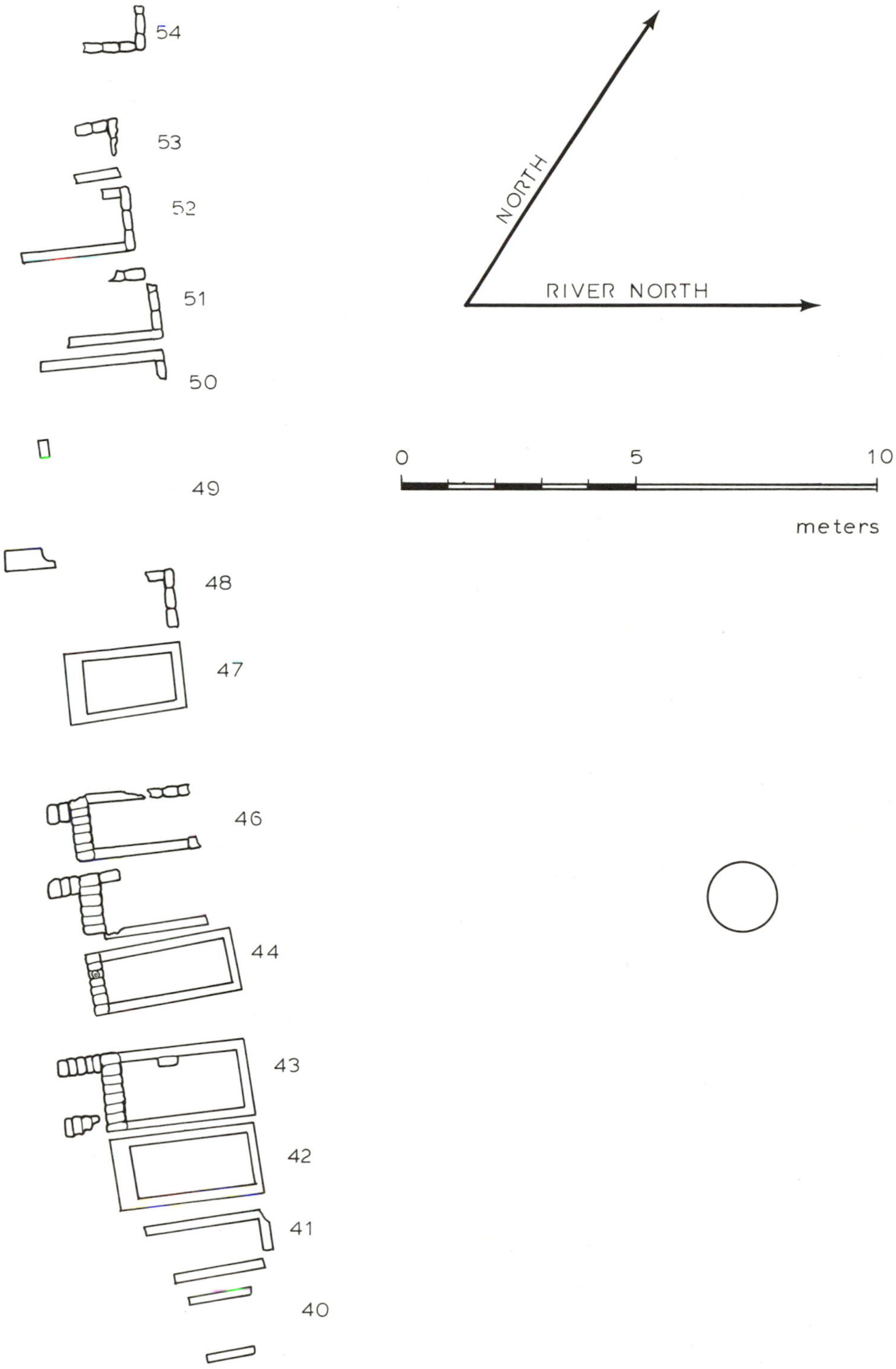

Figure 81. Plans of Chapels QC 40–54 and Associated Pit.

Table 40. Register of X-Group Finds in Cemetery Q (*cont.*).

Chapel	Description and Contents	Cairo	OIM	Figure/Plate
QC 55	Rectangular chapel just W of chapel 29 with thickened S wall. SE corner only remains			fig. 79

The chapel row for Qu. 48 seems to have begun in three places at an angle to the NE of the present axis of the chapels. Chapels begun or erected on this axis were superseded in one case, or possibly abandoned in favor of chapels that conform to the present axis. Larger than the chapels of Qu. 31, only one pair was built with a party wall. All of the chapels are slightly different, and it would be difficult to assign them to pairs with any confidence. Podia, less common than in Qu. 31 row, occur in different parts of this row, as do antae. Some groups may be identified, however, including the substantial chapels, often with wood fittings, in 1–14, and the chapels with stone fittings in the area 17–22.

Figure 82. Chapel Row QC, Associated Pits and Deposit Locations.

Table 40. Register of X-Group Finds in Cemetery Q (*cont.*).

Chapel/Pit	Description and Contents	Cairo	OIM	Figure/Plate

II. Qu. 48 Complex: Stone Objects and Fittings

QC 1–3	Fragment of door jamb with line in raised relief, probably the lower end of an "Isis garland," from top of shaft Q 267		20600	fig. 83

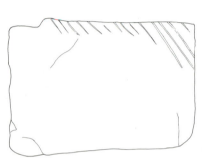

Figure 83. Fragment of a Jamb from Chapels QC 1–3 (OIM 20600). Scale 1:4.

QC 11	Offering table		20444	fig. 85a
QC 17	Door jamb with "Isis garland" in raised relief, fragment, 62 × 12.8 × 8.5		21305	
QC 17—2	Obelisk, with socle, four sides smoothed and whitewashed, 76 × 10 × 14, broken in the middle, socle indicates an object set into platform on R side of entry		21303	fig. 85b

The following objects were found at the tops of shafts Q 383 and Q 384

QC 20	Door jambs or obelisks, two sides finished, whitewashed and plastered, pt., found with bricks, 9–10 × 16–17 × 35–36, and *tibn*, 14–16 × 12 × 70, 15 × 12 × 71 cm, at top of shaft Q 355		Disc.	
QC 22	Lintel and two stone jambs, finished on two sides: lintel: 77 × 14 × 8–9 cm, jambs: 102 × 10–11 × 11 cm, rings of soil near lower ends; stones showed remains of white pt. and possibly plaster, Head of sphinx, R side		20811	fig. 84a
QC 44(?)	Offering table (from shaft Q 345), 15 × 22		20843	

III. Qu. 48 Complex: Circular Pits Associated with Cult

Q 304, pit cutting shaft, N of QC 9 (see OINE VIII)			31885	

Irreg. circular pit with plaster 4 cm thick, loose cb. toward N

Post-Meroitic sherds:

    A. X-Gr. ord. goblet I—A, purple and wh. pt. swags

    B. X-Gr. ord. cup I—G2–3, bk. and wh. pt. vine in pairs

    C. X-Gr. ord. cup I—G, base

    D. X-Gr. ord. goblet

  E–I. X-Gr. ord. goblets

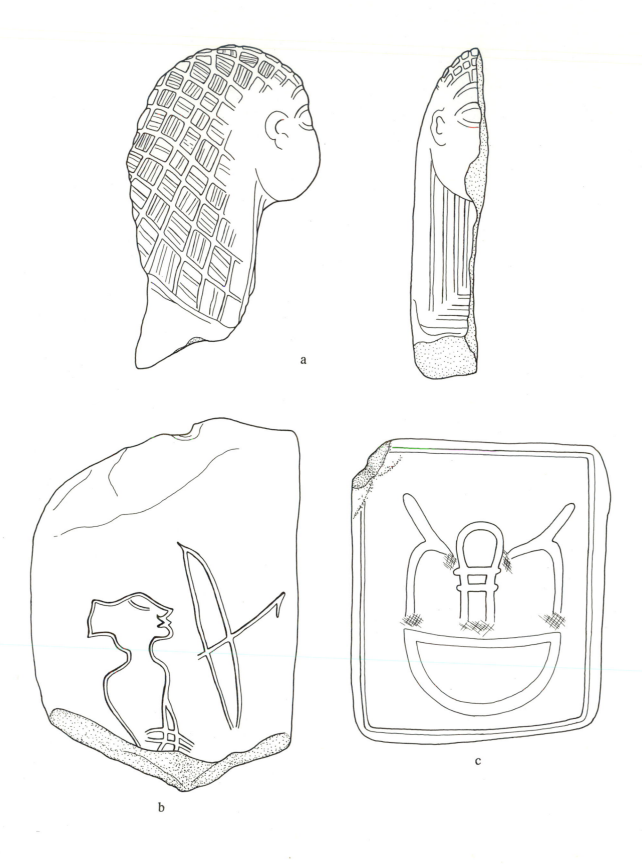

Figure 84. Fragment of a Stone Sphinx and Fragments of Incised and Painted Plaques:
(*a*) Sphinx Fragment, QC 22—4; (*b*) Incised Plaque Fragment, QF 11—1;
(*c*) Painted Plaque Fragment, QF Chapel Row, Object 1. Scale 1:2.

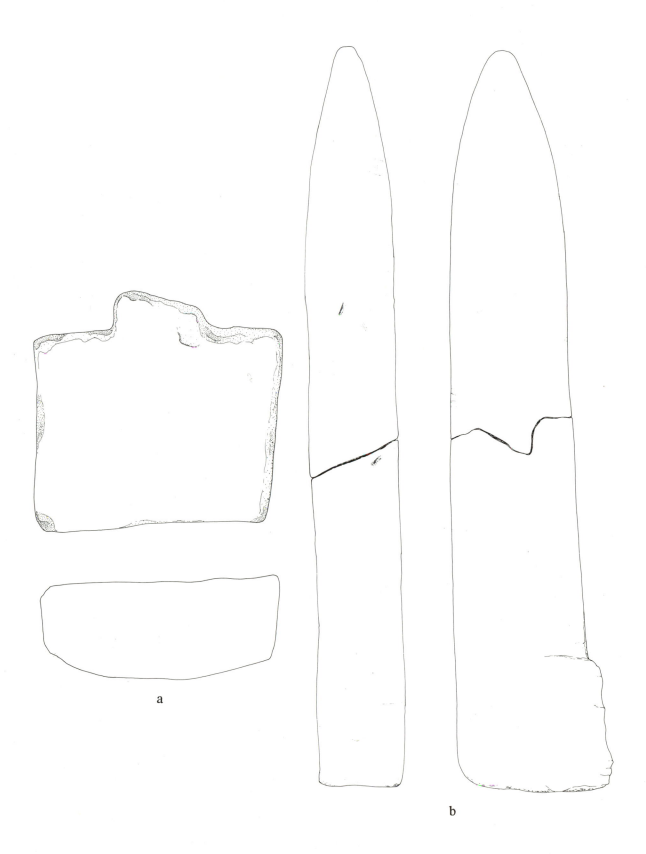

Figure 85. Objects from Chapels QC 11 and QC 17: (*a*) Offering Table, Chapel QC 11;
(*b*) Obelisk, QC 17—2. Scale 1:4.

Table 40. Register of X-Group Finds in Cemetery Q (*cont.*).

Pit	Description and Contents	Cairo	OIM	Figure/Plate

Q 304, pit cutting shaft, N of QC 9 (*cont.*)

Post-Meroitic sherds (*cont.*):

    J. X-Gr. ord. goblet I—A

    K. X-Gr. ord. goblet I—A

    L. X-Gr. ord. bowl I—C1 (rib below rim), wh. pt. rim band

    M. Coptic period Eg. utility, ribbed

    N. Unc. handle, bk. pt.

    O. X-Gr. storage-utility jar I—B, wh. and bk. pt.
          blob beads at neck

    P. Unc. jar, incised band at shoulder, vert. zigzags

    Q. Unc. rib-rim, discolored

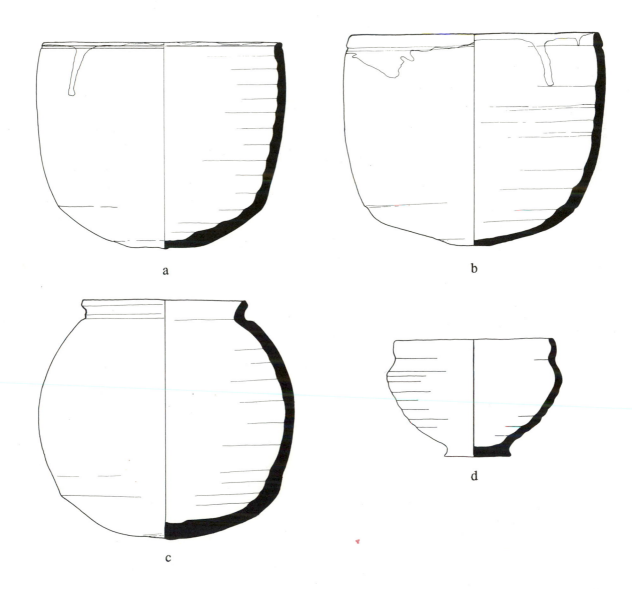

Figure 86. Pottery from Chapel Row Q*C*: (*a*) X-Gr. Ord. Bowl I—A2, Q 140—1;
(*b*) X-Gr. Ord. Bowl I—A2, Q 140—2; (*c*) X-Gr. Ord. Convex Jar I—C,
Q 328—3; (*d*) X-Gr. Ord. Goblet I—B, Q 328—X-Gr.—B. Scale 2:5.

Table 40. Register of X-Group Finds in Cemetery Q (*cont.*).

Chapel	Description and Contents	Cairo	OIM	Figure/Plate
Q 328, pit cutting shaft, N of QC 14				
	Circular pit: 2.00 × 0.60 m; inside coated with mud plaster			
	Inside pit to the N was a small area with fragments of textiles and bone, slightly to the SE were two roughly formed bricks turned on edge at R angles to one another, next to them were uncertain objects, sherds(?), and at the S edge was a bowl-shaped mud object			
	Objects:			
	1. Textile fragments (CAT Mer.)		Disc.	
	2. Mud container		Disc.	
	3. X-Gr. ord. convex jar I—C, with modeled rim, caked outside with carbon, greasy carbonized mass inside bottom		20713	figs. 12, 86c
	Sherds (see OINE VIII):		31902	
	A. X-Gr. ord. bowl I—A2, wh. pt. rim band			
	B. X-Gr. ord. goblet I—B, rim			fig. 86d
	C. X-Gr. ord. bowl I—A?, rim, discolored and caked with carbon			
	D. X-Gr. ord. goblet I—B, base			
	E. X-Gr. ord. goblet I—B			
Q 317, pit cutting shaft, N of QC 15–14				
	Circular pit: 1.54 × 0.45 m			
	Objects:			
	1. X-Gr. ord. goblet I—B1c; caked remains inside of white pt., height 8.4		20747	
	2. X-Gr. ord. goblet I—B1c; neck missing, remains of gn. pt., height 8		20746	
	3. Truncated cone of pk. stone (indurated clay?) with hole bored in center		20850	fig. 159d
	Post-Meroitic sherds from Q 317 (see OINE VIII):		31896	
	A. X-Gr. ord. goblet I—B			
	B. X-Gr. ord. goblet I—A, wh. pt. vine			
	C. X-Gr. ord. goblet I—A, bk. and wh. pt. swags and tassels			
	D. X-Gr. ord. goblet, base			
	E. Unc. ord. bowl			
	F. Unc., probably post-X-Gr. bowl rim			
	G. Unc. ord. crater or jar, rib rim, beveled top			
Q 324/Q 368 area, N of QC 16				
	Circular pit, no dim.			
Q 333, pit cutting shaft, N of QC 19				
	Circular pit: 1.9–2.0, diam.; coated inside with mud plaster			
	Objects:			
	1. X-Gr. ord. goblet I—A1bi *alpha*		20769	fig. 87b, pl. 41a
	2. X-Gr. ord. goblet I—B1c, with potter's mark, height 9.3		20781	
	3. X-Gr. ord. goblet I—B1c, height 8.2		20783	
	Sherds (see OINE VIII)		31904	
Q 492, pit cutting shaft, SE of QC 30				
	Circular pit: dia. unc., coated inside with mud plaster "on the surface were found bones of a sheep"			

Table 40. Register of X-Group Finds in Cemetery Q (*cont.*).

Pit	Description and Contents	Cairo	OIM	Figure/Plate

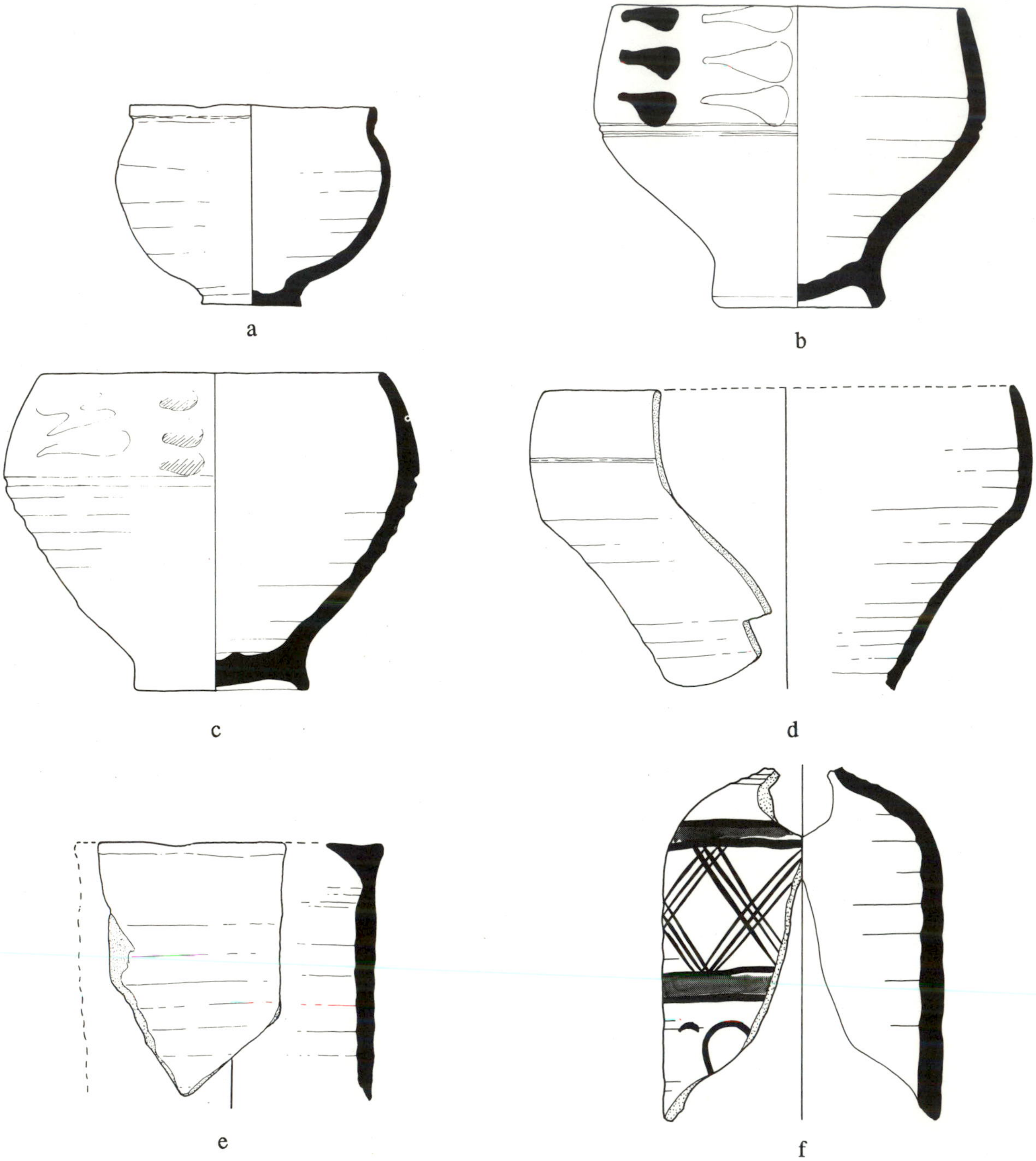

Figure 87. Pottery from Chapel Row Q*C* (*cont.*): (*a*) QC 17—G, (*b*) Q 333—1, (*c*) Q 416—1 [surface], (*d*) Q 176—A, (*e*) Pipe, Q 433—A, (*f*) Q 401—A. Scale 2:5.

Q 140, S of Q*C* 36–37   pls. 21–22
　　Circular pit, elongated NE: 2.10-2.45 × 0.40 m
　　A pile of small stones was placed in the center;
　　　　fragmentary remains of animal(s) were place on the
　　　　stones, parts of a jaw, lower leg with a hoof, and
　　　　some hair. The bones appear to be from two different
　　　　individuals. Sherds were mixed with the bones.

Table 40. Register of X-Group Finds in Cemetery Q (*cont.*).

Pit/Tomb	Description and Contents	Cairo	OIM	Figure/Plate
Q 140, S of QC 36–37 (*cont.*)				
Objects:				
	1. X-Gr. ord. bowl I—A2, wh. pt. band at rim		20271	figs. 10a, 86a
	2. X-Gr. ord. bowl I—A2; wh. pt. band at rim		20272	fig. 86b
	3. Ostrich egg fragment		20263	
	4. Date pits		Disc.	
	5. Textile fragments (CAT unc.)		Disc.	
Sherds:			32090	
	From shaft and bones		Disc.	

Both vessels were blackened on the outside with fire and on
the inside with greasy carbonized material.

Q 241, N of QC 44
Shallow circular pit

Q 480/486, pit cutting shafts S of E end, QC chapel row
Circular pit, 1.70 × 0.50
Three cb. near surface of Q 480 may be part of the
pit arrangements.

IV. Qu. 48 Complex: Meroitic Tombs and Associated Surface Loci with X-Group Material Attributed to Cult Activity

Pit/Tomb	Description and Contents	Cairo	OIM	Figure/Plate
Q 175, in tumulus trench				
Sherds, Q 175 (see OINE VIII):			31830	
	A. Mer. ord. bottle-jar, very short neck; late			
	B. X-Gr. ord. goblet I—A			
	C. Eg. bowl rim, Meroitic?			
	D. Unc. ord. globular jar, red coat			
S of Q 175, on face of alluvium:				
Object:				
	1. X-Gr. ord. goblet I—B, interior caked with residue of gn. pigment			
Sherds (see OINE VIII):			31830	
	A. X-Gr. ord. jar, bk. spot bead below rim			
	B. X-Gr. *qadus*, bottom			
	C. X-Gr. *qadus*, rim			
	D. X-Gr. ord. goblet I—A, bk. and wh. pt. swags			
	E. X-Gr. ord. goblet I—A			
	F. X-Gr. ord. goblet I—B, rim			
	G. X-Gr. ord. goblet I—B, base and body			
	H. X-Gr. ord. goblet I—B			
	I. X-Gr. handmade cooking pot, rim, blackened			
	J. X-Gr. handmade cooking pot, body			
	K. Unc. Coptic period Eg. utility jar, gray, ribbed			
	L. Unc. Utility-storage jar, rim			
	M. Post-X-Gr.? ord., ring base			
	N. Mer. ord. jar, red coat, bk. pt. outline, large lt. oval			
	O. Unc. ord., bk. and red			
	P. Post-X-Gr. fine gray, base and rim			
	Q. Post-X-Gr. ord. bowl with ye. interior			
	R. Post-X-Gr. pk. jar			
	S–V. Unc. ord.			
Q 230, under QC 2				
Sherds, Post-Meroitic (see OINE VIII):			31841	
	A. Unc. ord. stump base of bowl?, irreg. wh. spots of pt.			

Table 40. Register of X-Group Finds in Cemetery Q (*cont.*).

Tomb	Description and Contents	Cairo	OIM	Figure/Plate
Q 254, N of QC 4				
	Sherds, Post-Meroitic (see OINE VIII):			
	A. X-Gr. ord. cup, base		31855A	
	B. X-Gr. ord. goblet I—B		31855B	
	C. Coptic period Eg. amphora with squared rim, bitumen lining (Emery and Kirwan 13a, Firka 5)		31855C	
Q 165, S of QC 4–7, on surface				
	Sherds, Post-Meroitic (see OINE VIII):		31824	
	A. Unc. cup base, abraded			
	B. Unc. handmade bowl with red coat			
	C. Post-X-Gr. orange with bk. pt.			
	D. Post-X-Gr. orange with bk. pt.			
Surface S of Q 175, at QC 5–7				
	Object (see OINE VIII):			
	1. X-Gr. ord. goblet I—B1c, interior encrusted with gn. pigment, height 8.6		20474	
Q 635 at QC 9				
	Sherds, Post-Meroitic:			
	A. X-Gr. ord. goblet I—B			
	B. Unc. ord. gray			
Q 414, S of QC 12				
	Sherd, Post-Meroitic (see OINE VIII):		31943	
	A. X-Gr. storage jar, wh. pt. beads at neck, very sloppy, vine in pairs (possibly bottle jar)			
Q 433, S of QC 12				
	Sherd, Post-Meroitic (see OINE VIII):		31954	
	A. Tubular pipe or stand of storage jar pottery (see pipe or stand from Ballana enclosure)			fig. 87e
Q 367, S of QC 13				
	Sherds, Post-Meroitic (see OINE VIII):		31924	
	A. X-Gr. ord. goblet			
	B. Bn. amphora with bitumen			
Q 297. between QC 14 and 15				
	Sherds, Post-Meroitic (see OINE VIII):		31879	
	A. X-Gr. ord. goblet I—A, bk. and wh. pt. swags			
	B. X-Gr. ord. goblet I—B, base			
	C. X-Gr. ord. goblet I—B			
	D. X-Gr. ord. goblet I—B			
	E. Unc. ord. jar; spout, wh. coat			
Q 383, at QC 16–17				
	Sherds, Post-Meroitic (see OINE VIII):		31930	
	A. X-Gr. ord. goblet I—B			
	B. Post-X-Gr. wh. coat, purple swags and chain			
	C. *Qadus*, rim			
	D. Unc. ord., gray-red			
Q 384, at QC 16–17				
	Sherds, Post-Meroitic (see OINE VIII):		31932	
	A. X-Gr. ord. goblet, base			
	B. X-Gr. ord. bowl, wh. pt. rim band			
Q 330, N of QC 18				
	Sherd, Post-Meroitic (see OINE VIII):		31903	
	A. X-Gr. ord. goblet I—A; base, fire blackened			

Table 40. Register of X-Group Finds in Cemetery Q (*cont.*).

Tomb	Description and Contents	Cairo	OIM	Figure/Plate
Q 470, six meters S of QC 20				
	Sherds, Post-Meroitic (see OINE VIII):		31969	
	A. X-Gr. ord. goblet I—A, later type, wh. pt. vine, in groups of five			
	B. X-Gr. ord. goblet I—A			
Q 310, N of QC 21–22				
	Sherd (see OINE VIII):		31890	
	A. X-Gr. *qadus*			
Q 540, N of QC 28				
	Sherd, Post-Meroitic (see OINE VIII):		31998	
	A. X-Gr. ord. goblet I—A, bk. and wh. pt. vert. lines			
Q 618, N of QC 27				
	Sherds, Post-Meroitic (see OINE VIII):		32026	
	A. X-Gr. ord. (with bk. core) bowl I—A, wh. pt. vert. lines			
	B. X-Gr. ord. goblet I—B, low rim			
Q 578, NNE of QC 31				
	Sherds, Post-Meroitic (see OINE VIII):		32011	
	A. X-Gr. ord. goblet I—A			
	B. X-Gr. ord. goblet I—A, with low rim			
Q 353, at QC 33				
	Sherds, Post-Meroitic (see OINE VIII):		31919	
	A. X-Gr. ord. goblet I—B, rim			
	B. X-Gr. ord. goblet I—B			
	C. X-Gr. ord. goblet I—A, carination, bk. and wh. vert. lines			
	D. X-Gr. ord. bowl, wh. spot beads			
	E. X-Gr. ord.			
Q 347, N of QC 33				
	Sherd, Post-Meroitic (see OINE VIII):		31915	
	A. Deep concave base, chaffy ord., gray to bn. coat			
Q 573, N of QC 55				
	Sherds, Post-Meroitic (see OINE VIII):		32008	
	A. X-Gr. ord. jar I—, wh. pt. spot bead			
	B. X-Gr. ord. jar I—			
	C. Handle, worn			

V. Qu. 48 Complex: Meroitic Tombs and Associated Surface Loci with X-Group Material with no clear Attribution to Cult Activity

Tomb	Description and Contents	Cairo	OIM	Figure/Plate
Q 173, EW at QC 41–42				
	Sherds, Post-Meroitic (see OINE VIII):		31828	
	A. X-Gr. ord. goblet I—A, large			
	B. X-Gr. ord. bowl I—, fire blackened			
Q 176, EW at QC 37				
	Sherd, Post-Meroitic (see OINE VIII):		31831	
	A. X-Gr. ord. goblet I—A, very large			fig. 87d
Q 240				
	Surface object:			
	1. X-Gr. ord. goblet I—B1c, height 8.2		20885	
Q 303, EW at QC 32–33				
	Sherds, Post-Meroitic (see OINE VIII):		31883	
	A. Unc. crater fragment, abraded			

Table 40. Register of X-Group Finds in Cemetery Q (*cont.*).

Tomb	Description and Contents	Cairo	OIM	Figure/Plate
Q 303, EW at QC 32–33 (*cont.*)				
Sherds, Post-Meroitic (see OINE VIII) (*cont.*):				
	B. Unc. buff-orange amphora or *qadus* with button base			
	C. Unc. handmade jar, coarse			
	D. Unc. handmade coarse bowl			
Q 339, EW at QC 1				
Sherds, Post-Meroitic (see OINE VIII):			31910	
	A. Unc. ord. jar			
	B. Unc. gray-pk. jar with beveled rim, vestigial handles and two grooves			
Q 401, Christian tomb				
X-Group sherd from shaft:				
	A. Eg. fine ord jug? with bk. pt. bands frame crossed parallel zigzags		31934	fig. 87f
Surface at Q 416				
	1. X-Gr. ord. goblet I—A1aii *beta*		21244	fig. 87c

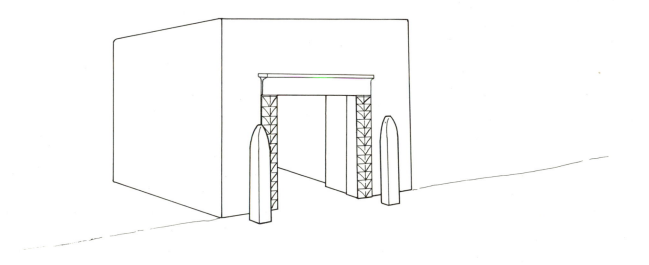

Figure 88. Conjectural Reconstruction of Chapel QC 17.

Table 40. Register of X-Group Finds in Cemetery Q (*cont.*).

Tomb	Description and Contents	Cairo	OIM	Figure/Plate
Q 512, EW 20 m S of QC 30				
Sherd, Post-Meroitic:				
	A. X-Gr. ord. bottle jar I—A (3?), simple rim, single wh. band on shoulder			
Q 513, Meroitic tomb				
Sherd, Post-Meroitic (see OINE VIII):			31992	
	A. X-Gr. ord. bottle jar I—A(1?), simple rim and shoulder; lt. ye. band, late X-Gr.			
Q 571, QC chapel row ca. 5 m E at 20 m S				
Sherd, Post-Meroitic (see OINE VIII):			32007	
	A. X-Gr. ord. goblet, bk. and wh. pt.			
Q 649, at chapel QC 15				
Sherds, Post-Meroitic (see OINE VIII):			32039	
	A. Unc. gray-pk. ord. convex crater with rect. rim			
	B. X-Gr. ord. goblet I—A			

Figure 89. Conjectural Reconstruction of Chapel QC 22.

Table 40. Register of X-Group Finds in Cemetery Q (*cont.*).

Chapel	Description and Contents	Cairo	OIM	Figure/Plate
	QU. 56 COMPLEX			
QE 1				fig. 90
	Rectangular brick enclosure, destroyed at the NE and SE sides, oriented N-S, with a single course. An extension led to the S from an opening, only the W side of which was preserved. An L-shaped structure, with signs of burning and ash, was located W of the opening. The interior and the area to the W may have had a mud paving. Brickbats were scattered in the area.			
	Pottery associated with this structure was assigned to a surface locus near Q 338.			
	Surface finds 2 m E of NE corner of shaft:			
	1. X-Gr. ord. goblet I—A1aii *beta*, wh. pt. vine in pairs (2.5YR 5/4, 2.5YR 6/6, 5YR 6/4)	20867		fig. 91d
	2. X-Gr. ord. goblet I—B1c	20868		fig. 91a
	3. X-Gr. ord. bowl I—A2, red ct., wh. rim band blackened	20869		fig. 91g
	4. X-Gr. ord. goblet I—A1aii *beta*, wh. pt. vine in pairs	20871		fig. 91e
	5. X-Gr. ord. goblet I—B1c (2.5YR 6/4, 5YR 5/4), height 9.1	20872		
	6. Amphora base	Disc.		fig. 91f
	Surface finds S of Q 360, directly beyond wall extension:			
	1. X-Gr. ord. bowl I—A, ribbed, bk. and wh. vert. lines	20766		fig. 91b
	2. X-Gr. ord. handmade bowl/cup—A, red ct., very small	21088		figs. 19a, 91c
	3. X-Gr. handmade cooking pot, mud plastered bottom, blackened	22292		fig. 92
	Field note concerning vessel 3 indicates that six objects were found in this location (no information on other five).			
	Surface SW of Q 422:			
	1. X-Gr. ord. cup—D4a, dk. and wh. pt. bands (2.5YR 5/6, 2.5YR 4/4, 7.5YR 7/4, 2.5YR 4/6)	21328		fig. 165c
	2. X-Gr. ord. goblet I—B1a, height 9	21329		
	3. X-Gr. ord. goblet I—A1g, wh. plaster, height 6.9	21371		

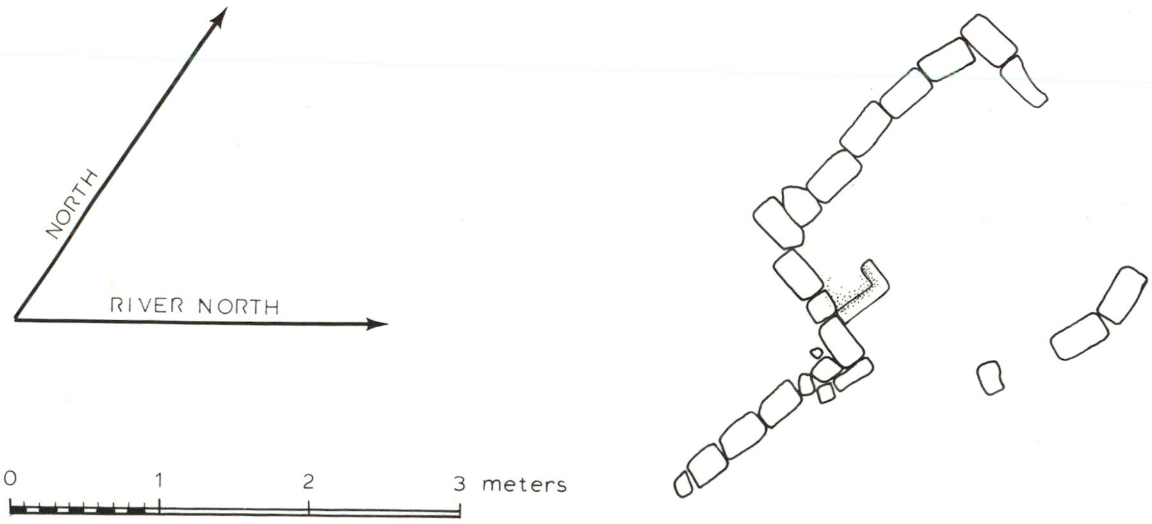

Figure 90. Chapel QE 1.

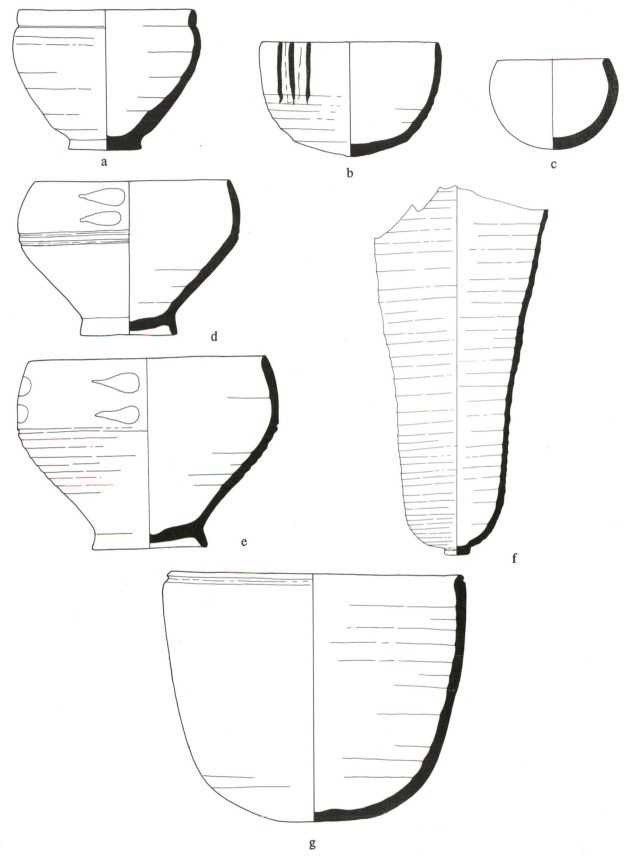

Figure 91. Pottery from Chapel Row Q*E* Deposits: (*a*) X-Gr. Ord. Goblet I—B1c, Q 338 E—2; (*b*) X-Gr. Ord. Bowl I—A, Q 360 S—1; (*c*) X-Gr. Ord. Handmade Bowl/Cup—A, Q 360 S—2; (*d*) X-Gr. Ord. Goblet I—A1aii *beta*, Q 338 E—1; (*e*) X-Gr. Ord. Goblet I—A1aii *beta*, Q 338 E—4; (*f*) Amphora Base, Q 338 E—6; (*g*) X-Gr. Ord. Bowl I—A2, Q 338 E—3. Scale 2:5.

Table 40. Register of X-Group Finds in Cemetery Q (*cont.*).

Tomb	Description and Contents	Cairo	OIM	Figure/Plate
QE 1				
Sherds:				
	A. Mer. Eg. jar			
	B. Mer. fine/ord. cup, red coat			
	C. Unc., possibly X-Gr. *qadus* rim			
	D. Fine orange with bk. pt. spiral			
QE 2 (such a locus otherwise unknown)				
Sherds:			33151	
	A. Mer. Eg. utility cook-pot rim			
	B. Unc. coarse open jar or bowl			
	C. X-Gr. ord.? coarse bowl, with broad bottom			
	D. Post-X-Gr. pk., carinated base			

Figure 92. A Plastered and Blackened Cooking Vessel, Q 360 S—3, from a Q*E* Deposit. Scale 2:5.

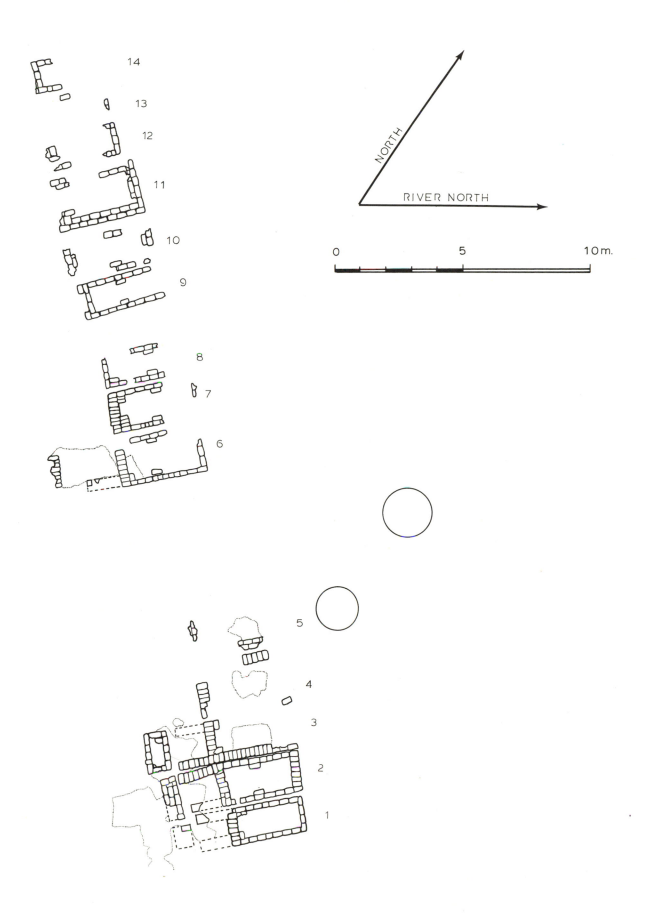

Figure 93. Plans of Chapels QF 1–14 and Associated Pits.

Table 40. Register of X-Group Finds in Cemetery Q (*cont.*).

Chapel	Description and Contents	Cairo	OIM	Figure/Plate

QU. 36 COMPLEX

I.   CHAPELS QF
II. ANIMAL SACRIFICE BURIALS

I. COMPLEX QU. 36: CHAPELS QF   pls. 9, 24a

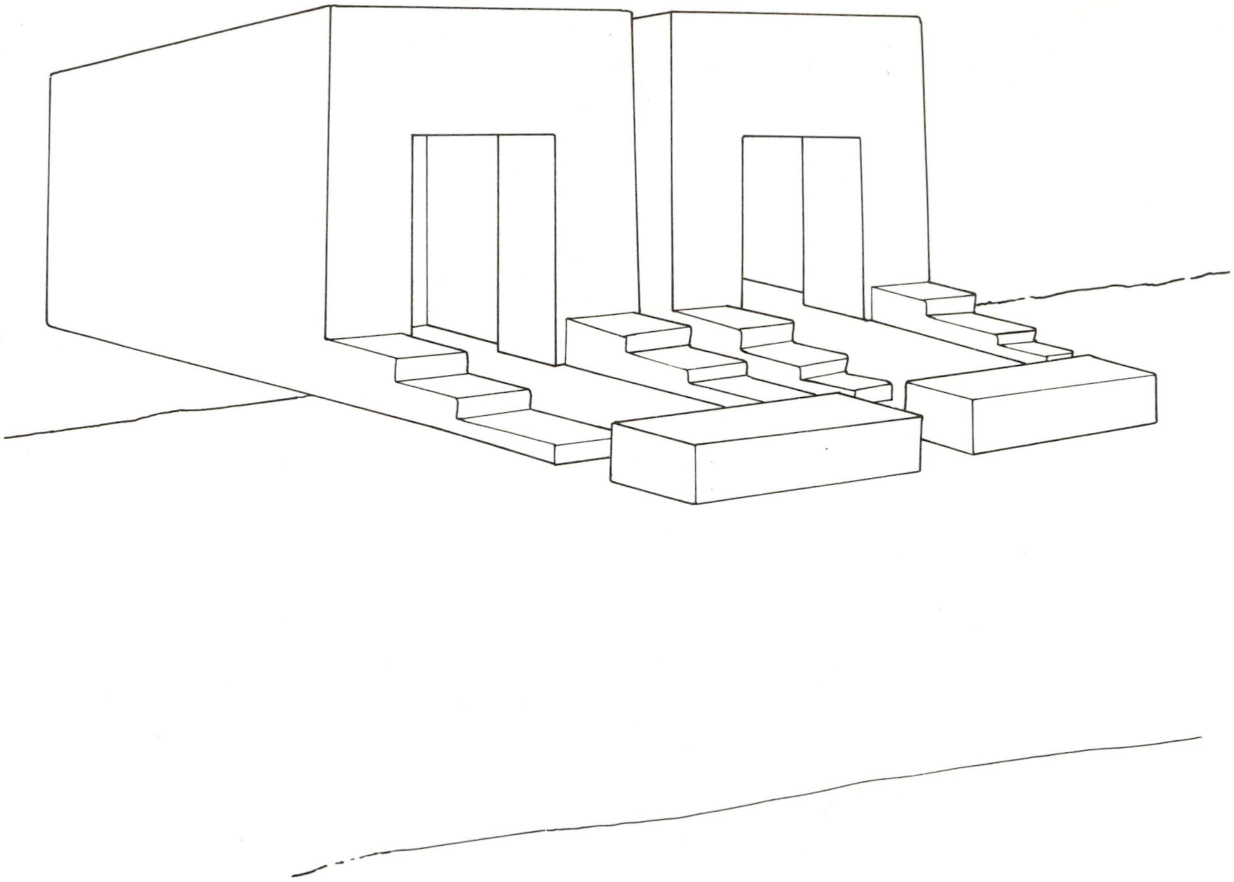

Figure 94. Conjectural Reconstruction of Chapels QF 1 and 2.

QF 1	Rectangular chapel with thickened S wall (headers, reinforced S corners and long antae) mostly destroyed. One brick from a long podium remained.		figs. 93, 94, pl. 23a, b
QF 2	Rectangular chapel with thickened S and N walls (headers), buttresses on the side walls, and antae. A long podium three cb. thick was constructed on the paving just beyond the antae.		figs. 93, 94, pl. 23a, b
QF 3	Rectangular chapel with wall foundations of headers, side walls continuing to the S, as antae (E only preserved). Just opposite antae was long podium. The N and W walls were destroyed, but paving inside and to the podium was preserved.		fig. 93, pl. 23a, b
QF 1–3	The podia were surrounded by mud paving.		
QF 4	Rectangular chapel row with wall foundations of headers and mud paving inside. The N, E, and most of the W wall were destroyed.		fig. 93
QF 5	Rectangular chapel with mud paving inside; fragments of the E and S walls only		fig. 93

Table 40. Register of X-Group Finds in Cemetery Q (*cont.*).

Chapel	Description and Contents	Cairo	OIM	Figure/Plate
QF 6	Rectangular chapel with buttresses on the side walls and thickened S wall (headers). The SE corner was reinforced with a stretcher; the W corners were destroyed. Remains of a long anta were preserved to the E, and a long podium was directly opposite. Remains of mud paving was preserved inside and between chapel and podium.			fig. 93
QF 7	Rectangular chapel with buttresses on the side walls, thickened S wall, and reinforced S corners. Most of the N and parts of the side walls were destroyed.			fig. 93, pl. 24b
QF 8	Rectangular chapel with buttresses on the side walls and reinforced NE corner. The other corners were destroyed, with the N and parts of the side walls.			fig. 93, pl. 24b
QF 9	Rectangular chapel with buttresses on the side walls, and single bricks reinforcing the outside of the S corners. The N wall was destroyed.			fig. 93
QF 10	Fragmentary remains of rectangular chapel with buttress on the E wall and thickened ends.			fig. 93
QF 11	Rectangular chapel with double thickness walls; the S wall was mostly destroyed			fig. 93
	Object:			
	1. Fragment of sandstone door jamb? or plaque with incised archer		21085	fig. 84b
QF 12	Rectangular chapel with thickened S wall, the S and sidewalls are fragmentary.			fig. 93
QF 13	Fragments of N and W wall of chapel			fig. 93
QF 14	Part of S and side walls of rectangular chapel, slightly off axis to NE			fig. 93
	Object, 3 m S of chapel row ("fourth rectangle"):			
	1. Stone plaque with pt. hieroglyphic group		21084	fig. 84c
	Sherds:			
	a. Chapels QF 3–5:		33152	
	A. X-Gr. ord. goblet I—B, rim, sharply profiled			
	B. X-Gr. ord. goblet I—B, rim rounded			
	C. X-Gr. ord. goblet I—B, low rim			
	D. X-Gr. ord. jar (open), with ridges, discolored			
	b. Chapels QF 5–6:		33153	
	A. X-Gr. ord. goblet I—A, rim vert., sharp carination			
	B. X-Gr. ord. goblet I—A, base			
	C. X-Gr. ord. goblet I—A, carination			
	D. X-Gr. ord. goblet I—B, base			
	E. X-Gr. ord. goblet I—B, rim, sharply profiled			
	F. X-Gr. ord. goblet I—B, rim			
	G-H. NID			
	c. Chapels QF 7–14:		33154	
	A. X-Gr. ord. goblet I—B, rim			
	B. X-Gr. ord. goblet I—B, base			
	C. X-Gr. ord. goblet I—B, rim-shoulder, ribbed			
	D. X-Gr. ord. goblet I—A, med.-tall, bk. pt. vine, in pairs			
	E. X-Gr. ord. goblet I—B, rim			
	F. Unc. ridged gray amphora			
	G. Unc. pk. amphora handle			

Table 40. Register of X-Group Finds in Cemetery Q (*cont.*).

Pit	Description and Contents	Cairo	OIM	Figure/Plate

The chapels of Qu. 36 were built in three small rows at
slightly varying axes: 1–5, 6–8 and 9–14. Antae were found
on 1–3 and 6, associated with long podia, here approx. the
width of the chapel frontage. Chapels here were closely
spaced.

Pits were found near this chapel row, but they appear to be of early date.

II. COMPLEX QU. 36: ANIMAL SACRIFICE BURIALS

Q 264, Animal Pit   pl. 27a

Shaft: 2.89 × 2.15 × 1.76 m

Burials: Five camels, A–E

"three certainly killed by blow on skull, probably two male,
one female; bones of at least one camel spongy as if
diseased or undernourished"

Objects:

		Cairo	OIM	Figure/Plate
1.	Saddle (actually blanket, on A)	20929		
2.	Bell on strap (unc. animal, B, C?)	20887		fig. 95a, pl. 83g
3.	Bridle ("of bk. or bn. cloth with dk. red 'bosses' still on skull; traces of bn. cloth adhering to forehead")	Disc.		
4.	Ropes (loose in shaft)	Disc.		
	Stomach contents	20889		

Sherds:

A. Unc. gray with wh. coat

B. Unc. red-gray jar rim

Figure 95. Objects from Animal Pits Q 264 and Q 265: (*a*) Bell, Q 264—2;
(*b*) Arrowhead, Q 265—3. Scale 1:2.

Q 265, Animal pit   pl. 27b

Shaft: 2.74 × 1.87 × ca. 1.69 m

Burials:

A. Head E

B. Head W, in NW corner

C. —

D. —

E. —

Table 40. Register of X-Group Finds in Cemetery Q (*cont.*).

Pit	Description and Contents	Cairo	OIM	Figure/Plate
Q 265, Animal pit (*cont.*)				
Bodies:				
A.	Horse			
B.	Horse			
C.	Chestnut Arabian stallion, ca. 8 years			
D.	Arabian stallion, 8–11 years			
E.	Arabian stallion, 8–11 years			
Objects:				
1.	Wooden cinch attachment (near head of B)		20963A	figs. 57c, 60 pl. 72a
2.	Trappings (in fill)		20963B	
	a. Iron ring			fig. 57d
	b. Matting			
	c. Ropes			
	d. Beads		20940	
	e. Leather		20940	
3.	Arrowhead		20936	fig. 95b
Sherds:				
A.	X-Gr. ord. goblet I—A, carination			
B.	Coptic period Eg. red utility *amphoriskos*-jug, handle area			
C.	Unc. bn. ribbed			
D.	Coptic period Eg. utility, ribbing on lower body			

COMPLEXES WITHOUT CULT STRUCTURES

Qu. 3 Complex

Pit	Description and Contents	Cairo	OIM	Figure/Plate
Q 5, Animal pit				pl. 25a, b
Shaft: rectangular, E-W, cut to bedrock				
Burials: dismembered, pit filled with surface sand and two layers of mixed and broken up animal skeletons and trappings, the upper layer was at -1.00/-1.30, the lower at -1.70/-2.00 -1.90/-2.20 m				
Bodies: incomplete and jumbled. "Lack of corresponding horse skulls suggests incomplete skeletons being deposited."				
Hooves:				
	Horses: 58			
	Donkeys: 9			
	Unc. small hooves: 9			
Skulls:				
	Camels: 3			
Objects:				
1.	Textile remains (balls), av. 3.0 x 2.5 (CAT 36?)		19979	
2.	Bronze cup fragments, height 7.0		19980	
3.	Textile remains (balls), CAT 36		19898	
4.	Rope remains, large thickness 1.7; small 0.4		19981	
5.	Silver studs		19982	fig. 96a
6.	Copper pendant on ring, $7.5 \times 4.5 \times 0.05$		19983	
7.	Knife blade or bar (iron), length 16.3		19984	
8.	Iron ring fragments		19985	pl. 73f
	a. Fragments of bits, four pieces			
	b. Fragments of rings, four pieces, 5 cm × 1 cm			
	c. Fragments of block-like tool or rectangular harness-tube, four pieces			

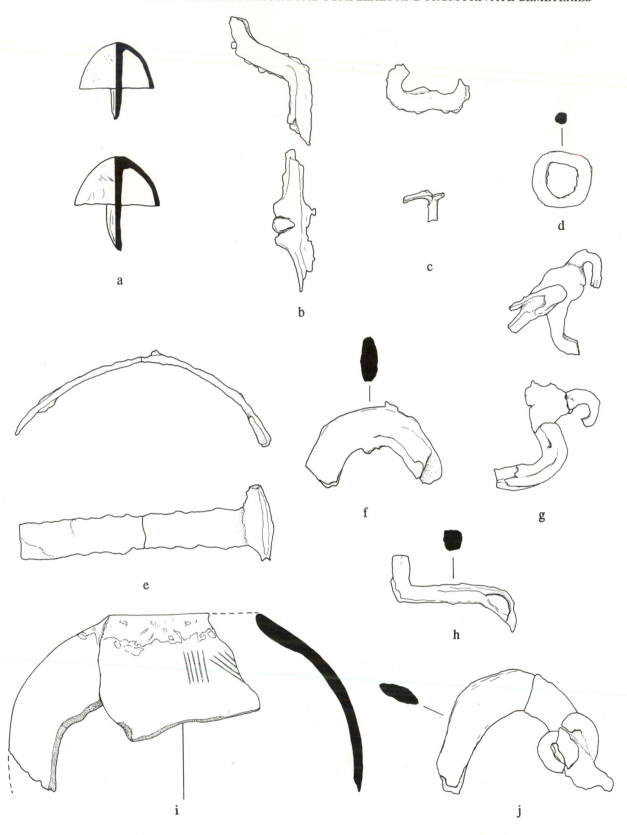

Figure 96. Objects from Animal Pit Q 5: (*a*) Silver Studs, No. 5; (*b*) Iron Fragments from Harness (Bit), No. 9a; (*c*) Iron Fragments from Harness (Rings), No. 9c, d; (*d*) Iron Fragment from Harness (Ring), No. 9e; (*e*) Iron Fragments from Harness (Uncertain Strap), No. 9j; (*f*) Iron Fragment from Harness (Uncertain), No. 9i; (*g*) Iron Fragments from Harness (Rings), No. 9k; (*h*) Iron Fragment from Harness (Bit), No. 9b; (*i*) X-Gr. Handmade Cooking Pot, No. A; (*j*) Iron Fragments from Harness (Uncertain Strap), No.9l. Scales: (*a*) 2:1; (*b–d, f, g, j*) 1:2; (*e, i*) 2:5.

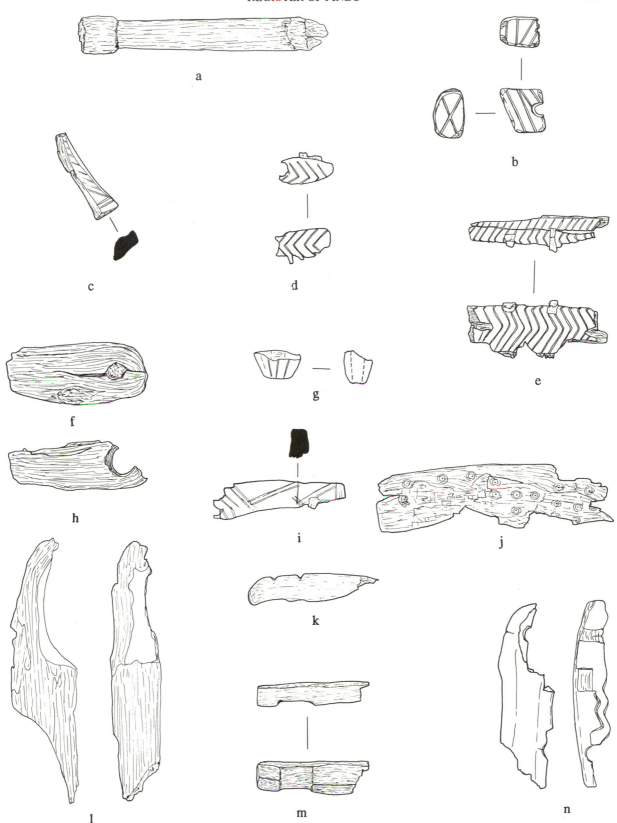

Figure 97. Remains of Saddles from Animal Pit Q 5: (*a*) End of Seat Rod, No. 12f; (*b*) End of Cinch Bar with Hole, No. 12c; (*c*) Cantle Fragment, No. 12a; (*d*) End of Cinch Bar, No. 12b; (*e*) Twin Sockets from Cinch Bar with Remains of D-ring, No. 12e; (*f*) End of Cinch Bar with Rope in Hole, No. 14a; (*g*) Socket Projection from D-ring in Cinch Bar, No. 12d; (*h*) End of Cinch Bar with Large Rope Hole, No. 14b; (*i*) End of Cinch Bar with Ring Attachment (?), No. 18a; (*j*) Cinch Bar with Ring Attachment (?), No. 18c; (*k*) End of Cinch Bar with Grooves, No. 18b; (*l*) Pommel Fragment, No. 12h; (*m*) End of Seat Rod?, No. 18d; (*n*) Cinch Bar Fragment, No. 12i. Scale 2:5.

Table 40. Register of X-Group Finds in Cemetery Q (*cont.*).

Pit	Description and Contents	Cairo	OIM	Figure/Plate
Q 5, Animal pit (*cont.*)				
9.	Iron fragments from harness		19986	fig. 96b–h, j
				pls. 73b–c, 75a–l
a.	Bit fragments (two)			fig. 96b
b.	Bit fragment			fig. 96h
c.	Double ring?			fig. 96c
d.	Rod end of cinch ring?			fig. 96c
e–h.	Rings			fig. 96d
i.	Unc. flat curved piece			fig. 96f
j.	Unc. metal strap			fig. 96e
k.	Bit fragment?			fig. 96g
l.	As j?, with two rings attached to one end			fig. 96j
	(and various unidentified fragments)			
10.	Textile fragments, CAT 37		19987	
11.	Stomach contents		19988	
12.	Wooden saddle fittings		19857	figs. 57b, 97a–e
			19989	g, l, n; pl. 72b
a.	Cantle fragment			
b.	End of cinch bar		19857	fig. 97d
c.	End of cinch bar with hole		19989	fig. 97b
d.	Socket projection for D-ring in cinch bar		19989	fig. 97g
e.	Twin sockets from cinch bar with remains of D-ring		19989	fig. 97e, pl. 72b
f.	End of seat rod		19989	fig. 97a
g.	"Bar with notches," 32.0 × 1.7 × 3.5		19857	
h.	Pommel fragment		19989	figs. 57b, 97l
i.	Cinch bar fragment		19989	fig. 97n
13.	Bronze vessel fragments		19990	
14.	Wooden saddle fittings		19991	fig. 97c, f, h
a.	End of cinch bar with rope in hole			fig. 97f
b.	End of cinch bar with large rope hole			fig. 97h
15.	Bronze bowl fragments, dia. 11.0		19992	
16.	Silver pendant, 8.4	89877		
17.	Iron rings, diam. 4.5		19993	
18.	Wooden saddle fittings		19994	fig. 97i–k, m
a.	End of cinch bar with ring attachment?			fig. 97i
b.	End of cinch bar with grooves			fig. 97k
c.	Cinch bar with ring attachment?			fig. 97j
d.	End of seat rod?			fig. 97m
19.	Rope remains, length 17.0		19996	
20.	Knife blade (iron), 15.5 × 2.5 × 3.5		19858	
Sherds:			33155	
a.	From second bone layer:			
A.	X-Gr. handmade cooking pot			fig. 96i
b.	From first bone layer:			
B.	X-Gr. ord. jar, abraded			
C.	X-Gr. ord. jar			
D.	*qadus*			
c.	From sand fill:			
E.	*Qadus*, knob			
F.	Coptic period Eg. ord./utility handle			
G.	Unc. coarse jar, everted neck rim			
H.	Unc. gray jar, red and bk. band with bk. ball beads			

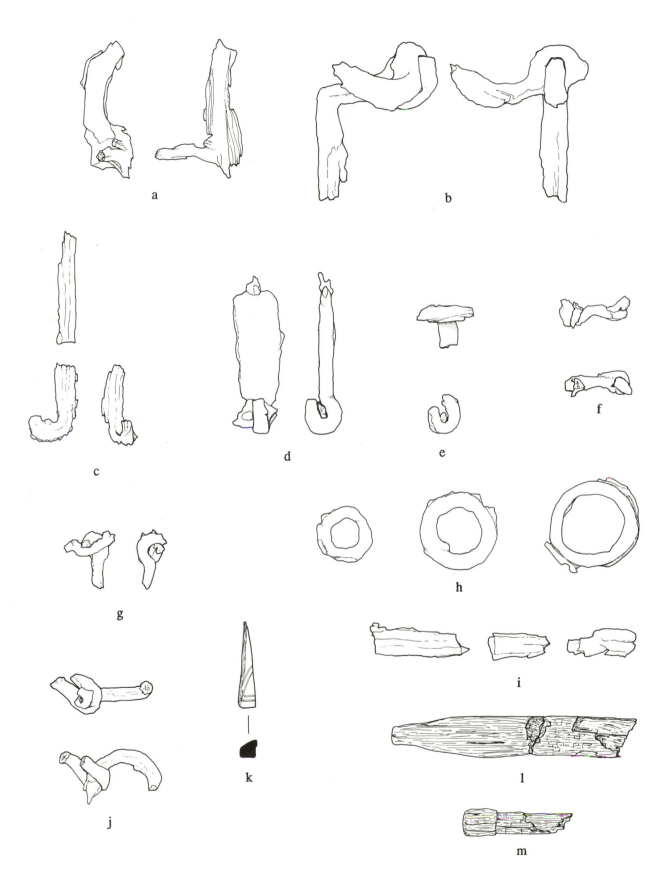

Figure 98. Iron Trappings and Wooden Saddle Fittings from Animal Pit Q 20: (*a*) No. 5a; (*b*) No. 5b; (*c*) No. 5c; (*d*) No. 5d; (*e*) Nos. 5e, g; (*f*) No. 5n; (*g*) No. 5f; (*h*) Nos. 5h, j-k; (*i*) Nos. 5m, o; (*j*) No. 5l; (*k*) No. 4c; (*l*) No. 4a; (*m*) No. 4b. Scale 2:5.

Table 40. Register of X-Group Finds in Cemetery Q (*cont.*).

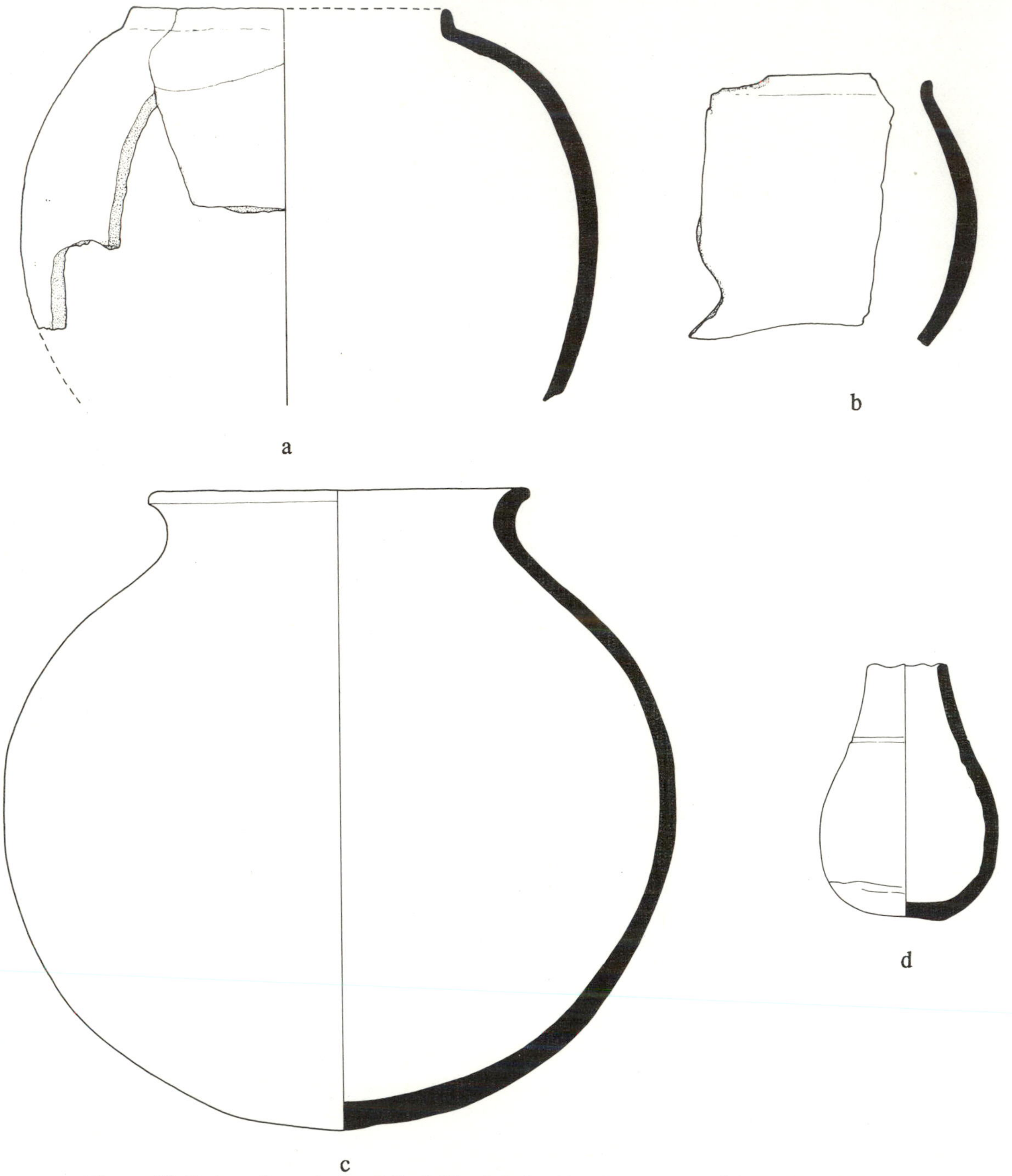

Pit	Description and Contents	Cairo	OIM	Figure/Plate

Figure 99. Pottery from Animal Pit Q 20: (*a*) Cooking Pot, No. B; (*b*) Cooking Pot, No. C; (*c*) X-Gr. Handmade Jar—C, No. A; (*d*) X-Gr. Handmade Jar—B2, No. 8. Scale 2:5.

Q 5, Animal pit (*cont.*)

    Sherds (*cont.*):

        c.   From sand fill (*cont.*):

            I.   X-Gr. ord. bowl, carinated

          J–N. Unc.

    Note that a mass burial at Meroe, east of temple KC 102 contained more than thirty individuals, many of them deliberately dismembered; see Shinnie 1984, p. 503

Table 40. Register of X-Group Finds in Cemetery Q (*cont.*).

Pit	Description and Contents	Cairo	OIM	Figure/Plate
Q 20, Animal pit				pl. 26
	Shaft: rectangular, E-W; steps cut in W end			
	Burials: dismembered, pit filled with surface sand alt. with two layers of bones at -1.30/-1.50/-1.60 and -1.80/-2.00 m, above the upper layer was a jumbled mass of brickbats and stones at -0.90/-1.00.			
	Bodies: incomplete and jumbled: "Lack of corresponding horse skulls suggests incomplete skeletons being deposited."			
	Hooves:			
	Horses: 68			
	Donkey: 1			
	Very small horses: 8			
	Skulls:			
	Camels: 7			
	Objects:			
	1. Copper or bronze cup fragments (scattered)		20092	
	2. Remains of iron rod (first bone layer), length 11		20091	
	3. Wooden saddle fittings (second layer)		20093	
	4a–c. Wooden saddle fittings (first layer)		20094	fig. 98k–m
	5. Remains of iron harness fittings (second layer and below)		20096	fig. 98a–j, pl. 74
	a. Fragment of bit, L-shaped around cheek, with six fragments.			fig. 98a
	b. Fragment of bit (?). With a curve, three pieces, one with loop at end.			fig. 98b
	c. Strap or band, three pieces, one narrowed at end and bent up to secure ring.			fig. 98c
	d. Rings attached to loops, four pieces.			fig. 98d
	e. Rings, six complete or large fragments, nine small fragments.			fig. 98e
	f. Uncertain fragments, three pieces (found with and below second bone layer).			fig. 98g
	6. Textile remains (second layer and below; CAT X-Gr)		20088	
	7. Tassels (second layer and below)		20089	
	8. X-Gr. handmade jar—B2		20069	figs. 20d, 99d
	9. Woven straw (first layer), $10.0 \times 6.2 \times 2.8$		20090	
	10. Stomach contents		20095	
	11. "Linen and leather in alt. layers of animal trappings"		20097	
	Sherds:			
	A. X-Gr. handmade Jar—C		24251	figs. 20c, 99c
	B. X-Gr. handmade Cooking pot		33156	fig. 99a
	C. X-Gr. handmade Cooking pot		33156	fig. 99b
Q 26, Animal pit				pl. 28a
	Shaft: three rectangular pits, arranged E-W			
	A. To W, long axis N-S, incomplete, dug only to -0.20 m			
	B. To E, long axis E-W, -1.00 deep			
	Burials: four horses, complete, dumped into shaft from NE corner, found lying as they fell			
	Bodies: horses, no further information			
	Objects:			
	1. Remains of rope, knotted through leather, longest 8.5×0.7		20105	
	2. Hair sample		20103	
	3. Stomach contents		20104	
	Sherds		33169	

Figure 100. Plan, Section, and an Object from Animal Pit Q 79: (*a*) Plan and Section,
(*b*) Wooden Cinch Bar, No. 2b. Scales: (*a*) 1:40, (*b*) 2:5.

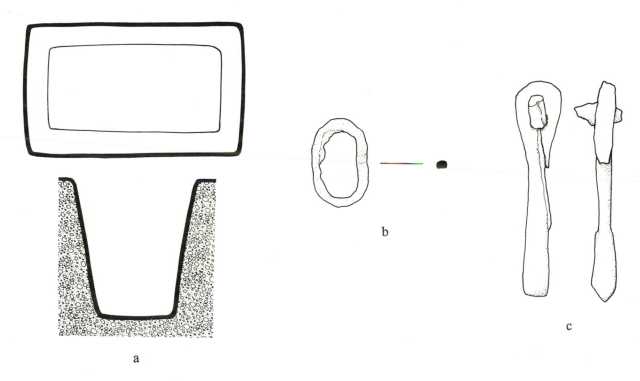

Figure 101. Plan, Section, and Objects from Animal Pit Q 73: (*a*) Plan and Section;
(*b*) Ring, No. 3b; (*c*) Buckle, No. 3a. Scales: (*a*) 1:40; (*b, c*) 1:2.

Table 40. Register of X-Group Finds in Cemetery Q (*cont.*).

Pit	Description and Contents	Cairo	OIM	Figure/Plate
QU. 54 COMPLEX				
Q 73, Animal pit				fig. 101a
	Shaft, N-S rectangle; 1.85–2.30 × 0.90–1.35 × 1.45 m			
	Burial: scattered			
	Body: animal, NID			
	Objects:			
	1. Rope remains (various lengths and thicknesses)		20134	pl. 71
	2. Textile remains (CAT X-Gr.)		20134	pl. 71
	3. Iron buckle, ring, and other fragments		20165	fig. 101b–c, pl. 73e
	4. Leather fragments		Disc.	
	See also Q 26., 77, 79, and 39; the metal of no. 3 is uncertain.			
QU. 60 COMPLEX				
Q 77, Animal pit, not excavated				
	Sub-rectangular pit: 1.55–1.75 × 1.20–1.55 × —			
QU. 4 COMPLEX				
Q 79, Animal pit				fig. 100a
	Sub-rectangular shaft: 1.60–2.05 × 0.80–0.95 × 1.10 m			
	Burial: —			
	Body: disarticulated bones, one animal			
	Objects:			
	1. Leather water bag? remains		20222	pl. 69
	2. Harness remains			
	a. Leather fragments		20223	
	b. End of wooden cinch bar		20223	fig. 100b
	3. Sherds		—	
QU. 10 COMPLEX				
Q 39, Animal pit				pls. 28b, 29
	Shaft: rectangular with rounded ends			
	Burials: four Animals, bones dist. or animals buried disarticulated as Q 5 and 20			
	Bodies: —			
	Hooves:			
	Horses: 3			
	Donkeys: 3			
	Other bones:			
	Camels: possibly two individuals			
	Objects:			
	1. Textile trapping remains, CAT 61		20098A–C	
	2. Textile remains ("saddle rug")		20480	
	3. Harness remains		20476	pl. 29c
	a. Metal rings			
	b. Leather straps			
	c. Iron ring			
	d. Wooden fragment			fig. 57a
	4. Animal horns, possibly from bit (three)		20481	
	5. Saddle		20374	fig. 56, pls. 29a–b, 70
	6. Stomach contents		20483	
	7. Leather bag (38 × 32) and other fragments		20484	pl. 29d

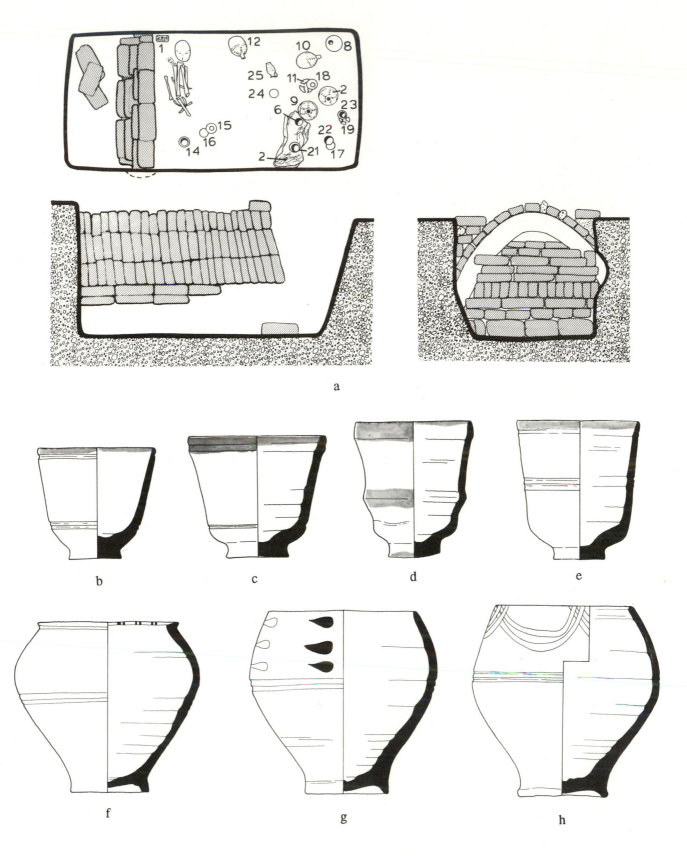

Figure 102. Plan, Sections, and Pottery from Tomb Q 1: (*a*) Plan and Section; (*b*) X-Gr. Ord. Cup I—D5a, No. 23; (*c*) X-Gr. Ord. Cup I—D5a, No. 22; (*d*) X-Gr. Ord. Cup I—D5bii, No. 21; (*e*) X-Gr. Ord. Cup I—D5bi, No. 19; (*f*) X-Gr. Ord. Goblet I—B2aiii, No. 15; (*g*) X-Gr. Ord. Goblet I—A1ci, No. 16; (*h*) X-Gr. Ord. Goblet I—A1ci, No. 14. Scales: (*a*) 1:40; (*b–h*) 2:5.

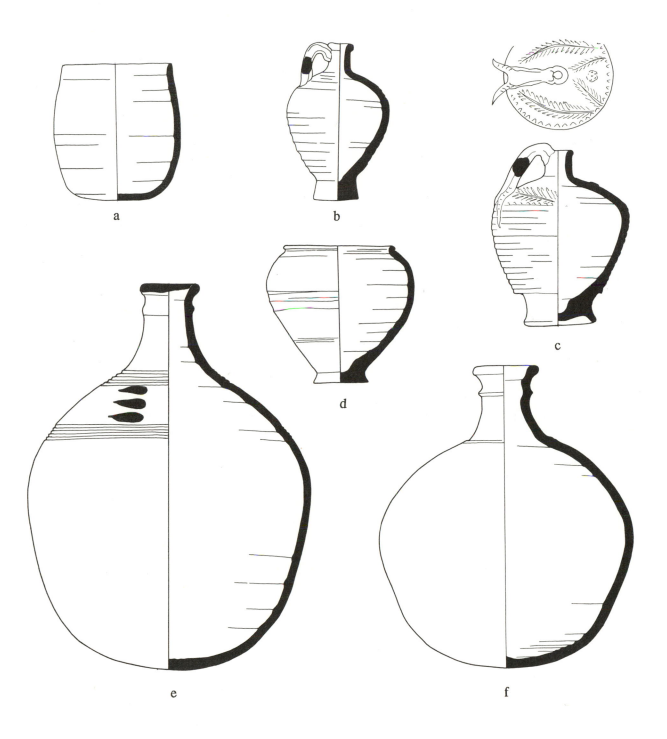

Figure 103. Pottery from Tomb Q 1: (*a*) X-Gr. Ord. Cup I—G1b, No. 17; (*b*) Coptic Period Egyptian Fine/Ord. Juglet I—C2, No. 25; (*c*) Coptic Period Egyptian Fine/Ord. Juglet I—A2a, No. 24; (*d*) X-Gr. Ord. Goblet I—B2aii, No. 18; (*e*) X-Gr. Ord. Narrow-Necked Bottle-Jar I—A2, No. 10; (*f*) X-Gr. Ord. Narrow-Necked Bottle-Jar I—E3, No. 8. Scale 2:5.

Table 40. Register of X-Group Finds in Cemetery Q (*cont.*).

Tomb	Description and Contents	Cairo	OIM	Figure/Plate
	AREA QA			
Q 1				fig. 102a
	Shaft with brick vault			pl. 35a
	Shaft: rect.; 2.00 × 1.40 × 1.80 m			
	Chamber: brick vault on ledges at -0.85, length 1.95 m; courses lean to the E			
	Blocking: brick			
	Burial: N/ "tightly contracted, dist.," bed fragments			
	Body: Mature male			
	Objects in chamber:			
	1. Bed leg and "extensive fragments"		Disc.	
	2. Miscellaneous leather and wood fragments			
	a. Quiver fragments		19932	fig. 32, pl. 59a
	b. Bow fragments		19932	
	c. Bag with grommets and stitching		19982	pl. 68b
	3. Beads		19928	
	4. Date pits		19929	
	5. Archer's loose, 3.6 × 2.7 × 3.9		19927	
	6. Scarab, 1.5 × 1.1		19930	
	7. Sandal, 25.5 × 13.8		19931	
	8. X-Gr. ord. narrow-necked bottle-jar I—E3		19873	figs. 14n, 103f
	9. X-Gr. ord. bottle-jar I—A2; wh. coat, bk. pt., vine, pairs, height 24.0		19880	
	10. X-Gr. ord. narrow-necked bottle-jar I—A2, wh. coat, bk. pt., vine, pairs		19877	figs. 14b, 103e, pl. 44c
	11. X-Gr. ord. bottle-jar I—A2, wh. coat, bk. pt., vine, pairs, height 25.2		19879	
	12. X-Gr. ord. bottle-jar I—A2, wh. and bk. pt., vine, in groups of three, height 25.4		19882	
	13. X-Gr. ord. bottle-jar I—A2, wh. and bk. pt., vine, in groups of three, height 24.5		19874	
	14. X-Gr. ord. goblet I—A1ci, wh. pt., swags (2.5YR 4/6, 7.5YR 8/2)		19887	fig. 102h
	15. X-Gr. ord. goblet I—B2aiii (10R 4/8, 10R 3/1)		19885	figs. 7u, 102f
	16. X-Gr. ord. goblet I—A1ci; wh. and bk. pt.; vine, in groups of three (10YR 5/6, 2.5YR N3, 5YR 8/2)		19886	figs. 7h, 102g
	17. X-Gr. ord. cup I—G1b (2.5YR 5/6, 2.5YR 4/6)		19890	figs. 9o, 103a
	18. X-Gr. ord. goblet I—B2aii		19878	fig. 103d
	19. X-Gr. ord. cup I—D5bi, wh. coat, red rim		19876	figs. 9j, 102e
	20. X-Gr. ord. cup I—D5a, wh. coat, red rim (7.5YR 8/4, 5YR 6/3), height 8.0		19888	
	21. X-Gr. ord. cup I—D5bii, wh. coat, red bands (7.5YR 8/2, 5YR 5/4, 7.5YR 8/6, 5YR 4/3)		19881	figs. 9k, 102d
	22. X-Gr. ord. cup I—D5a, wh. coat, red rim (7.5YR 8/4, 7.5YR 8/2, 5YR 4/4)		19889	fig. 102c
	23. X-Gr. ord. cup I—D5a, wh. coat, red rim		19875	figs. 9h, 102b
	24. Coptic period Eg. fine/ord. juglet I—A2a, incised on shoulder (5YR 4/6, 5YR 3/2)		19884	fig. 103c
	25. Coptic period Eg. fine/ord. juglet I—C2		19883	figs. 22 l, 103b
	Sherds, at surface:		33086	
	A. A-Group rippled jar, polished red coat, abraded			
	B. Post-X-Gr. orange bowl base			
	C. Post-X-Gr. or. with gray surface, base			
	D. Unc. brown surface, grooves			

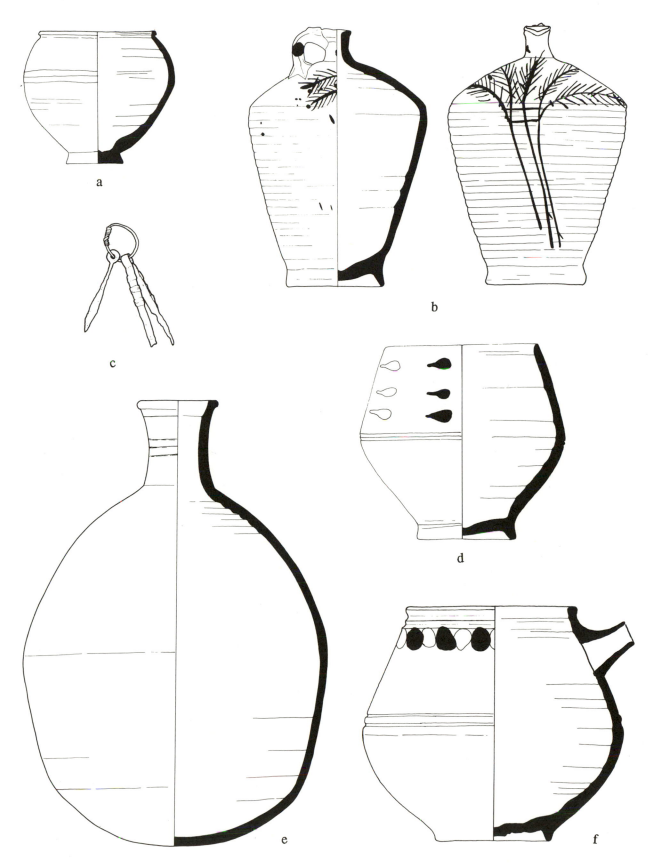

Figure 104. Pottery and an Object from Tomb Q 2: (*a*) X-Gr. Ord. Goblet I—B2ai, No. 7; (*b*) Coptic Period Egyptian Fine/Ord. Juglet I—A3a, No. 3; (*c*) Iron Tweezers and Probe on Ring, No. 14; (*d*) X-Gr. Ord. Goblet I—A1cii, No. 4; (*e*) X-Gr. Ord. Narrow-Necked Bottle-Jar I—D1, No. 1; (*f*) X-Gr. Ord. Spouted Jar I—B, No. 8. Scales: (*a, b, d–f*) 2:5; (*c*) 1:2.

Table 40. Register of X-Group Finds in Cemetery Q (*cont.*).

Tomb	Description and Contents	Cairo	OIM	Figure/Plate
Q 2				
	Shaft with chamber on the S side			
	Shaft: ca. 2.40 × 0.90–1.15 × 1.40 m			
	Chamber: 1.90 × −.70 × ca. 0.50 m; ca. 0.20–0.30 m overlap			
	Blocking: stone, dist. in chamber			
	Burial: W/R/—/—			
	Body: Adult, male?			
	Objects: in chamber:			
	1. X-Gr. ord. narrow-necked bottle-jar I—D1		19910	figs. 14i, 104e
	2. X-Gr. ord. bottle-jar I—D1, height 29.6		19911	
	3. Coptic period Eg. fine/ord. juglet I—A3a, bk. pt., branches on shoulder		19912	fig. 104b
	4. X-Gr. ord. goblet I—A1cii, wh. and bk. pt., vines, in groups of three		19916	figs. 7i, 104d
	5. X-Gr. ord. goblet I—B2ai (2.5YR 5/8, 2.5YR 4/6), height 8.9		19914	
	6. X-Gr. ord. goblet I—B2ai, height 9.1		19917	
	7. X-Gr. ord. goblet I—B2ai		19915	fig. 104a
	8. X-Gr. ord. spouted jar I—B, wh. and bk. pt., beads (2.5YR 5/4, 2.5YR 4/ , 5YR 8/4)		19913	fig. 104f pl. 42g
	9. Textile, CAT 35		19941	
	10. Beads		19938	
	11. Date pits ("1 pot found empty in pile of date pits and next to R foot")		19940	
	12. Sandal fragments		19942	
	13. Archer's guard, 8.5 × 4.8		19937	
	14. Iron tweezers and probe on ring		19939	fig. 104c, pl. 81b
	15. Textile (shreds of brown linen with red and white stripes)		19943	
	16. Sherds		33087	
Q 3				
	Shaft with chamber on the W side			
	Shaft: 2.20 × ca. 1.10 × 1.90 m			
	Chamber: 1.90 × .65 × 0.60–0.80 m; no overlap, floor lower than shaft			
	Blocking: stones, hor. in chamber, dist.			
	Plunderer's shaft: circular, to SW, incomplete			
	Burial: S/L/—/—			
	Body: Adult male			
	Objects in chamber:			
	1. Coptic fine/ord. juglet I—A2ai		19859	figs. 22d, 105g
	2. X-Gr. ord. narrow-necked bottle-jar I—A1, bk. and wh. pt., complex		19863	figs. 14a, 105e
	3. X-Gr. fine cup II—E1a, bk. pt. (5YR 8/3, 7.5YR 8/2, 7.5YR 4/4)		19861	figs. 9l, 105c
	4. X-Gr. ord. goblet I—B2aii		19860	fig. 105a
	5. X-Gr. ord. bottle-jar I—A1, bk. and wh. pt., complex		19864	fig. 105f
	6. X-Gr. ord. bottle-jar I—A1, bk. and wh. pt., complex		19862	fig. 105d
	7. Beads, some stringing preserved		19895	fig. 64j
	Sherds:		33113	
	A. X-Gr. fine cup I—, bk. pt., complex			fig. 105b
	B. X-Gr. ord. goblet I—A, worn			
	C. X-Gr. ord. goblet I—B, uncoated or worn			

Figure 105. Pottery from Tomb Q 3: (*a*) X-Gr. Ord. Goblet I—B2aii, No. 4; (*b*) X-Gr. Fine Cup I—, No. A; (*c*) X-Gr. Fine Cup II—E1a, No. 3; (*d*) X-Gr. Ord. Bottle-Jar I—A1, No. 6; (*e*) X-Gr. Ord. Narrow-Necked Bottle-Jar I—A1, No. 2; (*f*) X-Gr. Ord. Bottle-Jar I—A1, No. 5; (*g*) Coptic Period Egyptian Fine/Ord. Juglet I—A2ai, No. 1. Scale 2:5.

Table 40. Register of X-Group Finds in Cemetery Q (*cont.*).

Tomb	Description and Contents	Cairo	OIM	Figure/Plate
Q 3 (*cont.*)				
	Sherds (*cont.*):			
	D. X-Gr. ord. goblet I—B			
	E. Post-X-Gr. *qadus* with ridge rim			
	F. Unc. gray pottery, chaffy, globular shape, worn			
	G. Unc. gray pottery, V-shaped open bowl			
	H. Post-X-Gr. fine bowl with vert. side, side darkened			
	I. Unc. gray pottery, V-shaped open bowl			
	J. Unc. red alt., wh. coat, spout			
Q 4				pl. 33a–b
	Shaft with chamber on the W side			
	Shaft: 2.40–3.05 × 2.40 m			
	Chamber: 2.85 × 1.10 × 0.90 m; shelved 0.55 and 0.40 m at ends; floor flush			
	Blocking: stones, "loosely laid 0.30–0.40 m wide"			
	Plunderer's shaft: at NW end of chamber, 1.40 diam.			
	Burial: dist. in chamber			
	Body: Adult			
	Objects in chamber:			
	1. Bead		19924	fig. 62c
	2. Remains of wood		Disc.	
	3. Remains of leather		Disc.	
	Sherds:		33159	
	A. X-Gr. ord. jar			
	B. Mer. fine/ord. jar, bk. vine, red coat			
	C. X-Gr. ord. jar, bk. and wh. pt.			
	D. X-Gr. ord. goblet I—A, wh. pt. vine			
	E. X-Gr. ord. goblet I—A			
	F. X-Gr. ord. goblet I—B, rim			
	G. X-Gr. ord. goblet I—B, base			
	H. X-Gr. ord. goblet I—B, base			
	I. Post-X-Gr. pk., ribbed, small jar			
	J. Post-X-Gr. red-gray, wh. coat			
	K. Post-X-Gr. pk., darkened band			
	L. X-Gr.? Handmade cooking pot, everted rim			
Q 6				
	Shaft with chamber on the W side			
	Shaft: stepped, ca. 2.30–2.70 × 0.80–1.10 × 1.70 m; step to chamber, 0.60 m deeper			
	Chamber: 2.30 × 1.05 × 0.60 m (minimum), no overlap			
	Burial: —			
	Body: Mature male			
	Objects:			
	a. In shaft:			
	1. X-Gr. ord. med.-necked bottle-jar I—A1a, bk. and wh. pt., beads		19865	fig. 106d
	2. X-Gr. ord. med.-necked bottle-jar I—A1a, bk. and wh. pt., beads		19866	figs. 13a, 106e
	3. X-Gr. ord. goblet I—A1bi *beta*, wh. pt. (10R 4/6, 7.5YR 8/4, 7.5YR N8)		19867	fig. 106f
	4. X-Gr. ord. spouted jar I—A		20043	figs. 11, 106c

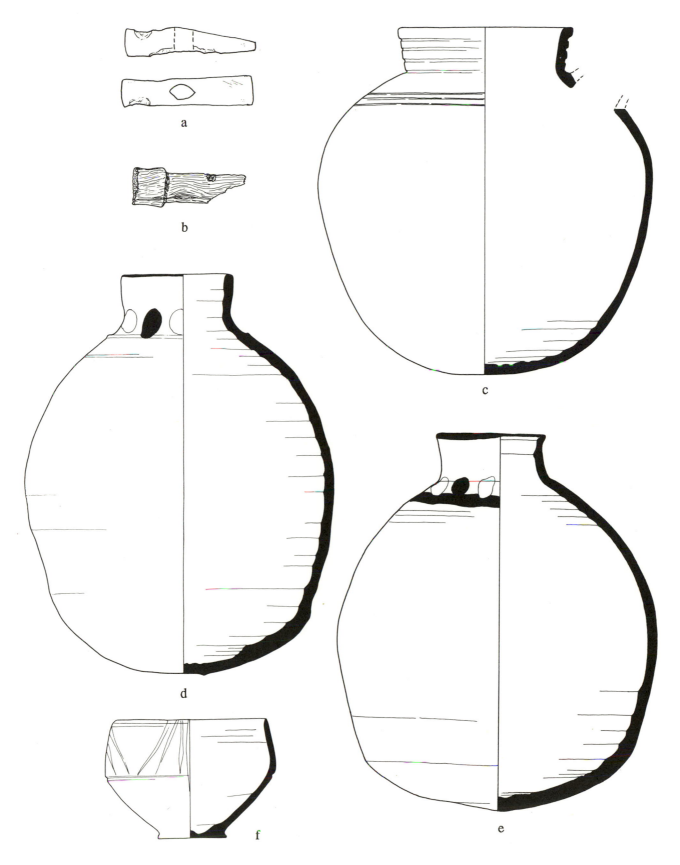

Figure 106. Pottery and Objects from Tomb Q 6: (*a*) Head of Iron Hammer, No. 5; (*b*) Wooden Rod, No. 7; (*c*) X-Gr. Ord. Spouted Jar I—A, No. 4; (*d*) X-Gr. Ord. Medium-Necked Bottle-Jar I—A1a, No. 1; (*e*) X-Gr. Ord. Medium-Necked Bottle-Jar I—A1a, No. 2; (*f*) X-Gr. Ord. Goblet I—A1bi *beta*, No. 3. Scales: (a) 1:2; (b–f) 2:5.

Table 40. Register of X-Group Finds in Cemetery Q (*cont.*).

Tomb	Description and Contents	Cairo	OIM	Figure/Plate
Q 6 (*cont.*)				
	Objects (*cont.*):			
	b. In chamber:			
	5. Head of iron hammer		19933	fig. 106a, pl. 83c
	c. At surface:			
	6. Remains of textile, CAT 38		19936	
	7. Wooden rod (shaft of 5?)		19934	fig. 106b
	8. Fragments of quiver		19935	fig. 33a–b pl. 60a–d
	Sherds:		33160	
	A. X-Gr. ord. goblet I—B, base			
	B. X-Gr. ord. goblet I—A, rim, purple and wh. pt. swags			
	C. Unc. gray jar, ribbed rim; small *qadus*? abraded			
	D. Post-X-Gr. with limy inclusions, some degraded; gray-ye. coat			
Q 7				
	Shaft with chamber on the E side			
	Shaft: 1.75–2.25 × 0.62–1.08 × 2.05 m			
	Chamber: 1.75 × ca. 0.63 × 0.55 m, floor flush			
	Burials:			
	a. In chamber:			
	A. —			
	B. —			
	b. In shaft at -0.95 m:			
	C. S/B/ext. /pelvis			
	Bodies:			
	A. Adult			
	B. Infant			
	C. Adult			
	Objects:			
	a. With C:			
	1. Textiles, CAT 39 (1a and b)		19956	
	2. Sherd on head		—	
	b. In shaft:			
	3. Portion of human hair		19954	
	c. At surface:			
	4. X-Gr. ord. goblet I—B1a(i)		19957	figs. 7p, 107d
	d. Unc. loc :			
	5. Remains of leather		Disc.	
	e. In chamber:			
	6. Textile remains (near A?)		Not Studied	
	7. Upper edge of bag with drawstring, leather, 6.0 × 4.7		19953	
	8. Matting fragment		Disc.	
	Sherds at surface:		33161	
	A. X-Gr. ord. bottle-jar, lt. ye. pt. crosshatched band			
	This tomb was reused in the Christian period (burials B and C).			
Q 8				
	Shaft with vaulted chamber on ledges built against the N end and a secondary chamber on the E side			
	Shaft: ? × 0.80–1.35 × 1.85 m			

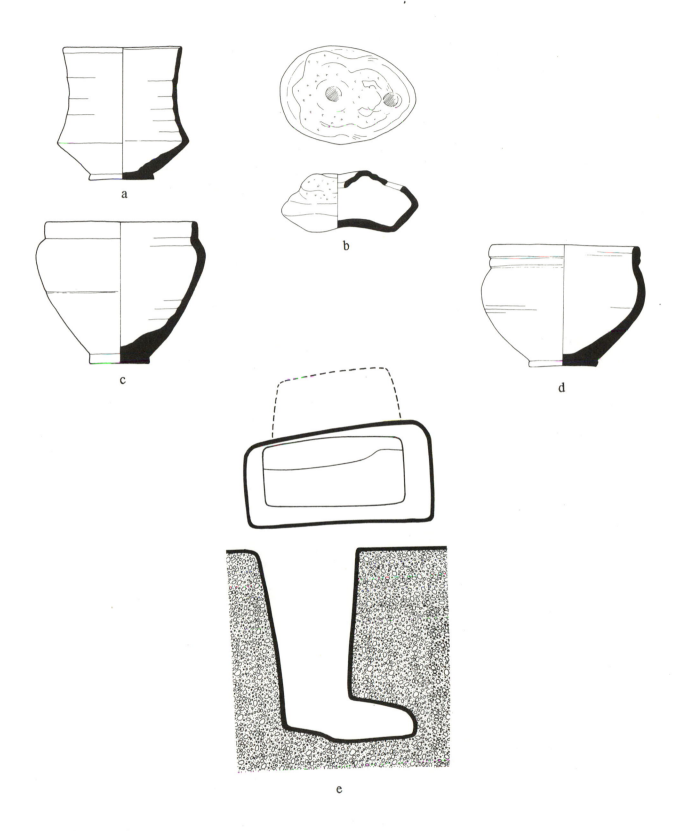

Figure 107. A Goblet from Tomb Q 7, Pottery and a Lamp from Tomb Q 8, and the Plan and Section of Tomb Q 11: (*a*) X-Gr. Fine Cup II—E2a, Q 8—1; (*b*) Lamp, Q 8—7; (*c*) X-Gr. Ord. Goblet I—B1c, Q 8—2; (*d*) X-Gr. Ord. Goblet I—B1a(i), Q 7—4; (*e*) Plan and Section of Tomb Q 11. Scales: (*a–d*) 2:5; (*e*) 1:40.

Table 40. Register of X-Group Finds in Cemetery Q (*cont.*).

Tomb	Description and Contents	Cairo	OIM	Figure/Plate
Q 8 (*cont.*)				
	Ledges: at 0.60 m from bottom, ca. 0.17 m wide			
	Chamber A: bricks leaned to N, 0.85 m remaining			
	Blocking: lower course on edge remains, cb. 0.09 × 0.17 × 0.30–0.32 m			
	Chamber B: 0.65 × 0.25–0.35 × ? m, floor below shaft on SE			
	Blocking: cb. on end			
	Chamber A:			
	Burial: N?/—			
	Body: Adult male			
	Objects:			
	1. X-Gr. fine cup II—E2a (10R 8/4, 7.5YR 7.4)		19973	figs. 9m, 107a
	2. X-Gr. ord. goblet I—B1c		19978	fig. 107c
	3. X-Gr. ord. goblet I—B1c, height 9.4		19976	
	4. X-Gr. ord. goblet I—B1c, height 9.0		19977	
	5. X-Gr. ord. goblet I—B1ai/B1c, height 8.3		19975	
	6. X-Gr. ord. goblet I—B1a, badly shaped, rim not prominent, height 8.6		19974	
	7. Terracotta lamp with frog design		19972	fig. 107b
	8. Leather remains		Disc.	
	9. Leather, some "knit with string"		19967	
	10. Beads		19963	
	Chamber B:			
	Burial: S/L/—/—			
	Body: Adult female			
	Objects:			
	1. Beads		19960	
	Sherds:		33162	
	a. Surface:			
	A. X-Gr. *qadus*; knob, rim			
	B. X-Gr. ord. goblet I—B, base			
	C. X-Gr. ord. goblet I—B, base			
	D. Unc. ord. utility-storage jar			
	b. Shaft:			
	E. X-Gr. ord. bottle jar or bowl			
	F. X-Gr. ord. jar, abraded			
	G. X-Gr. ord. goblet I—B, low rim			
	c. Chamber:			
	H. X-Gr. handmade cook-pot			
	I. X-Gr. ord. goblet I—B			
Q 9				
	Shaft with chamber on the W side			
	Shaft: ca. 2.55–3.50 × 2.05 (total with ch.) × 2.05 m			
	Chamber: 2.25 × ? × 0.70 m; floor at -0.30 m from shaft			
	Blocking: stone			
	Burial: S/—			
	Body: Mature male			
	Objects:			
	a. In chamber:			
	1. X-Gr. ord. goblet I—B1c, height 8.8		19891	
	2. X-Gr. ord. goblet I—B1c (2.5YR 5/6, 2.5YR 4/6)		19892	figs. 7r, 108b

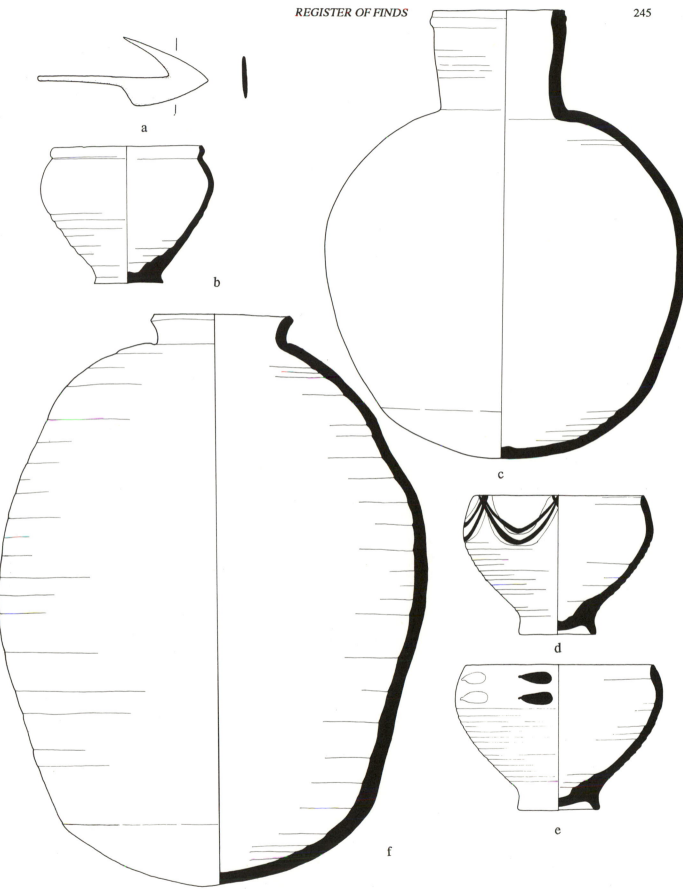

Figure 108. Pottery and an Arrowhead from Tomb Q 9: (*a*) Arrowhead, No. 8; (*b*) X-Gr. Ord. Goblet I—B1c, No. 2; (*c*) X-Gr. Ord. Medium-Necked Bottle-Jar I—B1, No. 6; (*d*) X-Gr. Ord. Goblet I—A1aii *alpha*, No. 3; (*e*) X-Gr. Ord. Goblet I—A1aii *beta*, No. 7; (*f*) X-Gr. Storage Jar III—C, No. 4. Scales: (*a*) 1:1; (*b–f*) 2:5.

Table 40. Register of X-Group Finds in Cemetery Q (*cont.*).

Tomb	Description and Contents	Cairo	OIM	Figure/Plate
Q 9 (*cont.*)				
	Objects (*cont.*):			
	a. In chamber:			
	3. X-Gr. ord. goblet I—A1aii *alpha*, bk. and wh. pt. swags (2.5YR 5/6, 2.5YR 4/4, 2.5YR 6/4)		19893	figs. 7b, 108d
	4. X-Gr. storage jar III—C		19894	fig. 108f
	5. X-Gr. goblet I—B1c		Disc.?	
	b. In shaft:			
	6. X-Gr. ord. med.-necked jar I—B1		19869	fig. 108c
	7. X-Gr. ord. goblet I—A1aii *beta*, bk. and wh. pt. swags (2.5YR 5/6, 2.5YR N4/, 5YR 8/1)		19868	figs. 7c, 108e
	c. In fill:			
	8. Arrowheads		19901	fig. 108a, pl. 64c
	9. Dates		19900	
	10. Beads		19899	fig. 63p, r, pl. 76d
	11. Leather fragments		19902	
	12. X-Gr. ord. goblet I—B1c, height 8.8		19891	
	d. At bottom of shaft:			
	13. Textile fragment (silk), CAT 40		19896	
	14. Cord, 11.0 × 0.3		19897	
	Sherds:		33163	
	A. X-Gr. *qadus*, rim			
	B. X-Gr. *qadus*, knob			
	C. Unc. ord. bowl			
	D. Coptic period Eg. fine-ord. juglet			
	E. Post-X-Gr. pk.-gray, wh. coat, body and handle			
	F. Post-X-Gr. pk. jar; rim, worn			
	G. Post-X-Gr. orange basin, repair hole, burnished, int. abraded			
	H. Post-X-Gr. fine bowl, red coat			
	I. Post-X-Gr. fine bowl, red coat			
	J. Unc. ord. ribbed			
	K. Unc. abraded rim			
Q 10				
	Shaft with chamber on the W side			
	Shaft: ca. 2.50–3.45 × ? × 2.05 m			
	Chamber: 2.55 × (1.90–2.05 with shaft) × 0.70 m; floor at -0.30 m from shaft			
	Blocking: stone			
	Burial: — (dist., contracted?)			
	Body: —			
	Objects:			
	1. Quiver fragments		19966	
	2. Textile remains, CAT 41–43		19958	
	3. Textile remains, CAT 44–45		19965	
	4. Four arrowheads		19961	fig. 109, pl. 65e
	5. Pendant (carnelian), 1.0 × 0.5		19962	

Figure 109. Arrowhead, Q 10—4. Scale 1:1.

Table 40. Register of X-Group Finds in Cemetery Q (*cont.*).

Tomb	Description and Contents	Cairo	OIM	Figure/Plate
Q 11				fig. 107e, pl. 34a

Shaft with chamber on the W side
    Shaft: 1.50–2.00 × 0.35–0.50 × 1.55–1.65 m
    Chamber: 1.50 × 0.95 × 0.25–0.55 m; 0.30 m overlap;
        floor at -0.35 m from shaft
    Blocking: present but uncertain material
    Pits: E of shaft, two round pits, dia. ca. 0.70 m × 0.30 m
        deep, filled with mud and stone chips, for making
        cb. or mortar
Burial: —
Body: Mature male
Objects:

Tomb	Description and Contents	Cairo	OIM	Figure/Plate
	1. Quiver fragments		19949	fig. 34
	2. Textile remains, CAT 46		19959	
	3. Beads (two)		19950	
	4. Textile remains, CAT 47		19951	
	5. Textile remains, CAT 48		19952	

Q 12

Shaft with chamber on the W side
    Shaft: 1.59 × 0.69–0.93 × 1.60 m
    Chamber: ? × 0.64 × ? m, floor at -0.13 m from shaft
Burial: — (present but dist.)
Body: —
Objects:

Tomb	Description and Contents	Cairo	OIM	Figure/Plate
	1. X-Gr. ord. goblet I—A1a *alpha*, bk. and wh. pt. bead pairs		20002	fig. 110e
	2. X-Gr. ord. bowl—C2 (2.5YR 4/6, 5YR 8/2)		20001	figs. 10d, 110c
	3. Remains of cord (rope), longest 5.8 × .3		19999	
	4. Bronze ring, 0.1 × 0.2		20000	
	5. Remains of leather, largest 24.0 × 18.2		19997	

Q 13

Shaft with chamber on the W side
    Shaft: 1.40–1.70 × 0.50–0.75 × 1.30 m
    Chamber: 1.40 × 0.60–0.70 × 0.30 m;
        floor at -0.10 m from shaft
    Blocking: stone slabs
Burial: — (jumbled in S end of chamber)
Body: Adult female
Objects:

Tomb	Description and Contents	Cairo	OIM	Figure/Plate
	1. Beads		19946	
	2. Horn of sheep, length 16.8		19947	
	3. Textile remains, CAT 49		19948	
	Sherds:		33164	
	A. X-Gr. ord. goblet I—B			
	B. Unc. wide *qadus*, rim and base			

Q 14

Shaft with chamber on the W side
    Shaft: 1.40–2.20 × 0.70–0.90 × 1.55 m
    Chamber: 1.65 × 0.50 × 0.20–0.45 m; floor at -0.05 m from shaft
    Blocking: stone slabs

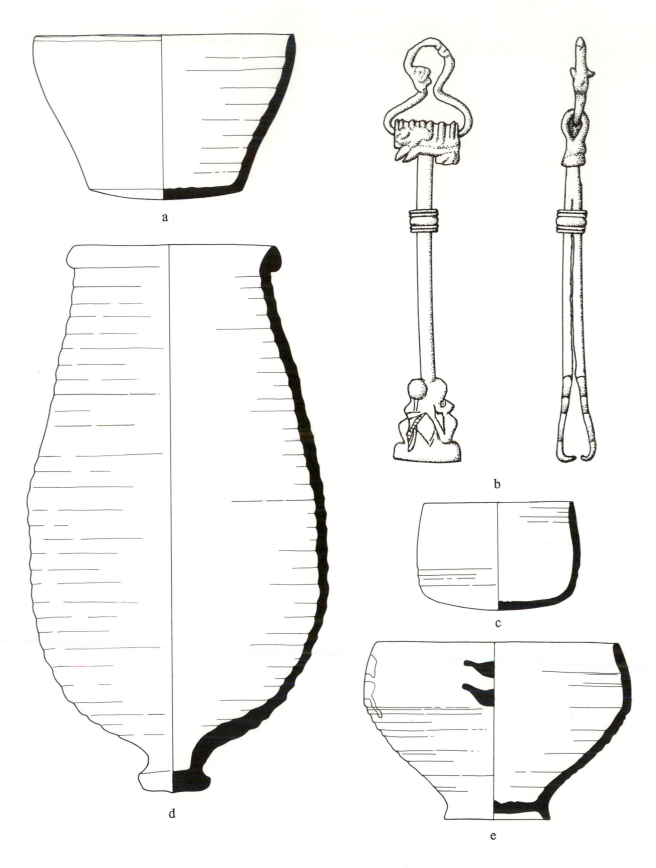

Figure 110. Pottery and Tweezers from Tombs Q 12, Q 14, and Q 16: (*a*) X-Gr. Ord. Bowl I—B1, Q 14—3; (*b*) Tweezers, Q 16—2; (*c*) X-Gr. Ord. Bowl—C2, Q 12—2; (*d*) *Qadus* Jar—A, Q 14—2; (*e*) X-Gr. Ord. Goblet I—A1a *alpha*, Q 12—1. Scales: (*a, c–e*) 2:5; (*b*) 1:1.

Table 40. Register of X-Group Finds in Cemetery Q (*cont.*).

Tomb	Description and Contents	Cairo	OIM	Figure/Plate
Q 14 (*cont.*)				
	Burial: S?/—/—			
	Body: Adult male			
	Objects:			
	1. Archery equipment			
	a. Quiver fragments		19968	fig. 35
	b. Fragment of bow, 8.0 × 1.0		19969	
	2. *Qadus* jar—A		19971	figs. 25a, 110d
	3. X-Gr. ord. bowl I—B1, wh. pt. rim		19970	figs. 10b, 110a
	4. Beads		—	
Q 15				pl. 35c
	Shaft with ramp, ledges, and vault			
	Shaft: 2.25–2.55 × 0.75 (bot)–1.15 (ledges)			
	× 1.20 m; ledges at -0.60 m			
	Ramp: at W end, 0.80 × 0.45–0.95 m			
	Vault: five cb., wedged with stones, top at surface			
	Blocking: cb. and stone			
	Burial: —			
	Body: Mature female			
	Objects:			
	1. Beads		19925	
	2. Textile remains, CAT 50		19926	
	Sherds:		33165	
	A. Mer. fine/ord. cup, red coat?			
	B. X-Gr. ord. jar, grooved			
	C. *Qadus*; knob			
	D. Post-X-Gr. dk., pk. surface, basin rim			
	E. Unc. body sherd			
Q 16				
	Shaft with ledges, vault, and ramp			
	Shaft: 2.30–2.65 × 0.85 (bot)–1.60 (top) × 1.35 m			
	Ledges: at-0.95, 0.15 m wide			
	Ramp: 1.20 × 1.20 m			
	Vault: four courses remaining			
	Blocking: stone and cb.			
	Burial: W/B/ext./pubis, R hand and arm encircle stone			
	(15 × 20 cm) on pelvis			
	Body: Mature male			
	Objects:			
	a. Under stone in hand:			
	1. Iron sickle-saw, length 11	Q 94, 89892		
	2. Tweezers (Ag.?)	Q 95, 89884		fig. 110b
	4. Date pits		Disc.	
	b. On body?			
	3. Textile wrapping (CAT X-Gr.)		Disc.	
	Sherds:		33166	
	A. X-Gr. ord. goblet I—B, abraded			
	B. X-Gr. ord. bowl			
	C. X-Gr. *qadus*, knob			
	D. X-Gr. handmade cooking pot			
	E. Unc. gray ribbed			

Table 40. Register of X-Group Finds in Cemetery Q (*cont.*).

Tomb	Description and Contents	Cairo	OIM	Figure/Plate
Q 16 (*cont.*)				
	Sherds (*cont.*):			
	F. Unc. fine/ord., red coat			
	G. Unc. jar, abraded			
Q 17				pl. 35b
	Shaft with ledges and vault			
	Shaft: 2.45 × 0.57–0.75 × 0.88 m			
	Ledges: ca. 0.10–0.15 m at -0.45 m			
	Chamber: 3½ cb. from E end, 1.60 m			
	Blocking: cb., ashlar on one course rowlock			
	Burial: W/B/vert. contracted/pubis			
	Body: Adult female, hair sample		19944	
	Objects:			
	1. Remains of textile, CAT 51		19945	
	Sherds		33167	
Q 18				
	Shaft with steps and chamber on the W side			
	Shaft: 2.00–2.45 × ? × 1.30 m			
	Steps: three, at 0.15, 0.15, and 0.25 m rises from chamber			
	floor, variable width 0.10–0.30 m			
	Chamber: 2.00 × 1.75–1.50 × 0.34–0.50 m; 0.35 m overlap,			
	floor flush			
	Burial: —			
	Body: Juvenile female			
	Objects:			
	a. From chamber:			
	1. X-Gr. ord. bottle-jar I—D3, bk. and wh. pt.,	19904		fig. 111f
	vine in groups of three, and rim band			
	2. X-Gr. ord. bottle-jar I—D2	19906		fig. 111e
	3. X-Gr. ord. narrow-necked bottle-jar I—C3, bk. pt. on rim	19909		figs. 14k, 111a
	4. Coptic period Eg. fine/ord. juglet I—A1a (5YR 5/4,	19905		fig. 111c
	5YR 4/3, 5YR 2.5/2)			
	5. X-Gr. ord. goblet I—B2ai (2.5YR 5/6, 2.5YR 6/2)	19908		fig. 111b
	6. X-Gr. ord. cup I—G1a, wh. pt. rim dots	19903		figs. 9p, 111d
	7. X-Gr. ord. goblet I—B2ai (2.5YR 5/6,	19907		
	2.5YR 4/6), height 8.2			
	b. From shaft:			
	8. Remains of textile		Disc.	
	9. Remains of hair (unc. whether part of body)		19922	
	10. Remains of textile, CAT 52		19923	
	11. Date pits		19921	
	12. Beads		19920	
Q 19				fig. 112a, pl. 36b
	Shaft with ledges, ramp, and vault			
	Shaft: ca. 2.50 × 0.95 (floor)–1.75 × 1.45 m, N-S			
	Ramp: 1.15–1.35 × 1.00–1.30 m; two bed grooves			
	ca. 0.30 m long near entrance			
	Ledges: at -0.95 m; ca. 0.17 m wide			
	Vault: twenty rings unc. no. cb. per ring, filled with			
	mud at sides and covered with cb.			
	Blocking: at bottom of ramp, stretchers, one course			
	rowlock, then ashlar and broadside			

Figure 111. Pottery from Tomb Q 18: (*a*) X-Gr. Ord. Narrow-Necked Bottle-Jar I—C3, No. 3; (*b*) X-Gr. Ord. Goblet I—B2ai, No. 5; (*c*) Coptic Period Egyptian Fine/Ord. Juglet I—A1a, No. 4; (*d*) X-Gr. Ord. Cup I—G1a, No. 6; (*e*) X-Gr. Ord. Bottle-Jar I—D2, No. 2; (*f*) X-Gr. Ord. Bottle-Jar I—D3, No. 1. Scale 2:5.

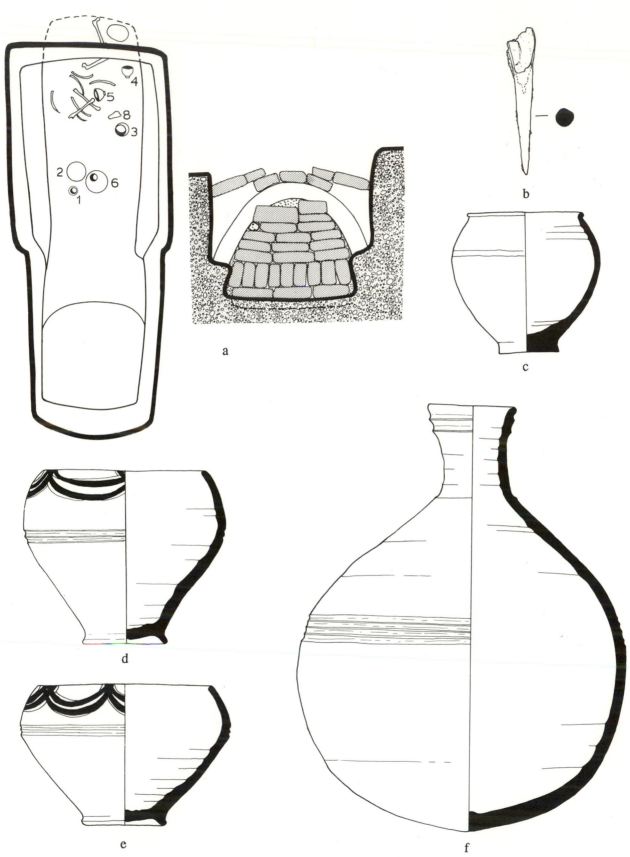

Figure 112. Plan, Section, Pottery, and an Iron Spear Butt from Tomb Q 19: (*a*) Plan and Section; (*b*) Iron
Spear Butt, No. 8; (*c*) X-Gr. Ord. Goblet I—B2aii, No. 5; (*d*) X-Gr. Ord. Goblet I—A1ci, No. 7;
(*e*) X-Gr. Ord. Goblet I—A1aii *alpha*, No. 2; (*f*) X-Gr. Ord. Bottle-Jar I—C3, No. 1.
Scales: (*a*) 1:40; (*b*) 1:2; (*c–f*) 2:5.

Table 40. Register of X-Group Finds in Cemetery Q (*cont.*).

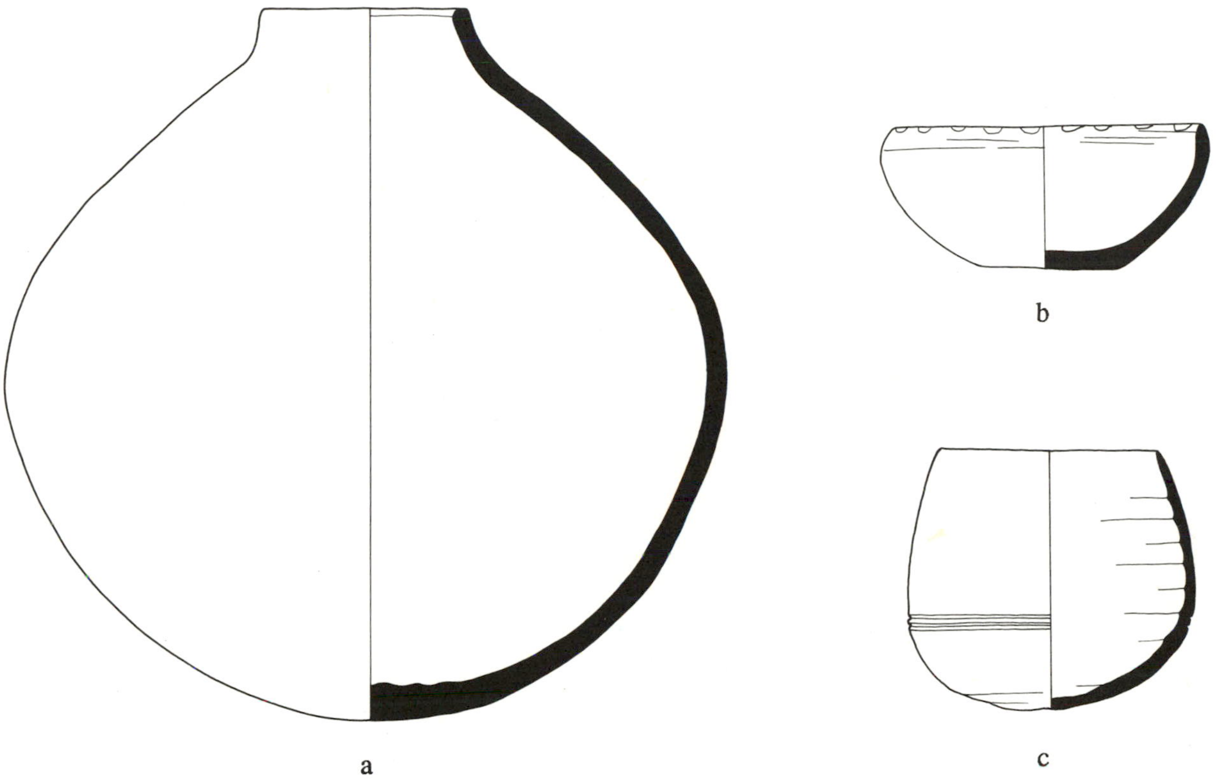

Tomb	Description and Contents	Cairo	OIM	Figure/Plate

Figure 113. Pottery from Tomb Q 19: (*a*) X-Gr. Handmade Jar IV—A2, No. 6; (*b*) X-Gr. Ord. Cup I—A2a, No. 3; (*c*) X-Gr. Ord. Cup I—G1, No. 4. Scale 2:5.

Q 19 (*cont.*)

Burial: —

Body: Adult

Objects:

		Cairo		Figure/Plate
1.	X-Gr. ord. bottle-jar I—C3	20007		fig. 112f
2.	X-Gr. ord. goblet I—A1aii *alpha*, bk. and wh. ptd. swags	20017		fig. 112e
3.	X-Gr. ord. cup I—A2a, wh. pt. rim dots (2.5YR 4/6, 2.5YR N2.5/)	20011		figs. 8c, 113b
4.	X-Gr. ord. cup I—G1	20006		fig. 113c
5.	X-Gr. ord. goblet I—B2aii	20009		figs. 7t, 112c
6.	X-Gr. handmade jar IV—A2	20008		figs. 20b, 113a
7.	X-Gr. ord. goblet I—A1ci, bk. and wh. pt. swags	20010		fig. 112d, pl. 41c
8.	Iron spear butt with blade fragments	20016		fig. 112b
9.	Textile remains, CAT 53	20015		

Sherds: 33168

A. X-Gr. ord. bottle-jar I—, grooved band, crosshatched wh. band

B. X-Gr. ord. goblet I—A, tall side, bk. and wh. swags

C. X-Gr. ord. goblet I—B, smooth curve, short rim

D. X-Gr. ord. goblet

E. Mer. Km. wm. bowl, lt. coat, bk. bands

F. Unc. fine red jar

G. Post-X-Gr. pk. base

H. Post-X-Gr. pk. base

I. Unc. red ribbed

Table 40. Register of X-Group Finds in Cemetery Q (*cont.*).

Tomb	Description and Contents	Cairo	OIM	Figure/Plate
Q 19 (*cont.*)				
	Sherds (*cont.*):			
	J. Unc. red			
	K. Unc. gray, wh. surface			
	L. Discolored by fire, thin			
Q 22				
	Shaft with chamber on the W side			
	Shaft: 1.15–1.60 × 0.65–0.85 × 1.20 m			
	Chamber: 0.70 × 0.35 × 0.30 m; floor slightly below shaft, no overlap			
	Blocking: stone slabs			
	Burial: —			
	Body: Juvenile female			
	Objects:			
	1. Remains of textile, CAT 54, 55		20003	
	Pottery was said to be present, but none was itemized.			
	Sherds:		33157	
	A. X-Gr.? handmade cooking pot			
	B. Post-X-Gr. jar rim with rib			
	C. Post-X-Gr. orange, sharp ribbing, narrow			
Q 25				
	Shaft with ramp, ledges, and vault, now removed, N-S			
	Shaft: ca. 2.20 × 1.15–1.60 × 1.20 m denuded at S end			
	Ledges: 0.20 and 0.25 at -0.30 m			
	Ramp: 1.40 × 1.15 m, grooved for bed			
	Bed pit: 1.70 × 1.00 m with grooves 0.20× 0.05–0.10 m deep			
	Vault: removed			
	Burial: —			
	Body: Adult			
	Objects:			
	1. Remains of iron tool (sickle-saw?), largest 6.0 × 2.4		19995	
	2. Leather fragments		Disc.	
	Sherds:		33158	
	A. Post-X-Gr. pk.			
	B. Post-X-Gr. gray with wh. surface			
	C. Post-X-Gr. gray with red surf, bar handle			
	D. Unc., very coarse, chaffy, red-bn.			
	E. Unc. bn. amphora, deep multiple grooves, bitumen			
Q 27				
	Shaft with chamber on the W side			
	Shaft: 1.40–2.20 × 0.50–0.85 × 1.75 m			
	Chamber: 1.70 × 0.75 × 0.60 m; overlap 0.20 m, floor at -0.30 m from shaft			
	Blocking: stone slabs			
	Objects, in shaft:			
	1. Beads		20004	figs. 62i, l, 65a, c
	2. Textile remains, CAT 56–57		20005	
	3. Goblet? (probably X-Gr. ord. I—A), height 8.6	Q 159	Disc.	
	4. Goblet? (probably X-Gr. ord. I—B), height 8.5	Q 160	Disc.	

Table 40. Register of X-Group Finds in Cemetery Q (*cont.*).

Tomb	Description and Contents	Cairo	OIM	Figure/Plate
Q 27 (*cont.*)				
	Sherds:		33170	
	A. Post-X-Gr. bn. with sand, jar, handle attachment, dk. pt., vert. trees, abraded			
	B. Post-X-Gr. gray-bn. globular jar, wh. pt.			
	C. X-Gr. ord. goblet I—B, open			
	D. Post-X-Gr. pk. band handle			
Q 28				
	Shaft with chamber on the W side			
	Shaft: 1.75 × 0.65 × 0.65 m			
	Chamber: 1.35 × 0.50 × 0.45 m; 0.08 m overlap, floor at -0.20 m from shaft			
	Burial: —			
	Body: "Infant II"			
	Sherd:		33171	
	A. X-Gr. storage jar III—			
Q 29				
	Shaft with chamber on the W side			
	Shaft: ca. 1.70–2.15 × 0.55–0.85 × 1.00 m			
	Chamber: 1.75 × 0.55–0.70 × 0.40 m; floor at -1.35 m; 0.35 m overlap			
	Blocking: stone slabs			
	Burial: —			
	Body: Adult			
	Objects:			
	1. Textile remains "ye." (CAT X-Gr.)		Disc.	
Q 30				
	Shaft with chamber on the W side			
	Shaft: 1.75 × 0.65–1.00 × 1.25 m			
	Chamber: 1.35 × 0.75–0.90 × 0.50 m; floor at -1.75 m, overlap 0.35 m			
	Burial: —			
	Body: Mature male			
	Objects in shaft:			
	1. Leather fragments with holes around edge, roughly rectangular, 7.7 × 5.3		20102	
	2. Beads		20099	fig. 63a
	3. Textile remains, CAT 58		20031	
	4. Sherds (see below)			
	5. Carpet remains, CAT 59 (note different OIM no.)		20030	
	Sherds: (unc. or post-X-Gr.):		33172	
	A. Eg. wh. (Kena) jar			
	B. Al sandy jar, red, discolored			
	C. X-Gr. ord. storage/utility jar III—			
	D. X-Gr. ord. storage/utility jar III—, neck, large			
Q 31				
	Shaft with chamber on the W side			
	Shaft: 1.25–1.55 × 0.60–0.85 × 0.70 m			
	Chamber: ca. 1.25 × ? × 0.35 m; floor at -0.80 m, overlap unc.			
	Blocking: stone slabs			

Table 40. Register of X-Group Finds in Cemetery Q (*cont.*).

Tomb	Description and Contents	Cairo	OIM	Figure/Plate
Q 31 (*cont.*)				
	Burial: — (remains of hair)			
	Body:"Infant II"			
	Objects:			
	1. Beads		20053	
	2. Textile ("rotted coarse linen with wide bl. stripe"; CAT X-Gr.)		Disc.	
	3. Human hair, blonde		20052	
	Sherd		33173	

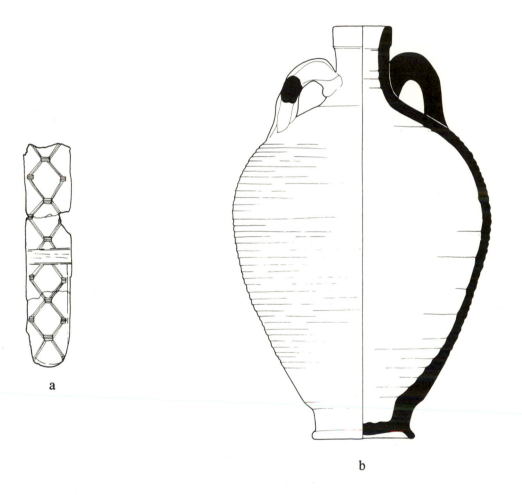

a

b

Figure 114. A Fragment of a Scabbard Cover and an *Amphoriskos*-Jug from Tomb Q 32: (*a*) Scabbard Cover Fragment, No. 3; (*b*) Coptic Period Egyptian Ord. *Amphoriskos*-Jug II—C, No. 1. Scales: (*a*) 1:2; (*b*) 2:5.

Q 32

Shaft with chamber on the W side
    Shaft: 1.85–2.65 × 0.80–1.20 × 1.70 m
    Chamber: ca. 1.60 × 0.90 × 0.75 m; floor at -0.30 m from shaft,
            overlap 0.25 m
    Blocking: stone slabs

Table 40. Register of X-Group Finds in Cemetery Q (*cont.*).

Tomb	Description and Contents	Cairo	OIM	Figure/Plate
Q 32 (*cont.*)				
Burial: —				
Body: "Infant II"				
Objects:				
1.	Coptic period Eg. ord. *amphoriskos*-jug II—C, wh. coat (7.5YR 8/2, 7.5YR 6/4, 10YR 8/3)		20024	figs. 21d, 114b
2.	Beads		20033	fig. 62j
3.	Silver scabbard cover fragment with embossed dec.		20032	fig. 114a, pl. 66b
Sherds:			33174	
A.	Post-X-Gr. hard pk.			
B.	Post-X-Gr. hard pk., wh. coat, sharp rect. rim			
C.	Post-X-Gr. brown-pink jar, smoothed, ring base			
D.	X-Gr. Coptic period Eg. fine/ord. juglet			

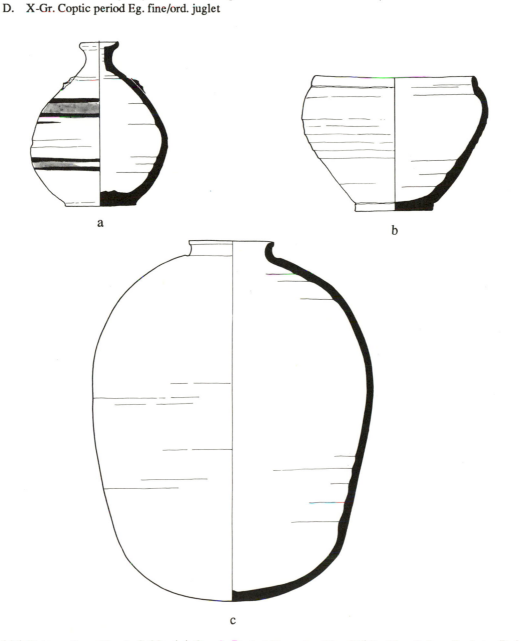

Figure 115. Pottery from Tomb Q 33: (*a*) Coptic Period Egyptian Fine White Handleless Juglet—D, No. 1; (*b*) X-Gr. Ord. Goblet I—B1a(i), No. 2; (*c*) X-Gr. Storage Jar III—C, No. 3. Scale 2:5.

Table 40. Register of X-Group Finds in Cemetery Q (*cont.*).

Tomb	Description and Contents	Cairo	OIM	Figure/Plate
Q 33				
	Shaft with chamber on the W side			
	Shaft: 1.50–2.95 × 0.70–1.30 × 1.75 m			
	Chamber: 1.50 × 0.95 × 0.60 m; floor at -0.10 m			
	from shaft, overlap 0.50 m			
	Blocking: stone slabs			
	Burial: S/R/90 degrees/face, legs folded			
	Body: Mature			
	Objects:			
	1. Coptic period Eg. fine wh. handleless juglet—D with two handle attachments; bk. and red pt. bands (10YR 7/4, 10YR 3/1, 2.5YR 5/8, 7.5YR 7.4)		20026	figs. 22n, 115a
	2. X-Gr. ord. goblet I—B1a (i)		20027	fig. 115b
	3. X-Gr. storage jar III—C, coat (2.5 YR 5/4–6/4, 2.5 YR 5/6–6/8)		20028	fig. 115c
	4. Sandal fragments		Disc.	
	5. Six fragments of iron, blade?, largest 7.8 × 2.4		20035	
	6. Beads		20034	figs. 62d, 63c
	7. Date pits		Disc.	
Q 34				
	Shaft with chamber on the W side			
	Shaft: 1.00-1.65 × less than 0.75 × 1.15 m			
	Chamber: 1.15 × 0.55 × 0.35 m; floor at -0.15 m from shaft; overlap?			
	Blocking: stone slabs			
	Burial: —			
	Body: "Infant I"			
	Objects:			
	1. X-Gr. utility storage jar III—A, red coat		20025	figs. 16a, 116c
	2. Beads		20037	
	Sherds:		33175	
	A. Coptic period Eg. globular handleless juglet I—, (pomegranate)			
	B. Coptic period Eg. fine-ord. juglet I—, red coat, incised dec.			fig. 116a
	C. X-Gr.? storage utility jar III—, rim			
Q 35				
	Shaft with a chamber on the W side			
	Shaft: 1.50–2.20 × 0.50–0.85 × 1.20 m			
	Chamber: 1.65 × 0.55 × 0.35 m; floor at -0.10 m from shaft, overlap 0.15 m			
	Blocking: stone slabs			
	Burials:			
	A. —			
	B. S/B/ext./pubis (Christian)			
	Bodies:			
	A. Mature			
	B. Mature			
	Objects:			
	1. Date pits		Disc.	
	With A:			
	2. Lamp		20038	fig. 116b
	With B:			
	3. Textile remains, coarse linen brown with red and wh. stripes, CAT 176		20039	

Table 40. Register of X-Group Finds in Cemetery Q (*cont.*).

Tomb	Description and Contents	Cairo	OIM	Figure/Plate

Figure 116. Pottery and a Lamp from Tombs Q 34 and Q 35: (*a*) Coptic Period Egyptian Fine/Ord. Juglet I— (Q 34—B); (*b*) Lamp (Q 35—2); (*c*) X-Gr. Utility Storage Jar III—A (Q 34—1). Scale 2:5.

Q 36

Shaft with chamber on the W side

Shaft: 1.45–1.70 × ca. 0.50–0.80 × 1.25 m

Chamber: 1.20 × ca. 0.80 × 0.35 m; floor at -0.10 m
from shaft, overlap 0.20

Blocking: stone slabs

Burial: —

Body: "Infant II"

Objects:

1.	"Large fragmentary jar"		Disc.	
2.	Beads		20036	

Q 37

Shaft with chamber on the W side

Shaft: 1.90–2.65 × 0.90–1.35 × 2.10 m

Chamber: 1.80 × 1.05 × 0.90 m; floor at -0.30 m from shaft,
overlap 0.30 m

Blocking: stone slabs, laid horizontally

Burial: —

Body: Juvenile

Objects:

1.	X-Gr. ord. med.-necked bottle-jar I—B2, bk. and wh. pt. beads		20082	figs. 13e, 117c
2.	Coptic period Eg. amphora IV—, dk. and wh. pt. complex (2.5YR 5/4–6/4, paint ca. 10R 3)		20083	fig. 117b

Table 40. Register of X-Group Finds in Cemetery Q (*cont.*).

Tomb	Description and Contents	Cairo	OIM	Figure/Plate
Q 37 (*cont.*)				
	Objects (*cont.*):			
	3. Ivory pyxis fragment, four		20054	
	4. Beads (two)		20055	
	Sherds:		33176	
	A. Unc. pk.-drab jar base; amphora? (cf. Q 38—A)			
	B. Unc. pk.-drab jar base			
	C. Bn. wine-jar with bitumen, unc.			
	D. Hard pk., sandy handle			
	F. X-Gr. fine			
	G. Gray-bn. sandy globular jar; twelve sherds, tools			
	H. Coptic period Eg. jug			fig. 117a

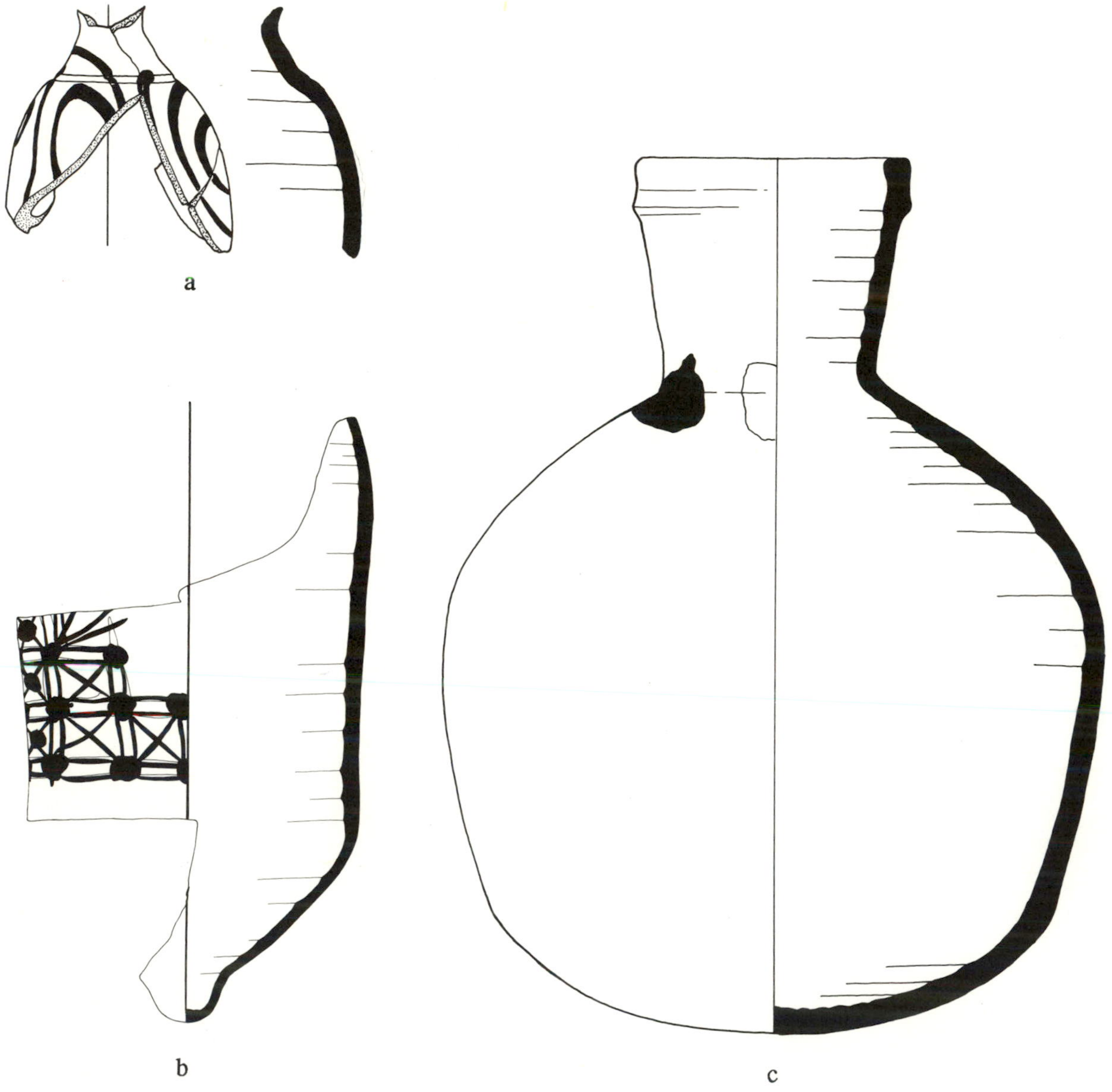

a

b

c

Figure 117. Pottery from Tomb Q 37: (*a*) Coptic Period Egyptian Jug, No. H; (*b*) Coptic Period Egyptian Amphora IV—, No. 2; (*c*) X-Gr. Ord. Medium-Necked Bottle-Jar I—B2, No. 1. Scales: (*a, c*) 2:5; (*b*) 1:5.

Table 40. Register of X-Group Finds in Cemetery Q (*cont.*).

Tomb	Description and Contents	Cairo	OIM	Figure/Plate

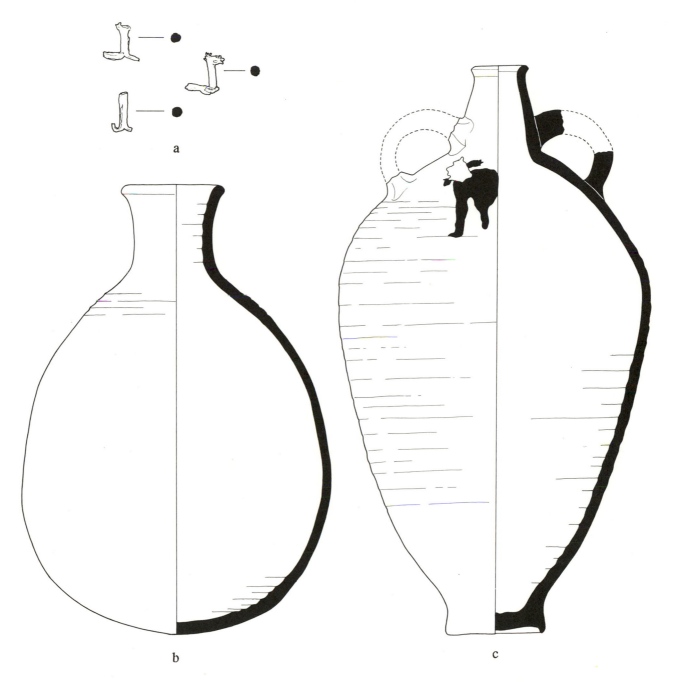

Figure 118. Pottery and Iron Fragments from Tomb Q 38: (*a*) Iron Fragments, No. 2a; (*b*) X-Gr. Ord. Medium-Necked Bottle-Jar I—C1, No. 3; (*c*) Coptic Period Egyptian Utility *Amphoriskos* III—C, No. 4. Scale 2:5.

Q 38

    Shaft with chamber on the W side

        Shaft: 1.80–2.00 × ca. 0.90–1.55 × 2.30 m

        Chamber: ca. 2.00 × 1.20 × 0.80 m; floor at -0.15 m, overlap ca. 0.40 m

        Ledge to W: 0.35 wide × 0.10 m high, with two circular

            depressions for bed legs

Table 40. Register of X-Group Finds in Cemetery Q (*cont.*).

Tomb	Description and Contents	Cairo	OIM	Figure/Plate
Q 38 (*cont.*)				
	Blocking: cb., 0.36 × 0.17 × 0.10 m; jumbled			
	Burial: —			
	Body: Adult			
	Objects:			
	a. In shaft:			
	1. Carpet remains, CAT 60		20084	
	2. Iron		20086	
	a. Fragments			fig. 118a, pl. 73a
	b. Arrowheads			pl. 64e–f
	b. In chamber:			
	3. X-Gr. ord. med.-necked bottle-jar I—C1		20044	figs. 13h, 118b
	4. Coptic period Eg. utility *amphoriskos* III—C, bk. and wh. pt. crude beads		20045	fig. 118c
	c. Unc. loc.:			
	5. Beads		20402	
	6. Silver earring		20085	fig. 61b, pl. 76g
	7. "Leather fragments (sandals?)"		Disc.	
	Sherds:		33177	
	a. From chamber		Disc.	
	b. From shaft:			
	A. Coptic period Eg. pk-drab amphora with bk. and wh. lines and spots showing altar (cf. Q 37—A)			

AREA Q*B*

Qu. 7				
	Tumulus and shaft subordinate to royal cemetery (see Emery and Kirwan 1938, p. 43; and see pl. 5 below)			
	Objects:			
	1. Remains of hide used to wrap burial		20467A	
	2. Sandal		20467B	
	3. Bead		20478	fig. 63t
Q 59				
	Shaft with chamber on the N side			
	Shaft: 2.80–3.35 × 1.10–1.25 × 1.60 m			
	Chamber: 2.70 × 1.20 × 0.70–0.80 m; floor flush			
	Blocking: cb. headers			
	Burial: N/R/90 degrees folded/face; on bed			
	Body: Mature male			
	Objects:			
	1. Bed remains		20247	pl. 50a
	2. Shards of glass bottle		20245	
	3. Same		20245	
	4. Beads		20246	
Q 60				
	Shaft with chamber on the W side			
	Shaft: 1.95–2.40 × 0.65–1.00 × 1.40 m			
	Chamber: 1.95 × 0.85 × 0.50 m; floor flush			
	Burial: S/R/thighs ext., legs 90 degrees/ under chin			
	Body: Adult male			

Table 40. Register of X-Group Finds in Cemetery Q (*cont.*).

Tomb	Description and Contents	Cairo	OIM	Figure/Plate
Q 60 (*cont.*)				
	Objects:			
	a. In chamber:			
	1. Textile wrapping (blue linen with red stripe, CAT X-Gr.)		20114	Disc.
	2. Twisted leather cord (hanging over shoulder) and seven strands at waist		20114	Disc.
	b. In shaft:			
	3. Sherd			
	c. Unc. Loc.:			
	4. Leather bottle, some remains of side and bottom with residue		20133	fig. 38a
	Sherds:		33178	
	A. X-Gr. ord. jar (no. 3)			
	B. X-Gr. ord. goblet, probably I—B			
	C. Coptic period Eg. utility II?, ribbed			
Q 61				
	Shaft with vault and brick-lined chamber on the E end			
	Shaft: ca. 1.70–2.25 × ca. 0.80–1.10 × 1.50 m			
	Chamber: ca. 1.25 × 0.37–0.90 (inside lining) × 0.80 m; shelf for cb. at ca. 0.09 m from floor, floor flush			
	Vault and lining: —			
	Burial: W/B/ext./pelvis (tomb reused?)			
	Body: Mature male			
	Objects:			
	a. Outside entrance and under some of the bricks in threshold:			
	1. Beads (some strung)		20203	
	2. Beads, red (some strung)		20203	
	3. Tweezers	Q 363, 89883		fig. 119a
	4. Coptic period Eg. juglet I—A2aii, incised dec. on shoulder		20198	fig. 119c
	b. In fill of chamber:			
	5. Leather objects		20204	
	a. Archer's guard, 10.0 × 5.0 × 0.5			
	b. Bow fragments			
	6. Arrowhead, length 4	Q 364, 89883		
	c. Beside and above legs and feet of burial:			
	7. X-Gr. ord. bottle-jar I—E3		20199	fig. 119b
	8. X-Gr. ord. goblet I—A1bi *alpha*, wh. pt., vine in groups of three (5YR 5/4, 5YR 5/3, 5YR 8/4), height 11.3		20200	
	9. X-Gr. ord. goblet I—A1bii, wh. pt., vine in groups of three, height 10.8		20201	
	10. X-Gr. ord. goblet I—A1bi *beta* (5YR 5/3, 5YR 4/2, 5YR 8/2), height 10.5		20202	
	d. Uncertain location:			
	11. Coptic period Eg. juglet (5YR 5/6, 5YR 3/2, 5YR 4/4), height 12 (as preserved) (see no. 4)		20198	
	Sherds from shaft:		33179	
	A. X-Gr. ord. goblet?			
	B. X-Gr. handmade cooking pot			

Table 40. Register of X-Group Finds in Cemetery Q (*cont.*).

Tomb	Description and Contents	Cairo	OIM	Figure/Plate

Q 61 (*cont.*)

Sherds from shaft (*cont.*):

    C. Unc. coarse utility, gray-bn. surface, chaffy, ribbed

    D. Post-X-Gr. sandy pk. with greenish

             white surface (firing zone)

Note a discrepancy between the sketch which indicates pelvis,
and the record which indicates chest. The tomb was reused,
objects 1–6 belonging to the earlier burial, which was early X-Gr.

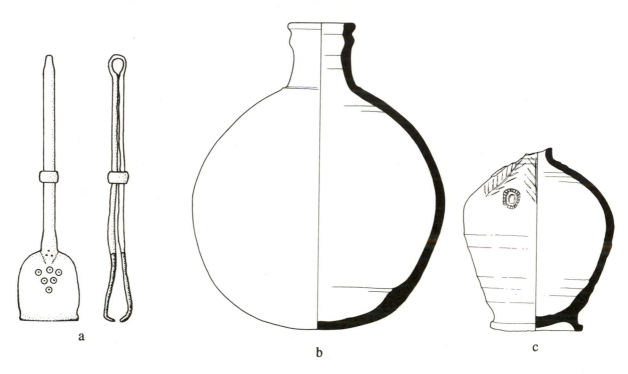

a   b   c

Figure 119. Pottery and Tweezers from Tomb Q 61: (*a*) Tweezers, No. 3; (*b*) X-Gr. Ord. Bottle-Jar
I—E3, No. 7; (*c*) Coptic Period Egyptian Juglet I—A2aii, No. 4. Scales: (*a*) 1:1; (*b, c*) 2:5.

Tomb	Description and Contents	Cairo	OIM	Figure/Plate
Q 62				pl. 39b

Shaft with ledges, vault, and niche at the W end

    Shaft: ca. 3.00 × 0.80–0.90 × 1.85 m

    Ledges: undercut, ca. 0.20 m wide, at 0.45 m from floor

    Niche: 0.95 × 0.90 × 1.00 m

    Vault: broken, leaned W

Burial: —

Body: Adult

Objects, in vault and niche:

		Cairo	OIM	Fig./Pl.
1.	Leather and bow fragments			
	a. Quiver	20398A		figs. 39, 40
	b. Fragment, gr., with wh. stitching; emblem?			fig. 121b
	c. Bow fragments	20398B		pl. 62b
2.	Leather armor fragment with rosettes, largest 7.4 × 5.7	20232		
3.	Stud or "tack"	20231		fig. 65k
4.	Textile remains, CAT 64–67	20178		
5.	Coptic period Eg. utility *amphoriskos* II—C, wh. coat, red pt. floral (2.5YR 6/4, 7.5YR 8/4, 7.5R 4/4)	20136		fig. 122a, pl. 46f

Figure 120. Pottery from Tomb Q 62: (*a*) X-Gr. Ord. Goblet I—A1bi *beta*, No. 18; (*b*) X-Gr. Ord. Goblet I—A1aiii, No. 9; (*c*) X-Gr. Ord. Goblet I—A1aii *beta*, No. 12; (*d*) X-Gr. Ord. Goblet I—A1bi *beta*, No. 7; (*e*) X-Gr. Ord. Goblet I—A1bi *beta*, No. 19; (*f*) X-Gr. Ord. Goblet I—A1bi *beta*, No.11; (*g*) X-Gr. Ord. Goblet I—B1c, No. 16; (*h*) X-Gr. Ord. Bottle-Jar I—E2, No. 10; (*i*) X-Gr. Utility Storage Jar III—B, No. 8. Scale 2:5.

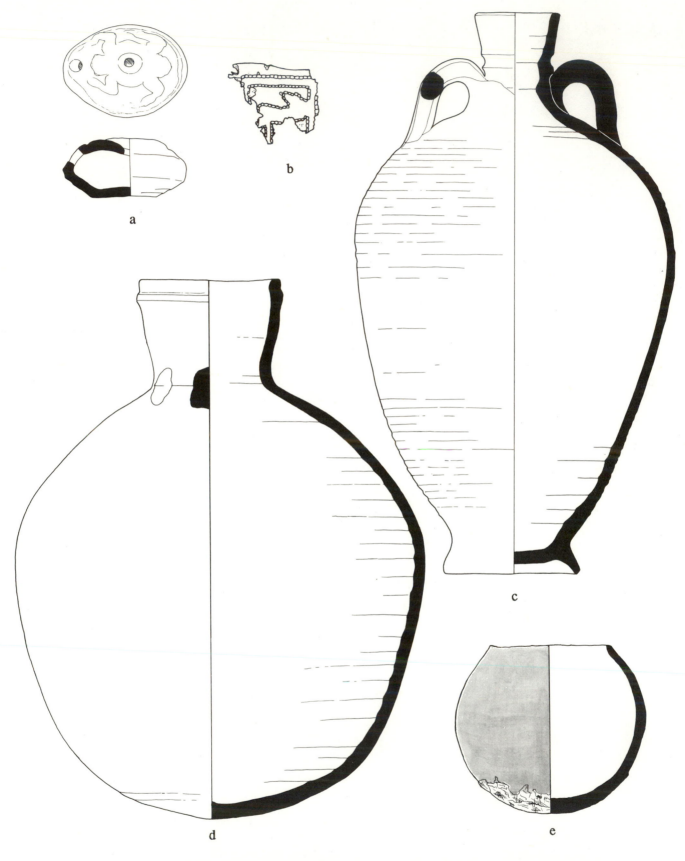

Figure 121. Pottery (*cont.*) and Objects from Tomb Q 62: (*a*) Coptic Period Egyptian Lamp, No. 17;
(*b*) Leather Fragment, No. 1b; (*c*) Coptic Period Egyptian Utility *Amphoriskos* II—C, No. 6;
(*d*) X-Gr. Ord. Medium-Necked Bottle-Jar I—B2, No. 20; (*e*) X-Gr. Handmade
Cooking Pot—B2, No. 13. Scales: (*a, c–e*) 2:5; (*b*) 1:2.

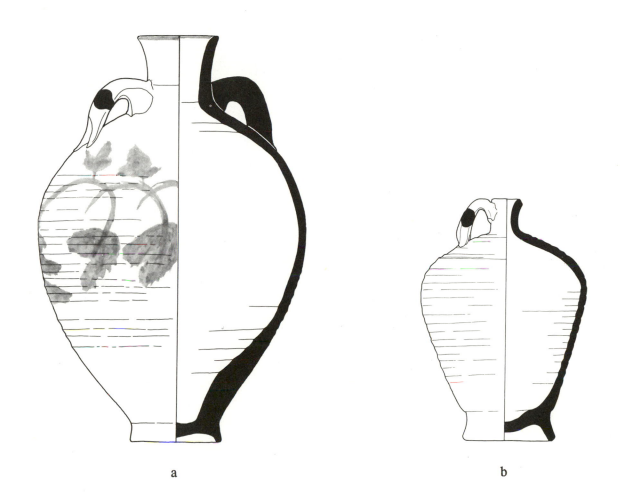

a   b

Figure 122. Pottery from Tomb Q 62 (*cont.*): (*a*) Coptic Period Egyptian Utility *Amphoriskos* II—C, No. 5;
(*b*) Coptic Period Egyptian Juglet I—A3a, No. 14. Scale 2:5.

Table 40. Register of X-Group Finds in Cemetery Q (*cont.*).

Tomb	Description and Contents	Cairo	OIM	Figure/Plate
Q 62 (*cont.*)				
	Objects, in vault and niche (*cont.*):			
6.	Coptic period Eg. utility *amphoriskos* II—C, lt. coat		20137	figs. 21c, 121c, pl. 46g
7.	X-Gr. ord. goblet I—A1bi *beta*		20138	fig. 120d
8.	X-Gr. utility storage jar III—B, red coat		20139	fig. 120i
9.	X-Gr. ord. goblet I—A1aiii, wh. pt. swags and tassels		20140	figs. 7d, 120b, pl. 41b
10.	X-Gr. ord. bottle-jar I—E2		20141	fig. 120h
11.	X-Gr. ord. goblet I—A1bi *beta*, wh. pt. swags		20142	fig. 120f
12.	X-Gr. ord. goblet I—A1aii *beta*, wh. pt. swags (5YR 5/4, 2.5YR 5/6, 2.5YR 4/4, 7.5YR 8/4)		20143	fig. 120c
13.	X-Gr. handmade cooking pot—B2, blackened, bottom encrusted		20144	figs. 19b, 121e
14.	Coptic period Eg. juglet I—A3a		20145	figs. 22g, 122b
15.	"Small cook-pot of bn. ware discolored bk. inside and out"	Q 304	Disc.	pl. 45c
16.	X-Gr. ord. goblet I—B1c (5YR 5/4, 5YR 8/1, 5YR 4/4)		20146	fig. 120g
17.	Coptic period Eg. lamp		20163	fig. 121a
18.	X-Gr. ord. goblet I—A1bi *beta*, bk. and wh. pt. vine in pairs		20233	figs. 7f, 120a
19.	X-Gr. ord. goblet I—A1bi *beta*, bk. and wh. pt. vert. bands (2.5YR 5/6, 5YR 8/2, 5YR 4/2, 2.5YR 4/6)		20234	fig. 120e
20.	X-Gr. ord. med.-necked bottle-jar I—B2		20235	fig. 121d
21.	Iron fragments (two), one in wood, including large spearhead, 3.2 × 0.9 and 10.7 × 4.8 × 1.6		20446	
22.	Beads		20231	
23.	Textile remains, CAT 68		20399	
24.	Date pits		Disc.	
	Note that a plunderer's passage enters the chamber from S.			
	Sherds:		33180	
A.	X-Gr. ord. goblet I—A2, very large, little if any color			
B.	X-Gr. ord. cup or goblet			
C.	X-Gr. ord.?, candlestick rim, (discolored)			
D–E.	X-Gr. ord.?			
F.	X-Gr. ord.?, candlestick rim, worn			
G.	Coptic period Eg. pk.-wh., ribbed (near Q 622)			
Q 68				
	Shaft with chamber on the W side			
	Shaft: 1.75–2.40 × 0.75–0.95 × 2.70 m			
	Chamber: 1.95 × 0.75 × 0.55–0.80 m			
	Blocking: present, but type not specified			
	Burial: —, on bed			
	Body: Mature male			
	Objects:			
1.	*Qadus*		20125	fig. 123d
2.	X-Gr. handmade jar—D3, with modeled rib at neck		20126	figs. 20h, 123c, pl. 45d
3.	Textile remains, CAT 69–71		20132	
4.	Two javelin points (iron; 4a and 4b)		20173	fig. 123a–b
5.	Beads		20175	fig. 64a
6.	Silver earrings with carnelian pendant		20174	fig. 61f
7.	Sandals (one on L foot), 23.5 × 7.5 × 8.0		20176	
8.	Bed remains		20177	pl. 50b
	Sherds:		33181	
A.	Post-X-Gr.? hard pk. chaffy deep basin, grooved rim			

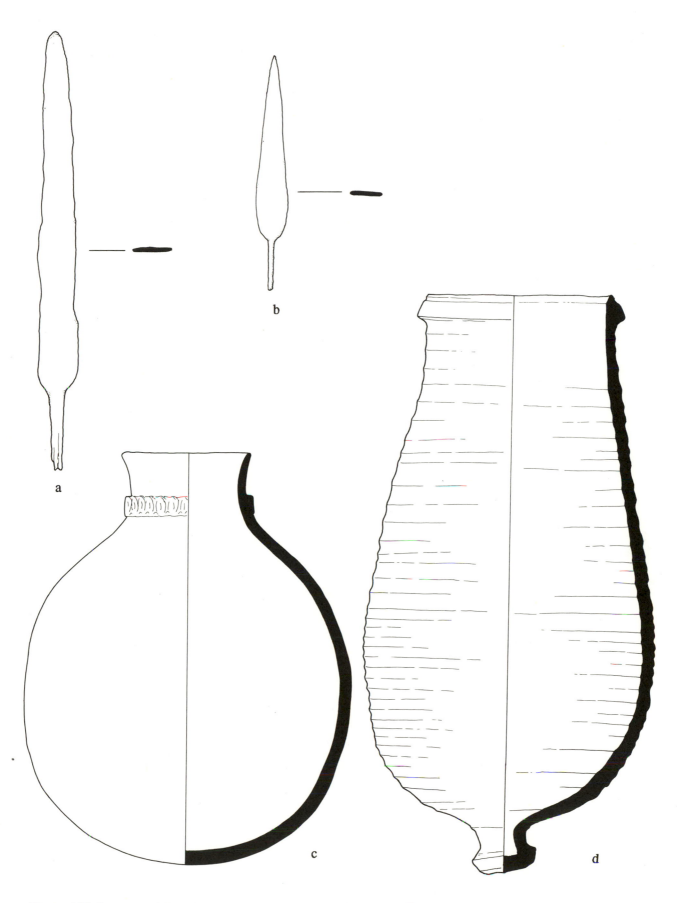

Figure 123. Pottery and Javelin Points from Tomb Q 68: (*a*) Javelin Point, No. 4a; (*b*) Javelin Point, No. 4b; (*c*) X-Gr. Handmade Jar—D3, No. 2; (*d*) *Qadus*, No. 1. Scales: (*a*, *b*) 1:2; (*c*, *d*) 2:5.

Table 40. Register of X-Group Finds in Cemetery Q (*cont.*).

Tomb	Description and Contents	Cairo	OIM	Figure/Plate
Q 69				
	Shaft with chamber on the W side			
	Shaft: ? × ? × 1.10 m (small)			
	Chamber: ? × 0.60 × 0.50 m			
	Burial: —, wrapped (?)			
	Body: —			
	Objects:			
	1. Textile remains (on body, CAT X-Gr.)		Disc.	
	2. Beads ("in a string arranged gn. and three orange in color over cloth on body")		20191	
Q 70				
	Shaft with chamber on the N? side			
	Shaft: 1.60 (minimum) × 0.65 (minimum) × 1.15 m			
	Chamber: 1.75 × 0.70 × 0.45 m			
	Blocking: stone slabs			
	Burial: —			
	Body: Adult male			
	Objects:			
	1. X-Gr. ord. goblet I—B2bii (inverted on 2; 2.5YR 5/6, 2.5YR 5/4), height 9.2		20149	
	2. X-Gr. ord. bottle-jar I—D1, height 27.3		20150	
	3. Coptic period Eg. juglet I—A2? (no neck) (2.5YR 2.5/0, 2.5YR 3/6, 2.5YR 5/6, 5YR 7/3), height 11.4 (as preserved)		20151	
	4. X-Gr. ord. goblet I—B2bii (5YR 4/6, 5YR 5/3), height 9.1		20152	
Q 71				
	Shaft with chamber on the W side			
	Shaft: 1.70–2.15 × 0.65–0.85 × 1.20 m			
	Chamber: 1.70 × 0.85 × 0.35 m; floor flush			
	Burial: —			
	Body: Mature female			
	Objects:			
	1. Remains of textile (CAT X-Gr.)		Disc.	
	2. Leather fragments		Disc.	
Q 72				
	Shaft with chamber on the N side			
	Shaft: 2.30 × 0.70 × 1.50 m			
	Chamber: 1.70 × 0.45 × ? m			
	Blocking: stone slabs			
	Burial: W?/—			
	Body: Senile female			
	Object:			
	1. Textile remains (CAT X-Gr.)		Disc.	
Q 74				fig. 124a, pl. 38b
	Shaft with chamber on the W side			
	Shaft: 2.65 × 0.85–1.50 × 1.95 m			
	Chamber: 1.75 × 1.65 × 0.95 m; 0.45 m overlap, floor at -0.75 m from shaft			
	Blocking: stone slabs			
	Burial: —, (probably contracted)			

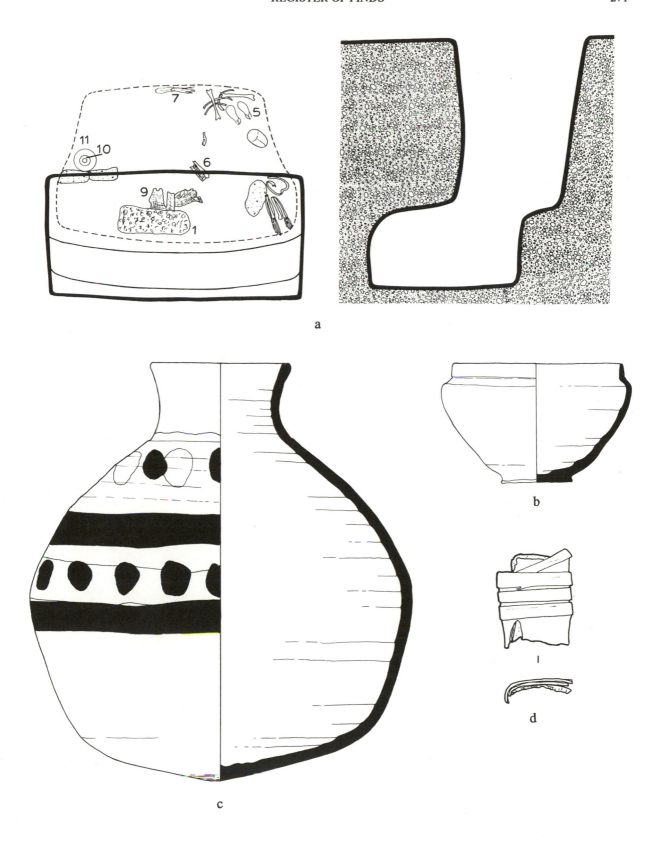

Figure 124. Plan, Section, Pottery, and a Sheath Liner from Tomb Q 74: (*a*) Plan and Section; (*b*) X-Gr. Ord. Goblet I—B1c, No. 10; (*c*) X-Gr. Ord. Medium-Necked Bottle-Jar I—A2, No. 11; (*d*) Sheath Liner, No. 2b. Scales: (*a*) 1:40; (*b, c*) 2:5; (*d*) 1:2.

Table 40. Register of X-Group Finds in Cemetery Q (*cont.*).

Tomb	Description and Contents	Cairo	OIM	Figure/Plate
Q 74 (*cont.*)				
	Body: Adult male			
	Objects:			
	a. In shaft:			
	1. Textile remains, CAT 72		20135	pl. 38a
	2. Archery equipment			
	a. Quiver		20184	fig. 41a–b, pls. 38a, 57b, 59c
	b. Sheath liner		20184	fig. 124d
	3. Arrowhead			
	4. Leather remains			
	a. Edge of bag with drawstring holes		20184	fig. 42b, pl. 68a
	b. Equipment belt or bag edge remains		20185	fig. 42c, pl. 67b
	c. Part of bow? (see 7b)		20184	fig. 42a, pl. 38b
	b. In burial chamber:			
	5. Sandals		20187	pl. 79d
	6. Quiver		20186	
	7. Leather remains		20186	
	a. Parts of bag			
	b. Bow			
	c. Armor fragments			
	d. Ornament in shape of "bee" or "fly" from quiver, belt or sandals			fig. 55
	8. Arrowheads		20183	pl. 64g–h
	9. Textile remains, CAT 73–74; as object no. 1			
	10. X-Gr. ord. goblet I—B1c (2.5YR 4/6, 2.5YR 6/2)		20196	fig. 124b
	11. X-Gr. ord. med.-necked bottle-jar I—A2, bk. and wh. pt.; wh. rim and neck, alt. beads at neck, wh. band with bk. beads at waist flanked by bk. bands		20197	fig. 124c
	12. Beads		20190	
	13. Silver earring		20182	fig. 61c, pl. 76f
	Sherds:		33182	
	A. X-Gr. utility storage jar III—A (small)			
	B. X-Gr. ord. goblet I—B			
	C. Unc. pk. storage jar, bk. pt. bands and lattice			
	D. Unc. pk. Coptic period Eg., ribbed			
Q 75				
	Shaft with chamber on the W side			
	Shaft: 1.75 × 0.65–1.00 × 1.75 m			
	Chamber: 1.45 × 0.85 × 0.45 m; floor at -2.00 m, overlap 0.25–0.30 m			
	Blocking: mentioned, type not specified, removed to N			
	Burial: —			
	Body: Adult male			
	Objects:			
	a. In shaft:			
	1. Sherds		33183	
	2. Leather bag (?) fragments, largest 28.0 × 20.5		20436	
	a. Sword sheath wrapping fragments		20229	fig. 125a, pl. 66a
	b. Bow fragments			

Table 40. Register of X-Group Finds in Cemetery Q (*cont.*).

Tomb	Description and Contents	Cairo	OIM	Figure/Plate
Q 75 (*cont.*)				
	Objects (*cont.*):			
	a. In shaft:			
	3. Quiver		20229	fig. 43
	4. Bag remains, largest 34.5 × 8.0		20230	
	b. In fill:			
	5. Earring		20226	figs. 61e, 65l, pl. 76e
	6. Beads		20226	
	7. Six arrows		20225	fig. 125b, pl. 64d
	8. Textile wrapping (around remains of body; CAT X-Gr.)			
	9. Cords (of different colors), length 9.6		20227	

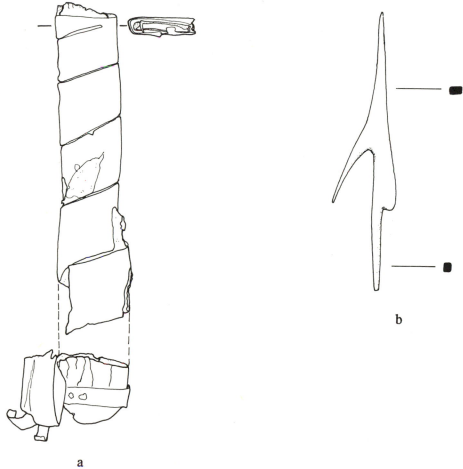

a

b

Figure 125. Objects from Tomb Q 75: (*a*) Sword Sheath Wrapping Fragments, No. 2a;
(*b*) Arrowhead, No. 7. Scales: (*a*) 1:2; (*b*) 1:1.

Q 76

Shaft with the chamber on the W side
    Shaft: 1.30–1.80 × 0.50–0.75 × 1.80 m
    Chamber: 1.40 × 050 × 0.40 m; floor flush
    Blocking: mentioned but not specified, removed from S

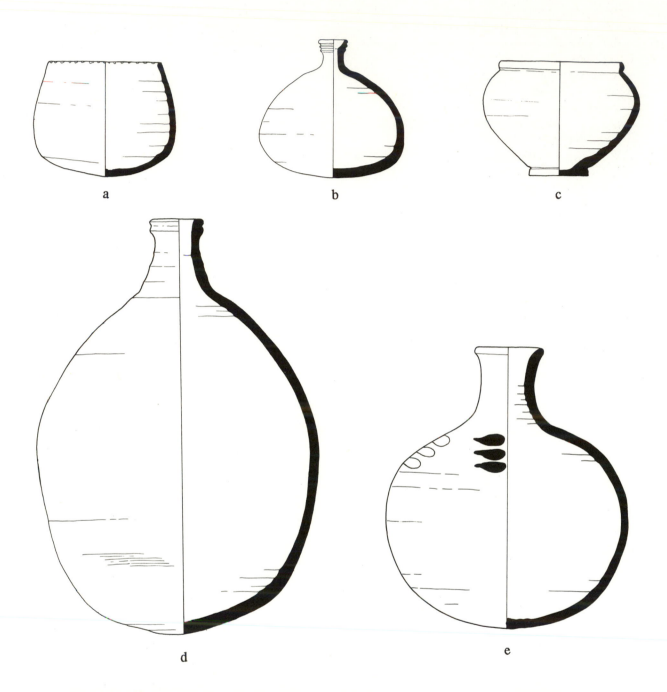

Figure 126. Pottery from Tomb Q 78: (*a*) X-Gr. Ord. Cup I—G1b, No. 1; (*b*) X-Gr. Ord. Min. Bottle-Jar—B2a, No. 4; (*c*) X-Gr. Ord. Goblet I—B2ai, No. 2; (*d*) X-Gr. Ord. Bottle-Jar I—D3, No. 5; (*e*) X-Gr. Ord. Narrow-Necked Bottle-Jar I—E1a, No. 3. Scale 2:5.

Table 40. Register of X-Group Finds in Cemetery Q (*cont.*).

Tomb	Description and Contents	Cairo	OIM	Figure/Plate
Q 76 (*cont.*)				
	Burial: —			
	Body: Adult male			
	Objects:			
	1. Quiver fragments		20256A	
	2. Bow fragments		20256B	
	3. Two beads		20257	
	4. Four arrowheads, length 5.6	Q 420, 89879		
	"Bones of a jackal found beside the body, but it is not sure that it was buried at the same time, hair on tail indicates a later date." Hair occurs on earlier burials, and dog burials do occur in X-Gr. (see Hofmann 1967, p. 478). Note also possible fragments of bag and a sandal with object no. 1.			
Q 78				
	Shaft with niche at the N end and vault			
	Shaft: ca. 1.80–1.95 × 0.65–1.05 × 1.00 m			
	Ledges: at 0.50 and 0.45 m from floor, 0.15 m wide			
	Niche: 0.65 × 0.65 m			
	Vault: four cb, 0.90 m from N end, top broken			
	Blocking: lower course rowlock;			
	above, four courses piled flat			
	Burial: —			
	Body: Adult female			
	Objects:			
	1. X-Gr. ord. cup I—G1b, wh. pt. rim dots (2.5YR 5/6, 2.5YR 4/6)		20214	fig. 126a
	2. X-Gr. ord. goblet I—B2ai (2.5YR 5/6, 2.5YR 4/6)		20215	fig. 126c
	3. X-Gr. ord. narrow-necked bottle-jar I—E1a, wh. pt. and bk., vine in groups of three		20216	figs. 14l, 126e
	4. X-Gr. ord. min. bottle-jar (handleless juglet)—B2a, red coat (2.5YR 4/4, 2.5YR 4/6, 2.5YR 4/2)		20217	figs. 15d, 126b
	5. X-Gr. ord. bottle-jar I—D3		20218	fig. 126d
	6. Sherds		33184	
	7. Date pits		Disc.	
	8. Textile wrapping remains, CAT 75		20250	
	9. Leather cord, longest 7.0		20249	
	Sherds:		33184	
	A. X-Gr. ord. bottle-jar, worn			

QC

Tomb	Description and Contents	Cairo	OIM	Figure/Plate
Q 40				fig. 127a
	Shaft with chamber on the W side			
	Shaft: 2.05 × 0.80–1.35 × 2.05 m			
	Chamber: 2.15 × 1.10 × 0.65 m, extended to W ca. 0.30 × 1.70 m; two holes in W ca. 0.40 diam. (oval) × 0.10 m (deep)			
	Blocking: indicated but not described			
	Burial: N/B/ext./(removed), on bed			
	Body: Adult male			
	Objects:			
	a. In shaft:			
	1. Coptic period Eg. fine/ord. juglet I—A4		20042	figs. 22i, 127c
	7. Leather fragments (see object no. 2)		21505	

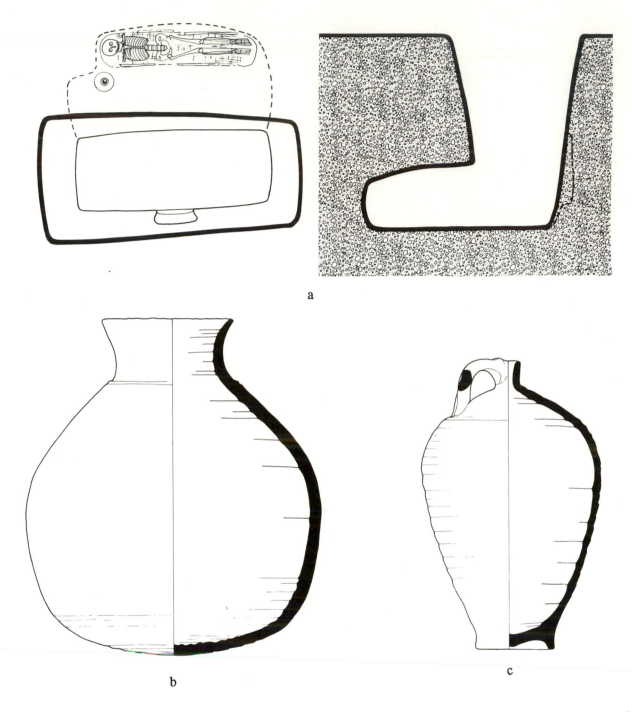

a

b

c

Figure 127. Plan, Section, and Pottery from Tomb Q 40: (*a*) Plan and Section; (*b*) X-Gr. Ord.
Medium-Necked Bottle-Jar I—B3b, No. 3; (*c*) Coptic Period Egyptian Fine/Ord.
Juglet I—A4, No. 1. Scales: (*a*) 1:40; (*b, c*) 2:5.

Table 40. Register of X-Group Finds in Cemetery Q (*cont.*).

Tomb	Description and Contents	Cairo	OIM	Figure/Plate
Q 40 (*cont.*)				
Objects (*cont.*):				
b.	In chamber:			
	2. Leather remains, largest ca. 45.0 × 12.0		21505	
	a. Quiver fragments			fig. 36, pls. 58, 59b
	b. Compound bow fragments			
	c. Sheath for short sword fragment			
	3. X-Gr. ord. med.-necked bottle-jar I—B3b, red coat		20029	fig. 127b
	4. Textile remains, CAT 162		20012	
	6. Bed (matting with a wooden frame)		—	pls. 37a, 49
	7. Sherd		33202	
c.	In fill:			
	8. Two dates on a cord		20014	
Q 41				
Shaft with chamber on the W side				
Shaft: 2.10–2.20 × 0.70–0.95 × 2.20 m undercut at ends near the bottom; depressions cut to insert bed				
Chamber: ca. 2.30 × 0.80 × 0.65 m; floor at -0.35 m from shaft, overlap ca. 0.20 m				
Bedpost holes: ca. 0.20 m dia., ca. 1.70 center to center × 0.60 m width				
Blocking: present but dist.				
Burial: S/B/ext./R side, L chest; wrapped				
Body: Adult female				
Objects:				
a.	In shaft and chamber:			
	1. Beads (some still strung)		20058	figs. 62o, 65i
b.	Unc. loc :			
	2. Berries and wheat stalk		20059	
c.	With body:			
	3. Five bracelets (on R. arm)		20061	
	4. Earring (from R. side), diam. 1.6		20060	
	5. Five beads, orange (under bed)		20259	
	6. Textile wrappings (CAT X-Gr.)		Disc.	
	7. Remains of bed		Disc.	
Q 42				
Shaft with ledges and vault (Knudstad's map shows chamber on west)				
Shaft: —				
Ledges: —				
Vault: destroyed, originally in E				
Blocking: single row of cb. headers				
Burial: W/B/ext./—				
Body: —				
Objects:				
a.	From chamber:			
	1. X-Gr. ord. goblet I—B2bii, height 9.5		20020	
	2. X-Gr. ord. bottle-jar I—C3, wh. coat		20019	fig. 128a
	3. X-Gr. ord. cup I—G1		20018	fig. 128d
	4. X-Gr. ord. bottle-jar I—C3, height 24.2		20021	
	5. X-Gr. ord. bottle-jar I—C3		20022	fig. 128b
	6. X-Gr. ord. bottle-jar I—C3, height 24.2		20023	
	7. Beads		20101	

Table 40. Register of X-Group Finds in Cemetery Q (*cont.*).

Tomb	Description and Contents	Cairo	OIM	Figure/Plate
Q 42 (*cont.*)				
	Objects (*cont.*):			
	b. From shaft:			
	8. Bead		20100	
	It remains possible that this tomb was reused after the removal of the vault.			
	Sherds: (mostly worn):		33185	
	A–C. X-Gr. and post-X-Gr. cook-pot, two heavy, one thin			
	D. X-Gr. ord. goblet I—B			
	E–G. Mer. or X-Gr. fine/ord., red coat			
	H. Unc. brown sandy, thin			
	I–K. Brown sandy amphorae, abraded			
Q 43				
	Shaft with ledges and vault			
	Shaft: 2.65–2.80 × 0.80–1.10 (ledges)/1.30 (outer) × 1.48 m			
	Ledges: ca. 0.15–0.18 wide × ca. 2.35 m			
	Vault: toward N; five cb. first course, then seven, chinked with stones, 0.45 above ledges (0.95 m above floor), leaned N., plastered?			
	Burial: S/L/ca. 135 degrees/knees			
	Body: Adult male			
	Objects: —			
	Sherds, from shaft above vault:		33186	
	A. Unc. brown, sandy, surface ribbed			
	B. Red-brown, organic, rim with two ridges			
	C. Post-X-Gr. pink-brown, ribbed			
	D. X-Gr. ord. goblet I—A rim			
	It is difficult to believe this simple burial is original in this tomb which must have been made for a much wealthier individual. See Q 45.			
Q 44				
	Shaft with chamber on the W side			
	Shaft: 1.90 × 0.70–0.90 × 1.95 m (slightly undercut to N)			
	Chamber: 1.95 × 0.75 × 0.60 m; floor at -0.05 m, no overlap			
	Blocking: cb., filling lower shaft? 0.38 × 0.18 × 0.80 m			
	Burial: —			
	Body: Juvenile female			
	Objects:			
	a. In shaft:			
	1. Textile remains, CAT 62		20040	
	2. Beads		20041	pl. 76c
	b. In chamber:			
	3. X-Gr. ord. med.-necked bottle-jar I—B3b, red coat		20046	figs. 13g, 128e
	4. X-Gr. ord. cup I—D1b, wh. pt. rim band		20047	fig. 128c
	5. Textile remains, CAT 63		20051	
	Sherds:		33187	
	A. Mer.? Roman period Eg. fine/ord. jar, bn. surface			
	B. Post-X-Gr. gray-bn.			
	C. X-Gr. Coptic period Eg. fine/ord. juglet, candlestick rim			
	D. X-Gr. Coptic period Eg. fine/ord. juglet, with pinched rim			
	E. Post-X-Gr. coarse chaffy basin, rect. rim, abraded			

Figure 128. Pottery from Tombs Q 42 and Q 44: (*a*) X-Gr. Ord. Bottle-Jar I—C3, Q 42—2; (*b*) X-Gr. Ord. Bottle-Jar I—C3, Q 42—5; (*c*) X-Gr. Ord. Cup I—D1b, Q 44—4; (*d*) X-Gr. Ord. Cup I—G1, Q 42—3; (*e*) X-Gr. Ord. Medium-Necked Bottle-Jar I—B3b, Q 44—3. Scale 2:5.

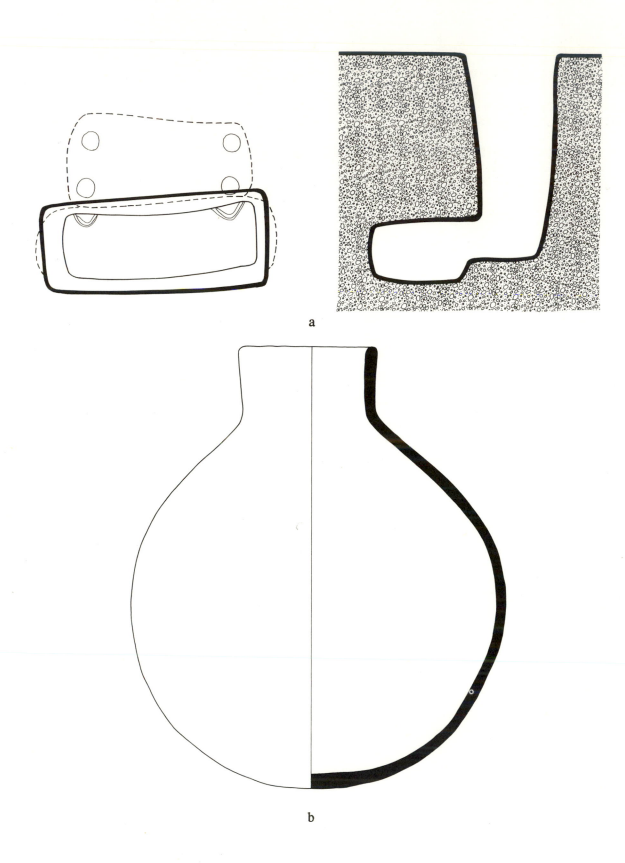

a

b

Figure 129. Plan, Section, and Pottery from Tomb Q 49: (a) Plan and Section;
(b) X-Gr. Handmade Jar I—D1a, No. 1. Scales: (a) 1:40, (b) 2:5.

Table 40. Register of X-Group Finds in Cemetery Q (*cont.*).

Tomb	Description and Contents	Cairo	OIM	Figure/Plate
Q 49				fig. 129a
	Shaft with chamber on the N side			
	Shaft: 1.60–2.30 × 0.50–0.70 × 1.25 m			
	Chamber: 1.80 × 0.60 × 0.50 m; floor at -0.15 m from shaft, overlap ca. 0.10 m			
	Blocking: stone slabs			
	Burial: —			
	Body: Adult male			
	Objects:			
	a. In chamber:			
	1. X-Gr. handmade jar I—D1a		20048	figs. 20f, 129b
	2. Sandals (one in shaft)		20087	pl. 78a
	b. Unc. loc.:			
	3. Leather cords		20057	
	4. Bead		20057	
Q 51				fig. 130a
	Stone slab with votive deposit of goblet and min. cups, E of Q 51A			
	Objects:			
	1. X-Gr. ord. goblet I—A2b		20049	fig. 130b
	2. X-Gr. min. cup, as 19, 2.8 × 3.6		20050-2	
	3. X-Gr. min. cup, as 5, 2.9 × 3.7		20050-3	
	4. X-Gr. min. cup, as 11, 2.8 × 5.0		20050-4	fig. 17g
	5. X-Gr. min. cup		20050-5	figs. 17a, 130c
	6. X-Gr. min. cup, as 22, 2.6 × 5.4		20050-6	
	7. X-Gr. min. cup, as 14, 3.2 × 4.4		20050-7	
	8. X-Gr. min. cup, as 22, 3.1 × 5.5		20050-8	
	9. X-Gr. min. cup, as 5, 2.4 × 4.4		20050-9	
	10. X-Gr. min. cup, as 19, 4.9 × 3.0		20050-10	
	11. X-Gr. min. cup		20050-11	fig. 130c
	12. X-Gr. min. cup, as 22, 2.9 × 4.7		20050-12	fig. 17e
	13. X-Gr. min. cup, as 5?, 3.0 × 5.2		20050-13	
	14. X-Gr. min. cup, 3.0 × 4.8		20050-14	figs. 17c, 130c
	15. X-Gr. min. cup, as 5, 2.6 × 5.3		20050-15	
	16. X-Gr. min. cup		20050-16	figs. 17b, 130c
	17. X-Gr. min. cup, as 22, 3.0 × 6.2		20050-17	
	18. X-Gr. min. cup, as 16, 1.9 × 3.6		20050-18	
	19. X-Gr. min. cup		20050-19	fig. 130c
	20. X-Gr. min. cup, as 5, 3.1 × 5.0		20050-20	
	21. X-Gr. min. cup, as 22, 2.8 × 5.0		20050-21	
	22. X-Gr. min. cup		20050-22	figs. 17d, 130c
	23. X-Gr. min. cup, as 22, 3.0 × 6.0		20050-23	
	24. X-Gr. min. cup, as 19, 2.5 × 4.2		20050-24	
	25. X-Gr. min. cup, as 22, 3.0 × 6.4		20050-25	
	26. X-Gr. min. cup, as 22, 3.2 × 4.8		20050-1	
Q 51A				
	Shaft with chamber on the N side			
	Shaft: —			
	Chamber: floor flush			
	Burial: W/—/ext./—			
	Body: Mature male			

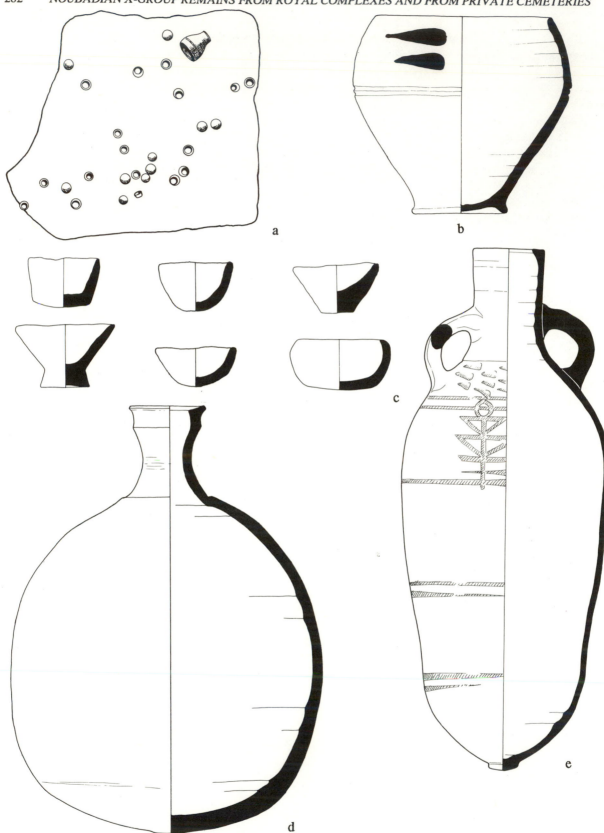

Figure 130. Plan of Vessel Deposit and Pottery from Tomb Q 51 and Pottery from Tomb Q 51A: (a) Tomb Q 51, Deposit and Vessels (Conjectural Reconstruction); (b) X-Gr. Ord. Goblet I—A2b, Q 51—1; (c) X-Gr. Min. Cup, Q 51—14 [Upper Left]; X-Gr. Min. Cup, Q 51—19 [Upper Middle]; X-Gr. Min. Cup, Q 51—16 [Upper Right]; X-Gr. Min. Cup, Q 51—5 [Lower Left]; X-Gr. Min. Cup, Q 51—11 [Lower Middle]; X-Gr. Min. Cup, Q 51—22 [Lower Right]; (d) X-Gr. Ord. Bottle-Jar I—D3, Q 51A—3; (e) Coptic Period Egyptian Amphora IV—, Q 51A—1. Scales: (a) 1:20; (b–d) 2:5; (e) 1:5.

Table 40. Register of X-Group Finds in Cemetery Q (*cont.*).

Tomb	Description and Contents	Cairo	OIM	Figure/Plate
Q 51A				
	Objects:			
	a. In shaft:			
	1. Coptic amphora IV—, bk. pt., potter's mark		20219	fig. 130e, pl. 47c
	2. Leather			
	a. Quiver		20228A	fig. 37a
	b. Bow fragments		20228B	
	c. Quiver fragments		20228C	fig. 37b
	d. Bow fragments, largest 8 × 1		20228D	
	e. Bag edge with tie hole		20228E	
	3. X-Gr. ord. bottle jar I—D3		20220	fig. 130d
	b. In chamber near or under body:			
	4. Sandal, 10.0 × 8.3		20255	N/A
	5. Beads		20224	
	Sherds:		33188	
	A. X-Gr. ord. goblet I—B (tall, open)			
	B. X-Gr. ord. bottle-jar I—, with simple rim and single rib at neck			
	C–I. X-Gr. ord. bottle jar I—, sherds			
	J. Unc. handmade cooking pot, small			
	K. Mer.? storage jar with bk. band			
	L. Mer.-X-Gr. Coptic period Eg. fine/ord. with brown surface			
	M. Unc. mottled coarse chaffy jar (organic)			
Q 52				
	Shaft with chamber on the N side			
	Shaft: 1.80–2.25 × 0.80–1.05 × 1.50 m			
	Chamber: 1.75 × 0.80 × 0.70 m			
	Blocking: stone slabs			
	Burial: —			
	Body: Juvenile			
	Objects, from chamber:			
	1. Mortar, 6.5 × 24.6 × 29.8		20081	
	2. Pestle, 7.4 × 4.2 × 5.8		20080	
	3. Iron rod or probe, length 6.5		20107	
	4. Beads		20108	
	5. Woven straw(?)		20106	
	6. Lamp		20072	fig. 131c
	7. X-Gr. ord. med.-necked bottle-jar I—B3(b), bk. and wh. pt. vine in groups of three (two)		20073	fig. 131g, pl. 43c
	8. Coptic period Eg. juglet I—A2c, incised vert. branches		20077	figs. 22f, 131f
	9. X-Gr. ord. goblet I—A1bii, bk. and wh. pt. vine		20074	figs. 7g, 131d
	10. X-Gr. ord. goblet I—A1bii, bk. and wh. pt. swags (3–4)		20075	fig. 131e
	11. X-Gr. ord. goblet I—B2ai (3–4)		20076	figs. 7s, 131a
	12. Min. cup (one?)		20078	fig. 131b [below]
	13. Min. cup (one?)		20079	fig. 131b [above]
	Sherds:		33189	
	A. X-Gr. Coptic period Eg. jar, ring base, bk. pt. bands, brown surface			
	B. A-Group Eg. hard pk. bowl, open burnish			
	C. Post-X-Gr. orange jar, ring base			
	D. Post-X-Gr. orange jar, rim			
	E. Uncertain			

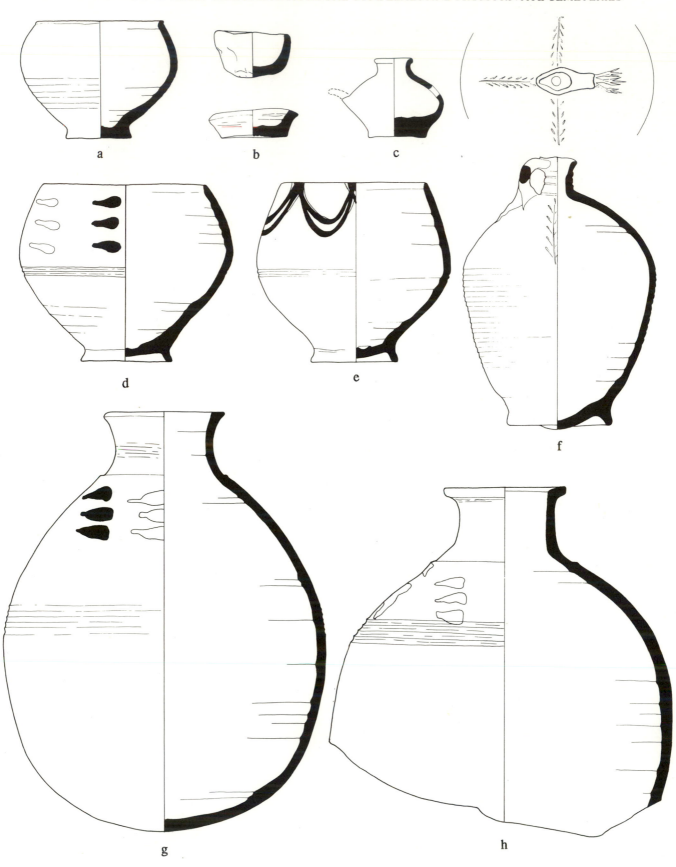

Figure 131. Pottery from Tomb Q 52: (*a*) X-Gr. Ord. Goblet I—B2ai, No. 11; (*b*) Min. Cup No. 13 [Above];
Min. Cup No. 12 [Below]; (*c*) Lamp, No. 6; (*d*) X-Gr. Ord. Goblet I—A1bii, No. 9; (*e*) X-Gr. Ord. Goblet
I—A1bii, No. 10; (*f*) Coptic Period Egyptian Juglet I—A2c, No. 8; (*g*) X-Gr. Ord. Medium-Necked
Bottle-Jar I—B3(b), No.7; (*h*) X-Gr. Ord. Medium-Necked Bottle-Jar I—B3, No. H. Scale 2:5.

Table 40. Register of X-Group Finds in Cemetery Q (*cont.*).

Tomb	Description and Contents	Cairo	OIM	Figure/Plate

Q 52 (*cont.*)

Sherds (*cont.*):

F.	Red to bn. chaffy, unc.			
G.	Post-X-Gr. straight-neck jar, hard pk., rect. rim and rib below			
H.	X-Gr. ord. med.-necked bottle-jar I—B3 (as object no. 7)		33214	fig. 131h

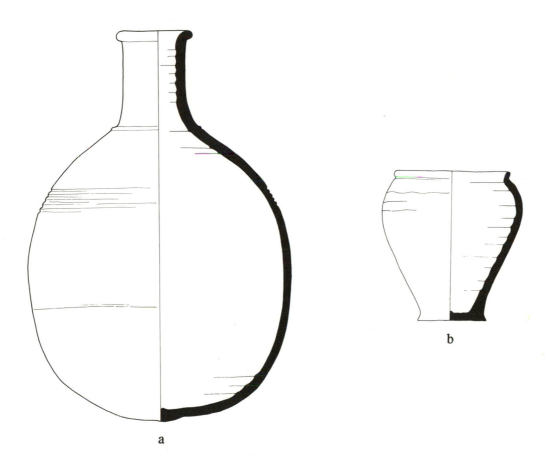

Figure 132. Pottery from Tomb Q 53: (*a*) X-Gr. Ord. Narrow-Necked Bottle-Jar I—E1b, No. 2;
(*b*) X-Gr. Ord. Goblet I—B2bii, No. 1. Scale 2:5.

Q 53

Shaft with chamber on the N side

Shaft: —

Chamber: —

Burial: W/L/90 degrees/hips, dist.?

Body: Senile female (gray hair)

Objects, near feet:

1.	X-Gr. ord. goblet I—B2bii		20064	fig. 132b
2.	X-Gr. ord. narrow-necked bottle-jar I—E1b		20063	figs. 14m, 132a

Sherd, on surface: 33190

A.	Unc. Coptic period Eg. base of pk. amphora with dk. surface, ribbing

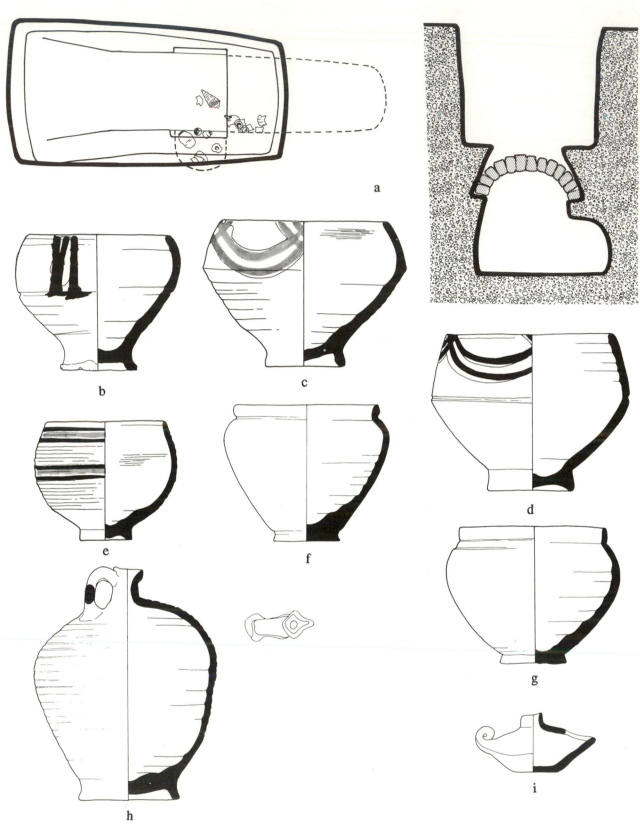

Figure 133. Plan, Section, and Pottery from Tomb Q 54: (*a*) Plan and Section; (*b*) X-Gr. Ord. Goblet
I—A1aii *beta*, No. 4; (*c*) X-Gr. Ord. Goblet I—A1bi *alpha*, No. 10; (*d*) X-Gr. Ord. Goblet
I—A1bi *beta*, No. 9; (*e*) X-Gr. Fine Cup II—C2, No. 6; (*f*) X-Gr. Ord. Goblet I—B1c,
No. 5; (*g*) X-Gr. Ord. Goblet I—B1b, No. 3; (*h*) Coptic Period Egyptian Juglet
I—A1b, No. 7; (*i*) Lamp, No. 2. Scales: (*a*) 1:40; (*b–i*) 2:5.

Table 40. Register of X-Group Finds in Cemetery Q (*cont.*).

Tomb	Description and Contents	Cairo	OIM	Figure/Plate
Q 54				fig. 133a
	Shaft with ledges, vault, chamber at the N end, and niche on the E side			
	Outer shaft: 1.20–1.30 × 2.70–2.90 × 1.30 m			
	Inner shaft: ? × 0.85 × 1.35 m			
	Ledges: at 0.85 m from floor, 0.20 m wide, undercut, 0.60 m long			
	Niche: ca. 0.50 × 0.35 × 0.60 m			
	Vault: up to twelve cb. laid lengthwise			
	Blocking: cb.			
	Chamber: 1.65 × 0.85 × 0.65–1.05			
	Burial: —			
	Body: Mature			
	Objects:			
	a. In shaft:			
	1. X-Gr. ord. narrow-necked bottle-jar I—C1 (neck and shoulder [object no. 7] below)		20124	figs. 14e, 134a
	2. Lamp		20117	fig. 133i
	3. X-Gr. ord. goblet I—B1b		20118	fig. 133g
	b. In chamber and niche ([1–6] in niche):			
	4. X-Gr. ord. goblet I—A1aii *beta*, bk. and wh. pt. swags (?)		20115	fig. 133b
	5. X-Gr. ord. goblet I—B1c (4–5)		20119	fig. 133f
	6. X-Gr. fine cup II—C2, bk. and red pt. bands (two)		20123	figs. 8e, 133e, pl. 42f
	7. Coptic period Eg. juglet I—A1b; red coat		20116	figs. 22b, 133h
	8. Coptic period Eg. amphora IV—A (13a)		20122	figs. 24a, 134c
	9. X-Gr. ord. goblet I—A1bi *beta*, bk. and wh. pt. swags		20120	fig. 133d
	10. X-Gr. ord. goblet I—A1bi *alpha*, bk. and wh. pt. swags		20121	fig. 133c
	11. "Small cooking pot of brown ware, incomplete," height 10.7 (as preserved)	Q 278	Disc.	
	c. In chamber:			
	12. Beads	Q 269, 89990		
	13. Jar (probable error in identification here, for 20113 was in niche)			
	14. X-Gr. utility storage jar III—C (1)		20113	figs. 16d, 134b
	Q 54—1 (7), —3 (8)?, —2 (10)? found in vault, with amphora base of —8 (9).			
Q 55				
	Shaft with ledges and vault, ramp, N-S			
	Shaft: 2.55–3.05 × 0.75–1.40 × 1.25 m			
	Ramp: 0.70–1.00 m from S end			
	Ledges: ca. 0.15–0.17 m at 0.70 m from floor of shaft			
	Chamber: 1.65, leaned against N end, four cb. on end, two lengthwise as keys			
	Niche: in NW corner of shaft, 0.60 × 0.10 × 0.50 m			
	Blocking: stone slab on end			
	Burial: S/R/R 130 degrees, L 90 degrees/knees			
	Body: Mature male			

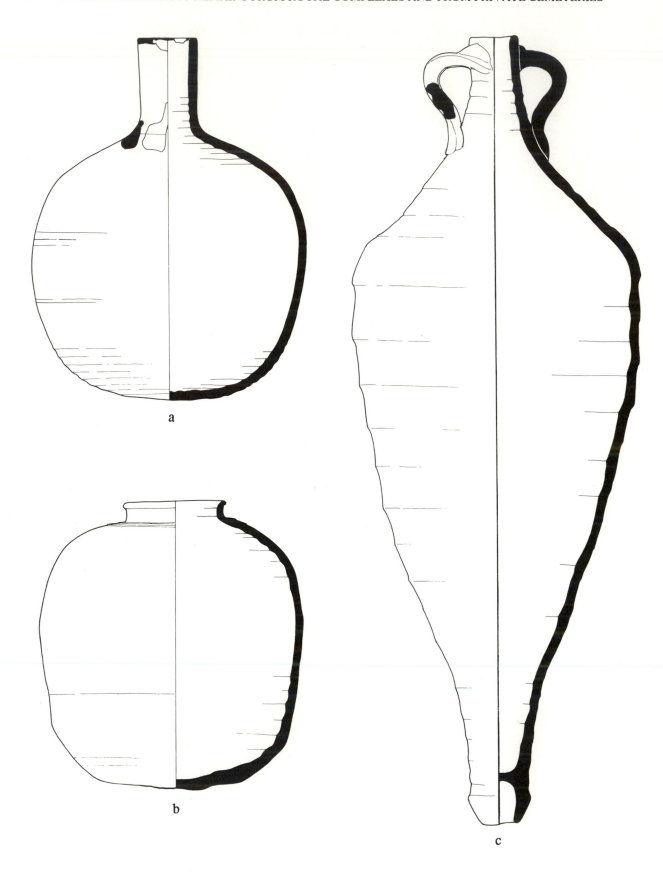

Figure 134. Pottery from Tomb Q 54: (*a*) X-Gr. Ord. Narrow-Necked Bottle-Jar I—C1, No. 1;
(*b*) X-Gr. Storage Jar III—C, No. 14; (*c*) Coptic Period Egyptian Amphora
IV—A, No. 8. Scales: (*a*, *b*) 2:5; (*c*) 1:5.

Table 40. Register of X-Group Finds in Cemetery Q (*cont.*).

Tomb	Description and Contents	Cairo	OIM	Figure/Plate
Q 55 (*cont.*)				
	Objects:			
	1. Leather with "strings," possibly garment for head		Disc.	
	2. Textile remains		Disc.	
	3. Remains of sandals		20212	
	A large piece of leather, with strings around the shoulders. As fragments of cloth were found fixed to these, this leather might have been used on the upper part of the body.			
Q 56				
	Objects:			
	1. Small jar—B1, with painted "scene" in red and wh.		20068	figs. 24c, 135c
	2. Dried leaf inside 1		20056	
	3. Bead inside 1		20172	

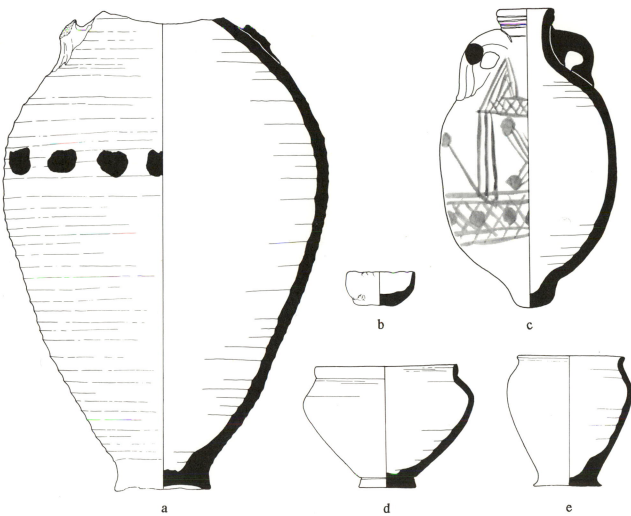

a   b   c   d   e

Figure 135. Pottery from Tombs Q 56, Q 57, and Q 58: (*a*) Coptic Period Egyptian *Amphoriskos* I—C, Q 57—1; (*b*) Min. Bowl, Q 57—3; (*c*) Small Jar—B1, Q 56—1; (*d*) X-Gr. Ord. Goblet I—B1c, Q 57—2; (*e*) X-Gr. Ord. Goblet I—B2bii, Q 58—1. Scale 2:5.

Table 40. Register of X-Group Finds in Cemetery Q (*cont.*).

Tomb	Description and Contents	Cairo	OIM	Figure/Plate
Q 57				
	Irregular, possibly shaft with chamber on the W side			
	Shaft: ? × 0.70 × 0.85 m			
	Chamber: ? × 0.35 × 0.30 m; floor flush			
	Burials:			
	A. —			
	B. —			
	Bodies:			
	A. Juvenile female			
	B. Infant			
	Objects:			
	1. Coptic period Eg. *amphoriskos* I—C		20070	fig. 135a
	2. X-Gr. ord. goblet I—B1c		20071	fig. 135d
	3. Miniature bowl		20171	fig. 135b
	4. Leaf		Disc.	
	Sherd:		Disc.	
Q 58				
	Shaft with chamber on the N side			
	Shaft: 1.70–2.50 × 0.50–0.90 × 1.10 m			
	Chamber: 1.70 × 0.35–0.40 × 0.45 m; floor at -1.45 m			
	Blocking: stone slabs? removed to W			
	Burial: W/B/ext./sides-pelvis			
	Body: Mature female; dist., wrapped			
	Objects, at E end of chamber:			
	1. X-Gr. ord. goblet I—B2bii		20065	figs. 7w, 135e, pl. 41g
	2. X-Gr. ord. bottle-jar I—C3, height 25.5		20066	
	3. X-Gr. ord. bottle-jar I—A1, height 23.2		20067	
	4. Textile wrapping (CAT X-Gr.)		Disc.	
	5. Date pits (beside head)		Disc.	
	6. Beads		20221	
Q 63				
	Shaft with chamber on the N side			
	Shaft: 1.60–2.00 × 0.55 × 1.25 m			
	Chamber: 1.75 × 0.55 × 0.45 m; floor at ca. -0.20 m, overlap 0.35 m			
	Blocking: stone slabs			
	Burial: E/B/ext./—, dist.			
	Body: Adult male			
	Objects: —			
	Sherds: Plunderer's tools reported.			
	The tomb is actually undated by the contents.			
Q 64				
	Shaft with chamber on the N side			
	Shaft: 1.55–2.00 × 0.60–0.80 × 1.50 m			
	Chamber: 1.65 × 0.70 × 0.50 m, floor flush			
	Burial: —			
	Body: Infant-juvenile			

Table 40. Register of X-Group Finds in Cemetery Q (*cont.*).

Tomb	Description and Contents	Cairo	OIM	Figure/Plate
Q 64 (*cont.*)				
Objects:				
a.	In chamber:			
	1. Ring, diam. 2.2		20110	
	2. Beads		20112	fig. 62b, pl. 76h
	3. Arrowheads		20111	pl. 64b
b.	In shaft:			
	4. Sherds			
Sherds:			33191	
A.	Mer. Eg. fine/ord., dk. surface, dk. bands			
B.	X-Gr. ord. goblet I—A?, no pigment			
Q 65				
Rectangular shaft: 0.80 × 0.75 × 0.50 m				
Burial: S/R/90 degrees/—, legs folded				
Body: "Infant I"				
Objects:				
	1. Textile remains, brown with yellow stripes (CAT X-Gr.)		Disc.	
	2. Stone (placed W of body)			
Q 66				
Shaft with chamber on the W side				
Shaft: 2.05 × 0.90 × 1.30 m				
Chamber: 1.60 × 0.70 × 0.45 m; floor flush				
Blocking: stone slabs				
Burial: —				
Body: Adult male				
Objects, in shaft:				
	1. X-Gr. ord. goblet I—B1c (5YR 5/3, 5YR 4/4), height 8.0		20131	
	2. Quiver fragments, largest 15.0 × 4.0		20166	
	3. Textile remains (CAT X-Gr.)		—	
Sherds, from shaft: —				
Q 67				
Shaft with chamber on the W side				
Shaft: 2.80–3.90 × 1.80 m				
Chamber: 2.65–1.00 × 0.60–0.70 m				
Blocking: stone slabs, possibly laid horizontally				
Burial: S/B/ext./—, dist.				
Body: Senile				
Objects:				
a.	In fill of shaft:			
	1. *Qadus*		20127	fig. 137
	2. X-Gr. ord. med.-neck jar I—A1c, height 23.7		20128	
	3. X-Gr. ord. goblet I—A1aii *beta*		20129	fig. 136b
	4. X-Gr. ord. goblet I—A1aii *alpha*		20130	fig. 136a
b.	Bottom of the shaft at the S end:			
	5. Miscellaneous			
	a. Wooden box fragments with ivory inlay		20188	pls. 51, 52, 53
	b. Strings of ostrich eggshell beads (with 5a)		—	
c.	In chamber, scattered at S end:			
	6. X-Gr. storage jar III—C		20153	fig. 136g
	7. X-Gr. ord. med.-necked bottle-jar I—A1c		20155	figs. 13c, 136f
	8. Coptic period Eg. juglet I—A1a (contents intact)		20154	fig. 136e

Figure 136. Pottery from Tomb Q 67: (*a*) X-Gr. Ord. Goblet I—A1aii *alpha*, No. 4; (*b*) X-Gr. Ord. Goblet I—A1aii *beta*, No. 3; (*c*) X-Gr. Ord. Goblet I—B1b, No. 10; (*d*) Coptic Period Egyptian Juglet I—A1c, No. 9; (*e*) Coptic Period Egyptian Juglet I—A1a, No. 8; (*f*) X-Gr. Ord. Medium-Necked Bottle-Jar I—A1c, No. 7; (*g*) X-Gr. Storage Jar III—C, No. 6. Scales: (*a–f*) 2:5; (*g*) 1:5.

Table 40. Register of X-Group Finds in Cemetery Q (*cont.*).

Tomb	Description and Contents	Cairo	OIM	Figure/Plate

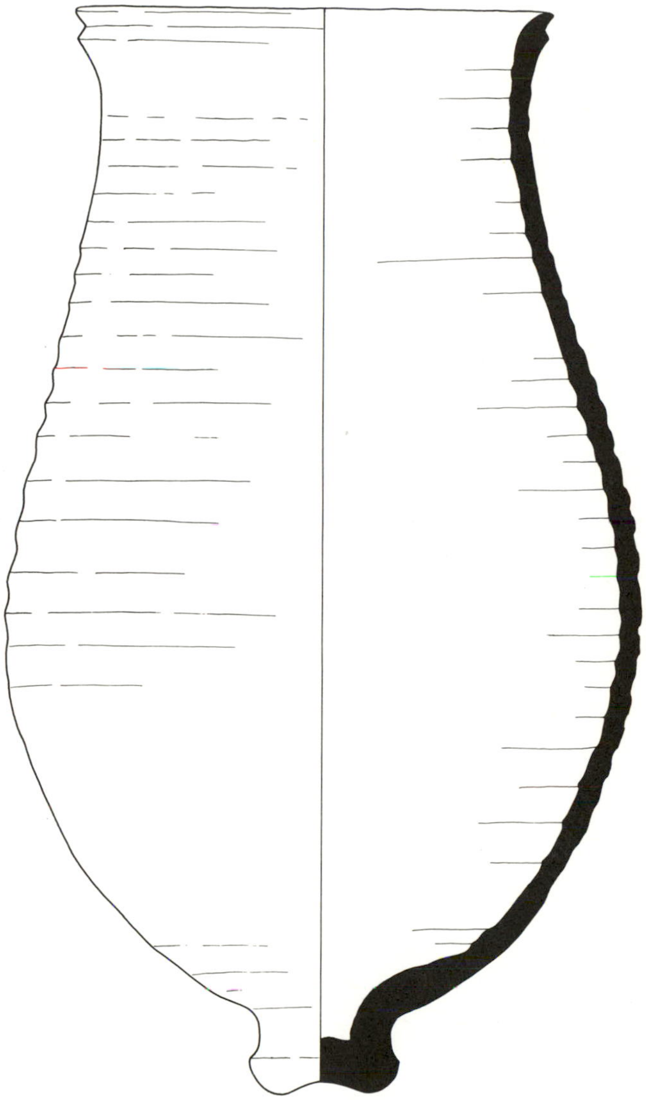

Figure 137. *Qadus*, Q 67—1. Scale 2:5.

Q 67 (*cont.*)
  Objects:
      c. In chamber, scattered at S end:

		Cairo	OIM	Figure/Plate
9.	Coptic period Eg. juglet I—A1c (contents intact)	20156		figs. 22c, 136d
10.	X-Gr. ord. goblet I—B1b (5YR 5/4, 7.5YR 6/4)	20162		figs. 7q, 136c

      d. In fill:

		Cairo	OIM	Figure/Plate
11.	Seeds of grapes?	20194		
12.	Sandals, length ca. 20	20189		
13.	Beads on string	20192		fig. 64o
14.	Bead	20195		

  Sherds: 33192

      A. Coptic period Eg. chaffy utility jug III—, base
      B. X-Gr. ord. bottle-jar; bk. pt., vine in pairs
      C. X-Gr. ord. bottle jar, bk. and wh. band and
           spot-beads or pseudo-vine
      D. X-Gr. storage jar III—C
      E. X-Gr. storage jar III—C
      F. X-Gr. storage jar III—C

Table 40. Register of X-Group Finds in Cemetery Q (*cont.*).

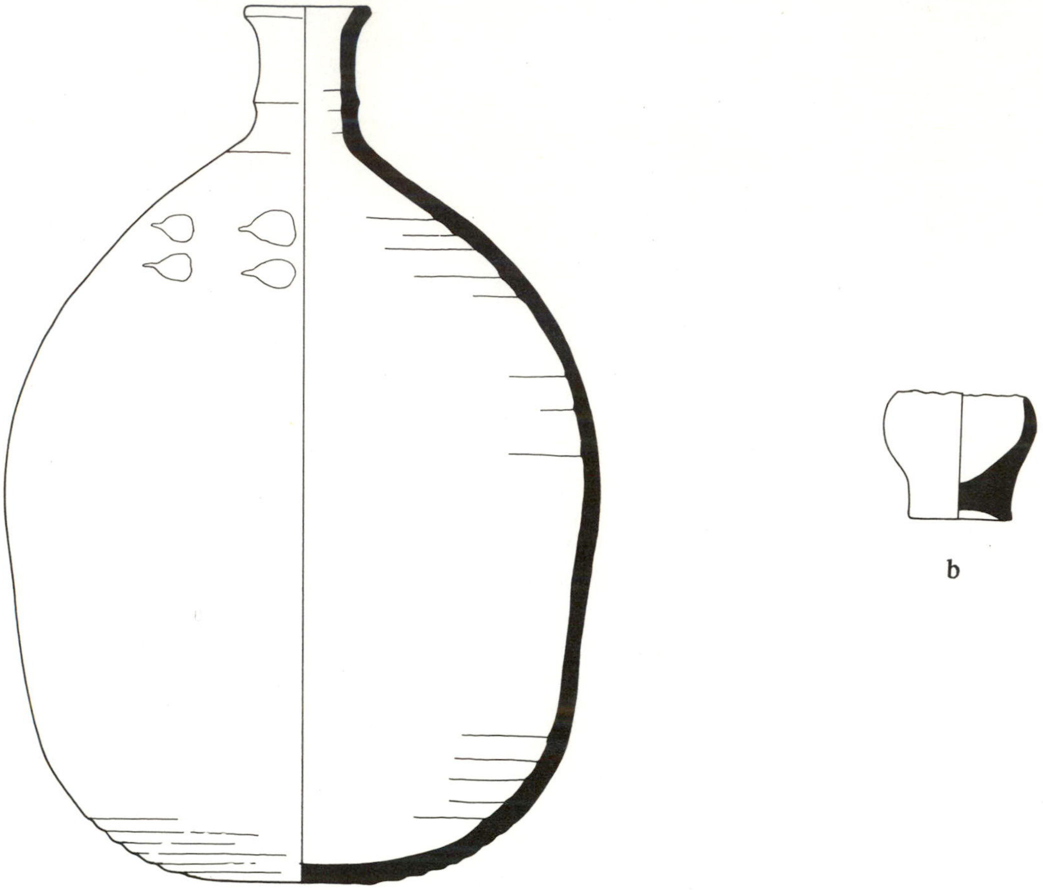

Tomb	Description and Contents	Cairo	OIM	Figure/Plate

a

b

Figure 138. Pottery from Tomb Q 227: (*a*) X-Gr. Ord. Narrow-Necked Bottle-Jar I—D2, No. 4;
(*b*) Min. Cup No. 4 (on Surface 2 m E of Tomb). Scale 2:5.

Q 227

Shaft with chamber on the N side
   Shaft: 2.40 × 0.70–0.85 × 1.35 m
   Chamber: 2.00 × 0.95 × 0.70 m; floor at -1.75 m,
        0.25–0.35 m overlap
   Blocking: stone slabs
Burial: —
Body: Adult female
Objects:

			Cairo	OIM	Figure/Plate
a.	In chamber:				
	1.	Bead bracelet		20387A	
	2.	X-Gr. ord. goblet I—B2ai, height 8.9		20363	
	3.	X-Gr. bowl with incised band below rim, height 12	Q 528		
	4.	X-Gr. ord. narrow-necked bottle-jar I—D2, wh. pt., vine in pairs		20364	figs. 14j, 138a
	5.	X-Gr. ord. bottle jar I—D2, wh. pt., vine in pairs, height 29.3		20365	
b.	In shaft:				
	6.	Bead bracelet (under blocking)		20387B	fig. 63g

Table 40. Register of X-Group Finds in Cemetery Q (*cont.*).

Tomb	Description and Contents	Cairo	OIM	Figure/Plate
Q 227 (*cont.*)				
	Sherds:			
	a. Surface, 2 m to E (S of Q 51):			
	Deposit of fourteen min. cups		20389	fig. 138b (cup 4)
	b. In shaft:		31845	
	A. X-Gr. ord. goblet I—B, large parts of rim			
	B. X-Gr. ord. goblet I—B (small sherds)			
	C. X-Gr. handmade cooking pot			
	D. X-Gr. handmade cooking pot, thick			
	E. Unc. thick red-bn. bowl, much organic material			
	F. Eg. or Coptic period Eg. fine/ord. jar, ring base			
	G. Post-X-Gr. orange with wh. on rim and body			
Q 501				
	Shaft with chamber on the W side			
	Shaft: 2.10–2.85 × 0.70–1.25 × 2.30 m			
	Chamber: 1.95 × 1.15 × 0.65 m; floor flush			
	Blocking: stone slabs			
	Burial: —			
	Body: Juvenile female			
	Objects:			
	a. From corner of shaft, dist.:			
	1. X-Gr. ord. utility storage jar III—A		21589	fig. 139e
	2. X-Gr. ord. goblet I—B1b		21590	fig. 139b
	3. Sandal, length 17.6		21652	
	b. In chamber:			
	4. Beads		21629	
	5. Silver ring		21627	fig. 61g, pl. 76j
	6. Pair of shoes, length 20.5		21651	
	7. Textile remains, CAT 142		21646	
	c. In shaft:			
	8. Sherds (see below)			
	9. "Sole of shoes"			
	Sherds:		31988	
	A. X-Gr. min., lamp, coarse mud, with pinched lip			
	B. Copt. Eg. ord. *amphoriskos* jug I—D1, ridge rim, neck, carinated shoulder, bk. pt., vine in groups of three		31987	fig. 139a
	C. X-Gr. ord. bottle-jar I—B1			
	D. Unc. utility-storage jar			
	E. X-Gr. ord. goblet —B2biv		21618	
Q 502				
	Shaft with chamber on the N side			
	Shaft: 1.95–2.55 × 0.85–1.15 × 2.05			
	Chamber: 1.30 × 0.65 × 0.40 m; floor flush, but sloped			
	Blocking: cb., two ca. headers			
	Burial: —			
	Body: "Infant I"			
	Objects:			
	a. In chamber:			
	1. X-Gr. ord. med.-necked bottle-jar I—B3, (very small)		21592	fig. 139d
	2. Barrel-jar, height 18.3	Q 1828, 89959		

Figure 139. Pottery from Tombs Q 501, Q 502, and Q 503: (*a*) Coptic Period Egyptian Ord. *Amphoriskos*-Jug
I—D1, Q 501—B; (*b*) X-Gr. Ord. Goblet I—B1b, Q 501—2; (*c*) Lamp, Q 502—3; (*d*) X-Gr. Ord.
Medium-Necked Bottle-Jar I—B3, Q 502—1; (*e*) X-Gr. Ord. Utility Storage Jar III—A, Q 501—1;
(*f*) X-Gr. Ord. Cup I—D5a, Q 503—4; (*g*) *Qadus*-Related Jar B, Q 503—2;
(*h*) X-Gr. Ord. Bowl I—B1, Q 503—1. Scale 2:5.

Table 40. Register of X-Group Finds in Cemetery Q (*cont.*).

Tomb	Description and Contents	Cairo	OIM	Figure/Plate
Q 502 (*cont.*)				
	Objects (*cont.*):			
	b. In shaft:			
	3. Lamp		21591	fig. 139c
	4. Goat remains (?)		Disc.	
	Sherds, from shaft:			
Q 503				
	Shaft with chamber on the N side			
	Shaft: 1.60–2.05 × 0.70–0.95 × 1.80 m			
	Chamber: ca. 1.45 × 1.05 × 0.55 m; floor at -2.15 m, overlap ca. 0.40 m			
	Blocking: cb., one course stretcher, two rowlock? 0.36 × 0.18 × 0.08–0.09 m			
	Burial: —			
	Body: "Infant I"			
	Objects, from shaft:			
	1. X-Gr. ord. bowl I—B1, exterior darkened (2.5YR 3/4, 2.5YR 2.5/2, 10YR 6/3)		21594	fig. 139h
	2. *Qadus*-related jar B		21593	fig. 139g
	3. Textile wrapping remains, CAT 143		21665	
	4. X-Gr. ord. cup I—D5a, with pinched mouth, (uncoated; 5YR 5/4, 5YR 5/3)		21684	fig. 139f
	5. Beads		21625	
Q 504				
	Shaft with chamber on the N side			
	Shaft: 1.40–1.85 × 0.75–1.00 × 1.50 m			
	Chamber: 1.60 × 0.70 × 0.45 m; floor at -1.75 m, overlap ca. 0.35 m			
	Burial: W/B/ext./dist.			
	Body: "Infant II"			
	Objects (all displaced):			
	1. X-Gr. ord. goblet I—A1ai, wh. pt. vert. line groups (2.5YR 4/6, 5YR 5/4, 5YR 8/3), height 10		21617	
	2. X-Gr. handmade jar—A1, red coat, wh. pt. vert. zones, spots		21643	figs. 20a, 140b
	3. Beads		21628	
	4. X-Gr. ord. bottle-jar (2.5YR 4/4, 2.5YR 5/4), height 13		21616	
Q 505				
	Shaft with chamber on the W side			
	Shaft: 1.80–2.10 × 0.80–1.00 × 1.55 m			
	Step (for blocking): 1.90 × ca. 0.50 m; floor at -1.85 m			
	Chamber: 1.80 × 0.60 × 0.60; floor at -2.05 m			
	Blocking: cb. in irreg. stack, 0.32? × 0.16 × 0.08 m			
	Burial: —			
	Body: Senile male			
	Objects (probably all displaced):			
	a. In chamber:			
	1. X-Gr. ord. storage jar III—B, 29.40 × 25.00		22293	
	2. Basket (leaning on jar, plunderer's tool)		Disc.	
	b. In shaft:			
	3. Coptic period Eg. *amphoriskos* jug II—C, wh. coat		21620	fig. 140a

Table 40. Register of X-Group Finds in Cemetery Q (*cont.*).

Tomb	Description and Contents	Cairo	OIM	Figure/Plate
Q 505 (*cont.*)				
	Objects (probably all displaced) (*cont.*):			
	b. In shaft (*cont.*):			
	4. Leather remains		21742	
	a. Quiver remains			fig. 51, pl. 57a
	b. Other leather			
	5. Coptic period Eg. fine/ord. juglet I—A1a, height 13		21683	

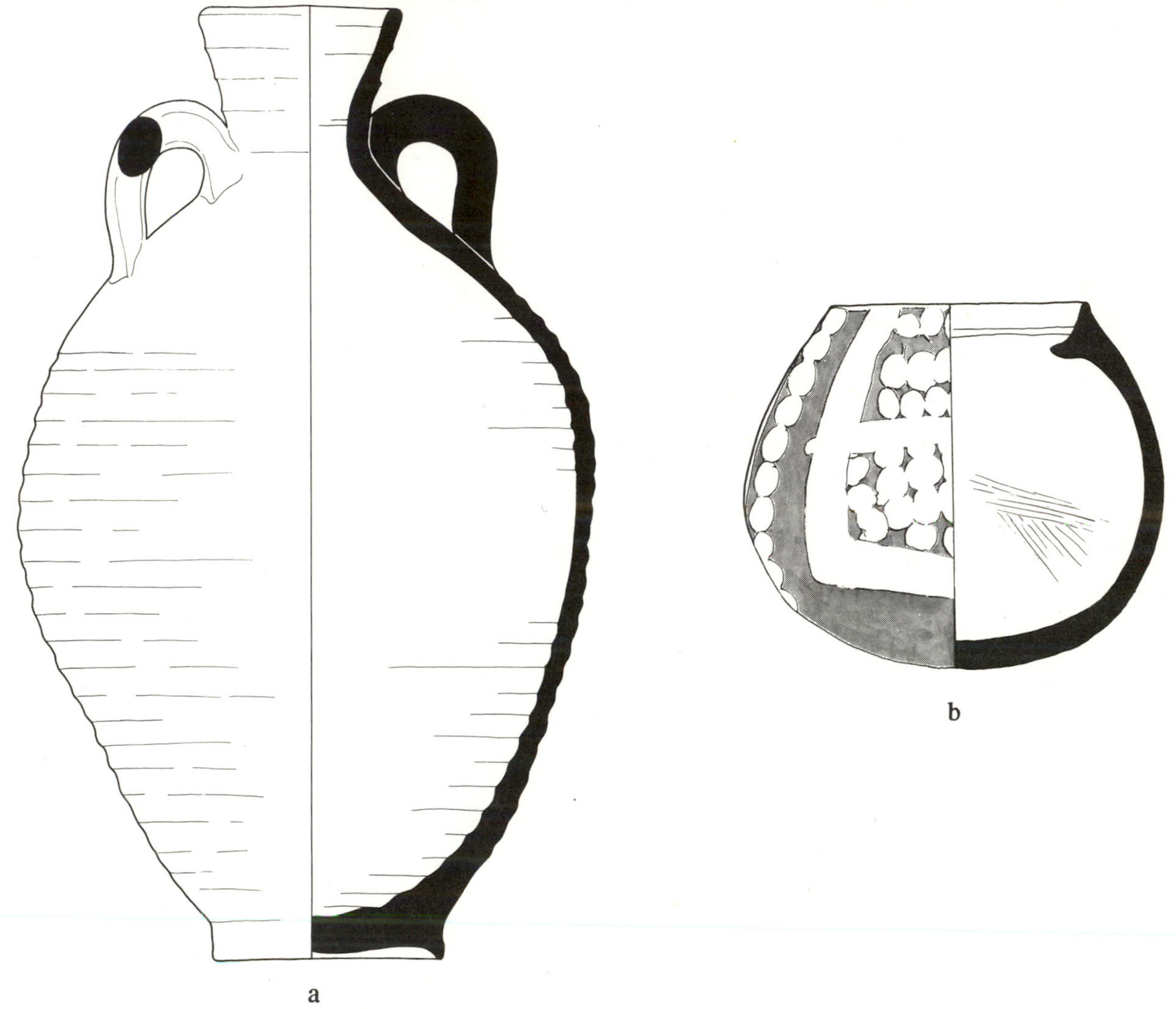

a

b

Figure 140. Pottery from Tombs Q 504 and Q 505: (*a*) Coptic Period Egyptian *Amphoriskos*-Jug II—C, Q 505—3; (*b*) X-Gr. Handmade Jar—A1, Q 504—2. Scale 2:5.

Q*D*

Q 82
    Shaft with chamber on the W side
        Shaft: 2.25–2.45 × 1.00–1.20 × 1.30 m
        Chamber: 2.25 × 1.15–1.30 × 0.65 m; floor at -1.90 m
        Blocking: hor. stone slabs
    Burial: —
    Body: Mature
    Objects:

	1. Coptic period Eg. handleless juglet I—E1 (5YR 3/1, 5YR 4/3, 5YR 5/3, 5YR 5/2)		20147	figs. 22o, 141a

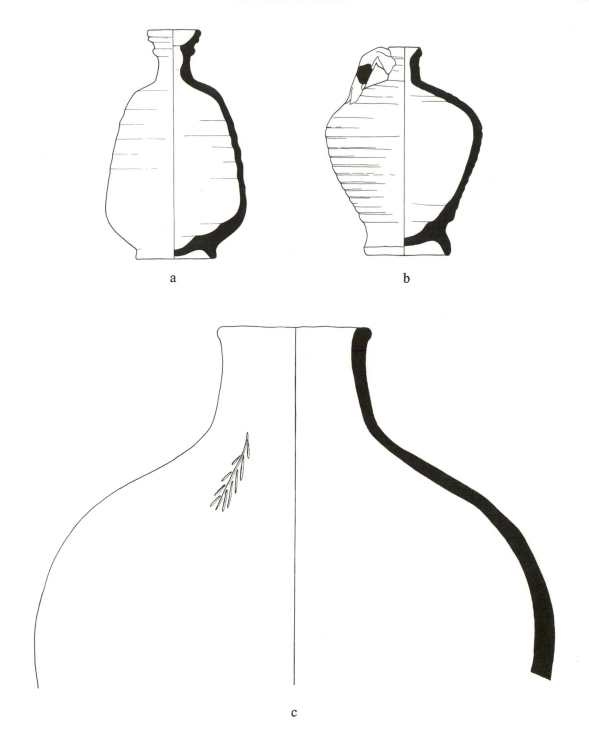

Figure 141. Pottery from Tombs Q 82 and Q 83: (*a*) Coptic Period Egyptian Handleless Jug I—E1,
Q 82—1; (*b*) Coptic Period Egyptian Juglet I—A2b, Q 82—2; (*c*) X-Gr.
Handmade Incised Jar Sherd, Q 83—2. Scale 2:5.

Table 40. Register of X-Group Finds in Cemetery Q (*cont.*).

Tomb	Description and Contents	Cairo	OIM	Figure/Plate
Q 82 (*cont.*)				
	Objects (*cont.*):			
	2. Coptic period Eg. juglet I—A2b (5YR 5/4, 5YR 5/3, 2.5YR 5/6, 2.5YR 4/2)		20148	figs. 22e, 141b, pl. 46b
	3. X-Gr. ord. goblet I—B1b (5YR 6/4, 5YR 7/2, 5YR 5/4, 5YR 6/6), height 8.2		20179	
	4. X-Gr. ord. goblet I—B2aii, height 9.2		20180	
	5. Beads		20205	fig. 64h
	6. Bead necklace		20168	
	7. Leather container fragment		20169	fig. 38b
	8. Twisted straw		20170	
	9. Textile remains, CAT 76 (renumbered, no. 11 in cat.)		20167	
	Sherds:		33193	
	A. X-Gr. ord. bowl I—, used as cooking pot			
	B. X-Gr. ord. jar I—			
	C. X-Gr. ord. bowl I—, wh. pt. rim band			
	D. Post-X-Gr.? red ord., wh. coat and whiter band			
	E. Mer. Km. wm. jar; bk. pt. "shark's tooth"			
	F. Unc. amphora, ribbed and bitumen			
	G. Neolithic, brown with earth temper, dotted line impression			
Q 83				
	Shaft with chamber on the W side			
	Shaft: 2.10–2.65 × 0.55–0.85 × 2.85 m			
	Step: 0.30–0.55 m at -1.35 m			
	Chamber: 2.10 × 1.00–1.10 × 0.85 m; floor flush			
	Blocking: cb.			
	Burial: —			
	Body: Mature			
	Objects:			
	1. Leather fragments		Disc.	
	2. X-Gr. handmade incised jar		33194	fig. 141c
	Sherd		33195	
Q 84				fig. 142a–b
	Shaft with broad step and chamber on the W side			
	Shaft: 1.95 × 0.80–0.95 × 2.50 m			
	Step: 0.95–1.60 × 0.60–0.90 × 0.95 m			
	Chamber: 2.45 × 0.85 × 0.70 m (inside blocking); floor at -3.10 m			
	Blocking: cb. in chamber and shaft overlap, laid over shaft floor, alt. flat and rowlock, 29 × 17 × 11 cm			
	Burial: —			
	Body: Adult female			
	Objects:			
	1. Rings (three)		20210	fig. 142c–e, pl. 65c
	2. Arrowheads (two; b is barbed)		20210	fig. 142f, pl. 65c
	3. Textile wrapping remains		Disc.	
	4. Beads		20209	
	5. Quiver remains		Disc.	
	6. Coptic period Eg. utility *amphoriskos* II—C, wh. coat		20213	fig. 142g

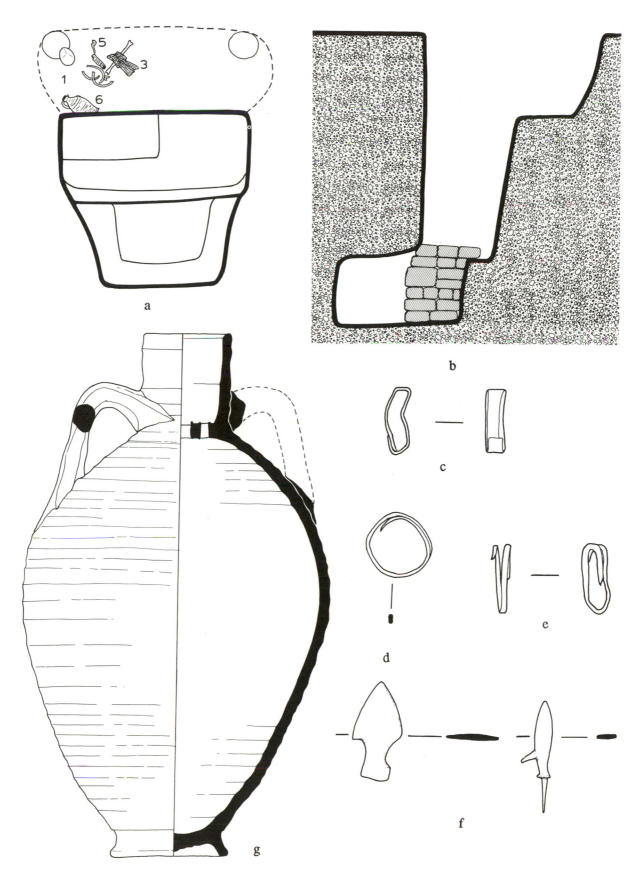

Figure 142. Plan, Section, *Amphoriskos*, and Objects from Tomb Q 84: (*a*) Plan, (*b*) Section, (*c*) Ring, No. 1c; (*d*) Ring, No. 1b; (*e*) Ring, No. 1a; (*f*) Arrowheads, nos. 2a, b; (*g*) Coptic Period Egyptian Utility *Amphoriskos* II—C, No. 6. Scales: (*a, b*) 1:40?; (*c–f*) 1:1; (*g*) 2:5.

Table 40. Register of X-Group Finds in Cemetery Q (*cont.*).

Tomb	Description and Contents	Cairo	OIM	Figure/Plate
Q 107				
	Shaft with chamber on the W side			
	Shaft: 1.50–2.15 × 0.70–1.00 × 1.95 m			
	Chamber: 1.50 × 0.90 × 0.50 m; overlap ca. 0.45 m, floor at -2.05 m			
	Blocking: cb., 0.10–0.11 × 0.17 × 0.36 m			
	Burial: —			
	Body: Juvenile-adult			
	Objects:			
	1. Quiver fragments (from shaft)		20253	fig. 44a–b
	2. X-Gr. ord. goblet I—B1aii (5YR 5/4, 5YR 4/4, 5YR 5/3), 9.0 × 11.2		20236	
	3. X-Gr. ord. goblet I—B1aii, 9.0 × 10.4		20237	
	4. Date pits		Disc.	
	5. Jewelry	Q 415, 89903		
	a. Three bone pendants			
	b. Ag. earring			
	c. Black faience bead			
	6. X-Gr. ord. goblet I—B1c, 9.5 × 10.5		20238	
Q 117				
	Shaft with chamber on the W side			
	Shaft: 1.80–2.00 × 0.75–0.90 × 1.70 m			
	Chamber: 2.10 × ca. 0.90 × 0.55 m; overlap 0.25 m, floor at -1.95 m			
	Blocking: cb., laid horizontally			
	Burial: —			
	Body: Mature female			
	Objects:			
	1. X-Gr. med.-necked jar I—B3b, red coat, bk. and wh. pt., vine in groups of three		20239	fig. 143a
	2. X-Gr. storage jar III—B, red coat, bk. and wh. pt., vine in groups of three, height 29.5		20240	
	3. X-Gr. ord. goblet I—B2bi, height 8.9		20244	
	4. Pot contents		20248	
	5. Leather fragments		Disc.	
	Sherds:		33196	
Q 119				
	Shaft with chamber on the W side			
	Shaft: 2.05–2.10 × 0.75–0.95 × 1.65 m			
	Chamber: 2.05 × 0.80–0.90 × 0.45 m; floor at -2.00 m			
	Blocking: cb., laid alt. header, stretcher, 0.36 × 0.17 × 0.08 m			
	Burial: —			
	Body: Mature male			
	Objects:			
	1. X-Gr. ord. goblet I—B1b		20241	fig. 143b
	2. X-Gr. ord. bottle-jar I—B1		20254	fig. 143c
	3. Textile remains, CAT 77-79		20251	
	4. Sandals		20252A	pl. 79e
	5. Quiver fragments		20252B	fig. 44c

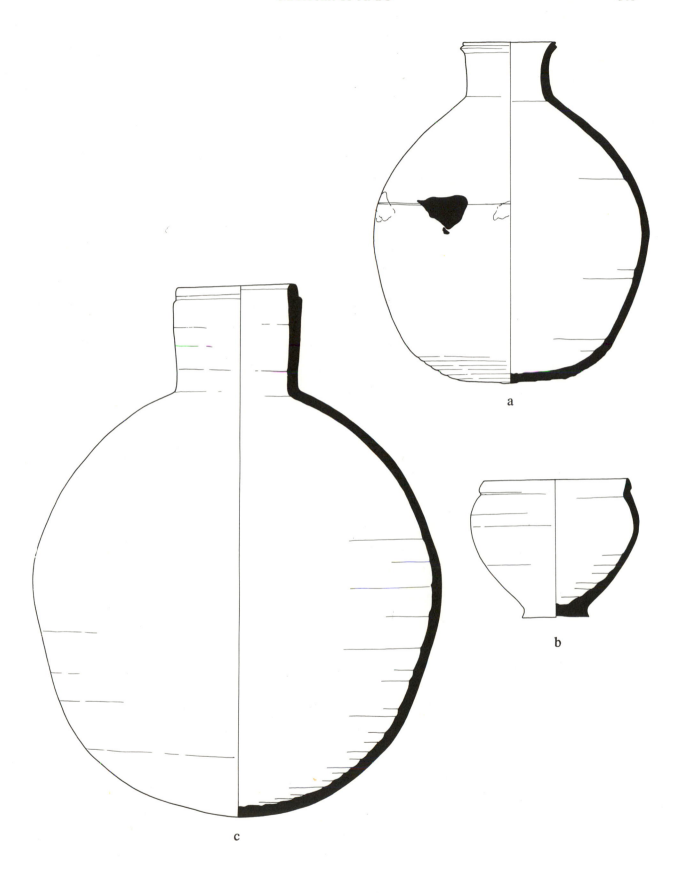

Figure 143. Pottery from Tombs Q 117 and Q 119: (*a*) X-Gr. Ord. Medium-Necked Jar I—B3b, Q 117—1;
(*b*) X-Gr. Ord. Goblet I—B1b, Q 119—1; (*c*) X-Gr. Ord. Bottle-Jar I—B1, Q 119—2. Scale 2:5.

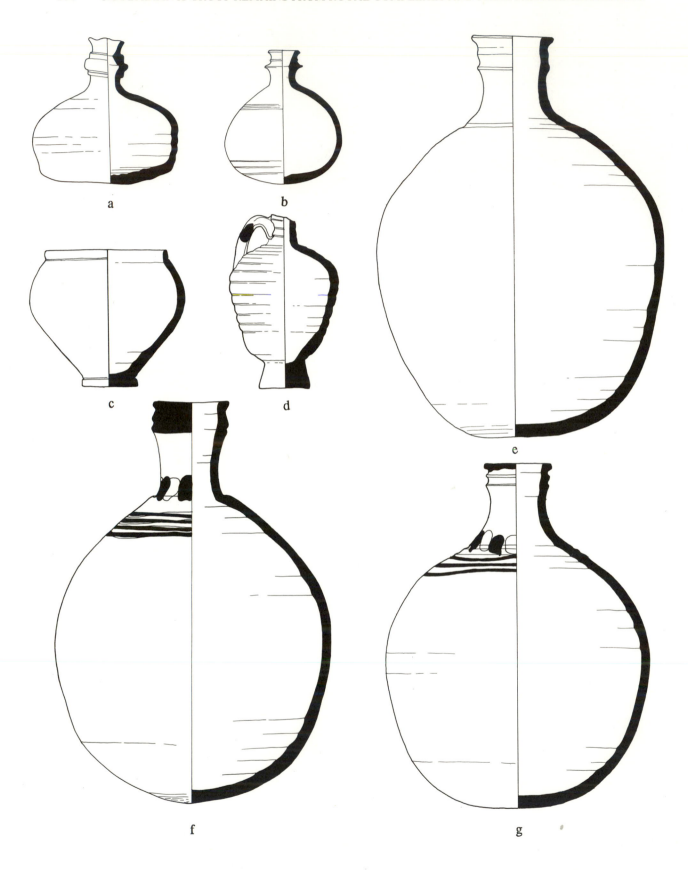

Figure 144. Pottery from Tomb Q 143: (*a*) Coptic Period Egyptian Handleless Juglet, No. 6; (*b*) X-Gr. Ord. Min. Bottle-Jar B1, No. 7; (*c*) X-Gr. Ord. Goblet I—B2ai, No. 4; (*d*) Coptic Period Egyptian Juglet I—C1, No. 5; (*e*) X-Gr. Ord. Bottle-Jar I—D3, No. 10; (*f*) X-Gr. Ord. Bottle-Jar I—D3, No. 11; (*g*) X-Gr. Ord. Bottle-Jar I—E3, No. 9. Scale 2:5.

Table 40. Register of X-Group Finds in Cemetery Q (*cont.*).

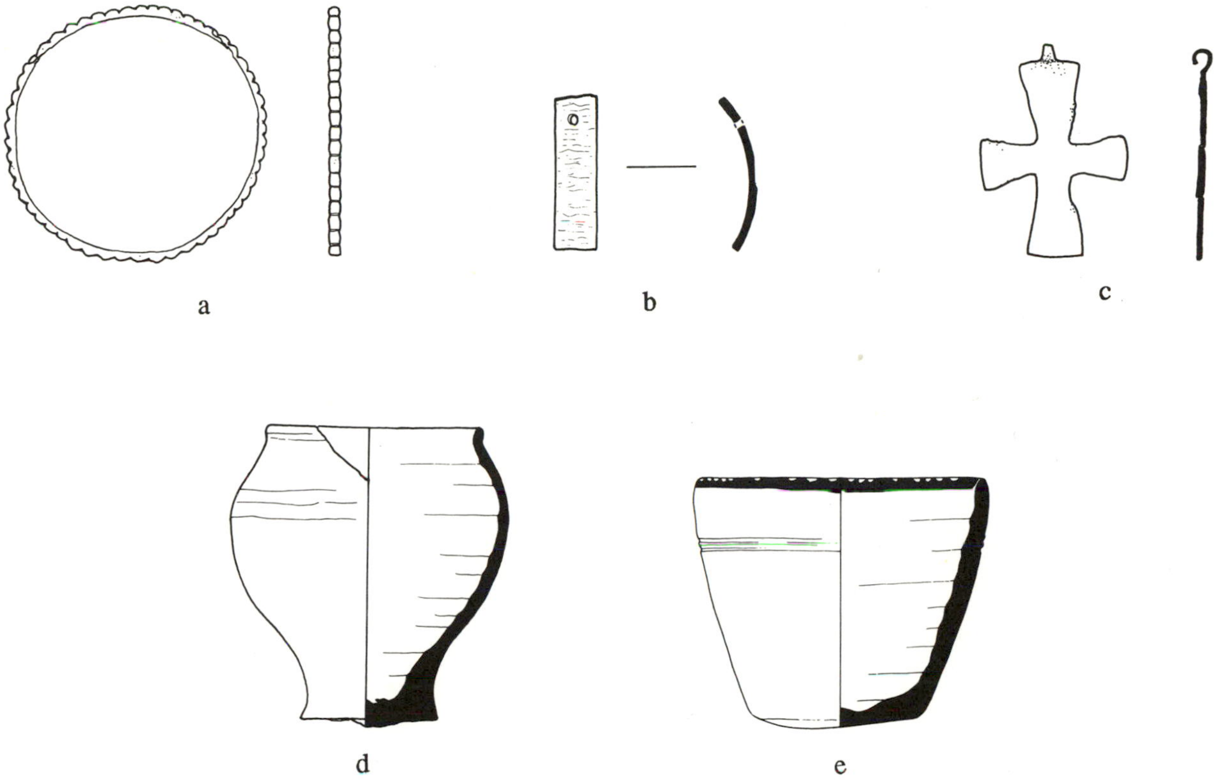

Tomb	Description and Contents	Cairo	OIM	Figure/Plate

Figure 145. Pottery and Jewelry from Tombs Q 143 and Q 144: (*a*) Iron Bracelet, Q 143—2; (*b*) Ivory Bracelet Fragment, Q 143—12; (*c*) Copper Cross Pendant, Q 143—13; (*d*) X-Gr. Ord. Goblet I—B2biii, Q 144—2; (*e*) X-Gr. Fine Cup II—D1b, Q 144—3. Scales: (*a*, *b*) 1:2; (*c*) 1:1; (*d*, *e*) 2:5.

Q 143

Shaft with chamber on W, ramp, ledges, vault,
and niche at the E end
Shaft: 2.30 (and ramp) × 0.90–1.20 (undercut)
× 0.90–1.15 m
Ramp: 1.20 × 1.00 × 0.65 m
Ledges: at -0.65 m; one cb. wide
Niche: 0.50 m deep
Chamber: Three cb.?, leaned E
Blocking: cb. on W
Burials:
    A.   W/B/ext./pelvis, on debris in vault
    B.   —
Bodies:
    A.   Mature
    B.   Mature
Objects, in layer of debris on floor with B:

		Cairo	Figure/Plate
1.	Beads (some strung)	20336	figs. 63d, 64e, 65m
2.	Iron bracelet	20334	fig. 145a
3.	X-Gr. ord. goblet I—B2ai, 8.15 × 9.4	20319	
4.	X-Gr. ord. goblet I—B2ai	20320	fig. 144c
5.	Coptic period Eg. juglet I—C1	20321	figs. 22k, 144d

Table 40. Register of X-Group Finds in Cemetery Q (*cont.*).

Tomb	Description and Contents	Cairo	OIM	Figure/Plate
Q 143 (*cont.*)				
	Objects, in layer of debris on floor with B (*cont.*):			
	6. Coptic period Eg. handleless juglet, miniature		20322	figs. 23b, 144a
	7. X-Gr. ord. miniature bottle-jar (handleless juglet)—B1		20323	figs. 15c, 144b, pl. 46d
	8. X-Gr. ord. goblet I—B2ai, height 7.5		20328	
	9. X-Gr. ord. bottle-jar I—E3, bk. and wh. pt.		20337	fig. 144g, pl. 43a
	10. X-Gr. ord. bottle-jar I—D3		20338	fig. 144e
	11. X-Gr. ord. bottle-jar I—D3, bk. and wh. pt. band at rim, beads at neck, bk. framed wh. bands at shoulder		20339	fig. 144f
	12. Ivory bracelet fragment		20334	fig. 145b
	13. Copper cross pendant		20335	fig. 145c
	14. Date pits		Disc.	
	Note that the tomb was reused in post-X-Gr. times. Nos. 1, 2, and 13 belong to the Christian burial.			
Q 144				pl. 36a
	Shaft with ledges and vault; bed burial			
	Shaft: 3.00 × 1.45 × 1.30–ca. 1.55 m			
	Ledges: at ca. 0.25 m from floor			
	Vault: on three courses. cb., vault 1.00 m above spring, 1.75 m to E end of shaft and 0.45 m length to base			
	Blocking: cb. laid rowlock; 0.37–0.38 × 0.19–0.20 × 0.08 m			
	Burial: —			
	Body: Mature			
	Objects:			
	1. Remains of bed		—	
	2. X-Gr. ord. goblet I—B2biii		20332	fig. 145d
	3. X-Gr. fine cup II—D1b (5YR 7/3, 5YR 7/4, 5YR 3/3)		20333	figs. 9b, 145e
Q 174, Meroitic tomb with intrusive burial				
	Structure: see OINE VIII			
	Burials:			
	A. see OINE VIII			
	B. "stuffed into B[urial] C[hamber] at W end, upper trunk as A" (W/B/—/—)			
	Bodies:			
	A. See OINE VIII			
	B. "Infant I" (female !)			
	Objects:			
	1–2. see OINE VIII			
	3. Beads			
	a. Pendant bead		20523B	fig. 63e
	b. Pierced spiral shell, length 6.2		20523A	fig. 65j
	4. Textile, CAT 163 (no. changed from 2)		20525	
Q 282				
	Stepped shaft with chamber on the W side			
	Shaft: 1.60–1.70 × 0.45–0.60/1.30 (incl. steps) × 2.35 m			
	Step 1: 1.20 × 0.30 at -1.10 m			
	Step 2: 1.20 × 0.30 at -1.45 m			
	Chamber: 1.85 × 1.15 × 0.60 m; floor at -2.75 m, ca. 0.20 m overlap			
	Blocking: cb., in chamber and lower shaft			
	Burial: —			
	Body: Mature			
	Objects: —			

Table 40. Register of X-Group Finds in Cemetery Q (*cont.*).

Tomb	Description and Contents	Cairo	OIM	Figure/Plate

QE

Q 133   fig. 146

    Broad-stepped shaft with chamber on the W side

        Shaft: 1.50–1.75 × ca. 2.85 × 2.05 m

        Step 1: 0.80 × 0.60 m at -0.60 m (max.)

        Step 2: 0.90 × 0.60 m at -1.30/-1.50 m (max.)

        Step 3: 1.05 × ca. 0.35 m at -2.05 m (flat)

        Chamber: 1.70 × 0.85 × 0.75 m; floor at -2.55 m,
                overlap ca. 0.30 m

        Blocking: mass of cb. laid in shaft and chamber
                opening to level of top of step 2 at -1.30

Burial: —

Body: Mature

Objects:

			OIM	
1.	Beads		20401	
2.	Leather fragments, decayed		20301	
3.	Textile remains (CAT X-Gr.)		20301	Disc.
4.	Arrowhead, 2.8 × 0.9		20362	

Sherds   33197

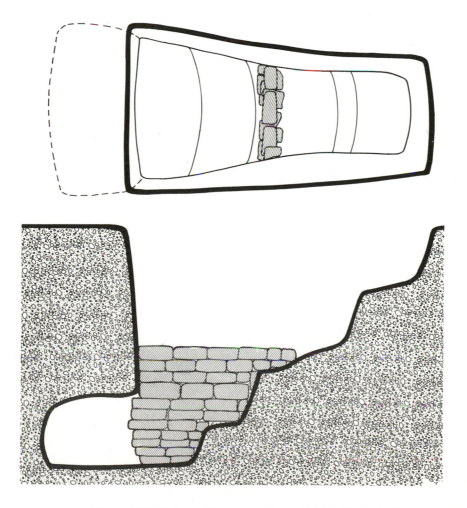

Figure 146. Plan and Section of Tomb Q 133. Scale 1:40.

Table 40. Register of X-Group Finds in Cemetery Q (*cont.*).

Tomb	Description and Contents	Cairo	OIM	Figure/Plate
Q 134				
	Broad-stepped shaft with chamber on the W side			
	Shaft: 1.30–2.05 × 2.30 (max.) × 1.50 m			
	Step 1: 1.00 × 0.60 m at 0.30 m at N side of shaft			
	Step 2: 1.30 × 0.35 m at -1.50 m (broad step downward)			
	Chamber: 1.90 × 0.95 × 0.70 m; floor at -2.40 m			
	Antechamber opening: 1.30 × 0.90 m			
	Blocking: mass of cb. filling shaft to -1.30 m			
	Burial: S/R/—/—, on bed			
	Body: Mature male?			
	Objects:			
	a. At feet of burial:			
	1. X-Gr. storage jar III—C, height 36.4		20287	
	b. Uncertain location:			
	2. Coptic period Eg. *monophora* IV—C (2.5YR 6/6, much mica)		20288	figs. 24b, 147b
	3. Arrowheads, average length 3.0		20346	
	4. Copper rings (five), average diam. 1.8		20347	
	5. Iron fragments, largest 2.2 × 2.1		20353	
	6. Coptic period Eg. utility *amphoriskos* II—D1, wh. coat (2.5YR 5/6, 10YR 8/6)		20289	fig. 147d
	7. X-Gr. ord. cup I—Fla (2.5YR 5/6, 2.5YR 4/8)		20292	figs. 9n, 147f
	8. X-Gr. ord. goblet I—A1aii *beta* (2.5YR 5/6, 2.5YR 6/4)		20294	fig. 147a
	9. Contents of jars 1 and 2		20341	
	10. Ivory bracelet, 1.2 × 0.2		20350	
	11. Coptic period Eg. juglet I—C2, red coat, (2.5YR 5/6, 2.5YR 4/6, 5YR 7/4, 5YR 2.5/1)		20369	fig. 147e
	12. Beads and shell fragment		20343	figs. 62q, 63l–n, 64n
	13. Copper wire ring		—	
	14. Copper spoon		20348	fig. 147c, pl. 80b
	15. Textile remains, CAT 82-84		20344	
	16. Leather fragments (see also nos. 22a, b)		20345 20354	
	17. Animal horn, 10.0 × 4.5		20351	
	18. Pendant		20352	fig. 65g
	c. With burial:			
	19. Bed remains, rectangular posts, unrecoverable			
	20. Shroud remains ("possibly bag-like with drawstring about head? plus inner finer lining, full length. Dk. colors not discernable"), unrecoverable			
	21. Shoes ("ankle high shoes with leather strings and cloth lining"), unrecoverable			
	22. Quivers:		20354	pl. 56a
	a. with streamers			fig. 45a
	b. base			fig. 45b
	Sherds:		33198	
	A. X-Gr. *qadus* (gray-pk.)			
	B. X-Gr. ord. bottle-jar I—A2, simple rib at base of neck; bk. and wh., vine in pairs			

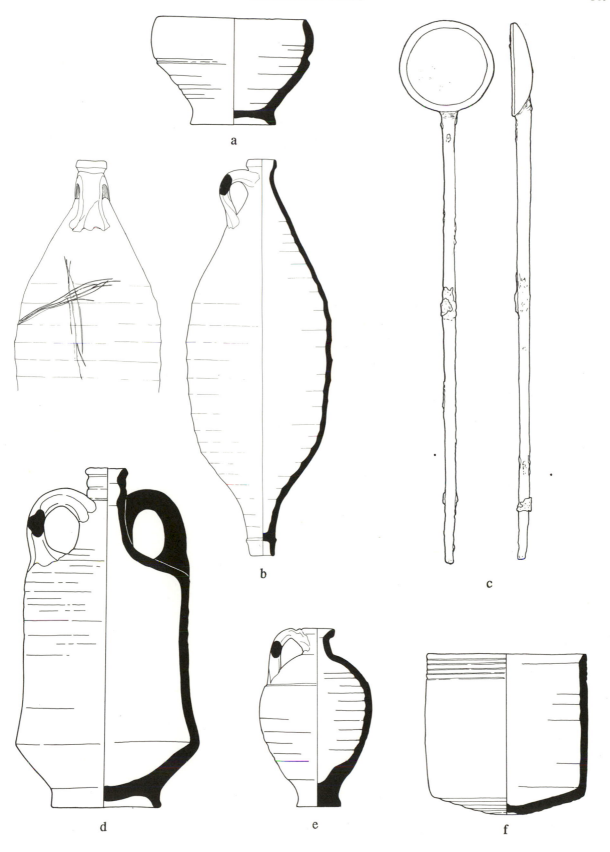

Figure 147. Pottery and Copper Spoon from Tomb Q 134: (*a*) X-Gr. Ord. Goblet I—A1aii *beta*, No. 8; (*b*) Coptic Period Egyptian *Monophora* IV—C, No. 2; (*c*) Copper Spoon, No. 14; (*d*) Coptic Period Egyptian Utility *Amphoriskos* II—D1, No. 6; (*e*) Coptic Period Egyptian Juglet I—C2, No. 11; (*f*) X-Gr. Ord. Cup I—F1a, No. 7. Scales: (*a, d–f*) 2:5; (*b*) 1:2, (*c*) 1:1.

Table 40. Register of X-Group Finds in Cemetery Q (*cont.*).

Tomb	Description and Contents	Cairo	OIM	Figure/Plate
Q 135				
	Broad-stepped shaft with chamber on the W side			
	Shaft: 1.40–1.70 × 2.10 (max.) × 2.80 m			
	Step 1: 1.10 × 0.70 × 0.70 m; even curve to drop to step 2			
	Step 2: 1.20 × 0.50 m; bottom at -1.65 m, hor.			
	Chamber: 2.20 × 1.10 × 0.80 m; floor at -2.80 m, flush			
	Blocking: cb., shaft filled to -1.30 m			
	Burial: —			
	Body: Mature			
	Objects:			
	a. From chamber:			
	1. Coptic period Eg. utility *amphoriskos* II—C, pk.	20295		fig. 148b
	wh. coat (2.5YR 6/4, 7.5YR 7/4-8/4)			
	b. Unc. loc:			
	2. Lamp, 3.7 × 7.4 × 9.9		20298	
	3. Fragment of *ba* statue, 33.0 × 14.3 × 20.0		20391	
	4. Textile remains, length 10.5		20357	
	5. Beads		20355	
	6. Iron arrowheads, average length 3.0		20356	
	7. Sandals, length 18.8		20358	
	Sherd:			
	A. Post-X-Gr. fine white juglet, interior discolored		32089	
	as though sherd used for lamp, ring base			
Q 136				
	Shaft in two stages and chamber on the W side			
	Shaft:			
	Outer: 1.80 × 1.40 × 0.40 m			
	Inner: to W, 1.00 × 0.85 × 1.86 m (from surface)			
	Chamber: 1.60 × ? × 0.50 m; floor flush			
	Blocking: cb., remains of headers in chamber and			
	on shaft floor			
	Burial: —			
	Body: Adult male			
	Objects in chamber:			
	1. Textile fragments, CAT 85–89		20326	
	2. Quiver fragments		20327	
	3. Leather bag fragments		20327	
	4. Coptic period Eg. ord. pitcher-jug I—B		20372	figs. 22j, 148a
	5. Beads		20359	figs. 63j, 64g, i
	6. Bone			
	a–b. Worked horn (two fragments)		20360	fig. 148c–d, pl. 83e
	Sherds:		32088	
	A. Unc. ord. jar, red coat, bk. pt. two bands			
	B. Unc. ord. jar			
	C. Post-X-Gr. beaker, ribbed			
	D. Post-X-Gr. ord. jar, angled bk. pt. band with palm branch			
Q 137				
	Shaft with chamber on the W side			
	Shaft: no dim.			
	Chamber: no dim.			
	Blocking: cb. headers			

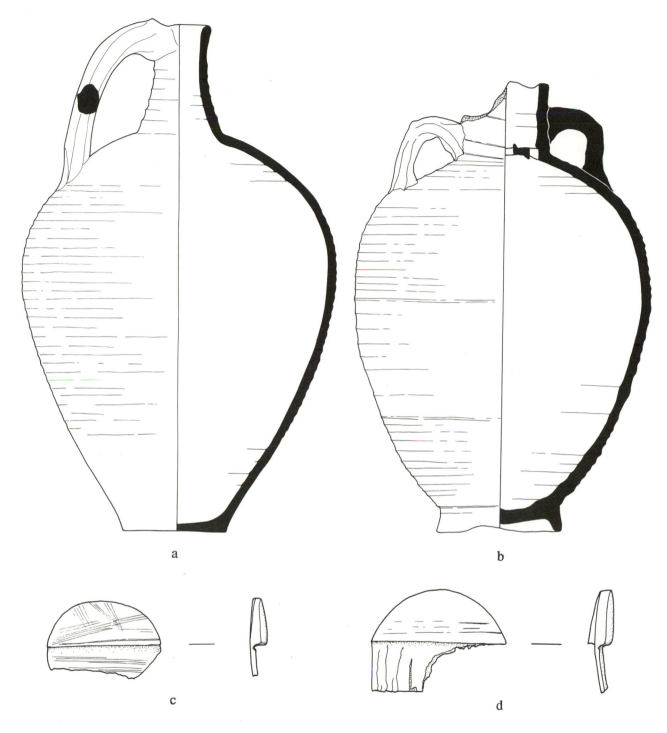

Figure 148. Pottery and Objects from Tombs Q 135 and Q 136: (*a*) Coptic Period Egyptian Ord. Pitcher-Jug I—B, Q 136—4; (*b*) Coptic Period Egyptian Utility *Amphoriskos* II—C, Q 135—1; (*c*) Worked Horn Fragment, Q 136—6b; (*d*) Worked Horn Fragment, Q 136—6a. Scales: (*a*, *b*) 2:5; (*c*, *d*) 1:1.

Table 40. Register of X-Group Finds in Cemetery Q (*cont.*).

Tomb	Description and Contents	Cairo	OIM	Figure/Plate
Q 137 (*cont.*)				
	Burial: —			
	Body: Adult male			
	Objects:			
1.	Ivory lion's head	Q 444, 89904		fig. 149c
2.	Textile remains, CAT 90		20285	
3.	X-Gr. storage jar III—, with four lug handles at neck		20274	fig. 149a, pl. 47a
4.	Beads		20282	
5.	Stud		20286	fig. 149d
6.	Arrowhead, longest 3.0		20284	
7.	Mer. fine cup I—, red rim band with bk. lines (5YR 6/4, 2.5YR 5/6, 2.5YR 2.5/4)		20368	fig. 149b
8.	Seeds		20283	
9.	Animal bone (from shaft)			
10.	Contents of no. 3		20281	
	Sherds:		32087	
A.	X-Gr. *qadus*, knob and bottom			
B.	X-Gr. ord., red coat, sharp, narrow ridges			

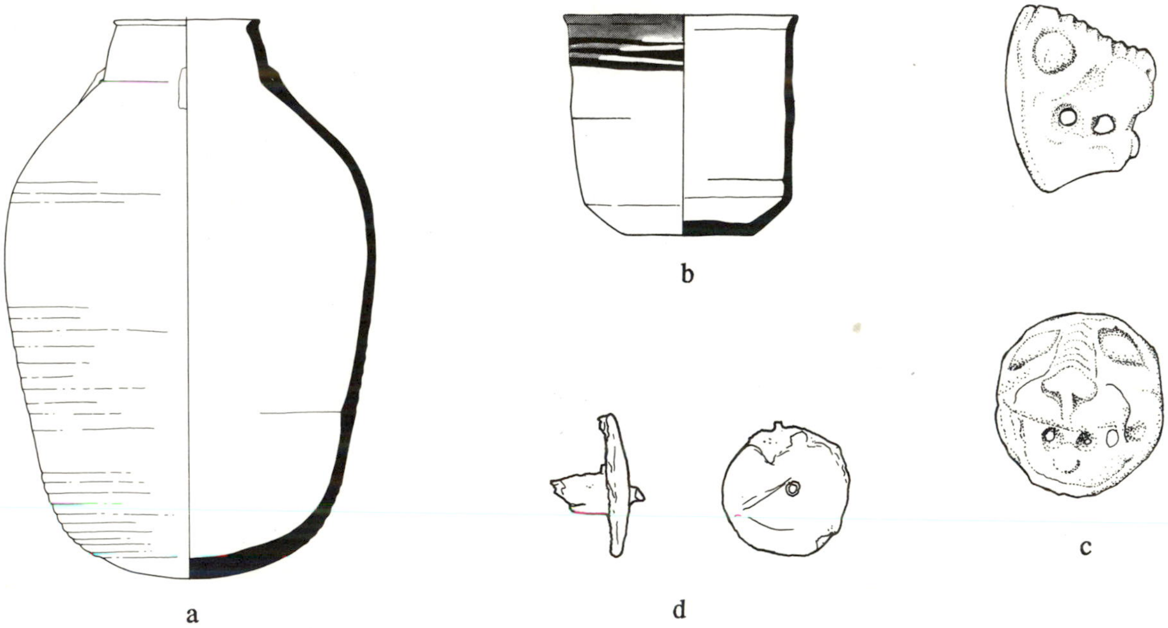

Figure 149. Pottery and Objects from Tomb Q 137: (*a*) X-Gr. Storage Jar III—, No. 3; (*b*) Mer. Fine Cup I—, No. 7; (*c*) Ivory Lion's Head, No. 1; (*d*) Stud, No. 5. Scales: (*a*) 1:5; (*b*) 2:5; (*c, d*) 1:1.

Q 141

Shaft with ledges and vault
Shaft: N-S, 1.35–1.65 × 0.50–0.75 × 1.20 m,
undercut at floor
Ledges: at -0.60 m, width of cb., cut from sides
Vault: Three cb., 0.33–0.35 × 0.17–0.18 × 0.33–0.35 m
(some sandy without *tibn*, some soft)
Burial: S/L/thighs 90 degrees, folded/chest
Body: Adult male

Table 40. Register of X-Group Finds in Cemetery Q (*cont.*).

Tomb	Description and Contents	Cairo	OIM	Figure/Plate
Q 141 (*cont.*)				
	Objects:			
	a. From shaft:			
	1. Sherds X-Gr. ord. storage jar I—B			fig. 150a
	b. With burial:			
	2. Beads, some on 3 (also 5)		20304	
	3. Textile wrapping remains, CAT 91–93		20305	
	4. X-Gr. storage jar III—C, height 26		20296	
	5. Beads (around neck)		20304	
	6. Two rings (on L hand)		20303	pl. 77g
	7. Gut string, average 9.0 × 0.3		20340	
	Sherds:			
	A. X-Gr. ord. goblet I—B, rim		31806	
	B. Post-X-Gr. worn pk.		31807	
	C. Unc. chaffy red-brown jar		31808	
Q 145				
	Shaft with chamber on the W side			
	Shaft: ca. 2.00–2.10 × 1.20 × 1.90 m; step at SE corner			
	Chamber: 2.00 × ca. 1.50 × 0.80 m; floor at -2.35 m, overlap ca. 0.50 m			
	Blocking: cb., filling chamber to ca. 0.95 m width, filled shaft to -0.55 m			
	Burial: —			
	Body: "Infant II"			
	Objects:			
	1. Beads		20468	
	2. Arrowheads, average length 1.8		20469	
Q 146				
	Shaft with chamber on the W side			
	Shaft: 2.15–2.45 × 0.90-–1.25 × 2.55 m; step at NE corner at -1.50 m			
	Chamber: 2.00 × ca. 1.40 × 0.70 m; floor at -2.95 m			
	Blocking: cb., L chamber ca. 0.70 m wide, filled shaft to unc. depth			
	Burial: —			
	Body: Present but no information			
	Object in chamber:			
	1. Coptic period Eg. handleless juglet (5YR 5/4, 2.5YR 5/8)		20311	figs. 23a, 150b
Q 147				
	Shaft with chamber on the S side			
	Shaft: unspecified dim.			
	Chamber: unspecified dim.			
	Blocking: unspecified			
	Burial: —			
	Body: Mature-senile			
	Objects:			
	1. X-Gr. ord. goblet I—B2 (inv. on 2; 5YR 4/6, 5YR 5/6)		20324	fig. 150c
	2. X-Gr. ord. bottle-jar I—D3, wh. pt. vine, blobs in groups of three, four sets, height 28.8		20325	
	3. Archer's loose		20302	fig. 150d, pl. 57c

Table 40. Register of X-Group Finds in Cemetery Q (*cont.*).

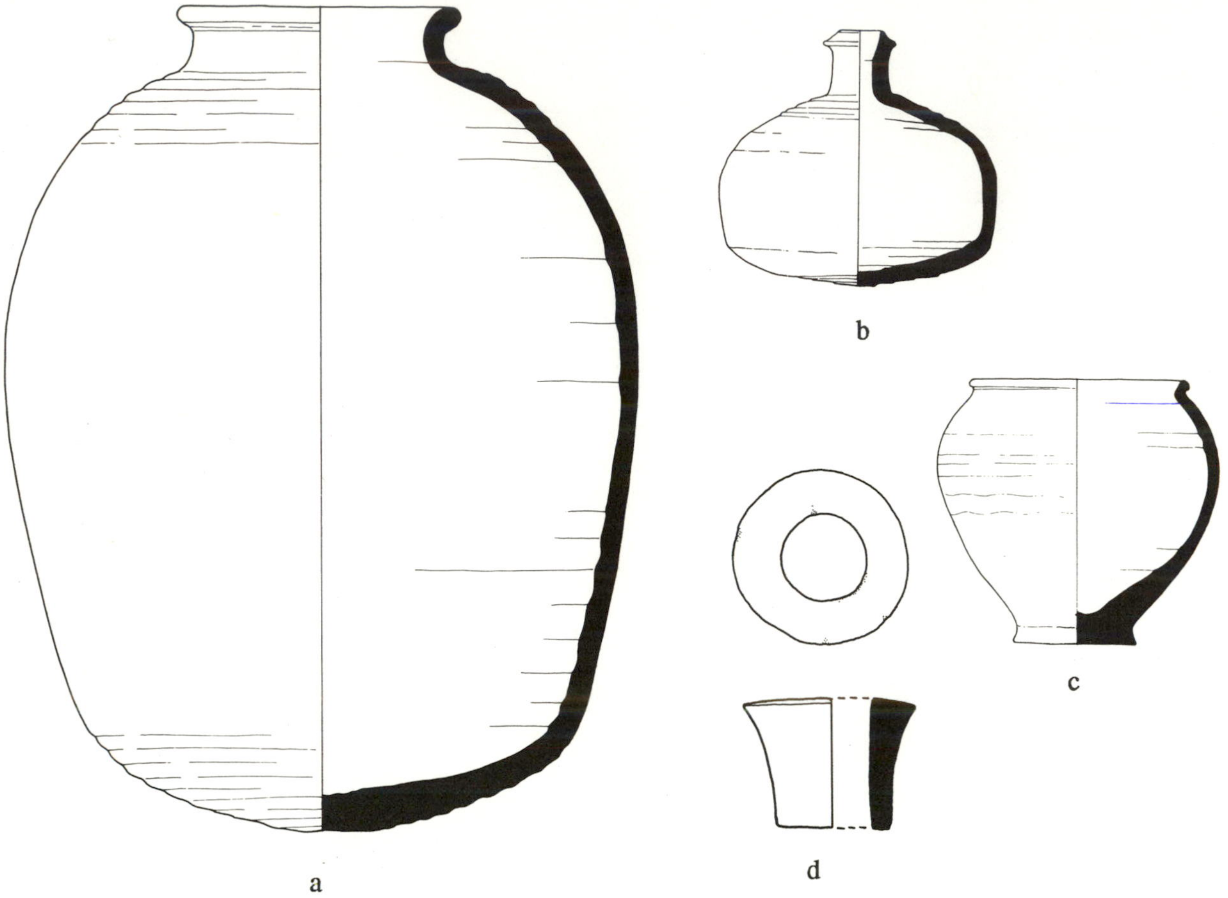

Tomb	Description and Contents	Cairo	OIM	Figure/Plate

Figure 150. Pottery and Archer's Loose from Tombs Q 141, Q 146, and Q 147: (*a*) X-Gr. Ord. Storage Jar I—B, Q 141—1; (*b*) Coptic Period Egyptian Handleless Juglet, Q 146—1; (*c*) X-Gr. Ord. Goblet I—B2, Q 147—1; (*d*) Archer's Loose, Q 147—3. Scales: (*a–c*) 2:5; (*d*) 1:2.

Q 148

Shaft with ledges and vault in the W end, bed burial

Shaft: 2.65–3.00 × 0.90–1.10 × 1.25 m, ramped at W end

Ledges: undercut 0.15 at -0.50 m

Chamber: Five cb. vault, 0.36 × 0.18 × 0.08–0.09 m

Burial: —

Body: Adult

Objects in chamber:

Tomb	Description and Contents	Cairo	OIM	Figure/Plate
	1. X-Gr. ord. narrow-necked bottle-jar I—A3		20312	figs. 14c, 151i
	2. X-Gr. ord. bottle-jar I—A2, wh. coat, bk. pt., vine in groups of three		20313	fig. 151h
	3. X-Gr. fine cup II—A1a (7.5YR 8/4, 7.5YR 8/6)		20314	figs. 8a, 151d
	4. X-Gr. fine cup II—D5a, red pt. bands, rim, waist (7.5YR 8/4, 5YR 4/4)		20315	figs. 9i, 151f, pl. 42a
	5. X-Gr. fine cup II—A1a (10YR 8/3, 10YR 8/4)		20316	fig. 151c, pl. 42e
	6. X-Gr. fine cup II—D1a, red pt. rim ticks (10YR 8/3, 5YR 5/6)		20317	figs. 9a, 151g, pl. 42b
	7. X-Gr. ord. cup I—D4b, wh. coat (7.5YR 8/6, 7.5YR 8/4)		20318	figs. 9g, 151e, pl. 42c

Figure 151. Pottery and Iron Fragments from Tomb Q 148: (*a*) Iron Fragments, No. 11a; (*b*) Iron Fragments, No. 11b; (*c*) X-Gr. Fine Cup II—A1a, No. 5; (*d*) X-Gr. Fine Cup II—A1a, No. 3; (*e*) X-Gr. Ord. Cup I—D4b, No. 7; (*f*) X-Gr. Fine Cup II—D5a, No. 4; (*g*) X-Gr. Fine Cup II—D1a, No. 6; (*h*) X-Gr. Ord. Bottle-Jar I—A2, No. 2; (*i*) X-Gr. Ord. Narrow-Necked Bottle-Jar I—A3, No. 1. Scales: (*a, b*) 1:1; (*c–i*) 2:5.

Table 40. Register of X-Group Finds in Cemetery Q (*cont.*).

Tomb	Description and Contents	Cairo	OIM	Figure/Plate
Q 148 (*cont.*)				
	Objects in chamber (*cont.*):			
	8. Bed remains (matting and wood), largest 7.1 × 4.8 × 2.5		20309	
	9. Leather remains		Disc.	
	10. Bead		20308	
	11. Iron			
	a–b. Fragments of iron		20310	fig. 151a–b, pl. 73d
	12. Date pits		Disc.	
	Sherds:			
	A. X-Gr. ord. bottle jar, bk. pt., vine in groups of three		31815	
	B. Unc. brown basin, rect. rim. (probably post-X-Gr.)		31809	
Q 149				fig. 152a, pl. 39a
	Shaft with chamber on the S side			
	Shaft: — × 1.05 × 1.25 m			
	Chamber: — × 0.65–0.85 × 0.65 m; floor at -1.65 m, ca. 0.50 m overlap			
	Blocking: cb. headers			
	Burial: W/L/90 degrees /at face			
	Body: Adult female			
	Objects:			
	1. Quiver (shaft)		20375	figs. 46, 47b, 48, 49; pls. 54, 55
	2. Quiver cover flap (shaft)		20375	figs. 46, 47a, 48, 49
	3. Archer's loose of wood (top of quiver)		20384	fig. 152b, pl. 57d
	4. X-Gr. ord. utility storage jar III—A, wh. coat, red pt. bands, two incised potter's marks on shoulder		20361	figs. 16c, 152c
	5. Sandals (on feet), length 29		20385	
	6. Two rings (third finger L)		20388	pl. 77d
	7. Beads		20386	
	8. Bowstring fragment, 1.4 × 1.3		20383	
	9. Textile remains, CAT 94–98		20382	
	Sherds:			
	A. Mer. fine cup I—G (1?), red and bk. pt., rim band, alt. red and bk. trefoil flower in double frame		31810	
	B. Mer. fine jar, red and bk. pt. shoulder, alt. red and bk. crescents above band of alt. opposed hatched triangles		31811	
	C. Mer. fine-ord. jar, lt. shoulder, red coat?		31812	
	D. Mer. ord. jar, bk. bands		31813	
	E. Mer. ord. jar		31813	
	F. Mer. ord. jar		31813	
	G. Mer. ord. jar, worn		31814	
	This tomb was probably reused.			
Q 152				fig. 152d
	Surface or irreg. shaft burial (E-W rectangular area with extension for feet)			
	Shaft: 1.40 × 0.60 × 0.35 m			
	Extension: 1.00 × 0.16 m			
	Burial: W/L/thighs ext., legs 90 degrees/face			pl. 37b
	Body: Adult male, turned almost on face			
	Objects:			
	1. Textile wrapping, CAT 99		20518	

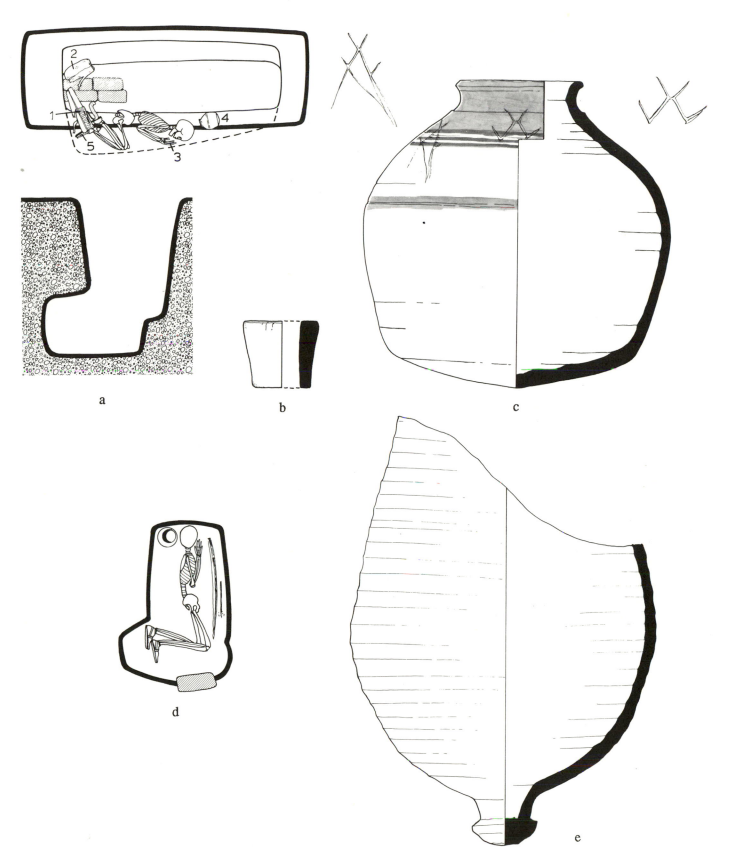

Figure 152. Plan, Section, Pottery, and an Archer's Loose from Tomb Q 149 and Plan and Pottery from
Tomb Q 152: (*a*) Plan and Section of Tomb Q 149; (*b*) Archer's Loose, Q 149—3; (*c*) X-Gr.
Ord. Utility Storage Jar III—A, Q 149—4; (*d*) Plan of Tomb Q 152; (*e*) *Qadus*,
Q 152—4. Scales: (*a*, *d*) 1:40; (*b*) 1:2; (*c*, *e*) 2:5.

Table 40. Register of X-Group Finds in Cemetery Q (*cont.*).

Tomb	Description and Contents	Cairo	OIM	Figure/Plate
Q 152 (*cont.*)				
	Objects (*cont.*):			
	2. Sandals (on feet), 15.0 × 8.0		20381	
	3. Silver anklet (L leg)		20376	pl. 77a
	4. *Qadus* (lower part only, SE of head)		20370	fig. 152e
	5. Wooden bow (ca. 1.20 m, with string)		20379	pl. 63a
	6. Arrow fragments and remains of fletching		20377	pl. 65f
	7. Beads		20378	

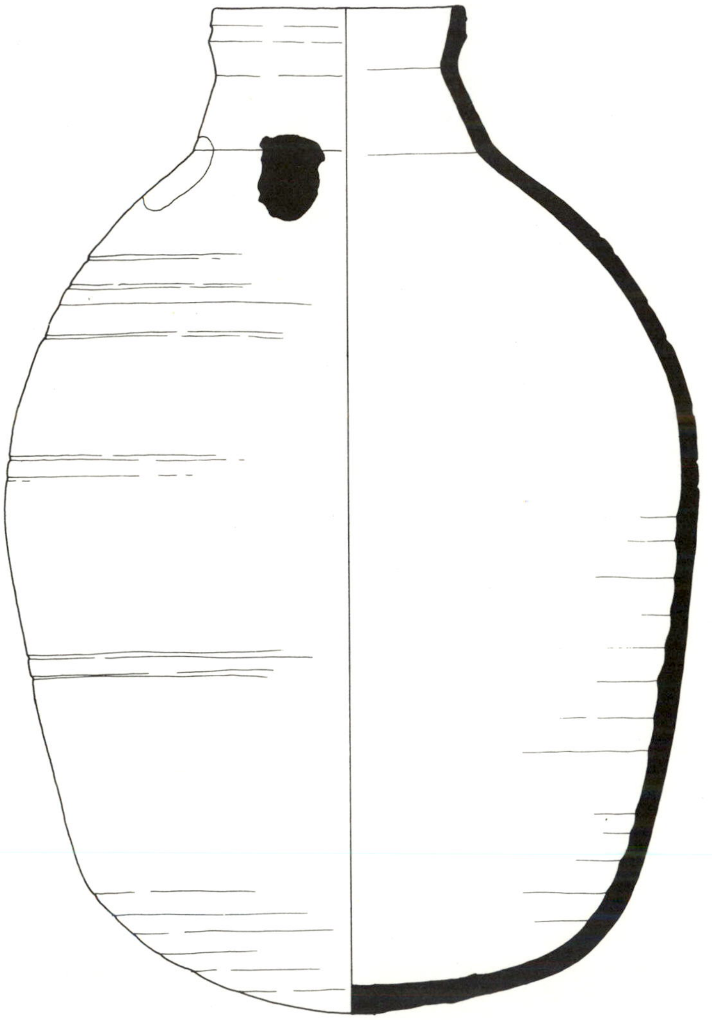

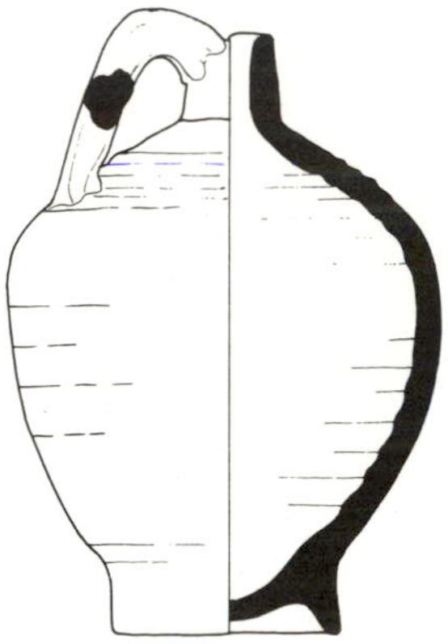

Figure 153. Pottery from Tomb Q 161: (*a*) X-Gr. Storage Jar III—C, No. 2; (*b*) Coptic Period Egyptian Juglet I—A1a, No. 5; (*c*) Coptic Period Egyptian Juglet I—A1a, No. 6. Scale 2:5.

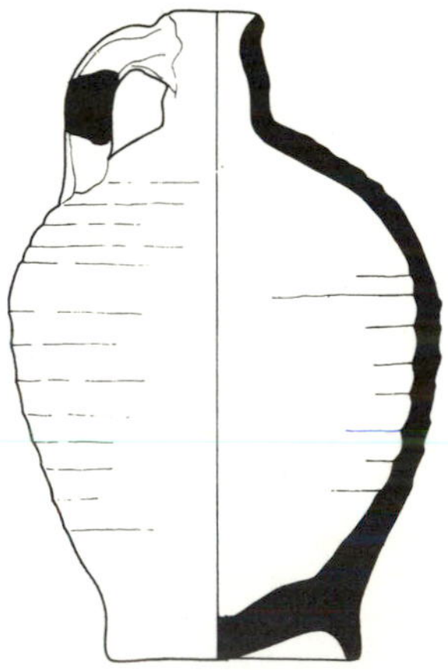

Q 161

Shaft with chamber on the W side
    Shaft: 1.85–2.20 × 0.70–0.90 × 2.00 m
    Chamber: 1.10–1.85 × 0.60–0.65 × 0.50 m; floor flush
    Blocking: stone slabs
Burial: S/L/thighs 45 degrees, legs 45 degrees/ R stomach, L side

Table 40. Register of X-Group Finds in Cemetery Q (*cont.*).

Tomb	Description and Contents	Cairo	OIM	Figure/Plate
Q 161 (*cont.*)				
	Body: Mature female			
	Objects:			
	1. X-Gr. ord. med.-neck jar I—B2, bk. pt. crude bands, height 33.8		20420	
	2. X-Gr. storage jar III—C, red coat, bk. and wh. blobs		20422	fig. 153a
	3. X-Gr. ord. goblet I—B1c (5YR 5/6, 5YR 7/1, 5YR 5/4), height 9.2		20419	
	4. X-Gr. ord. goblet I—B1c (5YR 5/4, 5YR 7/2), height 9		20421	
	5. Coptic period Eg. juglet I—A1a, red coat (2.5YR 5/6, 2.5YR 3/2, 2.5YR 3.5/0)		20423	figs. 22a, 153b
	6. Coptic period Eg. juglet I—A1a		20424	fig. 153c
	7. Beads		20400	
	8. Stone slab with incised offering table (blocking, reused?), 18 × 21 × 6.5		20482	
	9. Rock drawing (surface), 43 × 37 (see OINE VIII)		20396	
	The jars, each with a goblet inverted over the neck, were E of the feet of the burial; the juglets were in front of the face. They are not specifically identified.			
Q 164				fig. 154a
	Shaft with chamber on the N side			
	Shaft: 2.20–2.70 × 1.00–1.35 × 1.30 m			
	Chamber: 2.40 × 0.75 × 0.45 m; floor at -1.75 m, 0.35 m overlap			
	Blocking: no information			
	Burial: S/R/thighs 45 degrees, legs 90 degrees/face			
	Body: Adult female			
	Objects:			
	a. From shaft (probably Meroitic, see OINE VIII):			
	1. Wooden spindle shaft		20448	fig. 153c, pl. 83j
	2. Wooden whorls (two), 3.7 and 4.0		20461	
	b. From chamber:			
	3. Coptic period Eg. juglet I—C3 (5YR 2.5/1, 5YR 3/4)		20425	fig. 155d
	4. X-Gr. ord. goblet I—A1ai *beta* (5YR 5/4, 2.5YR 4/8)		20426	fig. 155b
	5. X-Gr. ord. med.-necked bottle-jar I—B3a, bk. and wh. pt. crude bands at neck, wh. bands bk. framed on body; rope band in relief at neck, height 30.8		20427	figs. 13f, 155f
	6. Coptic period Eg. juglet I—C3		20428	figs. 22m, 155e, pl. 46a
	7. Mer. fine/ord. cup I—G, red coat (dist.)		20441	fig. 155a
	8. Leather bag with hinges and lock		20447	pl. 67a
	9. Bronze bowl, 9.0 × 6.5	Q 625, 89887		
	10. Iron bracelet (R arm), 4.5 × 1.6		20459	
	11. Faience pendant, ram's head with sun disc		20454	fig. 65e, pl. 76b
	12. Iron kohl stick, length 29	Q 618, 89868		
	13. Ivory kohl tube		20449	fig. 154b, pl. 83i
	14. Cloth bag with lumps of galena		20450	
	15. Bronze earring		20458	pl. 77e
	16. Bead anklet		20451	
	17. Sandals, length 23.5		20453	

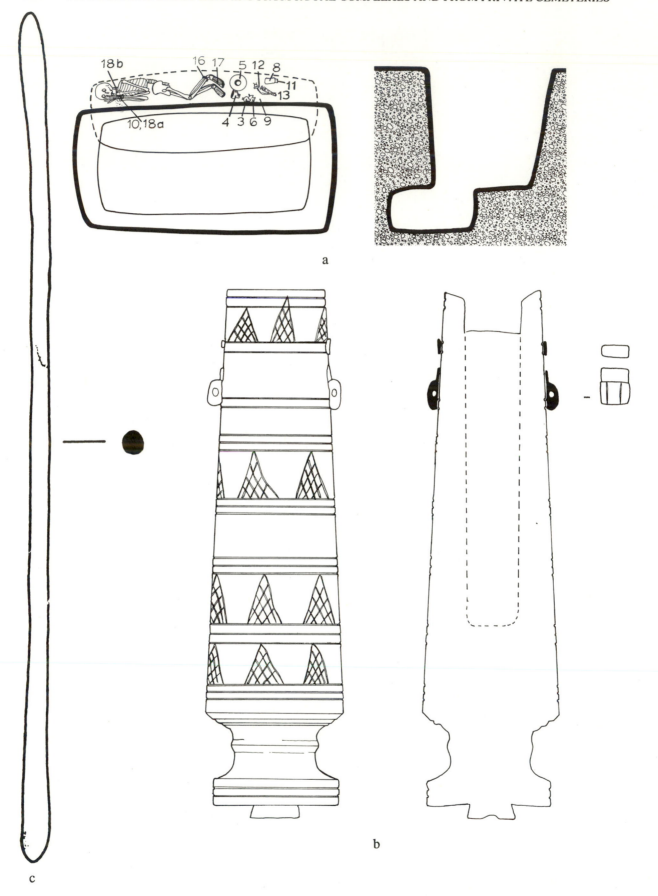

Figure 154. Plan, Section, Kohl Tube, and a Wooden Spindle Shaft from Tomb Q 164: (*a*) Plan and Section; (*b*) Ivory Kohl Tube, No. 13; (*c*) Wooden Spindle Shaft, No. 1. Scales: (*a*) 1:40; (*b, c*) 1:1.

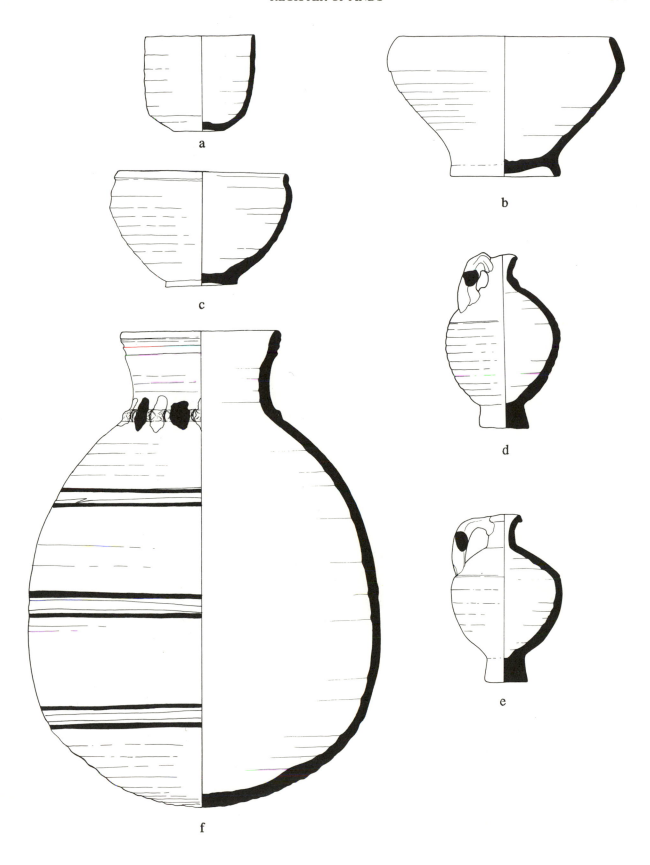

Figure 155. Pottery from Tomb Q 164: (*a*) Mer. Fine/Ord. Cup I—G, No. 7; (*b*) X-Gr. Ord. Goblet I—A1ai *beta*, No. 4; (*c*) X-Gr. Ord. Goblet I—B1a?, No. G; (*d*) Coptic Period Egyptian Juglet I—C3, No. 3; (*e*) Coptic Period Egyptian Juglet I—C3, No. 6. (*f*) X-Gr. Ord. Med.-Necked Bottle-Jar I—B3a, No. 5. Scale 2:5.

Table 40. Register of X-Group Finds in Cemetery Q (*cont.*).

Tomb	Description and Contents	Cairo	OIM	Figure/Plate
Q 164 (*cont.*)				
	Objects (*cont.*):			
	b. From chamber:			
	18. Beads:		20452	figs. 63h, k, o, 64p
	a. Bracelets (four?, L wrist)			
	b. Necklace			
	19. Textile wrapping, CAT 100–102 (renumbered from no. 20 in catalogue)		20456	
	20. Bronze fragment, 3.0 × 0.9		20462A	
	21. Seed		20462B	
	Sherds:		31827	
	A. X-G ord. cup I— , wh. pt., vine in groups of three			
	B. Unc.-coarse handmade open jar, red bur. coat			
	C. Same, very coarse (mineral/organic)			
	D. Unc. gray, chaffy jar, two bk. bands			
	E. Unc. red chaffy, wh. coat			
	F. Red-bk. carinated bowl, wide rim, rim red			
	G-I. Surface sherds			
	G. X-Gr ord. goblet I—B1a? (5YR 6/2, 5YR 6/3, 5YR 7/2)		20599	figs. 7o, 155c

This is a reused tomb of Meroitic IIIB–IV; objects 1, 2 and 7 belong to the original deposit.

Tomb	Description and Contents	Cairo	OIM	Figure/Plate
Q 184 (reused Meroitic tomb)				
	Shaft with chamber on the N side			
	Shaft: ca. 2.30–3.25 × 1.30–1.65 × 1.50 m			
	Chamber : 2.40 × 1.25 × 0.65 m; overlap 0.50–0.65 m, floor -0.65 m from shaft			
	Blocking: mix of stone slabs and cb.			
	X-Gr. use: on packed earth covered with stone slabs to 0.30 above floor			
	Burial: —, placed on leather			
	Body: Mature			
	Objects:			
	a. In chamber:			
	1. Coptic period Eg. utility *amphoriskos* II—C, wh. coat		20497	fig. 156a
	2. Beads		20567	fig. 64m
	3. Textile remains		Disc.	
	4. Sandal, largest 8.3 × 4.7		20564B	
	5. Pot contents from no. 7		20499	
	8. Leather (large piece, incomplete)		20564A	
	b. In shaft:			
	6. Beads		20567	
	c. Unplaced:			
	7. X-Gr. ord. bottle-jar I—?, bk. and wh. pt., spot beads at neck, wh. lines framed by bk. on body (neck broken away), height 24.7		20498	
	Sherds:		31834	
	A. A-Gr? handmade chaff-tempered V-Shaped bowl, bn. polished inside and upper exterior, worn			
Q 186 (reused Meroitic tomb)				
	Shaft with chamber on the N side			
	Shaft: 1.60–1.80 × 0.65–1.00 × 1.95 m			

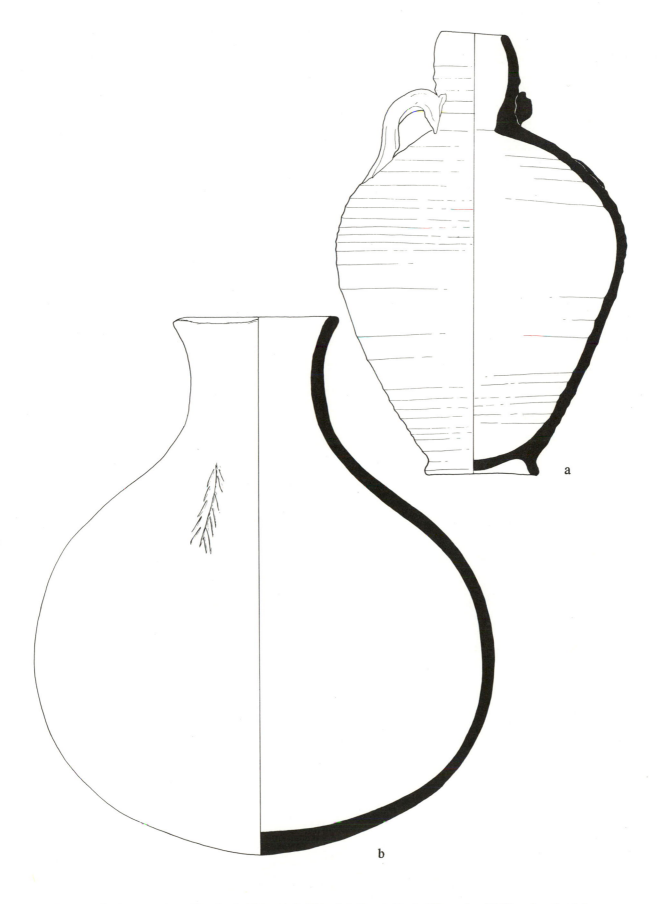

Figure 156. Pottery from Tombs Q 184 and Q 186: (*a*) Coptic Period Egyptian Utility *Amphoriskos* II—C, Q 184—1; (*b*) X-Gr. Handmade Jar—D2, Q 186—2. Scale 2:5.

Table 40. Register of X-Group Finds in Cemetery Q (*cont.*).

Tomb	Description and Contents	Cairo	OIM	Figure/Plate
Q 186 (*cont.*)				
	Chamber: 1.65 × 0.60 × 0.60 m; floor flush			
	Blocking: cb. 0.09 × 0.16 × 0.35 m			
	Burial: —			
	Body: Juvenile female, less than 12 years			
	Objects:			
	1. Beads		20565	
	2. X-Gr. handmade jar—D2, height 34.2		20557	figs. 20g, 156b
	3. Textile remains, CAT 164		20566	
	4. Date pits		Disc.	
	5. Sherd		—	
Q 192				
	Shaft with chamber on the W side			
	Shaft: ? × 0.60–0.80 × 1.15 m			
	Chamber: ? × 0.60 × ca. 0.60 m; floor at -1.65, sloped from step in shaft			
	Blocking: cb., broken to SW			
	Burial: N/R/"contracted"			
	Body: Mature female			
	Objects:			
	a. In shaft:			
	1. Sherds			
	b. In chamber (?):			
	2. Sandals		20542	pl. 78b
	3. X-Gr. ord. med.-necked jar I—B3, bk. and wh. pt. spot beads at neck, two sets wh. flanked by bk. lines		20536	fig. 157a
	4. Textile wrapping remains, CAT 104–105		20548	
	5. Beads and pendant		20546	
Q 196				
	Shaft with chamber on the W side			
	Shaft: 2.05–2.35 × 0.60–0.90 × ca. 1.70 m			
	Chamber: 2.05 × 0.75 × 0.55 m; floor flush			
	Blocking: stone slabs. many horizontal			
	Burial: —			
	Body: Adult male			
	Objects:			
	a. In shaft:			
	1. Archery equipment			
	a. Quiver		20507	fig. 50, pl. 56b–c
	b. Bow		20507	pl. 62d
	2. Bowstring frags., largest 30.0 × 0.3		20506	
	3. Wooden archer's loose	Q 679, 89885		fig. 157b
	4. X-Gr. ord. goblet I—B1c		20515	fig. 157d
	b. In chamber:			
	5. X-Gr. ord.utility storage jar I—B, red coat		20510	figs. 16b, 157e
	6. Coptic period Eg. *amphoriskos*-jug I—D2a, bk. pt.		20514	figs. 21f, 157c
	7. Beads		20509	
	8. Arrowhead		20522	pl. 65b
	9. Pot contents from no. 5		20511	

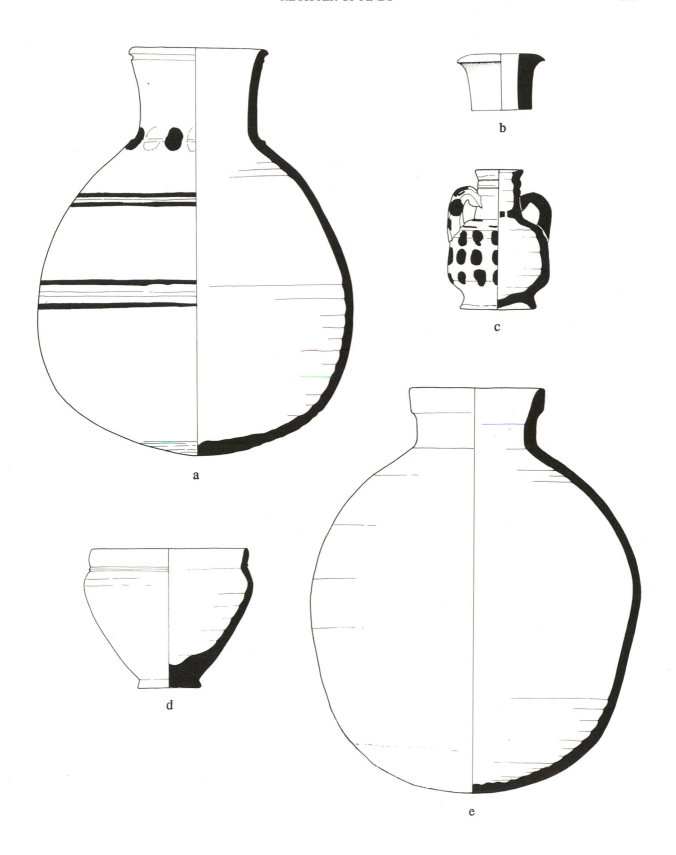

Figure 157. Pottery and Archer's Loose from Tombs Q 192 and Q 196: (*a*) X-Gr. Ord. Medium-Necked Jar I—B3, Q 192—3; (*b*) Archer's Loose, Q 196—3; (*c*) Coptic Period Egyptian *Amphoriskos* Jug I—D2a, Q 196—6; (*d*) X-Gr. Ord. Goblet I—B1c, Q 196—4; (*e*) X-Gr. Ord. Utility Storage, Jar I—B, Q 196—5. Scales: (*a, c–e*) 2:5; (*b*) 1:2.

Table 40. Register of X-Group Finds in Cemetery Q (*cont.*).

Tomb	Description and Contents	Cairo	OIM	Figure/Plate
Q 196 (*cont.*)				
	Sherds from shaft:		31839	
	A. Post-X-Gr. orange bowl, bk. pt. lines (abraded)			
	B. Post-X-Gr. orange bowl, pt. bands			
	C. Post-X-Gr. orange bowl, unpainted			
	D. Unc. gray-bk., abraded			
Q 231				
	Shaft with chamber on the W side			
	Shaft: ? × 0.70 × 0.45 m			
	Chamber: 0.80–? × 0.95 × 0.45 m; floor at 0.95 m			
	Blocking: cb.			
	Burial: contracted?			
	Body: "Infant II," male			
	Objects:			
	1. Textile remains, CAT 107–108		20521	
	2. Neck of jar		31843	
	Sherds		31844	
Q 279				
	Shaft with chamber on the W side			
	Shaft: 1.70–2.15 × 0.50–0.70 × 1.10 m			
	Chamber: 1.55 × 0.65 × 0.60 m; floor at -1.40 m, slight overlap			
	Blocking: stone slabs			
	Burial: —			
	Body: Mature male			
	Objects:			
	a. In chamber:			
	1. Quiver (bottom, straps and cord in shaft)		20593A	
	2. Two arrowheads (in no. 1)		20593B	pl. 64a
	3. Ornament or small bell, bronze?		20593C	fig. 158b, pl. 83f
	4. Leaves (as others in tombs)		Disc.	
	5. Date pit		Disc.	
	6. Textile remains (around head)(CAT X-Gr.)		Disc.	
	b. In shaft:			
	1. Parts of quiver no. 1			
	7. Remains of *ba* statue, 41.0 × 13.0 × 17.5		20754	
	Sherds from chamber:		31870	
	A. Mer. fine, bk. pt.			
	B. Unc. hard pk. sandy storage jar (from shaft)			
	C. Coptic period Eg. amphora, very worn (from shaft)			
	Surface E of Q 279:			
	1. X-Gr. ord. goblet I—B1c (worn surface), height 8.3		20743	
	Sherds from surface:		31871	
	D. Unc., coarse sandy handmade V-shaped bowl			
	E. X-Gr. handmade cooking pot, holemouth			
	F. X-Gr. ord. small jar			
	G. Unc., lt. colored, pedestal			
	H. X-Gr. storage jar III—C (E of Q 279)			
	I. Unc., mottled handmade jar			
	J. Unc., gray, coarse, chaffy			

Table 40. Register of X-Group Finds in Cemetery Q (*cont.*).

Tomb	Description and Contents	Cairo	OIM	Figure/Plate
Q 309				
	Shaft with chamber on the W side			
	Shaft: 1.65–2.15 × 0.60–0.85 × 1.55 m			
	Chamber: 1.70 × 0.65 × 0.45 m, floor flush?			
	Blocking: cb., 0.39 × 0.16 × 0.10, few stones			
	Burial: —			
	Body: "Elderly woman"			
	Objects:			
	a. In shaft:			
	1. Leather fragments		Disc.	
	2. Beads (many strung)		20686	
	b. In chamber:			
	3. Textile remains (CAT X-Gr.)		Disc.	
	4. X-Gr. ord. goblet I—B1b, height 8.3		20683	
	5. Matting		Disc.	
	6. X-Gr. ord. storage jar, height 33.4		20709	
	Sherds:		31889	
	A. Mer. fine/ord. jar, bk. pt. drop bead			
	B. X-Gr. *qadus*, surface dk. gray			
	C. X-Gr. handmade jar, smoothed, very thin red coat; band			
	of vert. zigzags deeply incised on shoulder			
	D. Unc. fine pk. jar, red coat			
	E. Post-X-Gr. fine pk. vessel, irreg. spout			
Q 316				
	Shaft with chamber on the W side			
	Shaft: 1.60 (top) × 0.60–0.80 × 1.20 m			
	Chamber: 1.40 × 1.00 × 0.40 m; floor at -1.40 m,			
	0.35 m overlap			
	Blocking: cb. 0.10–0.11 × 0.15–0.17 × 0.32 m; rowlock below,			
	stretchers above, in chamber, overlap: unc.			
	Burial: S/R/90 degrees/—			
	Body: Juvenile male?			
	Objects:			
	a. In chamber:			
	1. X-Gr. ord. med.-necked bottle-jar I—B1,		20711	figs. 13d, 158e
	bk. and wh. pt. spot beads			
	2. X-Gr. ord. med.-necked jar I—B1		20712	fig. 158c
	3. Dates (three, one date pit)		Disc.	
	4. Beads		20822	
	5. Textile wrapping remains (CAT X-Gr.)		Disc.	
	6. Wood remains		Disc.	
	b. In shaft			
	7. Coptic period Eg. utility *amphoriskos* II—C, wh. coat		20774	fig. 158d
	Sherd:		31895	
	A. X-Gr. ord. jug			
	No. 7 was reassigned from tomb Q 317.			
Q 320				
	Shaft with chamber on the W side			
	Shaft: 1.65 (top) × 0.70 × 0.75 m			
	Chamber: 1.30 × 0.75 × 0.35 m, floor at -1.00 m,			
	0.30 m overlap			

Figure 158. Pottery and Ornament/Bell from Tombs Q 279, Q 316, and Q 320: (a) X-Gr. Ord. Utility Storage Jar I—A, Q 320—1; (b) Ornament/Bell, Q 279—3; (c) X-Gr. Ord. Medium-Necked Jar I—B1, Q 316—2; (d) Coptic Period Egyptian Utility *Amphoriskos* II—C, Q 316—7; (e) X-Gr. Ord. Medium-Necked Bottle-Jar I—B1, Q 316—1. Scales: (a, c–e) 2:5; (b) 1:1.

Table 40. Register of X-Group Finds in Cemetery Q (*cont.*).

Tomb	Description and Contents	Cairo	OIM	Figure/Plate
Q 320 (*cont.*)				
	Blocking: cb., two courses, headers then stretchers, $0.28 \times 0.17 \times 0.09$ m			
	Burial: S/L/thighs 130 degrees, legs folded/at face			
	Body: Juvenile-adult female			
	Objects from chamber:			
	1. X-Gr. ord. utility storage jar I—A		20731	fig. 158a
	2. X-Gr. ord. goblet I—B1b (5YR 4/4, 5YR 3/4), height 8.7		20730	
	3. Coptic period Eg. utility *amphoriskos* II—C, wh. coat		20729	
	4. Textile remains (at waist; CAT X-Gr.)		Disc.	
	5. Thin copper wire and beads		21751	figs. 64f, 65h
Q 321				
	Shaft with chamber on the W side			
	Shaft: $1.00–1.65 \times 0.40–0.55 \times 0.75$ m			
	Chamber: $1.00 \times ? \times 0.40$ m; floor at -0.95 m, unc. overlap			
	Blocking: —			
	Burial: S/R/thighs 75 degrees, legs folded/chest			
	Body: Mature female?			
	Objects, from chamber:			
	1. X-Gr. ord. goblet I—B1c, height 8.8		20727	
	2. *Qadus*		20728	fig. 159a
	3. Textile wrapping remains, CAT 111–113		20818A–C	
Q 326				
	Shaft with chamber on the W side			
	Shaft: $2.15–2.55 \times 0.85–1.20 \times 1.70$ m			
	Chamber: $2.15 \times 0.70 \times 0.55$ m; floor flush			
	Blocking: stones, dist., one cb.			
	Burial: —			
	Body: Adult female			
	Objects:			
	1. X-Gr. ord. cup I—B1, red coat, wh. band on rim		20760	figs. 8d, 159c
	Sherds: —			
Q 332				
	Shaft with chamber on the W side			
	Shaft: $1.20–1.65 \times 0.40–0.70 \times 0.90$ m			
	Chamber: $1.20 \times$ slight $\times 0.30$ m, floor flush			
	Blocking: stone slabs			
	Burial: S/L/thighs 75 degrees, legs folded/—			
	Body: Juvenile			
	Objects:			
	a. In shaft:			
	1. Large sherd of *qadus* (tool)		—	
	b. Unc. loc :			
	2. Car. bead, hexagonal barrel		20808	
	c. In chamber:			
	3. Coptic period Eg. flask/juglet I—D2a		20789	fig. 159b, pl. 46c
	4. Beads		20808	
	5. Textile wrapping ("rug"), CAT 115–118		20812	
	6. Rings (third finger, L), diam. 1.9		20807	

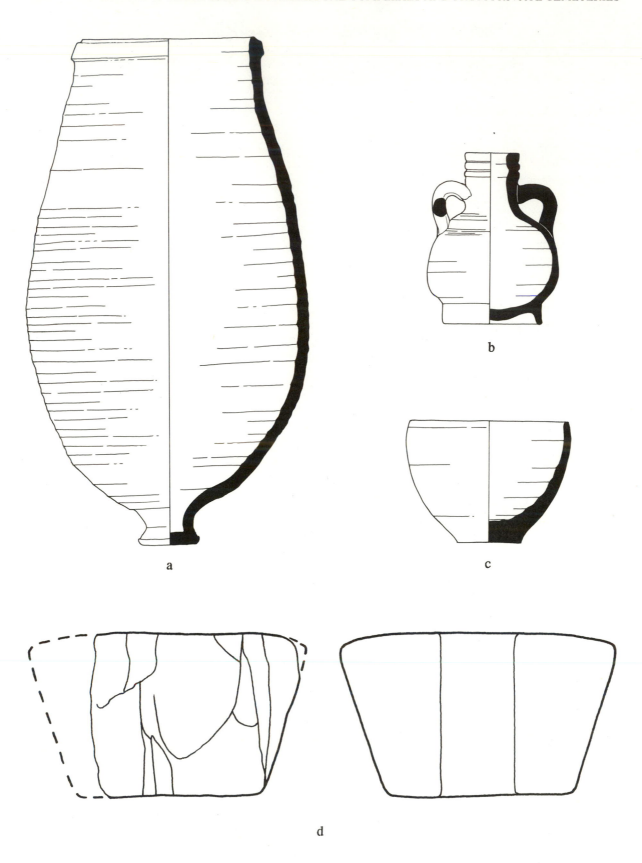

Figure 159. Pottery and Stone Object from Tombs Q 317, Q 321, Q 326, and Q 332: (*a*) *Qadus*, Q 321—2;
(*b*) Coptic Period Egyptian Flask/ Juglet I—D2a, Q 332—3; (*c*) X-Gr. Ord. Cup I—B1, Q 326—1;
(*d*) Truncated Cone of Pink Stone, Q 317—3. Scales: (*a–c*) 2:5; (*d*) 1:1.

Table 40. Register of X-Group Finds in Cemetery Q (*cont.*).

Tomb	Description and Contents	Cairo	OIM	Figure/Plate

Q 338

Shaft with chamber on the W side

Shaft: 0.75–1.10 × 0.45–0.55 × 0.35 m

Chamber: 0.75 × ? × 0.25 m; floor at -0.50 m; substantial overlap

Blocking: stone slabs

Burial: S/L/"contracted"/at face

Body: Infant

Objects:

1.	X-Gr. min. feeding cup (or lamp), dark ext (in no. 2)		20866	fig. 160b
2.	X-Gr. ord. goblet I—B1b		20870	fig. 160c
3.	Coptic period Eg. *amphoriskos* jug II—C, red coat		20873	fig. 160a
4.	Textiles, CAT 120–121		20815A–B	
5.	"Elaborate necklace," pendant average 1.0 × 0.8		20837	
6.	Bead string (around shroud at feet)		20836	
7.	Four bead bracelets		20804	
8.	Pendant/amulet, 1.8 × 0.9 × 0.5	Q 983, 89906		

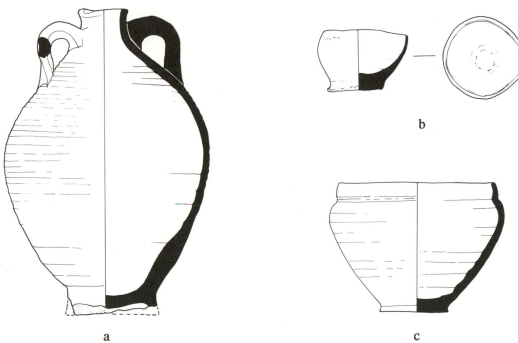

Figure 160. Pottery from Tomb Q 338: (*a*) Coptic Period Egyptian *Amphoriskos* Jug II—C, No. 3; (*b*) X-Gr. Min. Feeding Cup, No. 1; (*c*) X-Gr. Ord. Goblet I—B1b, No. 2. Scale 2:5.

Surface E of Q 338

Objects:

1.	X-Gr. ord goblet I—A1bi *alpha*		20867	fig. 7e
2.	X-Gr. ord. bowl A2		20869	
3.	X-Gr. goblet B1c		20868	

Q 343

Shaft with chamber on the W side and bed burial

Shaft: 2.30 × 0.65–0.90 × 1.65 m

Table 40. Register of X-Group Finds in Cemetery Q (*cont.*).

Tomb	Description and Contents	Cairo	OIM	Figure/Plate
Q 343 (*cont.*)				
	Chamber: 1.65–2.30 × ? × 0.75 m, floor flush			
	Blocking: cb.; see sketch, 0.34 × 0.18 × 0.10 m			
	Burial: S/L/ext./sides (displaced)			
	Body: Mature male			
	Objects:			
	a. From chamber:			
	1. Bed remains		21437	pl. 50c
	b. From shaft:			
	2. Leather wrapping		Disc.	
	3. Meroitic stela fragment, 25.7 × 17.3 × 9.7		20857	
	4. Fragment with face and shoulder in high relief, 21.2 × 13.0 × 9.0	Q 1049	Disc.	
	Sherds:		31909	
	A. X-Gr. storage jar III—, red coat			
	B. X-Gr. handmade cooking pot, blackened inside and out			
	C. Mer.? ord.			
	D. Mer.? fine cup, red coat			
Q 344				
	Shaft with chamber on the W side			
	Shaft: 1.25–1.60 × 0.50–0.70 × 1.20 m			
	Chamber: 1.00 × 0.75 × 0.40 m; floor at -1.50 m; 0.45 m overlap			
	Blocking: stone slabs			
	Burial: —			
	Body: "Infant I"			
	Objects:			
	1. X-Gr. ord. goblet I—B1a, height 8.5		20879	
	2. Textile remains		Disc.	
	3. Beads		20845	fig. 64b
	4. Silver earring		20846	fig. 61d
	5. Hair-ring-shaped pendant, 1.9 × 1.8		20845	
Q 345				
	Shaft with chamber on the N side; chamber begun to S.			
	Blocked with cb.			
	Shaft: 2.25 × 0.90 × 0.75 m			
	Chamber B: 1.40 × ca. 1.05 × 0.40 m; floor at -1.30, 0.35 m overlap			
	Blocking B: stone slabs, including stela with Meroitic text			
	Burial: W/L/thighs 90 degrees, legs folded/at face			
	Body: Adult male			
	Objects:			
	a. In shaft:			
	1. Offering table fragment with Mer. text, 26.0 × 23.2 × 7.6		20843	
	2. Sherds (surface)		31914	
	3. Stela, 53.0 × 21.0 × 7.5 (see OINE VIII, *Part 1*, p. 95 and *Part 2*, p. 64)		20842	pls. 17a, 100d (in OINE VIII)
	4. Beads		20946	
	5. Leather strap remains, largest 18.2 × 1.6		20961	
	6. X-Gr. min. "lamp" (burning, but like feeding cup; 5YR 2.5/1)		20880	figs. 18, 161c, pl. 45b

Table 40. Register of X-Group Finds in Cemetery Q (*cont.*).

Tomb	Description and Contents	Cairo	OIM	Figure/Plate
Q 345 (*cont.*)				
Objects (*cont.*):				
b. In chamber:				
	7. Bow fragments		20961	fig. 30, pl. 61
	8. Textile remains		Disc.	
	9. Coptic period Eg. *amphoriskos*-jug II—C (neck broken), height 30.1		20881	
	10. Bowstring fragment		20961	
	11. Sandals (on feet)		20955	pl. 79c
	12. Textile wrapping remains, CAT 122		20966	
	13. Archer's loose of wood	Q 1138, 89886		fig. 161b
	14. Two Arrowheads		20957	fig. 161a, pl. 65d
	15. Textile remains, CAT 123		20962	
	16. Beads		20958	fig. 65f
Sherds:				
	A. X-Gr. ord. bowl I—B1, angular side		31914	fig. 161e
	B. Unc., sandy red-gray bottle-jar rim			
	C. Post-X-Gr., wh. with bk. inclusions, red coat, carinated			
	D. Unc., sandy and org inclusions, red with gray surf, V-shaped bowl			
	E. Unc., worn pk. ring base			
	F. Mer. Ku. wm. bowl, bk. bands			
Q 348				
Shaft with chamber on the W side				
Shaft: 1.90–2.25 × 0.50–0.90 × 1.00 m				
Chamber: 1.90 × 0.35 × 0.30 m; floor flush				
Blocking: stone slabs, cb., and reused stela				
Burial: — (Christian, intrusive)				
Body: —				
Objects:				
	1. Reused stela		Disc.	
	2. Textile remains, CAT 167–168		20918A–B	
Q 349				
Shaft with chamber on the N side				
Shaft: 2.45–2.70 × 0.95–1.50 × 1.80 m				
Chamber: 2.60 × 1.00 × ca. 0.70 m; floor sloped to -2.10 m				
Blocking: stone with mud				
Burial: —				
Body: Juvenile				
Objects:				
	1. *Qadus* sherds		Disc.	
	2. Wood remains		Disc.	
	3. Textile remains		Disc.	
	4. Ring with key attachment, diam. 2.1		20891	
	5. Wood and leather remains from sword sheath, 5.4 × 0.9		20892	
	6. Sherds		31916	

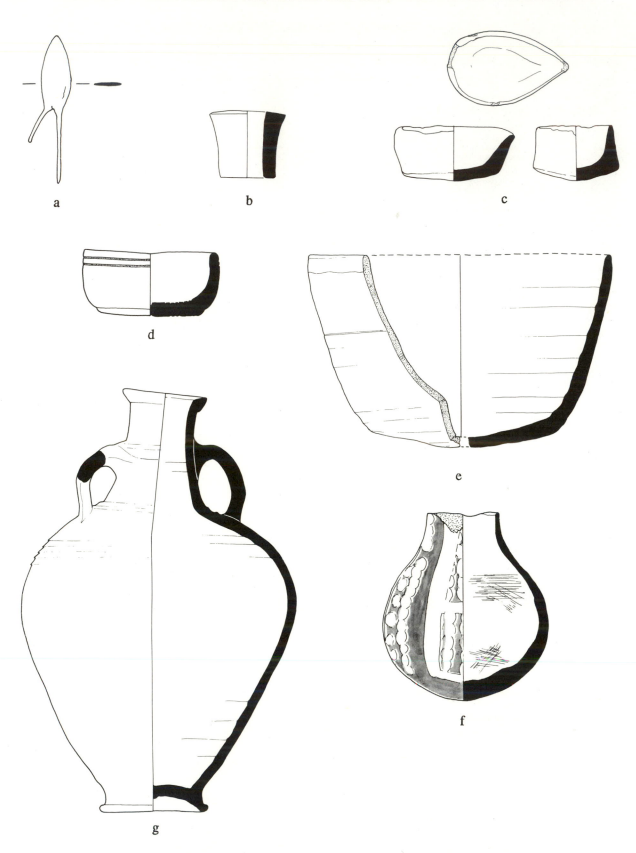

Figure 161. Pottery and Objects from Tombs Q 345, Q 350, and Q 356: (*a*) Arrowhead, Q 345—14;
(*b*) Archer's Loose, Q 345—13; (*c*) X-Gr. Miniature "Lamp,"Q 345—6; (*d*) Wooden
Container, Q 350—2; (*e*) X-Gr. Ord. Bowl I—B1, Q 345—A; (*f*) X-Gr. Handmade
Jar—B1, Q 356—4; (*g*) Coptic Period Egyptian *Amphoriskos*-Jug II—B,
Q 356—3. Scales: (*a*) 1:1; (*b*) 1:2; (*c–g*) 2:5.

Table 40. Register of X-Group Finds in Cemetery Q (*cont.*).

Tomb	Description and Contents	Cairo	OIM	Figure/Plate
Q 350				
	Shaft with chamber on the W side			
	Shaft: 1.70–1.90 × 1.00–1.20 × 0.75 m			
	Chamber: 1.50 × 1.25 × 0.50 m; floor at 1.45 m, 0.60 m overlap			
	Blocking: cb.			
	Burial: S/R/thighs straight, legs 90 degrees/at face			
	Body: Adult male			
	Objects:			
	1. Remains of sealed jar Coptic period Eg. *amphoriskos* jug II—C, red coat, height 30.6 (as preserved)		20884	
	2. Wooden container		20917	fig. 161d, pl. 83h
	3. Contents of no. 2:		20916	
	a. Beads			
	b. Nut			
	c. Castor seeds			
	Sherds from shaft:			
	4. Jar also possibly vessel described as no. 1		20884	
	5. Beads		20914	
	6. Textile remains, CAT 124–127		20919	
	7. Hair-ring pendant		20914	
	8. Bead bracelets (R. arm), average diam. 5.7		20915	
	9. Coptic period Eg. juglet I—A1, height 12.9 (as preserved)		20883	
	10. Two rings (bronze), diam. 2		20921	
	11. Two bead necklaces		20914	
	12. Textile wrapping		Disc.	
	13. Beads		20919	
	14. Sandals, 23.0 × 9.4 × 6.5		20920	
	15. Sherd		31918	
Q 356				
	Shaft with chamber on the W side			
	Shaft: 1.10–1.35 × 0.35–0.75 × 1.40 m			
	Chamber: 1.10 × 0.55 × 0.35 m; floor flush			
	Blocking: cb. with stones piled above			
	Burial: —			
	Body: "Infant II"			
	Objects:			
	a. Unc. loc.			
	1. Beads		20928	
	b. Shaft:			
	2. Leaves		Disc.	
	c. In chamber:			
	3. Coptic period Eg. *amphoriskos*-jug II—B, red coat		20982	figs. 21b, 161g
	4. X-Gr. handmade jar—B1, red coat, vert. zones of spots (10R 5/8 [coat], 5R 8/1)		20981	figs. 20c, 161f, pl. 45a
	5. Date pits (from no. 4)		Disc.	
	6. Textile remains, CAT 128–130		20943	
Q 357 (Meroitic reused, see OINE VIII)				
	Shaft with chamber on the N side			
	Blocking: stones with mud mortar, cb. below			
	Burial: W/—/ext./—, dist.			

Table 40. Register of X-Group Finds in Cemetery Q (*cont.*).

Tomb	Description and Contents	Cairo	OIM	Figure/Plate
Q 357 (Meroitic reused, see OINE VIII) (*cont.*)				
Body: Adult female				
Objects:				
a.	From shaft:			
	1. X-Gr. ord. goblet I—B1c, height 8.9		21078	
	2. Two worked pieces of stone		Disc.	
b.	In chamber:			
	3. Coffin traces		Disc.	
	4. Textile remains		Disc.	
Sherds from shaft:			31921	
A.	Unc., handmade, chaffy, brown mottled surface, drab interior, bowl			
B.	Unc., handmade, chaffy, brown mottled surface, drab interior, bowl			
C.	Post-X-Gr. red-orange, prominent voids, basin (red coat)			
D.	Unc., worn rim			
E.	Mer.? Ku. wm. tapered neck, voids, rib rim			
Q 360				
Surface burial with "shaft," one side blocked with stones and mud				
Burial: S/L/contracted/R stomach, L side				
Body: Newborn				
Objects:				
	1. Textile wrapping, fastened by two strands of string at head (CAT X-Gr.)		Disc.	
	2. String with one bead (R wrist)		20971	
Q 361				
Shaft with chamber on the W side				
Shaft: 1.35–1.60 × 0.60–0.80 × 1.00 m				
Chamber: 0.85 × 0.50 × 0.35 m; floor at -1.25 m, 0.25 m overlap				
Blocking: large stone				
Burial: —, none found				
Body: none found				
Objects, from chamber:				
	1. *Qadus*		20978	fig. 162c
	2. X-Gr. ord. cup I—D4a (2.5YR 5/4 [closest], 5YR 4/2)		20979	figs. 9f, 162a
	3. Small wooden bowl, 3.8 × 7.0 × 4.4		20942	
	4. Beads		20941	
	5. Textile remains		Disc.	
Sherds			32057	
Q 377				
Shaft with chamber on W side				
Shaft: 0.75–1.40 × 0.50–0.67 × 0.65 m				
Chamber: 0.85 × 0.40 × 0.35 m; floor at -0.80 m, overlap				
Blocking: —				
Burial: —				
Body: Infant I				
Objects:				
	1. Few strands of cloth clinging to face			
	2. Beads from burial chamber (no record)			

a

b

c

Figure 162. Pottery from Tombs Q 361 and Q 379: (*a*) X-Gr. Ord. Cup I—D4a, Q 361—2;
(*b*) *Qadus*, Q 379—1; (*c*) *Qadus*, Q 361—1. Scale 2:5.

Table 40. Register of X-Group Finds in Cemetery Q (*cont.*).

Tomb	Description and Contents	Cairo	OIM	Figure/Plate
Q 378 (X-Gr. reuse of Meroitic tomb)				
	Superstructure (mastaba) and shaft, with chamber on the S and W? side (see OINE VIII)			
	Burial B: E/L/semicontracted/face			pl. 37c
	Body B: —			
	Objects with Burial B:			
	6. Textile wrapping (a), CAT 131		21234	
	7. Textile wrapping (b), CAT 132		21281	
	8. Remains of wooden self-bow and string		Disc.	
	9. Remains of basket		Disc.	
	10. Mer. fine/ord. jar (with original deposit), height 20.2		21034	
	11. Iron spear or javelin head, 16.0 × 0.4		21266	
	12. Iron arrowheads (four), average 4.9 × 0.3		21266	
	13. Fletching from no. 12		Disc.	
	14. Bracelet from R wrist, diam. 5.5		21267	
	15. Bead necklace from neck		21268	
	16. Anklet of string and feathers, R ankle		21269	
	17. Sandals on feet		21283	pl. 79a–b
Q 379				
	Shaft with chamber on the W side			
	Shaft: 1.10–1.65 × 0.50–0.65 × 1.00 m			
	Chamber: ? × 0.50 × 0.45 m; floor at -1.15, slight overlap			
	Blocking: stone slabs			
	Burial: dist. extended?			
	Body: "Infant I–II" male			
	Objects, in chamber:			
	1. *Qadus* (at S end)		20974	fig. 162b
	2. Beads		20927	
	Sherds, in shaft		31931	
Q 381				
	Shaft with chamber on the W side			
	Shaft: 1.15–1.40 × 0.95–1.20 × 1.15 m			
	Step: sloping, 1.15 × 0.45 m at -1.50 m			
	Chamber: 1.15 × 0.90 × 0.70 m; floor at -1.80			
	Blocking: cb., jumbled and reset			
	Burial: —			
	Body: Adult male			
	Objects:			
	a. In shaft:			
	1. Leaves		Disc.	
	b. In chamber:			
	2. *Qadus*-like jar—B		20976	figs. 25b, 163a, pl. 47d
	3. Beads (gn.)		20854	
	4. Beads (white)		20854	
	5. Arrowhead		20810	pl. 65a
	6. Bowstring fragment		Disc.	
	7. Leather cord remains (possibly bow?)		Disc.	
Q 385				
	Shaft with chamber on the W side			
	Shaft: 1.35–1.55 × 0.65–0.80 × 0.60 m			

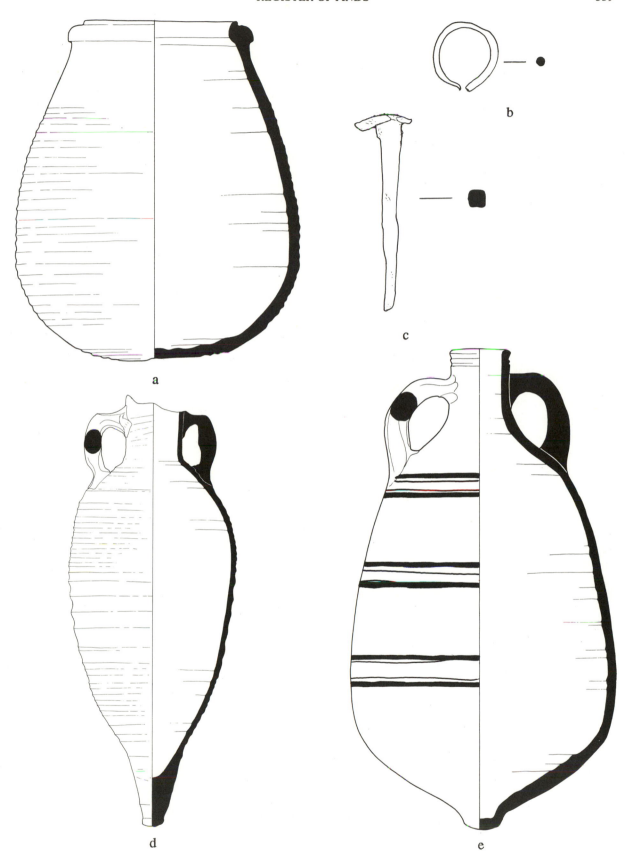

Figure 163. Pottery and Objects from Tombs Q 381, Q 385, Q 387, and Q 388: (*a*) *Qadus*-like Jar—B, Q 381—2; (*b*) Iron Ring, Q 387—4; (*c*) Nail/Spike, Q 385—5a; (*d*) Coptic Period Egyptian Amphora, Q 385—1; (*e*) Coptic Period Egyptian Amphora—A4b, Q 388—5. Scales: (*a, e*) 2:5; (*b, c*) 1:1; (*d*) 1:5.

Table 40. Register of X-Group Finds in Cemetery Q (*cont.*).

Tomb	Description and Contents	Cairo	OIM	Figure/Plate
Q 385 (*cont.*)				
	Chamber: 1.25 × 0.85 × 0.65 m (max.); floor at -1.25, ca. 0.20 overlap			
	Blocking: cb.			
	Burial: —			
	Body: Mature female			
	Objects, from chamber:			
	1. Coptic period Eg. amphora (bitumen) (2.5YR 6/4)		20996	fig. 163d
	2. X-Gr. ord. small bottle jar I—, (neck missing), height 14.7		20997	
	3. Beads		20855	
	4. Textile wrapping remains (CAT X-Gr.)		Disc.	
	5. Metal objects			
	a. Iron nail or spike		20856B	fig. 163c, pl. 83d
	b. Rim of bronze bowl		20856A	
Q 387				
	Shaft with chamber on the W side			
	Shaft: 1.35–1.65 × 0.85–1.05 × 0.90 m			
	Chamber: 1.20 × .50 × 0.40 m; floor at -1.10 m; 0.15 m overlap			
	Blocking: cb., leaned, dist. 0.32 × 0.14 × 0.10 m			
	Burial: S/L/thighs ext., legs folded/at face, dist.			
	Body: Adult male			
	Objects:			
	a. From shaft:			
	1. Sherds of cup		31894	
	2. Basket (small), diam. 11		21257	
	b. In chamber:			
	3. Textile wrapping remains, CAT 133–134 (no. changed from 1)		20968	
	4. Iron ring (second toe R)		20989	fig. 163b, pl. 76k
	5. Bead		21238	
Q 388				
	Shaft with chamber on the W side			
	Shaft: 1.50–2.05 × 0.60–1.00 × 1.10 m			
	Chamber: ? × 0.40 × 0.45 m; floor at -1.25 m; overlap			
	Blocking: cb.; hor., based on single course of stretchers in shaft			
	Burial: —/—/"contracted"			
	Body: Juvenile male			
	Objects:			
	1. Date pits		Disc.	
	2. Textile remains, CAT 135		20969	
	3. Beads		20986	
	4. X-Gr. ord. goblet I—A1aii *alpha*, height 8.5		20994	
	5. Coptic period Eg. amphora—A4b, bl. and wh. bands framed bk., three sets, red coat		20995	figs. 24d, 163e
Q 389				
	Shaft with chamber on the N side			
	Shaft: 1.00 × 0.85 × 0.70 m			
	Chamber: 0.90 × 0.65 × 0.30 m; floor at -0.95 m, 0.35 m overlap			

Table 40. Register of X-Group Finds in Cemetery Q (*cont.*).

Tomb	Description and Contents	Cairo	OIM	Figure/Plate
Q 389 (*cont.*)				
	Blocking: cb., one large stone cb.; $0.35 \times 0.18 \times 0.08$			
	Burial: W/L/thighs 90 degrees, legs 110 degrees/before face			
	Body: Juvenile			
	Objects:			
	1. Leaves		Disc.	
Q 390				
	Shaft with floor-chamber and vault			
	Shaft: N-S			
	Chamber: no dim.			
	Vault: three cb., leaned N, blocked with stretchers at S end			
	Burial: S/R/thighs 90 degrees, legs folded/— dist.			
	Body: Mature male			
	Objects:			
	a. From shaft:			
	1. Sherds		—	
	b. From chamber:			
	2. Textile remains, CAT 136		21232	
	3. Sherds		—	
	4. X-Gr. ord. goblet I—B2bi		21243	fig. 7v
	Sherds:		31933	
	A. Post-X-Gr. red-gray sandy, ye.-wh. coat			
	B. Unc. Coptic period Eg. *amphoriskos*? wh. coat			
Q 391				
	Shaft with deepened floor chamber on the W side			
	Shaft: no dim.			
	Chamber: no dim.			
	Blocking: none present			
	Burial: —			
	Body: Infant or premature			
	Objects:			
	1. Remains of textile (CAT X-Gr.)		Disc.	
Q 393				
	Shaft with chamber on the W side			
	Shaft: $1.55–1.90 \times 0.70–1.05 \times 1.60$ m			
	Chamber: $1.55 \times 0.75 \times 0.45$ m; floor at -1.75 m, overlap			
	Blocking: cb.			
	Burial: N/L/thighs 45 degrees, legs 90 degrees/—			
	Body: Adult female			
	Objects:			
	a. From shaft:			
	1. Sherd		—	
	b. In chamber:			
	2. Textile wrapping remains, CAT 137		21237	
	3. Handle of jug		—	
Q 394				
	Shaft with chamber on the W side			
	Shaft: $1.75–2.00 \times 0.70–0.90 \times 1.50$ m			
	Step: sloped			

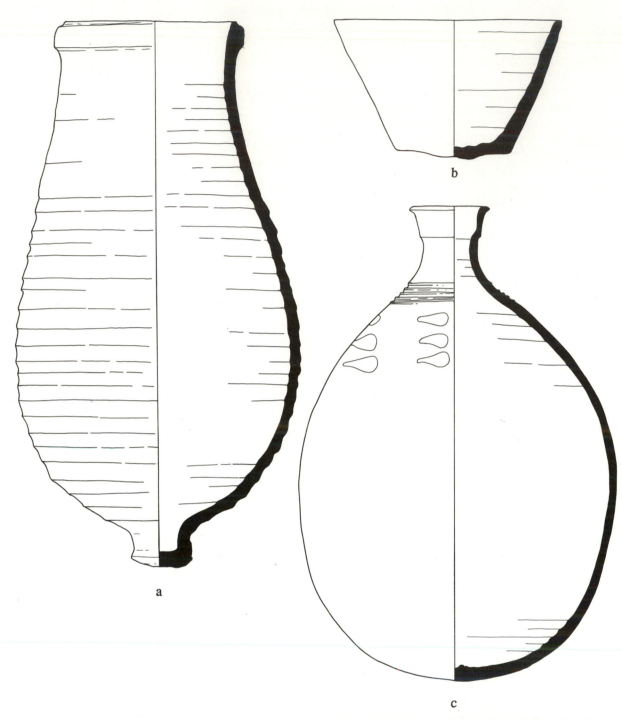

Figure 164. Pottery from Tombs Q 405 and Q 410: (*a*) *Qadus*, Q 410—4; (*b*) X-Gr. Ord. Bowl I—B, Q 410—3; (*c*) X-Gr. Ord. Bottle-Jar I—D3, Q 405—2. Scale 2:5.

Table 40. Register of X-Group Finds in Cemetery Q (*cont.*).

Tomb	Description and Contents	Cairo	OIM	Figure/Plate

Q 394 (*cont.*)

Chamber: 1.70 × 1.05 × 0.75 m; floor at -2.05, substantial overlap

Blocking: cb., laid alt. header-stretcher (two wide), some mud plaster

Burial: S/L/thighs 30 degrees, legs 100 degrees/—

Body: Adult male

Objects:

a.	In shaft:			
1.	Sherds		—	
2.	Textile remains		Disc.	
3.	Leather remains		—	
4.	Leaves (also in chamber)		Disc.	
5.	Tubular sherd (amphora frag.?), 56.0 × 12.4		21253	
b.	In chamber:			
6.	Textile wrapping, CAT 138, disintegrated		21233	
7.	Sandals remains		Disc.	
8.	*Qadus*, 39.0 × 18.5		22361	

Q 400

Shaft with chamber in the floor

Shaft: N-S, no dim.

Chamber: 1.10 × 0.40 × ? m

Blocking: stone slabs

Burial: S/L/thighs 75 degrees, legs folded/at face

Body: Juvenile-adult

Objects:

a.	In chamber:			
1.	Jar, broken		Disc.	
2.	Textile remains, two types		Disc.	
b.	Chamber and shaft:			
3.	Dates, fifty-eight in shaft		Disc.	
4.	Unfinished sandstone stela in shaft		Disc.	

Q 405, tumulus recorded — pl. 34b

Shaft with chamber on the N side

Tumulus: marked with circular trench

Shaft: 2.05–2.55 × ? × 0.65 m

Chamber: 1.80 × 0.50 × 0.40 m; floor at -1.05,
step in shaft at -0.80 m, mostly overlapped

Blocking: stone slabs

Burial: —

Body: Adult or older

Objects:

1.	X-Gr. ord. goblet I—B2a, height 8.6		21370	
2.	X-Gr. ord. bottle-jar I—D3, wh. pt., vine in groups of three		21400	fig. 164c

Sherd:

A.	Post-X-Gr. wh., hard pk., ribbed, red coat		31937	

Q 410

Shaft with chamber on the W side

Shaft: 1.40–1.80 × 0.75–0.95 × 1.20 m

Chamber: 1.45 × ca. 0.55 × 0.50; floor at -1.40 m; overlap

Blocking: cb., one course stretchers, three courses rowlock

Burial: S/R/thighs 30 degrees, legs folded/stomach

Table 40. Register of X-Group Finds in Cemetery Q (*cont.*).

Tomb	Description and Contents	Cairo	OIM	Figure/Plate
Q 410 (*cont.*)				
	Body: Mature male			
	Objects:			
	1. Textile wrapping remains (CAT X-Gr.)		Disc.	
	2. Textile band at head (secured wrapping)		Disc.	
	3. X-Gr. ord. bowl I—B		21496	fig. 164b
	4. *Qadus*		22362	fig. 164a
	Sherd:			
	A. X-Gr. ord. cup convex base, carinated lower side			
Q 422				
	Shaft with chamber on the S side			
	Shaft: 1.70–2.35 × 0.70–0.95 × 1.45 m			
	Chamber: 1.70 × 0.80 × 0.50 m; floor at -1.85 m;			
	overlap 0.40 m			
	Blocking: cb. headers on one course stretchers closed			
	by course rowlock			
	Burial: W/R/thighs 90 degrees, legs folded/L. thigh			
	Body: Mature male			
	Objects:			
	a. In chamber:			
	1. Textile wrapping, CAT 139–140 (no. changed from 3)		21230A–B	
	b. In shaft:			
	2. Two sherds		31947	
	3. Remains of leather		Disc.	
	Sherds:			
	A. A-Group? drab-bk. int, red coat, V-Shaped, chaffy			
Q 425				
	Shaft with floor chamber			
	Shaft: 1.90–2.25 × 0.80 × 0.30 m			
	Chamber: 1.90 × 0.35 × 0.45 m; floor at -0.75 m			
	Blocking: stone slabs			
	Burial: W/B/ext./pelvis, dist.			
	Body: Mature			
	Objects:			
	a. From chamber			
	1. Leaves and straw (near head)		Disc.	
	2. X-Gr. ord. goblet I—B2aii (near head), height 8.6		21250	
	3. Sherds			
	4. "Several types of string, 5 strips			
	of one type stuck to L side of head,			
	white string near waist"			
	5. Textile and sheepskin, CAT 170–173		21308	
	b. From shaft:			
	3. Sherds		Disc.	
	6. Textile remains		Disc.	
	Sherd:			
	A. X-Gr. ord. jar, red fabric with organic inclusions; ye.-wh. coat		31948	
Q 434				
	Shaft with chamber on the N side			
	Shaft: ? × 0.50–0.75 × 0.95 m			

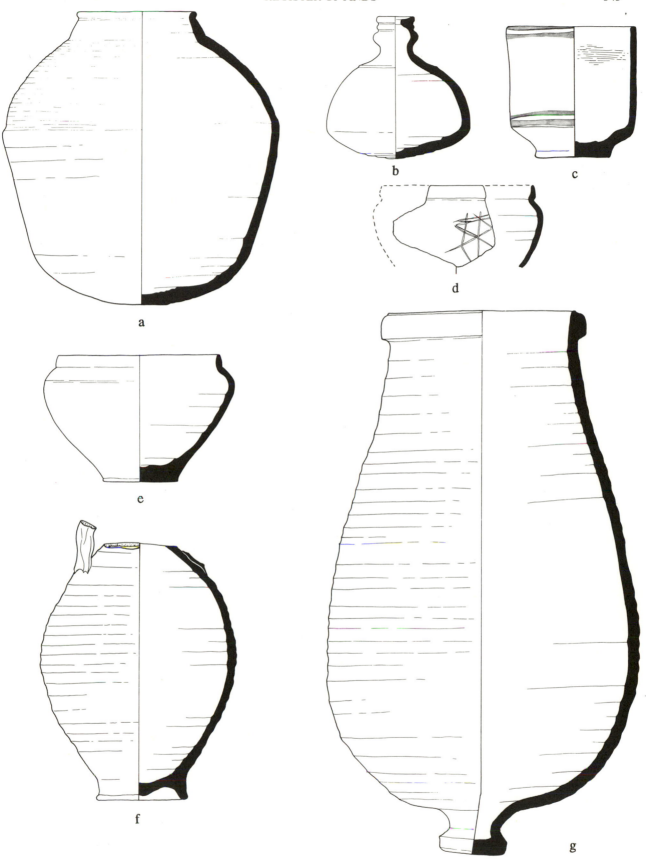

Figure 165. Pottery from Tombs Q 422 (Surface), Q 434, Q 446, Q 468, and Q 479: (*a*) X-Gr. Ord. Utility Storage Jar III—A, Q 434—3; (*b*) Coptic Period Egyptian Handleless Juglet, Q 434—5; (*c*) X-Gr. Ord. Cup—D4a, Q 422 SW—1; (*d*) X-Gr. Ord. Goblet I—B, Q 468—A; (*e*) X-Gr. Ord. Goblet I—B1c, Q 434—1; (*f*) Coptic Period Egyptian Utility *Amphoriskos*-Jug II—?, Q 446—1; (*g*) *Qadus*, Q 479—1. Scale 2:5.

Table 40. Register of X-Group Finds in Cemetery Q (*cont.*).

Tomb	Description and Contents	Cairo	OIM	Figure/Plate
Q 434 (*cont.*)				
	Chamber: ? × 0.40 × 0.30 m; floor at -1.10 m, ca. 0.20 m overlap			
	Blocking: cb. and stone slabs; cb. two courses headers in shaft, one course leaned, stone toward one end			
	Burial: —			
	Body: "Infant I"			
	Objects:			
	1. X-Gr. ord. goblet I—B1c		21330	fig. 165e
	2. Dates in no. 1		Disc.	
	3. X-Gr. ord. utility storage jar III—A		21331	fig. 165a
	4. Textile wrapping remains (CAT X-Gr.)		Disc.	
	5. Coptic period Eg. handleless juglet		21332	fig. 165b
	6. Beads		21367	figs. 62a, e, g, k, 63f, i, 65b
Q 446, Infant burial cut in S end of QC 44				
	Shaft with chamber ? on the W side			
	Shaft: irreg. depths vary from 0.40–0.80 m			
	Chamber: no dim.			
	Blocking: two rows of cb. on end, two on side			
	Burial: wrapped, in position, but jumbled by removal			
	Body: "Infant I"			
	Objects, in chamber:			
	1. Coptic period Eg. utility *amphoriskos*-jug II— ?, rim and handles broken		21447	fig. 165f
	2. Textile wrapping remains		Disc.	
	3. Beads		21425	
Q 463				
	Shaft and chamber: see OINE VIII			
	Burials:			
	A. See OINE VIII			
	B. —, possibly slightly contracted, facing S			
	Bodies:			
	A. See OINE VIII			
	B. "Infant II"			
	Objects:			
	1. Decayed wood in burial chamber		Disc.	
	2. Beads		21448	fig. 65d
	Note that the tomb was Meroitic, but burial B was probably X-Group.			
Q 468				
	Shaft with chamber on the W side			
	Shaft: 0.70–1.10 × 0.35–0.60 × 0.70 m			
	Chamber: undercut ca. 0.15 m			
	Blocking: present but kind not indicated			
	Burial: —			
	Body: "Infant I–II"			
	Objects:			
	1. Textile remains		Disc.	
	2. Sherds (from shaft, one potter's mark)		—	
	Sherd:			
	A. X-Gr. ord. goblet I—B; open, with potter's mark, worn		31968	fig. 165d

Table 40. Register of X-Group Finds in Cemetery Q (*cont.*).

Tomb	Description and Contents	Cairo	OIM	Figure/Plate
Q 473 (between Q 647 and 646)				
	Shaft: N-S, no dim.			
	Burial: —			
	Body: "Infant II"			
	Objects: —			
Q 479				
	Shaft with chamber on the W side			
	Shaft: ? × 0.40–0.60 × 0.65 m			
	Chamber: ? × 0.45 × 0.30 m; floor at -0.80 m, overlap			
	Blocking: stone slabs			
	Burial: S/R/thighs 90 degrees, legs 120 degrees/at face			
	Body: "Infant II"			
	Object, at head end:			
	1. *Qadus*		21483	fig. 165g
	2. Textile remains, CAT 141		21487	
Q 545 (reused Christian?)				
	Shaft with chamber on the N side			
	Shaft: 1.60–2.40 × 0.55–0.75 × 1.60 m			
	Chamber: 2.10 × 0.75 × 0.75 m; floor at -2.00 m, variable overlap			
	Blocking: cb., three courses stretcher then alt. three header-stretcher			
	Burial: W/B/ext./—			
	Body: Mature (?) female			
Q 580				
	Shaft with chamber on the W side			
	Shaft: 1.30–1.40 × 0.45–0.55 × 1.15 m			
	Chamber: 1.30 × 0.45 × 0.45 m; floor at -1.55 m, overlap 0.15 m			
	Blocking: stone slabs			
	Burial: —			
	Body: Juvenile male			
	Objects:			
	1. Sherds of jar		32013	
	2. Textile remains		Disc.	
Q 582				
	Shaft with chamber on the N side			
	Shaft: 1.00–1.15 × 0.40–0.50 × 1.00 m			
	Chamber: 1.00 × 0.45 × 0.40 m; floor at -1.30 m, overlap 0.20 m			
	Blocking: mixed cb. and stone			
	Burial: —			
	Body: "Infant I"			
	Objects:			
	1. Leaves		Disc.	
	2. Date pits		Disc.	
	3. Textiles			
	a. Remains		Disc.	
	b. Remains		Disc.	
	c. Remains, CAT 144		21793C	

Table 40. Register of X-Group Finds in Cemetery Q (*cont.*).

Tomb	Description and Contents	Cairo	OIM	Figure/Plate

Q 583

    Shaft with chamber on the W side

        Shaft: 1.05–1.30 × 0.35–0.45 × 0.95 m

        Chamber: ? × 0.30 × 0.30 m; floor at -1.10 m,

            0.10 m overlap

        Blocking: cb.

    Burial: —

    Body: "Infant II"

    Objects:

        1.   Leaves   Disc.

        2.   Sherds   Disc.

Q 589

    Shaft with chamber on the W side

        Shaft: 1.65–1.85 × 0.55–0.75 × 1.05 m

        Chamber: 1.60 × 0.95 × 0.70 m; floor at -1.60 m,

            0.20 m overlap

        Blocking: stone slabs

    Burial: —

    Body: Senile male

    Objects:

        1.   Sherds   Disc.

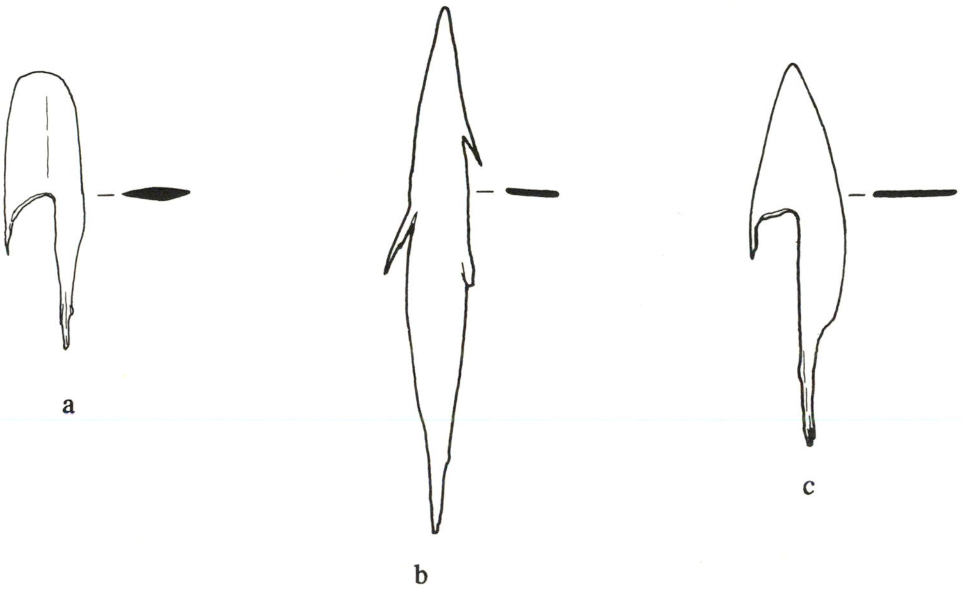

Figure 166. Arrowheads from Tomb Q 594: (*a*) No. 12, (*b*) No. 13, (*c*) No. 14. Scale 1:1.

Q 594, X-Gr. burial in Meroitic tomb

    Shaft with chamber on the S side (see OINE VIII)

    Burial: dist. in shaft

    Body: Adult male

    Objects (see OINE VIII):

        8.   Textile   Disc.

        9.   Remains of quiver   22026

      10.   Remains of bowstring, 53.0 × 0.2   22026

Table 40. Register of X-Group Finds in Cemetery Q (*cont.*).

Tomb	Description and Contents	Cairo	OIM	Figure/Plate
Q 594, X-Gr. burial in Meroitic tomb (*cont.*)				
Objects (see OINE VIII) (*cont.*):				
11.	Sherds		32017	
12–14.	Iron arrowheads		21890	fig. 166a–c

QF

Q 454, late X-Gr. bed burial removed, replaced by Christian burial				
Shaft with chamber on the N side				
Shaft: 2.45 × 1.05–1.45 × 0.70 m				
Chamber: 2.15 × 0.65 × ?; floor sloped, 0.25 m overlap				
Blocking: stone slabs				
Burial: W/L dist. /ext./pelvis				
Body: Mature female				
Objects:				
1.	Bed leg		Disc.	
2.	Textile remains (CAT X-Gr.)		Disc.	
Original burial was a bed burial, now removed.				

CEMETERY R

Table 41. Stages in Cemetery R.

1. Group of tombs to the N
   a. N-S shafts with W side chambers, dated early: 111, 118; other N-S shafts: 114, 116, 117, 107, 119
   b. E-W shafts with side chambers, dated to middle X-Gr.: 110; other E-W tombs: 109, 108, 106, 103, 115, 104, 102, 112, 105, 100

2. Scattered early to middle X-Gr. and one late X-Gr. tomb to the W
   a. Long E approach to N-S chamber: 1, 69, 74, 10
   b. E-W trench with end niche and vault?, dated late: 11

3. A large group of middle to late X-Gr. tombs to the S and E, presented in approximate order of position
   The following code is used:

[ ]	New Kingdom tombs
- -	Christian tombs
	N-S shafts
v	Vault-niche tombs
( )	Date indicated by contents

120,-77-, 82 (late), 103, <u>121</u>, [91],-101-, -30-, 14, [83],-97-, [81], 64v (late), 95 (late), 60 (middle), 66 (middle), 53, 49 (middle), 67, 37, [19], [20], [25], -12-, [13], [84], 15 (late), [17], 2 (late), 59 (middle), -113-, 92, 87, <u>65</u> (middle), 26, 68 (late), [79], 28, 24 (middle), -96-, [3], [4B], 4Av (middle to late), [94], <u>6</u> (middle to late), 89 (late), 50 (middle to late), [46], [45], [29], [52], [47], -80-, 22 (middle), -7-, -31-, [40], 27, 78, [76], [63], 48, [99], [33], [88], 23 (middle),-90-, [75], 18, 51 (late), [44], [58], [32], [42], [34], [38], [43], [39], [41], [35], 36, [61], 62 (middle), 8v (late), 16

New Kingdom tombs E of the house: [54], [56], [57], [55]

Child burials of uncertain date, with textiles only, extended: 113, 96, 80, 90

Table 42. Register of X-Group Finds in Cemetery R.

Tomb	Description and Contents	Cairo	OIM	Figure/Plate
R 1				
	Tumulus and shaft with chamber on the W side			
	Shaft: almost square, 1.50–2.05 × 1.05–1.65 × 1.40 m			
	Inner shaft or step: 1.60 × 0.55 × 1.30 m			
	Chamber: 2.25 × 1.15 × 1.40 m; ca. 0.20 m overlap, floor at -3.50 m			
	Blocking: stone slabs, in chamber			
	Burial: —			
	Body: Adult female			
	Objects:			
	1. Coptic period Eg. *amphoriskos*-jug I—D1a, red coat	20622	figs. 21e, 167b	
	2. X-Gr. utility-storage jar III—C	20623	fig. 167a	
	3. Beads	20624	figs. 63q, 64k	
	4. Braided leather cord, longest 8.0	20630		
	5. Two fragments of bone object, largest 2.2 × 2.4	20657		
	6. Two fragments of iron (arrowheads?)	Disc.		

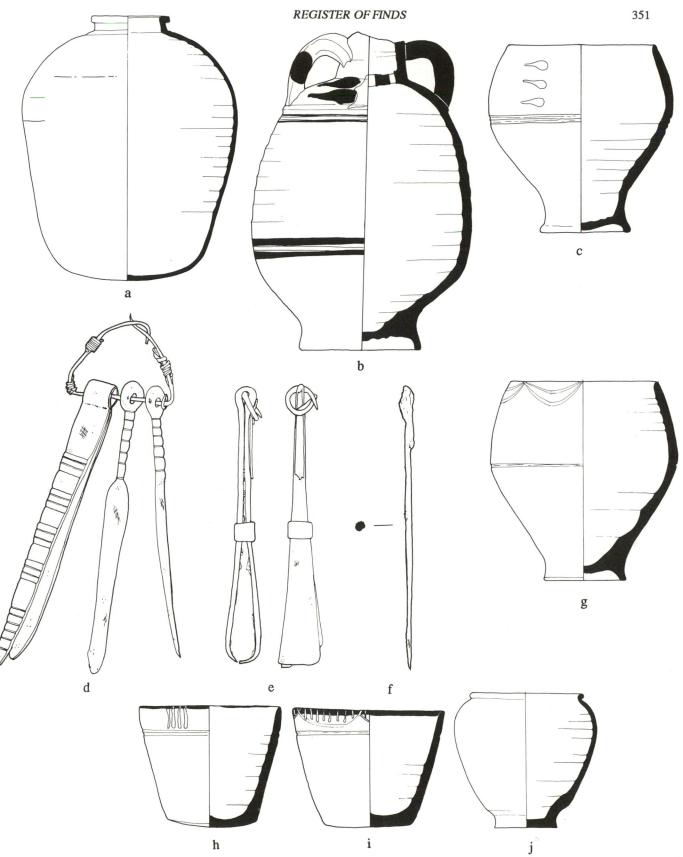

Figure 167. Pottery and Objects from Tombs R 1 and R 2: (*a*) X-Gr. Utility Storage Jar III—C, R 1—2;
(*b*) Coptic Period Egyptian *Amphoriskos*-Jug I—D1a, R 1—1; (*c*) X-Gr. Ord. Goblet I—A2ci,
R 2—4; (*d*) Ring with Tweezer and Two Probes, R 2—8b; (*e*) Broad Blade Tweezers,
R 2—8a; (*f*) Needle, R 2—8c; (*g*) X-Gr. Ord. Goblet I—A2b, R 2—3; (*h*) X-Gr. Ord.
Cup I—D1b, R 2—2; (*i*) X-Gr. Ord. Cup—D1b, R 2—5; (*j*) X-Gr. Ord. Goblet
I—B2biv, R 2—1. Scales: (*a*) 1:5, (*b, c, g–j*) 2:5, (*d–f*) 1:1.

Table 42. Register of X-Group Finds in Cemetery R (*cont.*).

Tomb	Description and Contents	Cairo	OIM	Figure/Plate
R 2				
	Tumulus and shaft with chamber on the N side			
	Tumulus: "with pebbles"			
	Shaft: 2.15 × 1.00–1.20 × 1.05 m			
	Chamber: 2.00 × 0.65–1.15 (expanded to E) × 0.75 m; floor at -1.50 m			
	Blocking: stone slabs			
	Burial: —			
	Body: Mature male			
	Objects:			
	1. X-Gr. ord. goblet I—B2biv		20625	fig. 167j
	2. X-Gr. ord. cup I—D1b, four groups of three wh. spots, four groups of five wh. vert. lines		20626	fig. 167h
	3. X-Gr. ord. goblet I—A2b, wh. pt. swags		20627	figs. 7k, 167g
	4. X-Gr. ord. goblet I—A2ci, wh. pt. vine in groups of three		20628	figs. 7l, 167c
	5. X-Gr. ord. cup—D1b, bk. rim band and swags with wh. fill		20629	fig. 167i
	6. Leather fragments, armor?, largest 4.7 × 4.5		20718	
	7. Quiver fragments		20658	
	8. Iron toilet objects		20697	pl. 80a
	a. Broad blade tweezers			fig. 167e
	b. Ring with tweezers and two probes			fig. 167d
	c. Two needles			fig. 167f
	9. Beads and pendant, pendant length 1.8		20803	
	10. Remains of wood		Disc.	
	11. "Bowstring"		Disc.	
	In other tombs, remains called bowstrings have also included braided cord.			
R 4A				fig. 168a, pl. 40a–b
	Tumulus and shaft with ledges and vault			
	Tumulus: 0.70 m high, with pebbles			
	Shaft: rectangular, NW-SE, undercut at E end, 2.40–3.05 × 1.00–1.40 × 1.55 m; rear niche at -0.65 m, 0.40 m deep			
	Ledges: undercut at -0.55 m, at -0.95, 0.20 m deep			
	Features: Two grooves at W end in access slope, 1.00 × 0.95 × 0.45 m, grooves 0.10–0.20 × 0.50 m			
	Vault: cb.			
	Blocking: mixed stone and cb.			
	Burial: —			
	Body: Mature male			
	Objects:			
	1. X-Gr. ord. goblet—A2b, wh. pt. vine, in groups of three		20631	fig. 169b
	2. X-Gr. ord. bottle-jar I—A2, height 25.9		20632	
	3. X-Gr. ord. bottle-jar I—A2		20633	fig. 169d
	4. X-Gr. ord. cup I—D2b, pk.-wh. coat		20634	figs. 9d, 170a
	5. X-Gr. ord. bottle-necked jar I—A2, height 25.4		20635	
	6. X-Gr. ord. bottle-necked jar I—A3		20636	fig. 169e
	7. X-Gr. ord. cup I—D3b, dk. rim with wh. spots (dec. not shown)		20637	figs. 9e, 170c
	8. X-Gr. ord. cup I—D4, same dec., height 9.1		20638	
	9. X-Gr. ord. goblet I—A2b, wh. pt. swags, height 13.2		20639	

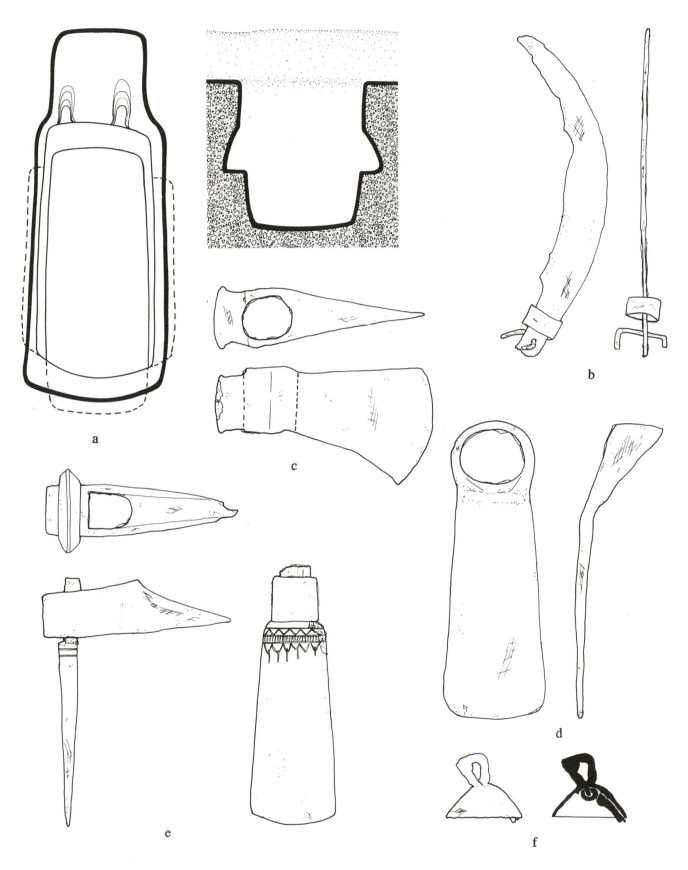

Figure 168. Plan, Section, and Objects from Tomb R 4A: (*a*) Plan and Section; (*b*) Sickle-Saw, No. 22; (*c*) Axe Head, No. 21; (*d*) Adze Head, No. 20; (*e*) Adze Head, No. 19; (*f*) Bell/Ornament, No. 26. Scales: (*a*) 1:40, (*b–e*) 1:2, (*f*) 1:1.

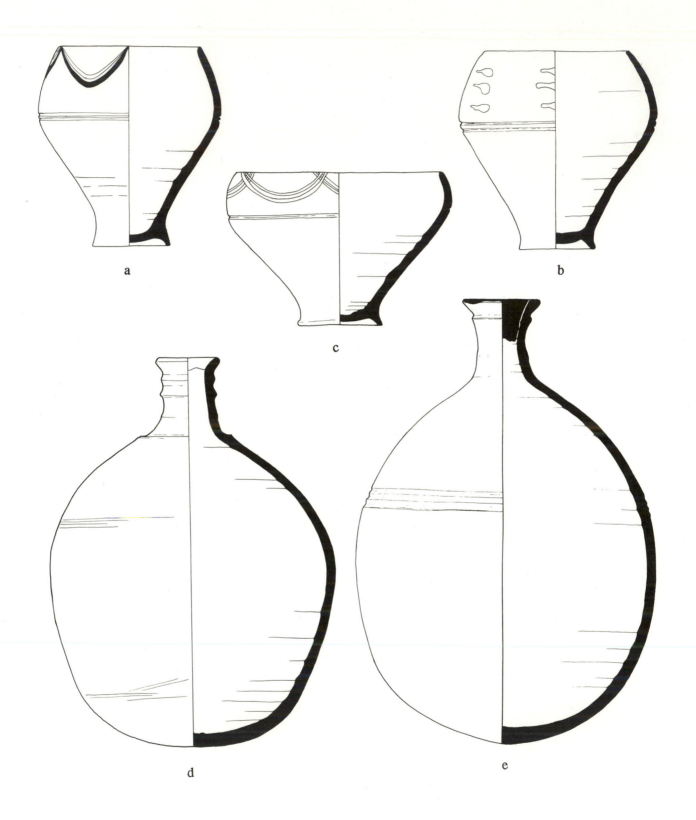

Figure 169. Pottery from Tomb R 4A: (*a*) X-Gr. Ord. Goblet I—A2b, No. 13; (*b*) X-Gr. Ord. Goblet—A2b, No. 1; (*c*) X-Gr. Ord. Goblet I—A2a, No. 18; (*d*) X-Gr. Ord. Bottle-Jar I—A2, No. 3; (*e*) X-Gr. Ord. Bottle-Necked Jar I—A3, No. 6. Scale 2:5.

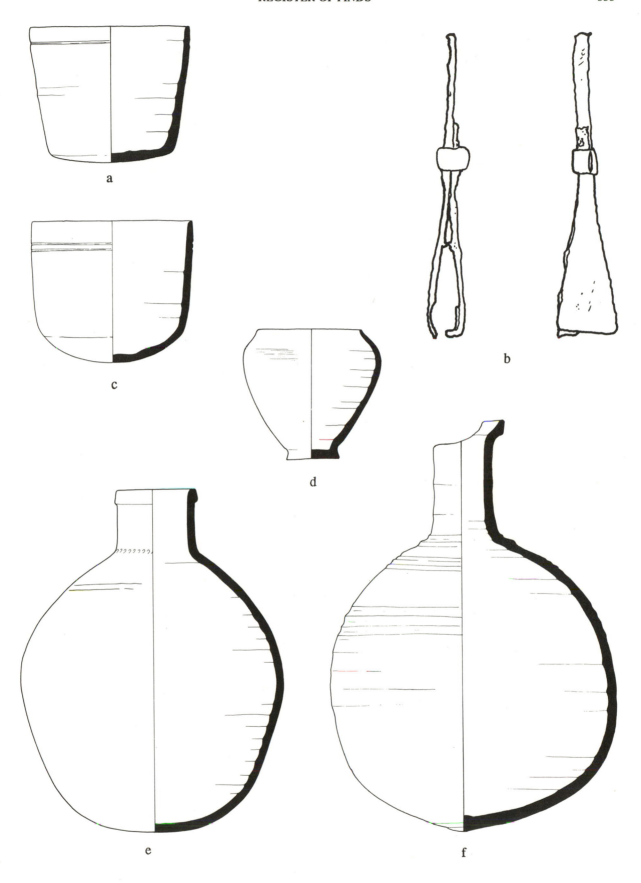

Figure 170. Pottery (*cont.*) and Tweezer from Tomb R 4A: (*a*) X-Gr. Ord. Cup I—D2b, No. 4; (*b*) Tweezer, No. 25; (*c*) X-Gr. Ord. Cup I—D3b, No. 7; (*d*) X-Gr. Ord. Goblet I—B2ai, No. 15; (*e*) X-Gr. Utility Storage Jar III—C, No. 14; (*f*) X-Gr. Ord. Narrow-Necked Bottle-Jar I—C2, No. 17. Scales: (*a, c–f*) 2:5, (*b*) 1:1.

Table 42. Register of X-Group Finds in Cemetery R (*cont.*).

Tomb	Description and Contents	Cairo	OIM	Figure/Plate
R 4A (*cont.*)				
Objects (*cont.*):				
10.	X-Gr. ord. goblet I—A2b, wh. pt. vine, in groups of three, height 12.6		20640	
11.	X-Gr. ord. cup I—D2b, pk.-wh. coat, height 8.7		20641	
12.	X-Gr. ord. cup I—D2b, pk.-wh. coat, height 8		20642	
13.	X-Gr. ord. goblet I—A2b, bk. and wh. pt. swags		20643	fig. 169a, pl. 41e
14.	X-Gr. utility storage jar III—C		20644	fig. 170e
15.	X-Gr. ord. goblet I—B2ai, polished		20645	fig. 170d
16.	X-Gr. ord. bottle-jar I—A3, height 27.1		20646	
17.	X-Gr. ord. narrow-necked bottle-jar I—C2		20647	figs. 14f, 170f
18.	X-Gr. ord. goblet I—A2a, wh. pt. swags		20732	figs. 7j, 169c
19.	Adze head, iron		20705	fig. 168e, pl. 82c
20.	Adze head, iron		20707	fig. 168d, pl. 82b
21.	Axe head, iron		20717	fig. 168c, pl. 82d
22.	Sickle saw, iron		20719a–b	fig. 168b, pl. 82a
23.	Archer's guard, width 7.0		20703	
24.	Quiver fragments, largest 27.5 × 15.5		20706	
25.	Broad blade bronze tweezers with gold locking band		20663	fig. 170b, pl. 81c
26.	Bell or ornament, iron?		20665	fig. 168f, pl. 83a
27.	Jar content		20696	
28.	Unc. stone object, possibly palette, 10.5 × 9.5 × 1.7		20720	
29.	Stone grinder (pestle), length 19.5		20721	
30.	Jar contents		20660	
R 5				pl. 40c
Shaft with ledges and vault (not on plan); no tumulus noted				
Shaft: no dim.				
Vault: no dim.				
Burial: —				
Body: Adult female				
Objects: —				
Sherds: —			33201	
R 6				
Shaft with chamber on the W side				
Shaft: 1.30–1.45 × 0.65–0.70 × 0.55 m				
Chamber: 1.30 × 0.45 m; ca. 0.10 m undercut; floor at -1.05 m				
Burial: S/R/"contracted"/under head				
Body: Mature male				
Objects:				
1.	Textile remains (bound around waist with 4–5 beads), CAT 147		20813	
2.	Coptic period Eg. utility *amphoriskos* jug II—C, wh. coat, height 23.4		20659	
3.	X-Gr. ord. goblet I—B2bii, height 9.2		20775	
4.	Ring with tweezers, two probes and blade	Q 847, 89892		fig. 171b–f
5.	Braided leather cord for no. 4		20698	fig. 171a, pl. 63b

Table 42. Register of X-Group Finds in Cemetery R (*cont.*).

Tomb	Description and Contents	Cairo	OIM	Figure/Plate

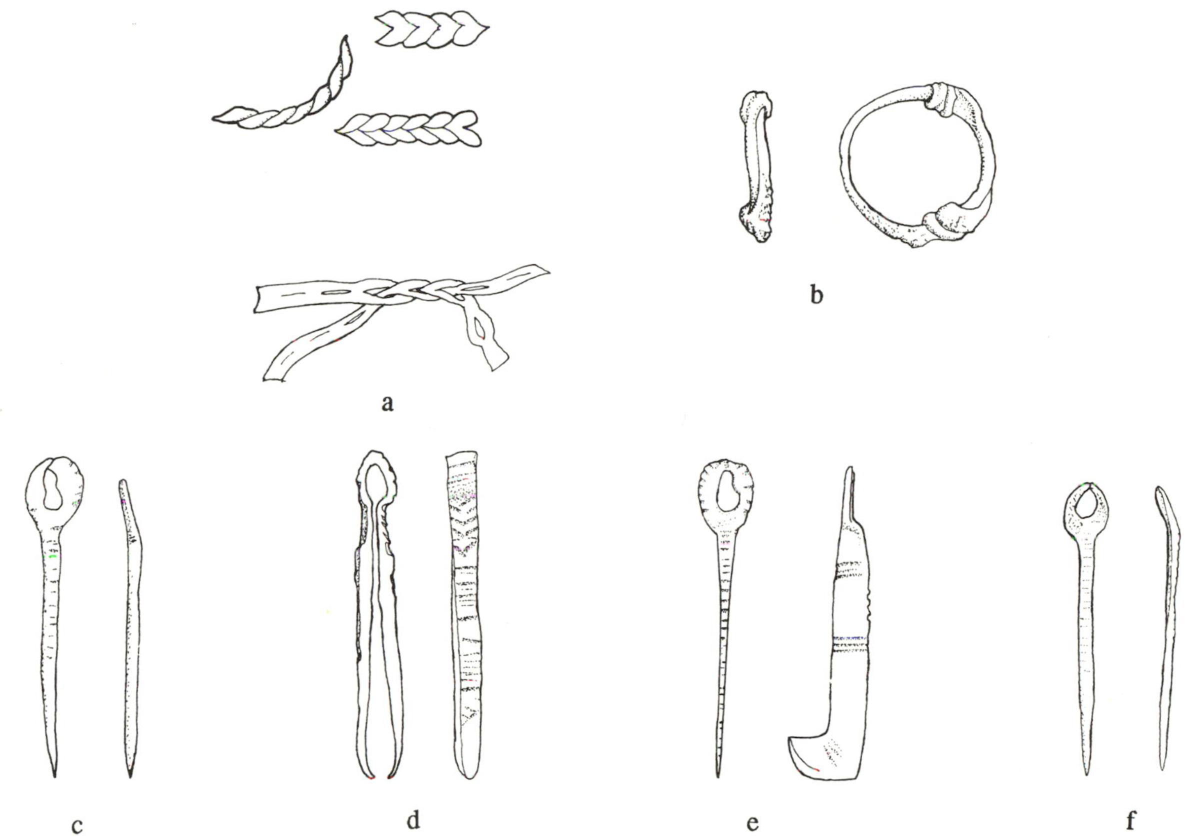

Figure 171. Cosmetic Ring from Tomb R 6: (*a*) Braided Leather Cord, No. 5; (*b*) Ring, No. 4; (*c*) Probe, No. 4; (*d*) Tweezers, No. 4; (*e*) Blade, No. 4; (*f*) Probe, No. 4. Scale 1:2(?).

R 7

Shaft with chamber on the N side
    Shaft: 1.95–2.30 × 0.70–1.00 × 1.45 m
    Step: shorter than shaft, at -1.65 m
    Chamber: 2.10 × 0.65 × 0.50 m; floor at -1.95 m;
        overlap ca. 0.20 m
Burial: W/B/ex /pubis
Body: Mature male?
Objects:

1.	Remains of textile (CAT X-Gr.)		Disc.	
2.	Wood remains (under body, bed?)		Disc.	

R 8   fig. 172

Shaft with ledges and vault
    Shaft: 2.00–2.30 × 0.55–0.93 × 1.35 m
    Ledges: undercut at -0.35 m; at-0.70 m; 0.20 m wide
    Access ramp: 1.10 × 0.60 × 0.65 m
    Vault: cb., few courses intact to E
Burial: W/B/ext./pubis
Body: Mature
Objects:

1.	X-Gr. ord. goblet I—B2bii, height 8.8	20656		

Table 42. Register of X-Group Finds in Cemetery R (*cont.*).

Tomb	Description and Contents	Cairo	OIM	Figure/Plate
R 8 (*cont.*)				
	Objects (*cont.*):			
	2. X-Gr. ord. bottle-jar I—C3, height 27.2		20701	
	3. Beads		20667	
	4. Textile wrapping remains (at chest and legs; CAT X-Gr.)		Disc.	

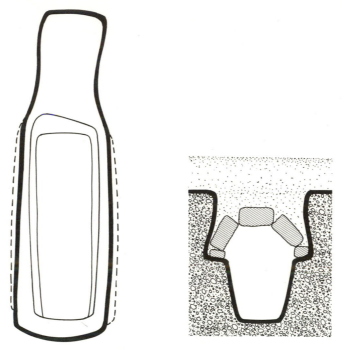

Figure 172. Plan and Section of Tomb R 8. Scale 1:40.

R 10

    Tumulus and shaft with ledges and vault, grooved ramp

        Tumulus: 0.10 m high

        Shaft: 1.95–2.45 × 0.85–1.05 × 1.75 m;

                undercut at W, ca. 0.15 m

       Ledges: undercut, at 1.15 m, ca. 0.20 m wide

       Ramp: 1.25–1.40 × 0.90 m; grooves 0.15 m wide

       Vault: Five cb., leaned W

    Burial: W/B ext./—

    Body: —

    Objects: —

R 11   fig. 173a

    Shaft with ledges and vault

       Shaft: 2.30–2.45 × 0.85–0.95 × 130 m

       Ledges: at -0.80 m, undercut 0.20 m

       Ramp: 1.00 × 0.85 × 0.45 m

       Vault: Five cb., 0.08 × 0.18 × 0.35–0.36 m

       Blocking: stone slab

    Burial: —

    Body: Senile male

    Objects:

        1. X-Gr. ord. bottle-jar I—B2b   20722   fig. 173f

Figure 173. Plan, Section, Pottery, and a Whorl from Tomb R 11: (*a*) Plan and Section; (*b*) Whorl, No. 7; (*c*) X-Gr. Ord. Goblet I—A2ci?, No. 5; (*d*) X-Gr. Ord. Goblet I—A2di, No. 3; (*e*) X-Gr. Ord. Goblet I—A2cii, No. 4; (*f*) X-Gr. Ord. Bottle-Jar I—B2b, No. 1; (*g*) X-Gr. Ord. Goblet I—D3, No. 2. Scales: (*a*) 1:40, (*b*) 1:1, (*c–g*) 2:5.

Table 42. Register of X-Group Finds in Cemetery R (*cont.*).

Tomb	Description and Contents	Cairo	OIM	Figure/Plate
R 11 (*cont.*)				
	Objects (*cont.*):			
	2. X-Gr. ord. goblet I—D3		20726	fig. 173g
	3. X-Gr. ord. goblet I—A2di		20723	figs. 7n, 173d
	4. X-Gr. ord. goblet I—A2cii, wh. pt., abraded, possibly vine		20724	figs. 7m, 173e
	5. X-Gr. ord. goblet I—A2ci?, height 11.8		20725	fig. 173c
	6. X-Gr. ord. goblet I— B2bii		20742	
	7. Steatite? whorl or disc with incised dec.		20824	fig. 173b

R 14

    Shaft with chamber on the N side

        Shaft: 1.60–2.20 × 0.60–0.80 × 1.00 m

        Chamber: 1.80 × 0.60 × 0.40 m; floor at -1.40;

                ca. 0.20 overlap

    Burial: S/R/"semicontracted"

    Body: Mature female

    Objects:

        1. Textile wrapping ("ye. colored"; CAT X-Gr.)   Disc.

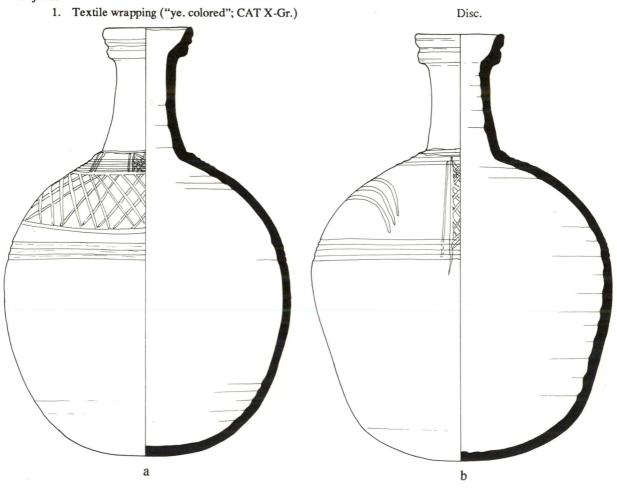

a   b

Figure 174. Pottery from Tomb R 15: (*a*) X-Gr. Ord. Bottle-Jar I—C3, No. 1;
(*b*) X-Gr. Ord. Bottle-Jar I—C3, No. 2. Scale 2:5.

R 15

    Shaft with vault

        Shaft: 2.56–2.85 (undercut 0.40 to S) × 1.15 × 1.45 m

Table 42. Register of X-Group Finds in Cemetery R (*cont.*).

Tomb	Description and Contents	Cairo	OIM	Figure/Plate
R 15 (*cont.*)				
	Grooves: parallel, to N for bed, 0.15 × 0.10 m			
	Chamber: built on four courses ashlar			
	Burial: —			
	Body: Mature female			
	Objects:			
	a. From niche:			
	1. X-Gr. ord. bottle-jar I—C3, wh. pt. complex		20752	fig. 174a
	2. X-Gr. ord. bottle-jar I—C3, wh. pt. complex		20753	fig. 174b
	3. X-Gr. ord. goblet I—A2b, vine, in groups of three[?], height 13.5		20755	
	7. Textile, CAT 148 (no. changed from 1)		20853	
	b. Unc. (chamber?)			
	4. X-Gr. ord. goblet I—A2b, vine, in groups of six, height 12.8		20761	
	5. X-Gr. ord. goblet I—B2bii, height 9.6		20762	
	6. Beads		20830	fig. 64c
R 16				
	Tumulus and shaft with chamber on the N side			
	Tumulus: ca. 0.30 m high, no pebbles			
	Shaft: 2.25–2.85 × 0.60–0.80 × 1.20 m			
	Chamber: 2.10 × 0.50 × 0.35 m; floor at -1.40 m, unc. overlap			
	Blocking: stone slabs			
	Burial: S/B/"extended"			
	Body: Mature female			
	Objects:			
	1. Iron ring (third finger, L)		20827	fig. 61j, pl. 77c
	2. Two iron rings (index L)		20826	fig. 61k, pl. 77b
	3. Beads		20828	
	4. Textile remains, CAT 149		20814	
R 18				
	Shaft with chamber on the N side			
	Shaft: 1.75 (max.) × 0.50–0.80 × 0.35 m			
	Chamber: 0.95 × 0.60 × more than 0.20 m (sloping floor); floor at -1.00/-1.15 m, overlap 0.30 m			
	Burials:			
	A. —			
	B. W/?/ext. "flexed at knees"			
	Bodies:			
	A. Juvenile			
	B. —			
	Objects: —			
R 21, tomb not located				
	Shaft: rectangular, no dim.			
	Burial: W/B/ext. "legs flexed at knees"/pubis			
	Body: "Infant II"			
	Objects:			
	1. Beads		20834	

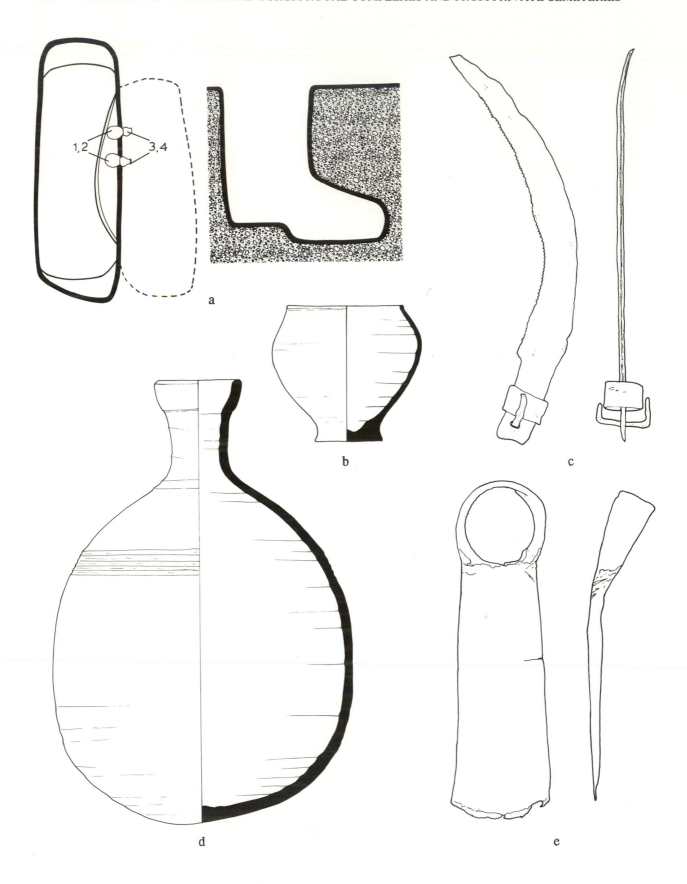

Figure 175. Plan, Section, Pottery, and Objects from Tomb R 22: (a) Plan and Section; (b) X-Gr. Ord.
Goblet I—B2aii, No. 3; (c) Sickle-Saw, No. 9; (d) X-Gr. Ord. Bottle-Jar I—D1, No. 1;
(e) Adze-Mattock Head, No. 7. Scales: (a) 1:40, (b, d) 2:5, (c, e) 1:2.

Table 42. Register of X-Group Finds in Cemetery R (*cont.*).

Tomb	Description and Contents	Cairo	OIM	Figure/Plate
R 22				fig. 175a
	Shaft with chamber on the N side			
	Shaft: 2.25–2.70 × 0.85 × 1.15 m			
	Chamber: 2.40 × 0.70–ca. 1.00 (overlap-expansion into shaft)			
	× 0.65 m			
	Blocking: none indicated			
	Burial: W/R/"contracted"/—			
	Body: Mature male			
	Objects, in chamber:			
	1. X-Gr. ord. bottle-jar I—D1		21071	fig. 175d
	2. X-Gr. ord. bottle-jar I—D1, 29.5 × 19.7		21072	
	3. X-Gr. ord. goblet I—B2aii		21069	fig. 175b
	4. X-Gr. ord. goblet I—B2aii, 9.5 × 9.2		21070	
	5. Leather garment or armor		20935	
	6. Archery equipment			
	a. Quiver		20964	fig. 52a
	b. Bag edge with grommets			fig. 52b
	7. Iron adze-mattock head		20934	fig. 175e, pl. 82f
	8. Beads (around neck of burial)		20937	
	9. Sickle saw, iron		20967	fig. 175c, pl. 82e
	10. Sandals, largest 18.5 × 8.8		20935	
	11. Remains of textile, CAT 150		20965	
R 23				
	Shaft with chamber on the N side			
	Shaft: 2.10–2.40 × 0.60–0.75 × 1.15 m			
	Chamber: 1.80 × 0.55 × 0.35 m; floor at -1.60 m,			
	overlap ca. 0.20 m			
	Blocking: stone slabs			
	Burial: W/B/ext./sides			
	Body: Mature female			
	Objects:			
	1. X-Gr. ord. bottle jar I—A2, ye.-wh. coat, bk. pt.,		20776	
	vine in groups of three, height 27.2			
	2. Textile remains (CAT X-Gr.)		Disc.	
R 24				
	Shaft with chamber on the N side			
	Shaft: 2.00–2.40 × 0.75–0.95 × 1.25 m			
	Chamber: 1.85 × 0.70 × 0.50 m; floor at -1.85 m,			
	overlap 0.25 m			
	Blocking: stone slabs			
	Burial: ?/B/ext./sides			
	Body: Mature female			
	Objects:			
	1. X-Gr. ord. bottle-jar I—E1b		20998	fig. 176d
	2. X-Gr. ord.bottle-jar I—, ye.-wh. coat		21000	fig. 176e
	3. X-Gr. ord. goblet I—B2bii		20999	fig. 176b
	4. X-Gr. ord. cup I—A1b, ye.-wh. coat		21002	figs. 8b, 176c
	5. Coptic period Eg. min. handleless juglet I—B1		21001	fig. 176a

Table 42. Register of X-Group Finds in Cemetery R (*cont.*).

Tomb	Description and Contents	Cairo	OIM	Figure/Plate

Figure 176. Pottery from Tomb R 24: (*a*) Coptic Period Egyptian Miniature Handleless Juglet I—B1, No. 5; (*b*) X-Gr. Ord. Goblet I—B2bii, No. 3; (*c*) X-Gr. Ord. Cup I—A1b, No. 4; (*d*) X-Gr. Ord. Bottle-Jar I—E1b, No. 1; (*e*) X-Gr. Ord. Bottle-Jar I—, No. 2. Scale 2:5.

R 26

    Shaft with chamber on the N side

        Shaft: 2.55 (max.) × 0.65–0.75 × 1.20 m

        Chamber: 2.00 × 0.70 × 0.50 m

        Blocking: —

    Burials:

        A. W/R/"semicontracted"/—

        B. —

    Bodies:

        A. Senile male

        B. Senile female

Table 42. Register of X-Group Finds in Cemetery R (*cont.*).

Tomb	Description and Contents	Cairo	OIM	Figure/Plate
R 26 (*cont.*)				
	Objects:			
	1. Textile (CAT X-Gr.)		Disc.	
	Shape, dimensions, and information on burial A are derived from the sketch on the back of the burial sheet, which is labeled R 61; a second sketch labeled R 61 is quite different.			
R 27				
	Shaft with side/floor chamber on the N? side			
	Shaft: 1.90–2.40 × 0.50–0.75 × 1.15 m			
	Groove for stones in wall: 0.35 × 0.10 m			
	Chamber: 1.95 × 0.25–0.45 × 0.40 m			
	Burial: W/B/ ext./pubis			
	Body: Mature female			
	Objects:			
	1. *Qadus*, wh. coat, very thin, carelessly applied		20858	fig. 180d
	2. Beads		20888	
R 28				
	Shaft: 2.15 × 0.60 × 0.60 m			
	Burial: W/B/"slight flex at knees"/—, at -0.50 m			
	Body: Senile male			
	Objects: —			
R 30				
	Rectangular superstructure, shaft and vault			
	Superstructure: headers, 0.88 × 0.65 m, on ca. 0.15 m sand			
	Shaft: 1.00–1.75 × 0.70 × 0.80 m			
	Vault: on two courses, stretchers, two cb.			
	Burial: —			
	Body: —			
	Objects: —			
R 31				
	Shaft with chamber on the N side			
	Shaft: 1.45 × 0.65–0.83 × 1.10 m			
	Chamber: 1.10 × 0.35 m, floor at -1.45 m			
	Blocking: stone slabs			
	Burial: W/"intact"			
	Body: Juvenile female			
R 36				fig. 177a
	Shaft with chamber on the W side			
	Shaft: 1.80–2.40 × 0.60–0.90 × 1.50 m			
	Chamber: 1.80 × 0.65 × 0.30 m			
	Blocking: stone slabs			
	Burials:			
	A. W/R/thighs 90 degrees, legs 120 degrees/face			
	B. W/B/ext./pubis, on blocking			
	Bodies:			
	A. Senile female			
	B. Mature female			

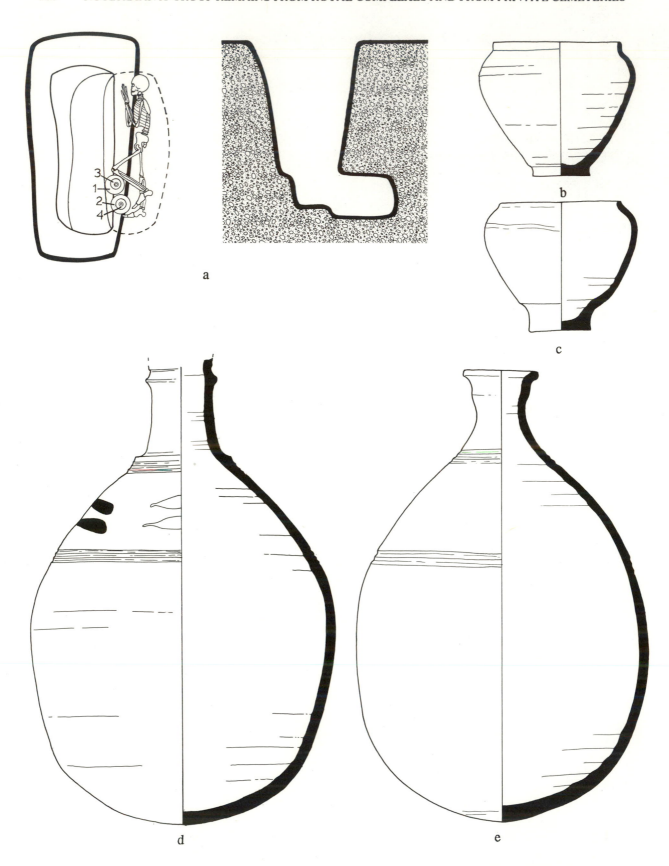

Figure 177. Plan, Section, and Pottery from Tomb R 36: (*a*) Plan and Section; (*b*) X-Gr. Ord. Goblet I—B2bii, No. 3; (*c*) X-Gr. Ord. Goblet I—B2biv, No. 4; (*d*) X-Gr. Ord. Bottle-Jar I—D2, No. 1; (*e*) X-Gr. Ord. Bottle-Jar I—A3, No. 2. Scales: (*a*) 1:40, (*b*–*e*) 2:5.

Table 42. Register of X-Group Finds in Cemetery R (*cont.*).

Tomb	Description and Contents	Cairo	OIM	Figure/Plate
R 36 (*cont.*)				
Objects:				
a.	From the chamber:			
	1. X-Gr. ord. bottle-jar I—D2, bk. and wh. pt., vine in pairs		21338	fig. 177d
	2. X-Gr. ord. bottle jar I—A3		21336	fig. 177e
	3. X-Gr. ord. goblet I—B2bii		21337	fig. 177b
	4. X-Gr. ord. goblet I—B2biv		21339	figs. 7x, 177c
	5. Beads		21377	
b.	From shaft:			
	6. Beads		21376	
	7. Textile wrapping of B (CAT X-Gr.)		Disc.	
R 37				
	Shaft with floor chamber			
	Shaft: 0.70–1.25 × ? × 0.80 m			
	Chamber: 0.70–0.85 × 0.40 × 0.20 m			
	Burial: W/B/ext./pubis			
	Body: "Infant I"			
	Objects:			
	1. Textile wrapping remains		Disc.	
	2. Incomplete cup		33212	
R 48				
	Shaft with chamber on the N side			
	Shaft: 1.50–1.85 × 0.50–0.86 × 0.70 m			
	Chamber: 1.40 × 0.45 × 0.40; floor at -1.30 m; overlap, ca. 0.30 m			
	Burial: —			
	Body: —			
	Objects: —			
R 49				fig. 178a
	Shaft with chamber on the N side			
	Shaft: 1.90–2.85 × 0.60–0.95 × 1.15 m			
	Chamber: 1.90 × 0.50–0.60 × 0.40 m; ca. 0.30 m overlap; floor at -1.50 m			
	Blocking: no information			
	Burial: W/B/ext./pubis			
	Body: Mature male			
	Objects:			
	1. X-Gr. ord. bottle-jar I—A2		21169	fig. 178d
	2. Iron tools			
	a. Sickle saw		21286	fig. 178c, pl. 82g
	b. Adze-mattock head		21285	fig. 178b, pl. 82h
	3. Beads		21287	
	4. Sandals, largest 17.6 × 7.8		21362	
	5. Leather archery equipment		21374	
	a. Quiver fragments			fig. 53a–b, pl. 60e
	b. Quiver fragments			fig. 53a–b
	c. Bow fragments			fig. 31, pl. 62a, c
	d. Bow fragments			
	e. Armor with studs			fig. 53c, e, f, pl. 66c

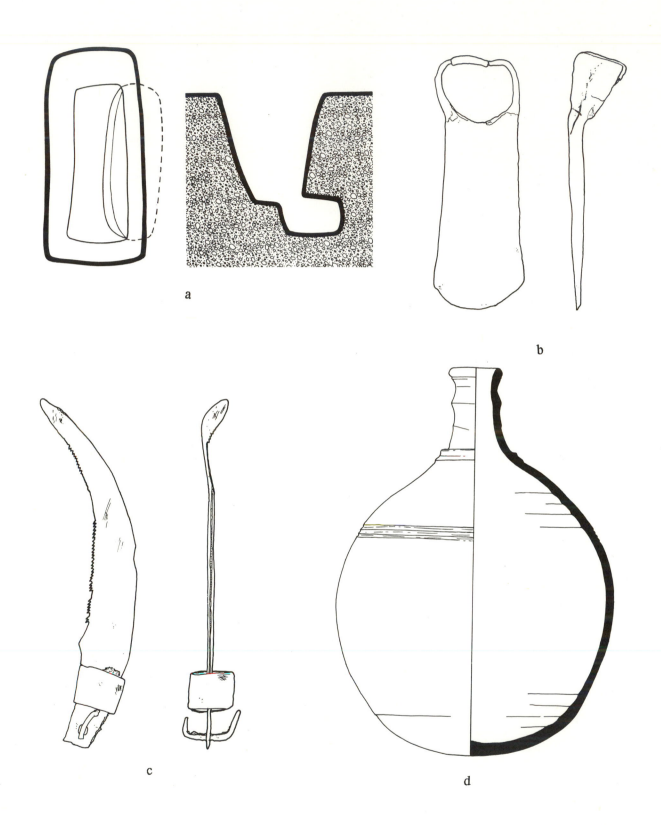

Figure 178. Plan, Section, Pottery, and Objects from Tomb R 49: (*a*) Plan and Section;
(*b*) Adze-Mattock, No. 2b; (*c*) Sickle-Saw, No. 2a; (*d*) X-Gr. Ord.
Bottle-Jar I—A2, No. 1. Scales: (*a*) 1:40, (*b, c*) 1:2, (*d*) 2:5.

Table 42. Register of X-Group Finds in Cemetery R (*cont.*).

Tomb	Description and Contents	Cairo	OIM	Figure/Plate
R 49 (*cont.*)				
	Objects (*cont.*):			
	6. Leather bag, remains of edging		21375	fig. 53d, pl. 67c
	7. Textile wrappings (CAT X-Gr.)		Disc.	fig. 53f
	a. Wrapping			
	b. Bands at head and pelvis			
R 50				fig. 179b
	Shaft with ramp and vault			
	Shaft: 2.25–2.30 × 0.70–0.96 × 1.15 m			
	Ramp: 0.50 × 0.65 × 0.35 m			
	Ledges: undercut, ca. 0.20 m			
	Vault: Four cb., 0.9–0.10 × 0.17 × 0.33 m (soft, with straw)			
	Blocking: cb., stretchers on one course rowlock			
	Burial: N/B/ext./pubis.			
	Body: Mature female			
	Objects:			
	a. In shaft:			
	1. Beads	20977, 20980		
	2. X-Gr. ord. goblet I—B2aii, 9.7 × 9.1		21251	
	3. Neck sherd of bottle-jar		33200	
	b. Unc. loc.:			
	4. Iron kohl stick		20983	fig. 179a, pl. 81f
	c. In chamber:			
	5. X-Gr. ord. goblet I—A2b, wh. pt., 13.1 × 12.2		21216	
	6. X-Gr. ord. narrow-necked bottle-jar I—B1a		21217	figs. 14d, 179f, pl. 44d
	7. X-Gr. ord. goblet I—B2aii		21218	fig. 179c
	8. X-Gr. ord. goblet I—A2b		21219	fig. 179d
	9. X-Gr. ord. goblet I—A2b		21220	fig. 179e, pl. 41d
R 51				
	Shaft with chamber on the N side			
	Shaft: 1.80–2.25 × 0.60–0.80 × 1.05 m			
	Chamber: 1.90 × 0.60–0.65 × 0.40 m; ca. 0.30 m overlap, floor at -1.40 m			
	Blocking: no information			
	Burial: no information			
	Body: no information			
	Objects:			
	1. X-Gr. ord. bottle jar I—C3, height 26.7		21168	
	2. X-Gr. ord. goblet I—B2bii, height 8.7		21173	
	3. Bronze tweezers and two probes on gold ring		21288	fig. 180a, pl. 81a
R 53				
	Shaft with chamber on the N side			
	Shaft: 1.30–1.60 × 0.50–0.60 × 0.95 m			
	Chamber: 1.10 × 0.35–0.45 × 0.20 (?) m; overlap ca. 0.17 m, floor at -1.30 m			
	Blocking: —			
	Burial: no information			
	Body: no information			
	Objects:			
	1. X-Gr. ord. min. bottle-jar I—A2, wh. pt., rib at neck		21170	figs. 15b, 180c, pl. 42d
	2. X-Gr. ord. bowl I—C1b, bk. band with wh. spots on rim		21249	fig. 180b, pl. 41h

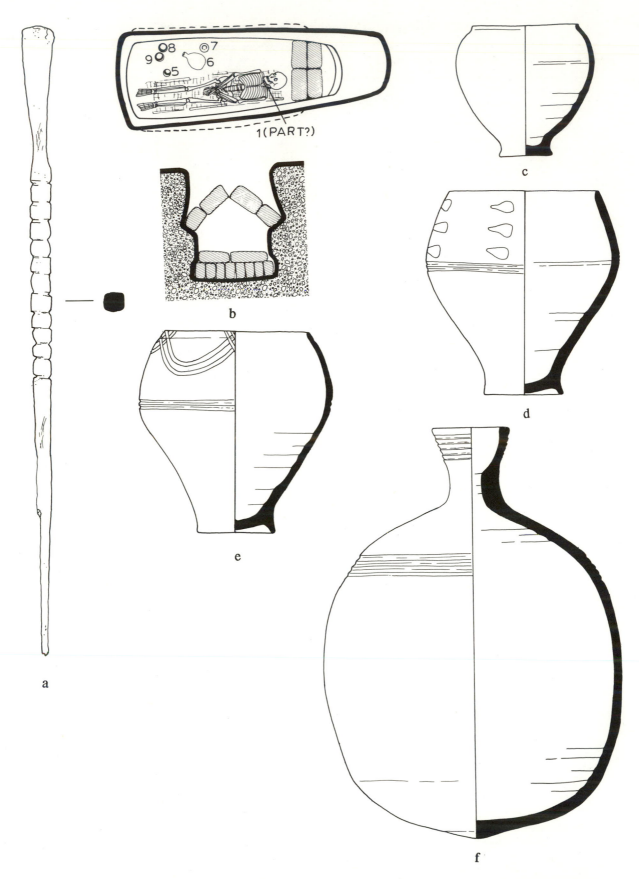

Figure 179. Plan, Section, Pottery, and Objects from Tomb R 50: (*a*) Kohl Stick, No. 4; (*b*) Plan and Section; (*c*) X-Gr. Ord. Goblet I—B2aii, No. 7; (*d*) X-Gr. Ord. Goblet I—A2b, No. 8; (*e*) X-Gr. Ord. Goblet I—A2b, No. 9; (*f*) X-Gr. Ord. Narrow-Necked Bottle-Jar I—B1a, No. 6. Scales: (*a*) 1:1, (*b*) 1:40, (*c–f*) 2:5.

Table 42. Register of X-Group Finds in Cemetery R (*cont.*).

Tomb	Description and Contents	Cairo	OIM	Figure/Plate

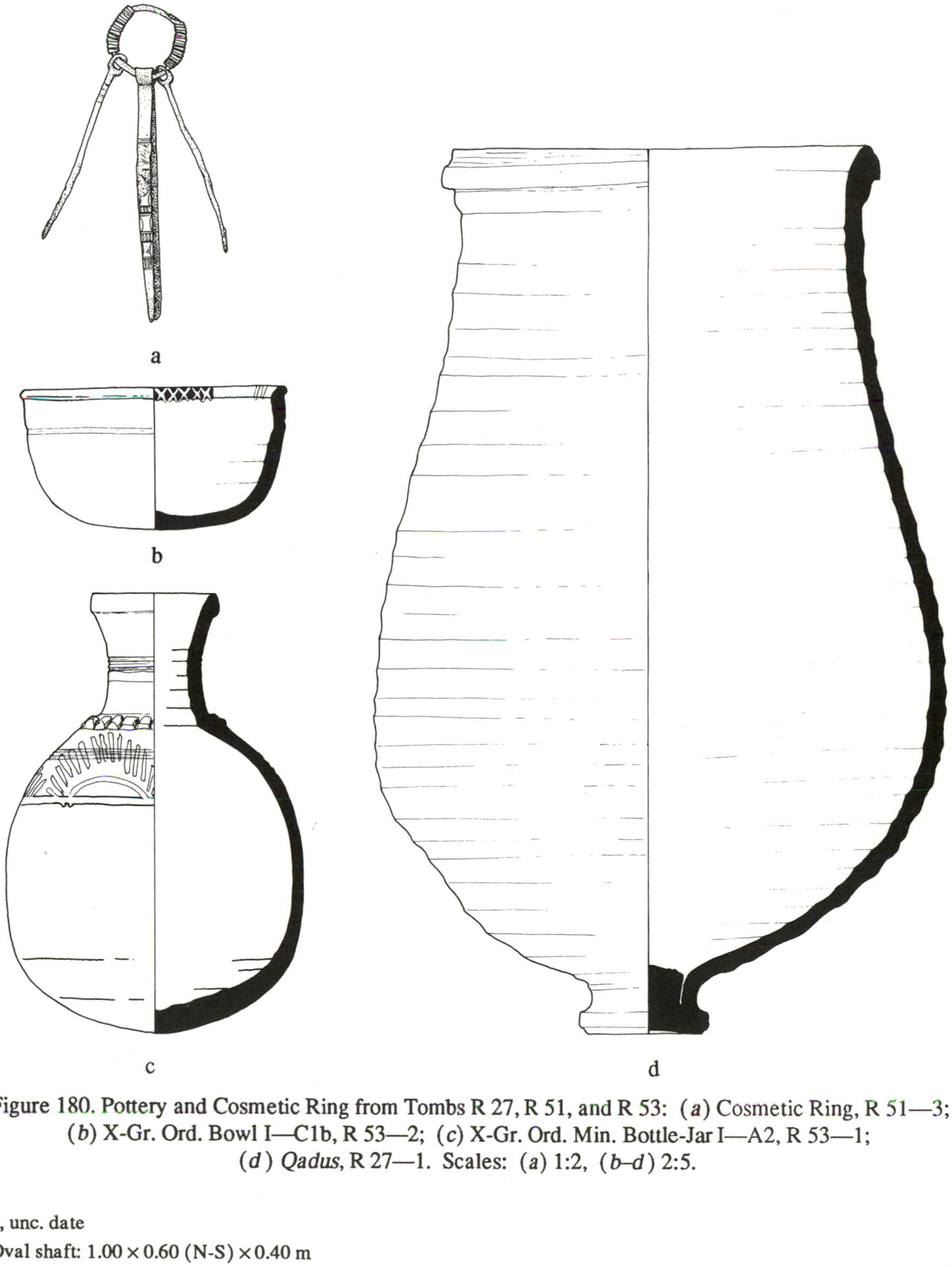

Figure 180. Pottery and Cosmetic Ring from Tombs R 27, R 51, and R 53: (*a*) Cosmetic Ring, R 51—3; (*b*) X-Gr. Ord. Bowl I—C1b, R 53—2; (*c*) X-Gr. Ord. Min. Bottle-Jar I—A2, R 53—1; (*d*) *Qadus*, R 27—1. Scales: (*a*) 1:2, (*b–d*) 2:5.

R 54, unc. date

Oval shaft: 1.00×0.60 (N-S) $\times 0.40$ m

R 55, unc. date

Oval shaft: 0.90 (E-W) $\times 0.40 \times 0.40$ m

R 59

Shaft with chamber on the N side

Table 42. Register of X-Group Finds in Cemetery R (*cont.*).

Tomb	Description and Contents	Cairo	OIM	Figure/Plate
R 59 (*cont.*)				
	Shaft: 1.95–2.35 × 0.50–0.75 × 1.00 m			
	Chamber: 1.55 × 0.50 × 0.50 m; overlap ca. 0.25 m, floor at -1.30 m			
	Burial: no information			
	Body: no information			
	Objects:			
	1. X-Gr. ord. bottle-jar I—A3, height 27.2		21167	
R 60				
	Shaft with chamber on the N side			
	Shaft: 1.70–2.15 × 0.65 × 0.95 m (floor collapsed into chamber)			
	Chamber: 1.70 × ? × 0.40 m; overlap ca. 0.45 m, floor at -1.15 m			
	Blocking: stone slabs			
	Burial: no information, in textile			
	Body: Mature female			
	Objects:			
	1. Cup (in fill)		—	
	2. X-Gr. ord. bottle-jar I—D1, height 24.6		21226	
	3. Beads (near pelvis)	21274, 21275		
	4. Textiles		21236A–B	
	a. Wrapping, CAT 151			
	b. Band, CAT 152			
R 62				
	Shaft with chamber on the N side			
	Shaft: 1.65–2.20 × 0.45–0.70 × 1.20 m			
	Chamber: 1.65 × 0.50 × 0.45 m; ca. 0.25 m overlap, floor at -1.60 m			
	Blocking: stone slabs			
	Burial: W/R/"contracted"			
	Body: Mature male			
	Objects:			
	1. X-Gr. ord. bottle-jar I—A2, ye.-wh. coat, bk. pt., height 27.4		21318	
	2. X-Gr. ord. goblet I—B2bii, height 8.7		21319	
	3. Textile wrapping remains (CAT X-Gr.)		Disc.	
R 64				fig. 181a
	Shaft with niche at the E end, ramp, and vault			
	Shaft: 1.90 × 0.70–0.75 × 1.35 m			
	Niche: 0.40 × 0.70 × 0.65 m			
	Ramp: 0.70 × 0.65 × 0.25–0.45 m			
	Ledges: undercut, one cb. wide			
	Vault: Four cb. with 4½ cb. laid flat above: slopes downward to niche, ca. 0.10 m; cb.: 0.08 × 0.17 × 0.34 m (soft, with straw)			
	Burial: —			
	Body: Mature male			
	Objects:			
	1. X-Gr. ord. bottle jar I—A2(?), ye.-wh. coat, bk. pt., vine, in groups of three (neck broken away)		21215	fig. 181d

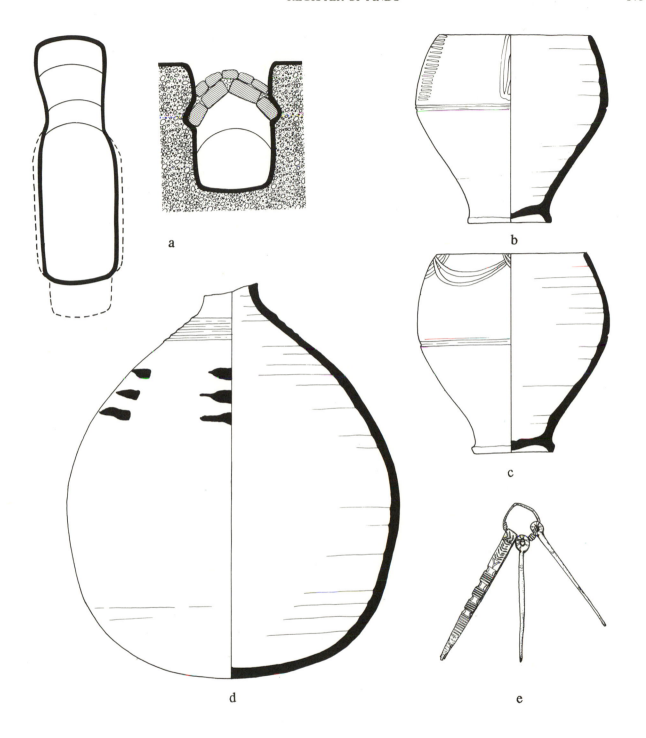

Figure 181. Plan, Section, Pottery, and Objects from Tomb R 64: (*a*) Plan and Section; (*b*) X-Gr. Ord. Goblet I—A2b, No. 3; (*c*) X-Gr. Ord. Goblet I—A2b, No. 4; (*d*) X-Gr. Ord. Bottle-Jar I—A2(?), No. 1; (*e*) Cosmetic Ring, No. 8. Scales: (*a*) 1:40; (*b–d*) 2:5; (*e*) 1:2.

Table 42. Register of X-Group Finds in Cemetery R (*cont.*).

Tomb	Description and Contents	Cairo	OIM	Figure/Plate
R 64 (*cont.*)				
	Objects (*cont.*):			
	2. X-Gr. ord. goblet I—A2b, wh. pt. double swags, 13.5 × 12.4		21212	
	3. X-Gr. ord. goblet I—A2b, wh. pt., vine in groups of eight, alt. with three vert. lines		21213	fig. 181b, pl. 41f
	4. X-Gr. ord. goblet I—A2b, wh. pt. swags		21214	fig. 181c
	5. Sandals, 22.4 × 10.6 and 20.0 × 6.8		21301	
	6. Glass cup fragments		21299	
	7. Unc. iron object, length 10.7	Q 1508, 89870		
	8. Ring with tweezers and probe		21298	fig. 181e, pl. 81d
	9. Beads		21300	
R 65				
	Shaft with chamber on the W side			
	Shaft: 1.65–2.20 × 0.55–0.80 × 1.00 m			
	Chamber: 1.40 × 0.45 × 0.55 m; floor at -1.40 m			
	Blocking: no information			
	Burial: —			
	Body: —			
	Objects:			
	1. X-Gr. ord. bottle-jar I—A3, height 28.4		21221	
	2. X-Gr. fine unfired pottery:		21252	
	a. Cup II—			pl. 48a
	b. Sherds			pl. 48b
	3. Archer's loose, 3.8 × 4.6		21291	
	4. Sandal fragments, largest 17.4 × 11.2		21294	
	5. Beads		21292	
R 66				
	Shaft with chamber on the N side			
	Shaft: 1.50 × 0.40–0.45 × 1.20 m			
	Chamber: 1.50 × 0.34–0.40 × 0.55 m; floor flush			
	Burial: W/L/"contracted"			
	Body: Mature male			
	Objects:			
	1. X-Gr. ord. narrow-necked bottle-jar I—C4, bar handle added, wh. pt. arches		21222	figs. 14h, 182a, pl. 42h
	2. Sandal fragments, largest 12.8 × 5.5		21270	
R 67				
	Shaft with ledges and slabs			
	Inner shaft: 1.25–1.50 × 0.35 × 1.30 m			
	Outer shaft: 0.55+ × 0.40+ m			
	Ledges: at -0.80 m, 0.10 m wide			
	Burial: Disturbed			
	Body: Mature male			
	Objects:			
	1. Scarab, 1.1 × 0.8 × 0.6		21379	
	2. Archer's guard, 9.5 × 4.0 × 0.4		21378	
	3. Remains of bowstring		Disc.	

Table 42. Register of X-Group Finds in Cemetery R (*cont.*).

Tomb	Description and Contents	Cairo	OIM	Figure/Plate

R 68

Shaft with chamber on the N side
    Shaft: 1.65–2.25 × 0.45–0.65 × 1.10 m
    Chamber: 1.65 × 0.50 × 0.30 m; overlap at 0.35 m,
        floor at -1.40 m
Burial: Extended, disturbed
Body: Senile
Objects:

1. X-Gr. ord. bottle-jar I—C3, wh. coat, red and bk. pt., complex of vert. and hor. framed bands on shoulder		21399		fig. 182b, pl. 44a

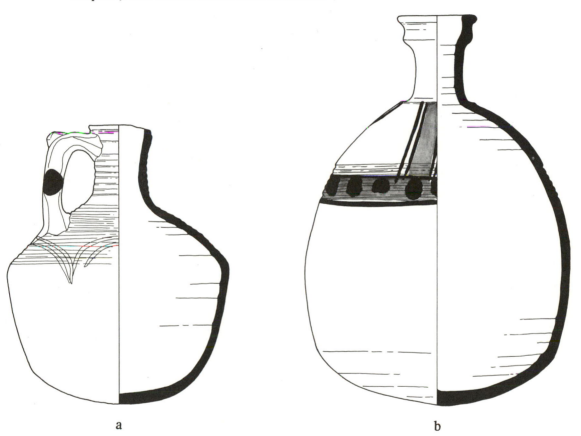

a   b

Figure 182. Pottery from Tombs R 66 and R 68: (*a*) X-Gr. Ord. Narrow-Necked Bottle-Jar I—C4, R 66—1; (*b*) X-Gr. Ord. Bottle-Jar I—C3, R 68—1. Scale 2:5.

R 69

Shaft with ramp, two steps, and a chamber on the W side
    Outer shaft: trapezoidal, more than 2.20,
        less than 1.40 × 2.35 × 3.15 m
    Ramp: 1.00 × 0.40 m
    First step: at -1.40 m, 0.35 m wide
    Second step: at -2.35 m, 0.40 m wide
    Floor: ca. 0.80 m wide
    Chamber: 2.15 × 1.10 × 0.80; floor at -2.60, no overlap
    Blocking: cb. stretchers (one course), headers, rowlock,
        headers rowlock, headers and rubble, piled in shaft
        0.08 × 0.17 × 0.33–0.35 (soft, with straw)

Table 42. Register of X-Group Finds in Cemetery R (*cont.*).

Tomb	Description and Contents	Cairo	OIM	Figure/Plate
R 69 (*cont.*)				
	Burial: S/?/"contracted"/dist.			
	Body: —			
	Objects:			
	1. Beads		22076	
	2. Five rings		22077	fig. 183a–c, pl. 77h
	3. Broken jar		Disc.	
	4. Broken "pitcher"		Disc.	

Intrusive burial excavated in the first step, chamber floor at -1.20 chamber 0.90 × 0.20, child.

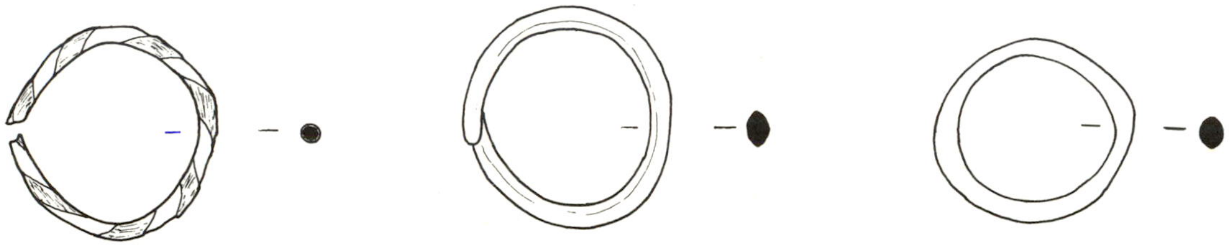

a   b   c

Figure 183. Rings from Tomb R 69: (*a*) No. 2a, (*b*) No. 2b, (*c*) No. 2c. Scale 1:1.

Numbers R 70–R 73 were not used.

R 74

Shaft with chamber on the NW side

Shaft: 2.50 × 0.74–? × 1.24 m

Chamber: 2.50 × 0.70 × 0.46 m; overlap ca. 0.44 m,
floor at -1.70 m

Blocking: stone slabs

Burials:

    a. In chamber:

        A. W/B/ext./hips

    b. In shaft at -0.65:

        B. W/B/ext./sides/—

Bodies:

    A. Adult male

    B. Adult female

Objects: with Burial B:

	1. Beads (R hand)		23502B	figs. 62n, p, 64l
	2. One silver earring (R ear)		23502A	fig. 61i

Probably very late X-Gr. or Christian.

R 82

Shaft with chamber on the N side

Shaft: 2.00 × 0.70 × 0.80 m

Chamber: 2.00 × ? × ? m

Blocking: stone slabs

Burial: W/B/ext./sides

Body: Mature female

Objects:

	1. X-Gr. ord. narrow-necked bottle jar I—C3, ye.-wh. coat, bk. pt., vine in groups of three, 26 × 18		23617	fig. 14g
	2. X-Gr. ord. goblet I—B2bii, 9 × 9		23607	
	3. Textile wrapping remains (CAT X-Gr.)		Disc.	

Table 42. Register of X-Group Finds in Cemetery R (*cont.*).

Tomb	Description and Contents	Cairo	OIM	Figure/Plate
R 89				
	Shaft with chamber on the N side			
	Shaft: 2.25 × 0.80 × ? m			
	Chamber: 2.25 × ? × ? m			
	Blocking: stone slabs			
	Burial: —			
	Body: Mature female			
	Objects, at E end of chamber:			
	1. X-Gr. ord. bottle jar I—C3, 27 × 19		23619	
	2. X-Gr. ord. goblet I—B2biv, (inverted on no. 1), 10 × 10		23606	
	3. X-Gr. ord. bottle jar I—C3, ye.-wh. coat, 28 × 20		23618	
	4. X-Gr. ord. goblet I—B2bii, (inverted on no. 3), 10 × 10		23626	
R 92				
	Shaft with chamber on the N side			
	Shaft: 1.31 × 0.65 × 0.90 m			
	Chamber: ca. 1.00 × 0.50 × 0.30 m; overlap 0.32 m, floor at -0.90 m			
	Blocking: —			
	Burial: W/R/thighs 75 degrees, legs 90 degrees/pelvis			
	Body: ca. 3 years			
	Objects:			
	1. X-Gr. ord. goblet I—B2aii, 8.5 × 9.0		23604	
R 95				
	Shaft with chamber on the N side			
	Shaft: 1.90 × 0.82 × 1.62 m			
	Chamber: 1.90 × 0.78 × ? m; overlap ca. 0.32 m			
	Blocking: stone slabs			
	Burial: E/B/ext./pubis			
	Body: Adult male			
	Objects:			
	1. X-Gr. ord. bottle-jar I—C3, 25 × 17		23615	
	2. X-Gr. ord. bottle jar I—C3		23616	fig. 184e, pl. 43b
	3. X-Gr. ord. goblet I—B2bii, lt. or pk. coat		23609	fig. 184b
R 100				
	Shaft with chamber on the N side			
	Shaft: 2.40 × 1.00 × 0.75 m (denuded)			
	Chamber: 2.40 × 0.30 × ca. 0.35 m; floor flush			
	Blocking: stone slabs			
	Burial: —			
	Body: Juvenile male			
	Objects:			
	1. *Qadus*		23621	pl. 47b
	The tomb is possibly Christian (?).			
R 102				
	Shaft with chamber on the N side			
	Shaft: 1.50 × 0.70 × 0.75 m			
	Chamber: 1.50 × ? × ? m; floor at -1.00 m			
	Blocking: —			
	Burial: W/L/thighs 35 degrees, legs folded/-			

Table 42. Register of X-Group Finds in Cemetery R (*cont.*).

Tomb	Description and Contents	Cairo	OIM	Figure/Plate
R 102 (*cont.*)				
	Body: 6.5–7.5 years			
	Objects:			
	1. Beads		Sample	
R 103				
	Shaft with chamber on the N side			
	Shaft: 1.50 × 0.70 × 0.70 m			
	Chamber: 1.50 × ? × ? m; floor at -0.95 m			
	Blocking: —			
	Burial: —			
	Body: 6 years			
	Objects:			
	1. Coptic period Eg. *amphoriskos*-jug II—A, abraded surface		23611	figs. 21a, 184a, pl. 46e
	2. Beads		Sample	
R 104				
	Shaft with step and chamber on the N side			
	Shaft: 1.30 × 0.60 × 0.60 m			
	Step: at -0.40 m, 0.17 m wide			
	Chamber: 1.30 × 0.25 × ? m; floor at -0.85 m			
	Burial: —			
	Body: ca. 3 years			
	Objects:			
	1. "Bottle"		Disc.	
R 105, no description available				
R 106				
	Shaft with chamber on the N side			
	Shaft: 1.40 × 0.60 × 0.70 m			
	Chamber: 1.40 × ? × ? m; ca. 0.20 m overlap, floor at -0.90 m			
	Blocking: stone slabs			
	Burial: W/R/legs 75 degrees/—			
	Body: 5–7 years			
	Objects:			
	1. X-Gr. ord. min. bottle-jar I—A1, bk. beads alt. with wh. vert. bands		23601	figs. 15a, 184c, pl. 44b
	2. Beads		Sample	
R 107				
	Shaft with chamber on the W side			
	Shaft: 2.00 × 0.90 × 1.28 m			
	Chamber: 2.00 × ? × ? m; floor below shaft			
	Burial: S/—/—/—			
	Body: Senile female			
	Objects: —			
R 108				
	Shaft with chamber on the N side			
	Shaft: 1.80 × 0.70 × 0.90 m			
	Chamber: 1.80 × ? × ? m; overhang of roof ca. 0.50 m, floor at -1.00 m			
	Burial: —			

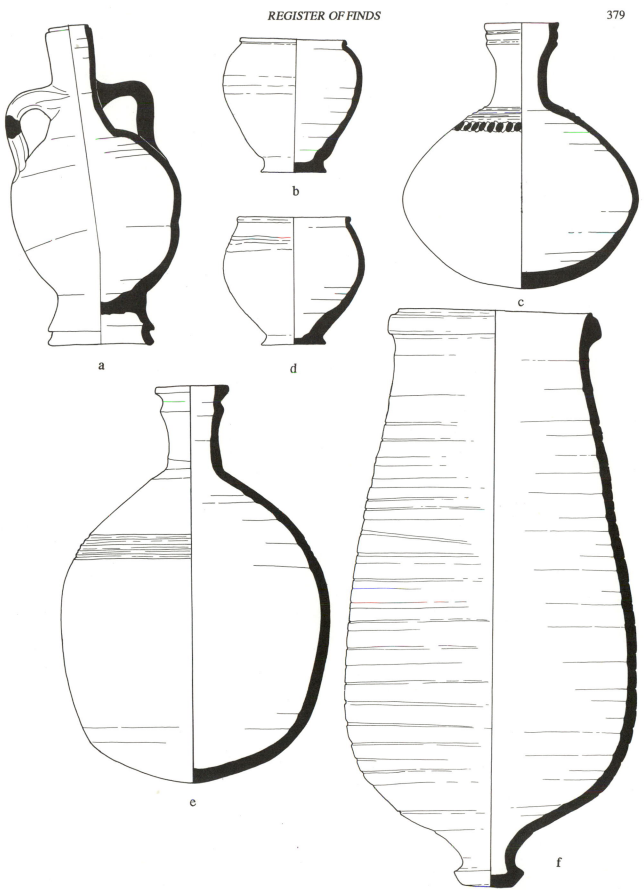

Figure 184. Pottery from Tombs R 95, R 103, R 106, R 108, and R 109: (*a*) Coptic Period Egyptian *Amphoriskos*-Jug II—A, R 103—1; (*b*) X-Gr. Ord. Goblet I—B2bii, R 95—3; (*c*) X-Gr. Ord. Min. Bottle-Jar I—A1, R 106—1; (*d*) X-Gr. Ord. Goblet I—B2aii, R 108—1; (*e*) X-Gr. Ord. Bottle-Jar I—C3, R 95—2; (*f*) *Qadus*, R 109—1. Scale 2:5.

Table 42. Register of X-Group Finds in Cemetery R (*cont.*).

Tomb	Description and Contents	Cairo	OIM	Figure/Plate
R 108 (*cont.*)				
	Body: Adult female			
	Objects:			
	1. X-Gr. ord. goblet I—B2aii		23608	fig. 184d
R 109				
	Shaft with chamber on the S side			
	Shaft: 1.90 × 0.80 × 1.00 m			
	Chamber: 1.90 × ? × ? m; floor below shaft			
	Blocking: stone slabs			
	Burial: W/B/—/pelvis?			
	Body: Adult female			
	Objects:			
	a. In shaft:			
	1. *Qadus*		23622	fig. 184f
	2. X-Gr. ord. goblet B1b, 8.0 × 11.5		23603	
	3. Goblet		Disc.	
	b. In chamber:			
	4. Sandals		33199	
R 110				
	Shaft with chamber on the N side			
	Shaft: 2.26 × 0.85 × 1.20			
	Chamber: 2.26 × 1.05 × 0.35 m; overlap ca. 0.50 m,			
	floor at -1.50 m			
	Blocking: stone slabs			
	Burial: W/B/ext./sides?, dist.			
	Body: Adult female			
	Objects in chamber:			
	1. X-Gr. ord. bottle jar I—D1		23620	fig. 185a
	2. X-Gr. ord. goblet I—B2ai		23610	fig. 185b
R 111				
	Shaft with chamber on the W side			
	Shaft: 1.95 × ca. 0.90 × 1.30 m			
	Chamber: 1.95 × 0.70 × ? m; floor flush			
	Blocking: stone slabs			
	Burial: N/B/ext./pubis			
	Body: Adult female			
	Objects, from chamber:			
	1. Large jar, probably *qadus*		Disc.	
	2. X-Gr. ord. goblet I—A1ai		23625	figs. 7a, 185c
	3. Textile wrapping remains (pelvis), CAT 153		23514	
R 112, no description available				
R 113, not on plan				
	Shaft: rect., 1.20 × 0.40 × 0.50 m			
	Burial: E/R/—/—, dist.			
	Body: Less than 7.5 months			
	Objects:			
	1. Textile remains, CAT 154–155		23707A–B	

Table 42. Register of X-Group Finds in Cemetery R (*cont.*).

Tomb	Description and Contents	Cairo	OIM	Figure/Plate
R 114				
	Shaft with chamber on the N side			
	Shaft: 1.50 × 0.75 × 1.00 m			
	Chamber: 1.60 × 0.65 × 0.45 m; floor approx. flush			
	Blocking: —			
	Burial: —			
	Body: 10–12 years			
	Objects:			
	1. X-Gr. ord. goblet I—B1b, 9 × 12		23605	
	2. Coptic period Eg. *amphoriskos* jug II—C?, red coat, neck broken, 31 × 19		23613	
R 115				
	Shaft with chamber on the N side			
	Shaft: 2.06 × 0.67 × 0.95 m			
	Chamber: 2.06 × 0.75 × 0.25 m (small)			
	Blocking: stone slabs			
	Burial: —			
	Body: Adult female			
	Object: —			
	Sherd: plunderer's tool, possibly Christian		33213	
	Note: position date only, possibly Christian			
R 116				
	Shaft with chamber on the W side			
	Shaft: 2.40 × 0.95 × 1.40 m			
	Chamber: 2.40 × 0.80 × ca. 0.70 m; floor at -1.80 m			
	Blocking: stone slabs			
	Burial: S/B/ext./sides			
	Body: Adult male			
	Objects: —			
	Note: burial possibly Christian			
R 117				
	Shaft with chamber on the W side			
	Shaft: 2.07 × 0.70 × 1.20 m			
	Chamber: 2.07 × 0.60 × 0.70 m; floor at -1.30 m			
	Blocking: not recorded			
	Burial: —			
	Body: Adult female			
	Objects:			
	1. Beads		23530	
R 118				
	Shaft with chamber on the N side			
	Shaft: 1.30 × 0.70 × 0.90 m			
	Chamber: 1.30 × ? × ? m; unc. overlap, floor at -1.80 m			
	Blocking: stone slabs			
	Objects:			
	1. X-Gr. ord. goblet I—A1ai *beta*, bk. and wh. pt. swags, 8 × 12		23602	
	2. X-Gr. handmade bowl B2, base mud plastered, surface fire blackened		23599	fig. 185d
	3. Textile remains, CAT 156–157		24877A–B	
	The measurements are questionable.			

Table 42. Register of X-Group Finds in Cemetery R (*cont.*).

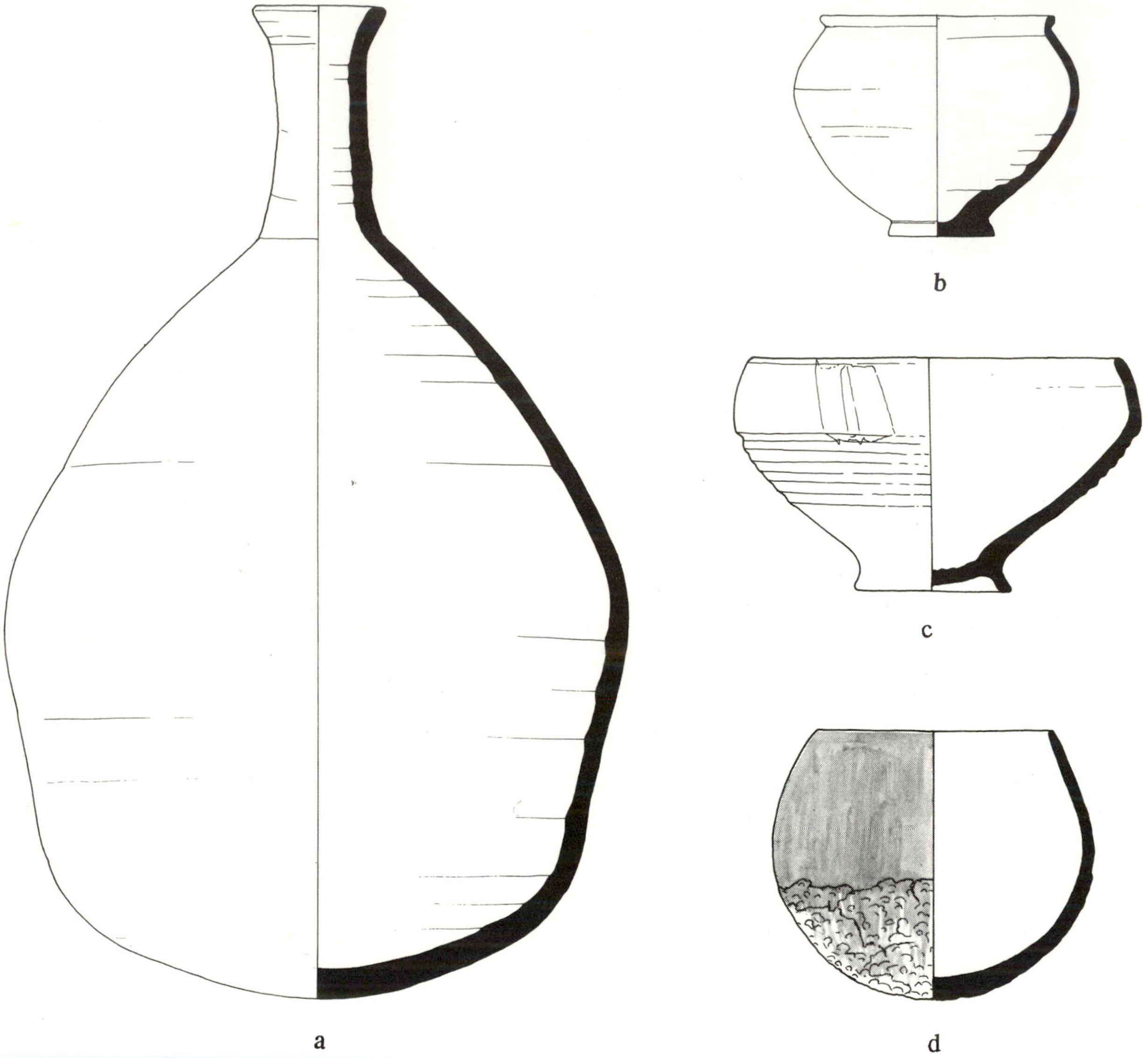

Tomb	Description and Contents	Cairo	OIM	Figure/Plate

a

b

c

d

Figure 185. Pottery from Tombs R 110, R 111, and R 118: (*a*) X-Gr. Ord. Bottle-Jar I—D1, R 110—1;
(*b*) X-Gr. Ord. Goblet I—B2ai, R 110—2; (*c*) X-Gr. Ord. Goblet I—A1ai, R 111—2;
(*d*) X-Gr. Handmade Bowl—B2, R 118—2. Scale 2:5.

R 119

    Shaft with chamber on the W side

        Shaft: 2.10 × 0.90 × 1.30 m

        Chamber: 2.10 × 0.68 × 0.50 m; overlap, floor at -1.55 m

        Blocking: stone slabs

    Burials: —

    Body: Adult female

    Objects:

			Cairo	OIM
a.	From shaft:			
	1.	Archer's loose	23535	fig. 186a
	2.	*Qadus* (on blocking)	23623	fig. 186c
	3.	Sheepskin (on blocking)	33200	
	4.	Leather strap fragments, 9.0 × 3.5	23529	

Table 42. Register of X-Group Finds in Cemetery R (*cont.*).

Tomb	Description and Contents	Cairo	OIM	Figure/Plate
R 119 (*cont.*)				
	Objects (*cont.*):			
	b. Unc. loc.:			
	5. Beads		Sample	
	6. Arrowhead, length 4.7		23536	
	7. Coptic period Eg. juglet I—A2, incised dec. on shoulder, neck broken		23612	fig. 186b
R 121, no description available				

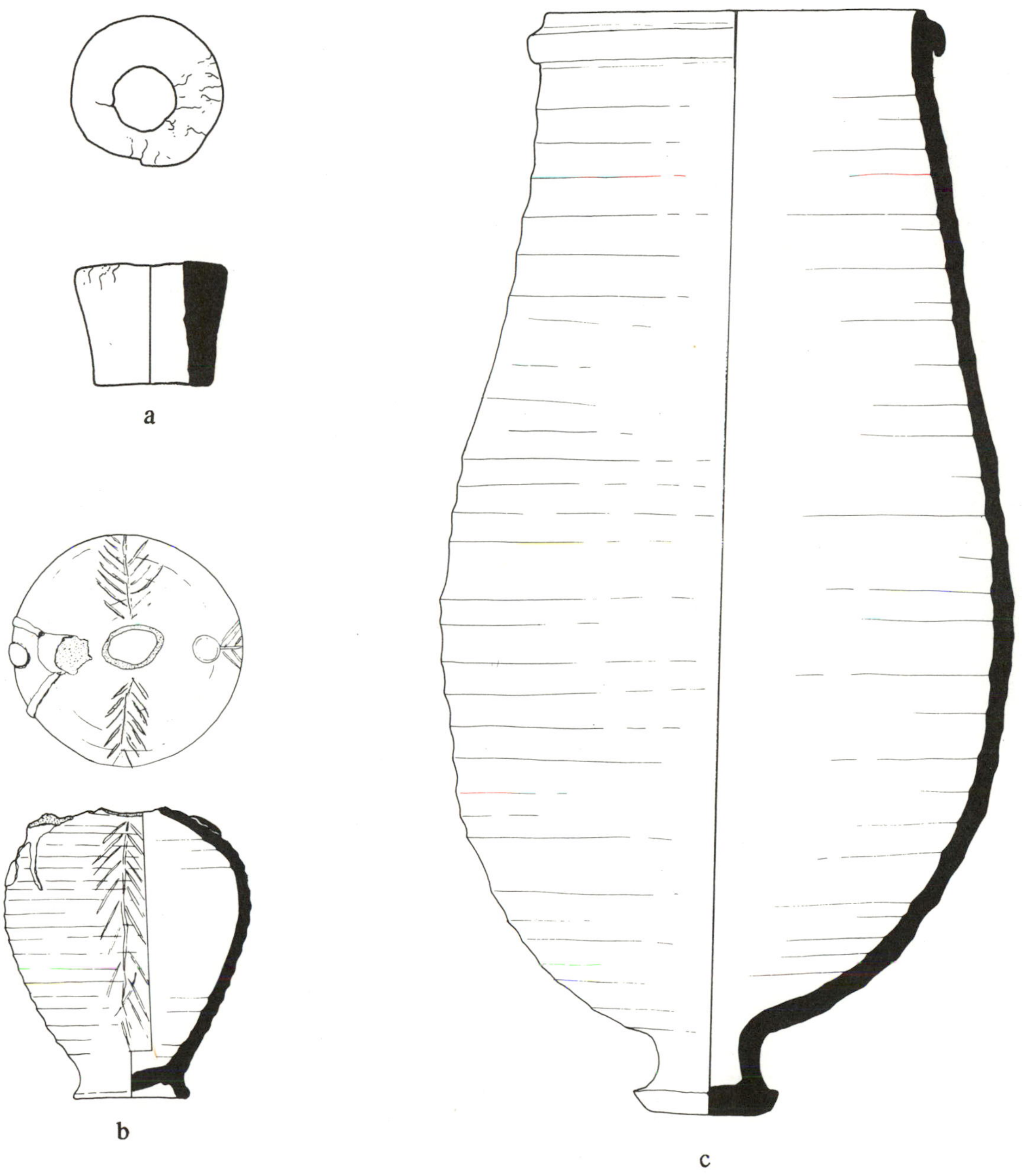

Figure 186. Pottery and an Archer's Loose from Tomb R 119: (*a*) Archer's Loose, No. 1; (*b*) Coptic Period Egyptian Juglet I—A2, No. 7; (*c*) *Qadus*, No. 2. Scales: (*a*) 1:2, (*b, c*) 2:5.

CEMETERY AREA VA

The tombs of VA were neither wealthy nor well-preserved. There were, however, contexts of different date which are noted in *Appendix A.*

Table 43. Register of X-Group Finds in Cemetery Area VA.

Tomb	Description and Contents	Cairo	OIM	Figure/Plate

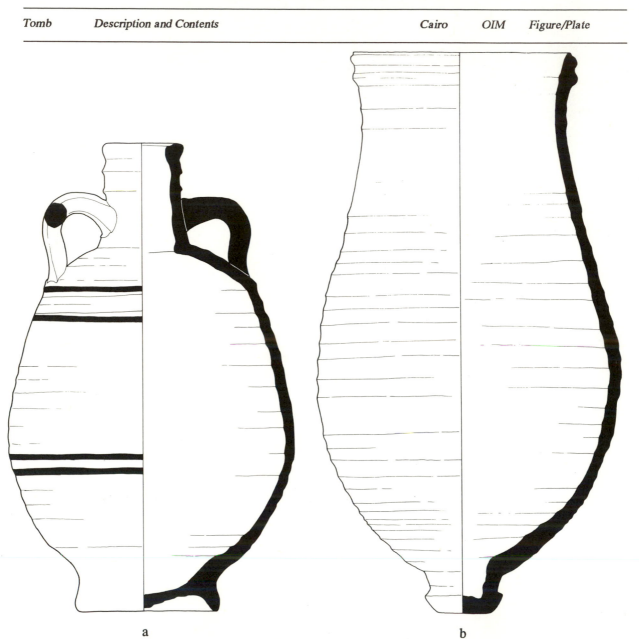

a   b

Figure 187. Pottery from Tomb VA 9: (*a*) Coptic Period Egyptian Jug I—D1a, No. 2;
(*b*) *Qadus*, No. 1. Scale 2:5.

VA 9
Shaft with steps and chamber on the W side
Shaft: no dim.
Steps: Two, no dim.
Chamber: no dim.
Blocking: cb., on end
Burials:
a. —
A. —

Table 43. Register of X-Group Finds in Cemetery Area VA (*cont.*).

Tomb	Description and Contents	Cairo	OIM	Figure/Plate
VA 9 (*cont.*)				
	Burials (*cont.*):			
b.	Blocked with stone slabs leaned above			
	B. S/R/ext./pelvis			
	Bodies:			
A.	Mature male			
B.	Mature female			
	Objects:			
a.	With A:			
1.	*Qadus*		21599	fig. 187b
2.	Coptic period Eg. jug I—D1a, red coat, bk. and wh. bands at shoulder and waist		21581	fig. 187a
3.	Quiver remains		21574	fig. 54
4.	Sandal heel with patch		21574	
b.	With B:			
5.	Iron earrings (at ear)		21543	fig. 61a, pl. 76i
6.	Beads		21576	
VA 12				
	Shaft with chamber on the N side			
	Shaft: 1.10 × 1.50 × 0.55–0.80 × 1.00 m			
	Chamber: 1.05 × 0.40 × 0.30 m; overlap 0.15 m, floor at -1.30 m			
	Burial: —			
	Body: "Child"			
	Objects:			
1.	Coptic period Eg. *amphoriskos* jug III— ?		Disc.	
2.	Miscellaneous objects			
a.	Silver (?) ring		22171	fig. 61h
b.	Beads		22171	
VA 13, reused Christian				
	Shaft with chamber on the W side			
	Shaft: 2.10–2.40 × 0.80–1.05 × 1.40 m			
	Chamber: 1.90 × 0.70 × 0.50 m; floor flush			
	Blocking: hor. stone slabs			
	Burials:			
A.	S/B/ext./sides			
B.	S/B/ext./pubis			
	Bodies:			
A.	—			
B.	—			
	Objects:			
1.	Large jar		Disc.	
2.	Bowl		Disc.	
3.	Beads (R hand A)		22162	
	The upper body is Christian in date.			
VA 14				
	Shaft with chamber on the N side			
	Shaft: 1.75–2.20 × 0.60 × 0.80 × 1.60 m			
	Chamber: 1.95 × 0.65 × 0.55 m; floor flush			
	Blocking: stone slabs on edge laid in mass across chamber			

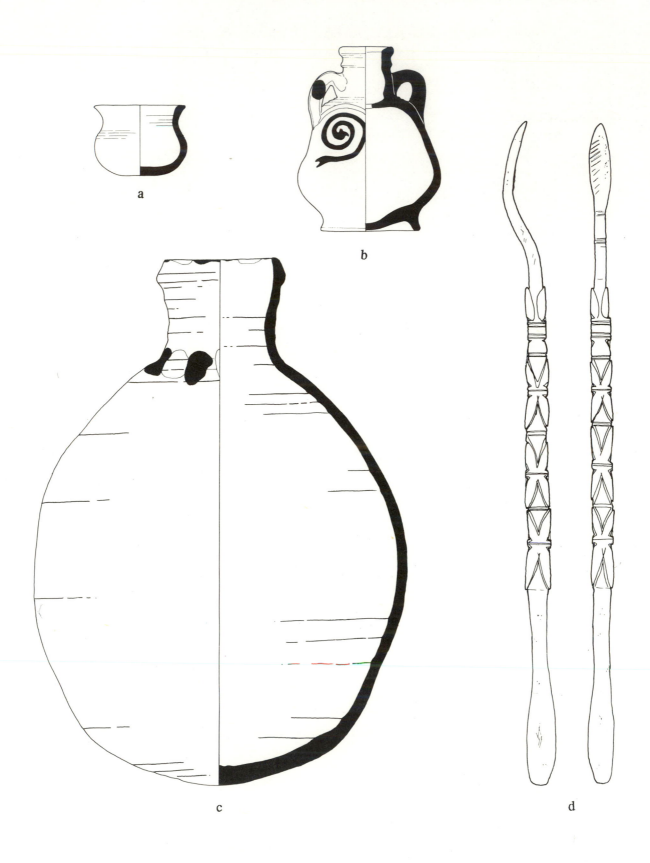

Figure 188. Pottery and Kohl Stick/Probe from Tomb VA 14: (*a*) Handmade Miniature Bowl, No. 7;
(*b*) Coptic Period Egyptian *Amphoriskos*-Jug I—D2b, No. 6; (*c*) X-Gr. Ord. Medium-Necked
Jar I—A1a, No. 1; (*d*) Iron Kohl Stick/Probe, No. 11. Scales: (*a–c*) 2:5, (*d*) 1:1.

Table 43. Register of X-Group Finds in Cemetery Area VA (*cont.*).

Tomb	Description and Contents	Cairo	OIM	Figure/Plate
VA 14 (*cont.*)				
	Burial: W/B/ext./sides, wrapped in textile			
	Body: —			
	Objects:			
	1. X-Gr. ord. med.-necked jar I—A1a, alt. rim spots bk. and wh., alt. spot beads on shoulder, one wh. drop-spill		22117	fig. 188c
	2. X-Gr. ord. bottle jar I— (Meroitic shape), wh. bands rim and shoulder		22118	fig. 189a
	3. X-Gr. ord. goblet I—B2ai, 8.5 × 10.8		22114	
	4. X-Gr. ord. goblet I—B2ai, 8.5 × 11.0		22115	
	5. X-Gr. ord. goblet I—B1a, height 7.5		22116	
	6. Coptic period Eg. *amphoriskos*-jug I—D2b, red coat, bk. pt. crude spirals		22119	figs. 21g, 188b
	7. Handmade miniature bowl		22150	figs. 17f, 188a
	8. Bead necklace		22157	
	9. Bead bracelet (at R hand)		22156	
	10. Ring (fourth finger, R)		22155	pl. 77f
	11. Iron kohl stick or probe (under feet)		22158	fig. 188d, pl. 81e
	12. Textile wrapping remains (CAT X-Gr.)		Disc.	

CEMETERY AREA VB

As indicated on the cemetery plan, Area VB comprised two loci, VB 70 of the X-Group, and VB 71, which dated to the New Kingdom. New Kingdom tomb VB 25, located north of the school near a well was also assigned to the area.

VB 70 is a stepped pit with a partial stone lining later used for an X-Group child burial. It is probably an X-Group cult installation of the type found in BA.

Table 44. Register of X-Group Finds in Cemetery Area VB.

Tomb	Description and Contents	Cairo	OIM	Figure/Plate
VB 70				fig. 189b
	Stepped pit lined with stone revetment on three sides; reused for X-Gr. contracted burial.			
	Pit: N-S (river), 1.60–2.10 × 1.80–2.00 × 1.20; in *gebel*			
	Steps: on NW and NE sides, 0.20, 0.25, and 0.35 wide; low is a shelf with a depression in the floor toward the S, 0.90 × 0.70 m			
	Revetment: three courses, small stone slabs			
	Burial: S/L/thighs 90 degrees, legs 90 degrees/pubis; at -0.35, cb. to E, stone slabs above			
	Body: Child			
	Objects:			
	1. Beads		21835	
	Note that the date of the burial is X-Gr. or earlier, possibly Dyn. XXV, though not likely. The structure of the pit lining resembles the great stone lined pit at Kerma, and the round building BA.			

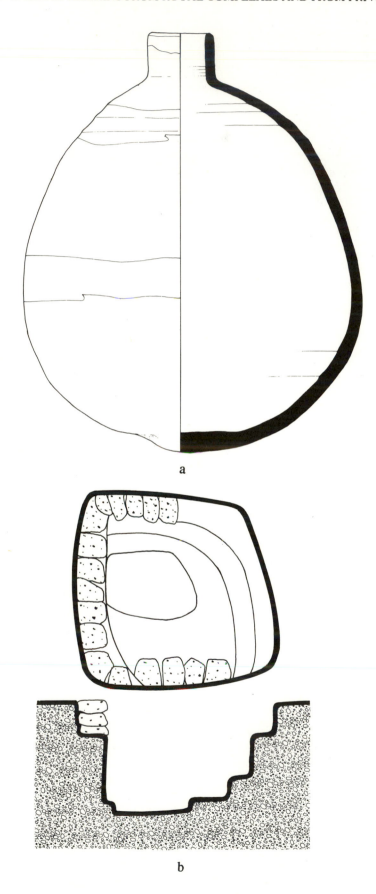

a

b

Figure 189. A Jar from Tomb VA 14 and the Plan and Section of Tomb VB 70: (*a*) X-Gr. Ord.
Bottle-Jar I—, VA 14—2; (*b*) Plan and Section of Tomb VB 70. Scales: (*a*) 2:5, (*b*) 1:40.

CEMETERY AREA VC

Table 45. Register of X-Group Finds in Cemetery Area VC.

Tomb	Description and Contents	Cairo	OIM	Figure/Plate
VC 41				
	Shaft with chamber on the W side, "no tumulus"			
	Shaft: $1.60 \times 0.60 \times 1.00$ m			
	Chamber: no dim. available; floor at -1.15 m			
	Blocking: stone slabs			
	Burial: S/L/slight bend/—; textile wrapping, bands on head and pelvis			
	Body: Juvenile female?			
	Objects:			
	1. *Qadus*		22363	fig. 190a
	2. X-Gr. ord. goblet I—B1c, height 9		21798	
	3. Textile wrapping remains (CAT X-Gr.)		Disc.	
	4. Beads (in no. 3)		Disc.	fig. 62r
VC 42				
	Shaft with chamber on the W side, "no tumulus"			
	Shaft: 1.40×0.60–0.71×1.00 (or 0.60?) m			
	Chamber: no dim. available; floor at -1.20 m			
	Burial: S/1/-/-; textile wrapping			
	Body: Juvenile male?			
	Objects:			
	1. *Qadus*, 35.3×19.7		22364	fig. 190b
	2. X-Gr. ord. goblet I—A1bi *beta*, bk. and wh. pt., vine in groups of three		21795	
	3. X-Gr. ord. cup I—G1; wh. pt.		21794	fig. 190d
	4. Textile wrapping remains (CAT X-Gr.)		Disc.	

CEMETERY AREA VD

No X-Group burials were found in Area VD; for tombs assigned to this area, see *Appendix A.*

CEMETERY AREA VE

Cemetery area VE consisted only of a plot of Christian tombs, VE 101–VE 109.

CEMETERY AREA VF

Table 46. Register of X-Group Finds in Cemetery Area VF.

Tomb	Description and Contents	Cairo	OIM	Figure/Plate
VF 68				
	Shaft with ramp and vault; tumulus not recorded			
	Shaft: 2.86–3.21×1.45–1.85×1.05 m (denuded)			
	Ramp: at N end, $0.65 \times 0.74 \times 0.55$ m			
	Vault: on one course cb. stretchers, multiple courses, leaned S			
	Blocking: at N, headers; cb. 0.07–$0.08 \times 0.18 \times 0.36$ m; soft, with straw			
	Burial: —			
	Body: —			
	Objects:			
	1. Three rings, dia. 1.8, 1.9, and 1.0		22000	
	2. Beads		22001	

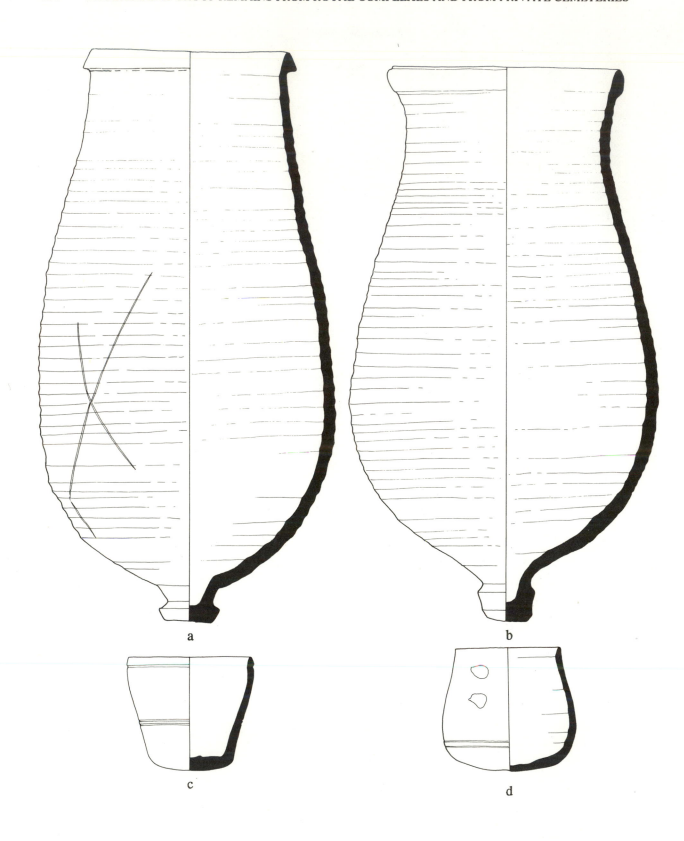

Figure 190. Pottery from Tombs VC 41, VC 42, and VG 97: (*a*) *Qadus*, VC 41—1;
(*b*) *Qadus*, VC 42—2); (*c*) X-Gr. Ord. Cup I—D2a, VG 97—1;
(*d*) X-Gr. Ord. Cup I—G1, VC 42—3. Scale 2:5.

CEMETERY AREA VG

Table 47. Register of X-Group Finds in Cemetery Area VG.

Tomb	Description and Contents	Cairo	OIM	Figure/Plate
VG 86				
	Shaft with chamber on the N side			
	Shaft: ca. 1.50 × 0.65 × 0.65 m			
	Chamber: 1.35 × 0.30 × 0.30 m; overlap ca. 0.20 m, floor at -0.75 m			
	Blocking: stone slabs			
	Burial: W/L/thighs 90 degrees, legs 90 degrees /pelvis			
	Body: Juvenile female			
	Objects:			
	1. X-Gr. ord. goblet I—A1ai *beta*, height 7.6		22085	
VG 89, reused for Christian burial				
	Shaft with chamber on the W side			
	Shaft: 1.40–1.65 × 0.70–1.00 × 1.05 m			
	Chamber: 1.60 × 0.60–0.75 × 0.45 m; ca. 0.30 overlap m, floor at -1.35 m			
	Blocking: stone slabs			
	Burial: none X-Gr.			
	Body: —			
	Object:			
	1. Incomplete X-Gr. *qadus*		Disc.	
	Note that a shallow cut 0.042 m deep made E-W at the S end indicates that recutting had begun, but the tomb was simply reused instead.			
VG 95				
	Shaft with chamber on the W side			
	Shaft: 0.90–1.15 × 0.50–0.65 × 0.50 m			
	Chamber: — × — × 0.30 m; overlap ca. 0.30 m, floor at -0.60 m			
	Burial: —			
	Body: "Infant II"			
	Objects:			
	1. X-Gr. ord. bowl I—C1, bk. and wh. pt. vert. bands, height 7.1		22080	fig. 10c
VG 96				
	Shaft with chamber on the N side			
	Shaft: 0.80–1.05 × 0.35–0.50 × 0.50 m			
	Chamber: ca. 0.80 × 0.35 × 0.30 m; overlap 0.20 m, floor at -0.65 m			
	Burial: —			
	Body: "Infant II"			
	Object:			
	1. X-Gr. ord. .goblet I—A1aii *beta*, bk. and wh. pt. vert. bands, height 8.5		22081	
VG 97, New Kingdom tomb				
	Object, X-Gr.:			
	1. X-Gr. ord. cup I—D2a		22120	figs. 9c, 190c

CEMETERY AREA VH

Table 48. Register of X-Group Finds in Cemetery Area VH.

Tomb	Description and Contents	Cairo	OIM	Figure/Plate
VH 122				
	Shaft with chamber on the W side			
	Shaft: rect., 2.90 × 1.30 × ? m			
	Chamber: 2.90 × 0.98 × ? m			
	Blocking: seven courses cb., alt. header, stretcher, top two stretchers			
	Burials:			
	a. In chamber:			
	A. —			
	b. In shaft:			
	B. S/B/ext./sides (dist.), probably Christian reuse			
	Bodies:			
	A. Adult female			
	B. Adult female			
	Objects with A:			
	1. Textile wrapping remains (possibly with B), CAT 158		23846	
	2. "Pot," jar or bottle		Disc.	
	3. X-Gr. ord. jar, 7.7 × 10.0		23966	
	4. Leather quiver		Disc.	

CEMETERY AREA VI

Tombs V 201–V 203 are not located on any plan. The numbers V 131–V 200 were not used.

Table 49. Register of X-Group Finds in Cemetery Area VI.

Tomb	Description and Contents	Cairo	OIM	Figure/Plate
V 201				
	Shaft with chamber on the N side			
	Shaft: 1.38 × 0.73 × 0.78 m			
	Chamber: 1.38 × 0.34 × 0.28 m; floor flush			
	Blocking: stone slabs			
	Burial: —			
	Body: —			
	Objects from shaft:			
	1. *Qadus*		Disc.	
	2. "Small red bowl with ring base, next to 1"		Disc.	
V 202				
	Shaft with chamber at the NE corner (NE-SW)			
	Shaft: — × 0.60 × 0.22 m (denuded)			
	Chamber: — × 0.30 × 0.25 m; floor at -0.48 m, overlap not specified			
	Blocking: —			
	Burial: —			
	Body: —			

Table 49. Register of X-Group Finds in Cemetery Area VI (*cont.*).

Tomb	Description and Contents	Cairo	OIM	Figure/Plate
V 202 (*cont.*)				
Objects:				
1.	Beads		Disc.	
	a. Blue tubes			
	b. White disc (alt.)			
	c. Blue-green drop-shaped pendant (not in string)			
2.	Earring, iron?		Disc.	
V 203				
	Shaft with chamber on the S side			
	Shaft: 1.85 × 0.87 × 1.12 m			
	Chamber: 1.85 × 0.27 × 0.43 m; floor flush			
	Blocking: stone slabs			
Burial: remains at W end of chamber				
Body: —				
Objects:				
1.	*Qadus* (deeply grooved "narrower than that of V 201")		Disc.	

CEMETERY W

No X-Group tombs were assigned to tombs 1–51, Cemetery W1, but one pit of uncertain date contained a *qadus*. Cemetery W2 consisted of two parts, a west and an east area. Most of the tombs in the west area were N-S shafts with chambers on the W side. Several were not late. Most burials were X-Group or Christian. However Christian tombs are normally oriented E-W; only one or two in Cemetery V had this orientation. Five tombs in this group were definitely X-Group, including two oriented E-W (W 80, W 88). Other burials are late X-Group or Christian (W 79, W 63, W 87). One tomb, W 74, was dated to middle X-Group, while W 57 and W 58 may have been middle X-Group. Even though most of the tombs contained no objects and had extended burials, most of Cemetery W2 is presented as an X-Group cemetery in this volume.

Table 50. Register of X-Group Finds in Cemetery W2.

Tomb	Description and Contents	Cairo	OIM	Figure/Plate
W 54				
	Shaft with chamber on the E side			
	Shaft: 1.60 × 0.61 × 0.46 m			
	Chamber: 1.60 × 0.65 × 0.39 m, 0.06 m overlap;			
	floor at -0.68 m			
Burial: N/R/dist./—				
Body: Adult female				
Objects:				
1.	Beads		23890	
2.	X-Gr. ord goblet A1aii *alpha*, bk. and wh. swags		23936	
3.	X-Gr. ord. goblet B1c		23937	
W 57				
	Shaft with chamber on the W side			
	Shaft: 2.05 × 0.75 × 1.00 m			
	Chamber: 2.05 × 0.65 × 0.27 m; overlap ca. 0.30 m;			
	floor at -0.27 m from shaft			
	Blocking: none noted			

Table 50. Register of X-Group Finds in Cemetery W2 (*cont.*).

Tomb	Description and Contents	Cairo	OIM	Figure/Plate
W 57 (*cont.*)				
	Burial: —			
	Body: Adult male			
	Objects, at SE corner of shaft:			
	1. X-Gr. utility storage jar III—A		23935	fig. 191a
	2. X-Gr. ord. goblet I—B1c, 9 × 11		23938	
W 58				
	Shaft with chamber on the W side			
	Shaft: 1.60 × 0.70 × 0.80 m			
	Chamber: 1.60 × — × — m; 0.45 m from edge of shaft,			
	floor at -0.30 m from shaft, denuded			
	Blocking: stone slabs			
	Burial: —			
	Body: Mature female			
	Objects:			
	1. X-Gr. ord. goblet I—B1c, 9.0 × 12.5		23939	
	2. *Qadus* (broken)		Disc.	
W 59				
	Shaft with chamber on the W side			
	Shaft: 0.96 × 0.47 × 0.30 m, denuded			
	Chamber: 0.96 × 0.30 × — m; floor at -0.45 m			
	Objects:			
	1. Beads		Sample	
W 60, reuse Christian				
	Shaft with chamber on the W side			
	Shaft: 1.80 × 0.80 × 0.80 m			
	Chamber: 1.80 × 0.88 × — m; floor at -1.05 m, overlap 0.24 m			
	Blocking: stone slabs			
	Burials:			
	a. Scattered?			
	A. —			
	b. Christian reuse:			
	B. W/L/ext./face; wrapped in brown textile			
	Bodies:			
	A. Adult female			
	B. Adult female			
	Objects:			
	1. X-Gr. utility storage jar III—A, 23.5 × 20.5		23963	
	2. Textile remains (from B; CAT X-Gr.)		Disc.	
W 61				
	N-S shaft: 1.22 × 0.55 × 0.40 m, rect. with rounded ends			
	Burial: —			
	Body: 15–18 years			
	Objects:			
	1. Beads		23888	
W 62				
	Shaft with chamber on the W side			
	Shaft: 1.20 × 0.60 × 0.30 m			
	Chamber: 1.20 × 0.55 × — m; overlap ca. 0.15 m			

Table 50. Register of X-Group Finds in Cemetery W2 (*cont.*).

Tomb	Description and Contents	Cairo	OIM	Figure/Plate

W 62 (*cont.*)
    Burial: —
    Body: 12–13 years, female
    Objects: —

W 63
    Shaft with chamber on the N side
        Shaft: 1.30 × 0.50 × 0.25 m
        Chamber: 1.30 × 0.55 × 0.33 m; overlap ca. 0.25 m; floor at -0.55 m
    Burial: —/B/"extended"
    Body: 7.5–8.5 years
    Objects: —

W 65
    Shaft with chamber on the W side
        Shaft: 1.10 × 0.50 × 0.30 m
        Chamber: 1.10 × 0.60 × 0.25 m; 0.25 m overlap, floor at -0.65 m
    Burial: —
    Body: 6 years
    Objects: —

W 66
    Shaft with chamber on the W side
        Shaft: ca. 1.30 × — × 0.25 m, denuded
        Chamber: 1.30 × 0.42 × — m; floor at -0.50 m
    Burial: —
    Body: 8.5–9.5 years
    Objects: —

W 67
    Shaft with chamber on the W side
        Shaft: 1.65 × 0.65 × 0.50 m
        Chamber: 1.65 × 0.40 × 0.30 m; floor at -0.75 m, 0.10 m overlap
    Burial: —
    Body: 7.5–8.5 years
    Objects: —

W 69
    Shaft with chamber on the W side
        Shaft: 1.80 × 0.60 × 0.65 m
        Chamber: 1.80 × 0.50 × 0.35 m; 0.10 m overlap, floor at -0.75 m
        Blocking: stone slabs
    Burial: —
    Body: Adult female

W 71, Christian
    Shaft with chamber on the N side
        Shaft: 1.60 × 0.70 × 0.70 m
        Chamber: 1.60 × 0.50 × 0.40 m; overlap ?, floor at -0.90 m
        Blocking: stone slabs
    Burials (Seele's order):
        A.   —, in textile
        B.   —, in textile

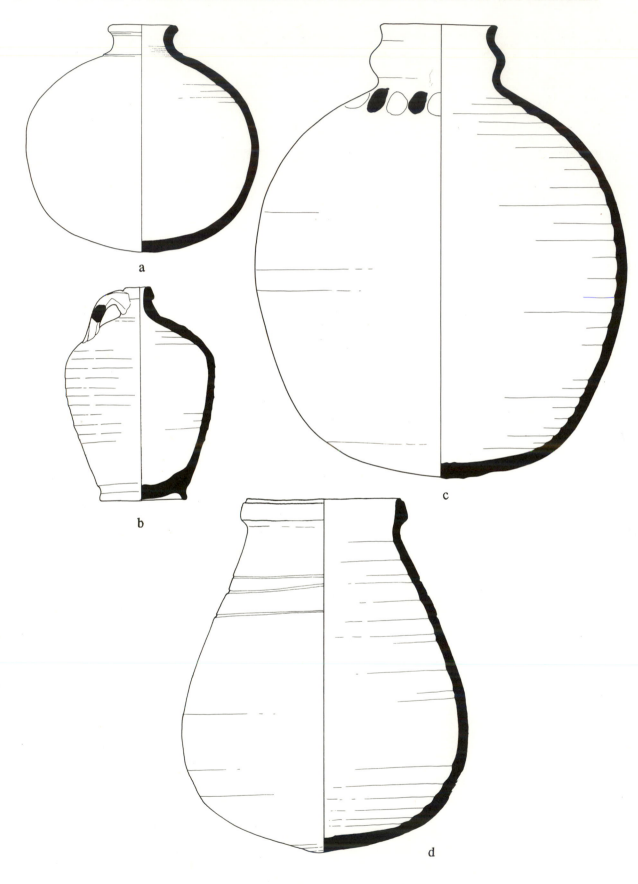

Figure 191. Pottery from Cemetery W: (*a*) X-Gr. Utility Storage Jar III—A, W 57—1; (*b*) Coptic
Period Egyptian Juglet I—A3b, W 74—5; (*c*) X-Gr. Ord. Medium-Necked Bottle-Jar
I—A1b, W 74—3; (*d*) *Qadus*-Shaped Jar, W 76—1. Scale 2:5.

Table 50. Register of X-Group Finds in Cemetery W2 (*cont.*).

Tomb	Description and Contents	Cairo	OIM	Figure/Plate
W 71, Christian (*cont.*)				
	Bodies:			
	A. 12 years, female?			
	B. Less than 7.5 months			
	Objects:			
	1. Textile remains from A		Disc.	
	2. Textile from B, CAT 161, ("tied with green string")		24878	
W 73, Christian				
	Shaft with floor chamber and slabs leaned against NW wall			
	Shaft: 1.65 × 0.62 × 0.70 m			
	Chamber: 1.65 × 0.42 × 0.19 m			
	Blocking: stone slabs, tops at -0.43 m			
	Burial: S/L/ext./L below body, R, pelvis			
	Body: Adult female			
	Objects: —			
W 74				
	Shaft with chamber on the W side			
	Shaft: 2.25 × 0.90 × 0.95 m			
	Chamber: 2.25 × 0.65 × 0.40 m; unc. overlap, floor deeper than shaft			
	Blocking: stone slabs			
	Burial: S/B/ext./—			
	Body: Mature female			
	Objects:			
	1. Necklace of bone beads		23894	
	2. Bead bracelets from R wrist		23895	figs. 62m
	3. X-Gr. ord. med.-necked bottle-jar I—A1b (bk. and wh. pt.)		23962	figs. 13b, 191c
	4. X-Gr. ord. goblet I—B2aii, blob of pt., wh., 9.0 × 10.5		23958	
	5. Coptic period Eg. juglet I—A3b, reddish coat		23950	figs. 22h, 191b
	6. Wooden box remains, round, 0.35 × 0.16, 0.03–0.06 thick (E of feet)		Disc.	
	7. Ring (in fill), 2 × 2		23891	
W 76				
	Shaft with chamber on the W side			
	Shaft: 1.95 × 0.65 × 0.80 m			
	Chamber: 1.95 × 0.75 × 0.40 m; overlap 0.20 m, floor at -1.25 m			
	Blocking: stone slabs			
	Burial: S/B/ext./pubis			
	Body: ca. 17 years, female			
	Objects:			
	1. *Qadus*-shaped jar, with no knob		23926	fig. 191d
	2. Cup, broken, on no. 1		Disc.	
	3. Beads		Sample	
W 79, probably Christian				
W 80				
	Shaft with chamber on the N side			
	Shaft: 1.70 × 0.60 × 0.60 m			
	Chamber: 1.70 × 0.60 × — m; 0.20 m overlap, floor at -0.80 m			
	Blocking: none mentioned			
	Burial: —			
	Body: Adult male			

Table 50. Register of X-Group Finds in Cemetery W2 (*cont.*).

Tomb	Description and Contents	Cairo	OIM	Figure/Plate
W 80 (*cont.*)				
Objects:				
1.	Coptic period Eg. *amphoriskos* I—C, ye.-wh. coat, 30 × 20		24042	
2.	Bowl or cup (near no. 1)		Sherds	
3.	Iron objects:		23893	
	a. Javelin/arrowhead			fig. 192a
	b. Arrowhead			fig. 192b
4.	Bead (from fill)		Sample	figs. 63b, s, 64d

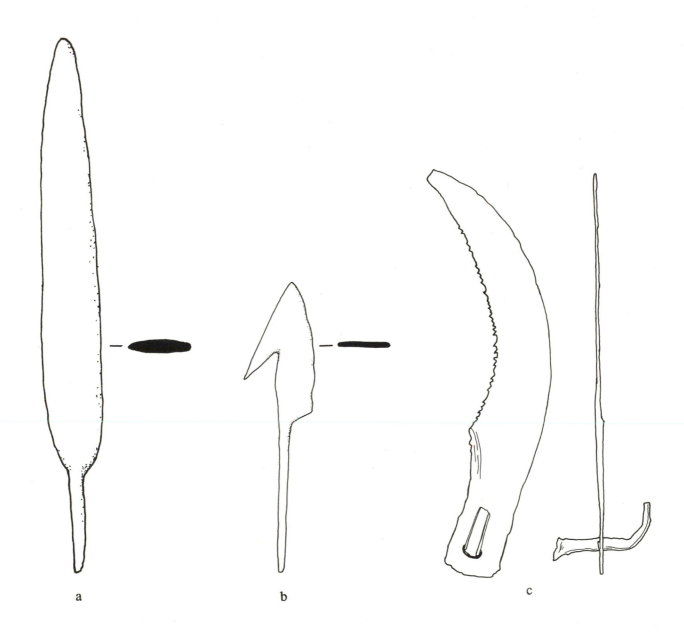

Figure 192. Iron Objects from Tombs W 80 and W 88: (*a*) Javelin/Arrowhead, W 80—3a;
(*b*) Arrowhead, W 80—3b; (*c*) Sickle-Saw, W 88—2. Scale 1:1.

Table 50. Register of X-Group Finds in Cemetery W2 (*cont.*).

Tomb	Description and Contents	Cairo	OIM	Figure/Plate
W 83				
	Shaft: rect., 1.45 × 0.66 × ? m			
	Burial: W/R/legs 80, thighs 45 degrees/before face			
	Body: Mature female			
	Objects:			
	1. Rect. slate or schist palette with hole in center from use, reused early object, 13 × 7 × 2 cm		23898	
	2. Textile remains from shaft (CAT X-Gr.)		Disc.	
	Note that this could be an early tomb.			
W 84				
	Shaft with chamber on the S side			
	Shaft: no dim.; denuded			
	Chamber: no dim.			
	Burial: —			
	Body: 14–15 years			
	Objects:			
	1. Beads		Sample	fig. 62f
W 87, Christian				
W 88				
	Shaft with chamber on the N side			
	Shaft: 1.97 × 0.47 × 0.60 m			
	Chamber: 1.97 × 0.40 × 0.40 m; overlap 0.21 m, floor at -0.85 m			
	Blocking: none mentioned			
	Burial: W/ext./pubis, in textile wrapping			
	Body: Adult female			
	Objects:			
	1. Leather (below head)		Disc.	
	2. Sickle saw (area of L hand)		23896	fig. 192c, pl. 83b
	3. Sandals (at feet)		Sample	
	4. Remains of textile (CAT X-Gr.)		Disc.	
	The leather was used as pillow; the designation "probably quiver" unlikely.			

CEMETERY J

Of the three X-Group tombs in J (3, 7, and 8), J 3 was oriented N-S; J 7 E-W, with a niche in the E end and no side chamber; and J 8 was a N-S brick vault. In addition, Cemetery J contained one C-Group (J 1) and four Christian (J 4, J 5, J 6, and J 9) burials. No record remains of tomb J 2.

Table 51. Register of X-Group Finds in Cemetery J.

Tomb	Description and Contents	Cairo	OIM	Figure/Plate
J 3				
	Shaft with chamber on the W side			
	Shaft: 1.45 × 0.65 × 1.00 m			
	Chamber: 1.25 × 0.55 × 0.47 m			
	Blocking: small stone slabs			

Table 51. Register of X-Group Finds in Cemetery J (*cont.*).

Tomb	Description and Contents	Cairo	OIM	Figure/Plate
J 3 (*cont.*)				
	Burial: —			
	Body: —			
	Objects, from shaft:			
	1. X-Gr. ord. cup I—D4a		23213	fig. 193b
	2. Same, 8.3 × 11.6		23216	
	3. Coptic period Eg. *amphoriskos*-jug I—C, bk. pt. unc. motif		23218	fig. 193a

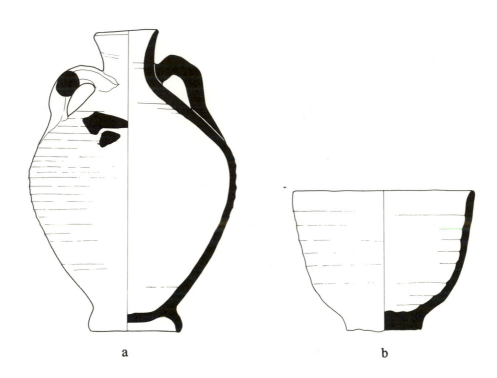

a   b

Figure 193. Pottery from Tomb J 3: (*a*) Coptic Period Egyptian *Amphoriskos* Jug
I—C, No. 3; (*b*) X-Gr. Ord. Cup I—D4a, No. 1. Scale 2:5.

J 7

Shaft with niche at the E end and vault, collapsed and denuded
    Shaft: 2.65 × — × 0.73 m, with ramp
    Niche: 0.68 m deep
    Vault: no dim.
    Blocking: cb., rowlock

J 8

Shaft with ramp and vault, probably niche
    Shaft: —, no dim. to -1.45 m
    Ramp: to -0.63 m, bed leg grooves 0.20 × 0.10 m deep
    Niche: no dim.
    Vault: sloped to E
    Blocking: three courses. cb., rowlock

TOMB M 1

Table 52. Register of Finds in Tomb M 1.

Tomb	Description and Contents	Cairo	OIM	Figure/Plate
M 1				
	A. Shaft with chamber on the W side			
	Shaft: 1.50 × 0.76 × 1.60 m			
	Chamber: 1.35 × 0.75 × 0.50 m; unc. overlap, floor at -1.77 m			
	Burial: S/L/135 degrees, folded/—			
	Body: Adult male			
	Objects:			
	1. Beads (at back of burial)		23653	
	2. Coptic period Eg. *amphoriskos* jug III—, 28 × 20		23614	
	3. Beads (below head of burial)		23653	
	4. Arrowhead, 3–4 cm		23654	
	B. Cut A; Shaft with chamber on the N side			
	Shaft: 2.05 × 1.03 × 0.50 m			
	Chamber: 2.05 × — × 0.55 m; unc. overlap, total undercut 0.35 m, floor at -1.05 m			
	Burial: —			
	Body: Adult male			
	Objects: —			

CEMETERY B

Table 53. Register of X-Group Finds in Cemetery B.

Tomb	Description and Contents	Cairo	OIM	Figure/Plate
B 176				
	Meroitic shaft with ledges and vault cut by X-Gr. tomb with N-S shaft			
B 176B, (cut Meroitic tomb B 176A)				
	Shaft with chamber on the W side			
	Shaft: dim. unc. ca. 1.50 × 0.70 × ? m			
	Chamber: ca. 1.35 × 0.60 × ? m			
	Blocking: cb.			
	Burial: —			
	Body: Adult female			
	Objects:			
	4. Bracelet of beads (L. arm)		22697	
	5. *Qadus*		22838	fig. 194c
	6. X-Gr. ord. goblet I—A1aii *beta*		22828	fig. 194b
B 190, Meroitic tomb, reused in X-Gr.				
	Shaft with ledges and vault (see OINE VIII)			
	Objects, X-Gr.:			
	4. X-Gr. ord. goblet I—A1aii *beta*		22830	fig. 194d
	5. *Qadus*-like jar, very irreg.		22659	fig. 194e
Cemetery B uncertain infant burial				
	Object:			
	1. X-Gr. rough feeding cup of buff ware, handmade, whole, found in shallow infant burial, 3.8 × 6.5		22609	fig. 194a

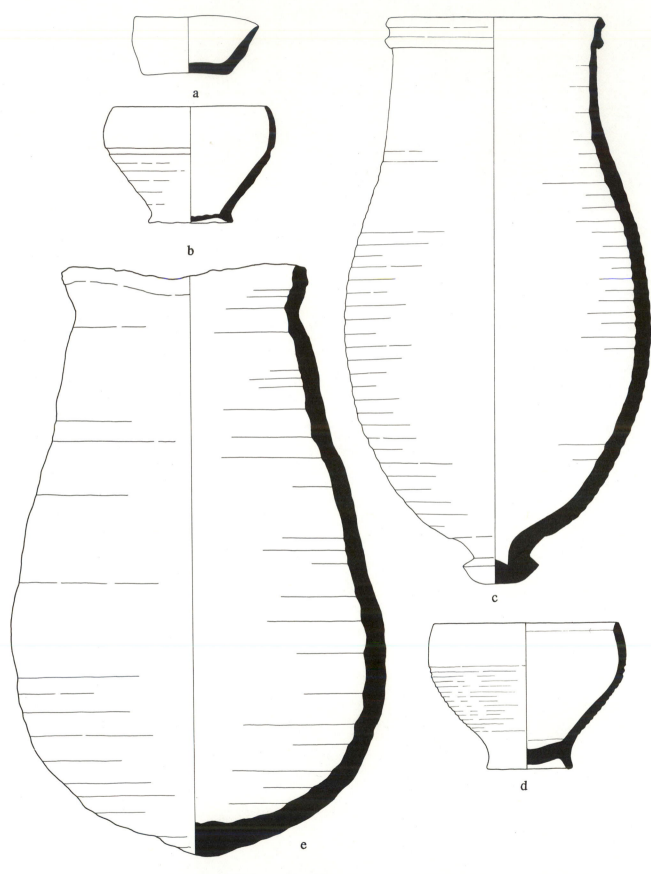

Figure 194. Pottery from Cemetery B: (*a*) X-Gr. Rough Feeding Cup, Uncertain Infant Burial, No. 1;
(*b*) X-Gr. Ord. Goblet I—A1aii *beta*, B 176B—6; (*c*) *Qadus*, B 176B—5; (*d*) X-Gr. Ord.
Goblet I—A1aii *beta*, B 190—4; (*e*) *Qadus*-like Jar, B 190—5. Scale 2:5.

CEMETERY 219

Table 54. Register of Finds in Cemetery 219.

Description and Contents	Cairo	OIM	Figure/Plate
Enclosure BA			fig. 195a; pls. 30a, b, 31, 32a, b

Note that the enclosure was found some 90 m E of a tumulus in Cemetery 219, the only area excavated in that cemetery. For the reason given in *Chapter 1*, it appears that this enclosure was E of tumulus Ba. 80 (the location is marked on pl. 1 according to a plan of Cemetery 219 prepared by Shafiq Farid).

Following is the description as given in the field notes:

"The circular cb. structure. The walls supported by buttresses, preserved 65 cm high in the W section." In the NE sections, remains of three walls:

    a. The innermost, apparently the earliest, was 33 cm thick at the base and 30 cm high.

    b. The middle one, built on a level 10 cm higher than wall a, preserved 41 cm high, 35 cm thick at the base.

    c. The outermost wall was the latest one, built on a level 10 cm higher than wall b. Preserved 115 cm high, 30 cm thick at the base.

Finds:

Description and Contents	Cairo	OIM	Figure/Plate
1. Offering table, badly weathered, found in debris 4 feet from the wall, about 77 cm above the floor of the enclosure; (in red)		Disc.	
2. Drainage pipe of pottery found 110 cm from the S wall, within the circle of the enclosure; (in red)	B 1086	23440	fig. 195b
3. Three jars, broken, found outside of the walls sherds: one saved, two disc.; (in red)			pl. 30
4. Stone cylinder found in debris, about 64 cm above the floor; (in red)		Disc.	
5. Three large stones and petrified wood found on the floor of the enclosure; (in red)		Disc.	
6. Large pottery object, broken, incomplete (brazier?); (in red)		sherds	

Note that objects like no. 2 occur in the area near Qu. 48 and they probably are related to cult activity, possibly as stands. Although the field staff believed that the enclosure was some part of a settlement, it is clearly not connected with any settlement remains.

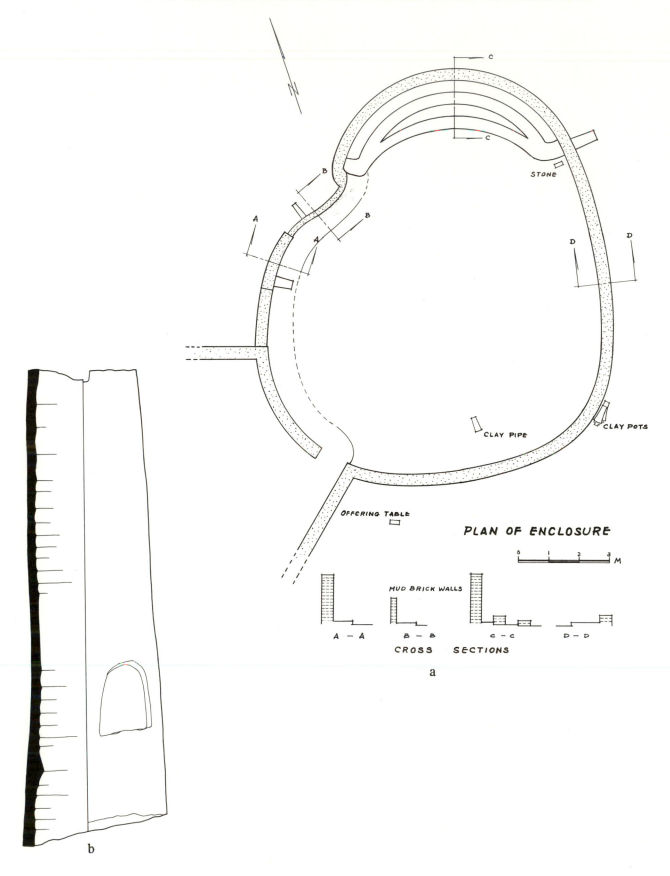

Figure 195. Plan and Pipe/Stand from Enclosure BA in Cemetery 219: (*a*) Plan of Enclosure BA in Cemetery 219; (*b*) Pipe/Stand, No. 2. Scales: (*a*) Scale Indicated, (*b*) 1:5.

INDEX

TUMULI, CHAPELS, ANIMAL PITS, AND TOMBS
LISTED IN THE REGISTER OF FINDS

Cemetery	Number	Type	Page	Cemetery	Number	Type	Page
219	BA	Structure	403	Q	30	Tomb	255
B	176	Tomb	401	Q	31	Tomb	255
B	176B	Tomb	401	Q	32	Tomb	256
B	190	Tomb	401	Q	33	Tomb	258
J	3	Tomb	399	Q	34	Tomb	258
J	7	Tomb	400	Q	35	Tomb	258
J	8	Tomb	400	Q	36	Tomb	259
M	1	Tomb	401	Q	37	Tomb	259
Q	1	Tomb	236	Q	38	Tomb	261
Q	2	Tomb	238	Q	39	Animal Pit	233
Q	3	Tomb	238	Q	40	Tomb	275
Q	4	Tomb	240	Q	41	Tomb	277
Q	5	Animal Pit	225	Q	42	Tomb	277
Q	6	Tomb	240	Q	43	Tomb	278
Q	7	Tomb	242	Q	44	Tomb	278
Q	8	Tomb	242	Q	49	Tomb	281
Q	9	Tomb	244	Q	51	Tomb	281
Q	10	Tomb	246	Q	51A	Tomb	281
Q	11	Tomb	247	Q	52	Tomb	283
Q	12	Tomb	247	Q	53	Tomb	285
Q	13	Tomb	247	Q	54	Tomb	287
Q	14	Tomb	247	Q	55	Tomb	287
Q	15	Tomb	249	Q	56	Tomb	289
Q	16	Tomb	249	Q	57	Tomb	290
Q	17	Tomb	250	Q	58	Tomb	290
Q	18	Tomb	250	Q	59	Tomb	262
Q	19	Tomb	250	Q	60	Tomb	262
Q	20	Animal Pit	231	Q	61	Tomb	263
Q	22	Tomb	254	Q	62	Tomb	264
Q	25	Tomb	254	Q	63	Tomb	290
Q	26	Animal Pit	231	Q	64	Tomb	290
Q	27	Tomb	254	Q	65	Tomb	291
Q	28	Tomb	255	Q	66	Tomb	291
Q	29	Tomb	255	Q	67	Tomb	291

Cemetery	Number	Type	Page	Cemetery	Number	Type	Page
Q	68	Tomb	268	Q	254	Tomb	214
Q	69	Tomb	270	Q	264	Animal Pit	224
Q	70	Tomb	270	Q	265	Animal Pit	224
Q	71	Tomb	270	Q	279	Tomb	326
Q	72	Tomb	270	Q	282	Tomb	306
Q	73	Animal Pit	233	Q	297	Tomb	214
Q	74	Tomb	270	Q	303	Tomb	215
Q	75	Tomb	272	Q	304	Animal Pit	207
Q	76	Tomb	273	Q	309	Tomb	327
Q	77	Animal Pit	233	Q	310	Tomb	215
Q	78	Tomb	275	Q	316	Tomb	327
Q	79	Animal Pit	233	Q	317	Animal Pit	211
Q	82	Tomb	298	Q	320	Tomb	327
Q	83	Tomb	300	Q	321	Tomb	329
Q	84	Tomb	300	Q	324/368	Animal Pit	211
Q	107	Tomb	302	Q	326	Tomb	329
Q	117	Tomb	302	Q	328	Animal Pit	211
Q	119	Tomb	302	Q	330	Tomb	214
Q	133	Tomb	307	Q	332	Tomb	329
Q	134	Tomb	308	Q	333	Animal Pit	211
Q	135	Tomb	310	Q	338	Tomb	331
Q	136	Tomb	310	Q	339	Tomb	216
Q	137	Tomb	310	Q	343	Tomb	331
Q	140	Animal Pit	212	Q	344	Tomb	332
Q	141	Tomb	312	Q	345	Tomb	332
Q	143	Tomb	305	Q	347	Tomb	215
Q	144	Tomb	306	Q	348	Tomb	333
Q	145	Tomb	313	Q	349	Tomb	333
Q	146	Tomb	313	Q	350	Tomb	335
Q	147	Tomb	313	Q	353	Tomb	215
Q	148	Tomb	314	Q	356	Tomb	335
Q	149	Tomb	316	Q	357	Tomb	335
Q	152	Tomb	316	Q	360	Tomb	336
Q	161	Tomb	318	Q	361	Tomb	336
Q	164	Tomb	319	Q	367	Tomb	214
Q	165	Tomb	214	Q	377	Tomb	336
Q	173	Tomb	215	Q	378	Tomb	338
Q	174	Tomb	306	Q	379	Tomb	338
Q	175	Tomb	213	Q	381	Tomb	338
Q	176	Tomb	215	Q	383	Tomb	214
Q	184	Tomb	322	Q	384	Tomb	214
Q	186	Tomb	322	Q	385	Tomb	338
Q	192	Tomb	324	Q	387	Tomb	340
Q	196	Tomb	324	Q	388	Tomb	340
Q	227	Tomb	294	Q	389	Tomb	340
Q	230	Tomb	213	Q	390	Tomb	341
Q	231	Tomb	326	Q	391	Tomb	341
Q	240	Tomb	215	Q	393	Tomb	341
Q	241	Animal Pit	213	Q	394	Tomb	341

Cemetery	Number	Type	Page	Cemetery	Number	Type	Page
Q	400	Tomb	343	QB	12	Chapel	184
Q	401	Tomb	216	QB	13	Chapel	184
Q	405	Tomb	343	QB	14	Chapel	184
Q	410	Tomb	343	QB	15	Chapel	184
Q	414	Tomb	214	QB	16	Chapel	185
Q	422	Tomb	344	QB	17	Chapel	185
Q	425	Tomb	344	QB	18	Chapel	185
Q	433	Tomb	214	QB	19	Chapel	185
Q	434	Tomb	344	QB	20	Chapel	185
Q	446	Tomb	346	QB	21	Chapel	185
Q	454	Tomb	349	QB	22	Chapel	185
Q	463	Tomb	346	QB	23	Chapel	185
Q	468	Tomb	346	QB	24	Chapel	185
Q	470	Tomb	215	QB	25	Chapel	185
Q	473	Tomb	347	QB	26	Chapel	185
Q	479	Tomb	347	QB	27	Chapel	185
Q	480/486	Animal Pit	213	QB	28	Chapel	185
Q	492	Animal Pit	211	QB	29	Chapel	185
Q	501	Tomb	295	QB	30	Chapel	185
Q	502	Tomb	295	QB	31	Chapel	185
Q	503	Tomb	297	QB	32	Chapel	187
Q	504	Tomb	297	QB	33	Chapel	187
Q	505	Tomb	297	QB	34	Chapel	187
Q	512	Tomb	217	QB	35	Chapel	187
Q	513	Tomb	217	QB	36	Chapel	187
Q	540	Tomb	215	QB	37	Chapel	187
Q	545	Tomb	347	QB	38	Chapel	187
Q	571	Tomb	217	QB	39	Chapel	187
Q	573	Tomb	215	QB	40	Chapel	187
Q	578	Tomb	215	QB	41	Chapel	187
Q	580	Tomb	347	QB	42	Chapel	187
Q	582	Tomb	347	QB	43	Chapel	187
Q	583	Tomb	348	QB	44	Chapel	187
Q	589	Tomb	348	QB	45	Chapel	189
Q	594	Tomb	348	QB	46	Chapel	189
Q	618	Tomb	215	QB	47	Chapel	189
Q	635	Tomb	214	QB	48	Chapel	189
Q	649	Tomb	217	QB	49	Chapel	189
QB	1	Chapel	181	QB	50	Chapel	189
QB	2	Chapel	182	QB	51	Chapel	189
QB	3	Chapel	182	QB	52	Chapel	189
QB	4	Chapel	183	QB	53	Chapel	189
QB	5	Chapel	184	QB	54	Chapel	190
QB	6	Chapel	184	QB	55	Chapel	190
QB	7	Chapel	184	QB	56	Chapel	190
QB	8	Chapel	184	QB	57	Chapel	190
QB	9	Chapel	184	QB	58	Chapel	190
QB	10	Chapel	184	QC	1	Chapel	195
QB	11	Chapel	184	QC	2	Chapel	195

Cemetery	Number	Type	Page	Cemetery	Number	Type	Page
QC	3	Chapel	197	QC	52	Chapel	204
QC	4	Chapel	197	QC	53	Chapel	204
QC	5	Chapel	197	QC	54	Chapel	205
QC	6	Chapel	198	QC	55	Chapel	206
QC	7	Chapel	198	QE	1	Chapel	218
QC	8	Chapel	199	QE	1	Deposit	220
QC	9	Chapel	199	QE	2	Deposit	220
QC	10	Chapel	199	QF	1	Chapel	222
QC	11	Chapel	199	QF	2	Chapel	222
QC	12	Chapel	200	QF	3	Chapel	222
QC	13	Chapel	200	QF	4	Chapel	222
QC	14	Chapel	200	QF	5	Chapel	222
QC	15	Chapel	200	QF	6	Chapel	223
QC	16	Chapel	200	QF	7	Chapel	223
QC	17	Chapel	200	QF	8	Chapel	223
QC	18	Chapel	201	QF	9	Chapel	223
QC	19	Chapel	201	QF	10	Chapel	223
QC	20	Chapel	201	QF	11	Chapel	223
QC	21	Chapel	201	QF	12	Chapel	223
QC	22	Chapel	201	QF	13	Chapel	223
QC	23	Chapel	201	QF	14	Chapel	223
QC	24	Chapel	201	Qu.	3	Tumulus	225
QC	25	Chapel	201	Qu.	4	Tumulus	223
QC	26	Chapel	203	Qu.	7	Tumulus	262
QC	27	Chapel	203	Qu.	10	Tumulus	233
QC	28	Chapel	203	Qu.	31	Tumulus	181
QC	29	Chapel	203	Qu.	36	Tumulus	222
QC	30	Chapel	203	Qu.	48	Tumulus	195
QC	31	Chapel	203	Qu.	54	Tumulus	233
QC	32	Chapel	203	Qu.	56	Tumulus	218
QC	33	Chapel	203	Qu.	60	Tumulus	223
QC	34	Chapel	203	R	1	Tomb	350
QC	35	Chapel	203	R	2	Tomb	352
QC	36	Chapel	203	R	4A	Tomb	352
QC	37	Chapel	203	R	5	Tomb	356
QC	38	Chapel	203	R	6	Tomb	356
QC	39	Chapel	203	R	7	Tomb	357
QC	40	Chapel	204	R	8	Tomb	357
QC	41	Chapel	204	R	10	Tomb	358
QC	42	Chapel	204	R	11	Tomb	358
QC	43	Chapel	204	R	14	Tomb	360
QC	44	Chapel	204	R	15	Tomb	360
QC	45	Chapel	204	R	16	Tomb	361
QC	46	Chapel	204	R	18	Tomb	361
QC	47	Chapel	204	R	21	Tomb	361
QC	48	Chapel	204	R	22	Tomb	363
QC	49	Chapel	204	R	23	Tomb	363
QC	50	Chapel	204	R	24	Tomb	363
QC	51	Chapel	204	R	26	Tomb	364

Cemetery	Number	Type	Page	Cemetery	Number	Type	Page
R	27	Tomb	365	R	115	Tomb	381
R	28	Tomb	365	R	116	Tomb	381
R	30	Tomb	365	R	117	Tomb	381
R	31	Tomb	365	R	118	Tomb	381
R	36	Tomb	365	R	119	Tomb	382
R	37	Tomb	367	R	121	Tomb	383
R	48	Tomb	367	V	201	Tomb	392
R	49	Tomb	367	V	202	Tomb	392
R	50	Tomb	369	V	203	Tomb	393
R	51	Tomb	369	VA	9	Tomb	384
R	53	Tomb	369	VA	12	Tomb	385
R	54	Tomb	371	VA	13	Tomb	385
R	55	Tomb	371	VA	14	Tomb	385
R	59	Tomb	371	VB	70	Tomb	387
R	60	Tomb	372	VC	41	Tomb	389
R	62	Tomb	372	VC	42	Tomb	389
R	64	Tomb	372	VF	68	Tomb	389
R	65	Tomb	374	VG	86	Tomb	391
R	66	Tomb	374	VG	89	Tomb	391
R	67	Tomb	374	VG	95	Tomb	391
R	68	Tomb	375	VG	96	Tomb	391
R	69	Tomb	375	VG	97	Tomb	391
R	70	Tomb	376	VH	122	Tomb	392
R	71	Tomb	376	W	54	Tomb	393
R	72	Tomb	376	W	57	Tomb	393
R	73	Tomb	376	W	58	Tomb	394
R	74	Tomb	376	W	59	Tomb	394
R	82	Tomb	376	W	60	Tomb	394
R	89	Tomb	377	W	61	Tomb	394
R	92	Tomb	377	W	62	Tomb	394
R	95	Tomb	377	W	63	Tomb	395
R	100	Tomb	377	W	65	Tomb	395
R	102	Tomb	377	W	66	Tomb	395
R	103	Tomb	378	W	67	Tomb	395
R	104	Tomb	378	W	69	Tomb	395
R	105	Tomb	378	W	71	Tomb	395
R	106	Tomb	378	W	73	Tomb	397
R	107	Tomb	378	W	74	Tomb	397
R	108	Tomb	378	W	76	Tomb	397
R	109	Tomb	380	W	79	Tomb	397
R	110	Tomb	380	W	80	Tomb	397
R	111	Tomb	380	W	83	Tomb	399
R	112	Tomb	380	W	84	Tomb	399
R	113	Tomb	380	W	87	Tomb	399
R	114	Tomb	381	W	88	Tomb	399

ORIENTAL INSTITUTE NUBIAN EXPEDITION

Cemeteries

Sites

Kasr el Wizz

OTHER EXCAVATIONS OR SURVEYS

Cemeteries   228   225   ○ 231

Sites   Set. A. 1.

MODERN CANAL SYSTEM

130

125

B

Meroitic Set.

219

River North

W 1   W 2

Vh

Q

220

140

150

B   Vh

Mer.
Set.

W 1   W 2

Q

500   1000 M

Plan of the Concession, X-Group Sites. The Small Cross in Cemetery 219
Indicates the Position of Structure BA.

PLATE 2

R I V E R

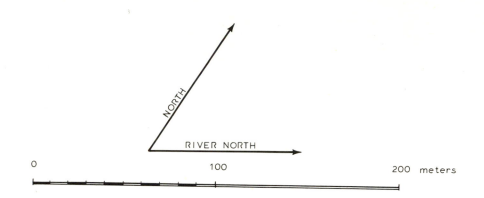

NORTH

RIVER NORTH

0   100   200   meters

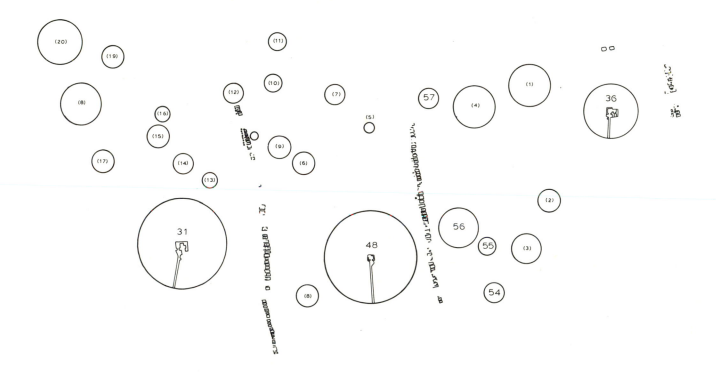

The Royal Cemetery at Qustul in X-Group. Site Plan of Cemetery Q.

PLATE 2

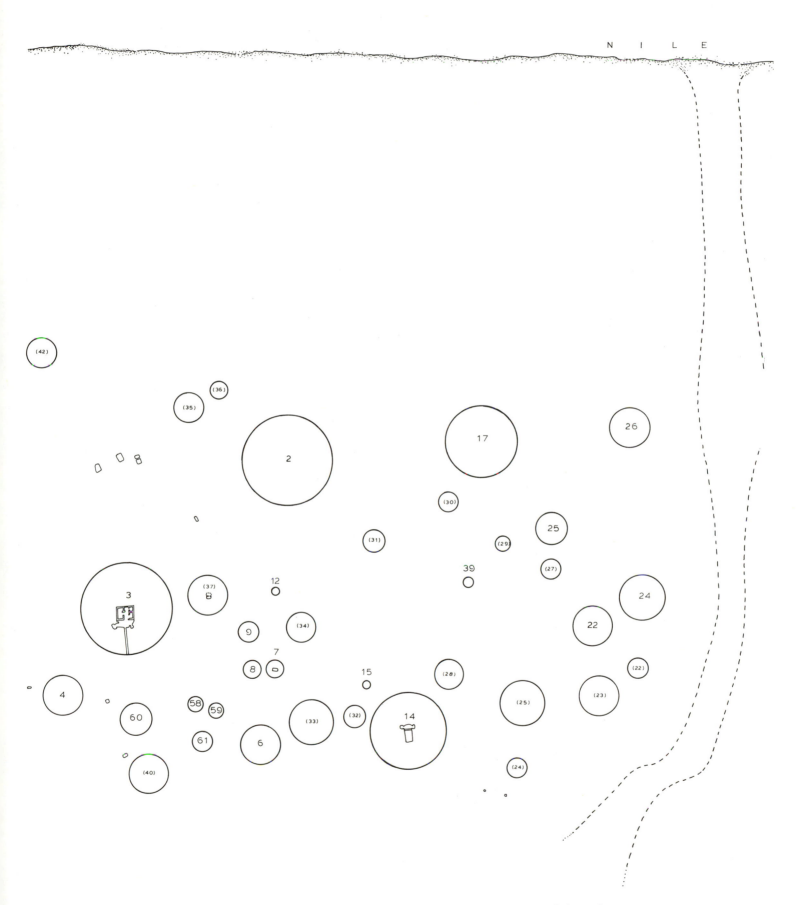

The Royal Cemetery at Qustul in X-Group. Site Plan of Cemetery Q (*cont.*).

PLATE 3

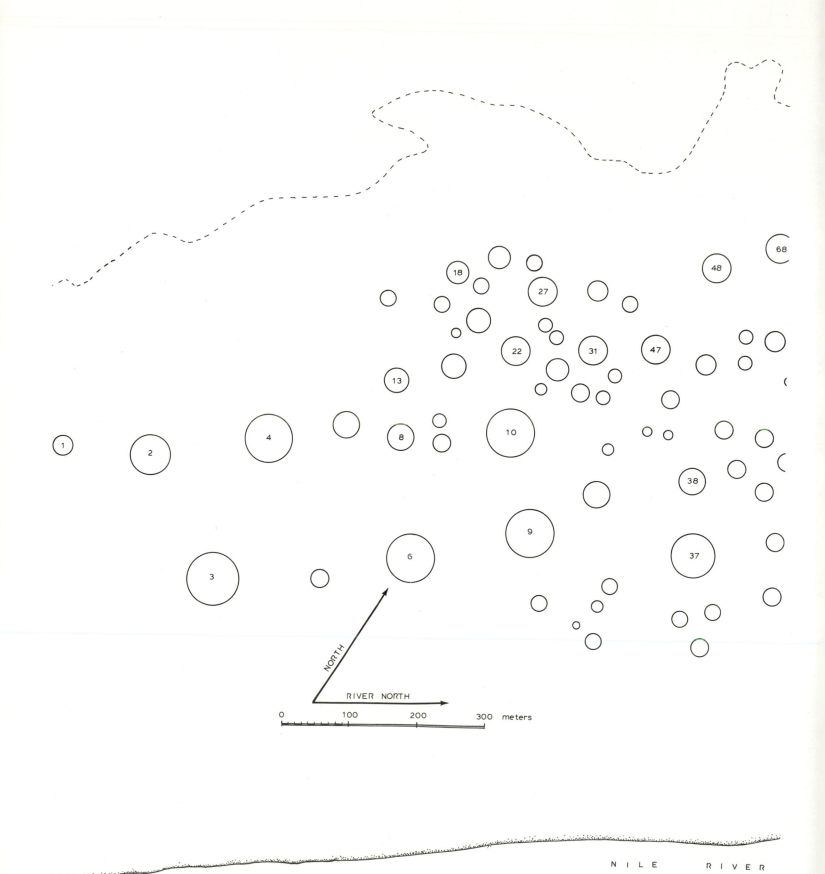

The Royal Cemetery at Ballana. Site Plan of Cemetery 219.

PLATE 3

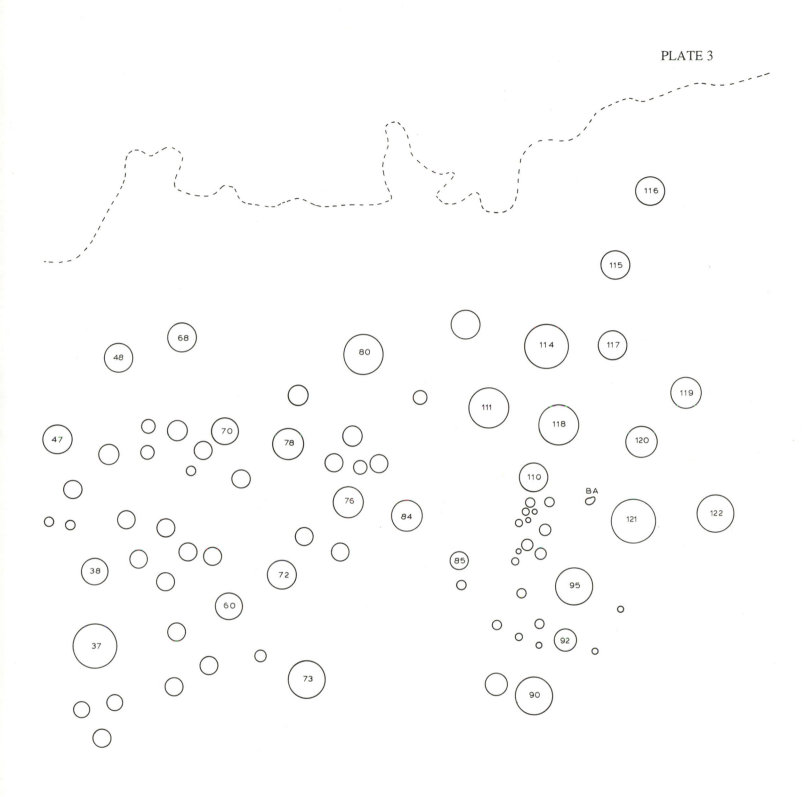

The Royal Cemetery at Ballana. Site Plan of Cemetery 219 (*cont.*).

PLATE 4

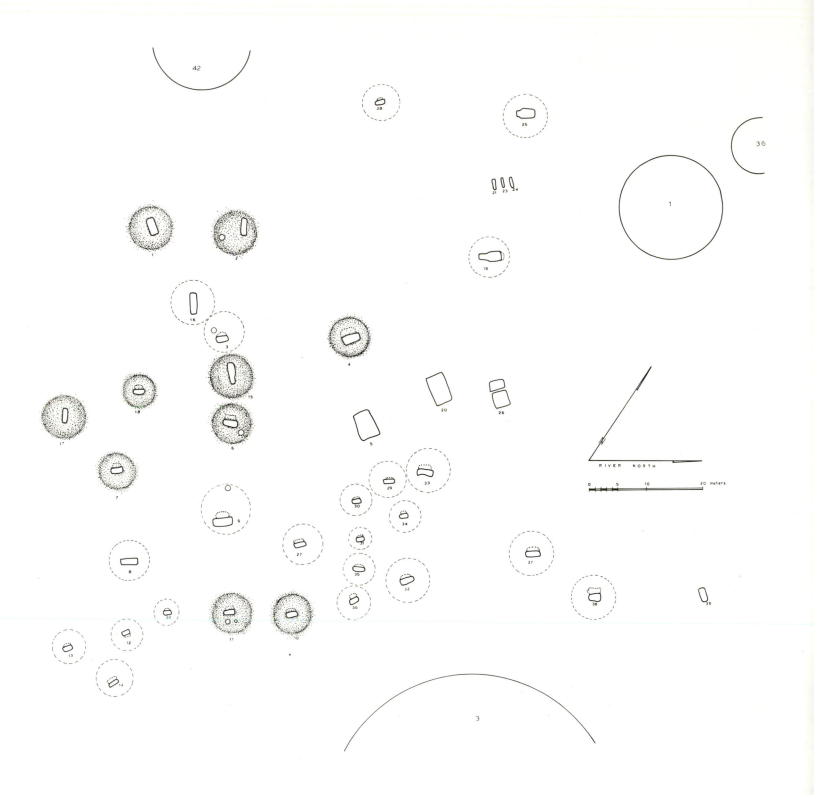

Qustul, Tumulus Qu. 3 Complex, Plan of Area QA. Solid Circles Indicate Tumuli Planned by Previous Expeditions. Stippled Circles Indicate Recorded Tumuli. Dashed Circles Indicate Restored Tumuli.

PLATE 5

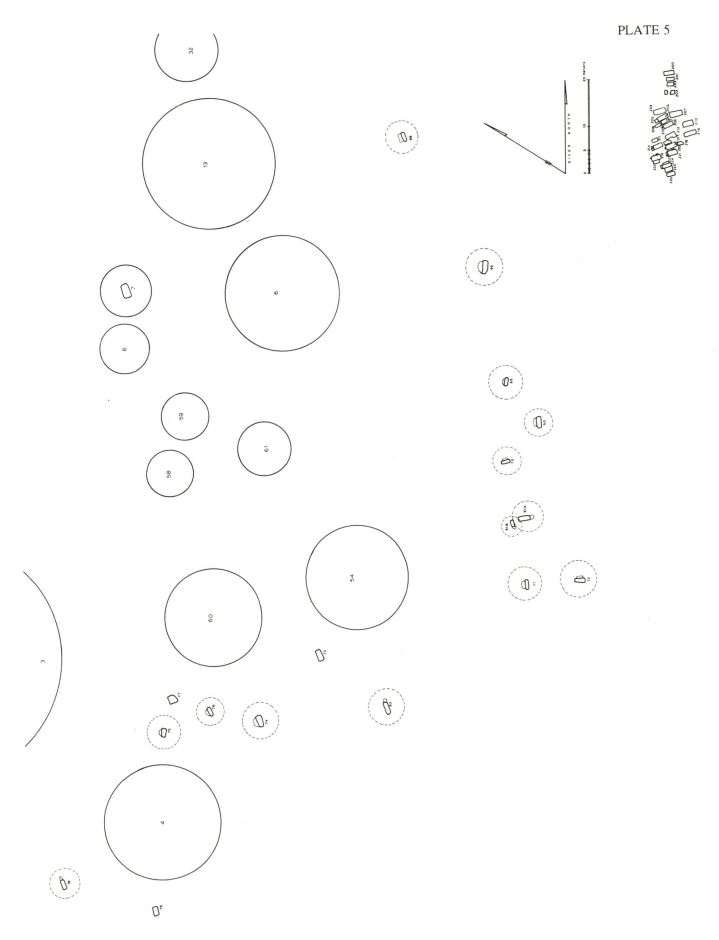

Qustul, Plan of Area Q*B*. Solid Circles Indicate Tumuli Planned by
Previous Expeditions. Dashed Circles Indicate Restored Tumuli.

PLATE 6

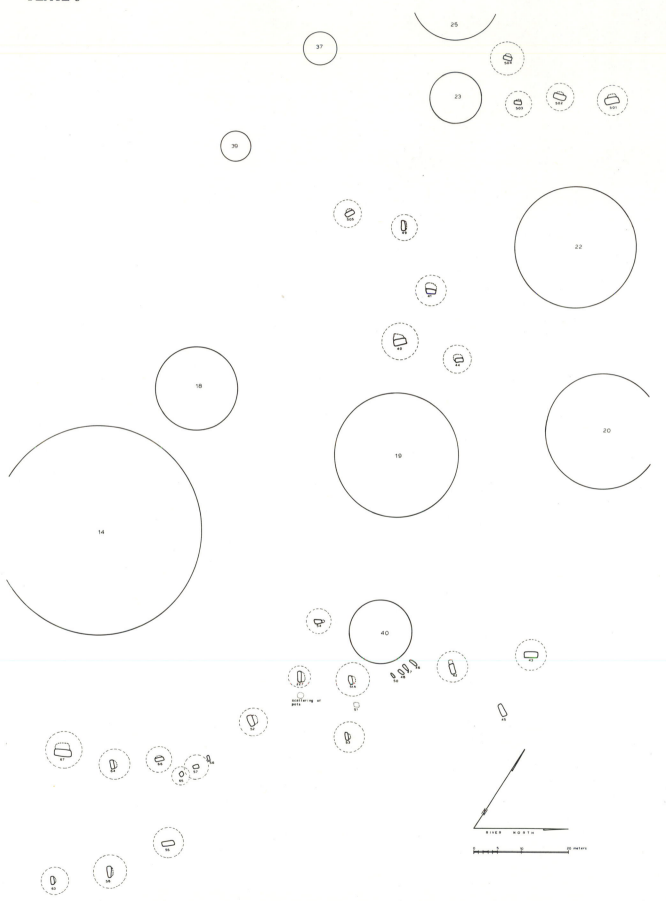

Qustul, Plan of Area QC. Solid Circles Indicate Tumuli Planned by
Previous Expeditions. Dashed Circles Indicate Restored Tumuli.

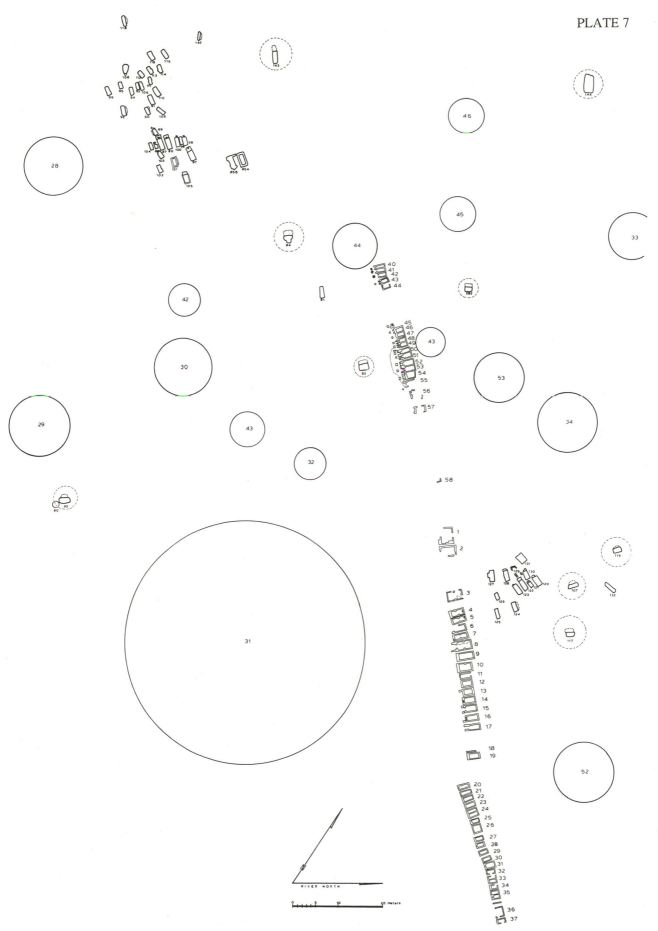

PLATE 7

Qustul, Plan of Area Q*D*. Solid Circles Indicate Tumuli Planned by
Previous Expeditions. Dashed Circles Indicate Restored Tumuli.

PLATE 8

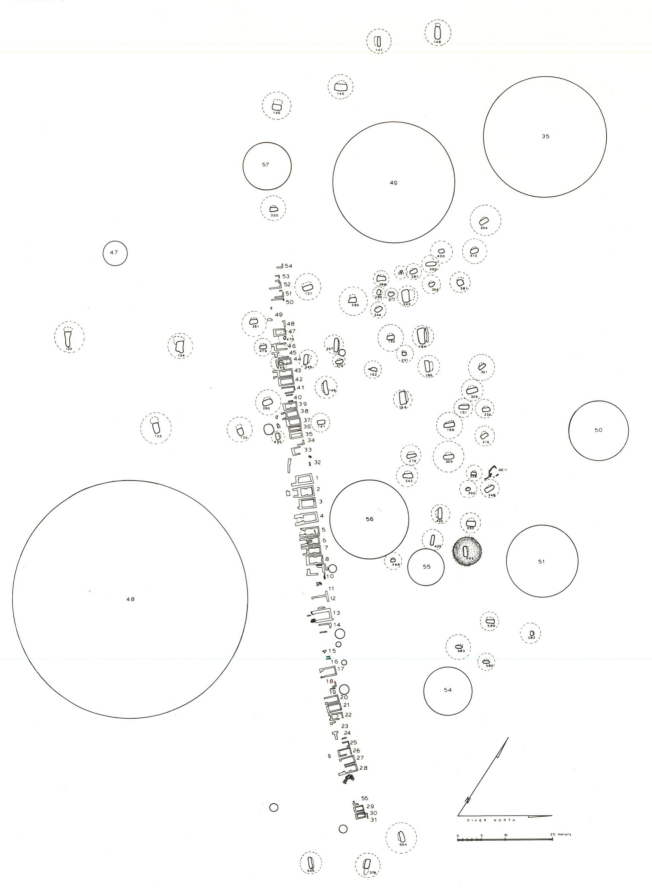

Qustul, Plan of Area QE. Solid Circles Indicate Tumuli Planned by
Previous Expeditions. Dashed Circles Indicate Restored Tumuli.

PLATE 9

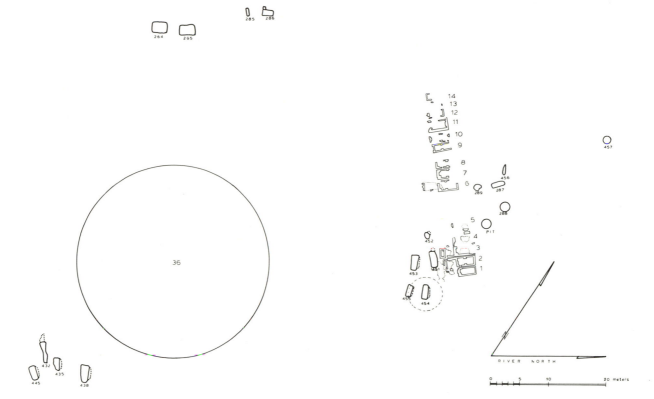

Qustul, Plan of Area Q*F.* Solid Circles Indicate Tumuli Planned by
Previous Expeditions. Dashed Circles Indicate Restored Tumuli.

PLATE 10

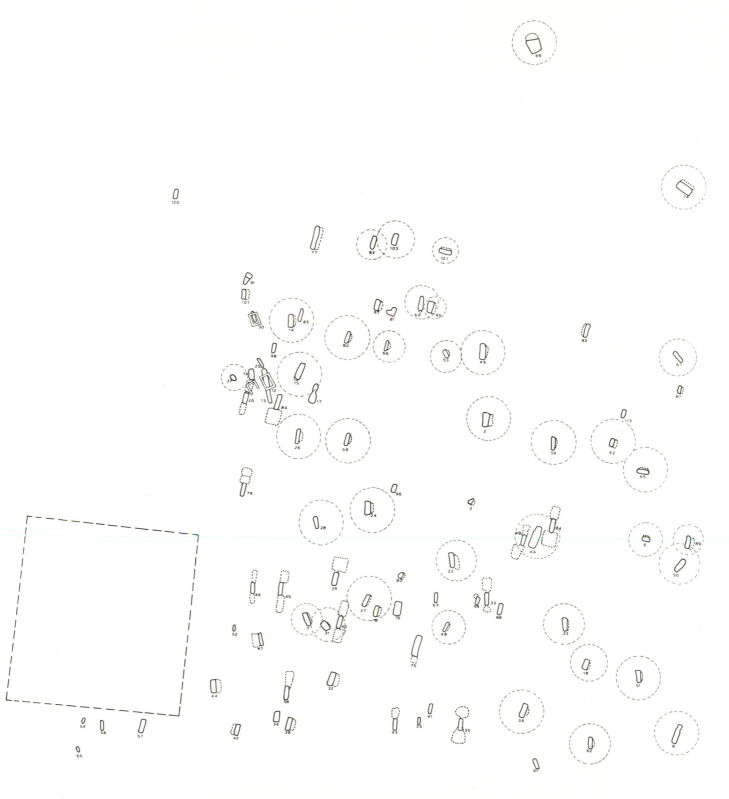

Qustul, Plan of Cemetery R. The Dashed Circles Indicate Restored Tumuli.

PLATE 10

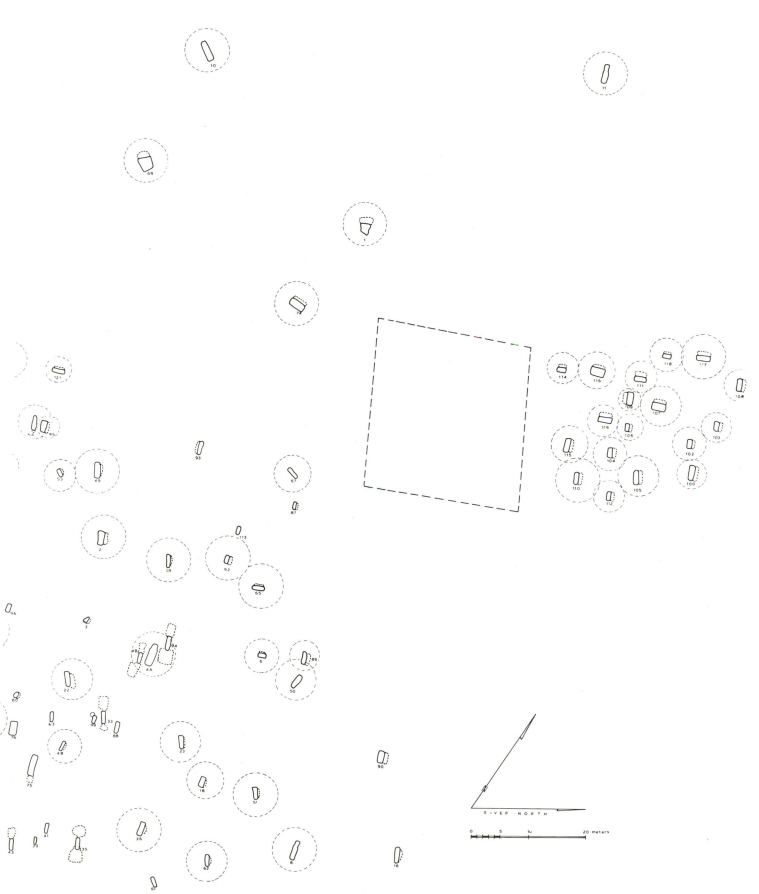

Qustul, Plan of Cemetery R. The Dashed Circles Indicate Restored Tumuli (*cont.*).

PLATE 11

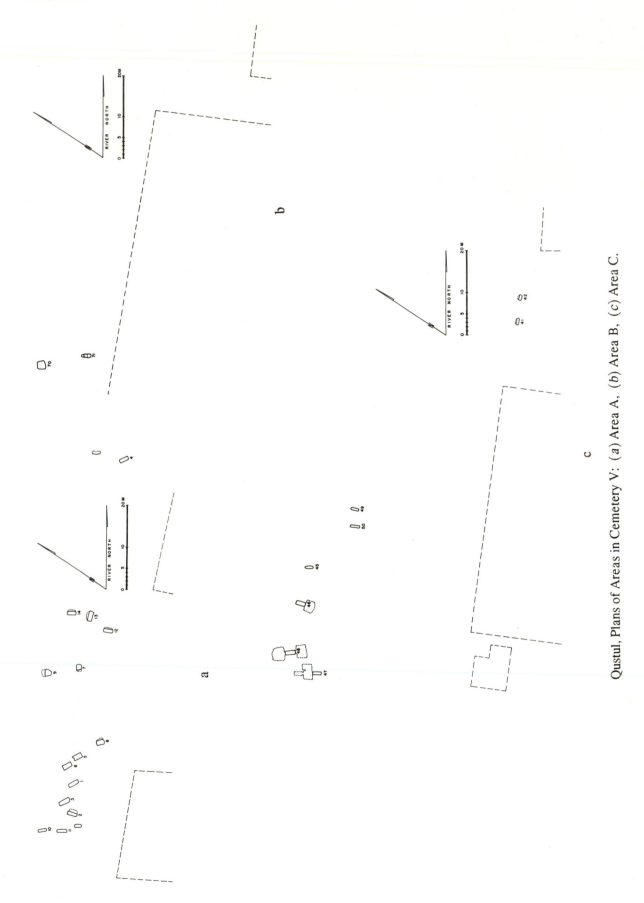

Qustul, Plans of Areas in Cemetery V: (a) Area A, (b) Area B, (c) Area C.

PLATE 12

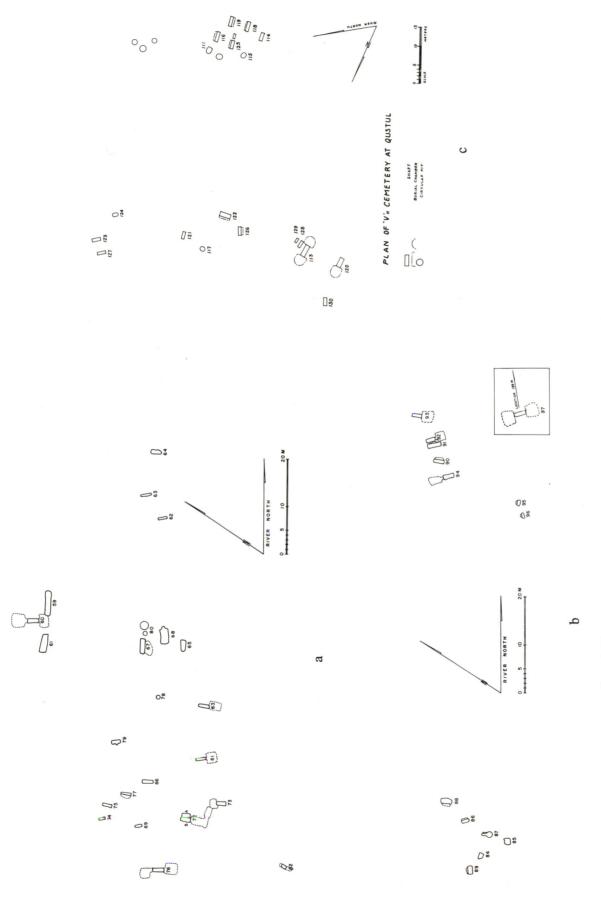

PLAN OF 'V'n CEMETERY AT QUSTUL

SHAFT
BURIAL CHAMBER
CIRCULAR PIT

c

RIVER NORTH

a

RIVER NORTH

b

Qustul, Plans of Areas in Cemetery V (*cont.*): (*a*) Area F, (*b*) Area G, (*c*) Area H.

PLATE 13

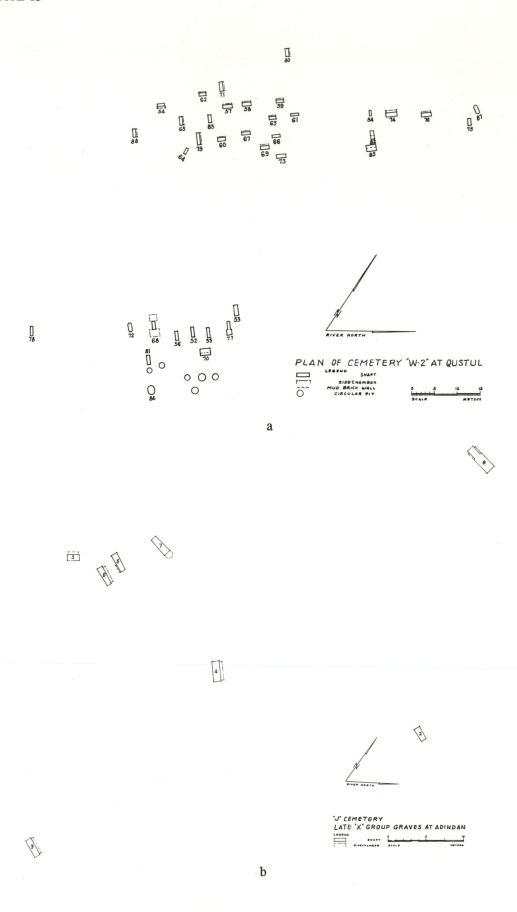

a

b

Cemeteries at Qustul: (*a*) Cemetery W 2, (*b*) Cemetery J.

PLATE 14

Qustul, Cemetery Q Toward the Northeast.

PLATE 15

a

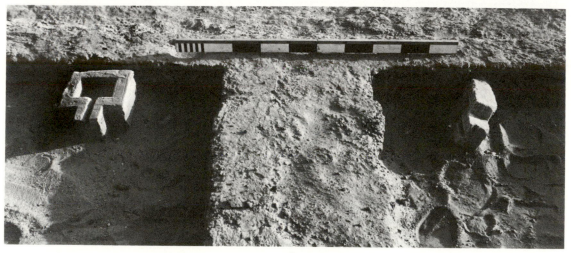

b

c

Qustul, Tumulus Qu. 31 Complex: (*a*) Chapels QB 40–43 from the South, (*b*) Offering Tables in Chapels QB 4 and QB 5, (*c*) Offering Table in Chapel QB 52.

PLATE 16

a

b

Qustul, Tumulus Qu. 31 Complex (*cont.*): (*a*) Chapels QB 45–49, (*b*) Chapels QB 49–53.

PLATE 17

a

b

Qustul, Tumulus Qu. 48 Complex: (*a*) Chapels QC 4–7 from the East, (*b*) Chapels QC 7–9 from the South.

PLATE 18

a

b

Qustul, Tumulus Qu. 48 Complex (*cont.*): (*a*) Chapels QC 8–9, (*b*) Chapels QC 19–20.

PLATE 19

The Door in Chapel QC 6: (a) Detail, (b) Context.

PLATE 20

Qustul, Tumulus Qu. 48 Complex (*cont.*): (*a*) Chapel QC 36, (*b–c*) Chapel QC 22, Jamb, Lintel, and Fragment of Sphinx.

PLATE 21

a

b

Qustul, Tumulus Qu. 48 Complex, Cooking Pit Q 140: (*a*) Pit with Pottery [in Situ],
(*b*) Deposit of Stones and Bones [in Situ].

PLATE 22

a

b

Cooking Pit Q 140: (a) Stone and Bone Deposit [detail], (b) Footprints in Mud Plaster Below Deposit.

PLATE 23

a

b

Qustul, Tumulus Qu. 36 Complex: (*a–b*) Chapels with Plastered Forecourts and Podia.

PLATE 24

b

a

Qustul, Tumulus Qu. 36 Complex (*cont.*): (*a*) Chapels from the West, (*b*) Chapels QF 7 and QF 8.

PLATE 25

a

b

Qustul, Tumulus Qu. 3 Complex: (*a*) Animal Pit Q 5 from the East,
(*b*) Animal Pit Q 5 from the North, (western half).

PLATE 26

Qustul, Tumulus Qu. 3 Complex, Animal Pit Q 20 from the North.

PLATE 27

a

b

Qustul, Tumulus Qu. 36 Complex (*cont.*): (*a*) Animal Pit Q 264 from the West,
(*b*) Animal Pit Q 265 from the East.

PLATE 28

a

b

Qustul, Animal Pits: (*a*) Q 26 from the North; (*b*) Tumulus Qu. 10 Complex, Pit Q 39 from the North.

PLATE 29

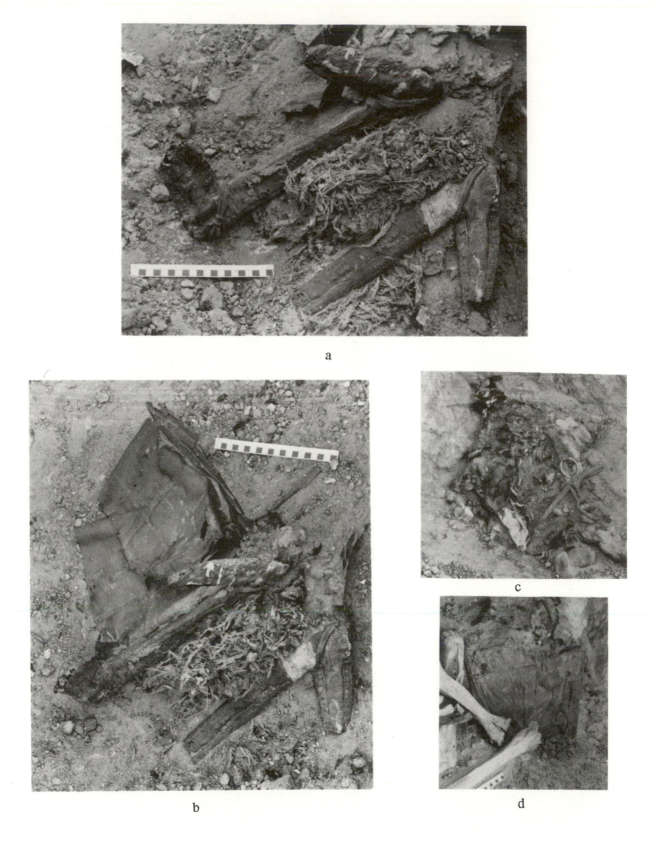

a

b

c

d

Details of Animal Pit Q 39: (*a*) Saddle [as cleaned], (*b*) Saddle with Seat [as uncovered], (*c*) Padding Below Leather [see plate 28b, left corner], (*d*) Detail of Leather [see plate 28b, center above].

PLATE 30

a

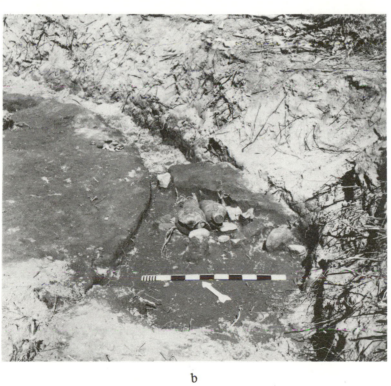

b

Cemetery 219, Structure BA in Cemetery 219: (*a*) Deposit of Amphorae, (*b*) Deposit from a Distance.

PLATE 31

Cemetery 219, Structure BA, Walls at the North End.

PLATE 32

b

a

Cemetery 219, Structure BA: (a) Doorway to the South, (b) Walls to the West.

PLATE 33

a

b

Tomb Q 4: (*a*) Tumulus and Shaft from the North, (*b*) Shaft and Blocking.

PLATE 34

a

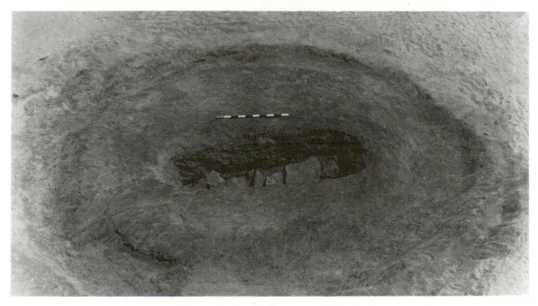

b

Tombs at Qustul: (*a*) Tomb Q 11 from the South, (*b*) Tomb Q 405 from the South.

PLATE 35

a

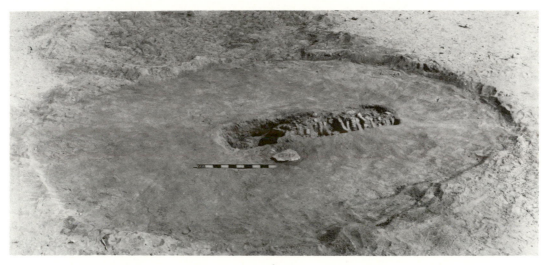

b

c

Tombs at Qustul (*cont.*): (*a*) Tomb Q 1 from the South, (*b*) Tomb Q 17 from the South,
(*c*) Tomb Q 15 from the North.

PLATE 36

Brick Chambers in Cemetery Q: (*a*) Tomb Q 144 from the West, (*b*) Tomb Q 19 from the South.

PLATE 37

b

a

c

Burials in Cemetery Q: (a) Bed in Tomb Q 40, (b) Tomb Q 152 from the North, with Bow, Arrow, and Hide Lining; (c) Tomb Q 378 [in situ].

PLATE 38

a

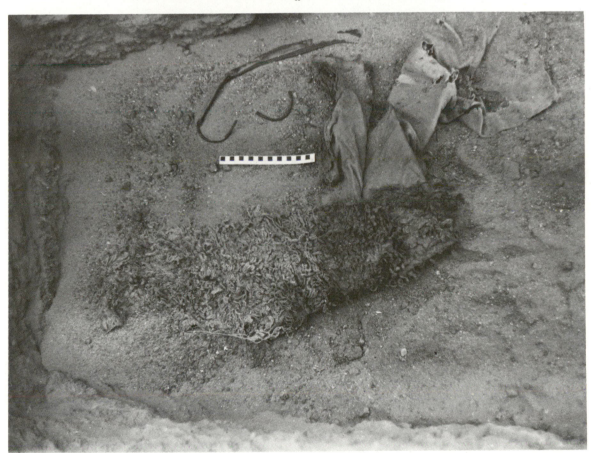

b

Objects in situ from Cemetery Q, Tomb Q 74: (*a*) Textile and Quiver,
(*b*) Tomb Viewed from the South, [remains of a bow are above].

PLATE 39

a

b

Objects in situ in Cemetery Q: (*a*) Tomb Q 149 from the East, Showing the Quiver,
(*b*) Tomb Q 62, with the Quiver and Vessels.

PLATE 40

a

b

c

Brick Structures in Cemetery R: (*a*) Tomb R 4A, (*b*) Tomb R 4A [opened], (*c*) Tomb R 5.

PLATE 41

X-Group Ordinary Goblets and Bowl: (*a*) Goblet I—A1bi *alpha*, Q 333—1; (*b*) Goblet I—A1aiii,
Q 62—9; (*c*) Goblet I—A1ci, Q 19—7; (*d*) Goblet I—A2b, R 50—9; (*e*) Goblet I—A2b,
R 4A—13; (*f*) Goblet I—A2b, R 64—3; (*g*) Goblet I—B2bii, Q 58—1;
(*h*) Bowl I—C1b, R 53—2. Scale ca. 1:3.

PLATE 42

X-Group Fine and Ordinary Pottery: (*a*) X-Gr. Fine Cup II—D5a, Q 148—4; (*b*) X-Gr. Fine Cup
II—D1a, Q 148—6; (*c*) X-Gr. Ord. Cup I—D4b, Q 148—7; (*d*) X-Gr. Ord. Min. Bottle-Jar
I—A2, R 53—1; (*e*) X-Gr. Fine Cup II—A1a, Q 148—5; (*f*) X-Gr. Fine Cup II—C2,
Q 54—6; (*g*) X-Gr. Ord. Spouted Jar I—B, Q 2—8; (*h*) X-Gr. Ord.
Narrow-Necked Bottle-Jar I—C4, R 66—1. Scale ca. 2:5.

PLATE 43

X-Group Ordinary Bottle-Jars: (*a*) I—E3, Q 143—9; (*b*) I—C3, R 95—2;
(*c*) I—B3b, Q 52—7. Scale ca. 2:5.

PLATE 44

a

b

c

d

X-Group Ordinary Bottle-Jars (*cont.*): (*a*) I—C3, R 68—1; (*b*) I—A1, R 106—1;
(*c*) I—A2, Q 1—10; (*d*) I—B1a, R 50—6. Scale ca. 2:5.

PLATE 45

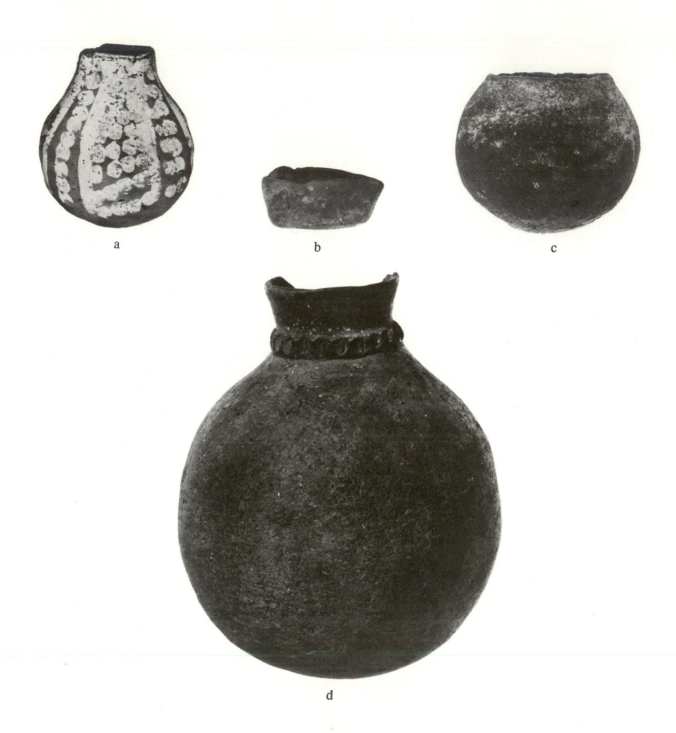

X-Group Handmade Vessels: (*a*) Jar—B1, Q 356—4; (*b*) Min. Lamp, Q 345—6;
(*c*) Small Cooking Pot, Q 62—15; (*d*) Jar—D3, Q 68—2. Scale ca. 2:5.

PLATE 46

X-Group Bottle-Jar and Coptic Period Egyptian Juglets and Jugs: (*a*) Juglet I—C3, Q 164—6; (*b*) Juglet I—A2b, Q 82—2; (*c*) Flask/Juglet I—D2a, Q 332—3; (*d*) X-Gr, Ord. Miniature Bottle-Jar—B1, Q 143—7; (*e*) *Amphoriskos*-Jug II—A, R 103—1; (*f*) Utility *Amphoriskos* II—C, Q 62—5; (*g*) Utility *Amphoriskos* II—C, Q 62—6. Scale ca. 2:5.

PLATE 47

X-Group Storage Jar, Coptic Period Egyptian Pottery, and *Qawadus*: (*a*) X-Gr. Storage Jar III—, Q 137—3; (*b*) *Qadus*, R 100—1; (*c*) Amphora IV—, Q 51A—1; (*d*) *Qadus*-like Jar—B, Q 381—2. Scales: (*a, c*), ca. 1:5; (*b*) ca. 1:3; (*d*) 2:5.

PLATE 48

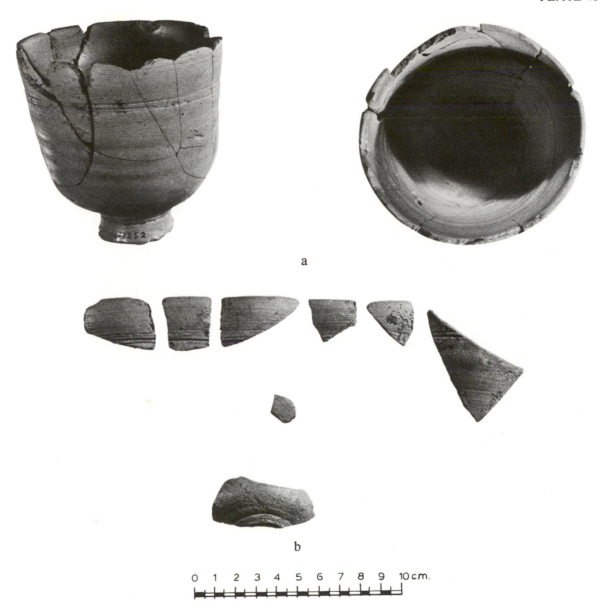

a

b

Unfired X-Group Fine Pottery: (*a*) Cup II—, R 65—2a; (*b*) Sherds, R 65—2b. Scale Indicated.

PLATE 49

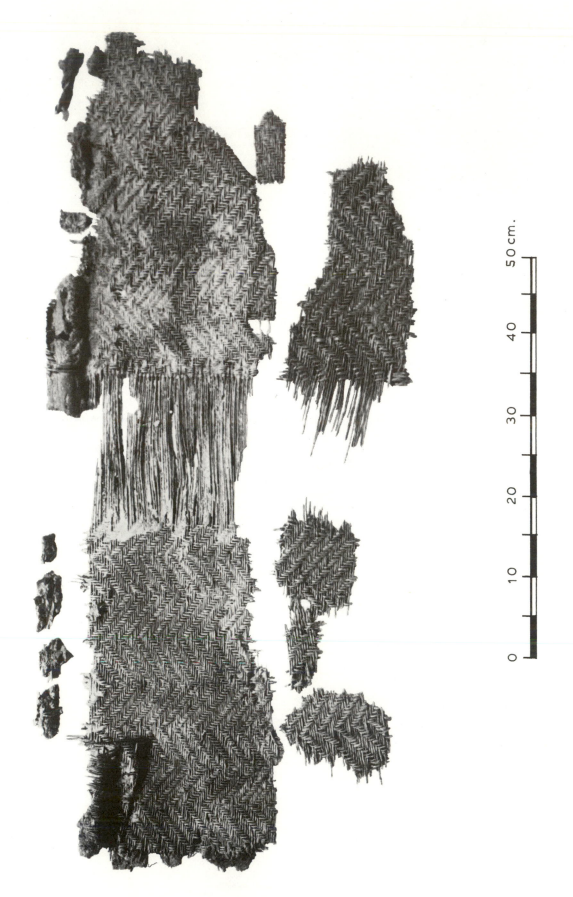

The Bed from Tomb Q 40. Scale Indicated.

PLATE 50

Remains of Matting from Beds: (*a*) Q 59—1, (*b*) Q 68—8, (*c*) Q 343—1. Scale ca. 1:1.

PLATE 51

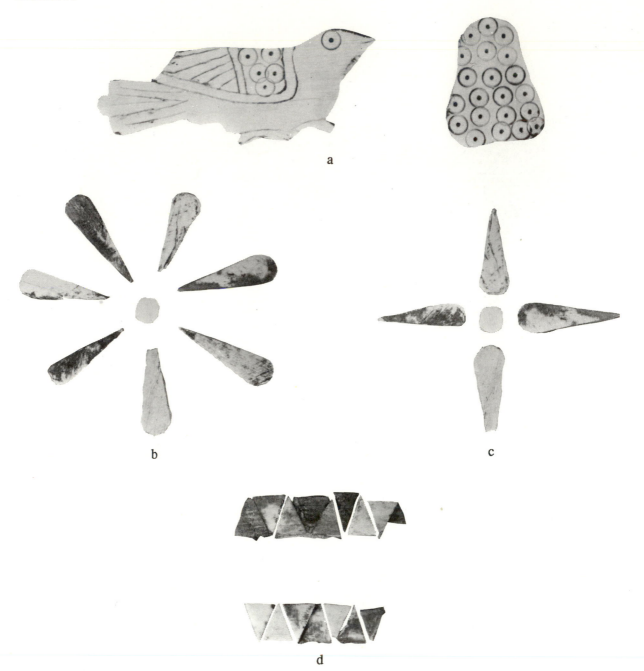

Inlays from Remains of a Box (*b* and *c* are Alternate Arrangements): (*a*) Q 67—5a, (*b*) Q 67—5a, (*c*) Q 67—5a, (*d*) Q 67—5a. Scale ca. 1:1.

PLATE 52

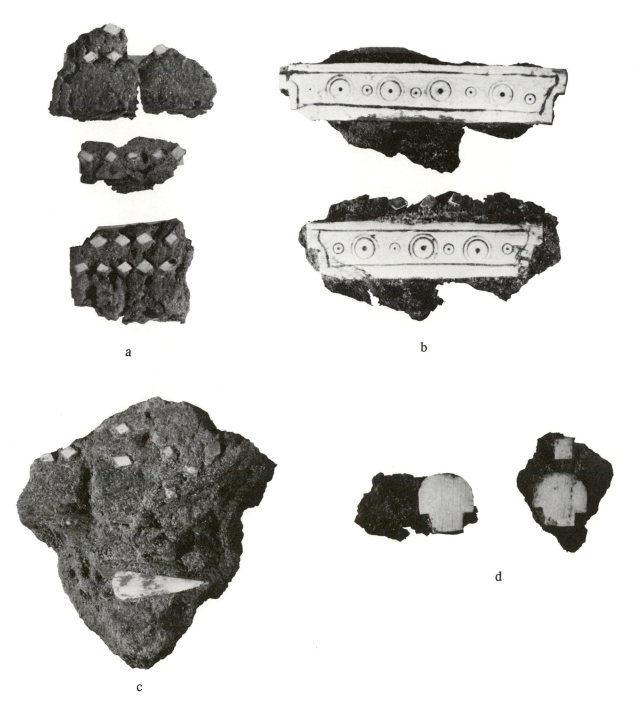

Fragments of a Box with Ivory Inlays: (*a*) Q 67—5a, (*b*) Q 67—5a,
(*c*) Q 67—5a, (*d*) Q 67—5a. Scale ca. 1:1.

PLATE 53

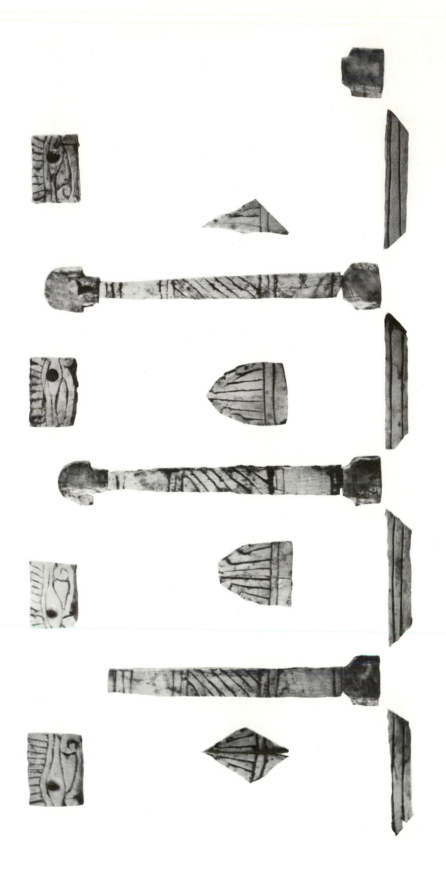

Ivory Inlays from Box Q 67—5a (in hypothetical arrangement): *Neb*–signs, Crowns, and Architectural Elements. Scale ca. 7:4.

PLATE 54

Quiver, Q 149—1. Scale Indicated.

PLATE 55

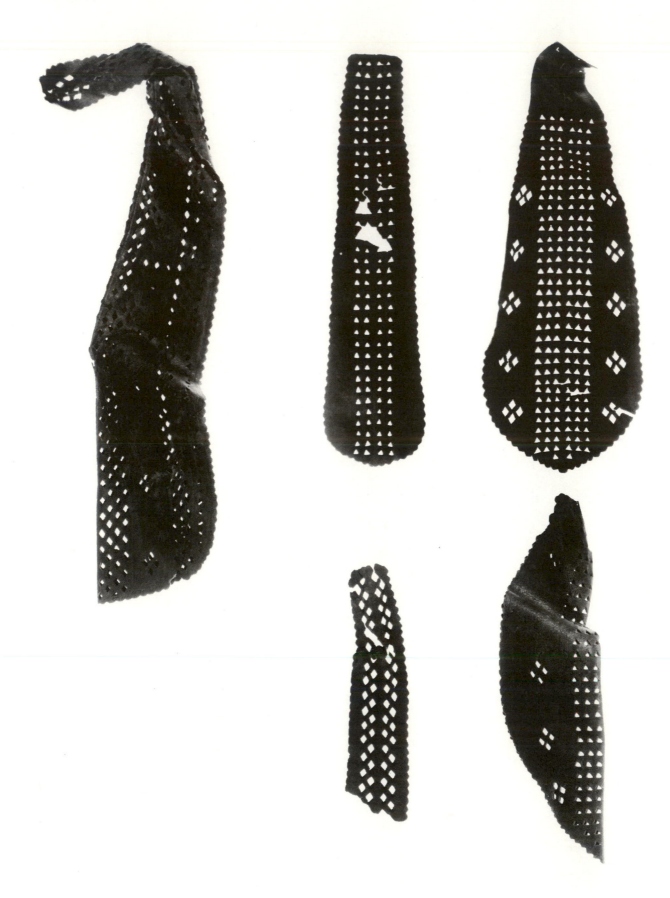

Flaps from Quiver Q 149—1. Scale ca. 2:5.

PLATE 56

Quivers: (*a*) Q 134—22, (*b*) Q 196—1a, (*c*) Q 196—1a. Scale ca. 2:5.

PLATE 57

Quivers and Looses: (*a*) Q 505—4a, (*b*) Q 74—2a, (*c*) Q 147—3 [Diorite], (*d*) Q 149—3. Scale ca. 1:1.

PLATE 58

Quiver, Q 40—2a. Scale Indicated.

PLATE 59

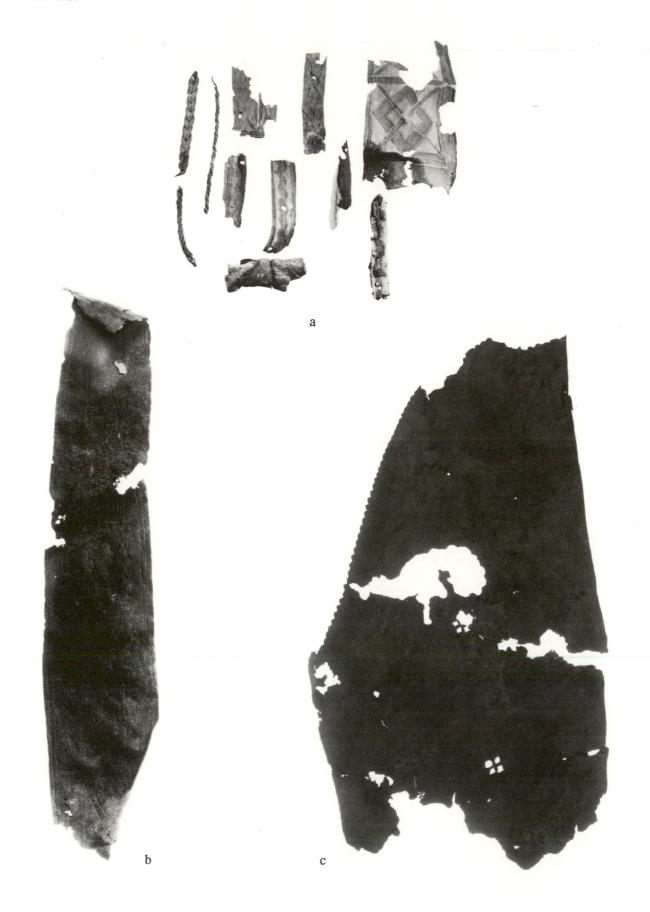

a

b   c

Quiver Fragments: (*a*) Q 1—2a, (*b*) Q 40—2a, (*c*) Q 74—2a. Scale ca. 1:1.

PLATE 60

Quiver Fragments (*cont.*): (*a*) Q 6—8, (*b*) Q 6—8, (*c*) Q 6—8, (*d*) Q 6—8, (*e*) R 49—5a. Scale ca. 1:1.

PLATE 61

Compound Bow, Q 345—7. Scale ca. 1:1.

PLATE 62

Compound Bow Fragments: (*a*) R 49—5c, (*b*) Q 62—1c, (*c*) R 49—5c,
(*d*) Q 196—1b. Scales: (a) ca. 1:2, (*b*–*d*) Not to Scale.

PLATE 63

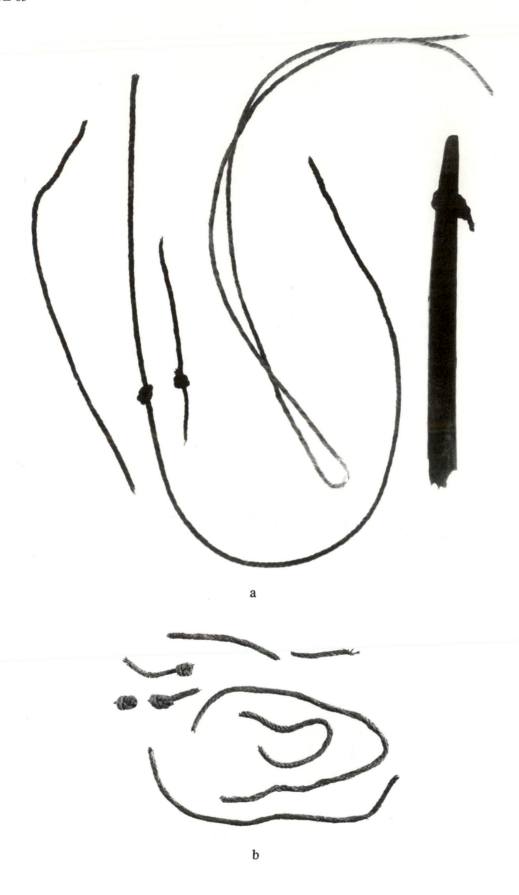

a

b

Bow Fragments and Thong: (*a*) String and Tip from Wooden Self-Bow, Q 152—5;
(*b*) Braided Cord from Cosmetic Ring, R 6—5. Scale ca. 1:2.

PLATE 64

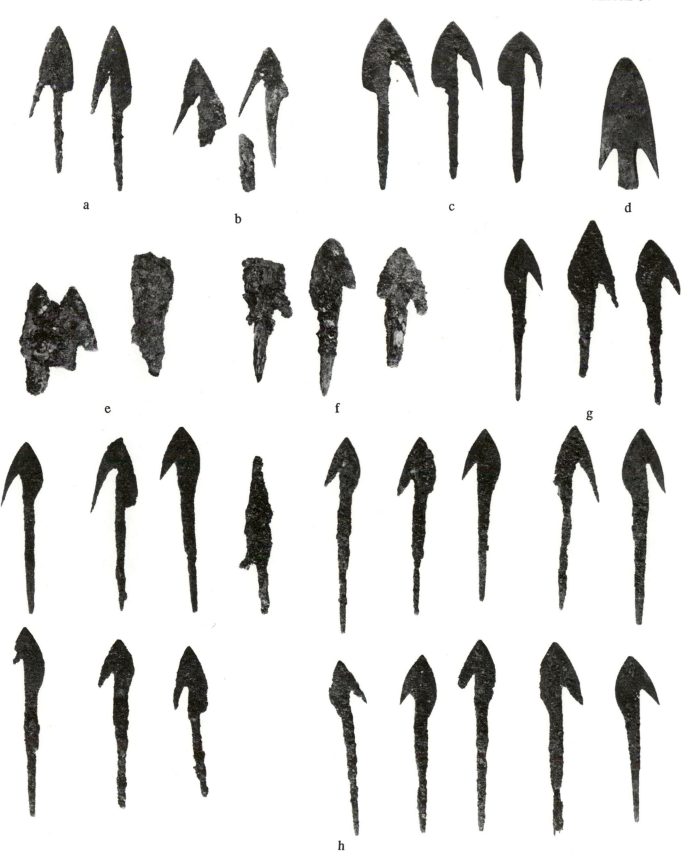

Arrowheads: (*a*) Q 279—2, (*b*) Q 64—3, (*c*) Q 9—8, (*d*) Q 75—7, (*e*) Q 38—2b, (*f*) Q 38—2b, (*g*) Q 74—8, (*h*) Q 74—8. Scale ca. 1:1.

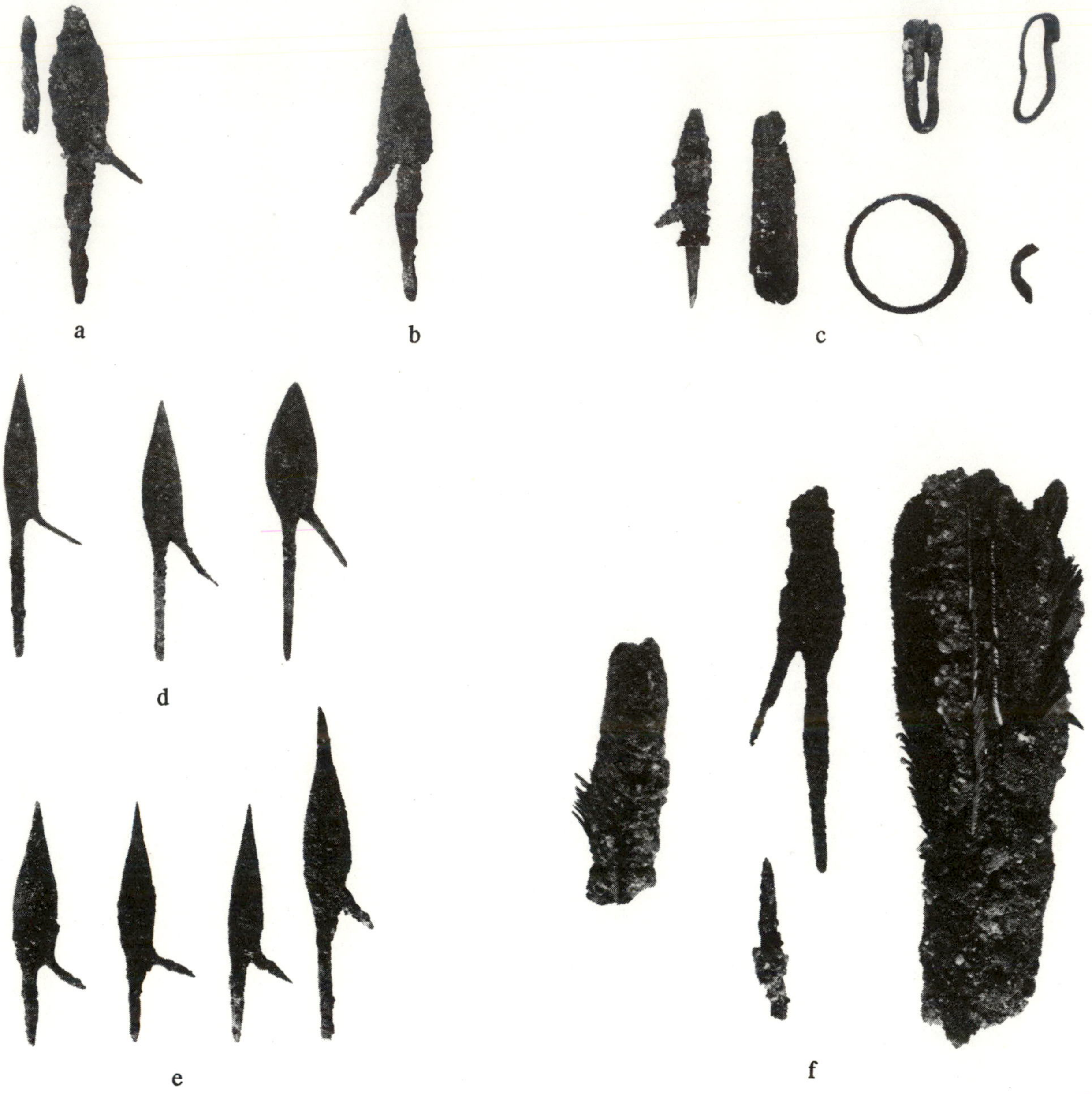

PLATE 65

Arrowheads, Rings, and Remains of Fletching: (*a*) Q 381—5, (*b*) Q 196—8, (*c*) Q 84—1, 2; (*d*) Q 345—14, (*e*) Q 10—4, (*f*) Q 152—6. Scale ca. 1:1.

PLATE 66

Armament: (*a*) Rawhide Scabbard-Liner, Q 75—2a; (*b*) Silver Scabbard-Cover Fragments, Q 32—3;
(*c*) Leather Armor[?] with Lead Rosettes, R 49—5e. Scales: (*a*) ca. 1:2, (*b, c*) ca.1:1.

PLATE 67

a

b

c

Remains of Bags for Water and Carrying: (*a*) Locking Bag, Top and Parts, Q 164—8; (*b*) Bag Edge or Equipment Belt, Q 74—4b; (*c*) Edge of Bag with Holes and Tab, R 49—6. Scale ca. 1:2.

PLATE 68

Remains of Bags: (*a*) Bag with Edge, Q 74—4a; (*b*) Bag with
Stitching and Grommets, Q 1—2c. Scale ca. 1:1.

PLATE 69

Water Skin(?), Q 79—1 (the sheen was produced by preservatives). Scale ca. 1:1.

PLATE 70

Saddle, Q 39—5 (the sheen was produced by preservatives). Scale ca. 2:5.

PLATE 71

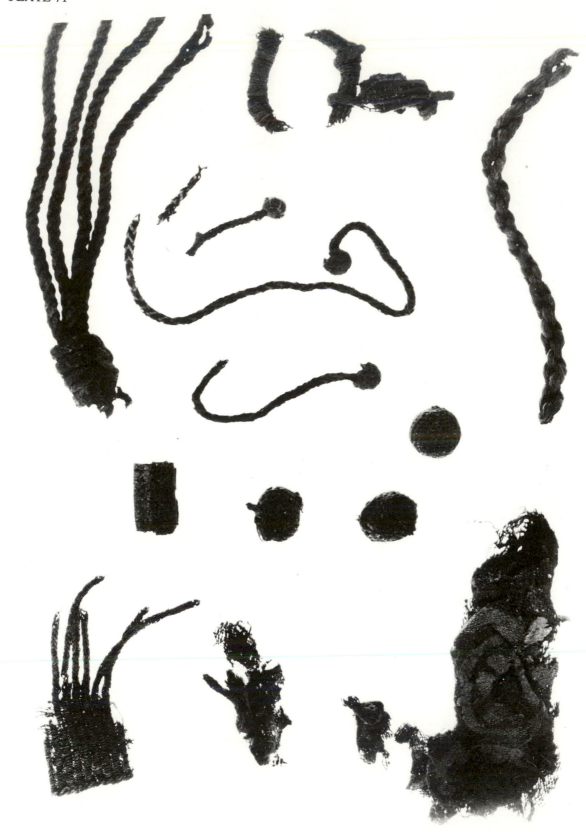

Cord and Textile Remains from Harness and Saddlery: Q 73—1, 2. Scale ca. 1:2.

PLATE 72

a

b

Cinch-Bars with Attachment Holes for Quarter Straps: (*a*) Q 265—1,
(*b*) Q 5—12d. Scales: (*a*) ca. 1:2, (*b*) ca. 1:1.

PLATE 73

Harness Fragments: (*a*) Q 38—2a, (*b*) Q 5—9, (*c*) Q 5—9, (*d*) Straps and Bar, Q 148—11; (*e*) Straps, Bronze Buckle, and Iron Rods, Q 73—3; (*f*) Rings and Fragments, Q 5—8. Scale ca. 1:2.

PLATE 74

Iron Harness, Rings, Bits, and Various Fragments, Q 20—5: (*a*) Various Harness of Bit Fragments,
(*b*) Possible Part of Bit, (*c*) Ring, (*d*) Possible Part of Bit. Scale ca. 1:2.

PLATE 75

Iron Harness Remains, Q 5—9: (*a–f*) Bit Fragments [*b*, two views], (*g, h*) Curved Strap,
(*i–k*) Saddle Fittings [*k* is the reverse of the lower fragment of *j*],
(*l, m*) Rings, Staples, and Other Fragments. Scale ca. 1:2.

PLATE 76

Jewelry: (*a*) Iron[?] *Ankh*, Surface North of Emery's Qu. 36—1 [not in *Register of Finds*]; (*b*) Faience Amun-Pendant, Q 164—11; (*c*) Beads with Pendants, Q 44—2; (*d*) Beads of Lead and Glass, Q 9—10; (*e*) Silver and Carnelian Earring, Q 75—5; (*f*) Silver Earring, Q 74—13; (*g*) Silver Earring, Q 38—6; (*h*) Beads, Q 64—2; (*i*) Large Silver Earrings, VA 9—5; (*j*) Silver Ring, Q 501—5; (*k*) Iron Toe Ring, Q 387—4. Scales: (*a–g, i–k*) ca. 1:1; (*h*) ca. 1:2.

PLATE 77

Jewelry (*cont.*): (*a*) Silver Anklet, Q 152—3; (*b*) Bronze Ring with Bezel in Unknown Material, R 16—2;
(*c*) Bronze Ring with Uncertain Bezel, R 16—1; (*d*) Two Bronze Rings, Q 149—6; (*e*) Bronze
Earring, Q 164—15; (*f*) Bronze Ring, VA 14—10; (*g*) Two Bronze Rings, Q 141—6;
(*h*) Five Bronze Rings, R 69—2. Scale ca. 1:1.

PLATE 78

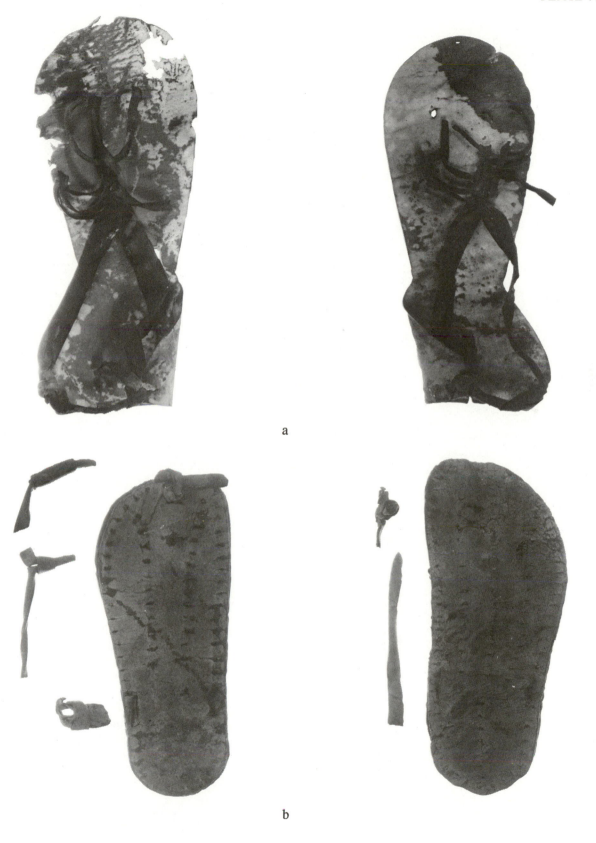

a

b

Pairs of Sandals: (a) Q 49—2, (b) Q 192—2. Scale ca. 2:5.

PLATE 79

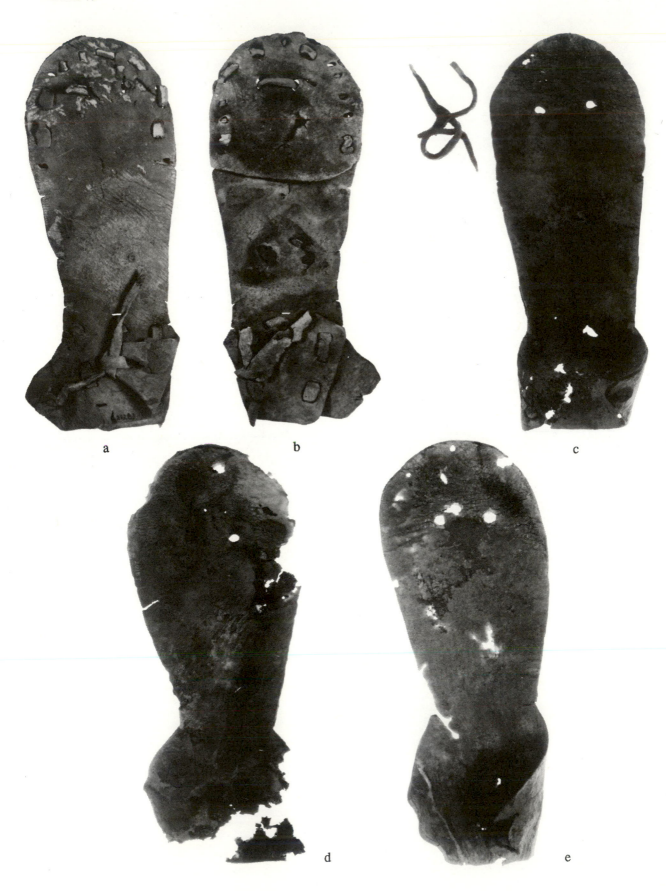

Sandals: (*a*) Q 378—17, (*b*) Q 378—17 [reversed], (*c*) Q 345—11, (*d*) Q 74—5, (*e*) Q 119—4. Scale ca. 2:5.

PLATE 80

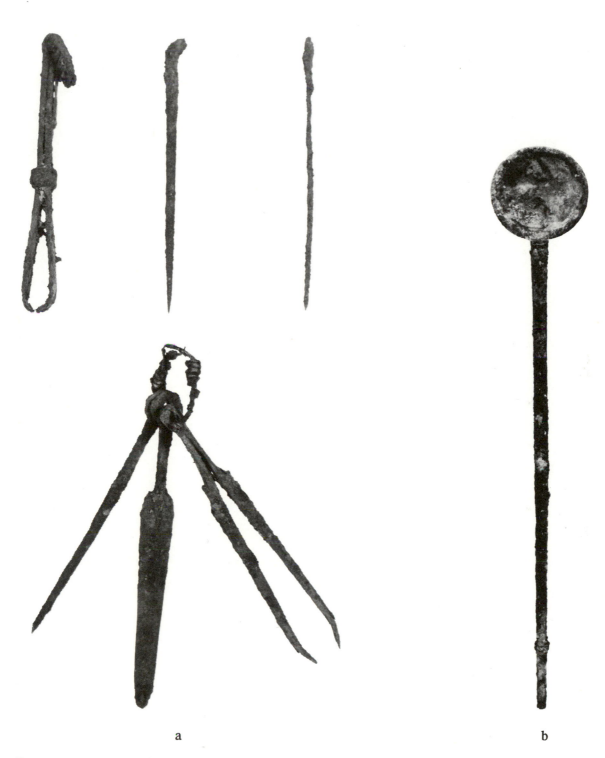

a   b

Cosmetic Implements: (a) Iron Toilet Objects, R 2—8; (b) Bronze Spoon, Q 134—14. Scale ca. 1:1.

PLATE 81

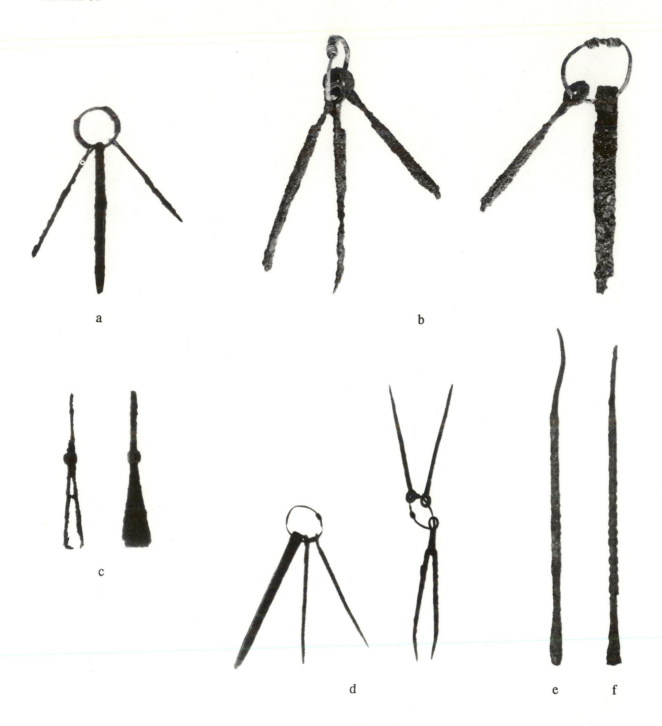

Cosmetic Implements (*cont.*): (*a*) Gold Ring with Bronze Tweezer and Two Probes, R 51—3; (*b*) Ring with Iron Tweezers and Probe, Q 2—14 [two views]; (*c*) Broad Tweezers (Side and Front), R 4A—25; (*d*) Ring with Tweezers and Probe, R 64—8; (*e*) Iron Kohl Stick, VA 14—11; (*f*) Iron Kohl Stick, R 50—4. Scales: (*a, c–f*) ca. 1:2; (*b*) 1:1.

PLATE 82

Iron Tools: (*a*) Sickle-Saw, R 4A—22; (*b*) Adze Head, R 4A—20; (*c*) Adze Head, R 4A—19; (*d*) Axe Head, R 4A—21; (*e*) Sickle-Saw, R 22—9; (*f*) Adze-Mattock Head, R 22—7; (*g*) Sickle-Saw, R 49—2a; (*h*) Adze-Mattock Head, R 49—2b. Scale ca. 1:2.

PLATE 83

Various Objects: (*a*) Iron Ornament/Bell, R 4A—26; (*b*) Sickle-Saw, W 88—2; (*c*) Hammer, Q 6—5;
(*d*) Spike, Q 385—5a; (*e*) Carved Bone, Q 136—6a–b; (*f*) Iron Ornament/Bell, Q 279—3;
(*g*) Bell, Q 264—2; (*h*) Wooden Container, Q 350—2; (*i*) Ivory Kohl Tube, Q 164—13;
(*j*) Wooden Spindle Shaft, Q 164—1. Scales: (*a, f*) 1:1, (*b–e, g–j*) ca. 1:2.

ORIENTAL INSTITUTE VOLUMES IN PRINT

Available from **THE ORIENTAL INSTITUTE**, Publications Sales

1155 East 58th Street, Chicago, Illinois 60637
Tel. (312) 702–9508, Fax (312) 702–9853

ASSYRIOLOGICAL STUDIES (AS)

21 *Computer-Aided Analysis of Amorite.* I. J. Gelb et al. 1980. Pp. xv + 657.

22 *Old Babylonian Letters from Tell Asmar.* R. M. Whiting, Jr. 1987. Pp. xiii + 177; 27 plates.

23 *Kaniššuwar—A Tribute to Hans G. Güterbock on His Seventy-Fifth Birthday, May 27, 1983.* H. A. Hoffner, Jr. and G. M. Beckman, eds. 1986. Pp. vii + 203; frontispiece [Professor Güterbock], 39 figures.

24 *The Hittite Instruction for the Royal Bodyguard.* H. G. Güterbock and T. P. J. van den Hout. 1991. Pp. xvi + 99.

25 *The Hittite State Cult of the Tutelary Deities.* G. McMahon. 1991. Pp. xxi + 302; 8 tables, 3 appendices.

CHICAGO ASSYRIAN DICTIONARY (CAD)

Volumes 1 (A, pts. 1 and 2), 2 (B), 3 (D), 4 (E), 5 (G), 6 (Ḫ), 7 (I/J), 8 (K), 9 (L), 10 (M, pts. 1 and 2), 11 (N, pts. 1 and 2), 13 (Q), 15 (S), 16 (Ṣ), 17 (Š, pt. 1), and 21 (Z)

CHICAGO HITTITE DICTIONARY (CHD)

Volume 3 (L–N): Fasc. 1 (1980), Fasc. 2 (1983), Fasc. 3 (1986), Fasc. 4 (1989)

MATERIALS AND STUDIES FOR KASSITE HISTORY (MSKH)

1 *A Catalogue of Cuneiform Sources Pertaining to Specific Monarchs of the Kassite Dynasty.* J. A. Brinkman. 1976. Pp. xxiv + 469; 11 plates.

ORIENTAL INSTITUTE COMMUNICATIONS (OIC)

23 *Excavations at Nippur: Twelfth Season.* McG. Gibson et al. 1978. Pp. xiv + 190; 92 figures, 16 tables.

24 *The American Expedition to Idalion, Cyprus: 1973–1980.* L. E. Stager and A. M. Walker, eds. 1989. Pp. xxiv + 516; 93 figures, 82 plates.

25 *Figurines and Other Clay Objects from Sarab and Çayönü.* V. B. Morales. 1990. Pp. xvi + 92; 2 catalogs; 30 plates.

ORIENTAL INSTITUTE NUBIAN EXPEDITION (OINE)

3 *Excavations Between Abu Simbel and the Sudan Frontier, Part 1: The A-Group Royal Cemetery at Qustul, Cemetery L.* Bruce B. Williams. 1986. Pp. xxxviii + 388; 190 figures, 100 plates, 43 tables.

4 *Excavations Between Abu Simbel and the Sudan Frontier, Parts 2, 3, and 4: Neolithic, A-Group, and Post A-Group Remains from Cemeteries W, V, S, Q, T, and a Cave East of Cemetery K.* Bruce B. Williams. 1989. Pp. xxvii + 141; 72 figures, 55 plates, 26 tables.

5 *Excavations Between Abu Simbel and the Sudan Frontier, Part 5: C-Group, Pan Grave, and Kerma Remains at Adindan Cemeteries T, K, U, and J.* Bruce Williams. 1983. Pp. xxvi + 235; 48 figures, 131 plates, 50 tables.

7 *Excavations Between Abu Simbel and the Sudan Frontier, Part 7: Twenty-Fifth Dynasty and Napatan Remains at Qustul: Cemeteries W and V.* Bruce B. Williams. 1990. Pp. xxvii + 83; 33 figures, 15 plates, 16 tables.

8 *Excavations Between Abu Simbel and the Sudan Frontier, Part 8: Meroitic Remains from Qustul Cemetery Q, Ballana Cemetery B, and a Ballana Settlement.* (2 volumes). Bruce B. Williams. 1991. Pp. xlvii + 458 (Part 1), xiii + 423 (Part 2); 308 figures, 114 plates, 33 tables.

ORIENTAL INSTITUTE NUBIAN EXPEDITION (OINE)

9   *Excavations Between Abu Simbel and the Sudan Frontier, Part 9: Noubadian X-Group Remains from royal Complexes in Cemeteries Q and 219 and from Private Cemeteries Q, R, V, W, B, J, and M at Qustul and Ballana.* Bruce B. Williams. 1991. Pp. xxxix + 502; 195 figures, 83 plates, 54 tables.

ORIENTAL INSTITUTE PUBLICATIONS (OIP)

3   *The Edwin Smith Surgical Papyrus, Volume One: Hieroglyphic Transliteration, Translation, and Commentary.* J. H. Breasted. 1930 (Reissued 1991). Pp. xxiv + 596; 8 plates.

4   *The Edwin Smith Surgical Papyrus, Volume Two: Facsimile Plates and Line for Line Hieroglyphic Transliteration.* J. H. Breasted. 1930 (Reissued 1991). Pp. xiii; 46 plates.

97   *Nippur II. The North Temple and Sounding E: Excavations of the Joint Expedition to Nippur of the American Schools of Oriental Research and The Oriental Institute of The University of Chicago.* D. E. McCown *et al.* 1978. Pp. xv + 105; 15 figures, 77 plates.

98   *Old Babylonian Public Buildings in the Diyala Region.* H. D. Hill, Th. Jacobsen, and P. Delougaz. 1990. Pp. xxxii + 257; 31 figures, 68 plates.

100   *The Temple of Khonsu I: Scenes of King Herihor in the Court.* The Epigraphic Survey. 1979. Pp. xxvii + 55; 110 plates.

102   *The Tomb of Kheruef: Theban Tomb 192.* The Epigraphic Survey. 1980. Pp. xx + 80; 3 figures, 88 plates (1 in color).

103   *The Temple of Khonsu II: Scenes and Inscriptions in the Court and the First Hypostyle Hall.* The Epigraphic Survey. 1981. Pp. xxiii + 93; 97 plates.

104   *Earliest Land Tenure Systems in the Near East: Ancient Kudurrus.* I. J. Gelb, P. Steinkeller, and R. M. Whiting, Jr. Two vols. (Text, Plates) 1989, 1991. Pp. xviii + 303; 166 plates.

105   *Prehistoric Archeology Along the Zagros Flanks.* L. S. Braidwood et al. 1983. Pp. ix + 695; 5 charts, 244 figures, 185 tables.

106   *The Great Hypostyle Hall at Karnak I, Part 1: The Wall Reliefs.* H. H. Nelson and W. J. Murnane. 1981. Pp. xxv; 267 plates.

107   *Reliefs and Inscriptions at Karnak IV: The Battle Reliefs of King Sety I.* The Epigraphic Survey. 1986. Pp. xxiv + 166; 2 figures, 50 plates.

108   *The Holmes Expeditions to Luristan.* E. F. Schmidt, M. N. van Loon, and H. Curvers, with contribution by J. A. Brinkman. 1989. Pp. xv + 594; 20 catalogs, 265 plates, 32 tables.

109   *Town and Country in Southeastern Anatolia I: Settlement and Land Use at Kurban Höyük and Other Sites in the Lower Karababa Basin.* T. J. Wilkinson et al. 1990. Pp. xix + 315; 90 figures, 4 plates, 20 tables.

110   *Town and Country in Southeastern Anatolia II: The Stratigraphic Sequence at Kurban Höyük.* G. Algaze, ed. Two vols. (Text, Plates) 1990. Pp. xl + 438; 139 figures, 169 plates, 50 tables.

STUDIES IN ANCIENT ORIENTAL CIVILIZATION (SAOC)

25   *The Comparative Archeology of Early Mesopotamia.* A. L. Perkins. 1949 (1977, Seventh Printing). Pp. xix + 200; 20 figures, 1 map, 3 tables.

36   *The Hilly Flanks and Beyond: Essays on the Prehistory of Southwestern Asia Presented to Robert J. Braidwood, November 15, 1982.* T. C. Young, Jr., P. E. L. Smith, and P. Mortensen, eds. 1983. Pp. xiii + 374, frontispiece [Professor Braidwood], 97 figures, 36 tables.

38   *The Demotic Verbal System.* J. H. Johnson. 1976. Pp. xv + 344; 51 tables.

39   *Studies in Honor of George R. Hughes, January 12, 1977.* J. H. Johnson and E. F. Wente, eds. 1976. Pp. xviii + 282; frontispiece [Professor Hughes], 52 figures, 1 photograph, 9 tables.

41   *Ecology and Empire: The Structure of the Urartian State.* P. E. Zimansky. 1985. Pp. xv + 143; 15 figures, 15 plates, 17 tables.

42   *The Road to Kadesh: A Historical Interpretation of the Battle Reliefs of King Sety I at Karnak.* W. J. Murnane. 1990 (2nd Ed. Rev.). Pp. xvi + 157; 3 maps.

STUDIES IN ANCIENT ORIENTAL CIVILIZATION (SAOC)

43 *A Neolithic Village at Tell El Kowm in the Syrian Desert.* R. Dornemann. 1986. Pp. xii + 89; 46 plates, 4 serial lists, 12 tables.

44 *Nippur Neighborhoods.* E. C. Stone. 1987. Pp. xviii + 294; 7 figures, 94 plates, 24 tables.

45 *Thus Wrote ʿOnchsheshonqy: An Introductory Grammar of Demotic.* J. H. Johnson. 1991 (2nd Ed. Rev.). In Press.

46 *The Organization of Power: Aspects of Bureaucracy in the Ancient Near East.* McG. Gibson and R. D. Biggs, eds. 1991 (2nd Ed. with Corrections). Pp. xii + 168; 15 figures, 10 plates, 1 table, 3 appendices

47 *Essays in Ancient Civilization Presented to Helene J. Kantor.* A. Leonard, Jr. and B. B. Williams, eds. 1989. Pp. xxxix + 393; frontispiece [Professor Kantor], 52 figures, 72 plates, 6 tables.

48 *Egyptian Phyles in the Old Kingdom: The Evolution of a System of Social Organization.* A. M. Roth. 1991. In Press.

49 *A Critical Study of the Temple Scroll from Qumran Cave 11.* M. O. Wise. 1990. Pp. xvii + 292; 2 figures, 8 tables.

50 *Subsistence, Trade, and Social Change in Early Bronze Age Palestine.* D. L. Esse. 1991. Pp. xvii + 219; 36 figures, 9 plates, 6 tables.

TITLES NOT IN ORIENTAL INSTITUTE SERIES

The Joint Istanbul-Chicago Universities' Prehistoric Research in Southeastern Anatolia 1. H. Çambel and R. J. Braidwood, et al. 1980. Pp. xv + 327; 49 plates, 26 tables.

Uch Tepe I: Tell Razuk, Tell Ahmed Al-Mughir, Tell Ajamat. McG. Gibson, ed. 1981. Pp. xi + 197; 9 figures, 116 plates, 8 levels/locus summaries, 27 tables.

Uch Tepe II: Technical Reports. McG. Gibson, ed. 1990. Pp. 140; 69 figures, 5 plates, 38 tables.

Quseir Al-Qadim 1978: Preliminary Report. D. S. Whitcomb and J. H. Johnson, *et al.* 1979. Pp. xii + 352; 57 figures, 89 plates, 15 tables.

Quseir Al-Qadim 1980: Preliminary Report. D. S. Whitcomb and J. H. Johnson, *et al.* 1982. Pp. xi + 406; 29 figures, 74 plates, 5 tables.

Available from **THE UNIVERSITY OF CHICAGO PRESS**

11030 South Langley Avenue, Chicago, Illinois 60628
Tel. (1–800) 621–2736, (312) 568–1550

ASSYRIOLOGICAL STUDIES (AS)

20 *Sumerological Studies in Honor of Thorkild Jacobsen.* S. Lieberman, ed. 1976. Pp. xiv + 316; frontispiece [Professor Jacobsen], 16 figures, 12 tables.

ORIENTAL INSTITUTE COMMUNICATIONS (OIC)

5 *Medinet Habu, 1924–28.* H. H. Nelson and U. Hoelscher. 1929. Pp. xv + 50; 35 figures.

7 *Medinet Habu Studies, 1924/28.* U. Hölscher and J. A. Wilson. 1930. Pp. ix + 33; 18 figures, 3 plates.

22 *Excavations at Nippur: Eleventh Season.* McG. Gibson et al. 1976. Pp. xi + 152; 3 catalogs, 90 figures.

ORIENTAL INSTITUTE ESSAYS (OIE)

The Intellectual Adventure of Ancient Man. H. Frankfort et al. 1946. Pp. vii + 401; 1 figure.

Kingship and the Gods. H. Frankfort. 1948. Pp. xxv + 444; frontispiece, 52 figures, 1 table.

ORIENTAL INSTITUTE NUBIAN EXPEDITION (OINE)

1 *The Beit El-Wali Temple of Ramesses II.* H. Ricke, G. R. Hughes, and E. F. Wente. 1967. Pp. xvii + 39; 6 figures, 49 plates (3 in color).

2 *Ausgrabungen von Khor-Dehmit bis Bet El-Wali.* H. Ricke. 1967. Pp. xvi + 70; 81 figures, 3 plans, 30 plates.

ORIENTAL INSTITUTE PUBLICATIONS (OIP)

10 *Prehistoric Survey of Egypt and Western Asia I: Paleolithic Man and the Nile-Faiyum Divide: A Study of the Region During Pliocene and Pleistocene Times.* K. S. Sandford and W. J. Arkell. 1930. Pp. xv + 77; 25 figures, 1 map, 11 plates.

24 *Sennacherib's Aqueduct at Jerwan.* Th. Jacobsen and S. Lloyd. 1935. Pp. xii + 52; frontispiece, 12 figures, 36 plates.

56 *Key Plans Showing Locations of Theban Temple Decorations.* H. H. Nelson. 1941 (second printing, 1965). Pp. xi; 38 plates.

70 *Persepolis III: The Royal Tombs and Other Monuments.* E. F. Schmidt. 1970. Pp. xxiv + 174; 38 figures, 105 plates, 9 tables.

74 *Reliefs and Inscriptions at Karnak III: Bubastite Portal.* The Epigraphic Survey. 1954. Pp. xiv; 1 figure, 22 plates.

76 *Studies in Arabic Literary Papyri II: Quranic Commentary and Tradition.* N. Abbott. 1967. Pp. xvi + 293; 27 plates.

77 *Studies in Arabic Literary Papyri III: Language and Literature.* N. Abbott. 1972. Pp. xvi + 216; 10 plates.

79 *Soundings at Tell Fakhariyah.* C. W. McEwan *et al.* 1957. Pp. xvii + 103; 87 plates.

84 *Medinet Habu VI: The Temple Proper, Part II: The Re Chapel, the Royal Mortuary Complex, and Adjacent Rooms with Miscellaneous Material from the Pylons, the Forecourts, and the First Hypostyle Hall.* The Epigraphic Survey. 1963. Pp. xix; 1 plan, 120 plates.

90 *Ptolemais: City of the Libyan Pentapolis.* C. H. Kraeling. 1963. Pp. xviii + 288; 74 figures, 22 plans, 64 plates.

91 *Aramaic Ritual Texts from Persepolis.* R. A. Bowman. 1970. Pp. xiii + 194; 2 figures, 36 plates, 1 table.

92 *Persepolis Fortification Tablets.* R. T. Hallock. 1969. Pp. x + 776; glossaries.

93 *Medinet Habu VII: The Temple Proper, Part III: The Third Hypostyle Hall and All Rooms Accessible from It with Friezes of Scenes from the Roof Terraces and Exterior Walls of the Temple.* The Epigraphic Survey. 1964. Pp. xl; 16 figures, 108 plates.

94 *Medinet Habu VIII: The Eastern High Gate with Translations of Texts.* The Epigraphic Survey. 1970. xxiii + 14; 10 plans, 70 plates.

95 *Excavations in the Plain of Antioch II: The Structural Remains of the Later Phases: Chatal Hüyük, Tell Al-Judaidah, and Tell Ta'yinat.* R. C. Haines. 1971. Pp. xiv + 66; 118 plates.

99 *Inscriptions from Tell Abu Salabikh.* R. D. Biggs. 1974. Pp. xii + 112; 30 figures, 183 plates.

STUDIES IN ANCIENT ORIENTAL CIVILIZATION (SAOC)

31 *Prehistoric Investigations in Iraqi Kurdistan.* R. J. Braidwood and B. Howe. 1960 (2nd Printing, 1966). Pp. xxviii + 184; 8 figures, 29 plates, 4 tables.

35 *Studies in Honor of John A. Wilson, September 12, 1969.* E. B. Hauser, ed. 1969. Pp. ix + 124; frontispiece [Professor Wilson], 8 figures.

37 *The Book of the Dead or Going Forth by Day: Ideas of the Ancient Egyptians Concerning the Hereafter as Expressed in Their Own Terms.* T. G. Allen, trans. 1974. Pp. x + 306.